A volume in the
DOUGLASS SERIES IN EDUCATION,
edited by HARL R. DOUGLASS, Ph.D.,
DIRECTOR OF THE COLLEGE OF EDUCATION,
UNIVERSITY OF COLORADO

Principles and Practices of

SECONDARY EDUCATION

VERNON E. ANDERSON
The University of Maryland

and

WILLIAM T. GRUHN
The University of Connecticut

Second Edition

THE RONALD PRESS COMPANY · NEW YORK

Library of Congress Catalog Card Number: 62–11648
PRINTED IN THE UNITED STATES OF AMERICA

To our many colleagues
in secondary schools and universities who are devoting
their lives to giving youth a fruitful educational experience, whose work has been an inspiration and a
source of information for the illustrations of forward-
looking practices in this book.

PREFACE

This book tells the story of secondary education in the United States, recording and evaluating the recent significant changes that have taken place. It has been written especially for the pre-service education student interested in keeping abreast of happenings in secondary education and in critically examining old and new practices. It will be equally useful, nevertheless, to the experienced teacher who is seeking information about current programs and trends in the schools.

Some of the newer trends examined in this book include the revision of the content of subjects; programs for the academically talented; the use of such new media and techniques of instruction as programmed learning, television, and language laboratories; team teaching; flexible size groups for instructional purposes; programs for special groups of pupils such as children of migrant workers; advanced placement plans; action research; national testing programs; and programs for handicapped pupils. Attention is given to practices in junior high schools, senior high schools, and community colleges.

The organization of the chapters describing school practices lends itself especially to these purposes. Principles basic to a modern program of secondary education are followed by descriptions of some common practices and trends, descriptions of specific secondary school practices that implement the principles, and discussions of crucial issues and problems facing secondary education. It is a basic tenet of the authors that, even though a point of view is stated, the student must make up his own mind on what position he will take. We are interested in preparing secondary school teachers who will attack problems critically and who, in turn, will encourage intelligent inquiry in their secondary school classes. The annotated references are selected with this purpose in mind. Students are urged to seek other references in recent professional periodical literature for arguments pro and con on current issues.

The plan of the book lends itself to practical use. The first part presents the purposes of the school in historical perspective, dis-

cusses the impact of American culture on school policies and procedures, and describes the nature and needs of the pupil population.
The next part takes up the many facets of curriculum and instruction.
The third part deals with administrative organization and leadership,
and outlines pupil services necessary for a good secondary school
program. The final part discusses how programs are evaluated for
high quality and looks forward to what the secondary school may
become.

In reading the text it is important to understand the reason for including certain practices in the sections called "Some Common Practices." Some of these are examples of good programs; many fail to
measure up to the principles advocated. They are neither average nor
typical practices unless so stated; they are actually in use in some
schools and classrooms. They give the student an idea of the variety
of situations teachers face so that he will be better prepared for what
he might encounter in his first position as a teacher.

The schools selected for the examples of new and forward-looking
practices in the sections "Implementation of the Principles" are not by
any means the only schools with such practices, nor are they necessarily the best practices to be found. These practices are representative of secondary schools with programs that show imagination, inventiveness, and a recognition of the need to change with the times.

The authors are indebted to many principals and other educators
for their cooperation and assistance in supplying information and materials for this volume. In particular we wish to pay tribute to the late
Paul R. Grim, former Director of Laboratory Experiences, University
of Minnesota, and co-author of the original edition of this book, for
his significant contributions which have left their imprint on this edition. We are deeply grateful to Urbane O. Hennen, Associate Professor of Education, University of Connecticut, for his preparation of
Chapter 3, American Culture and the Secondary School. We express
our appreciation to Harl R. Douglass, for his guidance and constructive criticisms; to Gladys A. Midura, for her willingness to permit us
to use in Chapter 2 information from her doctoral dissertation; and
to Alice P. Anderson and Myrtis Gruhn, for their valuable assistance
in editing and typing the manuscript.

VERNON E. ANDERSON
WILLIAM T. GRUHN

College Park, Maryland
Storrs, Connecticut

CONTENTS

Part I

FOUNDATIONS OF SECONDARY EDUCATION

Part II

CURRICULUM AND INSTRUCTION

Part III

ORGANIZATION AND LEADERSHIP

Part IV

IMPROVEMENT OF PROGRAMS

Part I

FOUNDATIONS OF
SECONDARY EDUCATION

1

BASES FOR JUDGING SECONDARY EDUCATION

One of the questions facing a secondary school teacher is how to judge whether or not a practice is good. He hears all kinds of opinions about the secondary schools in his community and in the country as a whole. Some critics are sharply in disagreement with current practices. Others believe that the system of secondary education is excellent. What makes a program good? Who decides whether to use a new idea?

An educator, a layman, a university professor, and a legislator may each have a different concept of what a good secondary school is like. Their values are a product of their backgrounds, their own education, and their accustomed way of making decisions. To a person with a European background, the kind of school program desired for his own and his neighbors' children may be vastly different from one considered as good by his neighbor, educated and reared in the tradition of the American public school.

Some persons make decisions about education based upon tradition, whim, personal interests and prejudices, or because "it is the thing to do." Others are content to follow a leader without thinking and without considering whether he is prejudiced or ignorant about education, a rabble-rouser, a hate-monger, or a well-informed person. Some arrive at their judgments after weighing the old or the new against the changing social scene and the values for which their own society stands.

By the same token, some teachers shop around for gadgets. At teachers' conventions they look for the latest tricks to help children learn what they have little desire to learn. Some teach "Macbeth" in the twelfth grade because it is accepted by English teachers in their region as the thing to do. Others are content to have outmoded texts prescribe outmoded mathematics content for their classes.

The strength of American secondary education lies in the fact

3

that the vast majority of educational leaders are thoughtful persons; good teachers in American secondary schools have a well-conceived purpose for what they do; and such a large proportion of the public are seriously enough concerned about their secondary schools to spend time and effort in studying and evaluating them. No program of secondary education can remain a strong, vital force in a nation where people think only in the past and remain blind to the rapidly changing world of the mid-twentieth century.

The important questions for us as teachers are: Where do we stand on issues about secondary schools? Upon what criteria do we base our judgments? It is of momentous consequence to the future of education whether or not future teachers establish the pattern of selecting valid bases for making choices. Every teacher has to make innumerable decisions every day. They cannot expect to run to a book or to the principal for information on what to do in regard to each disciplinary case as it arises, for each case will be different as long as young people differ. Nor can teachers continue practices that have been carried on in secondary schools simply because they have long existed. It is imperative that as teachers we have some guides for judging why we teach certain content or use particular methods.

In this chapter are outlined principles, based on accumulated research and information, that will help the teacher in making better judgments on the issues in the field of secondary education. If decisions concerning secondary schools are based on principles such as these, youth will find a greatly enriched program in their schools. The practices in secondary schools discussed in the rest of this book will be evaluated by the principles presented here. Students in teacher education classes are urged to examine school practices critically. It is not intended that anyone should accept these principles as his point of view without questioning them. In fact, it is hoped that all those who read this book will examine them on the basis of what they already know and can discover about the behavioral sciences and democratic principles.

PRINCIPLES OF TEACHING-LEARNING

The S-R bond theory of learning, the theory that learning takes place through establishing in the neural system a bond or connection between a specific stimulus and its response, is generally regarded as an oversimplification of the learning situation. Students of learning have expanded research into areas broader than the stimulus-response concept can describe. The organismic theory, which stresses that the whole organism reacts to stimuli in its environment, has contributed much to understanding the learning process in school situations.

Whether emphasis on rote learning resulted from the application of the stimulus-response bond theory, or from a misinterpretation of the theory, as some psychologists claim, makes little difference. This theory of learning has not fostered teaching-learning practices that result in effective learning of concepts and attitudes or in a real zest for learning. Many practices in schools today testify to this influence that has permeated secondary education. Both the critics and the proponents of modern secondary education, neither of which wants inefficient learning, can profitably examine these influences.

The influence of the organismic theory and recent research in learning is, however, increasingly evident in secondary schools. Examples of good practices described in this book indicate that teachers and administrators are applying a more functional concept of learning. The application of principles based on modern developments in the psychology of learning is found most frequently among teachers genuinely interested in keeping up with new developments in this field.

Throughout the text, "change of behavior" refers to changes in social skills, habits, attitudes, ideals and implicit mental activities, as well as in motor skills and overt, physical action. Changes in a pupil's conduct, his ways of meeting a situation, his understanding of a subject are examples of important changes that take place. These changes occur when a person is striving to attain his goals and is blocked in some way because his responses are inadequate to meet the new problem. Thus, the learning situation is essentially a problem-solving one. It is important to realize that learning is goal-seeking behavior, the result of the individual's working to achieve his goals.

The significant and lasting products of learning for living in a democratic society are attitudes, appreciations, skills, and understandings, not facts and information for their own sake. Facts are useful only as they form the basis for thinking through a plan, idea, or problem, or for understanding a process or event. By themselves they become as meaningless as nonsense syllables to the adult, or as words to the young child who has no experience background for understanding them. Used to clarify ideas or to substantiate a point, these bits of information become important factors in contributing to understandings. Studies show that learned generalizations, ability to make applications, and methods of solving problems are more permanent outcomes than factual information.

Teachers need to be concerned with "learnings" which, because they are understood and used, affect the behavior of young people. These are the attitudes that are built up toward people, things, or ideas; the appreciations or enjoyments of life; the understanding of life and man's attempt to control his environment and improve living conditions; the skills by which persons communicate, earn a living, or use tools of any kind. These are the only real learnings of value. The principles discussed here are concerned with the more lasting types of learning, not with those which have no permanence nor social significance.

The principles are stated in a form that may be readily applicable to teaching-learning practices, whether they be pupil-teacher, teacher-administrator, or school-community relationships. The following section is not intended to be a theoretical explanation of learning, but rather a statement of principles that can be used throughout the book as a basis for examining the secondary school in American society. A number of questions are raised to stimulate the student's thinking in regard to practices. In order to arrive at a further understanding of how people learn, the student may need to refer to other sources of information such as those listed in the bibliography for this chapter, which document these principles. It is important to understand that the principles are applied to a particular kind of social situation.

In any learning situation, the individual should accept the goals as worthy ones for him.

The purposes must be accepted by the learner as his own, not just someone else's purposes. The pupil should recognize the need for new ways of behaving and strive to change his behavior in certain ways. Just because the teacher has certain goals in mind does not mean that they are also the pupil's goals. What does this signify for school experiences of youth? Should the teacher alone make all the decisions as to how the group will proceed?

Untold amounts of a teacher's time and effort are spent in trying to get pupils to learn assignments which they do not see as important for them. How much more satisfactory it would be, and how much less time would be spent, if school tasks were related to youth's interests and needs! The interests and needs already existing and those that may be developed must be discovered and stimulated by the teacher. The real challenge is the expansion and broadening of interests and desire for knowledge.

If the goals are not accepted by the pupils, the learning will probably be incomplete and transitory. Such learning disappears as rapidly as items "crammed" for a final examination.

The learner should participate actively in the learning situation.

The laity show rather keen discernment of how learning takes place most effectively when they say, "Experience is the best teacher." High quality experiences for optimum learning involve maximum interaction between the person and his environment: people, written words, objects, living things, and ideas. These experiences do not need to be overt activity. If one is thinking, he is reacting to his environment. In judging a lecture or teacher-pupil planning as a learning experience, teachers need to determine how actively the individual is entering into the situation. In some classes the pupil copies verbatim, sees no purpose except to pass a test, listens half-heartedly, or engages in some other activity that interests him at the moment. There may be just as little intellectual stimulation in participation in a purposeless activity as there is in listening to a droning lecturer.

In observing high school classes, it is well to note the amount of goal-directed activity on the part of the pupils. Who does the participating, teacher or pupil? Is there any evidence of individual or small group activity, such as in a science laboratory? Are pupils given every opportunity to perform tasks or take charge of activities in the school day? Who profits most when the teacher always answers questions, reads notices, takes charge of room responsibilities, and makes decisions—the teacher or the pupils?

Learning experiences should be unified for the individual.

In a demonstration class of a state university summer workshop, the pupils had two consecutive classes in the same room. One class was English; the other was social studies. They were taught by different teachers. It was strikingly brought home to the observers that the pupils were often confused by the period or time barriers separating the two classes, since at times they did not recall which rules they had agreed upon for the particular class. The work was purposeful and related to their interests. The time divisions that represented a change of classes were artificial to them. If they had decided in the English class that they were to work on improving their speech, it was obviously ridiculous to forget about such a purpose when they were working on social studies problems.

Yet, in many schools, the barriers set up between classes are even more rigid and difficult to cross. Pupils may be told that "this is history; we are not concerned with literature." In taking principles of secondary education one hour and methods of teaching the next, is there unity for learning for the college student?

The unit organization of class experiences was devised to provide for unity in learning. Nevertheless, it is not uncommon to find a teacher talking about "unit teaching" when there is really no unity for the learner. There may be unity of content, but none whatsoever in the experiences that pupils have. Unity cannot be achieved without a concept of a clear, specific goal. In cases where there is real unity, there is no question of fear of treading on another department's or course's "territory." The teaching unit can only provide a means of facilitating unity and cannot assure a unified learning experience.

The individual has a desire for and an interest in gaining new ideas, developing new interests, acquiring new skills, and gaining knowledge that is new to him.

The normal adolescent—in the sense of one who is able to profit by formal education—is certainly not without interest in anything, as some teachers claim. The difficulty is that the teachers may have failed to develop the interests or to stimulate the learning of new interests. Teachers or student teachers who live with a youngster for a day on a camping trip, find that his joys, sorrows, and concerns stand out in bold relief. Every parent knows that young children have an insatiable curiosity and a desire to learn. Is this interest lost in the process of growing up?

Pupils are not easily interested if school work is repetitious and boring or has little meaning and relation to their past or present experiences or to clearly anticipated future needs. Effective learning takes place when they are no longer satisfied with a low-level performance. Teachers need to seek the kinds of experiences that present a challenge or fulfill a need. It may well be true, in the case of some young people, that school experiences have so conditioned them that they cannot enjoy activities in which the normal adolescent participates.

The learning products are many, since the individual responds as a totality in his learning.

The learning process involves many aspects of the individual's growth and development: physical, mental, social, emotional, and moral. Learning has no neatly classified pigeonholes, such as mathematics or science or civics. The feelings are brought along to the mathematics class. Even though the teacher may not be aware that attitudes are being formed, they are most certainly being learned. It is no secret to parents that a crabby, sarcastic teacher may contribute to their child's unhappiness more than to his understanding. Emotional blocks are severe handicaps to learning skills. How well can a pupil do in an examination when he has seemingly insurmountable worries?

One of the issues in the current debate concerning secondary education is whether or not the schools should be concerned with more than the intellectual development of the individual. Evidence from the field of psychiatry and mental hygiene indicate that teachers cannot afford the luxury of oversimplification of the extremely complex process of human growth. It is impossible to educate part of a child. The question is how to avoid unfortunate concomitant outcomes of learning activity.

Individuals differ markedly in their ability to learn.

Some pupils learn much more readily than others. Tests of intelligence and achievement have long indicated that individuals differ in rate and retention of learning. They vary considerably in how readily they learn abstract concepts or how they function in social situations such as getting along with others, conversing easily and making friends. Some may be able to acquire a high degree of skill in creativeness by use of brush, drawing pencil, or other art media. The ability of others can be highly developed along mechanical lines. Learning is a means by which the individual tends to push himself to his highest level of attainment, given a proper environment and encouragement.

It is indeed confusing for the student of education to hear advocated standards that all pupils are expected to meet, when it is a known fact that good instruction develops even greater differences among individuals. Standards should be individual, requiring a higher level if achievement from the most capable students and a lower level for the least capable. Requiring everyone to meet minimum standards, the same for all students, is a means of fostering mediocrity. The inconsistency of some practices in regard to ability grouping are readily apparent. Some schools group pupils according to ability and then continue to give each group the same type of experiences, the same books, and the same examinations. As puzzling to the uninitiated is the practice of having all thirty pupils in the same class use the same book, read the same stories, do the same exercises or problems.

Experiences are fruitful only when they have meaning for the learner.

Foreign languages are not really learned unless they become a part of the individual's means of communication. Being able to recite vocabulary meanings for a test and forgetting them the next week is not the kind of learning with which schools ought to be concerned. An experience in apparently meaningless diagraming of sentences or in the memorization of a grammatical rule may be confusing and irritating to a pupil who neither understands what he is doing nor sees any reason for doing it.

This is a rather obvious principle; yet, pupils do many tasks that to them do not make sense. They may prepare reports on the Industrial Revolution from encyclopedias or reference books too difficult for them to understand. As a result, most of the material is copied from the reference. What is the learning in such a case? Are these experiences fruitful in developing attitudes and understandings needed in our society? Are geometry theorems which are not really understood by pupils learned when they are memorized?

Learning results in changed behavior that can be discerned by the skillful teacher, whether it be understanding the most abstract ideas and relationships or adjusting to a difficult interpersonal situation.

Individuals learn most effectively when, by reason of their stage of development and previous experiences, they are mature enough to profit by the new experiences.

Young children who are forced to learn to read before they are ready for that new experience may develop maladjustments that often become serious handicaps in developing reading skills. Experiential background must be built up before formal reading begins. The same principle applies to older pupils. Consider the skills required for self-control. Are they acquired by giving a new freedom to pupils who have never had any experience in self-direction? Can cooperation be practiced by a secondary school group that has had no opportunity to use this skill in previous years? Maturation of the individual has a great deal to do with readiness to learn not only physical skills such as walking but also skills and understandings in other areas.

Trying to force pupils to learn beyond their present capabilities produces abnormal behavior, frustration, and tensions instead of producing early learning or acceleration of the process. In other words, the learning outcomes may be quite different from those desired. What does this mean with regard to the inauguration of a plan of student government? What does it mean as to the grade level at which certain concepts and skills should be taught? Is there any such thing as seventh-grade maturity?

Learning takes place only when a person is not threatened.

Fear is the antithesis of rational thought. No one can think clearly when he is threatened either by physical harm, by disease, or by inner fears that tend to disorganize his personality. Yet, threat is frequently used by teachers. They often impose upon the student the fear of failure as a stimulus to learning.

Moreover, when a person feels threatened, the range of ideas or facts that he considers significant narrows considerably. He develops what some call "tunnel vision." What he can perceive in a situation is constricted, for the elements that cause the fear unduly occupy his mind. Consequently, his learning is handicapped just as surely as if he were emotionally upset by some real or imagined crisis in his life.

Learning is unique to the individual.

Many studies of perception carried on in recent years indicate that a person's perceptions relate very definitely to his behavior. Experiences that a pupil has must have personal meaning of some kind in order to affect his behavior. Each person perceives a situation in terms of his own background, purposes, and needs. His behavior is the result of how things seem to him, his perceptions. He behaves in terms of his concepts of both himself and others. A teacher who thinks of himself as a taskmaster will behave quite differently from one who perceives himself as a guide and a facilitator of learning. These studies show, too, that a person's concept of himself may be quite different from the way others perceive him.

The learning situation should provide for continuity of experience.

Only if by previous experience a pupil is prepared for a new experience can there be any continuity *for him.* School systems often spend considerable effort to establish a sequential program of subject matter from grade level to grade level. Yet such a revision does not actually guarantee continuity. Is it reasonable to expect each of thirty or more different students to come out with the same level of understanding at the end of the year? Do courses of study built for the "average" pupil promote sequential growth from year to year for all pupils?

The principle that teachers should begin teaching a person where he is, rather than according to where they think he should be, is sound. In other words, at any stage, continuity can be provided for a student only if teachers build on what he has already learned, not on what he has "covered," for there is a tremendous difference between the two. Learning experiences need to be sequential, not merely repetitive. Programmed instruction through teaching machines endeavors to build such a sequence of learning.

Secondary school teachers sometimes blame elementary school teachers for pupil's lack of preparation; college teachers put the responsibility on secondary school teachers. When such remarks are made, do the teachers assume their responsibility for assisting the student? What does it show about their belief in how continuity can be obtained?

PRINCIPLES OF ADOLESCENT GROWTH

The nature, distinctive characteristics, and development of the adolescent boy and girl are of themselves no single guide to the content of the secondary school curriculum. But they are important criteria for determining the kinds of experiences that should be provided for youth in all facets of their school life. Almost any of the practices discussed in this book can be examined in the light of these principles of adolescent growth and development.

Important means of studying the adolescent to find out more about him include the investigation of research findings in adolescent psychology and the observation and study of adolescents in the classroom, playground, and home. Children can be understood only in relation to the culture in which they live. Fortunate indeed is the student preparing to be a teacher who has guided experience in the observation and study of elementary and secondary school pupils while studying about them.

It is assumed in this book that time will be spent in the teacher education program on this important phase of teacher preparation and that other references will be studied to achieve a more complete understanding of the adolescent. The authors have not attempted to include in the principles listed here all the facts about the adolescent's nature and growth, but rather have selected principles that they believe will serve to guide the teacher in his judgments.

No one of these principles appears as significant by itself as when seen in relationship to the others. When all are considered, far-reaching implications for the secondary school program become evident. What a secondary school looks like if all of the principles are applied effectively by the staff is one of the vital questions to be considered in subsequent chapters.

School experiences should recognize the adolescent's striving to achieve independence and adult status as a normal phase of growing up.

A normal part of growing up is the desire to gain independence from the family in matters of dating, money, dress, and other life activities. The adolescent wants to make decisions for himself. Often this desire may result in rebellion against interference with his plans or revolt against authority. For him it is a period of conflict in more than one way, since he is torn between loyalties to his friends and to his parents. Although this is a fortunate aspect of natural development, some parents fail to recognize it as such. Witness the unhappy individuals who are still "tied to mother's apron strings" after reaching adulthood and suffer serious emotional conflicts in their efforts to disentangle themselves.

If a pupil is misunderstood both at home and at school—if his parents or teachers regard these manifestations of growth as deviltry or rank disobedience—his chances of attaining desirable growth in attitudes and emotions will be considerably lessened. Should the adolescent-parent relationship happen to be particularly strained or unnatural at this period, the pupil will need all the more sympathetic understanding at school. Can the teacher help the pupil toward a more responsible use of newly gained freedom? Of what value are pupil activities in providing the needed experience that gives youth a feeling of being adult? Should the teacher apply repression and punishment for the critical attitude that usually accompanies this period of growing independence? The way these questions are answered will make a considerable difference in the kinds of experience pupils have in class and extraclass activities.

School experiences should assist the adolescent in achieveing a desirable relationship with his age mates of both sexes.

Approval and acceptance by one's peers are powerful determiners of behavior of adolescents. At this age, status with peers is more important than adult approval. Young people will imitate each other in dress, speech, and mannerisms in order to be accepted by the group. An example of this manifestation can be seen in the development of high school fraternities and sororities in spite of school opposition to them. Unfortunately, cheating and lying may be ways selected as adjustments to a normal growth process, for the group feeling may be so strong that these actions become a way of protecting one's friends. Can school situations be planned to minimize opportunities for such behavior?

Social recognition, and consequently the development of social skills, become important to school experiences. The teacher in his classes and activities can make use of this group spirit and desire for acceptance. How can the teacher help in preventing the formation of antisocial groups of adolescents which defy acceptance by the group as a whole? What responsibility does the secondary school have for providing varied social activities that appeal to young people?

The desire for status with the opposite sex and the groping for ways of solving these new relationships should be of concern to the school. Showing off may be just a desire for gaining the attention of the opposite sex. The beginning teacher may be particularly disturbed by the interest of adolescents in obscene jokes, although this may be simply another manifestation of seeking prestige with their classmates. His concern should be the seeking of socially acceptable ways through which such prestige can be gained and, at the same time, school purposes forwarded.

The school program should help the adolescent make adjustments to his changing body.

The adolescent is likely to have abnormal fears and worries about the rapid changes in his body that occur during puberty. Uneven growth or failure to develop may cause him to worry about whether he is normal. These factors call for a straightforward discussion of sex and well-trained teachers who can help pupils over the rough spots by giving friendly advice.

The need for development of physical coordination and skills that assist youth in gaining social recognition furnishes an important guide in the planning of physical education experiences. Does the school make use of these deep-seated interests and important needs for assistance in development? Can the school afford to slight these important phases of an adolescent's development? Should they be left to the home? What relation does a healthy body and a wholesome attitude toward the body have to success in intellectual activities?

Educational experiences should give the adolescent a sense of security and satisfaction with his own development as a person.

It is essential for the pupil to succeed in something and to know that he is accepted in at least a few ways important to him. He should feel that there are some things which he can do better than others can. Constant failure is a terrible load for any personality to carry. The results often are unfortunate or tragic. Teachers need to ask themselves if the curriculum includes enough opportunities for every boy and girl to succeed, for the individual is best able to deal with difficulties in the future if he has been successful in the past.

Security is closely related to the need for affection and for belonging to certain groups, such as a club, social "set", or group of young people who do things together. How secure does a child feel if he see no evidence that anyone cares what happens to him? As the hub of the school's guidance program, what will be the teacher's responsibility in this respect? What responsibility will the teacher have for helping pupils become active in extraclass activities?

A part of the business of growing up involves the building of a personal philosophy, a basic evaluation of self as a physical and social being, as a person. Satisfaction with one's own development and one's relations to others helps to build the right kinds of attitudes toward life. How much responsibility should the beginning teacher feel for helping to build such a philosophy? Perhaps it may be one of the most important tasks for him.

The successful teacher understands that normal adolescent behavior is not necessarily desirable nor pleasing from the point of view of the teacher or the adult.

The high school teacher is often inclined to look upon shoving or shouting in the halls or aggressive behavior of any type as something "abnormal" for boys. In fact, it may be the most normal type of adjustment for a boy in his desire to be admired or noticed. If he is not given proper opportunities in class to be somebody in the eyes of his classmates, he may engage in activities that are neither constructive nor wholesome.

Adolescents may develop codes of behavior to demonstrate their defiance of adults, such as being noisy to disturb the teacher. Particularly is this true in cases where the class is dominated by the teacher and the pupils have no say in establishing codes to regulate their own behavior in class, study halls, or halls. How many teachers accept as normal growth phenomena, stubborn or "tough guy" behavior, hiding real feelings by acting in the opposite way, or using the classroom as a place for social experimentation? Do you agree with this statement: "Behavior is desirable if it is a natural and necessary part of the growth process"? What are the implications for evaluation of growth?

Teachers should face realistically the fact that an adolescent in his relations with the school and the outside world lives in a confusion of double standards.

The moral code of the police department in a large city may not be the same as the standards set by the church. Young people are confused by what they hear professed and what they see adults doing. Political "deals" are very different from the idealism set for behavior in the school. Parents' standards of conduct may differ from those taught at school.

What is the young person going to do? If the school is totally blind to these confusions in culture, what will he do? Should mature young people actually delve into the facts and get at the basic issues? If pupils are not given an opportunity to make choices based on facts, how well will they be able to face these confusions as they grow up? Every teacher needs to deal with the impact that such confused standards makes on the adolescent.

Every adolescent behavior problem has a cause or causes that the school may be helping to alleviate or to aggravate.

Behavior problems of pupils have a relationship to every phase of school life: experiences in class, extraclass activities, guidance, and student government. The class as a social group may hinder as well as facilitate and support learnings considered desirable by the school.

The whole concept of discipline has changed to one based upon the understanding of behavior. Each case is a problem in itself into which the teacher must probe to find the causes. Defiance, bullying, and truancy, are not signs of inherent meanness, but are symptoms of the real trouble. Teaching that permits shy, quiet youngsters to isolate themselves from the rest of the group does irreparable harm to those individuals, for they are the real problem cases. The whole area of mental hygiene has a direct bearing on progress in learning.

Unless a child experiences acceptance and understanding by an adult, his intellectual growth may be stunted. Psychiatrists point out that personal warmth of parent or teacher relieves the anxiety of a child. Thus, sympathetic understanding may help free the pupil's mind for intellectual activity.

Growing up is regarded as a total, unified process for the adolescent.

In more recent years, teachers have been interested in the concept of the "whole child." Particularly in the primary grades, a definite attempt has been made to plan experiences for children to develop their total personalities. Good teachers know that the process of growing up has unity.

Significant studies, such as those by Olson cited in the references, have supported the idea of unified growth. Different types of development have been traced, such as dental, mental, height and weight development, and ossification of the bones. When growth in these areas is translated into age equivalents and charted, the different growth lines follow about the same pattern in a well-adjusted child.

Adolescents vary in the rate at which they grow and their ultimate level of growth.

Adolescents of the same age and grade may be found to differ by as much as six to seven years in their progress as measured by standardized tests. They vary as to their stage of maturation, physically and psychologically. Pupils are not alike; what will help one learn will not necessarily help another. Yet, mass production methods are used to an overwhelming degree in secondary school instruction.

Everyone is unique in his manner of growth. He grows at his own rate; forcing or attempting to speed up the process beyond a certain point results in maladjustment. The teacher with this point of view of growth understands that it takes much more time for some pupils to develop to a certain degree than for others. Moreover, some can never reach the degree of development possible for others.

Uniform assignments, single textbooks, rigid schedules, and minimum essentials for all, are thus called into question. Educators ought to examine critically what is happening to adolescents who spend the same time during the day on the same type of materials because they constitute what is known as English I, American history, or algebra.

PRINCIPLES OF DEMOCRACY

The principles of the democratic way of life discussed here attempt to define what democracy actually means. It is not only a form of government, as some persons think. It is not a way of living that never changes. It is, instead, a set of principles guiding the relationships of the individual to the group in a society, large or small. These principles, or this manner of living, apply to the classroom as well as to the school, the community, the nation, or a group of nations.

Those who advocate a European system of education for the secondary schools of the United States show little understanding of the relationship of education to the type of society which it seeks to perpetuate. Freedom and equality of opportunity are concepts dependent upon a free public school system universally available to all people.

Many of the practices in secondary schools fail to measure up to the principles of a democratic society. Differences in interpreting the meaning of a democracy have contributed to the confusion in implementing democracy in the schools. Lack of clear thinking about what democratic principles mean in practice has resulted in the apparent contradictions between theory and practice.

Concepts of school administration derived from business management have pervaded staff organization and various administrative practices for the past three or four decades. Only in the more recent years has the idea of democratic leadership gained a foothold. More schools are using teacher committees to share in determining policy. Interest in the group process and the function of leadership in the group is gaining momentum. Genuine democratic leadership will be apparent in many of the school situations described in this book.

The authoritarian teacher has thrived in the former type of environment. It is difficult for democratic teacher-pupil relations to develop in an atmosphere of autocratic administrator-teacher relationships. However, an increasing number of teachers live up to the full meaning of democratic principles in their work with pupils. Yet, beginning teachers will be sadly disillusioned if they expect to go into almost any school on their first job and carry out democratic practices in the classroom without receiving some severe jolts from the attitudes of fellow teachers.

Every person is regarded as worthy of optimum development of his potentialities, and his importance and contributions to society are fully recognized.

What is happening to the thousands of pupils who drop out of school every year because of a lack of interest in school, failure in school work, or a desire to go to work as soon as possible? Have these young people been considered by their teachers as worthy of the fullest development of their potentialities? Approximately one-half of the high school graduates in the upper quartile as to ability do not go on to college, and consequently, may never make their optimum contribution to society. Follow-up studies show that many students below average in academic ability drop out before graduation because high school holds no challenge nor interest for them.

A look at the barren offerings in the curriculum of some secondary schools reveals that the possibilities for a number of pupils to develop their potentialities are extremely slight. For example, in a curriculum without art, music, shop work, or advanced classes in mathematics, science, or the humanities, what chance has a pupil with special interests and talents to develop his potential creativity?

School programs should be examined with a critical eye to determine if equality of opportunity exists for pupils of all races, social classes, nationalities, or religions. Only if the individual is accepted as a person, if everyone is considered as important, is such equality present. The barriers are not all based on discrepancies in the amounts of money spent for schools in different localities. Segregation, unsuitable instructional materials, and outdated curricula all are as effective in producing inequalities. Schools that offer a curriculum for the average student only do not offer each pupil his maximum possibility of development of his abilities. The idea that everyone gets an equal dose of education is a perversion of democratic principles. A few other practices that need to come under a critical scrutiny are academic barriers to entering interscholastic activities, election to membership in pupil organizations, and the usual concept of failure. To help pupils develop maximum potentialities, attention needs to be paid to adequate health services, including psychiatric, dental, and medical services.

Differences in opinions, abilities, and interests among individuals are recognized and accepted as desirable and normal.

Teachers need to understand that growth of individuals comes through encouraging differences and that these differences are most essential to a democracy. Specialized interests and abilities are fundamental to the innumerable types of pursuits with which people occupy their time in our society; they are fundamental to invention and progress. What little progress would be made if everyone thought alike! Yet, that is the very practice encouraged by teachers who test for the answers in the book.

Should there not be a choice of experiences for different pupils or groups of pupils within a class? If teachers really value differences, they will not be afraid to trust pupils to think for themselves, to criticize, and to help evaluate what the teacher and pupils are doing in the class.

One of the threats to American democracy, pointed out by sociologists, is the apparent value placed upon conformity. The suburban community dweller who owns two cars, has an outdoor fireplace, belongs to a service club, votes the accepted party ticket, and attends teas and cocktail parties, is no iconoclast. He likes to be comfortable and avoids, like a plague, radical points of view. A communist society, in a much more extreme form, places a premium upon conformity in political thought. The pioneers who settled this country were, above all, independent thinkers and rugged individualists. The pioneers of this space age, the scientist, inventor, the creative writer, or political genius, can best develop in a school which does not stress conformity in the realm of ideas.

A democratic society is characterized by an ever-widening concern and responsibility for the welfare of others and for the social consequences of one's acts.

This principle is concerned with the development of a realization that privileges entail corresponding responsibilities. Studies of secondary school pupils' opinions about democracy seem to indicate that they are far more concerned about their privileges than about their responsibilities. Living in a school community, just as in a larger community, demands subjecting individual wishes to the good of the group.

Self-control is acquired in an atmosphere in which ample opportunity is given to exercise it. Pupils must realize that they are actually responsible for the welfare of others in study halls, corridors, lunchrooms, and other areas of school living, through being delegated full responsibility for control and management. Too often student government is a mere sham in this respect. Are competitive marking systems and competition through contests consistent with this principle? Is an autocratic form of teacher discipline conducive to developing a realization of the social consequences of what individual pupils do?

The principle also refers to the extension of common concerns to other groups. If young people are sent to exclusive schools, will they be concerned about the social classes who live across the tracks? Can teachers do more about extending interests into the community through use of field trips and the study of real social problems in their own community? On a wider scale, a democratic society shows a concern for the underfed and underprivileged in all nations and for an extension of the ideal of freedom throughout the world. Consequently, the secondary school of such a society has an obligation through its practices and curriculum to help students understand others of different cultural and ethnic backgrounds and be willing to extend to others the same privileges and economic advantages which they enjoy.

In a democracy, the control comes from inside the group concerned, not from the outside.

Group participation in making policies and rules that affect individuals in the group is basic to our democratic freedoms. Our country was formed out of rebellion against autocratic measures. Fundamental to the liberty of any people is a right to participate in making rules for their own living.

It is not difficult to find out if this principle is violated in different phases of the life of a secondary school. Examine the relations between administrator and teachers. Do they, as a group, determine policies regarding aspects of teacher welfare? Do they share in setting administrative regulations, the framework within which instruction takes place? Examine the classroom. Are pupils and teachers planning together, setting up their purposes together? Do pupils participate in making rules for classroom conduct? How much do pupils have to say in the management of the school, in the formation of policies for social functions, school activities, hall traffic, and other matters of living in their school community? It is extremely doubtful if democracy functions unless practices measure up to this yardstick of democratic living.

The democratic method necessitates determining all the facts and arriving at intelligent decisions cooperatively.

If a democracy is to function, people must have the attitude of inquiring critically into questions and problems of civic life. All sides of the question are examined and the decision is based on facts. Is this method of scientific thinking stressed in secondary school classes in social studies or science? Is there independent and group investigation of problems by students, a critical attitude in class discussions, and a readiness to defer judgments until all the facts are discovered?

The method of intelligence applied to problems is imperative in a secondary school program if it is to perform its function of developing competent citizens. What is happening in some schools regarding controversial issues? Can high school classes study about communism, about segregation, or about any heated issue without criticisms from some sources? Do pressure groups frighten teachers away from a frank and open consideration of social problems? Do social studies classes investigate what is happening in American life today because of fear and intimidation? Do they study school issues and local problems?

Future teachers need to be militant about freedom to express one's beliefs and to make inquiries without fear or reprisal. Even though community pressures against such open discussion are great, teachers can help students to question, to see what is happening in analagous situations comparable to their own, and to understand what repression means to the democratic way of life. Moreover, there are problem areas in which teachers can help students to take social action for the good of the school or community.

SUMMARY

Principles which can serve as guides to judging secondary school practices and the experiences pupils have in secondary schools have been presented in this chapter. It would be unfortunate, indeed, if these principles were regarded as points to be learned for a course in which this text is used. The principles are not the final word. They represent some guideposts for thinking through the problems and practices in secondary education, derived from information on how people learn, on adolescent growth and development, and on the democratic way of life. They draw upon data more extensively discussed in the following chapters of this section of the book. It is hoped that students will develop other principles throughout their study and investigation of the secondary school in this country, of its purposes, its nature, and its effectiveness as related to present-day society.

These principles are used as a means of evaluation of practices. Each chapter dealing with practices, in turn, lists further specific principles that apply particularly to the subject discussed. The most important outcome of the study of this book, and of others which may differ in point of view, should be the formation of a set of values or principles which students of education accept and will use as their own when they serve as teachers in secondary schools.

SELECTED REFERENCES

ASSOCIATION FOR SUPERVISION AND CURRICULUM DEVELOPMENT. *Fostering Mental Health in the Schools* (1950 Yearbook). Washington, D.C.: National Education Association, Chaps. 1, 6, 7.—These readable chapters on conditions of good mental health and the developmental tasks and their implications for the school are especially pertinent.

ASSOCIATION FOR SUPERVISION AND CURRICULUM DEVELOPMENT. *Human Variability and Learning*. Washington, D.C.: National Education Association, 1961, pp. 1-13 and 50-61.—These two sections of a useful pamphlet point out the different kinds of variability and their meanings for education and the relations between the individual learner and the classroom group.

ASSOCIATION FOR SUPERVISION AND CURRICULUM DEVELOPMENT. *Learning and the Teacher* (1959 Yearbook). Washington, D.C.: National Education Association, Chaps. 2, 3, 8.—Applications of what is known about learning to teaching. These particular chapters discuss how personality, experiences, and environment affect learning; the control the teacher exercises over learning.

ASSOCIATION FOR SUPERVISION AND CURRICULUM DEVELOPMENT. *Learning More about Learning*. Washington, D.C.: National Education Association, 1959, 88 pp.—The sections of this pamphlet dealing with personality theory, and its implications for learning, and perception give new insights into this area.

BERNARD, HENRY W. *Adolescent Development in American Culture*. New York: Harcourt, Brace & World, Inc., 1957, Chap. 2.—This chapter is especially pertinent; discusses principles of development.

BURTON, WILLIAM H. *The Guidance of Learning Activities*. New York: Appleton-Century-Crofts, Inc., rev. ed., 1952, Part I.—An excellent older reference on the application of principles of learning to the classroom, modern in its point of view and practical in its application.

EDUCATIONAL POLICIES COMMISSION. *Policies for Education in American Democracy*. Washington, D.C.: National Education Association, 1946.—Books I and II, published previously as separate bulletins, are most helpful references on the nature of the democratic way of life and its application to our society.

NATIONAL SOCIETY FOR THE STUDY OF EDUCATION. *Learning and Instruction* (Part I, Forty-Ninth Yearbook). Chicago: University of Chicago Press, 1952, 352 pp.—One of the older complete summaries of information on how children learn and on the application of these principles to instruction.

OLSON, WILLARD C. *Child Development*. Boston: D. C. Heath & Co., 2nd ed., 1959, Chaps. 1, 2, 7-9.—Written from the organismic and developmental point of view of growth. Deals with both children and adolescents. Stresses implications for the school situation. Contains significant studies on growth.

PRESCOTT, DANIEL A. *Factors that Influence Learning*. Pittsburgh: University of Pittsburgh Press, 1958, 77 pp.—The biological, emotional, and cultural factors that influence learning, written from a wealth of knowledge in field of human development.

STANLEY, WILLIAM B. AND OTHERS. *Social Foundations of Education*. New York: The Dryden Press, Inc., 1956, Chap. 8.—The democratic tradition and its meaning discussed by a number of prominent authors.

2

HISTORY OF THE AMERICAN SECONDARY SCHOOL

The secondary school of today had its beginnings during the colonial period of American history, more than three hundred years ago. During its early years it was influenced greatly by our European heritage, especially that of the English colonists. This was only natural because the educational system which was familiar to the Americans was that with which they had previous contact in Europe. With the development of social, economic, and political institutions that were more distinctly American, the educational system likewise changed to meet the needs of the people in this new country. An understanding of the secondary schools which served American youth of past generations is essential to any study of the secondary school as it exists in the United States today. It is the purpose of this chapter to describe the early secondary schools in America and their influence on the program of secondary education in existence today.

EUROPEAN INFLUENCES

THE FIRST SECONDARY SCHOOL. Early in the development of the American colonies it became apparent that some kind of organized program which would provide for education beyond the fundamental skills was necessary to prepare competent leaders for church and state. The colonists looked to England for the institution which would serve this purpose. With the English Latin grammar school as its prototype, the Boston Latin School, established in 1635, became the first secondary school in the American colonies. In Massachusetts, Charlestown and Salem quickly followed the example of Boston, while in Connecticut, Latin grammar schools were soon established in New Haven and Hartford. In the next few years,

24

other communities established Latin grammar schools, until by 1700 there were at least twenty-seven in New England alone.

The early Americans, however, did not intend to leave the education of children to the whim of their parents. Especially in Massachusetts, steps were taken early in the history of the colony to encourage the education of children and youth. In 1642 the Massachusetts Bay Colony recognized that many parents were neglecting the proper education of their children. It passed a law empowering local officers to find out whether parents and masters were teaching their children "to read and understand the principles of religion and capital laws of the country," and to fine those who failed to do so. This law was followed in 1647 by the "Old Deluder Satan Act," the first general school law enacted in the American colonies, which was concerned with both elementary and secondary education and which placed on the town rather than the parents and masters the responsibility for the education of children. The Massachusetts Law of 1647 provided that "it being the object of that old deluder, Satan, to keep men from the knowledge of the Scriptures," each town of at least fifty householders shall appoint someone to teach children to read and write, and each town of at least one hundred householders "shall set up a grammar school, the master thereof being able to instruct youth so far as they may be fitted for the university." The Law of 1647 imposed a penalty upon the town for failure to comply with the provisions of the law. The Massachusetts Law of 1647 was followed by a similar law in Connecticut in 1650, and it served as a guide for early laws on education in other colonies as well.

The first laws in the colonies which required the community to provide schools for the education of children and youth were not popular and were not well enforced. As late as 1700, there were many towns in Massachusetts alone which, though they were large enough, failed to provide secondary schools as directed by the Law of 1647. The fine for failure to comply with the law was increased in 1671 and again in 1683, but without satisfactory results. Furthermore, it should be recognized that the purpose of the early school laws was primarily religious rather than secular. Children were to be taught to read so they could read the Scriptures, while the Latin grammar school was designed to prepare youth for college, and ultimately for positions of leadership in church and state. Even so, the early laws on education passed by Massachusetts and other colonies revealed a recognition of the importance of education and set forth the responsibility of the community to provide for the education of children and youth through the secondary school.

CURRICULUM OF THE LATIN GRAMMAR SCHOOL. The Latin grammar school in America, like that in England from which it descended, offered instruction in Latin and Greek, with particular emphasis on teaching boys to read and write Latin. Since the early colleges based admission of boys primarily on their skill in Latin, the curriculum of the Latin grammar school, limited as it was, served the purpose for which the school was established. For instance, the admissions requirements for Harvard in 1643 stated that "a student should be able to understand Cicero, or a similar classical author, extempore, to make and speak Latin verse and prose, and to decline the Greek nouns and verbs."

Upon leaving the Latin grammar school, the boy "was usually ignorant of numbers, and was usually unable to write English with any degree of fluency or accuracy. He was, however, well schooled in the Latin tongue and usually, in the last years of the course, in the elements of Greek as well." That the curriculum of the Latin grammar school changed little over a period of many years is evident from the description of one offered in the Boston Latin School in 1712:

At that time the first three years were spent upon the elements of Latin, the declensions, conjugations, simple agreements, and vocabulary. In the fourth year Erasmus' *Colloquies* and Ovid were read. In the fifth year, these were continued and Cicero's *Epistles* were added. Cicero, Ovid, Lucius Florus, and Virgil were added in the sixth year. And in the seventh and last year a whole flock of authors, for the first time including Greek writers, were read.[1]

In other respects, also, the Latin grammar school was much different from the secondary school of today. The school day was long, often beginning at seven o'clock in the morning during the summer months, and eight o'clock in the winter, and extending to four or five o'clock in the afternoon, with a long noon intermission. The school building was sometimes built by the town, but often school was held in the home of the master. Some of the teachers were competent, but many belonged to a miscellaneous group, inadequately prepared, who taught school to keep from starving. The schools were attended only by boys, usually from the more prosperous families because tuition was charged. Pupils were very young compared with those in the secondary school today, being admitted at age seven or eight and leaving for college at fourteen or fifteen.

DEMISE OF A EUROPEAN INSTITUTION. Although the Latin grammar school may have been appropriate in European countries, it

[1] H. G. Good, *A History of American Education*, New York: The Macmillan Co., 1956, p. 56.

never was suited to the needs of youth in the American colonies. It was, furthermore, never popular among the American people. There were a number of reasons for this. The Latin grammar school was intended primarily for youth going to college, at a time when the college curriculum itself was designed especially for youth who planned to enter the ministry. The extreme emphasis on Latin grammar was not in harmony with the more practical demands of the kind of society which was developing in America. It catered to the "better" families, it made no provision for the education of girls, and in other ways it excluded a large part of the youth in a country where equal opportunity for all was emphasized.

The decline of the Latin grammar school in America began early in the eighteenth century. Its disappearance was by no means abrupt, since there were Latin grammar schools, especially in New England, throughout much of the eighteenth century. However, by the end of the eighteenth century the Latin grammar school had almost disappeared. It was rapidly replaced by other schools whose origin was more distinctly American and which were better suited to the needs of the times.

AN EARLY AMERICAN INSTITUTION

FRANKLIN'S ACADEMY. It was indeed appropriate that the first secondary school designed especially for the needs of American youth should have been introduced by Benjamin Franklin. Although there were other early schools which were called academies, Franklin's Academy in Philadelphia, which began instruction in 1751 with three organized departments—the Latin School, the English School, and the Mathematical School—is usually considered the first academy to have been established in America. Others followed rapidly. In Massachusetts, Dummer Academy opened for instruction in 1763 and Phillips Academy in 1780. Newark Academy in New Jersey opened in 1775 and Phillips Exeter in New Hampshire in 1783. By 1830 there were 950 incorporated academies in the United States, and by 1850, when interest in the academy was at its height, there was a total of 6085 for the entire United States, with more than 263,000 pupils enrolled. While the development of the Latin grammar school was limited largely to New England, the academy gained a firm hold throughout the eastern half of the United States, with many in New York, Pennsylvania, Massachusetts, Kentucky, Virginia, North Carolina, and Tennessee.

The academy was essentially a private school, many of them endowed by gifts or estates left by a will, while others were established by popular subscription from interested citizens. Practically all of the early academies charged tuition fees. The administration of the academy was usually in the hands of a private board of trustees which held corporate powers through a charter given by the state and was not responsible to the public. For some academies, members of the board of trustees were elected by citizens in the local community, often holding office for life, but in other cases the board was a self-perpetuating one, with the board itself electing members as vacancies occurred. As compared with the Latin grammar school, the academy in its administrative control was a private rather than a public institution, although in some states academies received financial aid from the state. In the East, they were attended only by boys, with similar schools called seminaries for the girls, but in the West some academies were coeducational.

BROADER OBJECTIVES. Franklin's Academy, as well as the others which followed it, was clearly established to provide a broader and more practical educational program than that which was being offered in the Latin grammar school of that time. Franklin's proposals for an academy suggested that it would be well if the students "could be taught everything that is useful, and everything that is ornamental." But since time limited what could be taught, he urged that "they learn those things that are likely to be most useful and most ornamental; regard being had to the several professions for which they are intended."

Franklin proposed that all students be taught penmanship, drawing, arithmetic, bookkeeping, geometry, astronomy, and the English language. The greatest stress was to be placed on English, with much reading of English authors. History, likewise, was to have an important place, as well as natural history, agriculture, commerce, industry, and mechanics. Franklin would have made this academy an English school. He yielded, however, to men of wealth and learning whose cooperation was needed, and included both ancient and modern languages. But the study of foreign languages was to be optional, with students selecting those which might be most useful in their respective professions.

It was Franklin's intention that the academy should offer a broad program with emphasis on English and other practical studies which would suit the needs of youth who were not going to college, as well as to prepare youth for college. It was not long, however, before the classical offerings dominated the curriculum in many academies. Since the academy absorbed the college-preparatory function of the

Latin grammar school, the growth in influence of the classical studies was to be expected. In any case, with the decline of the Latin grammar school by 1800, the academy became the college-preparatory school for the youth of that time.

The nature of the total curriculum in the academy of the early nineteenth century is revealed by the offerings at the Phillips Exeter Academy in New Hampshire in 1818:

Classical Department	English Department
Latin	Geography
Greek	Rhetoric and composition
Geography	Arithmetic
Composition	Geometry
Arithmetic	Algebra
Geometry	Declamation and forensic exercises
Algebra	History, U.S., ancient and modern
Declamation	Plane trigonometry
English grammar	Mensuration
History, Roman and ancient	Surveying
(Subjects grouped in four years,	Navigation
the last being parallel with the	Chemistry
first year of college)	Natural philosophy
	Moral philosophy
	Logic
	(Subjects grouped in three years)

CONTRIBUTIONS TO AMERICAN LIFE. The academy made a number of significant contributions to the development of secondary education in America. It was the first secondary school which was distinctly American both in its origin and purpose. Because of its immediate and widespread popularity, it demonstrated that Americans had the initiative and resourcefulness to develop educational institutions of their own, designed for the needs of youth in the democratic society which was emerging on this continent. Furthermore, with the decline of the Latin grammar school, the growth of the academy revealed a break with the influence of European traditions on American secondary education.

A significant contribution of the academy to American secondary education was its introduction of a broad program of education for youth who were pointing toward vocations other than the ministry, and which provided a place for both college- and non-college-bound youth. It gave status to English, rather than Latin, as the basic language for instruction in the American secondary school. The seminaries for girls in the East and South and the coeducational academies in the West provided for the extension of secondary education to girls as well as boys.

The academy also introduced and gave some respectability to

practical subjects, which earlier had no place in the Latin grammar school. It is true that the practical studies did not receive as much attention in the academy as Franklin had intended, but they were introduced in a sufficient number of academies to gain some recognition as a part of the program of secondary education. Science and mathematics, considered to be practical studies, also became an important part of the curriculum in the academy. The attention to English and the modern foreign languages was influenced by the practical value of these studies in business, foreign commerce, and government. Needlework, sewing, music, and art were taught in many of the early seminaries for girls, while surveying and bookkeeping were not uncommon studies in the academies for boys. The emphasis on history, including United States and modern history, was also a distinct departure from the curriculum offered in the Latin grammar school.

In the academy, there were also the beginnings of the extraclass activities which became such a significant part of the secondary school program a century or more later. The introduction of extraclass activities may have been influenced in part by the fact that the academy was often a boarding school, with the faculty responsible for the recreational activities of the students as well as their academic studies. The proposal for Franklin's Academy recommended sports activities, including "running, leaping, wrestling, and swimming." There was also much attention to the "art of speaking" with the offering of declamation and forensics, although these studies were often considered to be a part of the curriculum rather than extraclass activities.

A concern for the youth as a total personality therefore was a distinct contribution of the academy to American secondary education. This broad purpose of the academy was well expressed in the document setting forth the basis for the Phillips Academy at Andover, Massachusetts, in 1778, in which the donors proposed an "academy for the purpose of instructing youth, not only in English and Latin grammar, writing, arithmetic, and those sciences wherein they are commonly taught," but more especially in "the great end and real business of living." This broad purpose of secondary education in America, first set forth by the academy, has persisted to the present time.

DECLINE OF THE ACADEMY. In spite of its great contribution to the development of secondary education in America, the academy like the Latin grammar school had certain shortcomings. First, the academy was a private school, administered by a private board of trustees and financed largely by private rather than public funds. Although some were established as free academies, most of them required tuition fees of students to supplement income from endowments or public subscriptions. At a time in our history when family incomes were low, tuition fees made the academy a class institution, limited to the children of those who could afford it.

Second, although the academy originally was intended to offer a broad program to prepare youth for immediate entrance upon a vocation as well as for college, the college curriculum soon dominated the character of the entire academy. The reputation and prestige of individual academies were determined more by their college-preparatory programs than the practical studies which Franklin had considered so important. As a result, the practical studies offered by some of the early academies did not expand with the needs of the times, but in some schools actually declined.

The denominational character of the academy was a third undesirable characteristic of this institution in a country which came to emphasize the separation of church and state. Many academies were established by church groups and their programs were influenced by religious considerations. Academies established by individuals were also sometimes associated with a religious denomination, not in the admission of students, but in the qualifications for the headmaster and teachers and in the nature of the program of instruction. As the separation of church and state became a recognized policy in our governmental institutions, the denominational ties of academies were not as appropriate as in an earlier period.

The academy reached the height of its development in the decade before the Civil War, and thereafter declined rapidly in both numbers and influence. In the meantime, another secondary school had emerged in America which met some of the needs not served by either the Latin grammar school or the academy, and which soon replaced the academy in many communities.

PRESENT-DAY ACADEMIES. Although the popularity of the academy declined during the last half of the nineteenth century, unlike the Latin grammar school, it did not pass out of existence. Many academies continued to prosper and do so even to this day. Most of the academies which exist today serve primarily as college-preparatory schools, although some have programs for non-college youth as well. The academies today continue to be selective in their admission of students, both on the basis of scholarship and ability to pay tuition fees. Some of them are well-endowed, while others rely heavily on tuition fees for their incomes. They continue to be administered by a board of trustees which serves under a charter granted by the state. A few academies today are affiliated with religious denominations which contribute to their support. These academies are an important part of the program of secondary education, serving the needs of some youth more adequately than is possible in the public schools of their community.

In some communities, a private academy continues to serve as the only source of secondary education for youth. This is true especially in New England, where communities with well-established academies turned to the academy to provide secondary education for all youth, rather than build a public high school. Although these academies are administered by a private board of trustees, they accept all boys and girls who have completed the elementary school, with the board of education of the local school district paying the tuition fees. Usually a long-term contract between the academy and the board of education establishes the type of program of secondary education that is to be offered, the tuition fees to be paid by the board of education, and other conditions governing the relationship between the local school district and the academy. Although the number of academies which serve a community in this way is not large, some of them are making a significant contribution to the secondary education of youth.

The Norwich Free Academy, Norwich, Connecticut, established in 1856, with an enrollment today of more than two thousand pupils, is an example of an academy which provides for the secondary education of all youth in the community. It serves in every way as a public secondary school for the youth of Norwich, offering a broad educational program which includes college-preparatory, business, and general courses. The support of the Norwich Free Academy comes from income of endowed funds and tuition fees paid for the pupils by the board of education of the Town of Norwich. The curriculum, the extraclass activities, and the facilities of the Norwich Free Academy compare favorably with those of the better public secondary schools in New England. Except in its administrative and financial control, Norwich Free Academy serves youth much like any public high school.

THE PUBLIC HIGH SCHOOL

ESTABLISHMENT AND GENERAL PURPOSES. The first public high schools in the United States appeared during the period of most rapid growth and influence of the academy. For several decades these two institutions developed side by side, especially in the East, the public high school at first growing slowly, while the academy flourished and prospered. In some communities, however, it was evident early in the history of the academy that this institution did not serve all youth who desired education beyond the elementary school. It was in such communities that public high schools were first introduced, frequently with excellent academies also readily available.

It was indeed appropriate that Boston, where the first Latin grammar school was established, should also set an example to other communities by opening, in 1821, the English Classical School, as the first public high school was called. A year earlier a committee was appointed to study the advisability of establishing a secondary school which would provide a kind of education not offered in the academy. The purpose of the new school, as restated in 1833 in the *Regulations of the School Committee* (Boston), read as follows:

It was instituted in 1821, with the design of furnishing the young men of the city who are not intended for a collegiate course of study, and who have enjoyed the usual advantages of the other public schools, with the means of completing a good English education to fit them for active life and qualify them for eminence in private or public station.

At the beginning, therefore, the English Classical School was clearly intended for youth who did not plan to go to college. The school offered a three-year course for boys, who were required to be at least twelve years old and able to successfully complete an examination in reading, writing, English grammar, and arithmetic. The first public high school, like others for some years to come, therefore, had selective admission of pupils based on an examination administered by its faculty. The principal studies were English, declamation, science, mathematics, history, and logic, while no foreign language was to be offered. In 1824 its name was changed to English High School, which was perhaps suggested by a description of the High School at Edinburgh, Scotland, which appeared in an article in the *North American Review*, published in Boston, in January, 1824. Thus, the first free public high school made its appearance in America.

EARLY GROWTH. Other New England communities quickly followed the lead of Boston, with a high school established in Portland, Maine, in 1821; Worcester, Massachusetts, in 1824; and New Bedford, Salem, and Plymouth, all in Massachusetts, in 1827. In 1826, Boston also opened the first public high school for girls, but because there were so many applicants for admission that they could not be accommodated the school was abolished in 1828.

The Massachusetts Law of 1827 gave more encouragement to the early development of high schools in the United States than any other single event. This law required that a high school be established in every town in Massachusetts having five hundred families or more, and that the subjects should include United States history, bookkeeping, algebra, geometry, and surveying. The law specified further that any town with at least four thousand inhabitants should also offer instruction in Greek, Latin, history, rhetoric, and logic. The Law of 1827 not only formed the basis for other legislation on education in Massachusetts, but it also deeply influenced legislative action in other states.

It was not for long, however, that the curriculum of the public high school was limited to the English language and a program for youth who did not plan to go to college. The Massachusetts Law of 1827 went beyond such a limited curriculum when it required Greek and Latin to be taught in the larger towns. Some New England communities, notably Boston, offered the classical studies in a public Latin school, a continuation of the early Latin grammar school. But other communities early extended the curriculum of the public high school to include classical studies as well as the more practical subjects.

In spite of the tremendous interest in the public high school, its growth was slow until the Civil War. This was to be expected because the academy experienced rapid growth during the first half of the nineteenth century and did not reach its peak of development until the 1850's. Although in Massachusetts the Law of 1827 and subsequent laws required the towns to establish high schools, in most states only permissive legislation was passed. This legislation permitted the local community to decide whether it should establish a public high school and to determine the curriculum and standards of instruction. In some communities public high schools were established and later discontinued, usually because of the cost. In some New England communities where the Latin grammar school had continued from an earlier period, these schools were combined with the public high schools, thus offering a comprehensive program of secondary education in one school. The rapidly growing states in the Middle West and Far West showed much interest in the public high school, many of their cities establishing high schools during the 1840's and 1850's. However, by 1860 there were only 321 high schools in the entire United States, according to the *Report of the United States Commissioner of Education*, and more than half of these were in the three states of Massachusetts (78), Ohio (48), and New York (41).

GENERAL ACCEPTANCE OF HIGH SCHOOLS AFTER THE CIVIL WAR.
It was not until after the Civil War that the public high school became generally accepted as an essential and integral part of our
school system. The increasing demand by parents for better education for their children was one factor which, after the Civil War,
emphasized the need for public high schools. But there were others.
With the advent of the industrial revolution, opportunities for boys
to serve as apprentices to master-tradesmen declined. Other factors
favorable to the growth of public high schools after the Civil War
were higher family incomes, the decline in opportunities for suitable employment for children, the introduction in some states of
child labor laws, and the increased wealth for tax purposes of local
communities.

In many states, however, there were legal obstacles to the establishment of a high school by the community and its support by tax
funds. In some states the constitutionality of the public high school
or the taxation to support it was attacked in the courts. Such a case
in Michigan, commonly known as the Kalamazoo Case, attracted
wide attention not only in Michigan but in other states as well.
After the City of Kalamazoo, in 1872, voted to establish a public
high school and levied taxes for its support, one of its citizens
brought suit in the courts to prevent the collection of taxes for this
purpose. The Supreme Court of the State of Michigan, to which the
case was ultimately appealed, reviewed the educational legislation
of the State beginning with the first law on education passed in
1817. The Court concluded that there was no limitation on the
powers of the school district to provide instruction in the branches
of knowledge which their officers caused to be taught, or in the
grade of instruction, if their voters consented to bear the expense
and raise the taxes for the purpose. Similar cases were introduced
into the courts of other states. The decision in the Kalamazoo Case,
however, served as a precedent which was widely recognized and
led to the acceptance of the high school as a part of the public
school system in many other states.

After the Kalamazoo decision, public high schools were rapidly
introduced in many communities, especially in the North, the Middle West, and the West, though somewhat more slowly in the South.
The number of years included in the high school program varied at
first; it was usually three, four, or five years. By 1890 the idea of a
four-year school was generally accepted as the most desirable one.
By that time also the high school had become a recognized and accepted part of the public school system in all the states and was

then ready for the expansion in program, enrollments, and prestige which was to follow.

INTRODUCTION OF COMMERCIAL STUDIES. Although the high school's curriculum in its early years was extended to include offerings for college as well as for non-college students, by the close of the Civil War the only courses offered were the English and the classical, and in some schools an English-scientific and a general course. Both of the latter courses were really adaptations of the English course. The English, the English-scientific, and the general course were intended primarily for youth whose objective was immediate employment upon completion of high school, while the classical course was offered for college-bound youth. Some schools had extensive offerings in history, mathematics, science, modern foreign languages, and certain practical studies, but these were usually included as part of either the English or the classical course.

The introduction of commercial studies beginning in the 1880's constituted the first significant extension of the curriculum of the public high school. Although bookkeeping was offered in many of the early high schools, it was considered to be a part of the mathematics program. Some early high schools also offered other studies pointing toward the business vocations, such as the "mercantile" studies in the Boston English High School as early as 1823. It was not until after 1880, however, that serious attention was given to formulating a program of studies which was designed clearly to prepare youth for careers in business.

The expansion of the curriculum in the Springfield High School, Springfield, Massachusetts, is an example of the introduction of commercial studies in the 1880's. In 1885, the curriculum at Springfield was reorganized to include five courses—business, scientific, English, English-Latin, and classical. Although the business course was, in 1885, planned for the first time as a separate course, the only business studies offered were bookkeeping and commercial arithmetic, in addition to such general studies as English, mathematics, history, science, and mechanical drawing. In the revised program of 1885, "optional" studies also appeared for the first time in the Springfield High School curriculum, not only in the business course, but in other courses as well. The offering of mechanical drawing as a required subject in the business course was also unique to this program.[2] The business course offered by Springfield High School

    2 Gladys A. Midura, "A Critical History of Public Education in Springfield, Massachusetts," Unpublished Doctoral dissertation at the University of Connecticut, Storrs, Conn., 1961, pp. 414-20.

at the beginning was only a two-year course, as compared with four years for the other courses.

In the next decade few changes were made in the commercial course at Springfield High School, and for a short time it was actually discontinued. In 1896, however, an expanded three-year commercial course was introduced, which included bookkeeping, shorthand, and typewriting. In 1899, such courses as economics, industrial history, commercial law, commercial geography, office practice, and business correspondence were added to the commercial course, and it was recommended that pupils take four years to complete it. By 1899, Springfield High School had a broad business course which resembled those offered in public high schools today.

School systems other than Springfield introduced business programs before 1900. In 1898, Central High School of Philadelphia established a separate commercial school with a distinct curriculum to prepare youth for business vocations, and New York, Pittsburgh, Chicago, and Washington soon followed. By 1900, a well-organized commercial curriculum, which gave pupils both general education and specific preparation for business vocations, was considered to be an essential part of the total program of the public high school in the United States.

EXPANSION OF OTHER OFFERINGS. The late nineteenth century saw the introduction and expansion of other curricular offerings in the public high schools in many communities. The industrial revolution emphasized the need for skills in industry, and so encouraged the introduction of "manual-arts" or "manual-training" courses in the public high school. St. Louis, Cleveland, Baltimore, Toledo, Cincinnati, Philadelphia, and Omaha were among the cities which offered manual arts in high schools before 1890. In 1894, Massachusetts passed a law which required all cities with a population of thirty thousand or more to provide manual training in high schools. The early manual-training programs were intended to teach youth basic skills in the manual arts, as they were then called, rather than to develop specific vocational skills.

Springfield, Massachusetts, one of the leaders in the offering of "manual-training" courses, provides an example of these early programs. In September, 1886, a manual-training school was opened in Springfield on an experimental basis. It was a success from the start. It began as a two-year course, but by 1888 it was extended to four years. In addition to academic studies—English, science, and mathematics—the manual-training course included such subjects as carpentry, patternmaking, wood turning, filing, forging, brazing, soldering, and the use of machine-shop tools.[3] The manual-training program in Springfield, as in other communities, later developed into industrial-arts, technical-school, and trade-school programs.

With the development of industrial-arts programs for boys, offerings in domestic arts or domestic science, as the first homemaking courses were called, were introduced for girls. The Philadelphia High School for Girls offered courses in sewing in 1880; Toledo, Ohio, in 1886, introduced sewing, cooking, dressmaking, and millinery in its high schools; and Indianapolis included cooking, dressmaking, millinery, and art in its manual-training high school, established in 1889. By 1900, domestic-arts courses, like those in manual arts and business were accepted as an important part of the curriculum in public high schools in the United States.

The programs of public high schools late in the nineteenth century offered, in addition to courses in commercial, manual arts, and domestic arts, numerous other studies to give youth a broad program of secondary education. Among these were physical education, music, art, geography, and civics. Penmanship and spelling, usually considered today to be elementary-school studies, were also offered in many early high schools. By 1900, therefore, the program of the public high school in America was an exceedingly broad one, including instruction in the fundamental skills and knowledge, in college-preparatory studies, in some vocational subjects, and in numerous cultural subjects to prepare youth for better living.

INTRODUCTION OF PUPIL ACTIVITIES. In the public high schools, the extraclass activities, first introduced into the academy, were expanded and accepted as an important part of the total program of secondary education. In the early years of the public high school, attention was given especially to declamation, oratory, and dramatics. There were also sports activities in the early high schools, though not on the formal basis on which they are organized today.

Late in the nineteenth century, extraclass activities developed on the more extensive scale which has persisted in most high schools to the present time. Interscholastic athletic teams were formed in numerous sports. Springfield High School, for instance, in the fall of 1891, played football games with the teams of several neighboring high schools. In 1895, it had a baseball team which defeated most of its competitors, and by 1897, it had a Springfield High School Athletic Association, whose purpose was to promote sports

3 Midura, op. cit., p. 156.

activities. Before 1900, Springfield High School had interscholastic teams in basketball, football, baseball, polo, and track.[4]

School publications appeared in many high schools late in the nineteenth century, including yearbooks, papers, and literary periodicals. Debating societies, numerous clubs, and fraternities flourished. Secret societies were organized in many schools, and were soon deplored by teachers and parents. There were also social functions, sometimes on quite an elaborate scale. In at least one school, the social activities were discontinued in 1894 by direction of the school authorities because they were considered to be too expensive for all youth to participate, though they were renewed two years later. Student assemblies were held in many schools, and music programs, operettas, and dramatics productions were common. At the close of the school year, many high schools had class-day exercises, senior promenades, and graduation exercises. By 1900, the program of extraclass activities in many high schools was as broad as those which we find in our schools today.

CHANGES IN PRACTICES. Besides the changes in the curriculum and extraclass activities, there were many other developments in the public high schools by the end of the nineteenth century. During the first fifty years of its history, the public high schools admitted pupils from the elementary school only upon satisfactory performance on examinations administered by the high school faculty. By 1900, these admissions examinations were discontinued by most high schools and pupils were admitted upon the recommendation of their elementary school teachers.

In the early high schools all subjects were prescribed for a particular course. Once a pupil had chosen a course, he followed the pattern of required subjects, with no opportunity for elective courses as we know it today. However, in the late 1800's many high schools introduced more flexibility into their programs, with some elective offerings available. Usually the electives were quite limited, with pupils having a choice of only one or two subjects. But in some schools special courses were developed to give pupils broader programs, such as a combined English-Latin course or an English-scientific course. Some schools went even further and encouraged pupils who were enrolled in one course to elect studies listed in others, as in one school where pupils enrolled in the English or the classical course could elect typing or bookkeeping from the commercial course. Although the extensive offerings of elective subjects in most high schools were developed during the present century,

[4] Midura, *op. cit.*, p. 153.

the elective system by 1900 was recognized as a desirable practice.

The methods of teaching in some subjects were also modified by the close of the nineteenth century. That was especially true of the sciences. In the early high schools, the teacher and the textbooks, such as there were, served as the basis for the lecture-recitation activity that predominated in most classrooms. By the late 1800's, however, some high schools had begun to develop laboratories for experimental work in the sciences, especially in physics and chemistry. Although these facilities were quite limited in most schools, they were the beginnings of the more adequate laboratory facilities and equipment that have been provided in many of our high schools in recent years.

The lack of uniformity in the offerings of the public high schools in the United States was one of the annoying problems as this school developed, especially for the colleges and universities which had to examine the high school programs of students who applied for admission. This problem, and others related to college admission, led to the appointment in 1892 by the National Education Association of the Committee of Ten on Secondary School Studies, with Charles W. Eliot, president of Harvard University, as chairman.

In its report, presented in 1893, the Committee of Ten, as it is usually called, recommended that the numerous short courses which the public high school had adopted from the academy should be combined into fewer courses, each to be taught for a longer period of time; it made recommendations concerning the content that it considered appropriate for each of the high school subjects and suggested time allotments for each; and it recommended that the completion of high school courses should be measured in terms of a unit based on the amount of time devoted to a subject. Although the Committee of Ten was primarily concerned with those subjects which pupils might take as preparation for college, it had considerable influence in bringing about some uniformity in all high school courses, in improving the standards for the various subjects, and in pointing the way toward agreement on the unit of credit which later was accepted as the basis for measuring the work a pupil had completed in high school.

In the early years of the public high school there was considerable variation from school to school in the length of the program leading to graduation. Furthermore, within the same school courses also varied in length, with the commercial course sometimes two years long, the scientific course three years, and the English and the classical course four years. By 1900, four years was the usual length of time required to complete courses in most high schools of the United States.

In many respects, therefore, the administrative organization, the curriculum, and the extraclass activities of the public high school in the United States were well established by the late nineteenth century. Although there have been some administrative and curricular changes since that time, the high school program in the present century has been largely an expansion and further development of that which pertained about 1900.

GOALS STATED BY NATIONAL COMMITTEES. A historical study of aims of the secondary school would reveal a number of statements by educators. The best known of these, which has undoubtedly had significant influence on American secondary education, is the *Cardinal Principles of Secondary Education*, published in 1918 by the Commission on the Reorganization of Secondary Education, previously appointed by the National Education Association. The seven objectives of education formulated by the Commission were:

1. Health
2. Command of fundamental processes
3. Vocation
4. Worthy home membership
5. Citizenship
6. Worthy use of leisure
7. Ethical character

The Commission recommended several principles to carry out these objectives, some of which read as though they had been written today instead of more than thirty years ago. While the Commission made some attempt at interpreting these principles, it did not go far in translating them into educational practice or learning outcomes.

Twenty years after the publication of the *Cardinal Principles of Secondary Education*, the Educational Policies Commission of the National Education Association formulated a useful, easily understood statement of the purposes of education in American democracy. The Educational Policies Commission is a deliberative body of well-known educators appointed by the N.E.A. to consider general policies in American education. *The Purposes of Education in American Democracy*, published in 1938, was one of its important statements on the functions of education in our society.

The objectives of education formulated by the Commission are grouped under four headings, those of self-realization, human relationships, economic efficiency, and civic responsibility. The use-fulness of this statement lies in the fact that each of these objectives is defined in terms of what the educated person who lives up to these goals is like. The following lists the Commission's description of the educated individual:

THE OBJECTIVES OF SELF-REALIZATION

The Inquiring Mind. The educated person has an appetite for learning.
Speech. The educated person can speak the mother tongue clearly.
Reading. The educated person reads the mother tongue efficiently.
Writing. The educated person writes the mother tongue effectively.
Number. The educated person solves problems of counting and calculating.
Sight and Hearing. The educated person is skilled in listening and observing.
Health Knowledge. The educated person understands the basic facts concerning health and disease.
Health Habits. The educated person protects his own health and that of his dependents.
Public Health. The educated person works to improve the health of the community.
Recreation. The educated person is participant and spectator in many sports and other pastimes.
Intellectual Interests. The educated person has mental resources for the use of leisure.
Aesthetic Interests. The educated person appreciates beauty.
Character. The educated person gives responsible direction to his own life.

THE OBJECTIVES OF HUMAN RELATIONSHIPS

Respect for Humanity. The educated person puts human relationships first.
Friendships. The educated person enjoys a rich, sincere, and varied social life.
Cooperation. The educated person can work and play with others.
Courtesy. The educated person observes the amenities of social behavior.
Appreciation of the Home. The educated person appreciates the family as a social institution.
Conservation of the Home. The educated person conserves family ideals.
Homemaking. The educated person is skilled in homemaking.
Democracy in the Home. The educated person maintains democratic family relations.

THE OBJECTIVES OF ECONOMIC EFFICIENCY

Work. The educated producer knows the satisfaction of good workmanship.
Occupational Information. The educated producer understands the requirements and opportunities for various jobs.
Occupational Choice. The educated producer has selected his occupation.
Occupational Efficiency. The educated producer succeeds in his chosen vocation.
Occupational Adjustment. The educated producer maintains and improves his efficiency.
Occupational Appreciation. The educated producer appreciates the social value of his work.
Personal Economics. The educated consumer plans the economics of his own life.

Consumer Judgment. The educated consumer develops standards for guiding his expenditures.

Efficiency in Buying. The educated consumer is an informed and skillful buyer.

Consumer Protection. The educated consumer takes appropriate measures to safeguard his interests.

THE OBJECTIVES OF CIVIC RESPONSIBILITY

Social Justice. The educated citizen is sensitive to the disparities of human circumstance.

Social Activity. The educated citizen acts to correct unsatisfactory conditions.

Social Understandings. The educated citizen seeks to understand social structures and social processes.

Critical Judgment. The educated citizen has defenses against propaganda.

Tolerance. The educated citizen respects honest differences of opinion.

Conservation. The educated citizen has a regard for the nation's resources.

Social Application of Science. The educated citizen measures scientific advance by its contribution to the general welfare.

World Citizenship. The educated citizen is a cooperating member of the world community.

Law Observance. The educated citizen respects the law.

Economic Literacy. The educated citizen is economically literate.

Political Citizenship. The educated citizen accepts his civic duties.

Devotion to Democracy. The educated citizen acts upon an unswerving loyalty to democratic ideals.[5]

A more recent significant statement of goals of the school was also that of the Educational Policies Commission, published in 1961 by the N.E.A., *The Central Purpose of American Education*. In this statement the Commission identified the development of the ability to think, the rational power of man, as the central purpose which strengthens all other educational purposes. All the traditional purposes of the school can be better achieved as pupils develop the ability to think and learn to apply it to problems facing them. The statement reveals historically the change of emphasis in the functions of the school.

REORGANIZATION OF GRADES IN THE SECONDARY SCHOOL

The term of four years for the program of the public high school was hardly established before educators began to question its desirability. By 1900, a number of studies were already under way by various professional organizations to examine the grade organization of both the elementary and the high school, with particular attention to the age level when secondary education for youth might appropriately begin. The study of the grade reorganization of the elementary and the secondary school dominated most discussions of public education for the next two decades.

[5] Educational Policies Commission, *Policies for Education in American Democracy*, Washington, D.C.: National Education Association, 1946, pp. 192, 212, 226, 240.

EARLY NINETEENTH-CENTURY SCHOOLS. Because the movement to reorganize the grade arrangement of the secondary school had a direct bearing on the grade organization of the elementary school, it is important to understand the nature of the elementary school which had developed in America. Before 1800, the organization of the elementary school in the United States was a rather informal one, with no grade organization similar to the one that we have today. The monitorial school, which experienced a brief period of popularity in the United States between 1790 and 1820, was a highly organized school, but pupils were placed in groups on the basis of their progress in the fundamental skills, rather than in grades associated with the number of years a pupil had spent in school.

During the years from 1810 to 1830, the public elementary school experienced a rapid and extensive growth in all parts of the United States. It was during this period that the grade organization of the elementary school, as we know it today, was first introduced. Throughout the East, the Middle West, and the West, the practice of having eight grades in the elementary school was rapidly accepted. In other sections of the country, however, different plans of grade organization developed. In New England, many communities placed nine grades in the elementary school, while in the states from Maryland and south and west to Texas, the seven-year elementary school developed. By the late nineteenth century, therefore, the grade organization of the elementary and secondary schools in the East, the Middle West, and the West was the 8-4 plan, in New England the 9-4 plan, and in the South the 7-4 plan.

Educational historians do not know why these forms of grade organization developed in the United States. In the early nineteenth century the Prussian school system, which had eight-year elementary schools, was considered to be a model for other countries to follow. Since many American educators in the early 1800's visited Prussia to study its schools, it is possible that the eight-year elementary school in this country came about, in part, from the Prussian influence. That does not, however, account for the nine-grade elementary school in New England or the seven-grade school in the southern states. Neither are historians able to account satisfactorily for the four-year plan which developed in the American high school, since this certainly did not follow any European precedent. It is a fact, however, that by 1900 the 8-4 plan of grade organization prevailed throughout much of the United States, with the 9-4 plan in New England and the 7-4 plan in the South.

DISSATISFACTION WITH GRADE ORGANIZATION. The first evidence of dissatisfaction with the grade organization of the elementary and secondary schools did not come from either the educators in these schools or from the parents but from college and university leaders. As early as 1872–73, Eliot expressed serious concern over the fact that freshmen entering Harvard were increasingly older, thus delaying their completion of college and university studies and entrance into business or the professions. Eliot was more specific in his proposals to remedy this situation when he suggested at the annual meeting of the National Education Association in 1888 that the total period of elementary and secondary education be shortened. Several years later, the Committee of Ten on Secondary School Studies whose membership consisted in large part of college and university teachers, recommended that such high school subjects as algebra, geometry, science, and foreign languages be introduced in the upper elementary grades; or, as an alternative, that the secondary school period begin two years earlier, with elementary school limited to the first six grades.

Intensive study of the organization of the elementary and secondary schools followed the Report of the Committee of Ten, presented in 1893, with the result that other criticisms of the schools were added to those of the Committee. Educators suggested that elementary school studies and methods of teaching were continued too long; that pupils needed earlier the challenge of new subjects; that the seventh grade rather than the ninth marked the beginning of a new period in the physiological and psychological development of adolescents; that adolescents needed contact at an earlier age with men teachers; and that the transition from the elementary to the secondary school was too abrupt, resulting in the early elimination of too many pupils from school. These were some of the objections directed at the 8-4, 7-4, and 9-4 plans of grade organization.

DEVELOPMENT OF JUNIOR HIGH SCHOOLS. The most common proposal for reorganization of the public school system recommended by educators was that there be an equal division of time between the elementary and the secondary school, with a 6-6 plan of grade organization. It was not until 1910 that serious steps were taken to implement these proposals. Two school systems in that year —Berkeley, California and Columbus, Ohio—reorganized their schools so as to begin secondary education in the seventh grade. In both of these systems, however, the program of secondary education was divided into two administrative units—a junior and a senior high school—with three grades in each school, the total school program thus being organized on a 6-3-3 plan. The junior high school, however, was clearly considered to be a part of the secondary school.

The junior high school idea, first introduced in Berkeley and Columbus, immediately captured the interest of educators and parents throughout the country, with many other cities in the years after 1910 reorganizing their schools on the 6-3-3 plan. The junior high school, which usually included grades seven, eight, and nine, made it possible to meet many of the needs pointed out by critics of the 8-4 plan. Some of the features in the early junior high schools, most of which have persisted to the present time, included

1. Introduction of such studies as algebra, science, and foreign languages
2. Introduction of several new subjects, especially physical education, industrial arts, and home economics
3. Expansion of offerings in art and music
4. Provision for guidance and counseling of pupils
5. Emphasis on exploration in the school program
6. Development of broad programs of extraclass activities
7. Improvement of articulation between the elementary and secondary school programs.

RAPID GROWTH OF JUNIOR HIGH SCHOOLS. The development of the junior high school took different forms in different communities. In most urban communities, where total enrollments were sufficiently large to justify it, separate junior and senior high schools were established. Although most junior high schools included grades seven, eight, and nine, in some communities only the seventh and eighth grades were included because of local building or administrative considerations. In rural and small urban communities with low pupil enrollments, combined junior-senior high schools were most common, with grades seven through twelve in one building and under one administration. Whether the junior high schools were separate or were combined with the senior high school, the purposes to be achieved were the same, namely, to develop a well-articulated program of elementary and secondary education and to provide for a more effective educational program for early adolescents.

The most rapid growth of junior high schools has usually taken place during periods when total secondary school enrollments increased sharply, necessitating the construction of secondary school buildings, as was true in the 1920's and again in the years following

World War II. At such times communities have been encouraged to re-examine their total educational programs, including the plan of grade organization for their schools. By 1959, three-fourths of the secondary schools in the United States were reorganized on some basis which included the junior-senior high school plan. Because of the many communities in the United States with small pupil enroll-ments, the combined junior-senior high school is the plan which, in recent years, has been most widely introduced. With the rapid growth of the junior-senior high school plan in the United States, the number of four-year high schools has in turn shown a marked decline.

The development of junior-senior high schools over a period of years in the United States is revealed by statistics for different types of secondary schools, released by the United States Department of Health, Education, and Welfare, Office of Education, Washington, D. C., on December 2, 1960.

NUMBER OF PUBLIC SECONDARY SCHOOLS BY TYPE OF ORGANIZATION 1920-59

	1920 Number	1920 Percent	1952 Number	1952 Percent	1959 Number	1959 Percent
Combined Junior-Senior High Schools (6-6)	828	5.8	8,591	36.2	10,130	41.9
Separate Junior High Schools	55	.4	3,227	13.6	4,996	20.6
Senior High Schools (6-3-3)	15	.1	1,021	4.3	1,642	6.8
Reorganized 4-year High Schools (6-2-4)	7	.01	739	3.1	1,396	5.8
Unreorganized 4-year Traditional (8-4)	13,421	93.7	10,168	42.8	6,023	24.9
Total	14,326	100.0	23,746	100.0	24,187	100.0

SUMMARY

The early secondary schools in America all made a definite con-tribution to the program of secondary education which developed here in the past three hundred years. The concept of a public high school supported by public funds came from the Latin grammar school. A broad program of education which included mathematics, science, and practical studies and which emphasized the English language, was the unique contribution of the academy. The prin-ciple of secondary education for all youth, with studies suited to those of various ability levels and different educational and voca-tional goals, was introduced in the early 1800's by the founders of the public high school.

The public high school idea has been accepted throughout the United States, with comprehensive high schools in most communities offering studies in one school to meet the needs of all youth. Some cities, especially in the East, though they have broad programs of secondary education available, have specialized as well as comprehensive high schools, with the specialized schools offering studies in a limited area, either in a specific vocational field or for a group of selected pupils. Whether in one school, or in several, the concept of secondary education for all youth is recognized and accepted in all parts of the United States.

The program of secondary education for all youth is being continually extended in most communities. Through the consolidation of small high schools in rural areas, rural youth are being offered a broader program of secondary education. In medium- and large-size schools, programs are being developed more extensively for atypical pupils—the mentally retarded, the superior, the physically handicapped, and others—and vocational education programs are being constantly expanded. In some states, the concept of secondary education for all youth is being extended upward to include the public community college, with a broad program of studies for youth eighteen to twenty years old and for out-of-school youth as well. These developments in secondary education in America over a period of more than three hundred years are expressed in the program of secondary education which is provided for American youth today.

SELECTED REFERENCES

BROWN, ELMER E. *The Making of Our Middle Schools.* Boston: Longmans, Green & Co., 1902, 547 pp.—Presents a detailed account of the development of secondary education in America before 1900, with much valuable information for the student who wishes to pursue this subject in depth. Includes details on the Kalamazoo case.

CUBBERLEY, ELLWOOD P. *Public Education in the United States.* Boston: Houghton Mifflin Co., 1930, Chaps. 2, 5, 8, and 14.—These chapters present information that has a bearing on the development of secondary schools in the United States.

EDUCATIONAL POLICIES COMMISSION. *The Central Purpose of American Education.* Washington, D.C.: National Education Association, 1961, 21 pp.—A deliberative statement of the purposes of the school in American society.

GRIZZELL, E. D. *American Secondary Education.* New York: Thomas Nelson & Sons, 1937, Chap. 8.—Presents a good overview of the development of secondary schools in America, with particular reference to recent organizations and practices.

GRIZZELL, E. D. *Origin and Development of the High School in New England Before 1865.* New York: The Macmillan Co., 1923, 428 pp.—The entire volume presents a valuable statement of the development of secondary schools in New England before 1865, with examples of programs offered by schools at various times.

GRUHN, WILLIAM T., and DOUGLASS, HARL R. *The Modern Junior High School.* New York: The Ronald Press Co., 1956, Chap. 1.—Gives an overview of the reorganization of elementary and secondary education in the United States, with particular reference to the purposes and growth of the junior high school.

KNIGHT, EDGAR W. *Education in the United States.* Boston: Ginn & Co., 1929, Chaps. 4, 5, and 13.—These chapters give information concerning background for secondary education in America and the development of the secondary schools.

MIDURA, GLADYS A. "A Critical History of Public Education in Springfield, Massachusetts." Unpublished doctoral dissertation, Storrs, Conn.: University of Connecticut, 1961, pp. 153-56, 414-20.—Gives details concerning the development of commercial studies, other early vocational offerings, and extraclass activities in the Springfield schools before 1900.

MONROE, PAUL. *Founding of the American Public School System.* Volume I. New York: The Macmillan Co., 1940, Chaps. 6 and 12.—These chapters present a particularly good discussion of the development of secondary education in America, including the Latin grammar school, the academy, and the public high school.

NATIONAL EDUCATION ASSOCIATION. *Report of the Committee of Ten on Secondary-School Studies.* New York: American Book Co., 1894.—This is one of the most significant reports in the history of education in the United States which had much influence on the development of the public high school.

SMALL, WALTER H. *Early New England Schools.* Boston: Ginn & Co., 1914, Chaps. 1, 2, 11, and 13.—These chapters give a good description of the early secondary schools which developed in New England.

3

AMERICAN CULTURE AND THE SECONDARY SCHOOL

One aim of education in any society is to transmit from one generation to another its culture or way of life which is considered of fundamental value to that society. This is as true for totalitarian states as it is in free societies. The difference lies in what is considered "good" as defined by the culture. Because the function of the school is determined by the customs, aspirations, and ideals of the society which it serves, it is important to know what the differences mean to all institutions, including the schools.

Few would question that the United States and the free world are faced with a deadly menace by the Communist rulers of one-third of mankind. The struggle is more than a political and military conflict; it is a battle for "the minds of men" to preserve and promote radically different ways of life. No one doubts that education will be a vital factor in the ultimate outcome.

Even if, by some unlikely development, there should be total world disarmament, the United States and the schools would still be faced with extremely difficult and complex problems. The rapidly increasing gap between technological and scientific culture and social, economic, and political institutions is a serious problem. There has been more change in the twentieth century than in all previous history. The changes that are taking place in an age when the conquest of space has become a reality will inevitably create problems for secondary education.

With the stakes so high, free citizens must agree on the kind of education needed. However, great uncertainty exists in the United States over the purposes of education, the curriculum, and methods of teaching, especially in secondary education. One reason for this uncertainty is that many do not understand the culture and its implications for education nor the changes occurring in America and

50

throughout the world. Some Americans seem to favor educational policies which may eventually weaken or destroy those very aspects of our culture which we prize so dearly.

This chapter will view the changes in American culture and especially those aspects of it which bear on the problems of secondary education.

INFLUENCE OF THE CULTURE

A COMPREHENSIVE HIGH SCHOOL. The American secondary school is a product of American culture, growing out of the ideals and aspirations of the American people and greatly influencing other social institutions. The view of secondary education in its historical perspective in a previous chapter revealed how the comprehensive high school developed in this country to provide secondary education for all youth. This was a uniquely American contribution to education.

The American dream of equality of opportunity and freedom for the individual, as reflected in education for all youth in free public high schools, was brought about by a combination of social, political and economic forces. The absence of a feudal system and the freedom of the western frontier strengthened the concept of social and political equality. Too, American ideals of freedom and equality served as a magnet to draw immigrants from other lands where a different concept of secondary education pertained. Immigrant parents sought for their children a high-school education that would have been impossible in their native country. Serving pupils from many nations and cultures, the secondary schools in America thus became a unifying force to weld a diversity of nationalities, races, and religions into a single people.

As a result of the industrial revolution, the growth of factories, and the specialization of labor, a large wage-earning class came into existence. Workers viewed the schools as an important ladder by which their children could climb upward. Working men and women, especially through organized labor—small and weak as it was in early America—were and still are among the strongest supporters of free public education for all children. The belief that every individual in America should have an opportunity to improve his economic status through education, together with the achievements of public education, are among the major reasons why communism has found little support in the United States.

America's faith in democracy rests on a belief that a free people can and will act as responsible citizens. From the time of Jefferson, who asserted, "Whenever the people are well informed, they can be trusted with their own government," public schools have been considered fundamental to democratic government. The secondary schools in particular have directed a significant part of their program to preparing responsible citizens for self-government. The free public high schools, in opposition to the theory that only the elite should be educated to govern, make it possible for free men to govern themselves.

The secondary schools also have played an important role in perpetuating and strengthening other values and institutions in American society. Many of the face-to-face relations between people has become an important although informal aspect of education. A great deal of the socialization necessary for family living is learned in school. Appreciation for art and music, as well as other parts of our cultural heritage, has become an important function of secondary education. Religious tolerance, mutual respect among various cultural groups, and belief in fair play are patterns of behavior which must be learned; the schools share the responsibility with other institutions for transmitting these important moral and spiritual values.

The secondary school in America, as a product of American values and culture, has pursued two broad goals, (1) to meet the needs of individual youth so as to promote their fullest personal growth, and (2) to promote their effective participation in the society in which they live. These goals have also been those of a democratic society.

DEMAND FOR EXCELLENCE. The problems of universal public education, always a matter for public concern, have been aggravated since the end of World War II. As a result of Russia's lead in the missile race and the growing threat of military conflict, secondary education came under increasing pressures in the 1950's. The quality of secondary education and the drive for students for higher standards of academic achievement have been among the strongest of these pressures, recently expressed in the Rockefeller Brothers Fund, Report V, *The Pursuit of Excellence* as follows: "The demand to educate everyone up to the level of his ability and the demand for excellence in education are not incompatible. We must have both goals. We must seek excellence in a context of concern for all."

Such proposals represent widespread concern for the improvement of education and are indicative of faith in the public schools as an essential institution in our society. However, in their concern for quality and their stress on education of the gifted, some communities would turn the clock back. Certainly, no one would quarrel with the importance of placing emphasis on developing individual talent and on the pursuit of excellence, but this should apply to all youth and not to the intellectually elite alone.

It is a mistake to assume that the challenges faced by our society can be met merely by increasing the output of scientists, mathematicians, and technicians. If American society is to survive, the "pursuit of excellence" in developing responsible citizens must be given even greater emphasis. The secondary school provides the last formal education that the majority of our citizens receive. Franklin Patterson, reporting the results of a study of citizenship and youth development conducted by the Tufts University Civic Education Center, sums up the challenge this way:

> The future will demand of us much more than simply improved quality and output in professional and vocational training. The true test ahead will require a universally higher level of responsible, intelligent citizenship to deal with the revolutionary changes that science and technology bring about. It is a most critical task of the high school today and tomorrow to prepare citizens who understand and value the basic ideas of freedom, who are literate in political, economic, and social affairs, and who are ready and able to participate effectively in the civic life of a free nation.[1]

GOALS FOR A FREE SOCIETY. As a social agency, the school is not only one of the principal means for transmitting the essential aspects of the culture, but it is also an agent for changing and improving society. The educational system thus has two functions to perform: it serves as a mirror that reflects society as it is, and at the same time it is as an agent for social change and for the implementation of the ideals of society. To be effective, the school must understand the goals of our society and what is expected of the educational system in achieving those goals.

No one can turn to any one document for a statement of the ideals and goals of our society. The way in which people live and behave, the laws they adopt, the institutions they support, the statements they make, and the ideals they express are indicative of those goals. There are, however, many statements of democratic ideals from which insights can be gained regarding the premises or assumptions that the American people accept. One such expression is found in the report of the President's Commission on National Goals, titled *Goals for Americans,* which was presented to President Dwight D. Eisenhower in 1960 by a distinguished committee of citizens. The Commission's report states that the paramount goal of the United States was set long ago; it is to guard the rights of the

[1] Franklin Patterson, *High Schools for a Free Society,* Glencoe, Ill.: The Free Press, 1960, p. 17.

individual, to insure his development, and to enlarge his opportunity. To meet this goal, the Commission declares that "we must build a nation and help build a world in which every human being shall be free to develop his capacities to the fullest. We must rededicate ourselves to this principle and thereby strengthen its appeal to a world in political, social, economic, and technological revolution."

INFLUENCE OF SOCIAL CHANGE

ACCELERATION OF CHANGE. Our schools do not exist in a vacuum; they cannot escape being deeply influenced by the conflicts and pressures of their social, economic, and political environment. Before discussing how the schools are to adjust and function in an age of sweeping and revolutionary changes, some of the changes occurring in American life should be examined briefly to see how they affect secondary education.

It has been said that George Washington would have been more at home in ancient Rome than in modern America. The same is true for any person living in the early part of the twentieth century. When we consider that pupils entering secondary schools in the 1960's may live nearly a third of their lives in the twenty-first century, we can only guess what their future will be like. These pupils are growing up in an age of change, an age in which life is profoundly different from that of the first half of the twentieth century. If education is to be effective, the schools must change as society changes.

Yet the progress made in material culture has not been an unmixed blessing. Social developments have not kept pace with technological progress. No one has yet learned how to adapt technological advances to social living so that they will bring about a more satisfying life for all people and a more harmonious relationship between nations. Atomic warfare, economic depressions, broken homes, crime, racial conflicts, and unstable personalities are a few of the catastrophes resulting because technology has made great strides forward, while the ability to adjust to those changes has lagged behind.

URBANIZATION OF SOCIETY. As recently as 1900, approximately three-fourths of the American people lived on farms and in rural areas; today two-thirds of our people live in urban communities. This steady shift in population from rural to urban areas is expected to continue until 90 per cent of the nation's population resides in metropolitan centers. The metropolitan areas along the Eastern

Seaboard already overlap, forming one gigantic linear city that stretches for six hundred miles along the East Coast from Washington, D. C. to Portland, Maine, and including a population of over thirty million.

The growth of urban communities has deeply changed nearly ever phase of American life. Even rural life has been transformed by its becoming mechanized and in some respects urbanized. The city has become the dwelling place and workshop of modern Americans as well as the controlling center of the nation's leaders; its press, radio and television, and stage dominate public opinion; and it sets the pace for moral standards and intellectual pursuits.

Urbanization means more than merely the process by which people are attracted to the city. It is a set of attitudes and ideas— a way of life. The history of the United States has been the transition from a simple, slow-moving, rural way of life into one in which the city with its highly complex, heterogeneous, fast-moving, and rapidly-changing pattern plays the major role.

This shift from rural to urban living has come with phenomenal speed. Vast changes in how people live, greater than at any other time in history, have come within the lifetime of most people living today. The change from rural to urban ways of living is a continuous process because the city must draw much of its population from rural areas where the earlier folk society still persists. Consequently, many people living in cities are so bound by tradition, custom, superstition, and outworn institutions geared to the simple rural society of the past that they have been unable to cope with problems of urban living.

Youth who grew up in the simple agrarian society of the past had little difficulty integrating their personal lives into the life of the community. Life in rural communities changed little from generation to generation. The neighborhood was made up of people who knew each other intimately and were concerned with each other's welfare as neighbors. Life was closely knit and stable. There was a large degree of self-sufficiency and independence, with little need for highly developed governmental institutions beyond the occasional town meeting. Life was simple and slow moving, and it presented few problems other than those for which society had developed working patterns and in which each individual understood the part he was to play.

The schools, like other institutions, had become adjusted to the community life of the times. In the words of one observer:

In the old school the teacher simply instructed in a few basic skills, assigned lessons, heard recitations, and went home. Education was predominantly a function of the community. Its aim was to transmit the most vital elements of the cultural heritage, the patterns of the living present. Children learned by doing. The age itself was one of simplicity and stability, security and confidence. One knew what to do because one knew what was expected of him.[2]

Urbanization and industrialization have swept aside the simple living of the past. The closely knit unity of the community has been shattered. The warm and intimate primary group relationships are being replaced by secondary group contacts. Conflicting pressure groups, mass propaganda, and formal mechanisms of control are being substituted for the bonds of kinship and loyalty which were relied upon to hold the simple rural folk society together. A complex industrial economy with a high degree of interdependence has taken the place of the simple, small-scale, handicraft-agrarian system.

Of even greater importance has been the rise of skepticism and uncertainty regarding traditional values and codes of behavior. Urban dwellers are continually faced with choosing between a series of alternatives, but without such clearly agreed-upon values and common concerns as guided those who lived in an earlier time in the rural community. David Riesman in *The Lonely Crowd* has shown that, until recently, Americans have sought security in tradition and in conforming to parental, and particularly paternal authority, which permitted them to be "inner directed." Many middle-class urban dwellers today, however, seek social approval for the most part, not from their family and close personal friends, but from associates with whom they have secondary group relationships. Because they are constantly anxious to have the good opinion of their peer groups they become "other directed." The desire for acceptance leads them to conform to what others tell them to do, yet because contact with others is superficial, rather than warm and personal, they remain lonely members of the crowd. The school's culture, as a reflection of society, all too often reinforces conformity.

CHANGING PATTERNS OF COMMUNITY LIFE. America has gone through two great changes in its urban living patterns. The first occurred with the shift from a predominantly rural to an urban society. During the early period of urban living, beyond the city limits there were no large concentrations of population. But in the second change in our pattern of urban living, which has taken place in recent years, the twentieth century has witnessed a "metropolitan explosion." With the rapid growth of suburban areas and satellite towns surrounding the central city, a new kind of urban community is being created. This is the metropolitan area, which is as much

[2] Lloyd Allen Cook, *Community Background in Education,* New York: McGraw-Hill Book Co., Inc., 1945, p. 5.

suburban as urban. Technological advances, especially in transportation with the wide use of the automobile, have made possible a diffusion of homes, shops, and factories over a wide area around the older central city.

Boundaries of the metropolis are often hard to define, and they frequently change and expand. Its growth ignores the old city and town boundary lines, jumps over rivers and around lakes, and spills out in all directions from the central city. While its economic and social life is closely interrelated, the metropolitan area is not organized as a political or governmental unit, but is fragmentized into numerous separate and often competing and antagonistic units of government.

As the population of metropolitan areas has mushroomed and their economy has expanded, the problems of local government have become increasingly complex. As a result of population shifts, the older central cities face such problems as the loss of tax revenues as business moves to the suburbs, the loss of civic leadership, and the spread of blight and slums over wide areas. The suburban town governments also have faced problems because of the rapid growth of the school population, the need for new school buildings, and the expansion of various local governmental services.

It is understandable why the people living in the central city and those living in suburban towns do not identify themselves with each other's problems. Long-established governmental institutions and traditions support the idea of independent local governments. Suburban dwellers also tend to prefer independent governments because they fear taxes will be higher if they are brought under a metropolitan government. The problems of metropolitan growth cannot be solved until some coordination between the city and its suburban communities is achieved. A new dimension in local government is needed, as well as a broader concept of citizenship if we are to meet the problems of metropolitan growth.

The human relations aspects of the changing city have far-reaching implications for secondary education. The disappearance of entire sections of cities brought about by slum clearance and urban renewal have uprooted many families. This has resulted in frustration and resentment by many parents, as well as older people, who did not wish to move. Many become dissatisfied with their community. Such attitudes, of course, have an influence on the attitudes of their children.

GROWTH OF THE AMERICAN ECONOMY. The revolutionary developments in science and technology have affected every aspect of life in America, but especially our economic institutions. The old economic order has been virtually replaced by a new industrial system in which many of the principles basic to our traditional concept of a free enterprise system no longer hold. Due to the productivity of agriculture and industry, our economy today is no longer one of scarcity, but rather one of affluence. However, as John Kenneth Gailbraith of Harvard University, a noted economist, suggests in *The Affluent Society,* there has been a remarkable resistance to the changing economic ideas which once interpreted the world of mass poverty, and Americans are still guided by ideas that are relevant to another world. Thus, people do many things that are unnecessary and unwise, thereby increasing the threat to our affluent society itself.

Although it is difficult to isolate specific causes, many of the changes in the economy can be attributed to increasing consumer demands, the development of new products, the development of new methods of production which reduce costs, and the ability of labor to adapt to changing techniques of production. For example, 25 per cent of the profits of industry in 1955 were made on products that did not exist in 1940. In the decade following 1945, American industry, educational institutions, and government spent some 50 billion dollars on research—more than was spent on research in all the previous history of mankind.

Enormous increases in the amount of energy for production has come about in the past fifty years, until today less than 2 per cent of the energy of production in the United States comes from human labor. The nation's rapidly-rising productivity—the ability of workers to turn out an increasing amount of goods in an average hour's work—is the key to our economic growth and our high standard of living. Morever, the use of atomic energy has an enormous potential for increasing productivity even more, though as yet we have scarcely begun to use it for peaceful purposes.

It is obvious that some parts of our economy will expand more rapidly than others. For example, the shift away from agriculture to nonfarm work may be expected to continue. The fact that today's agricultural workers number about the same as in 1860, but produce food for a nation many times larger and with staggering surpluses, is evidence of the revolution in agriculture. The extent to which the federal government has been called upon to deal with the farm surpluses illustrates the difference between the classical economic theories of Adam Smith and those of today. The federal government today is spending more each year to store surplus agricultural products than all federal government activities cost per year prior to 1930. In general, the trends indicate that fewer people will be required to produce the basic necessities, while more will be employed in the service occupations. Secondary school teachers and guidance counselors need to take these trends into consideration when they help students with vocational and educational plans.

Since women now constitute about 36 per cent of the labor force in the United States, secondary schools should encourage girls to prepare for careers in order not to waste talent which the nation needs. Increasing numbers of married women are working outside the home. The secondary school, therefore, has a responsibility for providing education in family living so that boys and girls may be better able to cope with family problems when both parents are employed.

Growth of the American economy has been accompanied by shifts in the location of industry. The trend has generally been away from the older industrial centers in New England and the Middle Atlantic areas, and toward the South and the Pacific Coast. Such relocations of industry have far-reaching implications, especially for secondary schools, as the South becomes increasingly an industrial-urban instead of an agrarian and rural area.

The trend of industry from central cities to suburban areas will also have important influences on the secondary schools. A higher level of education is necessary for jobs requiring advanced technical knowledge and responsible judgment. Yet, while much attention is being focused on preparing pupils for college, less concern is shown for those who lack the ability to do college work. Many of these students should be prepared for the variety of technical positions available in business and industry. Many secondary schools have not kept up with the technological changes in industry and do not offer programs which prepare youth for the new occupations that industry and business offer. As a result too many youth become discouraged and may even leave school before completing their secondary education. The American economy cannot afford such waste of talent because the nation requires contributions of all individuals in many occupations and at all levels of achievement.

There needs to be a new perspective in secondary education, one in which success is measured not primarily in terms of academic grades or personal attainment, but rather in recognition of and respect for the worth of every individual, whatever his talents and abilities may be. The emergence of Soviet Russia as a great power, if nothing else, has taught the American people the importance of education for youth at all levels of ability and for all vocational goals.

INDIVIDUAL AND GROUP RELATIONSHIPS. In the transformation of our society from a simple rural agrarian-handicraft way of living to a highly complex industrial-urban society, it was inevitable that individual and group relationships should undergo great changes. An industrial society seems to require a great web of rules to secure the cooperation of people and to bind them together. There has therefore been some loss of individual freedom and the need to conform to regulations as the price for the benefits of industrialization. The institutions which fix the limits of the citizens' activities have become so generally accepted by most people that they seldom stop to think about the influence of these institutions. Yet, in this almost automatic conformity lies one of the greatest threats to a free society. How to balance individual rights and freedom against the conformity that is necessary in a society which requires increasing collective action is one of the greatest challenges faced by our citizens.

In pre-industrial society, the local community was the primary social and economic unit and individuals carried on many of their activities in face-to-face relationships. But in the industrial-urban society of today many special interest groups have developed in which people tend to associate with others of their own kind in order to gain a sense of belonging and to advance their own interests. Many of these groups have become strongly organized as centers of power which exert great influence on the government and other sectors of society. The movement to combine and centralize in order to gain greater benefits has led to big corporations, big unions, and big government.

Large corporations have become economic and social units of great power. A. A. Berle, Jr., professor of corporation law at Columbia University, says that today approximately 50 per cent of American manufacturing assets are held by about 150 corporations and that 500 corporations control two-thirds of the nonfarm economy, with a still smaller group having ultimate decision-making power. This is, he points out, the highest concentration of power in recorded history and represents a concentration of power which makes the "medieval feudal system look like a Sunday School party."[3]

The corporation has also become a social system. Its employees pursue careers in whatever part of the country they are sent and have little opportunity to become rooted in a local community. To gain a feeling of belonging, these employees need membership in a

[3] A. A. Berle, Jr., *Economic Power and the Free Society*, New York: The Fund for the Republic, 1957, p. 14.

group. The corporation offers its employees this needed psychological security.

Because of a lack of values for guidance, many people in a transitional society such as ours may never gain a sense of direction and purpose. They suffer from what sociologists call "anomie," a feeling of loneliness and hopelessness, because they are without standards to guide them. Whether by necessity or choice, many corporation officials come to live by what William H. Whyte, a noted sociologist, calls the "social ethic." By this Whyte means the acceptance of values that are made morally legitimate by the pressures of the corporation and society. The "organization man" who conforms to "corporate morality" is found not only in the corporation, but also in the union, church, school, and government.

With the growth of industrial and business corporations, labor also has found organization necessary. Organized labor's contribution in preserving and extending the ideals of democracy is an exciting and dramatic story which deserves more attention than it sometimes receives in the social studies program of the secondary school. To understand organized labor's struggle against great obstacles, it must be recognized that unions, like other institutions, are a product of American culture and that the social and economic forces which created modern America also gave birth to the labor unions. Unions have persisted in spite of efforts to destroy them; they have become strong and powerful because they meet certain of the workers' needs. Collective bargaining in labor-management relations is now an established institution in the United States.

EMERGENCE OF BALANCE OF POWER. While the major economic objective of the unions is collective bargaining, the economic and political environment in which they exist impels them to strengthen their bargaining position and gain other benefits for workers through legislation. Organized labor, together with business associations and other special interest groups, have become powerful pressure groups which act as a system of checks and balances on each other. If organized labor is to fulfill its functions in a free society, it must develop a degree of organizational strength and power commensurate with the strength and power which surrounds it. While this, of necessity, reduces the worker's individual freedom, it nevertheless creates a balance among private and public power centers which is essential in a pluralistic industrial society.

What has been said regarding the necessity of maintaining a balance of power between corporations and unions is also true of other large organized groups. President Eisenhower, in his fare-well address to the American people, was troubled by the influence which two such groups, the military forces and the arms industry, today have on the nation. His parting words are all the more sig-nificant because, for most of his life, he was closely associated with these two groups. Looking back, he recalled the day when the United States did not need to be forever girded for war; in looking ahead he cautioned:

. . . This conjunction of an immense military establishment and a large arms industry is new in the American experience . . . We must not fail to compre-hend its grave implications . . . We must never let the weight of this combina-tion endanger our liberties or democratic processes . . . Only an alert and knowledgeable citizenry can compel the proper meshing of the huge industry and military machinery of defense with our peaceful methods and goals, so that security and liberty may prosper together.[4]

The dangers inherent in this situation, with its threat to civil rights and individual liberties, must not be ignored. In our fear of the enemy and our race for survival, there is grave danger that we may become more like the enemy than we dare think. If the free society is to remain free, it must set limits upon what it asks for defense.

Loss of Individuality in Society. With the development of big business, big unions, big military establishments, and big gov-ernment, increasing numbers of people have come to be a part of large organizations. While it may be necessary for a large organiza-tion to have its own social structure, bureaucracy, and administra-tive organization to carry out the purposes of the group, it does not follow that the individual must lose his individuality in the group, nor lose his influence with the group. The school itself, in this sense, is a bureaucracy in which various groups are related according to a system of authority, rank, and prestige, with administrators, teachers, and students holding different roles in the system.

The word "bureaucracy" has a negative connotation in popular thinking, but the fact that an organization is bureaucratic does not in itself create a problem. The problem arises when the quality of interaction in its structure causes the individual to lose his unique-ness and creativity in the group. How can individualism and cre-ativity survive in the midst of ever-expanding organizations? How can the individual be important in economic, political, and social affairs as our society becomes more highly organized?

The secondary schools can do much to answer this challenge by

4 *The New York Times,* January 18, 1961.

developing in students those attitudes and abilities which may help preserve one's individuality and at the same time permit effective membership in a group. If secondary schools are to prepare students for effective citizenship in a democracy, they must help them learn how to participate in groups in a manner that will preserve individuality. Secondary schools can also help students become aware of the dangers of conformity by fostering classroom activities which promote creativity, individuality, and critical thinking. The growth of large organizations in American society and the membership of most citizens in such groups places new responsibilities on the secondary school.

SOCIAL CLASS AND SECONDARY SCHOOLS

CLASS AND CASTE. The existence of social classes seems to contradict the American creed of equality. Yet, all societies have some degree of social stratification, even those societies which presumably have eliminated social classes. The United States is no exception. Some sociologists would go even further to say that, because of the relegation of the Negro to an inferior position, America has both a class and a caste system.

A social class is not an organized group of people, but rather a broadly defined grouping of people into higher and lower status positions on a social scale. Social classes exist and can be identified because people in one social class differ from those in others in their attitudes, values, and customs. The amount of education a person has; his occupation, income, and economic and political power; where he lives, and with whom he chooses to associate, all influence the social class to which he belongs. People in one social class have a sense of belongingness to each other and of separateness from other classes.

A social caste exists when the individual's position is determined by birth, race, and other factors. In some areas, the Negro, regardless of education or income, has a lower position than the lowest white person; because he is a Negro, he is not permitted to enter the white social class system. Within the Negro system, however, a class structure exists similar to that of whites. There are other caste-like groups in the United States, such as the Mexicans, Puerto Ricans, Indians, Chinese, and Japanese. The problem of integrating these groups into the schools and the total social system is less difficult than that of the Negroes because there is less segregation between these groups and the majority groups.

A social class system can be reconciled with the ideals of democracy only so long as it is an *open* class system which permits social mobility with equal opportunities for all individuals to ascend the social ladder. Americans cannot under any circumstances, however, maintain a caste system and at the same time contend a democracy exists. The inconsistency between the expressed creed of equal rights, opportunities, and freedom on the one hand, and discriminatory practices on the other is one of the most serious and difficult problems America faces.

> The fact that our class system is extralegal means that . . . a program for change cannot appeal to the state for support through the passage of new laws or the enforcement of present ones . . . The state is one dimension of society and class another . . . If we start with the assumption that both the state and class dimensions are part of society, it will be possible to see that one supports the other in many ways, and that they also work at cross purposes.[5]

To overcome the restrictions on freedom and opportunity which a social class and caste system imposes, we must seek cultural changes throughout our whole society. Legislation and court action prohibiting discrimination are important contributions to change because they are a vital part of the culture. The secondary schools moreover have a responsibility to provide not only equal educational opportunities to all regardless of caste or class, but also to promote the ideals of our society and educate citizens for democratic intergroup relations. In so doing, they serve their function to improve society.

STUDIES OF SOCIAL CLASS. Sociologists have made numerous studies of the social class structure in various communities in different parts of the country. Some of these studies are listed at the end of this chapter for those students who may wish to investigate them further. One feature common to almost all these studies indicates that members of different social classes generally agree on a classification, both in reference to themselves and others, which makes it clear that class distinctions exist in our society. The sociologist, therefore, is able to draw up a social scale that represents upper, middle, and lower classes with differing values and ways of living for each class.

Lloyd W. Warner and Paul S. Lunt, two sociologists who made a study of a New England industrial community called "Yankee City," in their book, *The Social Life of a Modern Community,* subdivided each of the three conventional classes into upper and lower classes. The study shows that over 50 per cent of the population falls into

[5] A. B. Hollingshead, *Elmtown's Youth,* New York: John Wiley & Sons, Inc., 1949, p. 448.

the two lower classes, slightly under 40 per cent is in the middle class, and some 3 per cent belongs to the upper classes. Various criteria, including patterns of association within the community, were used in identifying the classes, with class alignment closely paralleling money income.

Two studies of social class in cities of the Middle West, described under the names of "Jonesville" and "Elmtown," show nearly the same stratification as found in "Yankee City." In *Elmtown's Youth*, Hollingshead illustrates the impact of social class upon adolescents with evidence that teachers and pupils discriminate against those pupils who come from lower-class families.

In a study of "Old City" in *Deep South*, sociologists found a social structure similar to that of other parts of the country except that in the deep South a large Negro population constituted a caste outside the recognized and accepted white social class system. The Negro social class system is similar to that existing among whites, although a much larger proportion of Negroes are classified by Negroes and whites alike as lower-class Negroes. Integration in the public schools of the deep South is further complicated because not only does this involve mixing caste and class, but also because wide-scale integration would include large numbers of Negro children from lower-class families.

SUBCULTURES IN AMERICA. While there is a general American culture cutting across all class lines, each class has its own subculture. Classes vary considerably in their beliefs concerning manners, politics, religion, sex, and education. The lower class outnumbers the middle and upper classes in most communities, but the middle class tends to set the pattern for the over-all culture. For example, many lower-class families accept middle-class values and imitate middle-class patterns of behavior because they hope that by doing so they or their children may rise to middle-class status. Upper-class people accept middle-class attitudes, or a middle-class ideology, because it is the middle-class system that also provides them with status. The mass communication media, especially advertisements in both the press and television, express middle-class characteristics. It is not improper, therefore, to refer to the United States as a middle-class nation.

Accompanying the vast changes now occurring in the United States are significant changes in the social class structure. Few studies have been made as yet on the effect of population shifts on social classes. An increase in the middle class may be expected as the population becomes better educated. Already more than half of the workers in the United States have at least a secondary school education, and it is predicted that eventually at least one-third of the population will be college educated. As education is an important factor in social mobility, it may be assumed that all college-educated people will become middle class.

At the same time, the technological revolution is providing employment opportunities for white-collar middle-class workers. C. Wright Mills, a noted sociologist, in his book, *White Collar*, calls white-collar workers the middle class, and points out that their numbers have been increased by professional men and women, junior executives, technicians, salesmen, and clerks, most of whom are educated, live in suburbia, and are increasingly identified with large organizations.

Members of the top social stratum in the United States form a compact social and psychological group. They come from the upper social class and marry within the same class. Their prestige comes from the position they hold in society. Prestige does not always go with wealth and power, but like wealth and power, it tends to be accumulative—the more one has, the more one can get.

As middle-class occupations require more schooling, education has become the principal means of providing opportunities for advancement in social class. Realizing this, many parents encourage their children to go further in secondary school and college. In many communities, the pressure which parents place upon their children and the secondary schools in order that their children will be accepted in college has become something of a panic, which may well be called a "status panic." Education provides not only higher status, but also the avenue for social mobility.

If our schools are to provide equal opportunities for all, then a child's educational opportunity should not be limited by his social background. Since the financial status of families is related to their cultural background and social class, the opportunity of children to continue in school is in effect limited by their social class.

A MIDDLE-CLASS CULTURE. The practices and policies of the secondary school are influenced by our social class system, and the secondary school in turn influences the system because it provides the opportunity for social mobility. Acting as a sorting and selecting agency, the secondary school encourages the more able and ambitious youth to improve their status. The secondary school may also discourage some students by not offering an educational program which meets their abilities and needs. One measure of the secondary school's success in a democracy is how well equal opportunities are provided for all children to improve their status, regardless of their social status, race, religion, nationality, abilities, and ultimate vocational goals.

The secondary school, itself, is a reflection of our middle-class culture and emphasizes those values which the middle class believes most important. The large majority of teachers come from middle-class families and naturally are influenced by their own subculture. The teaching profession provides many young people with an opportunity to rise from a lower to a higher position in status. This is one reason why many youth from low- and middle-class families become teachers.

School board members, moreover, not only come from the middle class, but they are often the most conservative element of the middle class and are careful to employ only "good" middle-class administrators and teachers. The school naturally develops a subculture that represents the beliefs and values of those who control its policies. Those beliefs and values in turn are imposed on all children in the community.

PUPILS FROM LOWER CLASS. Although the public school emphasizes middle-class values, the pupils in many schools come predominantly from the lower classes. In the country as a whole, some 60 per cent of the students in a typical school come from lower-class families.[6] In some districts, especially the slum areas, the proportion of school children from lower-class families may be much larger. Lower-class children may experience confusion and conflicts when they try to conform to middle-class standards imposed upon them by the school. Such conformity often means violating the standards of their families and friends, and is sometimes the reason for students becoming "reluctant learners," causing them to become discipline problems and to drop out of school before they graduate.

The school's culture that favors middle-class pupils is illustrated by the school's use of rewards and punishments. Pupils from the lower class receive a disproportionate amount of punishment and are rewarded much less frequently than children who come from middle-class families. Children growing up in lower-class families learn patterns of behavior different from those in middle or upper classes. Much of children's behavior—fighting, use of profanity, and the like—which many teachers consider "bad," may not seem wrong to many of the children themselves because that is the way they have learned to act at home and in their neighborhood. This

[6] W. Lloyd Warner, *American Life: Dream and Reality,* Chicago: University of Chicago Press, 1953, p. 177.

does not mean that teachers should accept this kind of behavior in the classroom. However, teachers too often do not understand the cause for it, and in an attempt to correct students they may unintentionally cause guilt, anxiety, and a feeling of rejection or frustration, all of them emotional disturbances which tend to lead to aggressive behavior. Moreover, by constantly being "looked down upon" by teachers and other students, some students come to accept themselves as being of little worth and may act accordingly.

Secondary school teachers have a responsibility to help pupils clarify their own thinking and values and what they want to get out of life. This is not a simple problem because children from different social classes have different values and goals which often result in a conflict between the child and the school. As long as a conflict of values and goals exists, learning new values and making changes in behavior is not likely to take place because the child cannot freely examine the consequences of his own values and behavior. While he may be forced to conform in school, no real change occurs in his thinking. It is important, therefore, that the differences in children's values and feelings should be respected and acknowledged in the classroom, not for indiscriminate condonement or acceptance, but in order to help them clarify their own thinking and propose alternatives for their choice. Only when pupils, regardless of differences in social class, feel that they are respected and accepted can they understand their own attitudes, beliefs, and values and learn more desirable goals and behavior.

GROUPING AND SOCIAL CLASS. Grouping pupils according to ability is common in secondary schools and to some extent is perhaps necessary. Although pupils of the same ability presumably are grouped together to facilitate teaching and learning, this practice tends to create groups that are likely to be homogeneous in social class as well as in ability to achieve in school. Pupils from lower social class families may have mental ability equal to those from the upper classes, but they are not as likely to be good students. The selection process generally begins when children enter school. By the time they reach secondary school the pupils themselves, as well as their teachers, may come to believe that they have less ability. Their lack of ability, however, may be due in part to the fact that they were not born into a "good" middle-class family. Since teachers generally feel that pupils from the best families do the best work, such pupils generally do.

In many sections of the country, pupils in the typical comprehensive secondary school are placed in groups according to the curriculum which they have chosen—college preparatory, commercial, general, or others. This practice usually places pupils in groups according to social class, with the college-preparatory group including pupils largely from the middle and upper social classes, while the general and vocational groups include pupils from the lower social class. If pupils of the lower class have a free choice of curriculum in a secondary school, this system provides an opportunity for social mobility. However, in many secondary schools the practice of placing pupils in groups according to their curriculum and courses leads to discrimination and the association of individuals with social class levels. In *Elmtown's Youth*, a senior girl summarizes the views of many students:

> If you take a college preparatory course you are better than those who take a general course . . . If you take a general course, you don't rate. It's a funny thing, those who take college preparatory set themselves up as better than the other kids. Those that take the college preparatory run the place. I remember when I was a freshman, mother wanted me to take home economics, but I didn't want to. I knew I couldn't rate, you could take typing and shorthand and still rate, but if you took straight commercial courses, you couldn't rate. You see you are rated by the teachers according to the course you take. They rate you in the first six weeks. The teachers type you in a small school and you are made in classes before you get there. College preparatory kids get good grades and the others take what is left. The teachers get together and talk, and if you are not in college preparatory you haven't got a chance.[7]

Unfortunately, some secondary school teachers have little understanding of and respect for the less able pupils. Although it is understandable that teachers should prefer to work with pupils of high ability who will achieve well in their studies, the lack of sympathy for and understanding of the slow pupils frequently leads to mutual hostility between teacher and pupils, and ultimately to difficult disciplinary problems and early withdrawal from school. In discussing problems of hostility in education, Arthur T. Jersild, professor of education, Teachers College, Columbia University, says:

> One general expression of hostility in the academic world is to treat difficulty in learning as a deliberate kind of rebellion, which should be punished. There is also an undercurrent of hostility in intellectual snobbery. We are venting our hostility when we feel contempt for people who are not as bright as ourselves or who, as we see it, have academic wares that are inferior to our own.[8]

Teachers may actually be expressing their own hostility when they express such undesirable attitudes toward pupils of low

[7] A. B. Hollingshead, *Elmtown's Youth*, New York: John Wiley & Sons, Inc., 1949, p. 169.

[8] Arthur T. Jersild, *When Teachers Face Themselves*, New York: Bureau of Publications, Teachers College, Columbia University, 1955, p. 115.

academic ability and often also of low social class. There is little wonder that youth from low social-economic homes drop out of school in greater numbers than those from more fortunate circumstances. The great majority of youth who withdraw from secondary school before graduation are from families of the two lowest groups (see Chapter 4).

Parents of low social class often encourage their children to leave school as soon as they can legally do so because they see little use for education in their way of life. There may be many reasons why pupils *want to quit school,* but the desire for education must be learned and many lower-class children have never really had a chance to learn to *want to go to school.* As long as the curriculum is not suited to the needs and abilities of all pupils, as long as some school practices and policies discriminate against pupils on the basis of social class, and as long as parents do not encourage their children to desire an education, the secondary school must assume some responsibility for encouraging pupils to want to go to school and to succeed there.

DESEGREGATION AND SOCIAL CHANGE. In one of the most important decisions in its history, the United States Supreme Court in 1954 declared racial segregation in public schools to be unconstitutional. In a unanimous decision, the Court declared that even though school facilities might be equal in segregated white and Negro schools,

> To separate them [Negroes] from others of similar age and qualifications solely because of their race generates a feeling of inferiority as to their status in the community that may affect their hearts and minds in a way unlikely ever to be undone . . .
> A sense of inferiority affects the motivation of a child to learn. Segregation . . . has a tendency to retard the educational and mental development of Negro children and to deprive them of some of the benefits they would receive from a racially integrated school system . . .
> We conclude that in the field of public education the doctrine of "separate but equal" has no place. Separate educational facilities are inherently unequal.

The Court did not order an immediate end to segregation, but it ruled that states must end compulsory racial segregation in the public schools "with deliberate speed." So began one of the most revolutionary changes ever to occur in American education. There is little need at this point to discuss in detail the social and economic causes of racial prejudice and discrimination. In discussing the race problem in America, Gunnar Myrdal, a Swedish sociologist who made an extensive study of the Negro problem in America, says in *An American Dilemma,* "The subordinate position of Negroes is perhaps the most glaring conflict in the American conscience and the greatest unsolved task of American democracy." As Myrdal points out, this is a moral issue and a conflict within the minds of men over belief in the American creed of liberty and equality with an attempt to rationalize racial prejudice and discrimination. It has existed from the beginning of our history and is now, in many parts of the nation, the cause of deep conflicts and confusion. It will, no doubt, continue to be a difficult problem for years to come, but if America is to move toward a fuller realization of democracy it must be solved.

To many people, education is the answer to the race problem in America. In the long run, education in its broadest sense is the hope for better understanding. However, it would be naïve to assume that the schools can go very far beyond the beliefs and practices sanctioned by the community. Education that is in the nature of propaganda or exhortation at the level of platitudes is largely ineffective. The solution to racial prejudice and discrimination will come about only when enough people understand the causes and costs of such prejudice and discrimination and are willing to do something about it. As long as racial segregation exists and is rationalized, racial prejudice will be perpetuated. This is why the Supreme Court decision ordering school desegregation is so important.

The mere mixing of whites and Negroes does not automatically overcome prejudices; it may even increase them. Certain kinds of contacts, however, have produced spectacular changes in attitudes. In the armed services, in employment, and in certain housing projects, integration of the races has not resulted in the dire consequences which many predicted. On the contrary, it has generally resulted in striking reductions in prejudices. Yet incidental and involuntary contacts in which a great deal of fear and tension has been created are likely to increase prejudice.

COMMUNITIES PREPARED FOR INTEGRATION. When a community has been carefully prepared for integration in its schools and law-enforcement officials have made it clear that they will tolerate no disorder, desegregation has usually come about without serious trouble. While it is true that a law is enforceable in a free society only when supported by public opinion, an intolerant minority in the absence of law can nullify the goodwill of the majority. Laws, therefore, are necessary because this reverses the role of the trouble-maker. Disorders are likely to accompany integration of races in the schools only when law enforcement officials indicate that they will not enforce the law. This principle was clearly demonstrated in the desegregation of the public schools of Washington, D. C., when the police in effect said to some potential troublemakers, "You may not like the law, but it is the law of the land and it will be enforced."

Successful integration of Negro and white servicemen in the armed forces revealed the importance of getting groups together for functionally important activities. As long as the army was segregated into white and Negro divisions, there was continual conflict between the races, but once they were integrated, prejudice and conflict were greatly reduced. When white soldiers experienced fighting side by side with Negroes, they overcame much of their prejudice; they had an experience which made it possible for them to think of the Negro as a fellow soldier rather than as a Negro. Prejudice becomes too high a price to pay if keeping alive depends upon cooperation between individuals.

Practically no desegregation in the public secondary schools has as yet taken place in the deep South and little in the mid-South, but in the border states integration is being achieved with little resistance. As areas become more urbanzied and industrialized and the proportion of Negroes becomes smaller, resistance to desegregation weakens. Although discrimination still exists throughout the nation, there are powerful forces at work against segregation. These forces cannot be stopped. The deep South eventually will be unable to preserve segregation at the cost of economic, political, and cultural isolation from the main currents of American life. The problem of the future is how to learn to live with the change.

In a very real sense, the world-wide struggle between communism and the free world is an intercultural conflict. Non-whites constituting more than half of the world's population will not take America's professions of freedom seriously until this country solves its problem of racial discrimination and segregation. Whether viewed locally or on a world scene, what America is reaching for is democracy at home and abroad. As Myrdal says, America is free to choose whether the Negro shall remain her liability or become her opportunity:

> In this sense the Negro problem is not only America's greatest failure but also America's incomparably great opportunity for the future. If America should follow its own deepest convictions, its well-being at home would rise immensely. The century-old dream of American patriots, that America should give to the entire world its own freedoms and its own faith, would come true. America can demonstrate that justice, equality and cooperation are possible between white and colored people.[9]

American secondary education has made many contributions to American life. One of the most significant of these is educating great

[9] Gunnar Myrdal, An American Dilemma, New York: Harper & Brothers, 1944, p. 1021.

numbers of youth from many different lands and cultures, with an understanding of America's historic heritage. The challenge for the secondary schools in this respect is greater today than ever before. The extension of greater opportunities in secondary education to Negro youth is the most serious challenge which has confronted the American secondary school throughout its history.

CULTURE OF THE SECONDARY SCHOOL

In analyzing the changes which are taking place in modern society, the secondary school itself must not be overlooked. The school is itself a social system with a subculture of its own—a complex set of beliefs, values, traditions, and ways of thinking and behaving. These, together with a network of interactions among students, teachers, administrators, and the community, enable the secondary school to function so as to achieve its objectives and perform its role as an agency of society.

STRUCTURE OF SCHOOL SOCIETY. The culture of the school is made up of a number of different elements—buildings and equipment, books and materials, curriculum, and pupils, teachers, and other school personnel. The ways in which these all interact, make it different from any other institution.

While it is recognized that the school's purpose is to "educate," and that education is carried on in various subjects in a formal way in the classroom, it is frequently overlooked that pupils learn many things in school in addition to subject matter. What pupils learn through informal approaches in school may be fully as important as learnings from textbooks. All school experiences, the school culture, and the adolescent subculture influence youthful behavior.

Without describing the culture of the school in detail, the activities which many teen-agers consider the most important part of school life serve to illustrate what Willard Waller, well-known for his early work in educational sociology, calls the internal culture of the school:

Teachers have always known that it was not necessary for the students of strange customs to cross the seas to find material. Folklore and myth, tradition, taboo, magic rites, ceremonials of all sorts, collective representations, *participation mystique,* all abound in the front yard of every school, and occasionally they creep upstairs and are incorporated into the more formal portions of school life.

There are, in the school, complex rituals of personal relationships, a set of folkways, mores, and irrational sanctions, a moral code based upon them. There are games, which are sublimated wars, teams, and an elaborate set of ceremonies concerning them. There are traditions, and traditionalists waging their world-old battle against innovators. There are laws, and there is the problem of enforcing them. There is *Sittlichkeit*. There are specialized societies with a rigid structure and a limited membership. There are no reproductive groups, but there are customs regulating the relation of the sexes. All these things make up a world that is different from the world of adults. It is the separate culture of the young, having its locus in the school.[10]

COLD WAR BETWEEN YOUTH AND ADULTS. The adolescent sub-culture and certain cultural conflicts will be dealt with only briefly, but one of the most challenging and difficult problems facing secondary schools today is the conflict between what youth expects of society and what the adult society expects of youth. The conflict is all the more difficult because of the confusion, contradictions, and conflicts in the adult society. While the adult is always excluded from teen-age society, adolescent culture reflects adult society and is a powerful agency for molding the values and behavior which youth will have as adults. The trouble is that too many adults continue to think and behave as they did when adolescents.

A normal youth wants desperately to "grow up" and win respect and recognition from adults. Yet the very nature of the changes that have come about in our society cuts him off from the rest of society and forces him inward toward his own age group. As a consequence, society finds itself no longer with a set of individuals to be trained toward adulthood but with a subculture which presents a united front against adults:

Thus the very changes our society is undergoing have spawned something more than we bargained for. They have taken not only the training-for-job out of the parents' hands, but have quite effectively taken the whole adolescent himself away and have dumped him into a society of his peers, a society whose habitants are the halls and classrooms of the school, the teenage canteen, the corner drugstore, the automobile, and numerous other natural habitats of Homosapiens, age sixteen.[11]

These conditions present both a problem and an opportunity. The problem is that adolescents who are cut off from their parents and adult society create spontaneous subcultures of their own; the opportunity is for the secondary school to handle adolescent societies so that they will generate their own civic responsibilities.

The teen-ager in many ways is an exploited and exiled adolescent minority. Except for finding an appropriate mate and serving in the army in time of war, adolescents generally find themselves kept

[10] Willard Waller, *The Sociology of Teaching*, New York: John Wiley & Sons, Inc., 1932, pp. 103-104.

[11] Franklin Patterson and others, *The Adolescent Citizen*, Glencoe, Ill.: The Free Press, 1960, p. 294.

out of adult society. They have no vote and few opportunities to work because of child labor laws and union regulations. They must prolong their dependency on adults over a longer period of time than has any previous generation. They are, however, compelled to go to school at least until they are sixteen. If they are poor in school or are not interested in formal education, it is not surprising that they drop out of school to become members of a teen-age gang.

Many youth who have not left school physically have "dropped out," however, as far as benefiting from formal education is concerned. Many of them have little interest in what the secondary school has to offer and respond unfavorably to pressures put on them to learn. How to succeed in teaching "reluctant learners" is a difficult problem. Usually, the more pupils resist, the greater is the pressure to make them conform. While this may succeed in getting some to learn, it only results in increased passivity or rebellion in others. In too many classrooms this "conflict of cultures" is at best a kind of "cold war" in which pupils and teachers form negative, if not hostile, concepts of each other.

Many adults, including teachers, have a negative stereotype image of teen-agers. This attitude can result in serious damage to healthy personality development, as well as reinforce resistant behavior and the separateness of the adolescent from society. A negative stereotype of youth provides a convenient scapegoat for the adult community. The increasing pressure placed on pupils in secondary schools today is undoubtedly motivated to some extent by adult fears of themselves.

Adults exhibit the same kind of negative behavior as teen-agers do when they are placed under the autocratic authority of others and are frustrated in achieving their goals. Adults, like teen-agers, form "little societies" or cliques and set up their own rules of conduct to protect themselves against the pressures of those in authority. In developing desirable behavior, much depends upon the nature of the relationship that exists between subordinates and those in authority. For the secondary school this means that the curriculum, the teacher, and the pupil must be so well correlated that the needs of the adult society and those of the youth in his subculture are satisfied in one unified living process.

The problem of the teacher is to understand adolescents so well that he can relate them to the school program in such a way that they will find answers to their hopes and expectations in school, and as a consequence react positively to learning. In this way, youth should make an easier and more positive transition from the adolescent subculture to adult society.

SUMMARY

The public secondary school in the United States, as a product of American culture, has its function determined by the ideals and aspirations of the society which it serves. In achieving its goals, the secondary school is committed to a policy of educating competent, responsible, intelligent citizens for a free society. The schools, however, cannot escape influences of the conflicts and pressures which exist in the social, economic, and political environment.

We are living in an age of almost incredible change, with many changes in our way of life occurring with accelerating speed. Industrialization and urbanization have swept aside old ways of living, while powerful special interest groups have greatly complicated and modified the individual's role in society. These changes have created new problems in school and community relations. Furthermore, we are caught up in a world-wide conflict of cultures, with many problems of social class and caste and intercultural conflict emerging in America. All of these developments emphasize the transitional nature of modern society. They in turn have serious implications for the organization and the program of the secondary schools.

In an age of such revolutionary change, it is inevitable that some confusion and conflict of values will exist because the alternatives which individuals have for choosing different values and courses of action are greatly multiplied. At a time when people are questioning traditionally held values and are searching for new values and goals, secondary education has greater freedom to determine its own direction and it has greater responsibilities for providing an effective program of education for youth. The future existence of a free society depends in large part upon the ability of the secondary schools to prepare citizens who understand and value the basic ideals of freedom and who can deal intelligently with the revolutionary changes brought about by developments in science and technology. It is within this framework that we should examine the principles and practices of secondary education in America.

SELECTED REFERENCES

ASSOCIATION FOR SUPERVISION AND CURRICULUM DEVELOPMENT. *Forces Affecting American Education*. (1953 Yearbook). Washington, D.C.: National Education Association, Chap. 2.—Charles S. Johnson discusses the culture affecting education.

ASSOCIATION FOR SUPERVISION AND CURRICULUM DEVELOPMENT. *What Shall The High Schools Teach?* (1956 Yearbook). Washington, D.C.: National Education Association, Chap. 2.—Deals with the influence of social changes on the adolescent subculture and the school as a social system.

DAVIS, ALLISON, GARDNER, BURLEIGH B., and GARDNER, MARY R. *Deep South.* Chicago: University of Chicago Press, 1941, Chaps. 2 and 10.—A discussion of the caste and class system in the South.

GAILBRAITH, JOHN KENNETH. *The Affluent Society.* Boston: Houghton Mifflin Co., 1958, Chaps. 1 and 2.—A discussion of new concepts for an economy of abundance.

HAVIGHURST, ROBERT J., AND NEUGARTEN, BERNICE L. *Society and Education.* Boston: Allyn & Bacon, Inc., 1957, 465 pp.—An excellent presentation of the social structure in America and its relation to education.

HOLLINGSHEAD, AUGUST B. *Elmtown's Youth.* New York: John Wiley & Sons, Inc., 1949, 453 pp.—A study of social class in a small mid-western city and its impact on adolescents and educational policies.

HORTON, PAUL B., and LESLIE, GERALD R. *The Sociology of Social Problems.* New York: Appleton-Century-Crofts, Inc., 1960, Chaps. 11, 12, and 13.—An excellent treatment of social class and race problems.

MYRDAL, GUNNAR. *An American Dilemma.* New York: Harper & Brothers, 1944. Chaps. 2, 3, and 45.—A discussion of the Negro problem in America and the opportunity it presents for a solution in harmony with democratic ideals.

NATIONAL COUNCIL FOR THE SOCIAL STUDIES. *Citizenship and a Free Society.* (Thirtieth Yearbook). Washington, D.C.: National Education Association, 1960, Chap. 2. —A discussion of the nature of the adolescent and his subculture.

PATTERSON, FRANKLIN, AND OTHERS. *The Adolescent Citizen.* Glencoe, Ill.: The Free 1960, 93 pp.—Deals with citizenship education in the secondary school within the context of revolutionary changes brought about by science and technology.

PATTERSON, FRANKLIN, AND OTHERS. *The Adolescent Citizen.* Glencoe, Ill.: The Free Press, 1960, Chaps. 1, 7 and 11.—Suggests new perspectives for secondary education as they apply to the adolescent citizen.

PRESIDENT'S COMMISSION ON NATIONAL GOALS. *Goals for Americans.* Englewood Cliffs, N.J.: Prentice-Hall, Inc., 1960, 372 pp.—A report of the President's Commission on National Goals and chapters submitted for the consideration of the Commission by noted scholars on American ideals and social, economic, and political problems.

RIESMAN, DAVID. *The Lonely Crowd.* New Haven: Yale University Press, 1950, Chaps. 1 and 2.—An analysis of the American character and its tendency toward conformity.

ROCKEFELLER BROTHERS FUND. *The Pursuit of Excellence: Education and the Future of America.* Report V, The Special Studies Project. Garden City, N.Y.: Doubleday & Co., Inc., 1958, 49 pp.—Deals with the challenges facing education in an age of crisis.

WARNER, W. LLOYD, HAVIGHURST, ROBERT J., and LOEB, MARTIN B. *Who Shall Be Educated?* New York: Harper & Brothers, 1944, 190 pp.—An analysis of social class influences on education.

WARNER, W. LLOYD, and LUNT, PAUL S. *The Social Life of a Modern Community.* New Haven: Yale University Press, 1941, 460 pp.—A picture of the social class structure of a New England community called "Yankee City."

WHYTE, WILLIAM H. JR. *The Organization Man.* New York: Doubleday & Co., Inc., 1957. Chap. 2.—Discusses the decline of the Protestant ethic in America.

4

THE SECONDARY SCHOOL PUPIL

This chapter shows the kind of population that exists in the secondary schools of the United States, what young people in secondary schools are like, how they differ from the pupil population of earlier schools and of schools in other countries, and other significant data concerning pupils. A considerable portion of the chapter is devoted to the question of the extent of democratization of secondary education in this country. Such factors as socioeconomic status, intelligence, racial and ethnic background, cost of attending high school, and underachievement are discussed. A final section of the chapter centers on the developmental tasks and the problems that youth face in the process of growing up.

These are not isolated data presented for their own sake. They represent information that persons must have to make intelligent statements about secondary education. The kind of population that a secondary school serves is closely related to the purposes of that secondary school system and to the program that it needs to present for the particular groups that it serves. For example, if a school system provides education for a large number of adults beyond the age of twenty who have not completed high school, it must relate its program to their demands and needs.

Since research and data are plentiful in these areas discussed, the chapter does not recount all the information that is found in studies. These studies are accessible through a number of publications on secondary schools. Succeeding chapters throughout the book indicate through descriptions of current practices how well the needs of pupils discussed in this chapter are being met. The student of education courses should constantly keep in mind that data concerning pupils as he evaluates present practices.

SECONDARY SCHOOL POPULATION[1]

The secondary school enrollments reflect the rise in birthrate. The population of the United States in 1960 had increased about 25 per cent since 1946, while the school-age population had increased about 50 per cent in the same period, or at approximately double the rate of the increase of the total population. Although from the period beginning in 1939-40 to 1949-50 the secondary school population actually decreased, it is now increasing rapidly. The three to four million children who were born annually in the years 1946 to 1960, as compared with approximately two and a half million early in the 1940s, have entered and will enter high school from 1960 to 1974. Thus the impact of the rising birthrate is being felt more and more in the secondary schools. Anyone living in a large suburban area is conscious of this fact through seeing the new secondary schools that are being built in that area.

In 1961–62 almost thirteen million youth were enrolled in public secondary schools as contrasted to about seven million in 1951–52. It is estimated that in 1965 about nineteen million youth will be enrolled in secondary schools. Because of the increasing population of the United States and the accompanying increase in interest of education for the children of the nation, the end of increased enrollments is nowhere in sight.

Nearly all youth of secondary school age are now enrolled in school. Approximately 90 per cent of youth fourteen through seventeen years of age are enrolled in school. In 1890, only 7 per cent of the young people of these ages were attending school. The pupil population in secondary schools practically doubled every decade from 1880 to 1940. The fact is of tremendous significance for the secondary school curriculum, guidance services, and other aspects of the secondary school program.

The figures for the proportion of high school youth enrolled in school vary for different sections of the country and for urban and rural areas. Some states of the Far West, Mid-west, and East have the highest proportion enrolled. In some states in the South, where support of education is not as favorable and larger percentages of

[1] Data in this section come from the latest United States Bureau of the Census Population Reports and the United States Office of Education Bulletins that present the statistics of secondary schools, especially the *Statistics of Education in the United States,* dated annually by school year, and in various *NEA Research Bulletins.* The National Education Association publishes from time to time graphically illustrated summaries of data concerning enrollments in secondary schools. The data in this chapter generally refer to the years 1958–59 or 1959–60.

the population have a low income, the lowest proportion is found. Density of population and the different types of life led by the people are factors of importance affecting school attendance. Rural areas, where school facilities are less easily accessible, have a smaller percentage of youth going to high school.

The majority of youth attend large high schools. With the increasing trend toward urbanization in the United States, it is not surprising to find that 55 to 60 per cent of young people of high school age live in urban areas. In fact, one of five live in large metropolitan areas consisting of one million or more people. About 20 to 25 per cent of youth live in villages and small towns, and about 28 per cent live on farms. This picture is constantly changing somewhat in favor of the higher percentages of those who live in urban and suburban areas.

There were in 1958-59 somewhat over twenty-four thousand public secondary schools in the United States. Although approximately 70 per cent of these secondary schools had an enrollment of less than 500 students each, over two-thirds of the secondary school pupils attend high schools having an enrollment of 500 or more.

It is interesting to note that in 1959 there were about four thousand secondary schools in this country with pupils numbering less than one hundred. The median size of the secondary school had risen considerably, however, in recent years to a figure of nearly three hundred pupils.

These facts point out that, even though the majority of young people attend large high schools, in discussing secondary education in this country one needs to consider the many small high schools that cannot possibly have the advantages of larger institutions. They do have some advantages peculiar to a small-sized school, however. This question is dealt with in another chapter.

There are increasingly fewer young people compared to the number of adults in the total population. Youth in the secondary school age bracket, fourteen to seventeen years of age, constitute about 10 per cent of the population of the United States. This proportion has been steadily diminishing and there are now fewer youths per 1000 adults than there were in the year 1900. The South, as a region of the country, has more youth per adult population than any other section.

These facts indicate some inequalities in the ability of various regions of the country to support secondary education, an argument used in favor of federal aid to education. Another important implication is related to the manpower situation and the consequent rise in the age of beginning employment which young people can look forward to. In other words, they compete against a larger number of adults than young persons did some twenty or thirty years ago.

Youth come from home backgrounds of all types. A high school education for their children has become the ambition of parents of all economic classes. The rapid democratization of secondary school education in this country is in striking contrast to the selective character of European secondary education. Here the people of semiskilled and unskilled occupational groups have found free public education a boon which provides greater opportunities for their children.

The increasing enrollment in public schools has brought together pupils from all walks of life, from various economic and social classes, from different religious and racial groups. This development in itself has been of utmost importance in giving the pupil a significant part of his secondary school education, that of learning to live together with all types of people. In most sections of the country, different racial groups attend classes together and form lasting friendships there. Pupils from the home of the plumber, the mechanic, the itinerant worker, the doctor, and the business executive go to the same high school. They come from broken homes as well as from homes where family harmony and solidarity give an added advantage. Their home may be an eighteen-room mansion overlooking the beach or a shack by the river. In spite of these facts, the greater proportion of children of the professional and managerial class remain in high school.

Some teachers and principals who look back with longing at the days when the secondary school could readily force out the "misfits" are bewildered by pupils who come from slum environments and broken, unhappy homes, bringing their many maladjustment problems with them to school. Teachers sometimes fail to realize that the pupils in today's secondary schools are different from those of the 1920's because they represent all groups in the American population.

The population in secondary schools is showing increasing mobility. It is common knowledge to the secondary school principal and teacher that more and more students are moving from one section of the country to another. The alert teacher capitalizes on this fact by using students from various sections of the country as resource persons. Such migration, of course, causes a good many headaches since students may come ill prepared from some small high schools in poor regions of the country, or constant transfer from school to school may cause severe emotional problems among the students affected.

The census data show that some 18 per cent of youth moved from the house in which they lived during the previous year. About 6 to 11 per cent of young people of high school age migrated to a different county. These rates of migration are considerably higher on the West Coast than in some other sections of the country.

A greater proportion of secondary school youth are married. The greatest change in marital status has, of course, been noticed at the college level, where it is becoming more common now for young people to be married before the man finishes his education. However, the trend is also noticeable in secondary schools. As one could guess, a greater proportion of girls than boys are married in high schools. About 6 per cent of the girls in the high school age group are married while less than 1 per cent of the boys are. These would be found largely in the upper grades of the high school.

This change in the social mores causes problems for secondary school administrators. However, youngsters who are married in secondary schools, in some cases may well be of an older age; in other cases, they may have the consent of the parents. Consequently, an intelligent approach to the problem would not regard these young people as deviants or in the same classification as juvenile delinquents.

The incidence of juvenile delinquency in recent years has been rising. Although legal and sociological definitions of juvenile delinquency differ, the statistics available show that since 1948 the rate of juvenile delinquency increased materially in the United States. In fact, the rate of increase is four times the increase of the population of the country. It has been estimated that some one and a quarter million teenagers will get into trouble in one year. However, this is only around one-eighteenth of the total population ten to seventeen years of age. About one-half million become involved each year in serious actions that are brought to the courts.

Other facts concerning juvenile delinquency are of even more importance for the schools. The greater incidence of delinquency occurs in the highly congested areas of population. The young person who becomes a delinquent is more likely to come from a home in which there are negative interpersonal relations, a home with substandard conditions in housing, family stability, supervision, and love.[2]

[2]William C. Kvaraceus, *Juvenile Delinquency, What Research Says to the Teacher,* Series No. 15, Washington, D.C.: Department of Classroom Teachers and American Educational Research Association, National Education Association, 1958, pp. 3-4, 12.

COMPARISONS IN SCHOOL POPULATION

A much greater proportion of youth attend high school than in the early American secondary school. It was indicated in a previous section of this chapter that nearly all youth of secondary school age are now enrolled in school as contrasted with but a small proportion at the beginning of the century. The ideal of a universal secondary education, the grand experiment of the century, has indeed been successful beyond the dreams of the early leaders in this country who first advocated this concept.

While in 1870 only about 2 per cent of youth of post high school age were graduates of high schools, at the present time better than two of three youth under thirty years of age are high school graduates. This figure is in startling contrast to the large number who dropped out and the fewer who finished secondary school in the latter decades of the last century, and even through the first quarter of this century.

These figures in themselves reveal the change in function of the American secondary school since its early beginnings. While at first it was a very selective school intended to train only a small proportion of youth for leadership positions in the particular culture of the times, the academy brought a changing concept of whom the secondary school was intended to serve. Since the establishment of the high school, the steady progression, every decade, of numbers of youth who have attended secondary schools has strongly underscored a firm belief of the American public in universal, free public education.

The American secondary schools serve children of all types and backgrounds as contrasted with European secondary schools. The early American secondary school was in many respects modeled after the schools which the imigrants coming to these shores had known in their European homelands. The highly selective nature of the European schools is still maintained in most nations in western Europe, although there is evidence of a change toward the direction of a universal public education, particularly in such countries as Russia, Sweden, and England.

Yet the European secondary school in most instances continues to serve the minority of the young people going through the schools of that continent. In western Europe, only about 20 per cent of the sixteen- to seventeen-year-olds are enrolled in the secondary schools. In fact, there are about as many secondary school students in our honor societies as there are in the total European secondary school group. This, of course, is an especially pertinent fact when we compare the curriculum of the American high school with that of secondary schools of other countries. European secondary schools accept about one-fifth of the children and about one-half of these persist to graduate. Fewer than one in twenty of European youth can complete secondary school and attend college, except in Russia where the figure is probably closer to one in ten, with the gradually increasing proportion finishing secondary school. The elite concept of European secondary education is well illustrated by the fact seven times as many of the age group attend high school in the United States as do in Europe.

The result of the rather rigid academic curriculum and examination system is that most of the high school youth in European countries will be from homes that are favored economically or from students in the higher intelligence brackets. There is also another significant difference. In the high schools of the United States, girls make up slightly over 50 per cent of the students while in Europe attending high school is still considered largely a masculine prerogative.

Reliable figures of school attendance in the Soviet Union have been difficult to obtain. However, in 1957 the United States Office of Education reported that there was a total of one-and-one-half million graduates of Soviet secondary schools as contrasted with one-and-three-tenths million graduates of American high schools.

There are considerable differences between American and European secondary schools in the proportion of youth going on to college. Following somewhat in the tradition of the European pattern of education, in 1870 less than 2 per cent of the youth of college age in this country were enrolled in college. The tremendous interest in education and the growing requirements for a good educational background both for intelligent citizenship and for participation in occupations has caused a rapidly rising rate of attendance in college. In the last half of the 1940's came a big increase in college enrollments with the enactment of the G.I. "Bill of Rights" which gave an unprecedented opportunity to veterans to attend college. The colleges and universities of this country are now facing what they term the "bulge" from the large number of children born in 1942-53, who are and will be in college from 1964–75.

In the 1920's and the 1930's it was not uncommon for perhaps one or two graduates of a small secondary school to be the only ones from the senior class who attended college. In those years approximately 10 to 20 per cent of high school graduates entered college. Today the figure is more than 50 per cent, and in some schools in wealthy suburban areas the percentage will run closer to 100 than to 50. The United States Office of Education estimates that about 40 per cent of youth eighteen to twenty-one years of age will be enrolled in college by the middle of the sixth decade of this century. It is interesting to note, too, that the predicted college enrollment for 1978 is over nine million while the enrollment in colleges in 1961-62 was almost four million.

Over one-third of the eighteen- to twenty-year-olds are enrolled in schools as compared with fewer than 10 per cent in the European countries. The USSR, it was estimated in 1956, had 8 to 12 per cent college-age students enrolled, full and part time. This figure again would be greater at the present time.

These figures must be taken into consideration when the function of secondary schools in this country as contrasted with the function in European countries is discussed. Function determines the curriculum, and the curriculum of the schools of any society is built to serve the young people of the society who attend its schools. If those young people are primarily college bound and intend to prepare for the professions and scholarly pursuits, the curriculum of the secondary school will, of course, be of a nature suited to that purpose. If secondary school youth are bound for all kinds of occupations within the society, the curriculum will be different in nature. It should be noted, however, that the secondary school of the United States is gradually becoming more of a college-preparatory school in function since the proportion of its graduates who go on to college is increasing and has increased in recent years. This is a fact that is often forgotten by those who think of the secondary school in terms of what it was like ten to twenty years ago.

EXTENT OF EDUCATIONAL OPPORTUNITY

Although the American secondary school has made rapid strides toward serving equally all the children of all the people, we need to examine additional data to determine whether it is genuinely democratic in providing equal opportunity for all youth. To what extent does the economic group into which a child is born determine his chances of receiving a high school education? Is American secondary education geared to all its youth except those who, because of severe mental or physical handicaps, cannot support themselves or take the responsibility for their own lives? What are the differences between those who complete high school and those who do not?

Approximately two-thirds of the young people who enter the ninth grade graduate from high school. The actual figures show that, in 1960, 60.4 per cent of those who had entered ninth grade in 1956 graduated. There is a gradually diminishing number remaining from year to year as the group progresses through high school. The number dropping out is significant. Evidently high school is not meeting the needs of these youth, or other circumstances in their environment prevent them from continuing.

Another set of figures indicate that somewhat over 60 per cent of the young people in the age bracket twenty to twenty-four have completed high school. Among the sixteen- and seventeen-year-old brackets approximately one-fourth of the young people are not enrolled in school.

Youth of higher intelligence levels have a better chance of survival through high school. As the question of why so many youth fail to complete high school is studied, results show that those from the lower brackets of intelligence (as measured by the verbal type of test) are more likely to drop out. Studies show that the average I.Q. of graduates is usually greater than that of drop-outs, but they do not indicate the differences in other types of abilities; mechanical, artistic, or social. Evidently, the secondary school has been selective by intelligence to some extent. The rest of this section presents some data that throw light on this question. In addition, many of the chapters in this book present evidence as to what kind of a program is being carried on in secondary schools. The student of education can study these and draw his own conclusions as to whether or not the secondary school program is geared to youth of all levels of academic ability and all backgrounds.

Youth from homes of low socioeconomic status drop out in greater numbers than those more fortunately situated. A number of studies show that the father's occupation is an extremely important factor in determining how long a boy or girl will attend high school. Whether a child is born into the home of a proprietor, a store manager, a doctor, a coal miner, a waiter, or a factory worker determines to a large extent his chances of being in line on commencement day, and consequently of attending college or securing certain types of employment. These studies show convincingly that the youth from the lower economic brackets do not have equal opportunity in attending high school. For example, such evidence as the following has been presented from time to time in the last twenty-five years:

1. A young person from a home in the highest economic level is five times as likely to complete high school as one from the lowest income group.

2. A smaller proportion of youth from underprivileged homes continue school after high school graduation as contrasted with those from the top of the economic scale.
3. One of the reasons given for dropping out of school is the need to work or the lack of money to stay in school.
4. Two of every three youth who drop out of school below the ninth grade are from homes in poor economic circumstances.
5. Juvenile delinquency is more frequent among drop-outs than among graduates.[3]

In the homes of the lower income group, the family members are usually many and the dollars few. Older children are needed at home on the farm or must begin earning money early to supplement the family income. There may be less encouragement for them to continue high school. Certainly, the father and mother often see little chance of their being able to send the children to college. The total family culture, including its mores and accepted patterns of living, is a powerful factor in determining how long a child will continue in school. (See Chapter 3.)

The cash cost of attending high school is a factor in determining whether youth will continue in school. The findings of research that has been done on the cost to pupils for textbooks, student tickets, dances, yearbooks, student supplies, gymnasium uniforms, class rings, and the like have raised the question whether the public high school is "free." The average cash cost per year as found in the different studies has varied from $10 to $400.

One notable fact in these studies is that children from the lower economic groups spend considerably less than the amount spent by children of homes in the upper brackets. These figures, in themselves, tell the story of the difficulty and sacrifices of parents from low income homes in order to send their children to high school. They do not tell of the heartaches and disappointments of many youth who are not able to be like other pupils in the school because of the lack of money to spend on clothes, dances, games, or "cokes" at the corner drug store.

Harold C. Hand, professor of education at the University of Illinois, in his Hidden Tuition Costs Study, found that in the 1930's, the average yearly expenditure of students for incidental expenses in connection with attending high school, not including food, clothing, shelter, or transportation, was $125. No pupil reported less than $25 spent per year. He notes that these studies were made in the years when 63 per cent of the American families earned less than

[3] The student who wishes to investigate these studies further will find a list of them at the end of the chapter.

$1,500 annually. Later studies show these expenses were even higher.[4]

Young people from certain racial and ethnic groups frequently do not have equality of opportunity in attending high school. In 1956 somewhat over 80 per cent of the non-white children fourteen to seventeen years of age were enrolled in school as contrasted to somewhat less than 90 per cent of the children of the whites. The inferior nature of the schools for Negroes, in sections of the country where segregated schools existed and still exist, has in the past been evident in many ways, although to the credit of the southern states, in recent years the facilities in these schools have been greatly improved. In many cases, teachers' salaries have been lower than those of teachers in the schools for white children; the pupil-teacher ratio has been higher; and the money spent for instructional materials, less. Teachers have not been as well prepared. In some instances, these conditions have also been improved. In the Southwest, children from Mexican parentage attend school in smaller proportion than children from the rest of the population. More children of native white parentage reach the twelfth grade than those of foreign-born parentage, according to census figures.

One of the tragedies in the educational picture in the United States in recent years has been the closing of secondary schools in some communities (for example, in Virginia and Arkansas) in order to avoid integration. This event has been especially unfortunate in view of the increased demands on the population for intelligent participation in civic affairs. In a time when educators have been concerned with improving secondary education, especially in the fields of science and mathematics, schools in some communities have remained closed to large numbers of children. Since the private secondary schools set up to take care of the children in communities where the public schools were closed have been for white children only, large numbers of Negro youth have not been able to attend schools. Thus, to some children in America, equality of opportunity for secondary education is still a dream.

The amount of money spent for education per pupil varies considerably among the different states in the union. It is a well-known fact that the states with the lowest per capita wealth generally have the greatest number of children to educate. Those who advocate federal aid for education point out that since the wealth is not distributed equally in various sections of the country, the federal government has a responsibility to the states in order to provide equality

[4] Harold C. Hand, *Principles of Public Secondary Education,* New York: Harcourt Brace and World, Inc., 1958, pp. 91-99.

of opportunity for the children throughout the United States. This argument has become particularly pertinent in recent years when more and more families migrate from state to state. At the same time, it is significant to note that the states with the lowest percentage of youth enrolled in the secondary schools were found largely in the South. According to the United States Office of Education, the total expenditure per pupil in average daily attendance in 1957-58 was about three times as large in the highest ranking state as in the lowest state. The actual amounts varied from $174 annual expenditure per pupil in Mississippi to $506 in New York State.

The place where the young person of high school age happens to live affects his chances of attending high school. As was indicated in the previous section, smaller proportions of the youth in the South generally attend high school than in other sections of the country. If a young person between fourteen and seventeen years of age happened to live in Virginia in 1950, for example, his chances of being enrolled in secondary school were not as good as they would have been if he had lived in the state of Washington at that time. In 1956, 53.5 per cent of the ninth-grade students entering school four years previously did not graduate in the state of Georgia as contrasted with 6.9 per cent for the same year in the state of Wisconsin.

If a young person lives in a rural area, some factors seem to operate that make his chances of attending secondary school somewhat less than those of children of families who live in urban areas. Undoubtedly many of these factors operating in these situations are complicated, but nevertheless they indicate that the place of residence of the parents has some relation to whether or not the child is likely to finish secondary school.

Youth from the upper economic and intellectual groups participate more frequently in extraclass activities. Hand has summarized a number of studies which indicate that high school students from the upper socioeconomic classes take greater part in the school's extraclass activities or belong to more clubs and school organizations. A greater proportion of the student leaders tend to come from the upper socioeconomic levels. The "Elmtown Youth" who came from the two lower social classes had by far the largest proportion of non-participators. There is no reason to believe that this situation has changed. Here again it is found that a segment of the youth population is deprived of some of the worthwhile experiences in secondary school. Although cost of participation is a factor, the culture pattern of secondary schools makes it impossible for pupils with failing marks in school subjects to participate in extraclass activities.

The opportunity for college attendance is related to the family's socioeconomic status. Approximately two-thirds of the children of fathers in professional and semi-professional occupations attend college after high school graduation as contrasted with about one-fourth of the children of farmers, factory workers, craftsmen, unskilled laborers, and other similar occupations.[5] In addition to being related to the father's occupation, the likelihood of attendance in college is related to the education of the parents, their financial ability, and the general culture status in the home. Since more scholarships are becoming available, there is more likelihood for a child from a poor home being able to attend college for the four years if he has the capacity to do so. However, where children are not encouraged to go to college and where the pattern of the culture in which they move is that of going to work and earning money as soon as possible, they are less likely to go on to school after high school graduation.

With the increase in the number of the junior colleges available to youth in their own home or nearby community, they are finding it financially easier to attend at least the first two years of college. The more forward-looking states in the country are planning coordinated programs of higher education whereby institutions of higher learning will be available to students in all sections of the state.

One of the problems of American society is the fact that almost 50 per cent of the most able high school graduates do not enter college. Many factors may enter into this situation, such as race, financial ability, the values in the home, as well as others. This is a serious waste of talent in a society that needs many well-trained individuals in a number of the professions. The profession of teaching is only one of these in which a shortage exists.

The problem of youth dropping out of school is related to the program of the school as well as to many other factors. The previous discussion showed that the drop-out problem is still a serious one in secondary schools of this country. About one-third of youth drop out between grades nine to twelve. Girls stay on to a somewhat greater extent, and the persistence through high school varies considerably by states. Youth begin to drop out in considerable numbers at age sixteen, when the compulsory school attendance period ends. For example, the 1950 census showed that 8.6 per cent of the fifteen-year-olds were not enrolled in school while the proportion mounted rapidly to 19.1 per cent of the sixteen-year-olds. The facts indicate also that those who drop out tend to be retarded, although several studies show that drop-outs come from among good as well as poor students.

[5] Commission on Human Resources and Advanced Training, *America's Resources of Specialized Talent,* New York: Harper & Bros., 1954, p. 160.

These data deserve careful study by school teachers and administrators who want to do something about the problem. The reasons that pupils give for dropping out of school are also important to consider. In most studies, dislike of school or lack of interest in school work ranks high among these reasons. Others include marriage, need for money in the family, desiring more spending money, perferring to go to work, entering the armed services, and poor attendance. When principals are queried about the reasons why pupils drop out of school they usually list low intelligence, retardation, desire for a job, parents' attitude, broken homes, and lack of interest in school, as well as poor study habits.

The Research Division of the National Education Association points out that "to keep youth in school, attention must be focused on a meaningful curriculum, enlightened guidance efforts, and a program of financial aids." The same article summarizes the characteristics of the drop-out as follows:

The average drop-out is 16 years old; often he has been marking time, waiting to reach the age when he may legally quit school. He is most likely to quit between the ninth and tenth, or between the tenth and eleventh grades. It is especially likely that he will not return after a summer vacation.

As a rule, the drop-out has shunned participation in extracurricular activities, and he may have failed to become part of a social group within the school.

Usually his relationships with his teachers and with many of his fellow students indicate tension, suspicion, and strain. His poor attendance record, lack of interest, and failure to cooperate have contributed to his being retarded by about two years. Before leaving school, he may have spent as many years there as one who graduates, but because he has probably been held back rather than promoted regularly, he will not have completed the full program by the end of his attendance period.

The typical drop-out's parents are unimpressed with the value of education; often they openly scorn "book-learning." In addition, the family is likely to regard school as a financial burden; not only does it cost something to keep a child in school, but the family is deprived of the money which the boy or girl could be contributing to the budget.[6]

All of the studies concerning the drop-out problem tend to support the idea that in many cases the secondary school did not meet the needs of the pupil who dropped out of school. At least as far as his own perceptions are concerned, he did not find school a satisfying or fruitful experience.

Many factors other than educational opportunity are related to underachievement. The problem of a large proportion of the most academically talented students not attending college has caused considerable concern and has prompted studies of underachievers in secondary schools.

[6] "High-School Drop-Outs," *NEA Research Bulletin,* 38:11, February, 1960.

A number of factors in underachievement have been found to be related to the cultural and social background. Pupils from the lower social class homes do not have as high academic interests, and their families and neighborhoods stress neither success nor schooling. The parents generally have not gone far in school. Thus, their home environment through its building of attitudes adverse to further education tends to deprive them of an equal opportunity with that of their equally gifted colleagues.

The studies, cited in the bulletin, *Freeing Capacity to Learn,* listed in the selected references, seem to indicate in a preliminary way that among the factors somewhat related to underachievement are sex, racial origin, geographic factors, religious background, occupational goals, emotional adjustment, and motivational factors. Boys outnumber girls among underachievers in high school. Social class seems to account for greater variability than ethnic origin. These studies also show that from 12 to 42 per cent of the academically talented in a school are underachievers.

It is well known to teachers, however, that a boy from an underprivileged family living on the "shanty" side of the tracks and a member of a minority group may well be an outstanding student. Other factors than the cultural ones are significant in whether or not a student achieves up to his capacity. Such motivations as a desire to achieve and to know are important. A person's perception of himself as a "student" will, to a large extent, determine how he will behave, given native capacity to be a high achiever. Underachievers tend to rate themselves less able to do school tasks, have less confidence in themselves, and are less eager to learn.

The values that are held by the home, the community, and the adolescent community are undoubtedly influential as to what a pupil in school will do with his talents. The immediate environment may not "cotton" to success, high marks, verbalization, and ambitions to attend college. Immediate pleasures and the approbation of friends who hold no high moral or intellectual standards may be the guiding forces. Underachievers tend to identify themselves with non-intellectual values in a community in which the intellectual values are non-existent.

ADOLESCENT NEEDS AND PROBLEMS

The period of adolescence from puberty to early adulthood is marked by important physical and psychological changes which are of profound importance to the teacher. The process of becoming an adult is a fascinating one. The body undergoes dramatic changes which distinguish the sexes, accompanied by the acquiring of the behavior of "male" or "female" demanded by the culture in which the adolescent lives. These changes in themselves are of interest to the teacher in order that understanding physical maturation can be incorporated at appropriate points into the curriculum.

Of even greater concern to the teacher sensitive to human beings are the psychological changes accompanying the attaining of adulthood. This period marks the further formation of attitudes and values (and, alas, solidification of attitudes in some cases). The unevenness of growth, the resulting awkwardness, and the individual differences in development among adolescents cause many heartaches and problems for the growing boy and girl. The new relationships expected between boys and girls may be frightening. The psychiatrist knows well what genuine problems are involved in the change that occurs during the adolescent period. Physical retardation, for example, may have adverse effects on one's personality.

These behaviors are by no means of a standard variety that can be catalogued for every pupil in the class. They differ for the boy and the girl. They differ for adolescents of the same age. They even differ according to the family social status in the community and the part of the world in which the child happens to be growing up.

When the child begins to become an adult, he finds that he must assume a more active social role and secure a social status of his own with his peers; thus, the well-known desire to conform in order to gain status. A knowing teacher can either regard this as a nuisance or put it to use for good ends. Adults tend to think of young people as "going to the dogs," a characteristic attitude toward youth in any age in the history of civilization.

These changes, far-reaching in their meaning for the individual and for society, are not discussed here in detail. The undergraduate student of education can find either courses or numerous books dealing with adolescent development. (See references at the end of the chapter.) But the meaning of the changes are basic to a secondary school.

The extent of understanding of adolescents' nature and problems influences the skill with which a teacher can provide a rich environment for intellectual and social development. This is the crux of the meaning of understanding adolescent development for curriculum. The teacher may create situations in which the desire to conform develops desirable behavior. Group activities can be planned within the scope of the pupils' total school curriculum in order to satisfy the adolescent's wishes to participate in group activities. The teacher who realizes that adolescence is a period of growth in reflective thinking will likely be more effective in teaching mathematics or social studies than the one who deplores the harmless antics of the teenager.

In order to help youth with their daily problems of adjustment to their environment, teachers of the secondary school should know youth. They should be familiar with the nature of adolescents' whims, fancies, worries, fears, and hopes. The competent teacher looks on much of the behavior in a classroom as social experimentation on the part of boys and girls in establishing themselves as "grown up." Such a teacher spends time in observing individual behavior and in trying to find ways to help pupils make the transition from childhood to adulthood. To him the characteristics of the adolescent boy and girl are displayed through their interests in conversation, reading, hobbies, radio, movies, and other daily activities. He knows that adolescents differ a great deal in their stages of physical, social, and psychological development. In other words, the teacher does not expect the same type of reaction or intensity of problems from young people of the same age.

The more that the teacher knows about the young people with whom he deals, the more he can help them with their problems of social maturation through understanding, encouragement, and advise. An environment rich in intellectual challenges is best nurtured by an understanding teacher whom a student respects, not only for his knowledge but also for his sensitivity to what it means to be an adolescent.

The competent teacher recognizes that the fulfillment of basic psychological needs is necessary to the welfare of the maturing individual. The basic psychological needs most often discussed by psychologists are: to be approved and accepted by one's peers, to be loved, to be recognized and valued as an individual, to be understood, to be respected by adults, to feel secure, to satisfy curiosity, to be independent, and to achieve success and have a sense of adequacy. These needs are related to physical and mental growth and are also social in their context.

These are the needs that are basic to the development of the individual's personality. Although the results of lack of fulfillment of these needs are not as dramatic as in the case of some physical needs, as much damage may be done to the growing boy or girl in his process of maturing into a contributing member of society. If deprived of these needs, a person's mental health and outlook on life will be twisted and warped. Complete adjustment is not the goal, for such a situation rarely results in great accomplishments or creativity. As someone has aptly said, the sharecropper may have been one of the best-adjusted persons *when he knew no better* and accepted his fate without question. Needs are never completely satisfied, but it is important that an adolescent make progress toward their satisfaction in order that he may continue to strive toward his goals.

In secondary schools, pupils may be given tasks which are far beyond their attainment. The slow student finds himself a misfit in an academic environment of symbols, formulas, and abstractions. He cannot "be somebody" in the eyes of his fellows through succeeding in assigned lessons; the school deprives him of accepted ways of receiving social recognition; and so he is likely to take recourse in means frowned upon by adults—boisterousness, rudeness, loudness, lying, vandalism, or other ways of gaining recognition that are within his grasp. The way in which these fundamental needs are satisfied will help to determine what kinds of attitudes youth will develop.

In his actions and attitudes, the young ninth-grader may belie his real feelings in order to avoid revealing his insecurity. He may be cocksure and defiant. Another pupil may resort to flights of fancy instead of facing realities of the classroom that are too much for him. In secondary schools where teachers understand these basic emotional needs, pupils are given important jobs so that they may demonstrate their ability—jobs in which they can succeed and which, at the same time, are challenging. This is at the very heart of academic accomplishment in history, mathematics, or home economics. When needs are more nearly satisfied, the potential for growth can be more easily realized.

The degree with which the school aids the adolescent in his developmental tasks of living and of becoming an adult is a measure of how well it serves the society for which it exists. These tasks are the problems of living that a person must work through and solve in each period of life. Thus, to the adolescent they are tasks of importance both for his own period of life and for the process of becoming an adult. Some children never solve them adequately at the adolescent stage and, consequently, remain children emotionally or in almost complete dependence for decisions and livelihood upon some adult in the family. These tasks are socially oriented with a rather close relationship to the person's social class. If a child is reared in a lower-class home, the task of achieving a set of socially desirable values is vastly different from that of a child reared in a middle-class home. These tasks are in a sense an adolescent's needs, just as they can be regarded as goals which he must meet. Some of the tasks were referred to in Chapter 1.

Havighurst's excellent statement of developmental tasks is one of the most widely known. His list of tasks follows:

1. Achieving more mature relations with age mates of both sexes
2. Achieving a masculine or feminine social role
3. Accepting one's physique and using the body effectively
4. Achieving emotional independence of parents and other adults
5. Achieving assurance of economic independence
6. Selecting and preparing for an occupation
7. Preparing for marriage and family life
8. Developing intellectual skills and concepts necessary for civic competence
9. Desiring and achieving socially responsible behavior
10. Acquiring a set of values and an ethical system as a guide to behavior.[7]

The concept of developmental tasks is a highly useful one for curriculum planning. Each task may serve as a guide to a center of interest or problem in the curriculum. Such a classification should be helpful in planning learning experiences for pupils at different stages of growth. It should also be recognized that each child's own stage of growth and background of experience determine which developmental tasks are important for him.

The teacher may find in these tasks suggestions for selection of problems and curriculum content in any field. Literature, science, psychology, physical education, vocational education, work-study programs, home economics, social studies, and advanced academic courses for the academically talented should offer especially good vehicles for helping students to accomplish these tasks successfully. The guidance program of the school has a big responsibility for helping pupils in these tasks. So does the student activity program.

They give some excellent leads for principles in planning the curriculum. For example, socially responsible behavior can better be achieved if students are given responsibility both in school classes and in community study and planning. The admission and study of values is important to acquiring a set of values. The operation of these tasks in curriculum development will become more apparent throughout the discussion in the rest of the book.

The adolescent in and out of school wrestles with problems of growing up which are of concern to the school. The adolescent's life is as full of thrills, sorrows, joys, and adventure as that of the adult. He must make adjustments to people and to established institutions and customs. Moreover, he has the added burden of making a tran-

[7] Robert J. Havighurst, *Developmental Tasks and Education,* New York: Longmans, Green & Co., Inc., 1952, pp. 33-71.

sition from childhood to adulthood, where accepted values and mores are different from those he has been accustomed to. The problem of growing up is in itself a difficult one.

Significant problems that youth face in their everyday living are outlined briefly here. They serve as a type of check list for the secondary school teacher. If youth work at these problems, they will see the need for developing communication skills, social skills, and other fundamental skills considered important by society.

Making friends and group contacts. Young people want to widen their contacts and have friends among their school group. Many have a real problem of making any friends at all because of their shyness, physical characteristics, or social maladjustments. Do the planned experiences of the classroom and activity program assist them in getting acquainted with new people? Do these experiences help youth to analyze themselves? What help is extended to the youngster who has just moved into the community, or the awkward and the shy?

Gaining the approval of one's peers. This is a potent factor in determining behavior, for being accepted by fellow pupils is far more important to youth than is social convention or the authority of a teacher who little understands what youth think or feel. It is of foremost importance to most pupils. Witness the many fads that high school pupils follow. Does the school put this knowledge of youth to work, or does it try to quell fads as "foolish"? How do teachers try to help youth gain status within the group?

Making adjustments to the family. Problems in this area may be minor, or they may be enormous and tragic in their consequences. They will vary from the ordinary adjustments to sisters and brothers to jarring emotional adaptations some adolescents are expected to make to broken and unhappy homes. Who helps these youth in school with the more difficult type of adjustments? Is there any flexibility in the program to meet their specific needs?

Planning for marriage and family responsibilities. The secondary school authorities used to frown upon the girl who married while in high school. In most cases, she was politely asked to leave school. What recognition does the school of today give to the fact that many youth in the upper high school grades, extended secondary schools, or junior colleges are soon planning to be married or are married? What are guidance services doing about them?

Establishing satisfactory relations with the opposite sex and maturing sexually. Questions of dating, going steady, having boy friends or girl friends, developing physically, and being attractive to the other sex are uppermost in adolescents' minds before serious thoughts of marriage arise. Some authors have said that youth spend most of their time working at the problem. Radio programs and young people's magazines deal with these questions. Do they have any place in curriculum content in the secondary school?

Differing in physical development from ones age-mates. At the age onset of puberty there are rapid spurts of growth among youth of both junior high school and senior high school age. In the more extreme variations, feelings of abnormality are frequent. Are these dissimilarities merely topics for ridicule by students in the hallways or are they matters of concern to the teachers?

Worrying about physical and mental health. Youth are concerned about such unsatisfactory health conditions as overweight, skin blemishes, frequent illness, tiring easily, and constant worries. Is the study of health in the secondary school concerned with these problems—the health of the boy or girl in the class—or only with classifying and memorizing diseases and bodily functions from a book?

Gaining independence from the family and attaining adult status. This problem discussed in Chapter 1 in itself causes many family misunderstandings; it is often a difficult adjustment for young people to make.

Formulating values acceptable to one's own group, to parents, and to the culture mores. Youth may find that the moral standards of adults and those of their own group vary considerably. They may be torn between receiving the approval of the "crowd" and following the accepted mores of the culture in which they live. These standards differ a good deal among groups of different social status. The question of necking or petting may be ridiculous to old-maid school teachers of both sexes, but it is real to youth. Do experiences that youth have in school help them to formulate an adequate philosophy to life and to adopt acceptable moral values?

Solving questions and doubts concerning religion and spiritual life. Youth are concerned about life and death. Many have serious doubts at times concerning the teachings of the Bible and their own faith. Some become intensely religious; others lose faith in religion. As previously mentioned, conflicts between religion and the life in which youth find themselves, or between religious teachings and adult actions, are puzzling to many. Is this an area of responsibility only for the church and the home, or is it also one for the school?

Securing money for spending and buying personal necessities. Some youth have difficulty in getting enough spending money to keep up with "the gang," to buy sodas, take trips with the team, bowl, go to the movies, or pay for the innumerable items included in the cost of attending high school. This problem is tied up with popularity and friendships. Some young people are faced with humiliating experiences because they are ashamed of their clothes, their home, their neighborhood, or their parents. Some have to contribute to the support of the family.

Maintaining a sense of personal achievement. Much has already been said about this obvious problem. Every youth wants to "be somebody," to develop himself, and to find himself. Is there sufficient consideration on the part of secondary schools to help all pupils attain this goal?

Establishing satisfactory relations with teachers and adjusting to school and its demands. The adjustment that some seventh grade youngsters must make in going from a self-contained classroom to an entirely departmentalized situation is often a formidable hurdle. Any high school youth works hard at making adjustments to four or five different teacher personalities and spends a good deal of energy in trying to figure out how to get good marks from each one. Pupils have difficulty in learning how to study, in getting into courses they want, in getting into clubs, in meeting homework demands, and in adjusting to a new school situation. Does the school help pupils with these real social problems of their own lives?

Choosing and buying clothes and other goods and services. In the life of youth, the selection of one's own clothing becomes a jealously guarded privilege. Adolescents also want to buy personal items by themselves. They are now becoming consumers in a new sense. Secondary schools have begun to recognize the need for knowing how to buy wisely. Should all pupils in the typical high school study how to become good consumers?

Finding something to do with leisure time and places to go with other youth. For the boy or girl in the small town, this is often a serious matter. They may wander the streets, drive to the next town, or perhaps travel fifty miles to a dance when they find nothing provided by church, school, or community for their evening's amusement. Churches may frown on dancing, an appealing form of recreation to youth. What obligation does the school have to provide desirable forms of recreation for young people?

Being accepted by the community. Where adults jealously hang on to political positions, community responsibilities, and the right to decide what is good for the community, young people indeed have a difficult time learning how to take an active part in community affairs. Should the school sponsor community participation activities for its pupils? Should social study end in social action?

Being concerned about improving world conditions. A high school teacher of social studies knows—if he has given pupils a chance—that youth are interested in current affairs. As young people mature, this interest grows and deepens, and idealistic youth will champion "causes" for human betterment. To what extent is this interest being carefully guided and stimulated?

Getting along with people. Not as broad in scope, but fully as important for effective democratic participation in community life, is the ability to meet people, to get along with fellow classmates, fellow workers, and others with whom youth are in daily contact. Young people are concerned about this matter. They are concerned about quarreling with friends, hurting others' feelings, helping others, and making a good impression. They are concerned about their relations with people of minority groups. Is the school also concerned?

Choosing a vocation and getting a job. This choice faces every secondary school pupil. He wants advice. Parents may insist on one type of occupation in which he is not interested. A girl may need to make the choice between marriage and a career. Some want to leave school to begin work. Many have unrealistic ambitions. All need help in knowing how to get a job and in finding one that is suitable and to which they are adapted. Do guidance services give the help needed? Is a ninth-grade course or unit in vocations sufficient to help solve the problem of choosing an occupation?

Planning what to do with regard to further education. The choice between work and further schooling is involved here. Youth often want to go to college when they have little chance of succeeding. Others find the financial barriers too great. Pupils in high school seek and rightfully expect advice on further educational opportunities from which to choose. The problem has become increasingly important in recent years. Does the secondary school, through its practices, encourage an interest in continued education? Does it help them to make wise choices in this area?

SUMMARY

The public secondary school in the United States has been committed to a policy of providing an education for all youth, the sons and daughters of rich and poor alike. An examination of the facts reveal that a number drop out before they graduate. Among the most potent factors for determining survival in high school are the economic ones. Youth from the Negro district, from "across the tracks," or from the foreign-born section have the poorest chances of surviving until they have amassed the needed units. Those who are fortunate enough to be able to handle with ease abstract concepts may find the high school program more palatable than those who have talents along the artistic, mechanical, or social lines. Many able youth stop their education early.

A number of youth's problems of living and growing up have been presented in this chapter as a guide to future teachers in deciding what they can do to make high school interesting and worthwhile for young people of all kinds, circumstances, and abilities. These problems are the concerns of the intellectually gifted and of the mentally retarded—problems of *all* youth. These concerns, and the facts about young people in secondary schools, should offer teachers a further yardstick for evaluation of secondary school practices.

SELECTED REFERENCES

ASSOCIATION FOR SUPERVISION AND CURRICULUM DEVELOPMENT. *Freeing Capacity to Learn.* Washington, D.C.: National Education Association, 1960, pp. 40-73.—A section entitled "Those Who Can Don't" discusses studies in underachievement of able students.

BEREDAY, GEORGE Z. F., BRICKMAN, WILLIAM W., and READ, GERALD H. (eds.). *The Changing Soviet School.* Boston: Houghton Mifflin Co., 1960, Chaps. 1 and 4.—An authoritative analysis of Soviet educational practices written by participants in an exchange mission to Russia, brought up to date to the year of publication.

BERNARD, HAROLD W. *Adolescent Development in American Culture.* New York: Harcourt, Brace & World Inc., 1957, Part II.—The adolescent's growth in relation to the forces of his culture. Emphasis both on the adolescent's growth and needs and the environmental factors which influence him.

CRUZE, WENDELL W. *Adolescent Psychology and Development.* New York: The Ronald Press Co., 1953, 557 pp.—A standard text on adolescent development, discussing psychological, physiological, emotional, and social problems of adolescents. Includes information on delinquency.

DOANE, DONALD C. *The Needs of Youth.* New York: Bureau of Publications, Teachers College, Columbia University, 1942, 142 pp.—Reviews the earlier literature on youth needs and problems, and has additional information on youth problems. It is especially helpful in clarifying what is meant by youth needs.

EDUCATIONAL POLICIES COMMISSION. *Manpower and Education.* Washington, D.C.: National Education Association, 1956, 127 pp.—Contains a number of charts and graphs on population distribution, levels of schooling, and growth of school enrollments discussed in relation to man power needs.

GARRISON, KARL C. *Psychology of Adolescence.* Englewood Cliffs, N.J.: Prentice-Hall, Inc., 5th ed., 1956, Chaps. 1-5.—A comprehensive and authoritative work in field of adolescent psychology.

HAND, HAROLD C. *Principles of Public Secondary Education.* New York: Harcourt, Brace & World, Inc., 1958, Chap. 5.—An excellent summary of studies of the holding power of the secondary school and the relation of socioeconomic status to school leaving.

HAVIGHURST, ROBERT J. *Developmental Tasks and Education.* New York: Longmans, Green & Co., Inc., 1952, 100 pp.—An outstanding reference on the concept of developmental tasks, which are listed and discussed.

HOLLINGSHEAD, A. M. *Elmstown's Youth.* New York: John Wiley & Sons, Inc., 1949, Part III and Chap. 13.—Presents a thought-provoking sociological study of adolescents, both in school and out, in a mid-western community, written in readable style, in such a manner that it will be enjoyed by students of education and laymen alike.

MORRIS, GLYN. *The High School Principal and Staff Study Youth.* Secondary School Administration Series, New York: Bureau of Publications, Teachers College, Columbia University, 1958, 102 pp.—For students who wish to read about, in concise and practical form, the ways of studying pupils used in schools.

"THE IMPERATIVE NEEDS OF YOUTH OF SECONDARY-SCHOOL AGE." *Bulletin of The National Association· of Secondary-School Principals*, 31:1-44, March, 1947.—A classic in the history of secondary education, stating the needs of youth.

U.S. DEPARTMENT OF HEALTH, EDUCATION, AND WELFARE, OFFICE OF EDUCATION. *Education in the USSR.* Bulletin 1957, No. 14. Washington, D.C.: Government Printing Office, 1957, 226 pp.—Education in the Soviet Union including primary, secondary, and higher education. Describes the system and includes some statistics as of 1955.

U.S. DEPARTMENT OF HEALTH, EDUCATION, AND WELFARE, OFFICE OF EDUCATION. "Statistical Summary of Education," *Biennial Survey of Education in the United States.* Washington, D.C.: Government Printing Office.—This summary chapter of the biennial survey of education in the U.S. contains statistics for a two-year span on enrollments, retention, number of graduates, etc. of public schools in this country. (Beginning in 1961, the new series is titled *Statistics of Education in the U.S.*, including data for 1958-59. The new series is dated annually by school year).

STUDIES FOR FURTHER INVESTIGATION OF THE TOPIC OF SCHOOL LEAVERS

1. BELL, HOWARD M.: *Youth Tell Their Story.* Washington, D.C.: American Council on Education, 1938.
2. DILLON, HAROLD S.: *Early School Leavers—A Major Educational Problem.* New York: National Child Labor Committee, 1949.
3. ECKERT, R. E. and MARSHALL, T. O.: *When Youth Leave School.* New York: McGraw-Hill Book Co., Inc., 1938.
4. EDWARDS, NEWTON: *Equal Educational Opportunity for Youth.* Washington, D.C.: American Council on Education, 1939.
5. HAND, HAROLD C.: *Principal Findings of the 1947-48 Basic Studies of the Illinois Secondary School Curriculum Program.* Springfield, Illinois: Office Superintendent of Public Instruction, 1949.
6. HECKER, STANLEY E.: *Early School Leavers in Kentucky.* Bulletin of the Bureau of School Service, Lexington: University of Kentucky, 1953.
7. HOLLINGSHEAD, A. B.: *Elmtown's Youth.* New York: John Wiley & Sons, Inc., 1949.
8. MONROE, WALTER S. (ed.): *Encyclopedia of Educational Research.* New York: The Macmillan Co., 1960.
9. NATIONAL EDUCATION ASSOCIATION, RESEARCH DIVISION AND DEPARTMENT OF CLASSROOM TEACHERS: *High-School Dropouts.* Discussion Pamphlet No. 3, Washington, D.C.: The Association, 1959.
10. REGENTS COUNCIL ON READJUSTMENT OF HIGH SCHOOL EDUCATION: *Dropouts—Cause and Cure.* Albany: New York State Department of Education, 1954.
11. SEGEL, DAVID and SCHWARM, OSCAR J.: *Retention in High Schools in Large Cities.* U.S. Department of Health, Education, and Welfare, Office of Education, Bulletin 1957, No. 15, Washington, D.C.: Government Printing Office, 1957.
12. WARNER, WILLIAM LLOYD: *Who Shall Be Educated?* New York: Harper & Bros., 1944.

Part II

CURRICULUM AND INSTRUCTION

5

CONCEPTS OF THE CURRICULUM

To the beginning teacher, the job of developing youth's values about democracy, human relations, cultural traditions and motivations, and people and meeting youth's needs may be extremely challenging, but may be puzzling as well. His own experience as a secondary school pupil may have had little relation to his needs as he perceived them. He may ask: What possible connection did these school experiences have with youth problems, social purposes, or democratic values? On the other hand, he may realize how many of his experiences in secondary school did apply directly to these concepts as they were discussed in the preceding chapters.

The student preparing to teach should realize that some school practices represent a point of view about education different from the philosophy expressed in a previous section of this book. It is the purpose of this chapter to present some basically different ways of thinking about curriculum and how teachers who hold these differing points of view plan the curriculum for their pupils. In order that the terms used in this book may be clearly understood, a portion of this chapter is devoted to definitions. It makes a considerable difference how we interpret the meaning of the word "curriculum." If the concept of curriculum as given in the following paragraphs is followed, attention is likely to turn more to what happens to pupils rather than only to what books we use or what outline of content is studied.

MEANING OF TERMS

The modern concept of *curriculum* is that it consists of the whole of the interacting forces of the environment provided for pupils by the school and the experiences that pupils have in that environment.

It is the school's job to plan and direct worthwhile activities that will help develop the type of behavior outlined in its objectives. The *quality* of the pupil's experience is the important factor. Definitely, the curriculum is not the inert material in the pages of a course of study. It is, instead, the things children do, plan, write, read, construct, talk about, react to, and think about. It includes their field trips, extraclass experiences, student council activities, the study of the community that they make, farm projects in connection with their agriculture courses, and work experience under school supervision. All these are significant learning experiences planned by the school to further the growth of pupils.

The *course of study* is a more limited term than curriculum, since it refers to the outline, bulletin, or written plan that serves as a guide to the activities that the teacher will plan for and with the pupils. It is not difficult to visualize how unlike the experiences might be for two groups of pupils under different teachers, different in temperament and background but following the same course of study. The modern term used frequently for published courses is "curriculum guide."

A *curriculum improvement program* refers to the plan of action adopted by a school, a state, or a committee in order to consider ways of providing better experiences for pupils. A school usually selects some phase of the curriculum for study by the faculty for the year, or over a period of years. "Curriculum revision," "curriculum building," "curriculum development program" are other terms used. In the past, some subject in the curriculum was invariably selected as the topic for study. In recent years, when school people have begun to think of the curriculum in terms of experiences provided for pupils, schools are more frequently attacking any significant problems that deal with the improvement of instruction and content. Generally, such study has yielded good results in actually improving the kinds of experiences that children and adolescents have. Examples of these types of problems studied in secondary schools follow:

1. Selecting instructional materials that promote good human relations and understanding of other pupils
2. Developing a program for the academically talented
3. Planning improved content in junior high school mathematics
4. Studying factors connected with underachievement
5. Making follow-up studies of secondary school drop-outs and graduates
6. Developing means of encouraging creativity in many fields

7. Using the community for pupil experiences
8. Experimenting with a research approach in industrial arts
9. Examining the best means of preparation for college

General education is the basic education needed by all youth in order to become effective, participating citizens who live fruitful lives and who have broad interests and concerns in humanity and the products of man's mind. The learnings essential for a general education are sometimes called "common learnings." These are the learnings considered important for intelligent citizens, competent members of a family, and well-disciplined individuals. Thus, the social studies, humanities, the sciences, and arts are considered vehicles through which activities in general education are planned. For example, in a democracy it is considered essential that people know how to make decisions based on facts and how to carry on discussions and social action as members of a civic group. Activities planned to promote these outcomes are a part of general education.

The *core curriculum* is a specific form or organization of the curriculum that cuts across subject fields and includes a greater block of time in the school day than the usual period. It refers to a way in which some of the important aspects of general education are organized within the secondary school curriculum. The core curriculum is a way of organizing some of the important experiences in the curriculum, centering around the problem-solving approach, using social and personal problems and other content significant to youth, and selecting subject matter from various areas to develop desirable behaviors. Usually English and the social studies are fused in the core, and the guidance function is always a part of the core. But since it consists of basic behavior patterns common to all and is based upon problem situations, it is not a mere fusing of subject matter. The core curriculum is explained in greater detail in Chapter 7.

Block time refers to an organization of schedule in which a longer period of time is blocked for the same group of students, usually in English and social studies, permitting correlation or use of aspects of the core. Other terms sometimes used in educational literature as synonymous with core curriculum are "unified studies," "general education," "basic program," "integrated English–social-studies curriculum."

These are some of the basic terms that will be used in a discussion of the curriculum. The student is referred to the *Dictionary of Education* for definitions of other terms he does not understand.

SIGNIFICANCE OF MODERN CONCEPTS

FOCUS ON QUALITY OF EXPERIENCE. The concept of the curriculum in terms of the experiences pupils have and the provision of an environment that permits such experiences, centers attention on what occurs in classes and in the school and on what teachers do to cause pupils to change their behavior in socially desirable ways. Parents are interested in what happens to children in school. They want to be assured that their children are learning. Both parents and teachers want pupils to have a high quality experience. Although current criticisms have been leveled against "play-acting," "wasting time," and "doing unimportant things," it is inconceivable that any sincere teacher would not want each of his pupils to develop to his highest potential.

If teachers concentrate on the course of study, it is assumed that learning what is in the course will follow. It may or may not, depending upon the teacher, the difficulty and level of materials and content, the equipment, and other conditions provided for learning. If teachers focus on the level of experience, they are concerned about whether school is a dull and frustrating or a challenging and inspiring experience for the pupil. All of the factors in the environment will be looked upon as important. The aim of all education is to change people's behavior for the better—"better" being defined by the society in which we live and its ideals and aspirations.

FOCUS ON SOCIAL PURPOSES AND ADOLESCENT NEEDS. The total environment as planned by the school, as well as that in life outside the school, affects what the pupil experiences and consequently learns. The secondary school is obligated to plan these activities to prepare pupils to live in a world of today and tomorrow, not for a world of 1870 or 1930. The rapid changes that proceed at jetlike speed in the mid-twentieth century make it impossible for a secondary school to stand still. Demands of scientific and technological advances are accelerating. Not always as obvious or dramatic, but fully as significant, are demands of new challenges in the political and social arena.

Not only does the world change because of new knowledge in sciences, but constant discoveries of research in the behavioral sciences give greater insight into human motives, actions, and ways of changing behavior. These are the heart of the teaching-learning process. As more is known about the adolescent, teachers can, with greater assurance of success, know how to deal with his problems and needs. Thirty years ago, little consideration was given to the different backgrounds, drives, and needs of children who came from homes of different socioeconomic classes. Today research in sociology has advanced to a point where there is no excuse for a teacher disregarding the information which can readily be obtained.

Thus, the social and psychological foundations dealt with in a previous section of this book have a direct bearing on what goes on in the school. They determine in a large measure what kinds of experiences pupils should have in dealing with the content studied. Ignorance of them may mean pupil experiences of a low quality. Up-to-date information about them and about the concepts, ideals, and structure of the subject taught, will likely mean a higher quality experience. That is the crux of the problem of improvement of the secondary school curriculum.

CONTRASTING BASIC APPROACHES

In his reading, the student of education will find reference to "the activity curriculum," "the child-centered curriculum," "the community-centered curriculum," "the integrated curriculum," and the like. No attempt will be made here to discuss what is meant by these various terms, for often several of them are used to mean approximately the same thing. Such a classification of the curriculum into types is more likely to confuse the future teacher than to assist him in understanding how he should function in developing the curriculum for his pupils.

Instead, this chapter will concentrate on the two fundamental approaches to curriculum development which represent different views of how the teacher should function, how content should be selected, what types of evaluation of progress should be made, and how books and other materials should be selected for the classroom. One is the subject-centered approach to curriculum development; the other is the experience-centered approach. Undoubtedly more secondary school teachers use the subject-centered approach in modified form but growing numbers who apply their knowledge of the principles of child and adolescent development are utilizing at least some aspects of the experience-centered approach. Actually, most teachers' practices indicate that their approach would be on a scale somewhat between the two extremes.

Both approaches represent definite points of view. A teacher who believes in the one approach acts differently in the classroom from one who believes in the other approach. It will be the purpose of this discussion to indicate how the teacher behaves if he uses one or the other. It should be understood, however, that this is not an either/or proposition. A person may, for example, be moving toward the experience-centered approach, accepting a number of its precepts that he feels he can carry out. The descriptive statements take the extreme form in order to highlight the contrasts between these points of view.

The subject-centered approach results in a subject-centered curriculum in which learning the facts of the subject is considered most important; the experience-centered approach results in an experience-centered curriculum in which the focus is on the kinds of experiences pupils have in learning generalizations and broad concepts of the subject matter. The inexperienced teacher needs to be warned, however, that the issue here is not subject matter versus experience, for the teacher using the experience-centered approach uses as much subject matter as any other teacher. The fundamental difference lies in the way subject matter is utilized and studied and what kinds of experiences are provided.

SUBJECT-CENTERED APPROACH. The student in education courses will be familiar with the subject-centered approach to curriculum development, for some modified form of it is predominant in secondary school courses and even more so in college courses. He experiences it when his entire course is structured by the textbook as the material to be learned. To the extent that a teacher does not follow these principles, he is moving away from the subject-centered approach toward the experience-centered approach. The statements which follow are not value judgments; these are statements explaining and illustrating an approach, or point of view, which some teachers believe in, and follow more or less, and some do not.

Subject matter in distinct compartments represents what is to be learned. Assignments are in blocks of subject matter which form the basis for what is done in class and what is evaluated in examinations. The recitation in class was founded upon this approach. Measurement of progress is by the amount of subject matter learnings acquired. Pupils pass or fail on this basis. Drill for college entrance examinations, makeup work, and review drill are all evidences of the concept of the subject-centered curriculum. Distinct lines are kept between subject departments in the school.

Even though the teacher may be sincerely interested in developing the character of young people, attitudes can receive attention only incidental to covering the subject matter. He is concerned that students learn the subject in the field that he is teaching.

The subject matter to be covered and the kinds of experiences pupils will have are determined before the course begins. These decisions are made without any knowledge of what the pupils will be like except that they will be in a specfic grade, of a general age level, and probably of a certain ability grouping. The books are selected first, and the teacher plans his work around the text. There may be an outline of what is to be covered in the course, with specific time limits for different sections, or a textbook that serves as the outline. If a course of study is provided, it prescribes what is to be taught. Teachers find that they can follow prescribed content and know that all teachers in the school system use the same plan.

Minimum standards and a predetermined pattern govern what is to be learned. Under the subject-centered approach, pupils are usually expected to achieve a set standard of learning in mathematics, English fundamentals, history, or any other field. This standard has been determined by the teacher or the school ahead of time for all pupils. All in a particular grade or class must meet these minimums in order to pass. Those who do not repeat the grade or course until they can meet the standard set for all. Individual differences are taken care of by eliminating students who cannot pass, by providing special schools or classes, or by repeating courses.

Students are required to conform to the predetermined pattern. English students may often write the same number of themes or do the same exercises. Social studies students often read the same textbook. Industrial arts or art students will probably make the same bookcases or draw the same object. Although these may be extreme practices with which we may not agree, they describe the extreme subject-centered approach.

Skills are taught as separate entities. Skills are taught directly by exercises at a set time, apart from the rest of the work. Drill periods are provided as a part of the planned course of study. Drill sessions, remedial work, coaching classes, and review are characteristic practices in the teaching of skills. The drill is often planned for certain days of the week without relation to what the pupil is writing, reading, or otherwise doing. Grammar, usage, and spelling are not deliberately related to the work that goes on in social studies, literature, or writing but the assumption is that these skills will transfer to the pupil's daily activities in school.

The teacher acts as the external authority who exercises control over the learning situation. Because so much subject matter must be learned in a certain period of time, the teacher acts as the authority on what is to be learned, how much time is to be spent on it, and what is to be done by the class. There is no time for planning together what is to be done because it takes too much time away from what must be done. The teacher makes the rules for classroom conduct. Discipline is a matter of control by the teacher as an authority.

Proponents of the subject-centered approach argue that its advantages are that its systematic organization is necessary for an effective interpretation of experience and that the subject-centered curriculum is simple in organization, readily adjusted, easily evaluated, and generally approved by teachers, students, and parents.

EXPERIENCE-CENTERED APPROACH. The experience-centered approach to curriculum development emphasizes the planning of experiences to develop behavior consistent with the goals of society. These experiences will be with subject matter, with the community, with school activities, with other pupils, with issues and problems. The essential difference from the subject-centered approach is that the pupil's development—how his behavior should be changed—is considered first; then, the experiences to develop those behaviors are planned and subject matter is used as a means of bringing about these changes.

Behavior changes include arithmetic skills; mathematics understandings; language skills such as writing, speaking, and spelling— just as much as changes in attitudes or habits. Behavior is changed if a person can speak and read a foreign language, write a thesis, or do an intricate piece of research. Good speech, correct mathematics skills and concepts, and wide reading are significant outcomes of the experience-centered approach to curriculum development. These behavior changes must be carefully planned for by the school and by the teacher.

The experience-centered approach, whose characteristics are described in the following paragraphs, is used by a number of teachers; again, generally in modified forms. Students of education often ask where they can find a school where they might see these ideas in action. Instead of looking around for schools with neatly tagged labels, the future teacher would do well to search out good teachers who give students a high quality experience. They can be found in many schools, among those who hold either point of view.

Subject matter is used as a means to an end, to lead to desirable outcomes in behavior changes. The teacher who follows the experience-centered approach uses subject matter to achieve the goals set up for the group. For example, subject matter from history aims toward an understanding that the struggle for freedom involves continuous conflict with reactionary forces bent on keeping special privileges for their own group. Or subject matter is selected that best lends itself to the skill of distinguishing between propaganda and reliable information. In the same way, subject matter is used to develop desired attitudes and appreciations. These are planned activities to achieve certain goals. The teacher uses as much or more subject matter than the one who uses the subject-centered approach.

Starting with desirable behavior changes as goals is as different from starting with a book or subject matter to be studied (the subject-centered approach) as night is from day. Unless this fundamental difference is understood, the student will probably not see the contrast between these two approaches clearly.

Attitudes develop in any learning situation whether or not they are consciously stressed. Dislike rather than appreciation of good literature may be the result of the study of some literary selections or the methods used.

In the experience-centered approach, the skills of finding sources of information, contrasting different points of view, and choosing more reliable data are developed through planned use of many sources, reading from different books, and checking for accuracy of facts. In other words, the experience is selected in terms of the objectives to be attained. A part of the experience is the use of subject matter that lends itself to achieving the desired aims. The experience-centered approach alone carries no guarantee, however, that attitudes and appreciations will be improved. It must be understood and intelligently used.

The development of the child or adolescent, his mind, body, emotions, and social nature, all are considered important. The child's development is of first and foremost importance. His balanced growth is the goal of the teacher. Improvement in skills and knowledge is recognized as dependent upon the physical and emotional state. The teacher is conscious of physical defects and health problems. As contrasted with learning to be stored for future use the situation calls for learning skills for present-day life, developing attitudes toward fellow pupils, and becoming a mentally curious and emotionally stable individual.

The content is a series of planned experiences growing out of the pupils' background, needs, interests, and daily living, and out of the social and physical environment. The pupils' nature and background and the society in which they live become the point of orientation for selection of learning activities. The social scene is an important source of problems and issues studied. The subject-centered approach would likely begin with the chronological starting point and go forward to present issues and concerns, under the assumption that the background gained would help to solve current problems.

The content grows out of pupils' daily living. It includes, in addition to issues of the day of world-wide significance, the immediate concerns of the pupil. The student council and problems with which it deals become important content. Rules and regulations of school and classroom are studied. Such problems as orientation to high school life, improvement of the lunchroom situation, the conflicts accompanying desegregation, the issues of world ideologies, and good citizenship in a school are considered. Adolescents' concerns about their own personality, their home, and their relations with others, receive attention. Writing or speaking activities grow out of ongoing activities in and out of school. The teacher looks for ways of relating classroom activities to the school, home, and community life of his pupils.

The teaching of the fundamental skills is done in relation to their use. The basic skills are extremely important in both the experience-centered and the subject-centered approaches. In the experience-centered approach it is the purpose for which these skills are taught and the use made of them that is of foremost significance in the teaching of these skills. Material used for drill purposes, where the teacher finds drill is needed, grows out of the subject matter used in the class rather than being studied from exercise booklets. The teacher is concerned with finding in the student's composition, history, science, or any other field in which writing and speaking is done, the opportunities for teaching the basic skills.

The act of planning itself provides many opportunities for practice in correct speaking, discussing, and writing. Pupils will need to increase speed and comprehension to read effectively from the many sources. Opportunities for writing letters, interviewing people, solving mathematics problems, using reference books, doing experiments, organizing information grow out of the classroom activities.

The experiences are selected cooperatively by teachers and pupils, based on a study and knowledge of those pupils and their previous experience. In the experience-centered approach, the subject matter is selected during the learning situation by those most directly concerned, within an over-all framework of plans made by teachers and the school. It will differ from year to year because pupils differ and the pressing current social issues, scientific discoveries or knowledge in any field may differ. This procedure contrasts with that of the subject-centered approach in which those who make the final selection of the subject matter may be far removed from the teacher. These may be the state department of education, the central administration of the school, the supervisor, a central committee, or the textbook writer.

A mistake often made by those who do not understand the difference, is that the experience-centered approach means a lack of planning and a selection of class activities based on the whims of the pupils at the moment. Haphazard planning is characteristic only of poor teaching, no matter what the approach. Much careful planning ahead of time is required by teachers cooperatively, by teachers and parents, by teachers and supervisors, and by individual teachers themselves in order to use effectively this approach. The difference is in the type of planning. It is not planning that merely decides on subject matter to be covered; it concentrates instead on aims in terms of pupil growth, types of materials and content to achieve that growth, kinds of experiences to be used, and means of evaluating progress toward the goals.

Cooperative planning in the classroom is planning by pupils and teacher. The teacher is the guide who, by virture of his greater experience and knowledge, helps pupils to select genuinely important problems. It is not an oversimplified process of asking "What are we going to do today?" Instead, skillful planning may take a number of days, and continues after a unit is under way. The group sets up the goals that it wants to achieve and then checks often on how well it is accomplishing those goals.

The teacher who uses the experience-centered approach successfully needs to have a good understanding of adolescents and life outside the classroom. Moreover, he needs to have a broad and well-grounded knowledge of subject matter. He must constantly study the behavior of his pupils to observe their growth and study their abilities, interests, and their previous school background. Also, he needs to be more expert in handling pupils in a cooperative classroom situation in which there is a greater degree of self-control expressed, for rules of the classroom are set up by the group as a desirable type of experience in learning self-control and democratic procedures. None of these are easily learned tasks to be tackled either by the indifferent or the insecure.

The teacher is concerned with the growth and development of each individual pupil rather than with preconceived ideas of what the mythical "average pupil" should know at a certain grade level. Each individual pupil is taken where he is and helped to grow from that point. Pupils are encouraged and helped to work independently, or with others of similar abilities and interests in a class, in order to progress at their own rate. In the experience-centered curriculum, minimum standards for the gifted pupil are not the same as for those who learn more slowly. The stress is on individual maximum standards which the child is capable of accomplishing. Appropriate activities, materials, and content are planned for individuals. English I includes skills and appreciations appropriate to the pupils in a specific class and may differ considerably in content from class to class or school to school. The objectives set up may be similar, but different expectancies will be evident for the different groups and individuals, depending upon their previous background and maturity. Emphasis on individuality, non-conformity of ideas, variability and difference are evident in the teacher's goals.

Proponents of the experience-centered approach argue that its advantages are that it takes into consideration pupils' needs and interests as well as social needs and that it is grounded in democratic values, is psychologically sound, promotes unity in school learning and studies, relates the school to the community, and deals with life's real problems of today.

SUMMARY

Curriculum is defined in terms of experiences that pupils have. Succeeding chapters describe the curriculum of secondary schools in these terms, for a discussion of courses offered in a high school program of studies tells very little about what is happening to boys and girls in the school. It would merely describe the externals, or the structure within which the curriculum operates.

In this chapter, a description of the extreme forms of the subject-centered approach and the experience-centered approach to curriculum development has contrasted how a teacher operates in planning a curriculum and the kinds of experiences he provides for pupils.

The student of education must decide for himself which approach he wishes to use, or which aspects of either approach he wishes to accept. He should search for evidence from the fields of learning, child and adolescent psychology, and the principles of a democratic society. However, a teacher must whole-heartedly accept an approach before he can use it effectively. The approach can be bungled badly if the teacher does not know how to plan learning situations or know the subject matter.

Beginning teachers may wish to move toward the experience-centered approach and attempt to use each year more practices that conform to the characteristics of the approach. They cannot expect to use all of these practices, nor may they wish to or be able to do so. They do not need to be discouraged because many of their colleagues use more of a subject-centered approach.

In this book, an attempt is made to illustrate what teachers and administrators who believe in this approach are doing. In the description of school practices in the following pages, it will be made clearer that the issue is not one of subject matter versus experience, but a question of how subject matter is used and what kind of subject matter is dealt with.

The experience-centered approach can be used most effectively in the areas of general education. In some areas of specialized learnings, it is more difficult to employ this approach, and perhaps aspects of it should not be applied. However, that does not give a teacher a handy excuse for failing to apply some of the principles. Moreover, there is no assurance that every teacher can use the experience-centered approach effectively, for unless it is so used the learning outcomes may be diminished rather than improved.

SELECTED REFERENCES

ALBERTY, HAROLD. *Reorganizing the High-School Curriculum.* New York: The Macmillan Co., rev. ed., 1953, Chap. 5.—Includes a good discussion of the two approaches and the arguments for and against each one.

ANDERSON, VERNON E. *Principles and Procedures of Curriculum Improvement.* New York: The Ronald Press Co., 1956, Chap. 4.—Explains at greater length the experience-centered and subject-centered approaches to curriculum development.

BURTON, WILLIAM H. *The Guidance of Learning Activities.* New York: Appleton-Century-Crofts, Inc., 2nd ed., 1952, Part III.—Contrasts traditional and modern practices in instruction and illustrates the two approaches in a discussion of experience and subject matter units.

DOUGLASS, HARL R. (ed.). *The High School Curriculum.* New York: The Ronald Press Co., 1956, 2nd ed., Chap. 3.—Explains the nature and the function of the curriculum, behavior as objectives, and the relation of the curriculum to growth.

GOOD, CARTER V. (ed.). *Dictionary of Education.* New York: McGraw-Hill Book Co., Inc., 2nd ed., 1959, 676 pp.—A dictionary of technical and professional terms in education useful to the student of education courses.

HOPKINS, L. THOMAS. *Interaction: The Democratic Process.* Boston: D. C. Heath & Co., 1941, Chap. 1.—Although not easy reading, this is one of the best single references on the topic of this chapter. Students who become interested in Hopkin's book are urged to read on for further clarification of the two approaches.

"THE EXPERIENCE-CURRICULUM IN ACTION." *Educational Leadership.* 6:194-244, January, 1949.—The entire issue is devoted to articles illustrating the experience-centered curriculum in public schools and teacher education programs, and to articles clarifying the nature of the experience-centered curriculum. Olson's and Parker's articles are best for the latter purpose.

THUT, I. N., and GERBERICH, J. RAYMOND. *Foundations of Method for Secondary Schools.* New York: McGraw-Hill Book Co., Inc., 1949, Chaps. 6, 7, 9, 10, 12, 13.—These authors contrast the daily assignment method, the subject-matter unit method, and the experience unit method and describe each of these methods in action. Essentially, the first two are the subject-centered approach and the third, the experience-centered approach. This book is written for undergraduate classes.

6

THE TEACHER'S ROLE IN CURRICULUM DEVELOPMENT

There are many adults who have some influence on the curriculum, including the teacher, the principal, the superintendent, the supervisor, the textbook writer, members of the state legislature, the curriculum committee, the public, and the consultant. The teacher's part in building the curriculum is considered in this chapter. The discussion centers around the importance of the teacher's values, knowledge, and understanding in the process called "curriculum making."

BASIC PRINCIPLES

The teacher is the one who largely determines the curriculum of the pupils with whom he works.

Although many persons affect classroom instruction through administrative decrees, legislative acts, or financial provisions, in the final analysis the teacher is by far the most influential of the curriculum makers. The day-by-day and year-by-year planning, or lack of it, is a basis for what the class will do. Whether pupils spend a great deal of time memorizing facts and unrelated information or search for information to solve significant problems depends upon the teacher's approach. He creates the type of learning situation that fosters the development of certain attitudes, understandings, skills, and appreciations. He has it within his control to give pupils experiences either in democratic participation in the classroom or in sitting and listening to orders. As the adviser, he sets the stage for what is going to happen in the club or the student council, although traditionally pupils have more freedom in these activities.

The teacher also determines what the curriculum will be like through the selection of materials to be used by the class. He may

118

participate in selecting books and learning aids to be purchased. At least, he can decide how to use those books, the school library, and other sources of information. The very attitude that he displays toward other persons and toward life, will have considerable influence on what kinds of experiences pupils will have.

The teacher should have an important part in making decisions concerning curriculum policies and practices.

Teacher-pupil planning of experiences will be nurtured best in an environment of cooperation among principal, other administrators and supervisors, and teachers. Many decisions that are made in schools affect the curriculum. Decisions need to be made about the content to be taught at specific grade levels, about the testing program, about the part that parents will play in curriculum making, about the extent to which experimentation by teachers will be encouraged, and about policy with regard to community excursions. In addition, the policies dealing with the budget for instructional materials and its management within the school system and with the selection of teachers and principals have a significant bearing on the curriculum.

Since his influence on the curriculum is substantial, the teacher should have a significant part in determining its polices.

The teacher should have freedom to experiment and plan the curriculum with pupils and colleagues, unhampered by inflexible courses of study or administrative fiat.

Curriculum change will result from teachers' experimentation with content, procedures, and materials under the guidance of competent leadership. Some teachers will be ready for limited types of experimentation with ideas new to them; others will be able to do more sophisticated testing of practices. Curriculum improvement occurs as individual teachers feel secure in trying out new procedures; whereas, insistence on uniform use of new practices by all staff members probably results in much unhappiness and frustration, and eventually in failure for the entire plan. There have been cases of such failure in secondary schools that have tried to put the core curriculum into practice as a school-wide experiment without giving time for the necessary teacher in-service growth.

Courses of study can serve either as a crutch or as a guide. Much planning together is necessary in each school. Rigid courses of study to be followed by all scarcely permit planning for individual needs. Such a practice assumes that all schools, pupils, and teachers are alike. We have but to visit two secondary schools in a single city or rural consolidated school district to realize the fallacy of this assumption. We know that pupils differ, but we would also see how communities differ: the reflection of different types of homes in pupil behavior, the differences in morale in the school, and the differences in the character of the school staff.

Courses of study and resource units used as guides and sources from which to gather ideas are helpful to the teacher in furnishing leads to units and in indicating the goals to be achieved, content and activities to achieve them, how to study pupils, and how to plan the curriculum with pupils. If the teacher wants to find references available on a unit, he should be able to go to the course of study as a source of information. Although the staff in a school agree on large areas of experience for pupils in a certain grade or class, such an agreement does not necessarily limit the teacher's freedom to develop units that grow out of classroom activities.

The teacher's point of view concerning education and the functions of the secondary school is of utmost significance as a basis for decisions concerning the kinds of experiences he will provide for pupils.

In the first chapter, certain principles were stressed as being fundamental for judging a good secondary school program. It was pointed out that school people who have not clarified for themselves the purposes of the secondary school are floundering around with no beacons to guide them. Such principles and purposes should be a part of every teacher's equipment. There are many decisions that a teacher must make each day. Only a philosophy developed through critical thinking about young people, about the society in which they will live, and about the application of facts of learning to the school situation, can assure consistent and wise choices.

In addition to holding some point of view, the teacher should clearly recognize its implications. It is here contended that a person should be open-mined to new ideas and ready to change his philosophy if he is convinced by the facts and by results as he finds them. The teacher who looks for tricks of the trade and tries them merely because they worked for someone else, without contemplating what the results may be, is indeed a dead weight on the progress of secondary education. An orientation, a point of view, is one of the important outcomes that can be developed by students in pre-service education courses. The study of methods and techniques means little unless an inexperienced teacher at the same time develops a philosophy to guide his procedures.

The philosophy he holds, whether or not coherently developed, guides the manner in which the teacher works with pupils. Consider the kinds of experiences pupils would have in the classes of two teachers who hold these different points of view:

Teacher A believes that all pupils should be brought up to relatively fixed standards of achievement during a year's time. In his classroom, pupils will be likely to do all the exercises in the book, no matter what their background or ability. As a student teacher remarked, "I get the feeling that these kids know all this material that we're working on in the grammar text." He had not given any pretest to find out what different pupils knew before he began teaching, but he had been told by the supervising teacher to assign certain chapters in the text. In teacher A's class, fixed assignments will be read by all. Objective tests will determine how much the pupils have attained. If some rank at the bottom of such tests, they will fail no matter how much progress they may have made.

Teacher B believes that each pupil should be considered as an individual and that standards are relative, depending upon the pupil's capacity. His pupils are more likely to study different short stories in literature, or read different books in social studies. He develops drill materials himself to use with his pupils. Each pupil works on materials which he is capable of learning, either as an individual or with a small group of other pupils. Pupils of outstanding ability are able to go ahead at their own pace. The progress of the individual student is evaluated by many means, to show what growth he has made over a period of time.

In the modern secondary school, curriculum building involves a knowledge of pupils, community, social trends, and principles of learning, in addition to knowledge of subject matter.

The student of education may have an instructor in a college course who says, "I am interested in education, but not in the art of teaching." Such a person, whether he teaches in high school or college, shows a profound ignorance of what good teaching involves. Enough is known about human behavior to indicate that a study of the behavioral sciences is basic to the teacher's development of a curriculum that will facilitate maximum pupil growth. A knowledge of the subject alone can no longer lead—or for that matter never has led—to a functional secondary school curriculum. Knowledge of subject matter in the modern world takes on a broader concept, for a background drawn from sociology, science, political science, anthropology, psychology, and other fields is necessary equipment for the teacher to participate effectively in curriculum making.

The secondary school teacher's many responsibilities in connection with planning a curriculum demand that he know the subject which he teaches, how to study boys and girls, what adolescents are like, under what conditions effective learning takes place, what the community in which he works is like, what subject matter is suitable for different maturity levels and interests, what are the newer developments in the subject he teaches, and how to evaluate progress toward goals. Only as the teacher is a student of these problems and conditions will he be able to plan worthwhile experiences that lead to significant goals. Such understanding calls for continuous study in summer schools, participation in school in-service programs, and individual reading.

SOME COMMON PRACTICES

In this section are described practices to indicate the extent of the teacher's freedom in the development of the curriculum and the opportunity to participate in curriculum policy-making in the typical secondary school.

LIMITATIONS UPON THE TEACHER. It should be recognized that the restrictions discussed here may or may not be desirable. They may serve the purpose of protecting children against the whims of imcompetent school administrators or teachers. They may be distinct aids to the teacher in his first year of teaching. They may also form the basis for the kind of uniformity that is advantageous to schools in the same community. On the other hand, when these restrictions limit the good teacher's possibilities for planning a curriculum suited to his pupils, they are a hindrance. Some of them, such as legal requirements of what should be taught in the schools, are built on the assumption that the schools' professional staff is not competent to develop the curriculum needed for the secondary schools of the state.

A number of limitations circumscribe the curriculum in the typical secondary school today, in addition to the limitations set by the education, experience, and vision of school personnel. Included are state laws and requirements by state departments of education and other accrediting agencies, local school policy, courses of study, attitudes of the teaching staff, attitudes of the community, and college entrance requirements.

1. *State Regulations and Accrediting Agencies.*

State Departments. State departments of education are established to carry out the laws of the state relating to education and to set general policies and regulations necessary for the good of the schools. In most cases, they plan legislation and state regulations with school people and work with them in a leadership capacity. Only in rare instances do they function mainly as an inspectorial agency.

Traditionally, state departments have exerted greater influence on the secondary school curriculum than on the elementary school curriculum. Most state departments of education, for example, determine the high school graduation requirements and the number of credits to be earned in certain subjects such as English, American history, science, and mathematics. State departments of vocational education exercise considerable control of the curriculum in courses coming under the federal acts mentioned in the next section, since they prescribe what the course should be.

State Legislation. States typically have some regulation of the curriculum through state legislation. The subjects most frequently required by law are these:

American history and the Constitution
Health and physical education
State history and government
Civics and citizenship
Driver training and education

Some laws specify definite areas of health education, such as teaching the effects of alcohol. Others prohibit certain practices such as giving religious instruction and using any subversive form of instruction. High schools that wish to receive federal aid under the Smith-Hughes Act, George-Deen Act, or other acts of Congress, must include such subjects as agriculture, home economics, or distributive education, since this aid is provided specifically for such vocational subjects.

State Examinations. A state-wide system of examinations where given to high school pupils in the different subjects, limits the curriculum. Teachers naturally try to include all subject matter on which pupils may be tested, since their teaching success is often judged by the proportion of pupils passing these tests. State-wide achievement examinations had nearly gone out of existence when in recent years some groups have strongly advocated a return to such examinations on the state and federal level and have been successful in at least one state. In 1961, the California state legislature enacted into law a requirement that each school district administer an achievement test chosen from tests prescribed by the State Board of Education.

State Courses of Study, and State Adopted Textbooks. State departments generally no longer publish courses of study that must be rigidly followed by the schools. Instead, state courses and curriculum bulletins of other types are intended as a service feature of the state department's supervision of the schools to give assistance and guidance to the schools and the teachers. A few states have a list of state-adopted textbooks, usually selected by a state commission on textbooks, from which schools must select books for their use. These regulations in most instances do not apply to large city school systems. In effect, this plan of selection of books may be as restrictive on the curriculum as prescriptive state courses of study. The pressures are great to re-establish the prescriptive type of course of study.

Accrediting Agencies. Regional accrediting agencies tend to work through state departments of education and exert leadership through promoting secondary school evaluations and publishing pertinent information on standards. These agencies receive reports from schools as a check on their meeting standards for accreditation. They compile lists of accredited schools for use by colleges and universities for admission purposes.

A means of supervising and evaluating secondary schools, used to a considerable extent in many states, is the *Evaluative Criteria* published by the National Study of Secondary School Evaluation. Using these criteria teams of evaluators are able to study and report on how well a secondary school meets acceptable standards. This process, described in some detail in Chapter 19, is the means by which the regional associations, such as the Middle States Association of Colleges and Secondary Schools, accredit high schools. They work in cooperation with state departments of education in carrying on the evaluative studies. Although the evaluation of the curriculum deals more with externals than with actual pupil experiences, these surveys have had considerable influence in improving the curriculum in secondary schools.

2. *Local School Policy.* The degree to which the teacher is permitted to plan the curriculum for his pupils is related to the policies established by the board of education, the superintendent, and any supervisors which the school may employ.

School policy relative to requirements for courses, school-wide achievement tests, the selection of textbooks, and the purchase of instructional materials may influence the teacher's opportunity to develop a functional curriculum. Most secondary schools require certain courses or specific units to be taught in courses taken by all pupils. An example of the latter is a unit in driver education added to some existing course. A rather common practice for larger school systems is to give achievement tests to all pupils in specific subjects. The value of this practice depends upon the emphasis given to the use of the tests. Often they are used only for survey purposes rather than mainly for instructional purposes. This practice may result in an undesirable uniformity and undue emphasis on learning the facts asked for in the test.

The type of supervision found in some schools that is properly termed "snoopervision" has as its main purpose to determine whether or not teachers are following the prescribed course and doing what the supervisor thinks is right. The practice, however, has been diminishing. The prevalent practice in larger systems is to use supervisors in the different subject fields; it is more common with special fields such as music and physical education.

3. *Courses of Study.* The type of course of study used in secondary schools has changed considerably in the last three decades. The change is away from an outline of content to be covered, toward the resource type of bulletin with suggested objectives, activities, means of evaluation, and materials. Some schools use rather brief outlines agreed upon by the teacher. Others do not use a course of study at all, but follow rather closely the textbooks selected by the school. In these cases the textbook becomes the course of study.

4. *Attitudes of the Teaching Staff.* A new teacher in a school finds that he can or cannot do certain things in his classes depending upon the attitudes of the other teachers. In certain schools, he will discover that teachers frown on "new-fangled" ideas and do all they can to discourage neophytes from using them. They realize that it requires more work to carry on the newer practices, or they may feel insecure in the face of new developments which they lack confidence in being able to carry out successfully. In other situations, beginning teachers may find that they are left to themselves. Other teachers do not know nor care what they are doing, and neither the principal nor fellow-teachers extend a helping hand to them. In other schools, beginning teachers are given help and encouragement by principal and fellow-teachers. The schools in which the staff works together with the principal in determining policy will generally have a high morale situation in which undesirable staff relations have less chance of developing.

5. *Attitudes of the Community.* The beginning teacher will find that the mores of the community influence what he can teach in the classroom. If the dominant group is one with an eye on the social calendar, there will be pressure exerted to have their children take courses merely for their status value. Many a secondary school

counselor knows what it means to have ambitious parents insist on the academic program for a child who has more talent for carpentry than for college.

Community attitudes toward sex education, toward liberal ideas, toward religion—toward manifold topics—help to determine what the secondary schools are teaching. If the majority of the more influential leaders in the community are not favorable toward labor unions, labor's position may not be fairly presented in the school, or labor-employer problems and relationships may not be studied at all. Sometimes the teacher is cautioned that he must go easy on a particular topic.

The community should play a vital part in determining what is to be taught in the school. In some communities teachers and parents rarely have the opportunity to meet for the purpose of discussing the school's program and policies in order to understand what the school is trying to do or should do. Instead, educators may try to please everyone and to stir up as little comment as possible, virtually keeping the school isolated from the community.

Pressure groups are found in every community. The difference is that some schools work with them and bring leaders from such groups together to develop the best solutions and to achieve a better understanding of the school's purposes; others try to ward them off as much as possible. Freedom of thought and investigation has often been encroached upon by supposed defenders of democracy who have but a twisted and warped idea of what democracy actually means. Throughout the history of American education, powerful groups in some communities have effectively prevented teaching about evolution, about Russia, or about the essential differences between democracy and communism. At times, they have been successful in keeping out of the schools some of the more liberal journals of opinion.

6. *College Entrance Requirements.* Colleges exert an influence on the high school curriculum by requiring certain subjects for college entrance, even though countless research studies have indicated that the pattern of high school subjects has no relation to subsequent college success. The college's influence on the content that teachers include in courses, although more indirect, is perhaps even more powerful. Literary selections for study in English are sometimes made with the thought in mind that college teachers expect all high school students to have read *Macbeth, Hamlet, Ivanhoe,* or the *Lady of the Lake.* Formal grammar is often emphasized in English classes because it is considered good preparation for college. As discussed in Chapter 18, a more enlightened attitude

toward cooperation between secondary schools and colleges has developed in recent years. The emphasis tends to be on the problem of articulation for the student of college ability and on the types of academic courses which will give him a good foundation for college.

College entrance examinations have had good as well as detrimental influence on the curriculum in secondary schools. When institutions of higher learning use these examinations for admission purposes, some teachers tend to plan their courses to fit the examinations, hold coaching classes in the afternoon, and strive to cover all the "essential" content which the examination may include. The more positive influences are described in Chapter 18.

TEACHER PARTICIPATION IN CURRICULUM DEVELOPMENT. The principles in this chapter indicate that the teacher as a curriculum maker controls pupils' experiences in one way or another. Many factors influence the teacher in his direction of those experiences as he works daily with his pupils. Those curriculum activities which are broader in scope than the work of the teacher and the pupils in individual classes are (1) the planning of the courses of study, course content, activities, and curriculum policy; (2) the selection of materials for use in classes; and (3) cooperative study of curriculum problems by the whole staff or a group of teachers. How do teachers take part in these aspects of curriculum development in the secondary school?

The development and use of courses of study. The new teacher is more likely to find courses of study to guide him if his first position is in a large city. Most school systems of cities with a population of 100,000 or more either have some type of organization for continuous curriculum study, or have produced courses of study spasmodically whenever a demand was felt. In the former, the emphasis is on the professional growth of the teacher in order to plan more effectively experiences for pupils; in the latter the emphasis is on providing outlines for the content to be taught in the classroom. Either plan may produce courses of study or curriculum bulletins. Many school systems produce resource units for teachers' use.

In the schools of medium size, there is more likely to be a mimeographed outline, usually briefer than the course of study published by large city systems or by state departments of education. However, the majority of secondary schools, including practically all the smaller ones, either depend upon the use of the state courses of study or have none at all.

In the large cities, teachers participate in course-of-study development to a considerable extent, usually as representatives of their departments. The number who serve on committees represents but a small proportion of all the teachers. In smaller school systems with only one high school, there is more opportunity for all teachers to take part. In most instances, in larger secondary schools, it is a departmental responsibility. For example, science teachers usually have little to do with developing the course for the social studies.

Most courses of study give suggestions for objectives, activities, content, and materials. Some are nothing more than a supplement to the textbook. The extremely long courses containing a detailed outline of subject matter content are declining in popularity. More suggestions relating to types of classroom activities and to materials of all types are being included.

The use made of a course of study is most important. Often it is expected to be followed as an outline of content, uniform in nature for all classes. Classes may be grouped homogeneously, but one course of study, geared either to high or average ability, is presumably supposed to fit all equally well. Voluminous courses, in the making of which teachers have had no part, gather dust on the shelves while good ideas for teaching go unheeded. In other cases the course of study is regarded as a source and a help, to be studied together by the staff and adapted to the local situation.

The selection and use of textbooks. Textbooks are most frequently chosen by the teacher in conference with the principal or superintendent. In the smaller secondary schools, there is less likely to be cooperative study of what the school is trying to do, how materials should be used, and what is needed in a text before it is selected. Insufficient consideration of the entire field of books available may result in a hasty choice.

In larger secondary schools, teachers, functioning through departments or committees, usually have the responsibility of recommending which books are to be purchased. Sometimes committees study what policy is most desirable for a good learning situation: a single textbook for the whole class, smaller sets of books for different levels of ability within the class, a text and supplementary books, or classroom libraries of single copies. Decisions are made on the basis of what practice will best further the desired educational goals.

The student of education may ask if the use of books in the secondary school has kept up with current knowledge of how to promote effective learning. A pupil cannot profit by reading materials that are too difficult for him. The gifted pupil is likely to find the typical textbook rather boring. Research shows that pupils in any one grade differ widely in their ability to read. Yet, there are countless pupils in secondary schools who fail in mathematics because they cannot understand the mathematical vocabulary, or who cannot master the books provided in social studies, or for whom some of the classics used are as bewildering as a new language to a student on his first day in class. There is a universal lag in the secondary school between what is known about reading ability and practice in selecting books that are suitable for the different levels of ability.

The study of curriculum improvement and problems. The teacher in all schools has an opportunity to discuss informally with colleagues or with the principal the experiences which he is providing for pupils. Some secondary schools carry on a continuous study and evaluation of the curriculum. Such study leads to a mutual understanding of purposes of the school, of the pupil needs in that school, and of the nature of the community. To reach that understanding requires a longer tenure of staff members than one or two years.

The situation that the beginning teacher is likely to find in a secondary school is illustrated by one or more descriptions of a number of different practices. Faculty meetings may be held once a month with the main consideration given to administrative matters, school functions, school regulations, or pupil conduct. In larger secondary schools, departmental meetings by subject areas are often held more frequently than general meetings of the entire staff or than meetings of small groups representing a cross-section of subject interests. In some schools, there are few meetings in which elementary and secondary school teachers work together on problems of common interest. In others, curriculum study is more often interpreted to mean the consideration of content of courses, selection of texts, course requirements in the program of studies, and course of study construction, than to include also problems dealing with adolescent development, recording behavior, adjustment problems, use of community resources, and pupil experiences in classes and activities. The teacher who is alert and interested professionally often volunteers or is usually called upon time and again for committee work; the teacher whose professional growth has come to a halt is but an infrequent participant in cooperative study. Teacher participation in local or university workshops is often confined to those who are working for graduate degrees or who are particularly interested in improving their work.

IMPLEMENTATION OF THE PRINCIPLES

Although the secondary school teacher may be hemmed in by regulations, straight-laced courses of study, and plain inertia, in an increasing number of forward-looking schools the principal considers it his responsibility to release and stimulate creativity in his teachers. Most principals facilitate, in many ways, experimentation and the building of the kind of curriculum that will make a difference in the lives of young people. In secondary schools, too, usually there will be teachers who are eager for knowledge, who have not forgotten how to try out new ideas, who can give leadership in curriculum improvement, and who use effectively the freedom they have by exercising imagination and resourcefulness in planning for pupil experiences.

EXPERIMENTATION IN THE CLASSROOM. Where teachers in secondary schools work in an atmosphere of relative freedom to experiment with new approaches to teaching or with revised content, the curriculum does not become stratified. There is likely to be considerable experimentation with content, activities, materials, and means of evaluation.

One of the more promising means of curriculum study and improvement is a process called "action research." It refers to a testing out of ideas in the classroom, done with a greater degree of care than the typical evaluation of an innovation. Thus, a greater degree of confidence for the particular school and classroom can be placed in the results of action research than is true of casual inquiry. The process is described more fully and illustrated in Chapter 19.

Teachers are directly involved in classroom experimentation and research, even though the project may be directed by outside consultants or by supervisors from the school system. Teachers help plan the project, define the problem, develop the hypothesis, gather data, and evaluate results. They are, in effect, attempting to improve their own practices by experimenting with their own classroom procedures.

A number of secondary schools are working with universities or colleges in this type of research. The Horace Mann–Lincoln Institute of School Experimentation of Teachers College, Columbia University, is an institute that cooperates with schools on action research projects. Another is the Institute for Child Study of the College of Education, University of Maryland.

USE OF RESOURCE UNITS. Resource units written by teachers are used as a source of information in developing the curriculum. Some schools have a file of resource units developed by teachers or secured from other schools, state departments of education, and organizations concerned with education.[1] These units are most appropriately named since they contain a rich fund of suggestions for goals, activities, problems, materials, and evaluation. Schools sometimes prefer to publish them in place of voluminous courses of study.

An example of a resource unit developed by a teacher is a unit entitled *Free and Equal? The Japanese-Americans in Oregon,* prepared in a workshop in intercultural education in the Portland Public Schools, Portland, Oregon. Since there was very little collected information on this topic, many facts were gathered from magazine articles, newspaper articles, personal interviews, and other original sources. A skeleton outline of this unit is given below:

  I. Introduction
 II. Objectives
III. Possible Methods of Approach
 IV. Outline of Subject Matter
    A. Japanese-Americans at War
    B. Characteristics of Japanese-Americans
    C. Problems of Integration into American Life
    D. History of Japanese in Oregon
    E. Period of Evacuation and Relocation
    F. Problems of Returning Japanese-Americans
       1. Myths and Prejudices
       2. Alien Land Law
       3. The Gresham Area
       4. The Hood River Area
       5. The Tigard-Sherwood Area
       6. The Portland Area
       7. Readjustment into Home Community
          a. The War Relocation Authority
          b. Citizen's Committee
    G. Conditions Today
  V. Suggested Activities
 VI. Possible Outcomes
VII. Bibliography, including books, magazine articles, pamphlets, miscellaneous; also personal interviews
APPENDIX I. Clarifying notes on the outline of subject matter
APPENDIX II. Clarifying quotations

MODERN COURSES OF STUDY. The trend in published courses, either mimeographed or printed, is toward including suggestions as

---

[1] Examples of units are those published by Louisville, Kentucky, Public Schools; Portland, Oregon, Public Schools; Fresno County, California, Public Schools; Center for Study of Intergroup Relations, University of Chicago; World Affairs Materials, Brooklyn, New York.

to methods and activities, well-annotated bibliographies of books and other teaching aids, and techniques on how to study pupils and evaluate their growth. The following outline of a course of study, *The English Laguage Arts: Secondary School Guide. The Program in Listening, Speaking, and Critical Thinking,* Stanislaus County Schools, Modesto, California, is an example. Under each of these headings are included specific suggestions for the teachers. Only the outline is presented here to illustrate what is included in a modern guide to the curriculum.

Section I. Teaching Critical Thinking
Point of View
What Is Critical Thinking?
When Does Thinking Start?
How Do We Teach Critical Thinking?
What Are the Basic Concepts Involved in Critical Thinking?
How Can the Basic Concepts of Critical Thinking Be Applied?
The Procedures for Problem Solving
What Are Some of the Factors that Condition Critical Thinking?
What Is A Good Climate for Critical Thinking?
Appendices

Section II. Teaching Speaking
Point of View
General Objectives for Speech Training
Development of Communication Skills
Kinds of Activities
Evaluation
Appendices

Section III. Teaching Listening
Point of View
What Is Listening?
What Are the Listening Needs of High School Students?
What Is A Good Listener?
What Are the Various Kinds of Listening and How Do We Teach Them?
How Do We Evaluate the Listening Program?
Bibliography

Other courses that students of education may wish to examine to see what the modern type is like are those published by school systems of Cleveland, Ohio; Montgomery County, Maryland; New

York City; Milwaukee, Wisconsin; Vancouver, Washington; Mt. Lebanon, Pennsylvania; Palto Alto, California. Often these can be found in the curriculum library of the institution at which the student is studying,

There is also a definite trend toward developing curriculum bulletins that deal with specific instructional problems. These bulletins may either supplement or supplant the traditional course of study. In the schools that publish such bulletins it is rightfully assumed that uniformity is achieved, not through printed courses, but through discussions about purposes and procedures to arrive at some agreements. These curriculum bulletins on specific problems are often used as a study guide for staff meetings and in-service classes and groups. Others serve as official guides for the subject areas.[2]

Policies concerning the use of courses of study are recognized as important. Good schools realize that teachers do better work when they do not have to follow course outlines rigidly. Such is the policy, for example, of the Battle Creek, Michigan, Public Schools:

We believe that the individual classroom is the basic unit for curriculum development. It is the individual teacher planning with her children who, in the final analysis, determines which experiences and needs will be selected for study. This planning is done, with help from the principal and supervisor, within the broad framework of educational goals established for the entire school system.

There are available for suggestion and help to the teacher the guides listed below. . . .

[2] See, for example:
Baltimore: City of Promise, Baltimore: Baltimore City Public Schools, 1953, 375 pp. (Produced by Senior High School Pupils).
Creative Music Education: An Instructional Guide. LaMesa, California: LaMesa—Spring Valley School District, 1959, 124 pp. (mimeo.)
Democracy and Its Totalitarian Competitors: Supplementary Materials, Grades 7–12, Resource Bulletin, Rockville, Maryland: Montgomery County Public Schools, 1957, 95 pp. (mimeo.)
Handbook for Core Teachers: A Core Program for Core Teaching, Curriculum Bulletin No. 1, Frederick, Maryland: Frederick County Public Schools, 1959, 85 pp.
Job Relations, Curriculum Bulletin 12, Grade 9, Cincinnati: Cincinnati Public Schools, 1958, 127 pp. (mimeo.)
Methods and Materials for Teachers of the Less Gifted, Cleveland: Cleveland Public Schools, 1959, 224 pp. (multilithed) (Outline of experimental work of a number of classroom teachers in four Cleveland junior high schools)
Parent-Teacher Conferences: Guide Book, Wichita Kansas: Wichita Public Schools, 1958, 49 pp. (mimeo.)
Reading and Library Skills, Grades 7-8, Curriculum Bulletin No. 20, New Orleans: New Orleans Public Schools, 1959, 114 pp. (mimeo.)
Successful Reading Techniques for Secondary Schools, Fallsington, Pennsylvania: The Pennsbury Schools, 1957, 88 pp. (mimeo.)
The School as a Social Institution and Home and Family as a Social Institution. Philadelphia: Philadelphia Public Schools, 1959, 116 pp. (mimeo.)
Trips to Take: Field Trips Handbook, Cuyahoga, Ohio: Cuyahoga County Schools, 1959, 29 pp. (mimeo.)

It is to be emphasized that these are guides and not rigid outlines to be covered. Teachers are encouraged to adapt from these guides if in so doing they are more adequately meeting the needs of their pupils.[3]

CONSULTANTS AND OUTSIDE ASSISTANCE. Schools often call upon experts in curriculum study and in the subject fields to help them in their curriculum revision. This is another type of resource that, in turn, assists the teacher to update himself in his field or in the field of professional education, to write teaching plans and materials, and to utilize the most recent advance in knowledge of the subject that he is teaching.

One of the most significant developments in curriculum making in recent years has been the close cooperation of professional educators and professors and other specialists in the academic fields to improve and modernize the curriculum, especially through the efforts of learned societies such as, for example, The American Association for the Advancement of Science. The several national curriculum studies in mathematics and the physical and biological sciences are described in Chapter 9. These groups give substantial aid in rewriting courses of study.

SELECTION OF INSTRUCTIONAL MATERIALS. In many outstanding secondary schools, teachers are responsible for choosing teaching aids, including books, maps, films and slides, library materials, and other types of materials that enrich the possibilities for learning and serve the purpose of instruction. In these schools, books are selected as an outgrowth of a study of the curriculum, not as a separate function.

One plan followed by a larger school system involves careful selection of textbooks. First, a committee of teachers and principals studied the recent trends in the fields in which books were to be chosen. Second, the committee set up criteria for the selection of the books on the basis of the purpose of the course. This included such policy decisions as whether one or more books would be used and whether there should be a selection of books of different levels of reading ability. These decisions were based on study and discussion with many teachers throughout the schools. Third, the committee developed an evaluation sheet, studied the books available, and rated them on the sheet. Book representatives met with the committee since city-wide adoptions of texts were being considered. Policies

[3] *Aims and Policies of the Instructional Program*, Battle Creek, Michigan: Division of Instruction, Battle Creek Public Schools, p. 5. (mimeo.)

were determined to govern the relations between publisher's representatives and the committee in order to avoid either any unfair advantages being given to certain publishers and any undesirable type of solicitation. The final decision of the committee was submitted to the administration for adoption by the board of education. Pupils had a part through the exploratory use of books in the classrooms of committee members and other teachers, who secured evaluation by pupils. The teachers then could select from the resulting list the books to purchase for their own classrooms. A number of larger city school systems follow a similar procedure.[4]

Teachers also participate in choosing audio-visual aids to be purchased by the school. They preview films and slides and recommend those aids that further the aims of the curriculum. Some schools have standing committees for this purpose; others receive recommendations from individual teachers. Teachers are called upon to recommend new library acquisitions each year, especially where the library is more of an integral part of classwork and is used extensively as a resource center.

DEVELOPMENT OF CURRICULUM POLICIES. Through committees and meetings, teachers have a part in determining curriculum policy and administrative matters that affect the curriculum. They participate through curriculum councils for the school system, through building or system-wide committees appointed to study specific phases of the curriculum, through planning by departments, and through in-service workshops. School system curriculum councils and committees serve as coordinating bodies for all of the schools in the system.

An illustration of how teachers take part in the policy-making of a large secondary school is the cooperative planning in Oakland High School, Oakland, California. The staff participates in different groups:

1. *The administrative staff*, composed of the principal, the vice-principals, and teachers elected by the faculty. This staff meets weekly to discuss and recommend administrative practices in the school.
2. *An instructional council* composed of the principal, vice-principals, curriculum assistants, and department heads. This council directs the over-all instructional problems of the school. The problems of different departments are brought to the attention of this group

[4] See mimeographed textbook adoption procedures of the Oakland public schools, Oakland, California, and the Denver public schools, Denver, Colorado, for good examples. Available in most good curriculum laboratories in teacher preparation institutions.

and, in turn, the department heads discuss with teachers in the department the curriculum problems for the entire school. Teachers meet once a week with their department heads.

3. *Interdepartmental meetings* of groups of teachers. The faculty is divided into groups; membership in each group is determined prior to the time the teacher has a conference period scheduled. These meetings are for the purpose of clarification of administrative, guidance, and curriculum practices. These groups also discuss reports on talks presented at faculty meetings of the total staff. Teachers bring up any problem upon which there is need for better understanding.

4. *Teacher committees* selected to study and recommend curriculum as well as other changes to the faculty. Examples of these are:

Committee on Home Rooms
Committee on Evaluation and Grading
Committee on Improvement of Family Life

5. *Monthly faculty meetings* to consider reports and hear talks by a teacher, the principal, or an outside consultant.

ISSUES AND PROBLEMS

By no means have all the questions regarding the teacher's role in curriculum development been settled. Some of them are fundamental to the controversies concerning education today. Not all teachers believe they should have a part in curriculum study and decisions. Some of the chief issues are pointed out briefly.

1. *Should the curriculum be determined by some centralized body or by local schools and communities?*

The authors of this book have taken the position that curriculum building occurs day-by-day in the classroom and that faculties of schools in a particular community can best determine the curriculum suited to the students of that school. In addition, there should be some type of coordination for the school system. Some people hold that the state should determine through prescribed courses of study what is to be taught. Others would go as far as to make the curriculum uniform for the entire nation. Some advocate a national curriculum commission as a coordinating body. The issue is fundamentally one of local autonomy in school matters. In the American tradition of control of education by board of education, under the broad powers of the state, a remarkable amount of uniformity has been achieved. But to what extent is uniformity desirable? Can uniformity in learning ever be achieved? What should be the role of the state or national governmental agency dealing with public schools? The whole question of federal versus state and local control is involved.

2. *Are teachers sufficiently well qualified to write courses of study and to develop the curriculum?*

To say that teachers should have a significant role in curriculum development implies their knowing the field that they teach, learning procedures, and the age-group's interests and peculiar characteristics. It also would indicate that they need to know something about the society in which they live. Not all teachers are thus qualified. As students in high school are well aware, some are not interested either in them or in improving their own knowledge.

Consequently, some persons argue that the teachers are not capable of writing courses of study and that this demanding task should be left to the experts in the subject fields and those who have a ready facility for writing. Less often do they recommend that experts in the field of teaching and learning and adolescent psychology join in the process.

But those who hold this point of view miss one important point. Teacher participation in curriculum study and course of study production is a two-edged instrument that develops not only the plan or the written material but also the person producing it. Experts in the learning process, in adolescent development, and in the subject field can be called in to work as a member of the team in the capacity of consultants. The process in itself is in-service training.

If curriculum study is confined to central committees in a large school system or country or state, this issue becomes even more complicated. In these instances, only a small proportion of the teachers derive the benefits that accrue from study and work on curriculum materials. If curriculum study is to be regarded as production of courses, bulletins, and guides, might it not be well to free the teacher from these duties and to employ someone particularly skilled in this purpose?

Should we expect to find within a school faculty teachers who are well prepared to serve as resource persons to curriculum study within school buildings?

3. *Does the curriculum consist of the pupils' experiences in the school or of the subject to be learned?*

This is a philosophic issue. Some educators believe that curriculum decisions involve only determining the subject matter to be studied. This is by far the most popular point of view among college faculties and has many proponents in high school faculties.

But this is also an intensely practical issue, more than something to be debated in academic circles. How does the teacher select and use subject matter in the classroom? How does he stimulate students to learn? How does he achieve a direction to learning in the class-room? How does he influence youngsters' behavior? These are fac-tors that determine the experiences that a student will have. The definition of curriculum affects the focus of curriculum study—whether it be on the subject matter alone or on the subject matter and the experiences which the student has with that subject matter.

Research specialists may argue that experience is a nebulous term, that it cannot be defined or classified with sufficient sharpness for research. Others say that a person's experience cannot be defined, for it is something intensely personal. The position taken in this book defines curriculum in terms of experience.

4. *Should state legislatures write into law the requirements of the curriculum?*

It is evident that many people feel this necessity for safeguarding the welfare of the children of the state. They want to be sure that American history, the dangers of alcohol, the effects of narcotics, or the history of the state is taught in the schools. Specific interests, appealing to patriotic sentiments or arguing on moral grounds, have brought into being these laws. The state, it is contended, must pro-tect its future citizens by seeing that these aspects are included in their education.

Those who argue against this position believe that it is inadvis-able to legislate the school curriculum. Such laws tend to make the curriculum inflexible and subject to political pressure rather than to the will of the people. State boards of education, composed of lay citizens, working with professional personnel in state departments of education, they argue, are better qualified to establish state require-ments as to what should be taught in the schools.

Who should set these requirements, the state or local commu-nities? Why have legislatures not required the teaching of modern world history, or the history of Asiatic countries, or the history of Russia, or modern foreign languages, important in a modern world? Are legislatures responsive to educational needs?

5. *Should teachers participate in developing policies for the school?*

There is a substantial group of teachers who believe that they should have no part in developing school policies; that these matters should be left to the school administration and the board of education. Included among these are some leaders in state teachers' associations.

On the other hand, there is a growing demand for teachers to take part in curriculum councils, advisory councils, and school committees dealing with many policies and questions other than salaries. They feel it is their right to participate in making decisions that affect them. Certainly, nothing in the way of school decisions affect the teacher's work in the classroom more than those which deal with the curriculum.

6. *Should the curriculum of the secondary school be determined by college admission examinations, national merit scholarship examinations, and examinations by a state or federal agency?*

The question of the effect of external testing programs on the secondary schools is an extremely live issue. As a result of the problems schools face with regard to these testing programs, three national organizations established a Joint Committee on Testing to collect data, make recommendations, and prepare publications. The organizations are the American Association of School Administrators, The Council of Chief State School Officers, and The National Association of Secondary-School Principals.

These external testing programs, which are national, regional, and state-wide in scope, are sponsored by some agency outside the local school district. There are approximately twenty such national testing programs, plus others state-wide in scope. The primary purpose of these tests is use for college admissions and scholarship selection. College admissions tests aid in the selection of students who are likely to succeed in college; for some colleges they assure the institution of only top-ability students. For these purposes, they have been used for some time with important refinements throughout the years of their use. The new dimension added to external testing programs is their use for talent search, such as merit scholarship programs.

The problems creating the issue as to the value of, or harm caused by, these programs lie in the use of the tests and in the lack of coordination of testing programs. These kinds of national or state tests influence the curriculum, because teachers tend to teach for the tests and programs are developed to help students pass the tests. One of the problems is the willingness of the public, especially, to place a blind faith in the infallibility of these tests. Schools report that these testing programs tend to exert an undue pressure because they are expected by the public to give them. Other problems which school principals report concern the time and costs of taking and giving the tests. The multiplicity of these tests makes it necessary for some students to take several of them.

The issue of interference in local educational programs by outside agencies promoting these testing programs is a serious one. Schools are likely to be rated on what proportion of students are selected on the basis of the test even though this was far from the intention of the testing agency. Should tests of this nature be used to judge the quality of an education? Can schools in low income areas be expected to compete with those in areas of higher economic and cultural status? Is the time spent on these tests justifiable in view of the fact that in some national programs less than two-tenths of one per cent of those tested are selected for scholarships? These are some serious questions for both secondary schools and colleges involved in these testing programs.

SELECTED REFERENCES

ANDERSON, VERNON E. *Principles and Procedures of Curriculum Improvement.* New York: The Ronald Press Co., 1956, Chap. 1 and Part III.—Teacher participation in curriculum study of various kinds.

DOUGLAS, HARL R. (ed.). *The High School Curriculum.* New York: The Ronald Press Co., 2nd. ed., 1956, Chaps. 15, 16, 17.—Discusses resource units, courses of study, giving further examples of modern courses, and the teacher's part in curriculum construction, in choosing textbooks, and in building and using courses of study. Many examples given.

EASTMOND, JEFFERSON N. *The Teacher and School Administration.* Boston: Houghton Mifflin Co., 1959. Chap. 8.—Discusses the teacher's relations to the administration of the school and his participation in administration.

HAND, HAROLD C. *Principles of Public Secondary Education.* New York: Harcourt, Brace & World, Inc., 1958. Chap. 11.—How teachers are involved in curriculum improvement and studies.

KEARNEY, NOLAN C. *A Teacher's Profession.* Englewood Cliffs, N. J.: Prentice-Hall, Inc., 1958. Chap. 6.—The teacher's participation in committees and workshops and his relationships with a democratic administration.

KRUG, EDWARD A. *Curriculum Planning.* New York: Harper & Brothers, 1950, Chaps. 1, 2, 4, 5, 7.—Indicates the role of teachers and others in curriculum planning, how a school faculty works together effectively, the use of the curriculum guides and units, and means of system-wide curriculum study. The teacher's part is stressed throughout, and the book contains good, concrete examples.

LEESE, JOSEPH, FRASURE, KENNETH, and JOHNSON, JR., MAURITZ. *The Teacher in Curriculum Making.* New York: Harper & Brothers, 1961. Part I and selected chapters.—This first complete book on the teachers' role in curriculum making furnishes a valuable reference for the student who wishes to dig deeper into the subject. Part II deals with the understandings a teacher needs for making wise curriculum decisions; Part III with the way the teacher works with both classes and extraclass activities in planning the curriculum; Part IV, with how he works as a member of a faculty in curriculum development.

Pritzkau, P. T. *Dynamics of Curriculum Improvement.* Englewood Cliffs, N.J.: Prentice-Hall, Inc., 1959, Chaps. 1 and 2.—In this section, and throughout the book, the student can find challenging ideas regarding the teacher's responsibilities in curriculum development in the classroom.

Romine, Stephen A. *Building the High School Curriculum.* New York: The Ronald Press Co., 1954, Chaps. 9–11.—Discussion and illustration of resource units and courses of study.

Saylor, J. Galen and Alexander, William M. *Curriculum Planning for Better Teaching and Learning.* New York: Holt, Rinehart & Winston, Inc., 1954, Chap. 12. —The use of resource units and illustrations of such units.

Spears, Harold. *Curriculum Planning Through In-Service Programs.* Englewood Cliffs, N.J.: Prentice-Hall, Inc., 1957. 350 pp.—A comprehensive account of how teachers participate in curriculum improvement and other kinds of in-service education, with illustrations from school systems.

Spears, Harold. *The Teacher and Curriculum Planning.* Englewood Cliffs, N.J.: Prentice-Hall, Inc., 1951, pp. 61-117.—Some principles regarding teacher participation in curriculum development.

7

ORGANIZATION OF THE CURRICULUM

Previous chapters have dealt with the approach that the teacher uses in directing the pupils' experiences and the teacher's part in curriculum planning. The discussion in this chapter will center on the way in which experiences and subject matter are organized for learning, both in the day's schedule and in the total program of studies. It is important to know how subject matter is arranged and used for most effective growth of pupils. The chapter includes a description of attempts of secondary schools to achieve an organization in which the relationships of different subject fields are made evident, and in which the experiences of pupils in school may form a more unified pattern. The course offerings of the school, the blocking of time for courses, and the organization of content within courses are all part of this topic.

BASIC PRINCIPLES

The curriculum should be organized in such a manner that it facilitates the student's seeing relationships among experiences in different subjects and activities during the school day.

There is little consistency with good learning principles in a policy of extreme departmentalization of subjects and few, if any, attempts made to coordinate the work done in various courses. The college student is well aware how limited is the coordination among his courses, how few are the attempts of instructors to help students integrate in their own minds information from various courses. Stress on learning the facts in each course without guiding students to use subject matter from all courses in solving questions and clarifying issues may serve to block such integration. Subject matter must serve a useful purpose, or learning will be of less than maximum efficiency.

Attempts of teachers to correlate English and history courses, that is, teaching related subject matter at the same time, and to fuse or combine geography and history into a single course in social studies illustrate how schools are trying to help the pupils see relationships or to correlate subject matter. Another illustration is a situation in which information from various subjects is drawn as needed to solve problems of significance. It is most commonly found in the elementary grades, where the teacher has the pupils in the room for the entire school day and time is taken to work on specialized phases of the curriculum, such as arithmetic or spelling, as needed. The core curriculum in the secondary school is designed to provide for an organization of the curriculum that permits more integrated experiences in the school day. Team teaching, as used by some schools, also has this objective.

The organization of the curriculum should be experimental and varied for individual goals and needs.

No stereotyped organization of experiences within the school day or in the classroom will best serve the purposes of the secondary school. Research on ways of organizing content to facilitate learning is needed. Organization of subject matter around problems will facilitate one kind of learning and will perhaps be better suited to certain pupils. Organization around the logical order of the subject may be best suited to developing the specialist in a field and better suited to other pupils. A promising way of studying the subject is by the means of discovery of knowledge used by the scholar in a particular discipline.

The unit organization of the curriculum around significant problems in general education areas facilitates the learning of desirable attitudes, appreciations, skills, and understandings for a democratic society.

The unit organization of the curriculum refers to the organization of activities, experiences, and subject matter around a central problem or purpose of a group or pupils. It is not correctly defined as merely a block of subject matter. The daily assignment-recitation type of teaching involves a certain type of organization of experiences in the classroom, including the teacher's planning of assignments by himself, discussion around assignments as decided by the teacher, and tests on material covered.

Problem-solving through the unit organization has certain characteristics of advantage in facilitating desirable learnings; presuming it is used by the skilled teacher:

The pupils have a chance to participate in setting their own goals, which have meaning for them.

The pupils plan together their experiences to meet their goals; they practice the skills in cooperative planning and living essential to democracy.

Several areas of subject matter are drawn upon to solve the problems involved, broadening the horizon of pupils' knowledge.

There is an opportunity for varied experiences, with different pupils doing the things most suited to their abilities and interests and using materials of varied difficulty.

The unit makes possible constant group evaluation of progress and a knowledge of the progress being made.

The investigation, weighing of information, interviewing people, evaluating sources, and reporting information are important skills encouraged by organization of learning around problems.

The principle does not preclude the study of subjects such as mathematics, foreign languages, and others in logical fashion. Specialized learnings may best be studied in that type of organization.

The program of studies in a secondary school should provide both common learnings for all pupils as a part of their general education for living and specialized learnings to develop diversified and unique interests and abilities.

Certain common learning experiences to develop skills, understandings, and attitudes that all intelligent citizens of a democracy need are a part of general education. They are not merely a compilation of required subject matter. Common experiences do not mean the same experiences. They should be suited to the maturity and abilities of the pupils. They would include, for example, learning how to communicate orally and in writing, developing civic and social skills, learning about one's own culture and that of other nations in the world, learning about scientific development, and development of cultural interests.

In addition to the common learnings, the secondary school must provide for the diversity that builds a strong democratic society, for the many interests, the special abilities, and the needs of those who are handicapped. A high quality experience in a secondary school demands content and learning activities that will challenge the best minds in the class and that will help youth to discover and develop special talents in mathematics and science, in the arts and crafts, in vocational skills, in business, and in many other fields.

The common elements of the program of studies should em-
body a well-balanced general education that includes provisions
for civic, intellectual, social, cultural, health, mental, and family-
life needs of every citizen no matter what his occupation will be.

Achieving a balance in the general education of the citizen for
community and family living is no easy task, but it is an important
goal of the secondary school. Civic responsibilities and intelligent
voting on issues are becoming more complicated in a world constantly brought closer to each individual through scientific inventions in transportation and communication, and made ever more
perilous through new and terrible instruments of destruction. Understanding the scientific and technological developments and learning to live on a higher cultural and aesthetic plane are clearly obli-
gations of a good general education.

General education should be broad rather than narrow in scope.
Every pupil—whether he intends to go to college, to business school,
or to get a job immediately after finishing high school—should have
some experiences in the areas of arts and crafts, science, mathematics, writing and speaking, literature, music, physical education,
and family living. He needs to give considerable thought to happenings in his world and to social, economic, and political questions. A
balanced education would not be complete unless he had a chance
to consider personal problems of his own living, health, and interpersonal relationships.

The total curriculum in the school day should be organized
so as to give each pupil maximum experiences in democratic liv-
ing.

The common learning experiences should include more than subject content. They should provide practice in democratic skills, experience in living in an atmosphere where mental health is valued
and fostered, and opportunity for developing attitudes and appreciations that go to make up a full and rich life—rich in friends,
beauty, interests, and satisfactions. The experiences should be consistent with the ideals of a democracy, in which each individual has
a share in deciding policy that affects his own welfare; where the
individual lives in an atmosphere in which he is regarded as important and respected for what he is as a person; which places a
great deal of value on concern for others and their welfare; and
which values individuality, creativity, and originality.

Segregation of pupils on a basis that places less value on any one
group of young people than on others is inimical to these democratic principles. The student of education should ask himself: How

were pupils in different curricula regarded in my school? Did these divisions, based on future plans, help pupils with less academic ability to achieve self-respect and security? Grouping for instructional purposes in order to assist pupils with particular learning difficulties or specialized abilities can be done effectively in many ways. But that is an entirely different matter from grouping students according to curricula. Any procedure that demeans the individual pupil by any kind of year-in and year-out segregation does not further the goals of a democratic society.

Parents who place their children in costly private schools to give them an exclusive social environment may actually be robbing them of the rich experience of learning to know and live with all kinds of people. Impoverishment of social skills is a serious deficiency that cannot be counterbalanced by enrichment of the social graces.

The curriculum should be so organized that there is good articulation in the learning experiences from one grade level to another.

One of the problems that faces a teacher is the previous preparation that his pupils have had in the subject that he is teaching. Pupils may become bored if subject matter is repeated from grade to grade without any sequence of progression to increasingly higher levels, new skills, or new topics. With the increasing amount of knowledge which makes it necessary for the school to be selective in what to teach, we can ill afford needless and purposeless repetition.

Articulation refers to establishing close relationships between what occurs in classes in a subject field from grade to grade. These relationships are attained by careful planning among teachers from different grades within a school unit and from different units, as described in Chapter 18. Setting down what is to be taught in a course of study will not alone solve the problem. Foreign language teaching, for example, will be effective only as teachers build upon the previous learnings of the pupils. If the school has a program in the third and fourth grades in a language, and then none until the ninth grade, the lack of articulation or sequence in opportunities to keep up the study of the language is obvious.

SOME COMMON PRACTICES

LOGICAL ORGANIZATION OF SUBJECT MATTER. In the typical American secondary school, the logical subject organization is the basis for organization of the curriculum. There has been little change in this respect during the history of secondary education in this country. The changes have been in new content added or substituted for the old, in line with new developments in American life. Just as Latin or Greek was taught quite separately from history or rhetoric in the early public high school, so English in most schools today is a distinct subject separate from home economics, world history, or social problems.

In the great majority of high schools, American history is taught as a chronological arrangement of events. Physics and chemistry are organized in a logical arrangement with new content added in keeping with scientific advances and a tendency towards a problems or research approach in the more modern laboratory practices. Foreign languages have generally begun with the simple vocabulary and grammatical structure, proceeding to a stress on reading in the advanced classes; but the concepts of teaching this field are changing radically in recent years to a conversational approach with more stress on speaking the language.

It is in the newer subjects, such as home economics, agriculture, business education, industrial arts, problems of democracy, the core, art, and music that the organization of experiences tends to be centered more around problems or larger units of work. Home economics classes generally organize experiences around such units as different aspects of food, child care, good grooming, the personal budget, and care of clothing. In agriculture, the projects on the boys' farms, along with regional aspects of farming, form a basis for organization of the work. Art and music also are more likely to acquire characteristics of the experience-centered approach to curriculum than the academic subjects. In these courses, projects are used more often as the basis of organization of subject matter and experiences. Many pupils may have little contact with these courses since they have traditionally not been considered as the basis for good preparation for college.

In academic subjects, such as English, science, and social studies, which constitute a large portion of the high school pupil's general education program, the unit organization of activities and content has gained little headway except in the junior high schools and problems of democracy courses in senior high school. The division of a textbook into units for these courses does not in itself assure unit teaching. Such units are merely divisions of subject matter, or a new name for chapters, not unified experiences in the true sense. In more specific skills subjects, such as mathematics, typewriting, and shorthand, which are sequential in nature, the unit organization is not as applicable.

DEPARTMENTALIZATION OF SUBJECTS. The following are some of the practices and trends that reflect the acceptance of departmentalization of subjects in secondary education. They may be good or bad depending on whether or not they promote desired learning.

1. Teachers tend to believe that their prerogative and responsibility is to teach only their own subjects and, consequently, hesitate to infringe on others' subject areas. Hence, the possible interrelationships are not developed.

2. The departmental organization with one teacher as a department head, commonly found in large senior high schools, promotes teacher planning mainly by departments. Jealousies have arisen over subject requirements and "intrusions" of some subjects in the list of required courses at the expense of others. Each group has fought to keep its hold on the curriculum.

3. City or country school supervisors have generally been subject supervisors. Only in recent years have general supervisors of secondary schools been appointed in a number of school systems. There is some trend to return to subject supervision.

4. Subjects in a single field are assigned to teachers. As the high school size increases, the teaching assignment is likely to consist of duplicate sections in English I or in American history.

5. The certification of teachers by many state departments of education is for the teaching of a specific subject or subjects.

6. The high school schedule of classes shifts pupils from one teacher to another at the end of each class period. There is little interchange among classes scheduled for the same period.

The beginning teacher may expect to experience difficulty in trying to use community resources effectively, for many teachers will resent any intrusion on the time scheduled for their classes. He will soon become conscious of the sharp divisions that actually exist between subjects, the many teachers who know little about what is happening in other departments, and the subtle rivalry between subject matter groups. The trend seems to be toward greater departmentalization in the junior high schools.

INCREASE IN COURSES OFFERED. The list of courses offered by secondary schools has continued to multiply since the days of the Latin grammar school. For example, Van Dyke found in a study of course offerings in thirty-five schools that the total number of different courses had increased from 828 in 1908-11 to 1,683 in 1929-30, doubling in about a twenty-year period.[1] The last thirty years have seen another substantial increase.

Undoubtedly, the addition of new courses has given secondary school youth an improved program. Often these courses provide for significant experiences that have had a difficult time infiltrating the established academic curriculum. However, it represents a faith that addition of new courses will meet youth needs without the necessity of changing the orientation and content offered in existing courses. It also implies the assumption that differentiation cannot be provided within courses. The actual situation is that many students are not affected by these new courses since they usually are found in the elective rather than the required category.

MULTIPLE CURRICULA. The list of subjects offered in the secondary school, grade by grade, is known as the program of studies. Two general arrangements of courses within the program of studies are found in secondary schools. There are variations of these patterns, but they represent the typical situation. The first organizes subjects into "curricula," "courses," or "tracks"; the second lists the required and elective courses for all students.

One of the common ways of organizing the program of studies in secondary schools is the grouping of subjects into different combinations (called "curricula" or "courses") around future vocational or educational objectives. This plan, known as the multiple curriculum type of organization, was popular in the early academy and high school. It was intended to meet varying needs of pupils, for both the college preparatory and non-college groups. In the late nineteenth and early twentieth centuries, this method of differentiation in the curriculum grew to ridiculous proportions, ten or twelve curricula being offered by many schools. The number of curricula offered has decreased in the past thirty years.

The practice is still prevalent in the large senior high schools. It is more typical in eastern areas than in the Midwest, West, or South. Curricula most commonly found are the college preparatory or academic, general, commercial or business, and vocational. Further breakdowns of the academic into classical and scientific curricula are sometimes made, emphasizing different groupings of subjects for the college preparatory students. Required and elective subjects are listed for each curriculum.

This type of organization, which has many advocates among sec-

[1] G. E. Van Dyke, "Trends in the Development of the High School Offering. II," *School Review,* 39: 737-47, December, 1931.

ondary school people, served as a means of introducing new emphases into the program of studies for large numbers of pupils whose high school education was terminal. It may have been the most effective plan of guiding pupils in taking the needed courses for their vocational or educational objective at a time when guidance was in the infant stage, but it can be questioned as fitting the needs of the modern secondary school on several counts.

Often a large proportion of the high school pupils enroll in the college preparatory curriculum since it has prestige value with parents, teachers, and pupils. In effect, this defeats the purpose of the plan, since a number of pupils are obviously misfits in that they are not college bound. In many schools, strict adherence to a pattern of courses within one of these curricula is a barrier to a student who wishes to take some subject, such as art or typewriting. The rigidity and inflexibility that often result do not serve the guidance function.

One result of this differentiation is an unfortunate social distinction. Pupils of academic ability are guided into the college preparatory curriculum, and others into the general, commercial, agriculture, or industrial-arts curriculum. The consequence is to divide pupils into two groups. Pupils in the one group often become identified as the "dumbells," or other harsh terms used by high school pupils. As pointed out in Chapter 3, the school helps to accentuate social class distinctions that already exist. In effect, the result is often a form of ability grouping that continues throughout the three or four years and does not provide for different grouping for different purposes and skills. The criticism is not directed against grouping for instructional purposes but against inflexible grouping.

Another similar form of multiple curricula that has been established in a few larger cities is the "track" plan. It is not widely used. This is definitely a form of ability grouping rather than an organization of the curriculum around vocational objectives.

SINGLE CURRICULUM ORGANIZATION. The second typical kind of organization of the program of studies is a listing of prescribed courses and electives for each of the four years without regard for vocational or educational objectives, called the single curriculum or constants-with-electives type. This organization is generally found in the smaller secondary schools, where in many cases programs of offerings have been too limited to permit much differentiation. In fact, almost 80 per cent of the high schools, according to a study of the NEA Research Division, have only the single curriculum. Even among larger high schools, it has gained considerable favor in recent years. Two-thirds of the high schools of 1,000 students or more have the single curriculum plan.[2] In junior high schools, this type of "curriculum" is the one most frequently found.

In this plan, the program of studies includes certain required courses, considered as essential for the general education of all pupils. The schools depend upon the guidance program to help pupils make wise choices of courses each year. These required courses do not ordinarily include as balanced a program as is desirable. Often specific courses listed for certain grades are not open to pupils in other high school grades.

This type of organization, if accompanied by adequate educational guidance, permits greater freedom of choice of certain courses to fit special needs and interests; tends to give more pupils who plan to go to college an opportunity to elect subjects such as music, art, vocational subjects, and industrial arts; creates less of a distinction between academic and non-academic subjects; and does not label specifically the "non-college" and "college" groups.

PROVISION FOR GENERAL AND SPECIAL EDUCATION. The principle that a program of studies should provide for a well-balanced general education is quite generally accepted by secondary school people. The type of education that is common to youth in many small secondary schools does not measure up very well against this standard. There is also a more limited opportunity for electives to provide for special abilities and interests in these schools.

Two sources of data indicate what the majority of young people going through high school are experiencing as to a balanced education: (1) a study of courses that have been pursued by high school graduates, and (2) the existing graduation requirements.

The typical program of studies pursued by a pupil in one of the numerous small high schools of the country includes: English, four years; mathematics, one year; science, one or two years; social studies, two or three years; and other courses in business, foreign languages, industrial arts, physical education, agriculture, and home economics or—more likely—additional units in the academic subjects, six to ten units. Since the very small high school is limited in the number of subjects it can offer, the pattern is largely college preparatory or academic in nature. Studies of credits earned by secondary school graduates indicate that about three-fourths of the subjects taken were of the academic type. In the junior high school, the pupil is more likely to get a broader program: art, music, industrial arts, or home economics are frequently a part of the common learn-

[2] "High School Graduation Requirements," *NEA Research Bulletin,* 37:121, December, 1959.

ings of all pupils. The practice there is to offer some of these subjects one, two, or three times a week.

Sixteen units, or full-year courses, are most frequently required for high school graduation, counting units earned in grades 9 through 12 as most schools do. There has been a notable tendency in recent years to extend this number in order to make it possible to include both a broader general education and opportunity for more specialized courses. By 1960–61, eleven states required from seventeen to twenty units for high school graduation, and in a sampling of thirty-nine cities, twenty-two required from seventeen to twenty units (see Chapter 18).

These figures do not tell the complete story, however, for many students take from seventeen to twenty-three units in the four years, ninth through twelfth grade. In Maryland, for example, three of five high school graduates in 1958 earned twenty or more units in the course of four years.[3] Credits in physical education and "extracurricular" activities have often been added to the basic sixteen. Many schools schedule pupils in five or six classes a day.

James B. Conant, former president of Harvard University, concluded from his study of the American high school that the number of small high schools should be drastically reduced by district reorganization. He found that few small high schools could offer the advanced subjects in mathematics, science, and foreign languages effectively for the academically talented student. He also found a lack of balance in the programs of the more able students, boys often specializing in mathematics and science and neglecting foreign languages, English, and social studies. Able girls often avoided mathematics, science, and foreign languages.

IMPLEMENTATION OF THE PRINCIPLES

Attempts to improve the organization of the curriculum in secondary schools have centered around three general purposes: providing for a general education, achieving a situation in which pupils can more readily relate their learnings from different subject fields, and providing opportunities for taking care of individual needs and abilities. Secondary schools are experimenting with a better organization of content of the general education of pupils. Although schools seek how to provide the common elements, they also recognize that provision must be made for specialization.

[3] Maryland State Department of Education, *A Study of the Relationship between Subjects Taken and Other Selected Factors for the Class of 1958, Maryland Public High Schools,* Baltimore: The Department, 1959, p. 76.

The different aspects of the organization of the curriculum will be discussed in this order: first, organization of content and activities into units; second, organization of subject content into courses that are broader in nature than many typical courses; third, coordination among courses; fourth, provision for common learnings and special interests in the total program of studies; and fifth, special means used for organization of content and activities in general education.

UNIT ORGANIZATION OF THE CURRICULUM. The unit organization of learning activities in the classroom is used by teachers in growing numbers, especially in the general education areas where it is more applicable than in other fields, that is, the social studies and the core curriculum. The kind of unit considered here is an organization of activities and content around a central problem or purpose of importance to the group, developed cooperatively by teachers and pupils, exemplifying the experience-centered approach.

In this type of unit, pupils draw on many areas of subject matter to find information to the solution of a problem. For example, a group may plan to study the problem of what forces operate in disagreements between the United States and the Soviet Union. Information would need to be drawn from history, government, and economics to understand what are the basic differences and the causes for them. The study of propaganda and human relations would be involved. The place of science and technology and their influence on the modern world would be of fundamental importance. At the same time, pupils would be speaking, writing, and using tool skills in gathering information.

Examples of units that draw from various subject fields for information to solve problems are those included in the seventh-grade social studies program at Ohio State University School, such as, Understanding My Body and How Columbus Protects Its People; and those studied by senior high school core groups, such as, The Problems of Earning a Living and The Bases for Determining Values by Which to Live.

BROADENED BASE OF COURSES. In many schools courses with a broader base of subject content have replaced narrower courses in some fields. In junior high schools, this trend is particularly noticeable. Geography and history are usually combined into social studies in the junior high schools. General science draws its content from many of the fields of science. The course in problems of democracy, usually offered in the twelfth grade, is another example. Most schools have changed from ancient history to community civics or a broader course in social studies for the ninth grade. In the latter, subject matter may be selected from the areas of community government, economics, history, sociology, problems of the school society, and personal-social problems of the pupils.

Newer courses that have been added to the high school curriculum to meet the needs of youth in the modern world often center around current problems or developments in society and around life problems that face youth. When a course deals with problems of such nature, it necessarily draws from a wider area of subject matter, cutting across the traditional fields. Examples of such courses are the following, taken from the programs of studies of selected high schools:

Honors seminar	Applied science
Mass media of communication	International relations
Consumer education	Social problems
Contemporary history	Family living

BREAKING DOWN DEPARTMENTAL BARRIERS. In spite of a trend toward departmentalization of subjects, one of the growing practices in order to provide for developing relationships among the various kinds of subject matter taught and to break down compartmentalization, is the scheduling of classes to meet for a block of time of two or more class periods. These block-time classes include two or more subjects that are required of all pupils, usually under one teacher. Most frequently, the combination is English and social studies. The United States Office of Education reported that this practice of blocking classes in the schedule, which includes the core curriculum, occurred in approximately one-fifth of junior and junior-senior high schools in 1956-57, an increase of about 10 per cent over 1949. This practice is much more common in the junior high school grades than in the senior high school, and occurs most frequently in seventh- and eighth-grade programs. Other studies have reported that from 30 to over 40 per cent of the junior high schools included in the study had block-time classes in their schedules. A study of the New Jersey secondary schools found that 51 per cent of the junior high schools and junior-senior high schools had a block-of-time program,[4] and a study of Illinois junior high schools reported that 61 per cent had block-time classes.[5]

---

[4] "Block of time Programs in Junior High Schools and Six-Year High Schools in New Jersey," *The Secondary School Bulletin*, No. 2, Trenton, N.J.: State Department of Education, March, 1960, p. 1.

[5] Illinois Superintendent of Public Instruction, *Block-of-Time Scheduling Practices in Illinois Junior High Schools*, Springfield, Ill.: Research Department, Office of the Superintendent, 1960, 35 pp.

When one teacher has both classes in a block, the situation encourages correlation and unit teaching around problems that draw subject matter from the two or more areas concerned.

In other schools, where the classes are not blocked in the schedule under one teacher, there is an attempt to correlate the subject matter taught under two different teachers. Other evidence of moving away from compartmentalization includes weekly planning together by teachers who teach a common group of pupils; part-time cooperative education programs in which pupils work half a day and relate much of their program to the job during the other half of the day; meetings between department heads and the principal to plan for coordination on an all-school basis; team teaching.

JUNIOR HIGH SCHOOL PROGRAMS OF STUDIES. Since each of the major subject areas has been divided into specific courses, the question that confronts the secondary school staff is how to assure each pupil a balanced program of general education and still leave him time for specialization.

In junior high schools, a major portion of the program of studies is generally included as required subjects, especially in the seventh and eighth grades. The trend is to require a large block of general education courses in the ninth grade as well, with provision for individual differences within the courses.

The program of studies at the Great Neck Junior High School, Great Neck, New York, is basically all common learnings in the seventh grade, with English and social studies in a block program:

Seventh Grade

Required Subjects:	Periods Per Week
English ⎱ Social Studies ⎰	10
Mathematics	5
Science and Health	5 (half-year)
Art	5 (half-year)
Home Economics (Girls) or Industrial Art (boys)	5 (half-year)
Music	5 (half-year)
Speech	2
Library Skills	1
Work-Study Skills	1
Physical Education	3
Total	32
Electives:	
Band	2
Orchestra	2
Glee Club	2

The program of studies of the Hixson Junior High School, Webster Groves, Missouri, which has a core program in the seventh and eighth grades, illustrates the general plan in junior high schools to allow a greater number of electives in the ninth grade:

Seventh Grade	*Eighth Grade*	*Ninth Grade*
Core {Language Arts / Social Studies	Core {Language Arts / Social Studies	Required: Language Arts Social Studies
Mathematics	Mathematics	Mathematics
Science	Home Economics	Algebra
Physical Education alternating with Vocal Music	or Shop	or General Mathematics
	Science (1 semester) and	Annual Electives: (elect 1)
Electives: (elect 1)	Health (1 semester)	General Science
Arts — Crafts — Speech		Home Economics
Arts — Crafts — Developmental Reading	Physical Education alternating with:	Shop
Spanish	(elect 1)	Art
French	Instrumental Music	Spanish
Instrumental Music	Vocal Music	French
	Spanish (Prerequisite 7th Spanish)	Latin
	French (Prerequisite 7th French)	Semester Electives: (elect 2) Art
	Arts and Crafts	Crafts
	Dramatics	Geography
	Developmental Reading	Speech
		Typing
		Physical Education alternating with: (elect 1) Instrumental Music Vocal Music Dramatics Plastics & Related Art Developmental Reading

In many cases, pupils are scheduled in classes for the full day rather than in study halls for a part of the day. In almost all junior high schools a well-balanced program of general education is attained through offering certain courses for less than five periods a week or for one semester only.

HIGH SCHOOL PROGRAMS OF STUDIES. The trend in secondary schools is toward requiring more courses in the academic fields for all students. This is especially true for the fields of mathematics and science. This section illustrates the opportunities for a well-balanced curriculum of both general and specialized education as indicated by the required and elective courses.

1. Provision for general education in graduation requirements.

One way of determining the areas of general education is

through examining what courses are required for graduation from high school. The majority of secondary schools require four years of English for the four years 9 through 12. Most schools require two to three years of social studies, one year of mathematics, one year of science, and one to four years of health and physical education. More are beginning to require two years each of science and mathematics. Graduation requirements have also increased in social studies.

Few secondary schools require music and art for graduation, although these subjects are considered by many educators to be important phases of general education. The following are examples of secondary schools that include either fine arts or practical arts in their graduation requirements:

Tulsa Central High School, Tulsa, Oklahoma
(Three Years)

	Units*
English	4
History	3
Science	2
Industrial Arts, Art, Homemaking, Music, Typing, Vocational Education	1
Mathematics	1
Physical Education	1
	12
Electives	7
Total	19

Total program must include two majors (3 units in the same subject) and two minors (2 units in the same subject).

* Unit is defined as a course taken daily, five days a week, for a full year.

Renton High School, Renton, Washington
(Four Years)

	Credits*
COMMON LEARNINGS	
Language Arts	6
Social Studies	6
Mathematics	2
Science	2
	16
HEALTHFUL LIVING	
Physical Education	5
Safety, Driving, First Aid	1
Elective (Physical Education or Health)	2
	8

VOCATIONAL TRAINING
Shop Drawing (boys)	2
Homemaking (girls)	2
Music, Business, Arts and Crafts, Home Economics, Science, or College Preparation (credits in single vocational field)	6
	8

AVOCATIONAL INTERESTS
Electives	8
	40

* 40 required for graduation

The trend toward requiring for graduation more than sixteen units (thirty-two credits) in the four-year high school, or more than twelve units in the senior high school, can be noted in the above illustrations.

2. Provision for general education in multiple curricula.

Often, secondary schools require additional subject matter within the various curricula in order to provide a well-rounded education. An example is the General Curriculum of Burnell and Stratford High Schools, Stratford, Connecticut, which are senior high schools requiring eighteen units for graduation.

Stratford High School, Stratford, Connecticut
(General Curriculum)

	Units
Tenth Grade	
Common Learnings	
English	1
World History	1
Biology	1
Physical Education	¼
Electives	1 or more
Eleventh Grade	
Common Learnings	
English	1
U.S. History	1
Physical Science (Boys) } Foods or Clothing (Girls) }	1
Physical Education	¼
Electives	1 or more
Twelfth Grade	
Common Learnings	
English	1
Problems of Democracy	1
Physical Science (Boys) } Home & Family Living (Girls) }	1
Physical Education	¼
Electives	1 or more

Students in the academic or college preparatory curricula are generally required to take more units in science, mathematics, social studies, and foreign languages than students in the other curricula.

3. Provision for special interests and needs.

In many high schools throughout the country, with the exception of the smaller ones, there is a rich opportunity for pupils to specialize in different areas or to take work in various fields of interest. Students with high academic aptitude, those with less competency in the verbal skills, and those who wish to prepare for specific vocations can find appropriate courses among the offerings.

Edwin O. Smith School, University of Connecticut, Storrs, Connecticut, which is the six-year high school for the surrounding community, is a smaller high school with a varied offering. Its program of studies lists the following course offerings for the four grades, 9 through 12.

English IX, X, XI, XII
Humanities
Introduction to Politics
World History
American Studies
World Problems
Earth Science
Biology
Chemistry
Physics
Applied Mathematics
Algebra I
Algebra II
Plane Geometry
Illinois Math I, II, III, IV
Solid Geometry and Trigonometry
Latin I, II, III, IV
French I, II, III, IV
German I, II, III, IV
Spanish I, II, III, IV

Junior Business Training
Bookkeeping
Stenography I, II
Office Practice
Note-hand
Business Law
Typewriting I, II
Home Economics I, II, III, IV
Family Living
New Techniques in Homemaking
  (twice a week)
Music I, II, III
Art I, II, III, IV
Industrial Arts I, II, III, IV
Driver Training (by arrangement)
Physical Education (twice a week)
Developmental Reading (by
  arrangement)
Work-Study Program (by arrangement)

College Level Courses
Humanities
English Composition and Literature
Advanced Mathematics
Advanced Physics and Chemistry
Western Civilization
Advanced French
Advanced Spanish
Advanced Latin

A large senior high school, Joliet Township High School, Joliet, Illinois, offers many opportunities for careful selection of electives under the guidance of the school. These are classified into fifteen categories:

Agriculture
- Agriculture I-II
- Agriculture III-IV
- Agriculture V-VI
- Agriculture VII-VIII
- Annual Agriculture Project
- Animal Husbandry I, II

Art
- Art I, II
- Drawing-Painting
- Studio Workshop
- Com. Art I, II
- Fashion Art I, II
- Fashion Art III, IV
- Rel. Art I-II
- Art Appreciation I, II
- Structural Art I-II

Business Education
- Basic Business I, II
- Bookkeeping I, II
- Bookkeeping III, IV
- Bus. Corr.
- Dis. Ed. I-II & Work Exp.
- Off. Pr. (cler.) I-II
- Off. Pr. (coop.) I-II & Work Exp.
- Off. Pr. (sec.) I, II
- Sten'g'hy (Shthd.) I, II
- Stenography III, IV
- Typewriting I, II
- Typewriting III

Driver Education
- Driver Training

English
- Dramatics I, II
- *English I-II
- *English III-IV
- *English V-VI
- English Lit. I, II
- World Literature I-II
- Journalism I-II
- Journalism III-IV
- Prep. English—English IV
- Radio Production I, II
- Remedial Reading
- Advanced Reading
- Speech I, II

Foreign Language
- French I-II
- French III-IV, V-VI, VII-VIII
- German I-II
- German III-IV, V-VI, VII-VIII
- Latin I-II
- Latin III-IV, V-VI, VII-VIII
- Spanish I-II
- Spanish III-IV, V-VI, VII-VIII

Homemaking
- Family Living
- Homemaking I-II
- Homemaking III-IV
- Homemaking V-VI
- Homemaking VII-VIII
- Home Economics Survey I-II

Mathematics
- *Algebra I-II
- Algebra III
- College Algebra
- *General Math, I-II
- *Plane Geometry I-II
- Solid Geometry
- Trigonometry

Music
- Music Appreciation & History I, II
- Theory I, II

Music Organization
- A Cap'la Choir
- Band
- Boys' Glee Club
- Fr. Chorus
- Soph. Chorus
- Orchestra

Physical Education
- *Boys' Phys. Ed.
- *Girls' Phys. Ed.

Reserve Officers Training Corps
- R.O.T.C.

Science
- Air Age Ed. I, II
- *Biology I, II
- Prep. Chem. I-II
- Chem. (Gen.) I-II
- Earth Sci. I-II, III-IV
- Geog. (Econ.) I, II
- Geog. (World) I, II
- Health
- Photog. I, II
- Physics I-II
- Physiology

Trade and Industrial Education
- Gen. Shop I, II
- Ind. Automechanics I, II

Automechanics III, IV
Automechanics V, VI
Mech. Drawing I-II
Drafting III, IV
Drafting V, VI
Ind. Elec. Shop I, II
Elec. Shop III, IV
Elec. Shop V, VI
Ind. Machine Shop I, II
Machine Shop III, IV
Machine Shop V, VI
Ind. Printing I, II
Printing III, IV
Printing V, VI
Related Art I, II
Related Drawing I, II

Ind. Woodworking I, II
Ind. Wood. III, IV
Woodworking III, IV
Woodworking V, VI

Social Science
American Government
Economics
History of Far East
Latin-American History
Social Problems
*Social Studies I-II
*U.S. History I-II
World History I, II
World Geog. I, II

* Required of all students.

In *The American High School Today,* Conant recommends that all students should be required to take four years of English, three or four years of social studies, one year of mathematics, and at least one year of science. For the academically talented, he recommends four years of mathematics, four years of one foreign language, three years of science, four years of English, and three years of social studies. This group he identifies as the upper 15 per cent of high school population on the national basis. For the highly gifted group (the top 3 per cent of the high school population academically), he recommends, in addition, one or more courses in the Advanced Placement Program, a program developed in recent years by secondary schools and colleges under the College Entrance Examination Board (see Chapters 11 and 18).

A number of secondary schools have planned special programs for the high ability students. Special seminars, enrichment classes advanced work in various subjects and other means of providing rich experiences for the academically talented are discussed in Chapter 11.

THE CORE CURRICULUM. Some junior high schools use the core curriculum to provide common learnings. This is one of the significant developments in recent years in the secondary school curriculum. It is an experimental approach in which the organization of the secondary school curriculum attempts to provide for improved learning experiences. According to the 1956-57 study of the United States Office of Education, approximately 6 per cent of the junior and junior-senior high schools in the United States have a core program. It is not as common as the block of time previously discussed, which is quite typical of seventh and eighth grades.

The core curriculum is a type of organization of school experiences in the school day. These experiences are regarded as important common learnings for all students. However, the core is not merely a form of organization; it has definite educational characteristics.

The core curriculum is generally scheduled for a longer block of time than one period a day, typically, two periods a day. In general, the core program is a junior high school development, with relatively few classes found in senior high schools. The longer block of time permits more teacher-pupil planning, field trips, and varied procedures in the class.

The content of the core classes is drawn from more than one subject field to solve problems of social and personal significance. Social studies and English are the areas most frequently drawn upon, but mathematics, science, art, and music are often sources of information and activities. Social studies and English are the subjects most often replaced as separate subjects by the core. Attempts to have the core take care of all experiences for mathematics, science, art, and music have not been very successful. Outside of the core classes, opportunity for specialization in other areas is possible, sometimes including the areas of social studies and English. Differentiation of content and activities to suit individual needs is taken care of within the class.

The content of the core in Prince Georges County (Maryland) junior high schools illustrates problems of personal and social significance:

Seventh-Grade Core	*Eighth-Grade Core*
Exploring Our Educational Opportunities	Discovering Maryland as America in
Achieving Good Intercultural Relations	Miniature
Maintaining Body Efficiency	The American Heritage
	Understanding and Improving Myself

Ninth-Grade Core

Democracy—A Balance Between Rights and Responsibilities
Living Together in Prince Georges County
Finding Our Place in the World at Work
Achieving and Maintaining Good Family Relationships

In the Great Neck Junior High School, Great Neck, New York, the units studied in the seventh grade include the following: People Helped New York Grow; Housing; New Yorkers at Home; New Yorkers Govern Themselves; and New York Contributes to the Culture of the World.

The concept of the core curriculum includes the use of the problem-solving approach to study questions of importance to youth and to society. Not all schools that label courses "core" use this approach, as indicated in research that has been made. Only about 12 per cent of the junior and junior-senior high schools which block their courses into two or more periods have what can be termed experience-centered core programs.

The core teacher and teachers from specialized areas spend considerable time planning together for each particular group of pupils. This is a type of planning that gives the teacher greater leeway and, at the same time, the confidence and background necessary for pupil-teacher planning of experiences in the classroom. In Merrill Junior High School, Denver, every teacher has one planning period a day. These periods are used to plan class work and to counsel with individual pupils. Referrals may be made to teacher counselors who also have a period a day assigned to seventy pupils. Most teacher planning meetings are held every two weeks before or after school.

In each core class are included pupils of different abilities and interests. The core curriculum concept does not include permanent grouping nor result in social segregation on the basis of future occupations. By and large in core classes, pupils are heterogeneously grouped. Grouping for instructional purposes occurs within the class. One of the essential experiences of the core program is learning how to live with others different from one's self in abilities, vocational objectives, social level, ethnic grouping, race, or family background.

The core curriculum is still in its experimental stage in American secondary education. It may go through many modifications as experimentation and evaluation continues. This is one of its advantages. Or it may be dropped by secondary schools under the pressures for "harder subjects." There is some evidence that this trend is occurring. Evaluative studies of the core program have generally indicated favorable results in improved attitudes, skills of critical thinking, and other skills, and student reactions to the core.[6]

CORRELATION AND FLEXIBILITY THROUGH TEAM TEACHING. In 1956, The Commission on The Experimental Study of the Utilization of the Staff in the Secondary School was established by the National Association of Secondary-School Principals to carry on experimental studies in secondary schools. With the aid of foundation funds, the Commission over a four-year period encouraged about a hundred

[6] Vernon E. Anderson and Arthur Goldberg, "Schools for Adolescents: Curriculum Content and Organization," *Review of Educational Research*, 24:32-33, February, 1954.

Edward Krug and Others, *Multiple-Period Curricular Organization in Wisconsin Secondary Schools*, Madison, Wis.: School of Education, University of Wisconsin, 1952, p. 43.

secondary schools to carry on experimental studies relating to staff utilization.[7] Under the leadership of J. Lloyd Trump, Associate Secretary of the National Association of Secondary-School Principals, this Commission undoubtedly has had considerable influence on the organization for instruction in American secondary schools. One of the outstanding types of experimentation by the schools working with the Commission has been in the use of team teaching, which has spread more rapidly than any other practice in staff utilization.

Teachers of varying competencies, of different backgrounds, and from different subject fields have been scheduled to work together as a team with a larger group of students than ordinarily found in a single class. These groups would generally vary from sixty to 150 students, although some schools have combined groups up to 400 for lecture sections. Two to four teachers are scheduled for the same period to work with this group of students in the ordinary size classroom group, in a total group, or in smaller groups for instructional purposes.

We are concerned here with this plan from the standpoint of how it allows teachers to plan together for achieving better coordination among two or three subjects, and how it permits flexibility in organizing the teachers' time for instructional purposes. The plan is related to the concept of core curriculum, in a sense, in that it focuses on cooperative planning by the faculty, and teachers may use some of the features of the core in planning work with pupils. It is an extension of the idea of block-time classes, with even more flexibility for independent study; group work; use of instructional media such as television, films and slides, tape recordings, and other audio-visual aids; use of resources; and a variety of instructional procedures.

One of its advantages is the better utilization of specialized skills and competencies of teachers. Thus, a teacher of social studies and a teacher of English may complement each other's knowledge and skills. It also permits flexibility of different size groups for different instructional purposes. Other advantages are cited as results of the studies.[8]

There are a variety of types of teams of teachers. One is the team of several teachers in one subject, who work together so that each may capitalize on the interests, backgrounds, and talents of the others. For example, in the Alfred Plant Junior High School, West

[7] J. Lloyd Trump, "Brief History and Recommendations of The Commission on the Experimental Study of the Utilization of the Staff in the Secondary School," *Bulletin of the National Association of Secondary-School Principals*, 45:275-81, January, 1961. See Chapter 8 for additional discussion of these studies.

[8] See the January, 1958, 1959, 1960, and 1961 issues of the *Bulletin of the National Association of Secondary-School Principals* for reports of these experimental studies.

Hartford, Connecticut, several teachers of general science form a team who help each other in planning and teaching various topics and units. In the junior high school, general science lends itself especially well to team teaching because it is difficult for teachers to be well prepared in all science areas. A physical science major may have little interest and preparation in botany and zoology, while the biology major may have had little college work in geology, astronomy, and oceanography. At the Alfred Plant Junior High School, the classes whose teachers form the science team are scheduled for the same period in the day so that pupils may be brought together for large-group instruction. Speakers may be brought in for the combined classes, movies shown, and demonstrations or presentations given by one of the teachers. The members of the team plan their work together, they work with the librarian and audio-visual director, and the teachers may exchange classes for activities in which one teacher is better prepared than the others.

The eleventh-grade teachers of Evanston, Illinois, Township High School work together with all of the students in the grade, teaching their specialty in creative and expository writing, poetry, or grammar to the combined group which meets twice a week for a lecture. On other days of the week, pupils meet in the regular-size classroom. Other teams within a field are in biology, business education, history of civilization, U. S. history, American problems, health education, driver education, general mathematics, and plane geometry. In the Urbana, Illinois, Senior High School, teachers work together as a team in English, one teacher particularly strong in literature and the other in grammar and composition.

A type of team illustrated by Urbana's plan works in different grade levels of a subject. The teacher of grammar and composition teaches these subjects two days a week to eleventh-grade pupils and three days a week to twelfth-grade pupils in Urbana Senior High School. The schedule of the literature teacher dovetails into this one for the two levels. The same type of team-teaching plan is used in the high schools of Jefferson County, Colorado, where, for example, three or four teachers are assigned to one large class in World History and another class in American History.

Teams composed of teachers of different subjects, which emphasize correlation of learning activities and outcomes, have been introduced in some schools. At the North Haven High School, North Haven, Connecticut, there are teams which include teachers in English, mathematics, social studies, and science, who have the same pupils in their classes. The teaching teams in North Haven emphasize cooperative planning among the teachers of these four subjects, the preparation of learning activities that cross subject lines, better understanding and guidance of pupils, and closer cooperation with parents. The teachers on a team have the same preparation period during the school day so that they can more readily work together. At McLean High School, Fairfax County, Virginia, about 100 pupils are taught American History and American Literature together as a course in American Civilization by a team of two teachers of English and two of history in the eleventh grade. This has the advantage of a block schedule, and at the same time utilizes the background strengths of the four different teachers. Mathematics, science, and geography for ninth-grade pupils are the subjects taught together by an instructional team, in a block of time varying in length for the days of the week. All three team teachers for this group of pupils are available to work with pupils for the twelve hours a week that they are scheduled together. General science, biology, and English are combined under three teams of two teachers each at Snyder, Texas, in the eighth grade. In the Wahlquist Junior High School, Weber County, Utah, language arts and social studies teachers are responsible as a team for a group of pupils. The one teacher, for example, takes over a combined class to teach them as a large group, while the remaining team members use this time for consultation with individual pupils or small groups in planning together.

Variations of the pattern and the purpose of team teaching is found in plans that use teams of professionally prepared teachers, instructional assistants with less preparation, and clerical aides, and teams of more experienced and less experienced teachers. Some schools have teams composed of master teachers, interns, and teacher's aides, for the purpose of using more effectively the talents of the master teacher, helping beginning teachers, and releasing teachers from the burden of reading pupils' papers, routine activities, and clerical work. The master teacher and the beginning teacher are both assigned classes, but they plan their work together, with the master teacher providing the leadership. The teacher's aide, if one is included on the team, reads pupil papers, records marks and attendance, and prepares records and reports. The O'Farrell Junior High School, San Diego, California, has such teams in several subjects. In typing, a teacher and an aide work together with seventy-five to eighty pupils in one class at a time but in two adjoining rooms. In English, the team is composed of two teachers and two aides, with two groups of pupils of approximately one hundred each. The teachers work together in planning and teaching, with the aides reading and correcting the written work of the pupils and assisting with records. The Jefferson County, Colorado, schools, which have carried on extensive and varied kinds of experimentation in staff utilization, use teams of a professional-in-charge, or teacher specialist, who has more preparation and leadership ability than others; professionals or general teachers, who are certificated, qualified teachers; "para-professionals" or teacher assistants, uncertificated persons with bachelor's degrees; and clerks. One of the purposes in this type of team is to extend the influence of a well-prepared teacher over a larger group of teachers and pupils and to meet the problem of the teacher shortage. These plans also serve as valuable in-service training for less experienced teachers.

In the Decatur-Lakeview Plan, on the teams of teachers in The Lakeview Junior-Senior High School, some teachers are designated as teacher presenter for large group instruction and others as teacher instructor serving as the small group leader. Instructional aids, general aids, and clerks also work with the teams. Thus, teachers use varying talents and skills in serving specialized functions. Groups range in size from large groups of 200 to small groups of seven. Large group instruction is scheduled for approximately 40 per cent of the student's time; small group instruction for approximately 40 per cent; and independent study for approximately 20 per cent. As time and space permit, students utilize resources in various subject areas during independent study time.

ISSUES AND PROBLEMS

It is evident that secondary school faculties are giving thought to how the curriculum can best be organized within the school day and in courses. The question of providing a balanced curriculum for all pupils and still giving sufficient opportunity for developing special interests and abilities presents a challenge. In a number of related issues, this is the all-pervading one.

1. *Should programs for secondary school students be predetermined or planned individually?*

The question concerns how much flexibility there should be in developing a program for an individual student. Granted that much in the secondary school curriculum is common to the program of all students; however, there also needs to be a differentiation to provide for the wide variety of abilities, interests, and future educational and vocational plans found among youth. This is consistent with the concept of educating all of the children of all of the people through universal secondary education.

There is a good deal of discussion over the value of the multiple curricula or "tracks," as they are sometimes called. The danger seems to lie in the inflexibility or the lack of adaption of a program to an individual's needs. Dr. Conant believes that every student should have an individualized program and that there should be no classification of pupils according to programs or tracks such as college preparatory and vocational. Differentiation in the curriculum is certainly important but fixed curricula may tend to make people fit into a single mold where there probably should be several molds.

One problem is that the greater the difficulty in breaking across curricular barriers to fulfill special needs, the more the risk of accentuating the socioeconomic class differences within a particular school.

2. *Will the change in organizational structure for instruction in and of itself improve learning?*

The experimental studies that have been made on utilization of the faculty in secondary schools have indicated favorable results. Most of them are not rigidly controlled studies but are more in the nature of action research. They represent some rather drastic changes in scheduling pupils and teachers during the day. It is doubtful, however, that the change in patterns of pupil-teacher contacts alone will improve pupils' learning. Undoubtedly, they will facilitate it. For too long, secondary schools have followed inflexible time patterns of the pupil's day and of the teacher's assignment without regard for individual differences.

The steps taken by a number of forward-looking schools are bold and imaginative. They recognize that the existence of individual differences is a basic fact that should govern instructional arrangements. But the essence of quality of learning depends upon many more factors: the teacher's knowledge, the content, the relationships within the classroom, the wealth of resources, the creativeness and imagination of the teacher, his understanding of human behavior, and others. In any organizational setting, mathematics may be a mechanical process; chemistry, a series of formulas; English, a stilted treatment of forms; foreign language, a study in how to translate words; history, an exercise in memory—all devoid of the human touches, the insights, and intellectual stimulation so necessary to rich and fruitful learning.

3. *How can the curriculum be organized so as to include in an already crowded program the rapidly growing body of knowledge?*

Knowledge is expanding rapidly in every field. New research, inventions, political changes, the growing importance of new nations on the continents of Africa and Asia, discoveries, the recognition of the importance of cultures of the world other than the European civilizations, and the importance of languages of these and other countries seem to create an impossible task for the school in providing a substantial base of general education needed to be an enlightened citizen of the world today, to say nothing of ten years from now. At the same time specialization demands a greater depth of knowledge.

How then can the secondary school expect to cope with this impossible situation? The addition of a greater number of subjects in a student's program is one way. The creating of instructional settings which help a student to move ahead at his own pace is another. Better integration among various subjects and activities will help. Improved articulation, eliminating wasteful duplication, is of importance. But it is doubtful that such combined measures even if well applied would solve the problem. For the expansion of knowledge is limitless. The answer would probably seem to lie in creating a sustaining interest in a field, an intelligent understanding of the processes characteristic of the field, and the skills for finding and organizing knowledge—those skills and motivations that go to make up the concept of independent study.

Nor can the secondary school act as though it were an isolated unit. Part of the job belongs to the elementary school, part of it to the college, and part of it to adult education, as formal units of schooling.

But the teachers and leaders in the secondary school also need to become more perceptive in selecting content that is not available to be learned through life in the market place, from television, and from other social institutions. Because the school can never do the job alone, and it now has many more supplementary informal co-agents of learning than it ever had before.

4. *Should departmentalization of subjects into compartments or fusion of subject matter into broader problems be encouraged?*

This issue concerns largely the junior high schools at the present time. There seems to be little demand on the part of educational leaders for any further fusion in the senior high school than has already been achieved.

There has been considerable argumentation for a return to greater departmentalization in the seventh and eighth grades, where the block-time classes and the core have made the greatest strides. The proponents of departmentalization argue that the teacher cannot be well versed in all fields, and his effectiveness is decreased by spreading his efforts over too many fields, all of which feel the effects of burgeoning knowledge.

The advocates of more of an experience-centered approach are discouraged at the signs of schools giving in to recommendations for greater departmentalization made by some national figures holding high status in the academic and educational world. They believe that the improved learning situation in problem solving argues for less, not more fragmentation and administrative and organizational barriers. Some see the decrease in interest in the core curriculum as tragic.

No doubt the core has been one of the really imaginative ways of organizing the curriculum in order to provide for the learning of skills, understandings, attitudes, and appreciations essential to a general education. Its effectiveness in practice has been largely with problems in the general areas of social studies, the humanities, and personal-life problems. However, its strength has been in its commitment to experimentation. The core at its best represented an idea not a form. It was a new approach to dealing with some of man's enduring issues and enigmas of the social-political sphere, a new approach to learning.

Those who think of the core curriculum as a form of organization only are likely to be the ones who do the most to destroy its effectiveness or influence on American secondary education. For they have forgotten the spirit, the idea, and look only at the form and the trappings. It may well be that secondary education will move beyond the core to forms which embody the basic ideas and concepts of the core but within a different framework, such as, team teaching. Above all, it should be remembered that the experimental attitude which will move secondary education forward does not rest on stratified arrangements of any type.

SELECTED REFERENCES

ASSOCIATION FOR SUPERVISION AND CURRICULUM DEVELOPMENT. *Developing Programs for Young Adolescents*. Washington, D.C.: National Education Association, 1954, 53 pp.—Discusses a variety of seventh, eighth, and ninth grade programs in junior high schools in the South and Middle West in the early 1950's.

ASSOCIATION FOR SUPERVISION AND CURRICULUM DEVELOPMENT. *Balance in The Curriculum*. (1961 Yearbook). Washington, D.C.: National Education Association, Chap. 7.—The book deals in part with balanced development for pupils and a balanced general education. Chapter 7 discusses "Problems in Organizing The School Program to Achieve Balance."

CHASE, FRANCIS S. and ANDERSON, HAROLD A. (eds.). *The High School in a New Era*. Chicago: University of Chicago Press, 1958, pp. 197-239.—Organizational innovations in the high school curriculum. Descriptions of practice and proposals for the future.

CONANT, JAMES B. *Education in the Junior High School Years.* Princeton, N.J.: Educational Testing Service, 1960, 46 pp.—Contains fourteen recommendations concerning the junior high school, relating to required subjects for all pupils, departmentalization, coordination, and other organizational matters.

CONANT, JAMES B. *The American High School Today.* New York: McGraw-Hill Book Co., Inc., 1959. 140 pp.—Contains recommendations for improving secondary education, based on visits to high schools, some of which deal with curriculum organization problems.

DOUGLASS, HARL R. (ed.). *The High School Curriculum.* New York: The Ronald Press Co., 2nd ed., 1956, Chaps. 12, 14, 20.—Integration, fusion, and correlation of the curriculum are considered. Further examples of organization of the curriculum pattern.

EDUCATIONAL POLICIES COMMISSION. *Education for ALL American Youth: A Further Look.* Washington, D.C.: National Education Association, 1952, 402 pp.—Two hypothetical secondary schools and communities, Farmville and American City, are described, indicating how a more closely integrated curriculum organization is achieved. An important landmark report in secondary education.

FAUNCE, ROLAND and BOSSING, NELSON. *Developing the Core Curriculum.* Englewood Cliffs, N.J.: Prentice-Hall, Inc., 1958, Chaps. 3-7.—Philosophy and characteristics of the core. Examples of programs in operation are given.

GRUHN, WILLIAM T., and DOUGLASS, HARL R. *The Modern Junior High School.* New York: The Ronald Press Co., 1947, Chap. 5.—Points out trends in curriculum organization in the junior high school. Contains additional sample programs of study.

KRUG, EDWARD A. *The Secondary School Curriculum.* New York: Harper & Brothers, 1960, Chap. 7.—Arguments for and against subject organization of classroom studies.

LURRY, LUCILE L. and ALBERTY, ELSIE J. *Developing a High School Core Program.* New York: The Macmillan Co., 1957. Chap. 6.—Describes a core program in action.

NATIONAL ASSOCIATION OF SECONDARY-SCHOOL PRINCIPALS, "Seeking Improved Learning Opportunities," *Bulletin of the National Association of Secondary-School Principals,* Vol. 45, No. 21, Washington, D.C.: National Education Association, January, 1961. 352 pp.—The final one in a series of reports in the experimental studies carried on by secondary schools. Describes team teaching in many of the studies and the results of evaluation of these studies. See also the January 1958, 1959, 1960 issues of The Bulletin.

THUT, I. N., and GERBERICH, J. RAYMOND. *Foundations of Method for Secondary Schools.* New York: McGraw-Hill Book Co., Inc., 1949, Chap. 4.—This chapter explores further the questions of the kind of curriculum organization appropriate to a democratic school philosophy.

TRUMP, J. LLOYD and BAYNHAM, DORSEY. *Focus on Change: Guide to Better Schools.* Chicago: Rand McNally & Co., 1961, 147 pp.—A readable pamphlet, a report on the four years of experimental studies under the Commission on the Experimental Study of the Utilization of the Staff in the Secondary School. Team teaching occupied an important place in these studies.

TRUMP, J. LLOYD. *New Directions to New Quality Education: The Secondary School Tomorrow.* Washington, D.C.: National Association of Secondary-School Principals, 1960. 14 pp.—A statement of specific recommendations for the secondary school of tomorrow regarding schedules, grouping, team teaching, staff patterns, and other organizational aspects.

WRIGHT, GRACE S. *Block-Time Classes and The Core Program in the Junior High School.* U.S. Department of Health, Education, and Welfare, Office of Education,

Bulletin 1958, No. 6. Washington, D.C.: Government Printing Office, 1958. 70 pp.—
Information from a survey of various type block-time classes in junior high schools of
this country.

WRIGHT, GRACE S. *Requirements for High School Graduation in States and Large
Cities.* U.S. Department of Health, Education, and Welfare, Office of Education,
Bulletin 1961, No. 12. Washington, D.C.: Government Printing Office, 1961, 29
pp.—Latest information at time of publication of this book on graduation requirements in the fifty states and in fifty large cities.

INSTRUCTIONAL PRACTICES AND RELATIONSHIPS

The instructional practices that are employed and the relationships that exist between teachers and pupils have a direct bearing on the effectiveness of any learning situation in the secondary school. If relationships between teachers and pupils are relaxed and friendly, an atmosphere that is conducive to effective learning is likely to pertain. But if the relationships between teachers and pupils result in tensions and unpleasantness pupils are not likely to do well in their studies. The instructional methods, devices, and materials likewise have much influence on the nature of the learning situation and the effectiveness of learning outcomes. How teachers work with pupils, the types of learning activities in which they engage, and the variety of instructional materials that are employed—all are important in promoting the most desirable learning situation in the secondary school. The present chapter is concerned with these instructional practices and relationships between teachers and pupils.

BASIC PRINCIPLES

Teacher-pupil relationships in the secondary school should be based upon mutual understanding, confidence, and respect among all those who participate in the learning situation.

Effective human relations are desirable in school as elsewhere in our democratic society. Desirable human relations are based primarily on mutual understanding and respect, confidence in the integrity of others, and respect for the dignity of the individual human being. This principle seems so obvious that it should hardly be necessary to mention it in a discussion for prospective teachers.

There are certain situations that pertain in the secondary school today, however, which impede achieving that understanding of and respect for each other which is basic to a desirable learning situation. The secondary school today is usually a highly departmentalized school, with a teacher having contact with as many as 150 pupils each day in groups of twenty-five or more, for periods of forty to sixty minutes. In medium-sized and large secondary schools several weeks may pass before the teacher even knows the names of all his pupils. Teachers seldom meet with pupils in a situation which helps them get acquainted, know each other's interests, and develop respect for one another as individual personalities. Mutual understanding, confidence, and respect among teachers and pupils is so important to the achievement of pupils in school and to their growth as individual personalities that more adequate provision should be made to foster the implementation of this principle.

Instructional practices should recognize the wide range of differences among individual pupils in personality and character qualities, interests, out-of-school backgrounds, and ability to achieve in school.

One of the serious difficulties faced by a secondary-school teacher in planning learning activities is the wide differences in personalities, interests, backgrounds, and abilities of his pupils. He may have some pupils from underprivileged homes, while others may come from home backgrounds that are desirable in every way; some of his pupils will be stable and secure in their personality qualities, while others may be emotionally immature; some may have high academic ability and motivation, while the ability and motivation of others may be average or below. This wide range of differences in the characteristics of individual pupils will always exist in any secondary school. It is important, therefore, to employ instructional practices which recognize these differences among pupils.

There is no simple formula for developing a learning situation which recognizes adequately the differences among individual pupils. In some schools this is accomplished in part by some form of ability grouping. But regardless of the pattern of grouping employed, teachers still need to work with pupils as individuals.

Secondary school practices should provide opportunities for developing understandings and skills in democratic approaches to group participation.

It is always a temptation for teachers to be authoritarian in their relationships with pupils. The authoritarian approach may, in fact, seem to lead more quickly and directly to desirable learning outcomes. However, the demands of our society for citizens with skill in democratic processes should discourage teachers from employing too frequently the authoritarian approach in dealing with pupils. Teachers need to show respect for the points of view of individual pupils; they should encourage pupils to show consideration for the beliefs, attitudes and cultural backgrounds of others; and they need to have the patience to establish democratic relationships in learning activities. In some subjects, such as language arts and social studies, emphasis on democratic relationships may be more readily achieved than in others. But in every subject, in every class, and in every learning activity, some attention needs to be given to helping pupils develop skill in working democratically with others in group situations.

The teacher in his relationships with pupils should emphasize self-discipline, courtesy, and consideration for others, and self-responsibility for one's actions, rather than authoritarian control, as the basis for pupil conduct and discipline in all school situations.

It is important that citizens in a democracy recognize the need for obedience to law and control by someone in authority. Without respect for law and constituted authority, anarchy would soon displace democratic procedures. Since school is preparation for life, the school needs to teach the importance of obedience to established law and authority. Even so, in the relationships between teachers and pupils should emphasize courtesy and considerations for others in learning situations. Teachers should help pupils respect the rights of others, show consideration for the interests and welfare of other pupils, and extend common courtesies to their classmates. Pupils should also learn the importance of assuming much responsibility for their own actions and conduct in any situation. They should develop the attitude that appropriate conduct is desirable whether or not it is imposed by the authority of the school. The aim of discipline should be the improvement of future behavior of the pupil, based on an understanding of the causes of the behavior. The teacher should work toward the goal of helping pupils to discipline themselves.

Instructional practices in the secondary school should make the unique talents of individual teachers available to the greatest possible number of pupils.

Even within the same subject, individual teachers have unique talents, interests, and backgrounds. In general science, one teacher may be interested in space science, another in astronomy, and still another in chemistry. In social studies, individual teachers may have interests and preparation in such different areas as Latin America, Africa, Western civilization, political science, geography, and current affairs. In art, music, industrial arts, home economics, and every other subject in the secondary school, individual teachers may be better prepared in some areas than in others in their respective subjects.

In medium-sized and large secondary schools, where there are several teachers in a subject area, it is desirable to have the unique talents of each one become available to as many pupils as possible. The departmentalized organization of the secondary school achieves this in part. However, even within a departmentalized school, special talents of individual teachers may not be adequately used. Instructional practices should be introduced and developed which will utilize to a maximum degree the strengths and backgrounds of individual teachers.

The instructional practices and teacher-pupil relationships in a secondary school should permit and encourage the use of a wide variety of human and material resources both within the school and from the community as a whole.

A desirable flexibility in the administrative and instructional practices should give pupils ready access to school laboratories, to instructional materials in the audio-visual center, to research and reference materials in the library, and to typewriters, teaching machines, reading equipment, and other mechanical aids to learning. Furthermore, pupils should have more frequent and ready access to teachers for individual help, for assistance with research projects, and for encouragement and guidance in learning activities.

Likewise, the instructional practices which are employed should make it possible to bring community resources into the school when these may contribute to the learning situation. Specialists from industry and business, teachers from nearby colleges and universities, and other resource people in the community can be used in this way. Pupils should also be able to capitalize on the resources of community agencies, industry, and business, as they engage in individual research activities and projects. Flexibility in the administrative and instructional practices that are employed has a direct bearing on the extent to which resources both within the school and from the community as a whole are used in learning activities.

The secondary school should encourage the use of a variety of learning activities and teaching methods in all aspects of the instructional program.

A recitation or class discussion led by the teacher and centered in the textbook continues to be the most common type of learning activity employed in secondary school classrooms today. The relationships between teachers and pupils in such a learning situation tend to encourage conformity to the teacher's point of view, memorization of textbook materials, and emphasis on facts and information rather than on problem-solving, research and independent study. The relatively short class period, the large number of pupils which a teacher meets daily, the rigidity of the daily schedule, and the inadequacy of resource materials all tend to encourage the use of teacher- and textbook-centered learning activities.

The individual differences which one finds among pupils in the secondary school make it essential that a variety of learning activities and teaching methods be employed. Gifted pupils, for instance, need to be challenged by independent study, small group seminars, and research activities in the library, school laboratories, and community agencies. Pupils with deficiencies in the fundamental skills should have the help of teachers in small groups, in individual study, and in other learning situations that may differ considerably from the typical teacher-centered classroom. The slow-learners, the physically-handicapped, the emotionally-disturbed, and the socially-maladjusted—all need individual attention that is not readily possible in teacher-centered classroom situations.

Teachers in their working relationships with pupils should not emphasize unduly the differences that one finds among pupils.

It is true, of course, that all pupils are aware that there are individual differences among their classmates in the secondary school. Pupils' names indicate differences in nationality backgrounds, their speech may reveal the influence of a foreign language spoken in the home, there may be differences in race and in the cultural backgrounds of pupils, and there are usually wide differences in their ability to achieve in school. The secondary school cannot eliminate these differences among pupils. They should, by all means, be recognized in instructional procedures, content, and materials. The point made here is that the differences that exist among pupils should not be unduly emphasized in the organization of pupils for instruction, the attitudes of teachers, and the individual relationship between teacher and pupil.

Some practices in secondary schools tend to overemphasize differences. Extreme forms of ability grouping, the segregating of pupils with low ability or physical handicaps, and the giving of names and labels to certain special classes are some ways in which attention is called to those pupils who differ distinctly in some characteristics from their classmates. The desirability of any instructional practice should be seriously questioned if it sets a group of pupils sharply apart from the rest of the school because of individual differences.

SOME COMMON PRACTICES

ABILITY GROUPING. In most secondary schools some plan of ability grouping is employed to arrange pupils in classes for instructional purposes. The practice is intended to reduce the range of differences in the abilities of individual pupils within a given class so that it is easier for the teacher to plan and carry on learning activities. Many different practices are used to achieve ability grouping. In junior high schools, pupils are usually arranged in groups on the basis of a combination of several criteria, such as I.Q.'s, previous marks, and teachers' judgments. A common plan is to place pupils in three broad ability groups, with pupils remaining in the same group for most or all subjects. Some junior high schools go a step further to reduce the range of abilities within groups by placing pupils into six, eight, or ten ability groups.

In senior high schools, pupils are usually placed in their class groups according to the curriculum in which they are enrolled, as described in Chapter 7. The grouping by curriculum is sometimes combined with ability grouping, especially in large schools where the enrollment of pupils is sufficient to justify having several groups.

Although some form of ability grouping is found in most secondary schools, there is no administrative practice which is more controversial today. The proponents of ability grouping contend that both the superior pupils and the slow learners are neglected in heterogeneous groups. They believe that it is easier for teachers to meet the needs of pupils of various ability levels if they are arranged in groups according to ability. The opponents of ability grouping contend that this practice is undemocratic; that pupils develop undesirable attitudes toward those of other ability levels; that the attitudes of pupils toward their studies may be adversely affected if they are placed in low groups; and that it is better for pupils to have contact in the school program with other pupils of all ability levels.

The disagreement among educators concerning the desirability of ability grouping has led to a number of studies on the subject. These studies suggest the following conclusions:

1. It is possible to place pupils for instructional purposes into class groups where they will be reasonably similar in ability in a given

subject. However, it is not possible to arrange pupils in groups which are completely homogeneous in ability.

2. Achievement is slightly higher in groups which are homogeneous as compared with those which are heterogeneous in ability. Ability grouping appears to be most effective in improving the achievement of pupils who are below average, next with average pupils, and least with pupils who are above average in ability. However, the evidence regarding the effect of ability grouping on achievement is not at all conclusive. Some recent studies show that ability grouping may be detrimental to slow and average ability children.

3. The evidence concerning the effect, if any, of ability grouping on the mental health of pupils is meager and inconclusive. The effect of ability grouping on the attitudes of slow learners probably is no more harmful than that of placing them in heterogeneous classes where they have little chance to equal the achievement of other pupils.

Educators have been giving much thought in recent years to ways of grouping pupils for instructional purposes. Some schools have developed approaches to grouping which are more in harmony with the principles presented in the first part of this chapter. Suggestions concerning desirable grouping practices will be given later in this chapter.

VARIETY OF INSTRUCTIONAL MATERIALS. There was a time in our secondary schools when each pupil had a textbook in every subject, but little or no other reference materials. That situation still pertains in many small schools in rural areas today. Most secondary schools, however, have a variety of instructional materials for those subjects in which they are needed. Libraries have been introduced in most secondary schools, schools have various kinds of audio-visual aids and materials, and they have special facilities and equipment in such subjects as science, art, industrial arts, and home economics. Although these materials are available in most medium-sized and large schools, many teachers do not make as wide use of them as they should. In most secondary school classes, teachers continue to rely on a basic textbook, with only occasional use of the many other instructional materials which are available.

In some schools, resources from the community are also being used in the learning activities in certain subjects. Community resources most widely used include professional, civic, industrial, and labor leaders; business, civic, and industrial agencies; public libraries, museums, and other community cultural centers; and nearby historical places. A few school systems provide teachers with lists of the available community resources. These schools may also assist teachers with arranging field trips to places of interest in the community and bringing community resources into the school. As with other instructional materials, however, community resources at present are not used in learning activities by secondary school teachers as widely as may be desired.

TEACHER-CENTERED CLASSROOM RELATIONSHIPS. As compared with European secondary schools, teacher-pupil relationships in our secondary school classrooms are more democratic, informal, and friendly. Pupils usually remain seated when they participate in class discussions, they feel free to approach teachers on both school and personal problems, and there is mutual courtesy and respect between them. However, the classroom situation in our secondary schools is largely teacher-centered. Although pupil seats are moveable, they usually are arranged in formal rows; class discussions are led by teachers, seldom by pupils; and the control of the classroom is centered clearly in the teacher.

Although there are advantages in having relationships in the classroom so definitely teacher-centered, this approach does not give pupils the experience they need in assuming responsibility for their own conduct and in working with teachers and other pupils in democratic situations. Pupil participation in planning learning activities; small group activities with pupils in charge; class discussions led by individual pupils, pupil committees, and panels; and informal arrangement of classroom furniture are some ways of making the human relationships in the classroom more pupil-centered. Activities such as these should be used in the secondary school more extensively than at present to give pupils experience in leadership and in democratic human relations.

IMPLEMENTATION OF THE PRINCIPLES

Considerable effort is being put forth in some secondary schools to introduce instructional practices and relationships that are in harmony with the principles presented earlier in this chapter. Faculties are re-examining their approach to the grouping of pupils; teachers are studying ways of working more effectively with pupils as individuals; teachers are working as teams in planning and carrying on learning activities; and other new approaches are being introduced in the instructional practices employed in secondary schools. Some of the new approaches now employed in secondary schools are discussed in this part of the chapter.

FLEXIBILITY IN GROUPING PUPILS. Although it is generally recognized that ability grouping for some purposes is essential in secondary schools, many educators and parents object to the inflexible approach to ability grouping which is being used so widely today. They suggest that pupils should spend a good part of each day in heterogeneous groups, where they can have contact with pupils of various backgrounds, interests, and abilities; that pupils should be grouped by ability only for specific purposes, with the composition of ability groups varying from subject to subject; that the nature of a group should not be emphasized by the use of numbers, names, or other means of identification; and that teachers should emphasize ways of working with individual pupils in whatever type of group they may be found.

In the Meadowbrook Junior High School, Newton, Massachusetts, pupils are placed in ability groups for approximately half the school day and in heterogeneous groups the rest of the time. Ability groups are used in mathematics, science, and reading because in these subjects the Meadowbrook faculty believes that ability grouping is especially helpful in meeting individual pupil needs. Pupils at Meadowbrook are placed in heterogenous groups in a block-time class, which includes the areas of English, social studies, and guidance, and in such other subjects as physical education, art, music, industrial arts, and home economics. Pupils remain with the same group throughout the day in these subjects where the heterogeneous approach is used, but the composition of groups is different for each of the subjects in which pupils are placed according to ability. In the Meadowbrook approach to ability grouping, both the content and methods of teaching are modified considerably from group to group.

The West Side Junior High School, Groton, Connecticut, achieves some of the advantages of flexibility in ability grouping by having three broad groups—with considerable overlapping in the abilities of pupils in the three groups. For instance, both the high and low groups include some pupils of average ability. The Groton plan of overlapping ability groups reduces the wide range of abilities in each group, and still it avoids the sharp distinctions between pupils in the various ability groups which exist in some of the other ability grouping plans.

Numerous other plans for grouping pupils are used in some secondary schools to achieve a satisfactory learning situation without the disadvantages that pertain to the more common plans of ability grouping. In some schools ability grouping is limited to honors classes for the intellectually talented and special classes for slow-learners, with all other pupils in heterogeneous groups. A few schools have special groups only for those pupils who are deficient in certain fundamental skills, such as reading and mathematics.

Even though some plan of ability grouping is used in a secondary school, teachers should not expect to lean too much on administrative practices like ability grouping to meet the instructional needs of individual pupils. More attention needs to be given in most secondary schools to methods of working with pupils as individuals regardless of the approach to grouping which is employed.

ACQUAINTANCESHIP WITH PUPILS. In Chapter 17 the importance of helping teachers get acquainted with their pupils as a basis for guidance activities is discussed at some length. It is equally important for teachers to become well acquainted with the pupils in all their classes in order to work with them as individuals in learning activities. Teachers in many schools have specific information about their pupils, such as their I.Q.'s, personality and character qualities, home backgrounds, extraclass participation, out-of-school activities, and previous achievement. They also have much specific information about individual pupils with respect to their own teaching fields. For instance, teachers of English are informed about each pupil's reading skills, his strengths and weaknesses in language usage, his reading interests, and those experiences of pupils which may be used as a basis for oral and written activities in the English class. Teachers of other subjects likewise gather specific information about the skills, backgrounds, and previous achievement of pupils as related to their subjects.

The practices employed for helping teachers get acquainted with individual pupils as a basis for working with them effectively in their classes include meetings of teachers with counselors who know the pupils well, meetings of sixth-grade with seventh-grade teachers to help them get acquainted with entering seventh-grade pupils, ready availability of cumulative records for pupils, and conferences by teachers with pupils and their parents. Some schools which are organized on the "little school" plan arrange the preparation periods of teachers so that they can meet frequently with the counselors for their help in understanding pupils better (see Chapters 15 and 17). Extensive testing programs are being used in some school systems to provide information about the learning needs of individual pupils in the various subject areas. These are some of the ways in which teachers obtain information about individual pupils as a basis for developing learning activities to meet their individual needs, interests, and abilities.

ASSISTANCE IN PUPILS' SOCIAL ADJUSTMENT. Most secondary schools have some pupils who are not well adjusted to the usual classroom situation. Although there may be only a few such pupils, one or two in a group may interfere seriously with the learning situation of the total group. In the past these pupils usually have been thought of as chronic discipline problems. Many educators today feel that these pupils have social adjustment problems and need special help to learn how to get along in school.

Some secondary schools today provide special help for these socially maladjusted pupils. In the Los Angeles City Schools, in a recent year, there were social-adjustment classes in thirty-two junior high schools and eleven senior high schools for pupils who persistently interfered with the work of regular classes. The purpose of the social-adjustment class, however, is not just to remove pupils who are disturbing regular classes, but to help them develop satisfactory classroom attitudes and behavior. In Los Angeles, it is not intended that these pupils be placed permanently in these classes, but rather to plan for their return to regular classes as soon as possible.

The social-adjustment classes in Los Angeles are much smaller than regular classes, ordinarily with only ten to eighteen pupils. Teachers are selected for these classes because of special preparation for and interest in this work. Teaching methods and materials are adapted to these pupils, there is much individual instruction, and there is emphasis on individual guidance and counseling. Pupils who do not improve in the social-adjustment classes are sometimes transferred to another school where they may begin in a totally new environment. In extreme cases they are sent to adjustment center high schools which are maintained for this purpose as part of the Los Angeles city school system.

Robert Fulton Junior High School, Van Nuys, California, which is a part of the Los Angeles City School District, for several years has had a program of social adjustment for pupils. At Fulton Junior High School, a teacher is assigned full time to the social-adjustment program. Pupils are placed in the program if their school citizenship has been consistently rated unsatisfactory. Some of the pupils report to the social-adjustment teacher periodically for counseling, but remain in their regular classes. Pupils whose conduct is decidedly unsatisfactory in certain classes may be placed in a social-adjustment class for part or all of the school day. However, the social-adjustment teacher counsels many pupils on school citizenship problems who have not been transferred to the social-adjustment class. At Fulton Junior High School, several years of experience with this plan has met with the approval of both teachers and parents.[1] A program in social adjustment, such as the one in Los Angeles, should do much to help pupils who frequently are a serious problem in secondary schools.

SPECIAL HELP FOR MIGRANT CHILDREN. Some schools have been confronted in recent years with a serious problem because of the large number of children of migrant workers whose attendance at school is decidedly irregular. Some communities with large numbers of migrant workers have many pupils who leave school in the early spring months and return after school opens in the fall. Because migrant families often remain in one place for only a short time, the children may not be in school at all during the months that the family is away from its home community.

It would not be so serious if the migrant children as a group were to leave school and return at about the same time, but the withdrawal and return of these pupils may be spread over a period of several weeks. One junior high school with a large number of migrant children, according to the principal, begins school in the fall with about 600 pupils. By late November the enrollment is about 900 pupils, and then beginning late in March it drops gradually again to 600 pupils by the close of the school year. Some pupils in this school are in attendance not more than a third of the school year.

The instructional problems created by migrant children are not confined alone to these pupils. The learning activities of other pupils may be seriously affected because of the help teachers need to give migrant pupils to become adjusted to school and to fit into the instructional program. The problems created by migrant children are especially serious in the elementary and junior high schools, since few of these children reach the senior high school.

Some schools are providing special help for migrant children. The schools of Palm Beach County, Florida, have such a program, which includes visiting teachers to provide liaison with the homes of these children; an area supervisor who assists schools and community groups with problems of educating migrant children; in-service education programs for teachers of migrant children; remedial instruction in fundamental skills for migrant children; and an advisory committee of principals, teachers, and public health officials to study problems of educating migrant children.

In the Dade County, Florida, Public Schools attention is also be-

[1] *Better Behavior Through the Fulton Plan of Adjustment,* Robert Fulton Junior High School, Van Nuys, California, February, 1961, 10 pp. (mimeo.)

ing given to problems presented by children of migrant workers. In the junior and senior high schools of Dade County, new pupils are distributed among different home rooms and classes so they will not band together in small groups; counselors interview each new pupil and try to help him fit into the school; resident pupils are encouraged to help migrant children; school lunches are provided for children who cannot pay for them; special abilities of pupils, such as the ability to use a foreign language, are recognized; pupils are helped with personal appearance; abilities of pupils are evaluated by a comprehensive testing program; and a special effort is made to get to know the parents. Programs such as those in Florida suggest ways of developing effective instructional practices for these pupils.

ATTENTION TO PUPILS OF LOW SOCIOECONOMIC STATUS. For some time, educators have been concerned about the influence of homes of low socioeconomic status on the motivation and achievement of pupils in school. Many pupils who come from poor cultural backgrounds apparently lack the motivation to continue in school beyond the compulsory attendance age. They are often underachievers during the years they remain in school. These pupils present a particularly serious problem in large cities with large numbers of families of low socioeconomic status, but similar problems exist, though on a smaller scale, in many small urban and rural communities. With these pupils in mind, a project was initiated at the Manhattanville Junior High School and the George Washington High School, both in New York City, which "was originally designed to identify, stimulate, and guide into college channels able students from low socioeconomic status homes." [2] Since the Higher Horizons Program, as the New York City program has come to be called, was originally intended for pupils with sufficient academic potential to go on to college, only the upper half of the student body as measured by various tests was included. This was soon changed, however, because it was recognized that the school would be split into the "haves" and the "have-nots," with possible ill effects on the attitudes of the student body as a whole.

Although in the beginning the Higher Horizons Program was thought of as a guidance project, it was soon extended to all aspects of the school program. Pupils in the Higher Horizons Program pursued the regular school curriculum, but they gave more attention to careers and career planning. Pupils visited research centers, professional schools, and hospitals to learn at firsthand about the educational

[2] Daniel Schreiber, "Raising Sights to Higher Horizons," *Strengthening Democracy,* 12:1-4, May, 1960. (Published by the Board of Education of the City of New York.)

requirements of different professions. Those who were deficient in the fundamental skills were given remedial help. Much was done also to raise the cultural interests of the pupils through attendance at Broadway shows, concerts, and the opera. Before attending such activities, time was devoted to preparing pupils to enjoy and appreciate them. Pupils in the program were given individual guidance and counseling, special help was provided in basic subjects for pupils who needed it, and frequent contacts were made with parents.

The success of the Higher Horizons Program in New York City is indicated by test records which reveal marked progress in the achievement of pupils in fundamental skills, improvement in attendance at school, reduced retardation of pupils during their three years in junior high school, improvement in school citizenship and conduct, graduation from high school by a larger percentage of these pupils, and sharply increased interest in attending college.[3] The Higher Horizons Program has been so successful that it has been extended to a number of other elementary schools and junior high schools in New York City.

CONCERN FOR NON-ENGLISH-SPEAKING PUPILS. Some school systems have large numbers of pupils who cannot speak English when they enter school. It is essential, therefore, to help these pupils make progress in the total curriculum of the school while they are learning the English language. These pupils present a particularly difficult problem in the secondary schools because they rapidly fall behind in the basic subjects due to their poor English.

In some schools special classes are provided for non-English-speaking pupils. In the junior and senior high schools of Dade County, Florida, such classes are taught by a bilingual teacher who helps pupils continue to make progress in the fundamental skills and at the same time teaches them the English language. These classes consist of not more than a three-period block of time, with pupils spending the remainder of the day in regular classes. It is intended that pupils should ordinarily remain in the orientation class not more than twelve weeks. The instructional program in the orientation classes for non-English-speaking children helps these pupils adjust more readily to the new school and make better progress in the total school program.

[3] Daniel Schreiber, "A School's Work With Urban Disadvantaged Pupils," *College Admissions 7: The Search for Talent.* The Proceedings of the Seventh Annual Colloquium on College Admissions of the College Entrance Examination Board, New York: The Board, 1960, pp. 57-66.

INDIVIDUALIZED ACTIVITIES FOR SUPERIOR PUPILS. The greatest change in the instructional practices of the secondary school have taken place in the classes for superior pupils. While learning activities in most classes continue to be teacher- and textbook-centered, in the classes for superior pupils there is a variety of learning activities, with much pupil participation in planning and carrying out those activitities.

Some indication of the nature of instructional practices in classes for superior pupils is revealed by an examination of practices in several communities. In Baltimore, resource people from the community assist with classes for superior pupils, they are conducted on a seminar basis, and field trips are taken when they may contribute to the learning activity. In Flint, Michigan, individual projects and research are emphasized. In Cleveland, Ohio, the major work classes have individual and small-group activities, with much pupil participation in planning those activities. In many senior high schools with advanced college placement programs, this work is offered on an individual basis with pupils doing much independent study. Individualized work, emphasis on independent study and research, and pupil participation in planning therefore constitute the basic approach to teaching in many of the programs for superior pupils in secondary schools. The types of programs are discussed at length in Chapter 11.

USE OF TELEVISION. Many school systems have been experimenting with teaching by television, some of them in large classes to reduce teaching costs and others in regular classes with television used to enrich the instructional program. The Oklahoma City public schools, which have their own local television station as well as the programs provided by the Oklahoma State Project in Educational Television, provide an example of the effective use of educational television. In Oklahoma City, television is used for (1) teaching in classes of normal size, (2) enrichment of the instructional program, (3) teaching to large classes, and (4) a team approach to teaching.

When television programs are used with classes of normal size, they contribute to the instructional program by providing learning activities which may not be available in any other form. They serve a purpose similar to that of movies, film strips, resource people, and other instructional resources. With large classes for television instruction, however, the teacher-pupil relationship is quite different from that in classes of normal size. Sometimes large classes have more than one teacher or have the help of a teacher's aide to assist with records and class routine. The basic subject content in these large classes is presented by television, but there are also other learning activities such as discussions led by the teacher, reports of individual pupils or pupil committees, and the study of textbook and other reference materials. Teams of teachers often bring several class groups together for television presentations to a large group, instead of several presentations to normal-size classes.

The most ambitious educational television program today is that known as the Midwest Program on Airborne Television Instruction, which, beginning in 1961, has broadcast programs to a potential audience of five million school and college students from an airplane flying 23,000 feet above the home base at Lafayette, Indiana. The Midwest Program was initiated because television broadcasts from an airplane can reach a much larger audience than the same investment in time and money can provide from TV stations on the ground. The MPATI, as it is commonly called, offers well-planned courses in Russian at the college level; in Spanish and French for elementary-school pupils; in general science for junior high school; and in history, music, and government for the senior high school. The program offers complete courses in subjects which cannot be offered in rural schools with a limited teaching staff, while in large schools with a broad program it provides opportunities for enrichment. The Midwest Program is designed especially for school use, but it also is available to others who have their television sets converted to the appropriate channels.

TEACHER-PUPIL RELATIONS IN PROGRAMMED LEARNING. Teaching machines and programmed learning are by no means new. As early as the 1920's, Sidney L. Pressey, professor of psychology at Ohio State University, developed a push-button device for automatic testing which, on multiple-choice tests, showed immediately whether the pupil's answer on a question was correct. Although there was much interest at the time in Pressey's automatic testing device, as well as in other mechanical teaching devices which he developed, it is only in recent years that teaching machines have attracted widespread enthusiasm from educators and the public. Today numerous automatic teaching machines from simple and inexpensive punchboard devices to complicated and highly expensive push-button equipment are available, many of them already being used experimentally in schools throughout the country.

Teaching machines may be said to "represent some form of variation on what can be called the tutorial or Socratic method of teaching. That is, they present the individual student with programs of questions and answers, problems to be solved, or exercises to be performed. In addition, however, they always provide some type of automatic feedback or correction to the student so that he is immediately informed of his progress at each step and given a basis for correcting his errors." [4] Continuous and active student response is required by the teaching machine, the student is informed immediately whether his response is correct, and he may proceed on an individual basis at his own rate.

Although much publicity has been given to teaching machines, few people are aware of the "programming" of a subject which these machines require. Much time must be devoted to developing in logical sequence the content of the subject which the pupil studies through the teaching machine. Some publishers are developing such materials in various subjects which, when produced in large quantities, should be available at a reasonable cost. Many educators believe, however, that these materials should be specifically designed for the needs of a given group of pupils, and therefore that they need to be developed by the teachers themselves. Whether the programmed materials are purchased or are prepared by the teachers in a school, the nature of these materials as well as the teaching machine have a direct influence on the effectiveness of the learning which takes place.

At present one cannot foresee how much teaching machines and programmed learning may affect instructional practices in the secondary school. Some enthusiasts believe that, in the future, teaching machines may become a basic instructional device in some subjects. Others believe that the use of teaching machines will be more limited, and that they will serve as only one more instructional aid, like films, film strips, recordings, and library materials. Certainly, teaching machines may be useful for individual work by pupils, but it is not clear at this time how extensively they may be used for group instruction. Present interest in mechanical teaching devices and programmed learning, however, suggests that instructional practices in the future may be greatly affected by them.

New Approaches to Staff Utilization. Some new approaches to the size of instructional groups, clerical help for classroom teachers, and ways in which teachers work together, are having a significant bearing on instructional practices in the secondary school. For many years, the desirable standard for class size in most secondary school subjects has been considered to be twenty-five to thirty pupils. The

[4] A. A. Lumsdaine and Robert Glaser, *Teaching Machines and Programmed Learning: A Source Book,* Washington, D.C.: National Education Association, 1960, pp. 5–6.

studies sponsored by the Commission on the Experimental Study of the Utilization of the Staff in the Secondary School have given attention to the use of different sizes of instructional groups and education by television, as well as to various approaches to the use of teaching teams and aides to assist teachers with reading papers and clerical work, discussed in Chapter 7.

One of the suggestions of the Commission concerns the normal size class of twenty-five to thirty pupils, which the Commission believes is too small for certain types of learning activities which can be carried on just as effectively in large groups, and also that it is too large for satisfactory group discussions and for the creative activity and individual study in which some pupils should engage. The Commission suggests that the present goals and content of the secondary school curriculum should be examined with these questions in mind: (1) What can students learn largely by themselves? (2) What can students learn from explanations by others? (3) What requires personal interaction among students and teachers? The Commission believes that, with the answers to these questions in mind, pupils should be placed in large groups, small groups, and normal-size groups, depending upon the needs of a particular learning activity; and, furthermore, for certain purposes that pupils should engage in individual study rather than work in class groups. In other words, the Commission believes that the secondary school can provide for more effective instruction and better utilization of the staff if the size of instructional groups is varied to meet the needs of different learning activities.

The suggestions of the Commission concerning large and small-group instruction and individual study are presently employed in a number of secondary schools. The Ridgewood High School, Norridge, Illinois, which opened in September, 1960, was designed for the new approaches to class size, with some rooms for large classes of 125 pupils and others for small groups of ten to fifteen pupils. There is also provision for individual study, with learning resource areas in the building where teachers help pupils with individual learning activities.

Many other junior and senior high schools in the United States are using large- and small-group classes and individual study. Newton High School, Newton, Massachusetts, for several years has had large-group classes in English, biology, and history. Wahlquist Junior High School in Weber County, Utah, has large-group instruction in history, language arts, and guidance. Evanston Township High School, Evanston, Illinois; Glenbrook High School, Northbrook, Illinois; and the secondary schools of Jefferson County, Colorado, are also using groups of different size for more effective teaching.[5]

The use of large and small classes and individual study, as recommended by the Commission on the Experimental Study of the Utilization of Staff in the Secondary School, has implications for the kinds of learning activities that teachers use. In large groups, where there is usually a presentation by a teacher or a resource person, much use is made of such visual aids as overhead projectors, charts, slides, films, and film strips. Television presentations, demonstrations by teachers and pupils, and pupil committees and panels are also employed frequently with large groups. Presentations for large groups need to be well organized, with careful attention to ways of maintaining the interest of all pupils.

The small groups are usually conducted on a seminar basis, with much pupil participation in planning and conducting learning activities. Teachers need to be well prepared for small-group instruction, but the plans for learning activities for small classes should be more flexible and informal than for large groups.

Even when pupils engage in individual study, they continue to need the help and supervision of a teacher who is well qualified in his subject. In individual study, pupils assume much responsibility for planning their own learning activities. They may use the library, school laboratories, and resources in the community. Individual study is most effective, however, if the pupil is responsible to a teacher, who in turn is available to assist him in organizing and completing his study activities. In the schools using the plan effectively, the pupil consults his teacher at regular intervals and feels free to request help at other times as it is needed.

LIBRARY AS A RESOURCE CENTER. The secondary school library is being used increasingly by pupils as a learning resources center for individual study, for committees and other small groups, and for an entire class group. Pupils find all kinds of instructional resources in the library, including reference books, film strips, tapes, slides, pamphlets, bulletins, pictures, charts, and newspaper and magazine clippings. There are also files which list the instructional resources that are available elsewhere in the community.

The physical facilities of the library likewise are undergoing changes to meet the needs of new approaches to teaching. A classroom adjacent to the library makes it possible to bring an entire class to the library to work under the supervision of the teacher and

[5] Reports of the experimental studies of large-group, small-group, and individual study are given in *The Bulletin of the National Association of Secondary-School Principals*, the January issues for 1958, 1959, 1960, and 1961.

a member of the library staff. In addition to a general reading area, the library has conference rooms where small groups of pupils may work together, a viewing room where film strips and slides may be studied, a small listening room where pupils may hear tape recordings, a typing area where pupils may do their written work, and a center for teaching machines and automated learning devices. The learning resources center of today need not be much larger than the library of the past, but it should have a variety of facilities which are appropriate for the kinds of learning activities in which teachers and pupils engage increasingly in the secondary school.

CAMPING ACTIVITIES. A few secondary schools have developed camping activities to give pupils experiences ordinarily not available in the classroom. Camping activities contribute greatly to instruction in science and conservation. Perhaps more important, however, is the opportunity which teachers have to develop relationships with pupils through camping activities that are not possible elsewhere in the program of the school. Pupils also develop certain desirable leadership, character, personal, and social qualities through participation in planning and carrying on camping activities. These qualities may be as important to the growth of the pupils as the subject-matter skills and knowledge which they gain from these activities.

The San Diego City Schools provide a week of camping activities for junior high school pupils at a camp in the mountains maintained by the school district especially for this purpose, with a qualified staff of teachers in charge. Science and conservation is studied outdoors, with attention to astronomy, meteorology, ecology, biology, and forestry. There are also activities which emphasize the social relationships among pupils, such as teaching them how to live and work together in groups, giving them an opportunity to develop a sense of self-responsibility, and helping them gain experience in group leadership. Although camping activities for secondary school pupils are offered in relatively few school systems in the United States, there has been much success with it in these schools.

ISSUES AND PROBLEMS

Educators and citizens recognize some problems in the instructional practices and relationships in the secondary school. The following are some of the more important ones.

1. *How can teachers be prepared to work effectively with adolescents in learning situations?*

For many years educators have been suggesting that teachers

should work with pupils in learning situations in a variety of ways, using many kinds of instructional materials and methods other than the class recitation and discussion. Educators also have stressed the importance of having teachers understand and work with pupils as individuals rather than as a group. However, these suggestions have had only a limited effect on instructional practices and relationships in secondary schools. The problem of helping beginning teachers employ a variety of approaches in teaching is especially difficult because the teachers whom they observe and with whom they study in their student-teaching experience often use only the recitation method and few materials other than the textbook.

The problem of helping teachers understand children, work with them as individuals, and employ a variety of learning activities and materials is both a pre-service and an in-service problem. In the teacher's pre-service education program, he should have the opportunity to study children and to observe some teachers who work effectively with individual pupils in a variety of learning activities. We must recognize, however, that in-service education should continue to provide teachers with such help and experiences.

2. *How can teachers be given the time that is necessary to keep up to date in their subjects, accumulate a variety of learning materials, and plan and carry on effective learning activities?*

Finding adequate time for teachers to plan their work, keep up to date in their subjects, and read the papers written by pupils is becoming an increasingly serious problem. In such subjects as science and social studies, developments are coming so fast that teachers need to devote many hours to reading and study. The preparation of laboratory work and demonstrations in science likewise takes many hours. For teachers of English, the pressure for improvement in the written work of pupils requires much time for reading and correcting papers. Planning learning activities to meet the needs of individual pupils, as suggested in this chapter, is likewise very time consuming. These are only a few of the activities of teachers which demand much of their time.

In a few schools, teacher's aides assist with clerical work. Parents sometimes read English papers for teachers, at an hourly wage paid by the school. In at least one school, teachers of English dictate their comments on pupils' papers, using a dictating machine and a stenographer to transcribe the comments. Some schools have pupils serve as laboratory assistants to science teachers, giving them credit for this experience. Many schools are examining the non-teaching tasks of teachers to see if some of these can be eliminated.

A few school systems have a sabbatic leave plan for teachers, so that they may take a semester or a year for study. Although efforts such as these are being made in a few schools to give teachers time for study, for planning learning activities, and for working with individual pupils, the fact remains that in most schools teachers do not have the time to do adequately the work which their teaching responsibilities entail. Secondary school administrators and faculties must continue to study this problem.

3. *How can needed buildings and other facilities be provided for new and flexible working relationships suggested by educators for secondary schools?*

Many principals and teachers would like to initiate some of the flexible approaches to teaching which are suggested in this chapter, but the school building in which they find themselves imposes definite limitations upon them. Large-group classes demand rooms that accommodate from 100 to 150 pupils, small discussion groups should have rooms for ten to fifteen pupils, and libraries need facilities which serve as an adequate resource and work center for pupils. In new buildings some of these facilities can be provided at little additional cost, but in old buildings it is difficult to provide such facilities.

Principals and teachers should study their present facilities to see if changes can be made which are appropriate for certain kinds of learning activities. The auditorium and the cafeteria may be used for large-group instruction, sometimes with little or no changes. Some classrooms may be converted into conferences or seminar rooms. In the school library, listening, viewing, and conference rooms sometimes can be built at low cost. In most secondary school buildings some ways can be found to adapt the facilities to the kinds of instructional practices and relationships suggested in this chapter.

4. *Are the newer media of instruction a threat to the teacher's importance in the learning situation or are they an aid to individualizing instruction and facilitating learning?*

This issue is often discussed at the emotional level. Teachers see themselves as losing jobs, losing status as a profession, or playing a role of declining importance in the schools. They may be thinking about television or teaching machines, rarely about other audiovisual devices such as radio, films, or recordings.

In analyzing this issue, there are a whole host of printed, mechanical, and electronic devices which should rightfully be included in any discussion of newer educational media: TV, programmed printed materials such as the scrambled textbook, the programmed text, the teaching machine, audio and video tapes, language laboratories, films, filmslides, radio, computers, calculators, and devices such as those used in teaching reading. In a sense all of these are relatively new. The types of electronic devices that will be developed in the next ten years cannot be foreseen. But all will undoubtedly affect instruction profoundly.

The proponents of the newer media, such as television and programmed learning devices, see in them a means of revolutionizing the teaching-learning process. They hail them as a solution to many educational problems, such as teacher shortages, inadequately prepared teachers, a rapidly expanding pupil population, lack of sufficient facilities, and difficulties in learning. They feel that now it is possible to develop sequential learning for the individual.

Those who take the opposite position feel that these media minimize the importance of the teacher. They fear that the development of the curriculum may be centralized and controlled and that a preselected, pre-organized curriculum which emphasizes facts and "right" answers will result. They hold that learning becomes passive without the stimulating interchange of questions and ideas. They question the desirability of having a master teacher lecture to a large group over a medium which requires a teaching procedure that may not be the most appropriate for the situation.

Much research is being done on the newer media. The research tends to show that learning can be improved with additional means of communicating to the student the concepts, ideas, skills, or processess to be taught. However, some of the research on this subject has been quite unscientific and of little value.

The basic question is to find out what these devices can help a teacher do better than he could without them. We scarcely have any choice but to be aware that we are living in an age of sweeping technological changes in communications, which so vitally affect teaching and learning and which may well wipe out some limitations on learning.

The responsibility is still the teacher's in learning to use these media and to program them effectively. If placing the pupil more on his own responsibility for learning is a desirable end, then any device that will help in so doing should be welcomed. Effectively used, some of the new media can free pupils for more independent study and permit teachers more direct contact with individual pupils. Not only must the teacher gain more skill and insight in the teaching-learning process but he must also be willing to change his role in that process.

SELECTED REFERENCES

Bush, Robert N. *The Teacher-Pupil Relationship.* Englewood Cliffs, N.J.: Prentice-Hall, Inc., 1954, Chap. 9.—Describes the results of case studies of teacher-pupil relationships.

Costello, Lawrence F., and Gordon, George N. *Teach With Television: A Guide to Instructional T.V.* New York: Hastings House Publishers, 1961, 192 pp.—A comprehensive discussion of television education in the schools, including facilities, costs, organization of programs, and planning for classroom use.

DeBernardis, Amo, Doherty, Victor W., Hummel, Errett, and Brubaker, Charles W. *Planning Schools for New Media.* Portland, Oregon: Division of Education, Portland State College, 1961, 72 pp.—Describes the building facilities which are needed in schools for instructional materials centers, language laboratories, radio, television, and other new media for teaching.

Erickson, Carlton W. H. *Administering Audio-Visual Services.* New York: The Macmillan Co., 1959, Chaps. 3-6.—A comprehensive discussion of the audio-visual services in elementary and secondary schools, including the kinds of materials and services, the facilities that are needed, the administration of the services, and use by teachers.

Galanter, Eugene. *Automatic Teaching: The State of the Art.* New York: John Wiley & Sons, Inc., 1959, 198 pp.—Presents papers delivered at a conference on automatic teaching, including teaching machines and programmed learning through specially prepared textbooks.

Goldman, Edward H. "A Day With the T.V. Teacher," *The Clearing House,* 35: 340-42, February, 1961.—Describes the work of the teacher in present educational TV programs.

Gruhn, William T., and Douglass, Harl R. *The Modern Junior High School.* New York: The Ronald Press Co., 1956, Chap. 10.—Suggests ways of working with individual pupils, including suggestions for ability grouping.

Lewis, Phillip. *Educational Television Guidebook.* New York: McGraw-Hill Book Co., Inc., 1961, 238 pp.—A comprehensive discussion of facilities and procedures for television education.

Lumsdaine, A. A., and Glaser, Robert, Editors. *Teaching Machines and Programmed Learning: A Source Book.* Washington, D.C.: National Education Association, 1960, Parts III, V.—Presents articles and reports of research studies on the use of teaching machines, covering the period of the 1920's to 1960.

Miles, Matthew B. *Learning to Work in Groups.* New York: Bureau of Publications, Teachers College, Columbia University, 1959, 285 pp.—Suggests ways of working effectively with people in groups which can be adapted for use in secondary-school classrooms.

Rigney, Joseph W., and Fry, Edward B. "Current Teaching-Machine Programs and Programming Techniques," *AV Communication Review,* 9:1-122, May-June, 1961.—Report of a survey of teaching-machine programs and programming techniques as they existed at the end of 1960.

Schramm, Wilbur (ed.). *The Impact of Educational Television.* Urbana: The University of Illinois Press, 1960, 247 pp.—Presents selected studies in educational television which were sponsored by the National Educational Television and Radio Center.

Smith, Mary Howard (ed.). *Using Television in the Classroom.* New York: McGraw-Hill Book Co., Inc., 1961, 118 pp.—Gives suggestions to teachers on the use of television programs which are broadcast as part of the Midwest Program on Airborne Television Instruction, which is broadcast from a plane over the states in the Midwest.

SUTTON, ELIZABETH. *Knowing and Teaching the Migrant Child.* Washington, D.C.: National Education Association, 1960, 147 pp.—Describes a project for working with and teaching the children of migrant families in Florida, Virginia, Texas, and Illinois.

TAYLOR, KENNETH I. "Instructional Materials Center," *The Nation's Schools,* 66:45-50, December, 1960.—Describes the combined library and audio-visual departments in the West Leyden High School, Northlake, Illinois, which provides facilities which are broader and more flexible than those in most schools.

TRUMP, J. LLOYD, and BAYNHAM, DORSEY. *Focus on Change: Guide to Better Schools.* Chicago: Rand McNally Co., 1961, 147 pp.—Describes instructional materials centers, large- and small-group instruction, independent study, team teaching, and other new practices in teacher-pupil working relationships in secondary schools.

9

EXPERIENCES WITH CONTENT IN GENERAL EDUCATION

The experiences that pupils have in their high school classes relate to various kinds of stimuli in their environment: to the teacher's behavior and attitudes, to other pupils in the classroom, to the facilities provided, and to the content studied. These multiple factors that influence what a class is like are interrelated to a high degree. What the teacher thinks about the value of having pupils take responsibility for class activities and participate in discussions will set the stage for how much interaction is possible. The content studied cannot be divorced from the extent to which individual differences are taken into consideration. Thus, the complex of factors—teachers, pupils, facilities, materials, subject matter, organization, and procedures—determine what a student's class experiences will be like.

In this chapter, the focus is on what the pupil studies and the kinds of experiences he has in dealing with the content that is considered as general education. General education by no means implies that all should have exactly the same experiences. For the factor of individual differences is as important in general education as it is in specialized education.

BASIC PRINCIPLES

The content of general education for all youth should challenge them to explore the world in which they live and their cultural inheritance.

General education which accomplishes its purpose of helping a person to become a better citizen, a better human being, and to live a richer life presents a challenge. It challenges the pupil to know more, to go beyond his present restricted and provincial orbit, to see possibilities for further learning. No secondary school curriculum can possibly encompass all knowledge important for a broad, general education. But it can provide the expanded interests and the tools for exploring the fascinating world of science, the social and political developments and their historical background, the records in story and song of man's development. It is the school's responsibility to stimulate, widen, and guide these interests.

The organization of the curriculum, discussed previously, provides the framework and insures a balance of exploration in the various areas of general education. The content and the experiences with that content furnish the richness of detail which cause the pupil to behave differently: to read more, to converse more intelligently, to examine issues, to enjoy more of mankind's abundant cultural legacy. None of this is aimed at helping him to specialize in order to make a living.

The content of general education should be dynamic, up to date, accurate, and continuously changing.

Nothing quite as exciting is happening in the secondary school curriculum as the long overdue efforts to update the content of a number of the subject fields. The explosion of knowledge through invention and research has made these changes imperative. Information taught in the sciences is no longer accurate unless it includes recent developments that led to the so-called "space age." The developments in communications research and technology make the language arts content of the last decade outmoded in a number of ways.

It is difficult in a shrinking world and in an expanding universe to conceive of what the developments will be even ten years hence. No area of general education is unaffected. The inventiveness of man extends into the forms of the creative arts, into political and economic arrangements. More is known about human behavior, prevention of disease, and effective ways of destroying as well as preserving life. The growing knowledge of how to produce 700 per cent more bushels of corn per acre has an impact upon the world-wide food supply. New nations in Africa and Asia must be studied as they come into prominence.

To say this is not to depreciate the old. It is to recognize the rapid changes in times which require an intelligent person to know more than he did in a society developing at a more leisurely pace. We have but to look at the new nations of Africa to realize how difficult it is for us to conceive of the kind of change from primitive to modern that skips hundred of years required for those changes by the older established nations of the West.

The study of the content in general education should go beyond facts to deal with meanings, relationships, concepts, and ideas.

If high quality learning is desired, it is not enough merely to know more about a subject. The basic question is what "knowing more" means. Surely, it is important to become acquainted with historical, cultural, and political developments of the regions of the world often neglected in textbooks. But the most searching kind of study that will lead to new understandings must go beyond the learning of unrelated facts to probe into meanings and principles, develop generalizations, and analyze concepts.

Each subject has some logical order, inherent relationships, and structure of its own. It has certain basic premises and concepts. It also has ways by which facts and concepts in that subject can be analyzed and evaluated. These become a part of the knowledge about a subject that is pursued with some depth and understanding. Nor should it be concluded that such understanding necessarily comes from studying the subject in its logical sequence.

The way the teacher can communicate those insights into a subject depend upon his own knowledge of it. In discussing a teacher's education, Smith has aptly said:

Now the depth of understanding to which a teacher must penetrate in the study of his subject is just this: First, he must know the content of his subject thoroughly, in its full range; he must know the basic elements of content at its foundations as well as those which are based and built upon it. Secondly, he must know this content in its logical structure; that is, he must see how the various elements to his subject are ordered and related together into a coherent whole, a logically organized body of knowledge. When these two aspects of his subject are understood in their interrelations, the teacher has grasped his subject in depth as well as in breadth.[1]

No matter what the intelligence level of the student, the teacher needs to deal with meanings of what is studied, of how it is related to daily life, of words, and of ideas. Deriving meanings is related to appropriateness of the content selected, the difficulty of the concepts discussed, and the vocabulary used. All of these are important considerations. But we should not sell the "general" student short in his ability to understand the reasons for doing things.

The experiences with content in general education should take into account the individual's previous progress in learning the concepts or skills of the subject.

[1] B. Othanel Smith, "A Joint Task: The Preparation of a Teacher," *The Journal of Teacher Education*, 10:192, June, 1959.

As the student progresses through the school years, a body of content has been allocated for him to learn in the various grade levels. In some areas of knowledge it has been possible to develop a sequential order of subject matter which depends upon what has been studied in the previous grades to a greater extent than in other areas. Mathematics and foreign languages are examples. But it should be noted that this learning can be sequential only for the individual himself. The order of study of the content facilitates this pyramiding of learning. In other areas, such as the social studies, the allocating of any sequence of subject matter to grade levels can be done with much less confidence that such order will be best for learning of the understandings desired. The present interest in so-called teaching machines for educational purposes arises largely from their potentiality for programming material to be learned in some sequential order that facilitates learning concepts and skills.

Continuity of learning any subject assumes that what the student has previously studied has had meaning for him. It also assumes that for him there has been a clarity of educational purposes so that he sees where he has been, has a concept of what he has learned, and an idea of what he still needs to learn to achieve the goal. It must be understood that each individual has unique objectives for himself related, to be sure, to the school's objectives. However, any hope to develop continuity of learning in a subject will fail unless the previous attainment of the student's progress toward the educational objectives are known for him, not for some mythical average pupil.

The common learning experiences should give attention to the problems youth face in their world of today.

In Chapter 4 it was pointed out that youth have a need for dealing with their developmental tasks. Any high school curriculum that neglects these tasks is likely to be bogged down by some deadwood of adult interests.

These are by no means the sole concern of general education, but they are problems that youth face in the process of growing up in an adult world that often seems to tolerate rather than value young people. To youth, life in their own school and non-school world is of utmost importance. Only as these concerns are interwoven with those of the adult world, can the schools be truly successful in reaching young people to effect a change of behavior that is more than surface manifestations.

They do not negate the study of the problems that society faces. In fact, they are often one and the same. Youth are vitally concerned about relationships with their fellow man, but to them to neglect the questions of segregation that they meet in their own living and to concentrate only on those which the African faces in his own nation is sheer hypocrisy. Moreover, for the school to overlook the issues of juvenile delinquency, the problems created in the home by divorce, the relationships with peers and family is to leave some serious gaps in a person's general education. The examination of values that youth hold may well be one of the most fruitful experiences they have.

The basic skills and concepts of communication and computation should be a part of the common learnings in the secondary school.

The Three R's are basic skills to which modern schools have added others. There is a need to continue improving skills in reading as well as in speech and writing during the high school years. Every class in science or social studies, for example, is rich in opportunities for explaining, relating experiences, reporting, reading, and writing. These skills can be improved in any learning situation in which they are used for a specific purpose. Much practice in writing and speaking is needed for the purpose of learning to organize and communicate ideas effectively.

In secondary school the skills in arithmetic taught in the elementary school need "refreshing" and extending, particularly in their application to complex life situations. Pupils in higher mathematics courses, as well as pupils who take little or no mathematics in senior high school, have been found to be deficient in such skills. The improvement of these skills is especially important in the junior high school years. Personal affairs demand ability to deal with mathematical computations. Even more important are the understandings basic to quantitative reasoning and to communicating by means of any kinds of symbols, verbal or mathematical. Problems of modern society which are increasingly technical and quantitative need citizens who understand mathematical concepts. The tools of communication are a vehicle for ideas. The educated person in this day and age needs to be able to communicate his ideas with some degree of facility.

General education in the secondary school should include varied experiences in creative self-expression.

Pupils should be able to express themselves through many media: art, crafts, dancing, dramatics and speech, music, creative writing. Although there should be opportunities to pursue specific interests and abilities in these fields, all pupils should have some experiences in these areas of self-expression.

The products of such experiences do not need to meet the social standards of creativity. Creativity has little chance to be nurtured in an atmosphere of uniformity. Creativity refers to a "fresh response, unique to the creator." When the pupil's joys, sorrows, and angers are repressed, when his individuality is not encouraged, then his desire to express himself in new ways is dulled.

Nor is creativity common only to the fine arts. Pupils can be creative in the realm of ideas, in action for school betterment, in their relations with others, in science, practical arts, or any field of endeavor. However, there is a definite need for creative experiences as a part of general education in the area of the arts.

General education in a democracy calls for opportunities to learn the civic skills through experiences in intelligent inquiry, investigating different points of view, decision-making, and other experiences that lead to wise choices and action.

The undergraduate student of education would probably recognize at once the difference between a classroom in which this principle is put into operation and one in which the textbook is the final word. In the latter, the teacher stifles inquiry by having pupils repeat what the textbook says, or squelches curiosity and initiative by taking an adamant position on controversial issues. In the other, the teacher leads youngsters to delve into new sources of information, analyze opinions, and investigate different aspects of the problems studied. Pupils learn how to question information and to seek the correct sources. These are the teachers who help to develop the inquiring mind.

Inquiry into unexplored nooks in the storehouse of mankind's knowledge will lead to interests in new fields of learning. The objective of a general education is to extend the person's curiosity and to open up new and exciting possibilities for knowing more about man's development.

But democracy demands action based on decisions. Pupils who merely study about things may see little relationship between what they study and the activities of their own lives. True, some classroom topics have little relation to contemporary life but many do, such as the study of intercultural education. In most instances, intergroup tensions exist in their own community, both in and out of school. Young people can be guided to decisive action for the improvement of the welfare of others. They need to see that these issues are related to themselves and their own school.

Right answers in written statements ought not satisfy teachers as demonstrating the student's ability and willingness to take the right course of action. Research has pointed out that such an assumption cannot be made. As a part of living and planning together in the classroom—particularly in the social studies and core classes—youth become more active participants in a gradually expanding community. The acquiring of civic skills cannot be expected to happen by magic as youth enter civic life. Studies of high school and college graduates have indicated that young people's participation in community affairs after they leave school cannot be taken for granted.

SOME COMMON PRACTICES

This section deals with the types of experiences with content found in some schools in courses serving as the medium for general education. To a large extent, these courses are English, social studies, science, mathematics, health and physical education. To a much lesser extent they include home economics (for girls), industrial arts (for boys), art, and music. In fact, in many communities, it is almost exclusively in the junior high schools that these latter courses are considered important enough to be included in the general education of the majority of pupils. In the examples in this section, there is much that is undesirable, as judged by principles of a good learning situation and adolescents' needs. These descriptions of practices are not intended to portray what is happening in any mythical "average" school. They are, however, some practices with which the beginning teacher may likely come in contact in schools. The student is referred to the next section of the chapter for the more recent promising trends.

NATURE OF CONTENT IN SOME OF THE ACADEMIC FIELDS. In the field of science, the content has tended to be descriptive in nature. Often the facts of science have been taught as specific, discrete items. On the other hand, until the 1960's little attention had been given to basic concepts, ideas, and principles. The nature of science, methods of science, and philosophy of science are not likely to be explored in most courses in secondary schools. There is considerable repetition from elementary school in general science courses in secondary school. A study made in Iowa in 1949 showed that about half the assignments were limited to a single text and the most common activity in the classroom was recitation. General science experiments were mostly of the demonstration type. Students in laboratories followed directions from the manual.[2] Fortunately, this picture has been changing in recent years as will be indicated in the next main section of this chapter.

[2] Burton E. Voss, "Status of Science Education in Iowa High Schools," *Epsilon Bulletin*, University of Iowa, Vol. 34, 1959, pp. 62-63.

Mathematics, too, has been undergoing a change. While mathematics used to be too frequently rules for memorization, the concepts and meanings are now receiving greater stress, as the next section will show. There are still, however, classes in mathematics which deal largely with methods of manipulating symbols with little attention to the meanings of the symbols and the abstractions they represent.

As yet, English courses give little evidence of being affected by the ideas from the field of linguistic science. English grammar is taught generally as a system of analysis. More stress is placed upon the parts of speech and learning rules that govern them than upon the skills and concepts involved in communication, such as, in organization and presentation of ideas.

The social studies are explored more fully in a number of the following sections.

STUDY OF YOUTH PROBLEMS. The homeroom, core classes, home economics classes, general science classes, ninth-grade social studies classes, and biology classes, have been the spearhead for consideration of youth's personal concerns and problems in most secondary schools, especially those courses taught in junior high school. Girls may have a chance to study about the care of clothing, good grooming, and personality problems. Biology and general science classes vary from those taught out of a book to those that consider scientific phenomena in everyday living, use the richness of the community life about them, and consider personal health problems as significant learnings for youth. Recent criticism of all that smacks of "life adjustment" has caused some schools to eliminate much of the content that deals with youth's social and emotional problems.

In some schools, the general education content makes little use of the concerns of youth. Sex education may be miseducation, received through friends and pornographic magazines. Literature that is full of examples of social and psychological problems of young people may be discussed entirely for its literary merits. The knowledge needed as a consumer of goods, the knowledge about care of pupil's own clothing, his own civic duties and responsibilities, and repairs in his home, may be left to the vocational schools, to the pupils in the home economics curriculum, or to the home.

SIGNIFICANCE OF INFORMATION STUDIED. One of the characteristics of the curriculum in some secondary school classrooms is the undue emphasis on relatively insignificant information for its own sake. There tends to be a quiz-program stress on facts. History classes have moved away from the detailed study of battles in the major wars, toward a consideration of historical trends and political and social movements, but the dull, unimaginative recitation of trivia still remains in a number of classrooms.

History is often studied as an end in itself. The stress is placed upon historical facts and events without any conscious attempt to bring those facts to bear on clarifying present happenings. The study of the history of the presidency of the United States to throw light on the presidential powers and relationships with Congress, or the study of the historical background of India to understand the change in that country, is still too infrequent a type of approach. More recent developments are often neglected or never reached at all in the history course. Some schools, in order to avoid this mistake, have instituted current event days once a week in history classes. Although the practice has brought contemporary material into the course, such content may still be unrelated to the study taking place the remainder of the week.

The rather close adherence to subject matter organization as the design for the curriculum experiences has tended to emphasize the remote and the past. The pupil lives in a fascinating world of scientific developments and world-revolutionary social changes; yet, he may spend most of his time on scientific formulas, outdated scientific principles, chronological history up to 1940, and English that ignores modern developments in communications. He lives in a golden age of profusion of magazines and books; yet, very little of his time may be occupied with current literature. He is condemned for reading trash, but nothing may be planned to help him choose the good from the poor among current publications.

In some cases, undoubtedly, these conditions are due to the teacher's lack of knowledge of the field of literature or the developments in science and technology and their significance for political and social institutions.

IMPROVEMENT OF FUNDAMENTAL SKILLS. In the main, the skills of reading and communicating and number skills have tended to be assigned to certain subject areas. For example, skills of speaking and writing have been placed in the English area, without much concern for them in other subject areas. Vocabulary study, of vital importance in reading materials in any subject, has been primarily the concern of English teachers.

When pupils work to improve speaking and writing skills, they may carry on the activities as isolated exercises unrelated to the subject matter in their high school courses. Speeches may be given simply to practice speaking, not to present important information or to sell an idea of significance to the pupil. Reading skills have received more attention recently especially in junior high schools. More senior high school English teachers are including reading and listening skills in their programs, but not enough are trained to improve such skills effectively. Too often reading is considered of value for only the slow readers, without a developmental program available to any pupil who wishes to improve his reading skills.

The junior high school in its mathematics courses may stress arithmetic skills, but pupils may have little opportunity to improve and maintain these skills during their senior high school years. Pupils in commercial curricula or shop courses often receive additional practice in arithmetic in a practical situation.

Study skills and work habits are frequently stressed, although at times apart from the study methods pertinent to the subject. The idea that so much ground must be covered in a year's course militates against good study habits. As a result of the haste to cover material without giving attention to how well the job is done, the habit of thoroughness suffers.

DISCUSSION OF CONTROVERSIAL ISSUES. Where pupils are not encouraged sufficiently to question, the end result may be conformity of ideas. Yet, one of the basic tenets of a democratic society is the value placed on the individual's right to differ in his views. Many pupils in secondary schools have a day-by-day experience of accepting without question the things that the teacher says.

Some teachers seem to be afraid of dealing frankly and honestly with controversial issues in the classroom, perhaps because such analysis might be a threat to their security. The reason may be the pressures from the community against such discussion or it may be that their lack of knowledge of the subject would be exposed. Clarifying problems, discussing issues, and probing into questions at some depth demands a good background in the subject. There is a security in sticking to answers derived from the book which appeals to those who lack the know-how that comes from continued study to keep informed.

While world-shaking events take place outside the school, pupils may confine their study to the textbook. The question of poverty is not real to pupils unless they investigate what their own community does for people and what has resulted from conditions of poverty. Labor-management relations have many sources of learning in any industrial community. The study of the nature of communism, corruption in local politics, and socialized medicine may be taboo because of the mistaken belief that keeping such facts from young people is the best way to help them develop into good American citizens.

In current affairs most textbooks are out of date with regard to controversial issues when they come off the press. If a school uses a text for five years in science or in social studies the information may be badly out of date. This situation makes the practice of confining study to what the textbook says unrealistic.

CONSIDERATION OF PUPILS' CULTURAL VALUES. Values are an inherent part of social interaction, social institutions, and human relations. They determine man's actions with regard to how he spends his money, how he treats his fellow-man, and how he participates in civic activities. Yet, the many opportunities for discussion of values in classes may not be utilized. In fact, it seems as though some teachers fear what will happen if pupil's values are admitted into discussion in the classroom. The pupil may find that the teacher obviously either is shocked by the values the pupil and his family holds or discourages by his actions their honest examination. As a result, he begins to regard school as something unreal. Since he has few contacts with others who may have different values, he has little chance to change or to examine his own critically.

The question of value admission has been well analyzed by Pritzkau, Director of the Curriculum Center, University of Connecticut, who states that "as children come to school, all are physically admitted. In terms of values which they hold, however, others are partially admitted, and a number are refused admission." [3] He describes the conditions in many schools in these terms:

> As the child comes to school, he will naturally tend to respond to situations in terms of the values which he holds. He soon discovers, however, that some of his responses are accepted by the teacher and others are rejected as not conforming to the established rules or wishes of the teacher or school. Furthermore, he discovers that the responses of some children are invariably accepted and those of others rather consistently rejected. The reason for rejection is not clarified because the values which were basic to the responses are not understood by the school and are, therefore, not brought under scrutiny. Those whose responses are not accepted soon find that they must make a decision between two alternatives, to conform or be ostracized. [4]

The frank and open discussion of the community's values, who holds them, and the power structure of the community that determines whose values will prevail are often regarded as out of bounds as topics on which pupils may stretch their minds.

[3] Philo T. Pritzkau, *Dynamics of Curriculum Improvement*, Englewood Cliffs, N.J.: Prentice-Hall, Inc., 1959, p. 171.

[4] *Ibid.*, p. 182.

LEVEL OF INTELLECTUAL INQUIRY. The contrast between a classroom in which intellectual inquiry is at a high level and one where thoughtful examination of facts and ideas simply does not exist is indeed startling. In a visit to the latter type of classroom, the teacher might be seen teaching the class from the front of the room with a book in hand, orally quizzing the pupils on page after page of the assignment, occasionally interspersing comments of his own to amplify the text. Pupils raise their hands and give answers as they recall them from the book. They strive to figure out the teacher's "system" of calling upon pupils. Their experience is one of memorizing facts, interpreting an author's meaning, outguessing the teacher, accepting the written or spoken word as truth, and accepting one person's point of view as final.

The careful examination of facts, testing of hypotheses, and independent inquiry and discovery needed for intellectual stimulation still occurs too infrequently in secondary school classrooms providing general education. The type of curriculum described above is a far cry from one that promotes scientific inquiry: weighing of information, suspending judgment, using many sources of data, reasoning from facts, and arriving at sound conclusions.

The use of sources other than the textbook is often confined to reports assigned by the teacher, for which the information is gathered from reference books and encyclopedias. Laboratory work in the sciences may consist of filling in manuals on experiments already laid out for the pupil. Few people in the school or the community may be questioned as to their opinion on the problem. There may be more copying than weighing of information.

ATTENTION TO APPRECIATION AND INTERESTS. Any subject taught in high school has opportunities for enjoyment, for fascinating and stimulating experiences, for extending interests. In too many instances, however, pupils are glad to "finish that course." New avenues, new interests in science in the world about them, have failed to be stimulated in an area full of possibilities. Wide reading about the world of today in social studies, or extended participation, reading, curiosity, and investigation in any area may be something that the teacher does not do and, consequently, cannot inspire his pupils to such ends.

In English classes there is a diminishing amount of minute analysis of literary selections, a practice that for many pupils ends forever the desire to read anything literary. Yet, including only certain classics as required study for everyone is prevalent, increasingly in condensed form. Pupils may not enjoy them but at least they should be exposed to them. Hundreds of fascinating and illuminating books go unread on library shelves because every class has thirty copies of one book instead of thirty different selections.

In glee clubs, more popular songs and folk music are being included. People like to sing for the sheer joy of singing. The bands, orchestra, and choruses are a unique contribution of American secondary education. In the area of music, there are appreciation classes where the mass experience may not produce the desired end of enjoyment of music in all of its forms.

In arts and crafts at the secondary level, emphasis frequently will be on perfection of the product judged by adult standards. This emphasis has enabled those with artistic abilities to derive pleasure from this creative medium, but it has left out the majority of pupils. Where stress has been placed on self-expression in the arts and crafts, all pupils have been able to participate to the benefit of their personal development.

EDUCATION FOR PHYSICAL FITNESS. In some schools, the quality experiences in recreation and physical activity are the privilege of the gifted few. Physical development and recreational skills and interests are closely related to mental health, especially in a society in which tension, hurry, and worry are characteristics of many people's daily occupations. In the increasing pressures for intellectual achievement, the time for developing the ability and desire to play may suffer serious losses.

Physical education has never had the prestige of some other subjects. Schools tend to give only half or quarter unit credits, instead of one credit as in other subjects, for an equal amount of time spent in physical education classes. In the small high schools, untrained teachers often are assigned these classes in addition to their regular classwork. In such classes, pupils may spend most of their time playing basketball or softball, and little attention is given to systematic development of recreational skills, bodily coordination, exercise, balanced physical development, and testing of growth. The fluctuation in emphasis from formal to extremely informal activities has served to give pupils going through high school at different times a different type of experience. The physical fitness emphasis during World War II served to improve the physical education program.

The practice still prevails of giving a disproportionate amount of staff time to interscholastic teams, with relatively less time and effort spent on intramural activities. This situation is particularly true in smaller high schools. In other words, those pupils who need special attention the most receive the least. High school pupils may become more familiar with group games that have little carry-over value than with games that can be easily participated in by adults, such as tennis, golf, badminton, or handball.

IMPLEMENTATION OF THE PRINCIPLES

The accounts in this section of what is happening in the fore-front are by no means intended to be all-inclusive examples of good practices in schools. Since specialized education often is a study of a subject at greater depth as an extension of general education, most of the examples of what is happening to the study of content in general education apply also to the more specialized and advanced phases of these subjects.

Content is changing appreciably in a number of fields, especially in mathematics and science, which as we have noted are becoming more frequently required in the senior high school as common learnings. One of the noteworthy changes in content in such fields as the sciences, the fine arts, and English is that there are fewer absolutes. Facts are more open ended since new discoveries may rapidly disprove some of the staid old theories; rules and regulations propounded when knowledge was in an earlier stage of development are found to be wanting; beauty is regarded as being governed by more than form and convention. Actually, these changes represent a profound revolution, which has not yet significantly affected the secondary school curriculum except in a few areas. When it does, the quality of experiences of a large number of students will be greatly enhanced. Some movement in that direction is portended by these illustrations.

The content is discussed in relation to the experience that pupils have in dealing with it. Note in the succeeding pages how the change in content is usually a change in the way facts that have previously existed are ordered and used. Studying mathematics or English to derive meanings and promote logical reasoning is a different way of looking at and using the subject. It makes for an entirely different kind of experience than does beginning with memorizing rules, tables, and formulas. These exciting changes in content mean a more stimulating experience for pupils.

CONTENT THAT DEALS WITH CONCEPTS AND PRINCIPLES. Students in an increasing number of high school classes are dealing with the basic principles of the subject and gathering information to arrive at generalizations. In the social sciences will be found many examples of the subject being studied from the standpoint of arriving at principles governing man's relationships and his relations to his environment. This has been particularly true in the courses in problems of democracy, in core classes, and in the teaching of geography in relation to its effect on the culture.

It is in the newer developments in the fields of the sciences and mathematics that the content stresses concepts and ideas. The recent significant changes in physics, biology, and chemistry, which are described under the next heading in this section of the chapter, show a definite trend toward teaching for understandings growing out of laboratory experiences.

The new courses in physics and chemistry aim at the development of understanding of conceptual patterns basic to these fields. Laboratory work is more of the experimental and problem-solving type to achieve these broader objectives. The President's Science Advisory Committee, a group of scientists, engineers, and educators appointed by President Eisenhower, stated that "education in science should have the objective of creating some understandings of how and why of observable phenomena and the methods of science itself." [5]

The *What Research Says to the Teacher* series, in the pamphlet on science, illustrates the development of generalizations, as follows:

> In and of themselves, however, facts should not be considered the ultimate objectives. The ultimate objective is an understanding of the generalization which makes clear the relationship of a number of facts to the interpretation of a natural phenomenon. For example, there are many incidents in which one animal may be observed eating some form of plant. There are many incidents in which one specific animal may be observed eating or otherwise using another animal to maintain itself. One may read that green plants use carbon dioxide in manufacturing food. Furthermore, one may read, or observe thru indirect means, that human beings give off carbon dioxide as a waste product. Each of these may be considered a fact of science and possibly an interesting fact. But these facts individually have little meaning or significance in understanding the environment, or in solving problems related to use of our biotic resources. On the other hand they can have meaning when, thru guided learning experiences, they are related to an important generalization of biology: Living things are interdependent. This generalization in turn has significance when it is applied with understanding in making decisions regarding such questions as: Should we kill off the hawks in our community? [6]

In mathematics, the elements of modern mathematics introduced into the high school curriculum move away from manipulating symbols toward becoming aware of the abstractions denoted by the symbols. At the University of Maryland, a group of mathematicians and

[5] President's Science Advisory Committee, *Education for the Age of Science*, Washington, D.C.: The White House, 1959, p. 16.

[6] J. Darrell Barnard, *Teaching High-School Science*, What Research Says to the Teacher Series, No. 10, Washington, D.C., National Education Association, 1956, pp. 6–7.

educators have developed a new approach to teaching mathematics in junior high schools, referred to as UMMaP, an abbreviation for University of Maryland Mathematics Project.[7] The UMMaP course for the seventh and eighth grades, stresses the concept of a mathematical system, properties of numbers, the understanding of the concept of numbers as distinct from the symbols used to represent the numbers, elementary set theory in arithmetic as in geometry, and the ability to use concepts and principles of mathematics to explore new situations.

Emphasis on structure and "big" ideas is one of the fundamental changes in mathematics and the physical and biological sciences, which involves a new approach as much as it does new content.

CONTENT THAT LEADS TO DISCOVERY. The developments in the fields of mathematics, science, and to some extent in English and industrial arts, serve to illustrate the trend in selecting and dealing with content toward the ends of deriving meanings and developing skills of logical reasoning. One curriculum specialist has discussed the significant place of linguistic and symbolic processes in knowledge, indicating that

> Should this conception prevail in the secondary schools much more emphasis would be placed upon logic, language and mathematics than is done at the present time. But the new program of instruction would entail a different entrance to logic, a different analysis of language, and a different approach to mathematics than we have seen before. For one thing, the study of linguistic analysis and logical processes would be built into the content of the social sciences, natural sciences, mathematics, and English. These fields would then become more meaningful and intellectually stimulating.[8]

1. *In mathematics.* The work of the University of Illinois Committee on School Mathematics (UICSM), the University of Maryland Mathematics Project (UMMaP), and The School Mathematics Study Group (SMSG) represents the revision of secondary school mathematics around the logic of mathematics and mathematics as a way of thinking. The use of precise language for communication of the concepts of mathematics is considered basic to the goal of understanding mathematics in order to replace much of what has been rote learning. Modern mathematics emphasizes relatedness of various aspects of mathematics. In the junior high school materials of the UMMaP project, for example, there is no artificial separation of

[8] B. Othanel Smith, "Basic Issues in American Secondary Education—1956," in *Frontiers of Secondary Education I,* Paul M. Halverson, ed., Syracuse: Syracuse University Press, 1956, p. 21.

[7] Similar types of projects have been developed at the University of Illinois Committee on School Mathematics Project and by the School Mathematics Study Group at Yale University.

algebra and arithmetic. Students are also led to make discoveries for themselves.

Such topics as properties of numbers, the concept of a mathematical system, mathematical structure, sets, intuitive geometry, and probability and statistics are included in the materials developed by these groups. Course materials which are mathematically sound and in accord with the developments in modern mathematics have been prepared as text materials for schools, tested in schools, and evaluated.

For example, the SMSG publication for junior high school grades seven and eight includes as the first five chapters: What is Mathematics? Numeration, Whole Numbers, Non-Metric Geometry, and Factoring and Primes.[9] The UMMaP materials for the seventh grade contain several topics, described as follows:

> Much of the traditional content of the seventh-grade course in mathematics is also a part of UMMaP's Mathematics for the Junior High School, First Book, but like the material on language is approached from a new point of view. No longer do we need achieve only skill in manipulating with numbers. In addition, the junior high school student is given the opportunity to recognize that the number systems we use are structured like any mathematical system, regardless of the nature of its elements. With this in mind, the Maryland course has, at its core, the concept of a mathematical system. Approximately one-third of the text concerns itself directly with this important idea. The four units which cover the topic are titled. PROPERTIES OF NATURAL NUMBERS, MATHEMATICAL SYSTEMS, THE NUMBER SYSTEM OF ORDINARY ARITHMETIC, and THE SYSTEM OF INTEGERS UNDER ADDITION. In the unit on Properties of Natural Numbers, the student is introduced informally to the three parts in the structure of a mathematical system, and to the language necessary for communicating about the system. A somewhat more formal treatment is used in the unit on Mathematical Systems, in which systems whose elements are not numbers are considered. With this background the students are ready to set up a mathematical system using the numbers of ordinary arithmetic (whole numbers, fractions) as the elements. Finally, in the unit on the System of Integers, the students are presented with the development of more rigorous definitions of operations and more rigorous proofs for the properties of the system. A more detailed description of the unit of Properties of Natural Numbers may serve to clarify the student's introduction to this concept.
>
> The three parts in the structure of a mathematical system consist of
> 1) definition of the elements of the set we wish to use
> 2) definition of the operation or operations we wish to use
> 3) proof that the elements and the operations have certain properties associated with them.[10]

[9] School Mathematics Study Group, *Mathematics for Junior High School*, Vol. I (Part I), rev. ed., New Haven, Connecticut: Yale University, 1960, 188 pp.

[10] Helen M. Garstens, M. L. Keedy, and John R. Mayor, "University of Maryland Mathematics Projects," *The Arithmetic Teacher*, 7:61-65, February, 1960. See also University of Maryland Mathematics Project, *Mathematics for the Junior High School*, College Park, Maryland: College of Education, University of Maryland, 1959, 318 pp.

All of this represents a new point of view in the way of looking at mathematics, the keynotes of which are discovery and understanding.

2. *In science.* Many high school students are having experiences that deal with discovery and understanding relationships in their science classes as a result of a number of projects for developing new classroom materials, spearheaded by scientists and scientific organizations. The pattern in these projects is generally one in which the scientists and competent teachers work together in preparation of materials and then test them in a number of pilot schools. One of these projects is that of the Physical Sciences Study Committee, which prepared radically different course materials to bring the subject up to date. Rational thought and analysis are stressed. Text materials, films, laboratory apparatus, manuals, tests, and booklists for additional reading were developed. Concepts of modern physics are included, such as theories of the atom, light, and energy.

The Biological Sciences Curriculum Study of the American Institute of Biological Sciences has prepared textbooks, laboratory manuals, and teachers' guides, which stress the development of major concepts and an understanding of the method of scientific inquiry. A laboratory block program provides for laboratory experiences in depth through six-week projects. In areas such as plant and animal growth and development, an integrated set of experiences are centered around the problem area through laboratory work, class discussion, and reading.

In the field of chemistry, the Chemical Bond Approach Project and the Chemical Education Material Study attempt a new approach to the introduction to the field. They are characterized by a more logical approach and a stronger base in experiments integrated with the text. Emphasis is placed on the experimental nature of chemistry. The nature of the Chemical Bond Approach course is described as follows:

In these chapters the student is presented with some examples of chemical reactions. In Chapter II particular emphasis is given to some of the kinds of observations that a chemist is interested in exploring. The student is introduced to equation writing as a shorthand device for describing chemical change. Throughout the discussion there is a point of view that a chemical change presents an intellectual problem whenever one asks how to understand what happens. In the laboratory several of the early experiments deal with what is called the "black box." This is first presented as an actual box with invisible contents to be described. Succeeding experiments are concerned with a variety of chemical reactions; in which one of the points made is that chemicals are similar to the black box, and the chemist observes their behavior in the laboratory, but tries to interpret this in terms of particles and processes concealed from direct view but susceptible to logical analysis.[11]

There are three noteworthy characteristics of these new course materials for secondary schools: (1) They contain the most recent content, such as advances in biochemistry, modern theories of the origin and evolution of the universe, atomic and nuclear theories, relativity, exploration of oceans, atomic-molecular nature of substances, concepts of behavior in terms of atomic theory; (2) they begin with an experimental approach to laboratory science in which the student makes discoveries for himself rather than follows the cookbook-recipe type of laboratory manual; and (3) they represent a new interest on the part of scientists in using their talents and knowledge to prepare high school study materials.

    3. *In English.* In a relatively few English classes, attention is given to linguistics, the structure of the English language including its phonology, morphology, and syntax. Analysis of the changing nature of the language, rather than a ready-made set of rules, becomes the focus for the basis of understanding the language structure and speech patterns. The linguistic approach of a descriptive analysis of the structure of a sentence and presentation of language as a structure or system of patterns provides more of an experience in discovery and study of relationships. A recent survey of The English language arts in secondary schools, found in the analysis of courses of study that recent courses of study in language arts seem to be moving away from propaganda analysis to a study of elementary semantics and the nature of language. Separate units of this type are to be found in bulletins produced by curriculum committees in Portland, Oregon; Rochester, New York; Tulare County, and Long Beach, California; Seattle, Washington; and the states of Iowa, New Jersey, and Minnesota; and other places.

    English teachers in California reported using composition assignments to help students develop ideas; evaluate ideas; learn processes of good thinking (criticizing generalizations, understanding the nature of rationalization, logical fallacies, ordering and arranging ideas, summarizing, studying how words affect thinking).[12]

    4. *In industrial arts.* Working with the University of Maryland's Department of Industrial Education, the Montgomery Hills Junior High School, Montgomery County Public Schools, Maryland, has

---

[11] *CBA Newsletter,* No. 8, Richmond, Indiana: Chemical Bond Approach Project, Earlham College, Nov., 1960, p. 1.

[12] M. E. Mushlitz and Others, *Practices in Teaching Composition in California Public High Schools,* Bulletin, Vol. XXVII, No. 5, Sacramento, California: State Department of Education, June, 1958, p. 5.

developed an industrial arts research laboratory in which students select a problem of interest that is solved through experimental procedures. The student determines the necessary approach, builds the apparatus needed, probes deeply into literature dealing with the research, and performs the experiment. This is a laboratory patterned after the research conducted in industrial processes. Such high level research as the following has been performed by these ninth graders: testing radio amplifiers under different temperatures, testing the effects of acids on woods, testing floor finishes under different conditions, experimenting with high-frequency induction heating, testing missile design for drag, testing movement of a rocket by camera. As background to these experiments pupils read widely in the pertinent areas of science.

CONTENT THAT DEALS WITH ANALYSIS OF SOCIAL ISSUES. In the classrooms of secondary schools where effective learning takes place, teachers realize that the adolescent's world is full of significant events, startling discoveries, and difficult problems. He lives in an environment of television, radio, newspapers, magazines, travel, the family, organizations, and expanding contacts with people. These teachers have learned to utilize this extraordinary potential for learning.

Classes in American history and world history study such problems as labor unions and their place in the improvement of living conditions, going back into history to throw light on conditions that exist today. The geographical facts about such a country as China, are studied to help clarify the development of its peoples, its institutions, its status today as a nation, and the question of the recognition of Communist China. The question of civil rights for all people in the United States involves a study of the Negro, his place in early southern society, the part played by Negroes in the reconstruction of the South, the tough issues of desegregation, and additional facts which generally have to be searched out from sources other than textbooks.

Courses in social problems study issues facing the United States in the last half of the twentieth century. A course dealing with contemporary world history, geography, and problems at Renton High School, Renton, Washington, organized on a problems approach basis, included such units as "The United States and World Affairs," "The Communist World," "The Conflict Is Global," "Science, Race, and Religion—Key Factors in Foreign Policy," "Man's Hope for Peace."

In the Hartford, Connecticut, public schools, high school students use a pamphlet developed in cooperation with The Greater Hartford Council on Economic Education, which discusses the water, mineral, soil, and human resources as they apply to the state or region. Some of the concerns regarding human resources are these:

Can we eliminate disease?

Can we establish freedom from want and fear of war?

Can the moral and spiritual values of our democratic society be made secure against the forces of delinquency?

Can we build attitudes toward our fields, forests and streams which will keep them good for man's use and enjoyment?

Will we provide educational opportunity for all the children of all the people?

Can all persons be given the kind of education best suited to make them productive members of society?

Will prejudice and class hate be conquered?

Will man have enough self-control and wisdom to use his knowledge of science to serve, rather than destroy mankind?

Will our laws, education, and way of life continue to release and develop the creative imagination and inventive genius of our people? Will our gifted children find opportunity to develop and use their talents? [13]

Units on current problems taught in the high school in Springfield, Vermont, include issues such as housing legislation and the outlawing of the Communist party. Pupils follow the elections, studying the policies of the parties and the speeches of the candidates. Among economic problems studied are crop price support and farm surpluses, developments in the price situation, and reasons for price increases. The group follows United States foreign policy in such matters as our attitudes toward China, the work of the United Nations, and the political and economic policies of the Soviet Union. A considerable amount of historical background necessarily is brought into the study of these questions.

One of the significant shifts in content in social studies classes is the increasing amount of attention devoted to the newer nations of Asia and Africa and Latin America, the international problems created by the surge for freedom in the former colonial areas of the world, and the cold war situation as it relates to the struggle for ideological control of these countries. Units on "Far East and India" and "Africa—South of the Sahara" are included in world history classes in Phoenix, Arizona, high schools. In a bulletin, *Curriculum*

[13] Ralph E. Keirstead, *We Look to Our Future*, Hartford, Connecticut: Hartford Public Schools, 1956, p. 39.

Suggestions and Teaching Aids for World Cultures, published by the Pennsylvania Council for the Social Studies, the major portion of the bulletin is devoted to non-western cultures, such as, the Soviet Union, China, Japan, India, Southeast Asia, The Islamic World, and Africa.

The problems facing the nation and the individual consumer are being given considerable attention in social studies classes. Topics such as these are studied: international significance of economic policy, issues relating to economic growth, monetary policy, economic security, financial institutions, investments, housing, protecting the consumer, the national income and national debt, credit, and the role of government in the utilization of natural resources. The Joint Council on Economic Education, the National Committee for Education in Family Finance, the Commission for the Advancement of Secondary Education of the National Association of Secondary-School Principals, and the Commission on Education for Economic Competence have been working to develop better teacher understanding of this field and materials for use by teachers.

Some of the issues that have been studied in the Portland, Oregon, public schools include: Should the city of Portland provide for its own system of collecting refuse from homes? How do propaganda and pressure groups influence our thinking on controversial issues? Should our civil liberties be restricted? Considerable attention is given to analysis of propaganda and the concepts of critical thinking about issues.

One of the issues studied in social studies classes at Norwich Free Academy, Norwich, Connecticut, is communism. Pupils do research in the different ideologies. The meaning and advantages of democracy are examined. The historical backgrounds of the Russian people, their experiences in thought control, the amount of democracy existing or lacking, and the present relations of our country with Russia form a part of the class research.

Projects such as the Citizenship Education Project at Teachers College, Columbia University, have helped teachers to focus on real live issues. Basic premises and goals are identified for American society. A card index of resource books and references is cross-referenced to the basic premises. In addition, teachers are provided with a resource file of laboratory practices that involve getting first-hand information and suggesting ways for dealing with the issues. Four basic ideas govern the citizenship laboratory practices:

1. It deals with real situations and issues, not make-believe or mock ones.
2. The students get information at firsthand, sometimes from books and

materials, sometimes by making a survey, sometimes by personal interviews or a field trip.

3. The practice should illustrate and illuminate one or more of the basic premises of democratic society.
4. Students take action.[14]

CONTENT THAT EXAMINES VALUES. The classes in general education fields in some secondary schools are attempting to combat the rather disconcerting picture presented by some studies that (1) indicate there were no significant differences between the values held by ninth-grade students and those held by twelfth-grade students.[15] or (2) report that "the adolescent prefers to be wrong with his gang or his peers rather than right with his parents and the adult world" and that high school students' beliefs on important current issues showed a "political and economic naïveté" and a "strong tendency toward group conformity and authoritarianism and repression of civil liberties." [16]

These classes deal with issues that are not only live but are "hot" issues in the state or local community. They examine critically the opinions and the facts concerning the federal government's relations with state government in school desegregation, anti-Semitic practices, the question of fair trade laws, corruption in elections, fluoridation of the city water supply, water pollution, wire tapping and other devices that may impinge on freedoms, censorship of books and movies, oil-depletion tax allowances, or any other public issue on which an intelligent citizen needs to be informed. They examine but do not propagandize. Students are encouraged to arrive at their own conclusions, which may or may not agree with those of the power structure of the community.

Obviously, these conditions of freedom of inquiry into the values held by various community groups exist only where courageous administrators support courageous teachers, and in turn are supported by parents who care enough about the thoughtful kind of citizens they want their sons and daughters to become. In conditions where parents are content with "suburbia-mindedness," "togetherness," and "other-directed values" for their children such open examination of values held by social groups has rough sledding indeed.

[14] Victor E. Pitkin, "Youth Development and Democratic Citizenship Education," in *Citizenship and a Free Society: Education for the Future* (30th Yearbook), Franklin Patterson, ed., Washington, D.C.: National Council for the Social Studies, 1960, p. 53.

[15] J. W. Getzels, "The Problem of Values, Value Change, and Personal Identity in Education: Some Recent Studies," in *Frontiers of Secondary Education IV*, Paul M. Halverson, ed., Syracuse: Syracuse University Press, 1960, p. 34.

[16] William C. Kvaraceus, "Tomorrow's Youth and Tomorrow's Citizens," in *Citizenship and a Free Society: Education for the Future, op. cit.*, p. 21.

Classes where pupils have a high quality experience also look at questions even closer to home. These are the personal values that pupils themselves hold about sex and marriage, about conflicts within a family, and about their philosophy of life. These are serious-minded discussions on an intellectual rather than an emotional level. They are a far cry from the innocuous discussions regarding dating and boy-girl relations led by some ill-informed teachers who have little concept of what they are attempting to do through such topics.

The learning situations which are structured in such a manner as to admit all children's values are of an unusually high order. Values are brought in to be examined in these situations, not to be condoned. They exist in a number of schools where the many questions relating to public policy, to human rights, and to the individual's concerns are accorded a significant place in the content of general education.

CONTENT THAT LEADS TO SOCIAL ACTION. Obviously, only some of the content of a secondary school curriculum will lend itself to taking action for the social good of either the school community or the community as a whole. Much of the content in general education is theoretical and informational in nature. Teachers know that it is difficult to have the study of civic problems lead to some action. In a curriculum where school and community problems may never arise, action as an end result is inconceivable.

But accounts of social action initiated through classes show that going further than reading about a problem is not an impossibility in a secondary school. During the war years, community service activities were sometimes given school credit in the high school program. School work camps have been successfully placed in areas where the underprivileged could be helped or run-down buildings could be restored. The pupils in the camp study about the social problems of the people and the institution or community with which they work, as an integral part of the camp experience.

Service activities to school and community often originate in classes through the insight of good teachers. School ground beautification projects are one example of this type. In Hanson High School, Hopkins County, Kentucky, a community recreation program developed from a discussion in the home economics class, as a result of which the girls realized the need for community recreational opportunities for themselves and adults. A recreation club was organized to develop a year-round recreational program.

In West Junior High School, Kansas City, Missouri, the housing situation was surveyed through the core classes in the ninth grade. The classes took pictures of houses in the community, met with the congressman for the district, and furnished him with information to use in his support of the housing bill in Congress. Junior high school pupils in this case took action for improved social conditions on a national scale.

In the Indianapolis public schools students completing home nursing classes are given a Red Cross Nursing Certificate. They volunteer for civil defense work in their community and are assigned a medical treatment station, where they report in case of disaster.

At Bedford Junior High School, Westport, Connecticut, a cooperative study by a ninth-grade English and a seventh-grade social studies class was carried on. Their objective was to modify the student government organization in the school. Trips were taken to other schools to study government, student council members were interviewed, and other data gathered. Recommendations were made to the administration and to the students in an assembly.

CONTENT THAT USES COMMUNICATION SKILLS. Many fine experiences are being provided for pupils in the language arts. Units in English or in core classes form the basis for development of communication skills. There are many occasions for reading, expressing one's thoughts orally, writing one's ideas, and listening with understanding. This is the functional approach to teaching these skills. In classes using this approach, there are informal class discussions of literature read or topics investigated. Panels and forums furnish plenty of opportunities for learning the skills of speaking. There is opportunity for oral reading in audience situations, for dramatization, for individual reporting, for conversation, and for planned programs given before school and community groups. Radio skits, minutes of class meetings, booklets, diaries, articles for the school paper, and summaries, all form an integral part of classroom study.

In these situations, the pupils deal with the mechanics of writing or speech in order to write a letter, organize a report, or give a speech before an assembly. The modern language arts classes organize writing and speaking about real-life situations. Topics to be investigated must be organized, developed in writing, or presented orally to the class. People must be interviewed, many kinds of books must be read, explanations need to be made, and letters must be written to ask for information or to thank visitors for the class.

Instruction in English usage is based upon needs as shown by standardized tests and subsequent individualized study of the weaknesses recognized. Spelling instruction grows out of the writing that pupils do for the class. Punctuation is related to the writing that is required to be done.

Speaking skills are a part of the class instruction with practice received both through class activities and through opportunities to speak at school assemblies, class meetings, and service clubs and other community organizations. Modern instructional media such as tape recorders are used to help pupils improve their enunciation, articulation, and quality and tone of voice. Many pupils are given special assistance with speech difficulties, using speech clinics where available.

Listening and viewing skills, too, have become important in language arts. Pupils learn to set standards of judgment for television and radio programs, motion pictures, and recordings. These experiences in listening are in turn tied in with the speaking and writing activities that pupils do.

The increase in the number of secondary schools having remedial or developmental reading programs has been rapid in recent years. In Illinois, for example, 64 per cent of the high schools in 1959 provided special reading instruction.[17] Organized reading programs are found more frequently in junior high schools than in senior high schools. Such programs include teaching skills in vocabularly, comprehension, speed of reading, skimming, outlining, interpreting what is read, using source materials, adjusting reading to purpose and type of materials used, locating main ideas.

Matilija Junior High School, the Norhoff Union High School District, California, alternates with science by semesters a developmental reading class in the seventh and eighth grades. At Washington Junior High School, Pasadena, California, any pupil of normal intelligence whose reading achievement is two years or more below his capability and who desires to improve his reading is given opportunity to do so. The duration of specialized reading instruction depends on the need and the progress of improvement. Lakewood, Ohio, High School has a reading center which pupils use during their study periods. No credits are given. The program is designed to help the pupil become a better reader in all kinds of material. (See Chapter 18 for further examples).

The Valley Regional High School in Deep River, Connecticut, has a program in reading under the direction of a reading consultant. The consultant assists teachers with procedures and materials designed to develop the reading ability of each student to its maximum. An in-service program directed by the consultant provides teachers on the secondary level with the background needed by

[17] M. Dale Baughman, "Special Reading Instruction in Illinois Junior High Schools," *Bulletin of the National Association of Secondary-School Principals,* 44:91, November, 1960.

them to provide their students with needed instruction in reading skills.

CONTENT THAT DEALS WITH CONCERNS OF YOUTH. Youth are given a chance to discuss with qualified teachers, school nurses, and doctors the results of medical examinations, diet in relation to health, questions regarding posture and appearance, clothing and health, body changes, body structure and function, and rest and sleep. Some of these experiences are in health classes; others, in biology classes; still others are offered through physical examinations and through conferences. Physical education programs pay attention to individual needs for exercise, recreation, and rest. Achieving physical fitness is accomplished through visits to health centers; diagnosis by doctor and dentist; investigation of information on diseases, quack medicines, and one's habits of living. It includes learning first aid, participating in healthful outdoor and indoor recreational activities, and testing one's progress in bodily coordination and muscular development.

In home economics classes, pupils are studying home duties and family responsibilities. In some schools, the girls actually receive experiences in cooperatively managing a practice home owned by the school; in decorating rooms; and in planning, preparing, and serving meals to selected groups of outsiders. In some schools, homemaking classes learn child care through conducting nursery schools for parents in the community.

In River Rouge High School, River Rouge, Michigan, boys and girls are together in a twelfth grade class in home planning. Here the problems studied deal with banking and insurance, broken homes, buying and furnishing a home, food preparation, child development, preparation for marriage, and other topics. The Cloonan Junior High School in Stamford, Connecticut, gives girls, as well as boys, experiences in home repair of electrical apparatus, care of household machines, and simple tool skills needed for the upkeep of the house.

The Ohio State University School's core program has as one of its major units "Problems of the Family as a Basic Social Unit." In these classes, pupils consider the causes of family tensions and how these conflicts can be solved; the family budget; adequate housing; and ways of making family living happier. In the tenth-grade core classes, questions of concern to youth are discussed, such as: "How democratic is our school?" and "Does it matter what you think?" Class discussions deal with problems of growing up when cultural background conflicts with the prevailing culture and with problems faced by youth on going into adulthood.

A course on literature and psychology at Milne High School, Albany State College, New York, studies human behavior through literature. Units are included on how the family influences behavior, how physical conditions influence behavior, how social organizations modify behavior, and how emotional conflicts affect behavior. Students study the concepts of behavior in psychology and apply these concepts to the literature studied.

CONTENT THAT INVOLVES ENJOYMENT OF CREATIVE ARTS. One of the high quality experiences that are a part of all pupils' general education in many types of secondary school classes is the enjoyment of products of imaginative minds. These areas of content are the substance of what make life more worthwhile: literature, music, drama, dance, drawing, painting, sculpture, design, and crafts of various kinds. They represent the products of man's attempt through the ages to create the unique and the beautiful.

Secondary schools whose programs are rich in the arts and the humanities, in English, music, art, physical education, industrial arts, and other courses, stress in the content the cultivation of understanding and literacy in the arts, as a part of the sheer enjoyment of the art forms. Deepened interests, better standards of tastes, and appreciation are the ends sought.

Music as a part of general education in the junior high schools includes general music supplemented by interests groups such as instrumental groups, choral groups, theory, music literature, informal singing groups. The content emphasis on consumer music education involves participation through assembly programs and community singing and listening, music history, the relation of music to the culture of people. The musical experiences include a balance of activities designed to create enjoyment in music.

General music classes at Noah Wallace Junior High School, Farmington, Connecticut, combine singing and listening activities and provide for individual differences and tastes. A unit may terminate in the class performing a musical play for the school assembly. All pupils participate in such a production regardless of ability. Assemblies growing out of work in general music classes are also found at the Troup Junior High School, New Haven, Connecticut. The programs given include community singing, soloists, guest artists, and varied musical programs.

The study of literature in the English classes that have well-defined objectives for general education aims at understanding one's culture, one's self, and the emotions and feelings of humanity in general. Literary criticism for the student who has a deeper interest in literary form is used as an aid to understanding, not as a formalized analysis which is an end unto itself. Pupils examine the basic meanings of a literary work, the author's purpose and basic ideas, and his means of expressing ideas.

The ninth- and tenth-grade classes at Milwaukee, Wisconsin, public schools organize the study of literature around the adolescent's interests in sports, in science and invention, in adventure, in the desire to know people and places, in an attempt to understand himself and his home and community. The pupils read different types of literature centered around such topics as "Enjoying Adventure," "Learning to Know One's Self," and "Following the Progress of Science and Invention." Abundant reading materials on each topic are found in the classroom and in the library—novels, newspapers, magazines, drama, biography, poetry, travel books, and documents. Pupils have an opportunity to select from materials suited to their needs and interests.

In the Minneapolis senior high schools, the study of world heritage in twelfth-grade English classes aims at the understanding of other cultures and enjoyment of their literature. Blocks of content may include the great epics, sagas, myths which have become a part of world culture, the cultures of peoples as revealed through literature, appreciation of the classics, appreciation of literary forms, the great spiritual leaders of the world, and great single names in world literature and what they stand for.

A course in humanities, offered in the twelfth grade at Milne High School, Albany State College, combines English, art, and music. Selected literature, music, painting, and architecture are studied as to their form structure, medium, and content.

CONTENT THAT EMPHASIZES SELF-EXPRESSION AND NON-CONFORMITY OF IDEAS. We can find many examples of creative talents put to use in art classes and in creative writing in secondary schools with an enriched curriculum. In these classes, pupils produce remarkably good sketches, painting, designs, or short stories.

In many subjects teachers can be found who place emphasis on freeing the individual to express himself, to experiment, and to develop new ideas. A permissive atmosphere, found in such classrooms, gives the pupil a sense of security and a desire to explore. English teachers give due credit for any attempt at originality and inventiveness. Social studies teachers encourage pupils to develop original ideas for the solution of school and community problems and to use and develop whatever talents they have in contributing to a group project. In music classes, pupils write the words and compose the music for songs to be used in operettas. Art classes often join them in the staging and costuming, or English classes in writing the script.

Original pageants or plays are produced by English classes or jointly by several groups. Dances and skits are developed by pupils. Pupils receive the experience of leading the orchestra; vocal or instrumental groups arrange their own music and think out new ideas for performances. Home economics classes stress originality in making clothing, rather than merely copying patterns, or in arranging furniture and decorating the home. Physical education groups develop dances that express individuality. Pupils in crafts or industrial arts classes are inventive in design and the use of wood, leather, or metal. Such conditions are found in the classes of creative teachers who themselves are independent, well-informed thinkers, non-authoritarian, and sympathetic with originality.

Non-conformity is related to the freedom for generation of ideas. During the adolescent years, the peer-group pressures for conformity are high. Teachers in any field who value original thought and inventiveness are careful to avoid behavior that makes students feel comfortable and safe if they agree with the opinions of the teacher or the textbook writer. They give pupils an opportunity to develop their self-esteem in the classroom, and support them in their efforts to dispute the popular opinions held by the peer group. They help the pupil become more independent in ideas and in ways of working and to be self-critical of his work.

Conducive to originality are the types of independent study activities encouraged in secondary schools. Evanston Township High School, Evanston, Illinois, through its seminars emphasizes independent study by students who do research on subjects of their choice. Jefferson County, Colorado, in its senior high schools has used increased independent study effectively (see Chapter 8 for further discussion and examples).

ISSUES AND PROBLEMS

There are a number of fundamental issues in the decisions to be made regarding the general education provided for youth in secondary schools. In determining the kinds of content and the experiences with that content, those responsible for the decisions must take a stand on them.

1. *Should the content of the secondary school curriculum be in harmony with immediate or long-range aims?*

Thoughtful persons generally believe that the school curriculum should change to meet the changing social and technological needs. The question here is really one of whether curriculum change should be an adaptation of expediency. Should school leaders watch the way the wind blows in the field of curriculum and make changes in order to be in the swing of things? Or should they initiate continuous studies of curriculum in order that there may be a continual adaptation to changing times? A case in point is the air-age courses that schools were urged from many quarters to adopt during and following the last World War. Although the air age has had an effect on the curriculum and has changed concepts and materials, this did not necessitate the adoption of new courses.

School leaders need to decide to what extent the immediate manpower needs determine which academic talents to nurture. It may be that when the children now in school go through college and get into civic and professional life certain talents will no longer be used. A continuous attempt must be made to assess the changes in American life as related to the world-wide situation in order to develop long-range aims for the school program. It is disturbing to find some who interpret the need for more technically trained individuals, such as engineers and scientists, as providing a license for neglecting the matter of general education. For certainly, the problems of the future lie not only in keeping up with or surpassing Russia in technical know-how, but even more so in surpassing her in insight in adjusting peoples ways of living to the rapid technological expansion and in insight into the skills of human relations. General education that stresses the values, attitudes, and understandings necessary to deal with such complex issues and to live in the world of today is a solid base of secondary education from which the specialized learnings stem.

2. *Should the curriculum common to all pupils in secondary schools center exclusively around knowledge from the scholarly disciplines and the traditional skills or should it also include the current civic, avocational, and social problems and concerns that society and youth face?*

There are some who hold that any content which meets the test of high quality is derived from the classics, contained in great books written in the past, or organized in the same way as content studied by the scholar in the accepted academic fields. This is the type of content with status in the scholarly world. Its study disciplines the mind, is rigorous and challenging. Others believe that any field of content that is worth the time for study lends itself to scholarly examination. They argue that home economics, music, art, political science, and sociology provide equal opportunity for high quality experiences in creativity and research.

Involved in this issue is the question of what is needed to make decisions in an intensely competitive world in social and political values. Involved, too, is the matter of whom we are educating to participate in the decisions to be made with regards to colonialism, foreign aid, economic policy, or the care of the aged. If we are content to leave these decisions to a select few, we need not be concerned about the general education for the many. But who is to select the few?

Rigorous examination of the questions that are crying for solution in the adult world and those which the adolescent faces in his developmental tasks calls for stretching the mind as well as the imagination. The here and now furnish means for learning the ways of scientific inquiry. Then, too, the staggering proportion of mental illness, the growing juvenile delinquency, and the change in nature of the family solidarity point toward a need for helping youth deal with problems that are as bewildering to them as they are to adults.

Some hold that the schools should "return to the fundamentals." They feel that more attention should be paid in general education to skills in reading, spelling, writing, arithmetic as interpreted a half-century ago, and less, or none, to the civic, recreational, social, and the fine arts studies that are the newer aspects of a general education. The battle that newer subjects have fought against being considered as fads and frills is by no means ended.

3. *Should the general education for citizenship contain content in the area of safe questions or that which is admittedly argumentative and controversial?*

No doubt the teacher's role will be an easier one if he assigns problems for which the answers have already been found or which were burning issues many years ago. It is easy to discuss the American colonist's fight for freedom in schools in areas where struggles for freedom are still going on. Many questions that are studied in general education courses are not controversial. It is in the realm of "man's inhumanity to man" that teachers may fear to tread. The Golden's and the Schweitzer's are all too few among teachers.

Right answers are comfortable. It is not popular to be on the "wrong" side or in the minority. Consequently, it should behoove every teacher who wants to help youth deal with controversy on an intellectual rather than on an emotional basis, to give young people the experience of arguing with their fellows on the merits of social issues. The arguments on the side of safe issues are evidently convincing, for one can find many more examples of research on such issues than on the controversial kind. They tend to center on the school's relationship with and support by the community. Yet enlightened teachers, administrators, and community members have demonstrated that the difficult local and national issues can be dealt with in a way that invites neither catastrophe nor censure.

4. *Should general education in secondary school be considered important for all youth whatever their abilities, educational interests, and vocational goals may be, or should it be primarily for the average and slow-learning pupils?*

There are those who believe that specialization should begin early as a preparation for future careers in scientific research and in engineering, as well as for other kinds of intellectual pursuits. They would have secondary school pupils study mathematics, science, English, a foreign language or two, and history or geography each year. It is well and good to teach the fine and practical arts and physical and health education to the poor student and the non-academically talented, but these subjects would crowd out more important content for the college-bound student.

Others believe that this is not general education, since it is specialization for specific vocational-educational purposes, not preparation for living that has common purposes for all. It could be more appropriately termed vocational education when it is aimed toward preparation for a future profession.

This argument relates to the notion that certain subjects have a vested birthright of status which makes them of greater value for any purpose. Moreover, the intellectual rather than the aesthetic and practical holds high priorities. The assumption that pupils who do not go on to college have no intellectual interests, or that those who continue with their education in college do not need nor want any practical, civic, social, or aesthetic education, has no basis in fact.

5. *Should certain subjects, such as foreign languages and typing be included in the program of general education for all or be considered as specialized education?*

Traditionally, both of these subjects have been considered as specialized fields, not common skills and knowledge that all should possess for civic competence and personal enrichment. The question is an issue in junior high school: Should all pupils in seventh and eighth grade, for example, study a foreign language or should it be an honors course for superior pupils?

There are no clear-cut answers to this question. Languages are becoming more essential to people who by virtue of easy travel are close neighbors to others in foreign lands. But will all persons in the future have need of another language as a communication skill, not vocationally but personally and culturally? Will a point be reached in the near future where all secondary school pupils will have the opportunity to use another language in their daily lives?

Some junior high schools do consider foreign language as general education, requiring a language of all pupils. Some senior high schools are encouraging the average and slow pupils to elect a language for communication purposes.

The same type of questions can be raised about typing. Is it a communications skill essential for all? Certainly, it has become a skill extremely useful for increasing numbers of people in their daily living. It is open to question whether the skill is in all cases non-vocationally oriented, as for example, in its usefulness for a college education.

SELECTED REFERENCES

AMERICAN ASSOCIATION FOR THE ADVANCEMENT OF SCIENCE AND AMERICAN ASSOCIATION OF COLLEGES FOR TEACHER EDUCATION. *Improving Science and Mathematics Programs in American Schools.* Washington, D.C.: The Associations, 1960, 41 pp.— Report of a joint committee of these two organizations dealing with the status of science and mathematics in public schools and in teacher education.

ASSOCIATION FOR SUPERVISION AND CURRICULUM DEVELOPMENT. *What Shall the High Schools Teach?* (1956 Yearbook). Washington, D.C.: National Education Association, 1956, Chaps. 3-6.—Requirements for graduation, selection of curriculum content, general education in the high school, and the concept of general education.

CHASE, FRANCIS S. and ANDERSON, HAROLD A. (eds.). *The High School in a New Era.* Chicago: University of Chicago Press, 1958, Sections III and VII and pp. 197-213.— Several distinguished authors discuss their concepts for redirection of the high school curriculum and changes in the mathematics and science curriculum.

EDUCATIONAL SERVICES INCORPORATED. *Review of the Secondary School Physics Program of the Physical Science Study Committee.* Watertown, Mass.: Physical Science Study Committee, 1960. 47 pp.—Description of the program of preparation of materials for the course, materials available and the course itself.

JEWETT, ARNO. *English Language Arts in American High Schools.* U.S. Department of Health, Education, and Welfare, Office of Education, Bulletin 1958, No. 13. Washington, D.C.: Government Printing Office, 1959, 122 pp.—Current development in the language arts curriculum, grades 7–12, as revealed in courses of study.

KRUG, EDWARD A. *The Secondary School Curriculum.* New York: Harper & Brothers, 1960, Chaps. 14-19.—These chapters discuss curriculum trends in the fine and practical arts.

McLENDON, JONATHAN. *Teaching the Social Studies.* What Research Says to the Teacher Series, No. 20. Washington, D.C.: National Education Association, 1960, 33 pp.—A brief resume of typical offerings, trends within courses, social learnings, and special problems in social studies.

MILLS, LESTER C. and DEAN, PETER M. *Problem-Solving Methods in Science Teaching.* New York: Bureau of Publications, Teachers College, Columbia University, 1960, 88 pp.—A monograph of the Science Manpower Project describing the problem-solving technique in the biological, physical, and earth sciences. Specific examples showing how a teacher works with a class.

NATIONAL ASSOCIATION OF SECONDARY-SCHOOL PRINCIPALS. "English Language Arts in The Comprehensive Secondary School." *Bulletin of the National Association of Secondary-School Principals,* 44:45-48, October, 1960.—A position statement on language arts developed by the Association's Curriculum Planning and Development Committee.

NATIONAL ASSOCIATION OF SECONDARY-SCHOOL PRINCIPALS. "Health, Physical Education, and Recreation in the Secondary School." *Bulletin of the National Association of Secondary-School Principals,* 44:29-86, May, 1960.—Although most of this issue is devoted to administrative problems, this section deals with some aspects of content and issues in health and physical education. Prepared in cooperation with the American Association for Health, Physical Education, and Recreation.

NATIONAL ASSOCIATION OF SECONDARY-SCHOOL PRINCIPALS. "Quality Science for Secondary Schools." *Bulletin of the National Association of Secondary-School Principals,* 44:3-210, December, 1960.—The entire issue, prepared by a committee of the National Science Teachers Association, is devoted to science teaching in junior and senior high school. Much of it deals with content of newly developed courses in the science subjects.

NATIONAL ASSOCIATION OF SECONDARY-SCHOOL PRINCIPALS. "The Place of Science and Mathematics in the Comprehensive Secondary-School Program." *Bulletin of the National Association of Secondary-School Principals,* 42:5-12, September, 1958. A position paper on mathematics and science developed by the Association's committee. Recommends mathematics and science as a part of the general education of all pupils in junior high school.

NATIONAL COUNCIL FOR THE SOCIAL STUDIES. *Citizenship and a Free Society: Education for the Future.* (Thirtieth Yearbook). Washington, D.C.: National Education Association, 1960. Chaps. 5, 7, 9, 11, and 13.—Stresses education of the citizen for participation in government, economic effectiveness, intergroup relations, world responsibilities, and responsible individualism.

NATIONAL SCIENCE TEACHERS ASSOCIATION. *New Developments in High School Science Teaching.* Washington, D.C.: The Association, 1960, 108 pp.—This pamphlet describes practices regarding science classes in secondary schools throughout the country, information gathered and summarized by one of the Association's committees. Has a valuable list of where additional information can be secured regarding these practices. Supplements Section 3 of this chapter.

NATIONAL SCIENCE TEACHERS ASSOCIATION. *Planning for Excellence in High School Science.* Washington, D.C.: The Association, 1961, 67 pp.—A position statement of beliefs regarding the science program.

NATIONAL SCIENCE TEACHERS ASSOCIATION. *Quality Science for Secondary Schools.* Washington, D.C.: The Association, 1960. Chaps. 3-6.—Emphasis is on improvement of the quality program in science in junior and senior high schools. The new courses and developments in secondary school science are described.

NATIONAL SOCIETY FOR THE STUDY OF EDUCATION. *Development in and through Reading.* (Sixtieth Yearbook, Part I). Chicago: University of Chicago Press, 1961. Chaps. 17, 18.—Reading programs in junior and senior high schools.

NATIONAL SOCIETY FOR THE STUDY OF EDUCATION. *Rethinking Science Education.* (Fifty-ninth Yearbook, Part II). Chicago: University of Chicago Press, 1960, Chaps. 2, 5, 9, 10.—A compendium of information on developments in science, its status in the school, facilities, problems and issues, etc. These chapters are especially pertinent.

PRITZKAU, P. T. *Dynamics of Curriculum Improvement.* Englewood Cliffs, N.J.: Prentice-Hall, Inc., 1959, Chaps. 6, 8, 9, 15.—Challenging ideas are presented concerning values, value admission, ideas, and high level thinking in the curriculum.

SNADER, DANIEL W. "Secondary School Mathematics in Transition." *School Life,* 42:9-13, March, 1960.—An explanation of modern mathematics content as developed in various programs discussed in this chapter.

10

PROVISION FOR SPECIAL INTERESTS AND TALENTS

Every pupil in secondary school should have an instructional program planned for his own particular needs. He has special skills and interests of his own, like those of other pupils to be sure, but in some respects differing in degree and kind. They are the academic interests and verbal skills. They are the vocational skills that characterize the occupational pursuits of society. They are those rare qualities that make up an inventive genius or a creative writer. They are the avocational pursuits for the leisure hours. They may be science, drama, painting, music, photography, basketball, agriculture, or research, any area of pursuit through which the individual may fulfill his own personal development.

Experiences are of high quality only if they are differentiated for individual goals. This differentiation occurs both within the areas of curriculum that provide the general education for all pupils and within the more specialized areas of the curriculum such as business education, agriculture, distributive education, foreign languages, and trade and industrial education. But subjects in themselves are not special or general. They may serve both purposes, no matter what the subject field. Art, music, mathematics, and science are obvious examples of fields which may be both general education and specialized education. Specialized education is an extension of general education. In any subject field, a pupil can specialize in depth and can have experiences of a high intellectual quality. Thus, the examples of changes in content presented in the last chapter, such as in mathematics, apply to both general education and the more specialized education.

This chapter presents the principles, some common practices, and issues and problems; the next chapter gives the examples of programs for quality experiences for individual pupils. These two complementary chapters and Chapter 8, which discusses instructional approaches and teacher-pupil relations in the classroom, all relate to adapting instruction and curriculum to individual interests and abilities through procedures used, the content of the courses, the materials used, and the types of experiences and courses provided.

BASIC PRINCIPLES

The secondary school curriculum should provide youth the opportunity to discover and pursue their special interests and talents.

Although there are many opportunities for the exploration of individual interests in the elementary school, the secondary school years is a time when these interests can be deepened and explored. During this period of formal education, youth should have an opportunity to discover their genuine interests and special talents that may be followed either vocationally or avocationally. The boy with a scientific bent should find in the secondary school a sympathetic encouragement and definite guidance in pursuing this interest. The girl who wants to sing should find in the curriculum a chance to develop her talents. There should be no barriers to youth who have a keen desire to invent, experiment, or explore some area of the world's culture.

As soon as a secondary school restricts its program, either by reason of limited offerings or through a highly prescribed curriculum, it fails to consider that young people differ in interests. There must be opportunity for searching further than many wish to go into the areas of mathematics, science, languages, literature, the arts, and history in the total program of the school. No highly regimented atmosphere will suffice to give them these opportunities. Exploration of interests also lays the basis for an intelligent selection of an occupation. Many secondary school courses can serve such an exploratory function.

Equality of opportunity in the secondary school means provision of an optimum program for all kinds of abilities, backgrounds, and educational and vocational goals.

Do experiences that youth have in secondary schools serve to bring out their potential abilities—yes, even develop their idiosyncrasies as strengths in their personalities—or do they bury these potentialities in a mass production of mediocrity? Special attention and assistance must be given to the gifted in speech, the gifted in mechanical ability, the gifted in verbal ability, the gifted in bodily coordination, and the gifted in mathematical reasoning. It is well known that there are vast differences in abilities of individuals. How to provide a curriculum that will allow each individual to run at his top speed is less well known.

The self-realization of the pupil who is talented academically is accomplished only by giving him opportunities that allow maximum development of his potentialities. Equal opportunity for him means the freedom to move ahead of his peers. It does not mean, as some have contended, that he must necessarily study the same content, be at all times with pupils of various abilities, or follow the same schedule that others do.

The chance for youth with mechanical abilities must be as real as for those with special ability in verbalization. In order to care for these varied needs, the secondary school must offer not merely a variety of courses but a greatly expanded flexibility within all courses.

For the smaller high school, this principle means even greater flexibility within a number of courses, since the offerings must necessarily be fewer. It may be that for some pupils the school day should be altogether different from that of the student who is taking courses as we now conceive them.

The provision for the special needs of the academically talented or of the handicapped pupils is an application of the principle of individual differences in learning. The school that applies this principle to instruction realizes that the "academically talented" and the "mentally retarded" are but convenient labels to use in discussing a general kind of pupil. Talented or retarded students are by no means a homogeneous group. Differences in talent within the top 20 per cent may be as great as in a so-called "average" group. To lump a group in a given category by means of one or more tests and then forget about individuality is a disservice to society.

Moreover, there is nothing undemocratic about special opportunities for individuals. It is only when these opportunities are considered satisfied by fixed groupings that the principle of individuality so basic to a democratic society is violated.

The secondary school should concern itself with pupils of outstanding ability in any field of human endeavor as a source of talent and leadership.

However, academic talents are not the only special abilities that a democracy prizes. Leadership in human relations, social skills, and political inventiveness are crying needs in a complex world faced by ideological struggles and a surge for freedom among subjected peoples. Leadership in cultural advances in music, art, and literature are probably needed as never before to provide a rational balance to the race for superiority in science and technology.

Thus, the teacher of any subject should concern himself with discovery and the nurture of talents in that field. Industrial arts, business education, agriculture, and home economics are fields of man's pursuits in which there is opportunity for creativity, for research, and for leadership. In an increasingly technological world, the industrial processes should occupy a much more important place in the school curriculum. The problems of the world's food supply will require specialists in research and agriculture. Labor, economic planning, education, business organization—any field one wishes to name —demand a reservoir of skilled leadership and talents. In order that such a goal will be attained, however, the specialized subjects must change with the changing times. Industrial arts that occupies itself solely with making bookcases and footstools, or home economics centered around cooking and sewing, is as unrealistic as physics that ignores the developments in atomic theory. Each of these subjects could be exciting to the inquiring mind of the pupil who wants and is permitted to discover and explore the new concepts and processes.

The times require that secondary schools devote more time to academic, creative, and special talents. The demands of learned societies and civic groups are but a reflection of social change that is propelled with increasing velocity.

The secondary school should provide for the special needs of handicapped youth who can profit from an education beyond the elementary school.

Most of the things that have been said about the talented pupil apply equally to the handicapped. The different kinds of handicaps —visual, auditory, mental, physical, and emotional—may be interwoven and extremely complex. The physically handicapped child may have become emotionally maladjusted, or he may be a mental genius. Visual handicaps may cause a youngster to appear mentally retarded. A Helen Keller obviously is a mentally gifted person. Yet how many schools are staffed to fulfill the potentialities of such an individual?

For the severely mentally retarded, the elementary school can provide all of the formal education that these children are capable of assimilating. But for the many who are retarded but able to learn social, civic, and manual skills, and to a lesser degree the verbal skills, the secondary school can provide for their special needs. The blind, partially sighted, deaf, hard of hearing, speech handicapped, crippled, brain injured, and the emotionally disturbed can be helped to become productive, contributing citizens through special services and specialized teachers who work with these pupils at least part of the day. Again, the principle of differentiation of experiences and content should be applied, geared to the rate of learning and the learning difficulty which may exist.

Any type of administrative or instructional device used for special groups of pupils should be judged by its effect on the quality of the learning experiences and the educational purposes that it serves.

The question of whether acceleration, enrichment, or special grouping should be the means by which the school provides for the gifted does not really get at the heart of the matter. For these are names we have invented for administrative or instructional devices. They do not describe the quality of experiences that pupils have if they are in accelerated or special groups or in regular classes where "enrichment" is practiced. Nor are they mutually exclusive. Unless the special honors class has an enriched curriculum, the grouping serves only the purpose of putting an elite group together for teaching. What really matters is the content taught to this group, the challenges presented, the opportunities to explore the unknown and the abstract. The alert, well-informed teacher can give high quality experiences in whatever organization the school happens to have for instructional purposes.

This is not to say that administrative devices cannot serve educational purposes. They can and do. It is not the device itself, but rather the use made of it as an opportunity to enrich experiences that counts. Putting pupils into advanced mathematics or foreign language classes are grouping devices to further instruction. Yet, many school leaders act as though a special class formed for a particular group ends their responsibility toward that group. Actually, it is only the beginning. For once a special group is formed, the administrator and the teacher are challenged to see that the experiences given to this group are *special*. The same old content and teaching procedures no longer will fit.

The educational experiences of the superior student should be characterized by intellectual stimulation and freedom to explore ideas.

Throughout this discussion the term "talented" or "gifted" is used to refer to talents in any field. The "academically talented" qualifies the term as applied to a general group with special abilities in learning verbal materials and abstractions. The "able learner" refers to the same group, defined by some educators as the top 15 to 20 per cent of the nation's school population in ability to master concepts in the academic fields. The "intellectually gifted" generally is used to define those in the top 1 to 3 per cent who are similarly endowed.

The child of superior academic talents is not a different species. He is different only in the degree to which he can master what is required to be learned in school. He tends to be superior also in physical ability and in personal adjustment.

The kinds of experiences planned for the academically talented or gifted should be, above all, intellectually stimulating. He should be encouraged to advance in a field to the extent of his capabilities. For some, this may mean studying content at a level of difficulty ordinarily associated with the college curriculum. Such encouragement can best be given in an atmosphere in which the student is free to read, explore, and experiment in the realm of ideas on his own, with a minimum of restrictions which cause him to perceive school as a place that limits his inventiveness. There are promising practices discussed in this book which allow such freedom. Others undoubtedly have not yet been conceived of as devices by which pupils may make individual progress; they may have little relation to credits, classes, or acceleration by advancement through school "years" or "units" more rapidly.

Education for specialized vocational needs of pupils in the secondary school should deal with occupational areas, be related to community needs, and be closely related to their use on the job.

It is the function of the secondary school to prepare some youth for entrance into vocations, but the curriculum would be hopelessly regimented, and the costs tremendously high, if specific vocational education were given for the many types of occupations into which these high school pupils are certain to go. Studies have indicated that specific vocational skills are common to many types of related jobs since the vast majority of jobs require no formal training. Vocational education at the secondary school level should prepare for fields of occupations and develop skills useful in a variety of jobs.

It is generally agreed by educational authorities and by employers that the vocational education offered by the schools should be of a broad nature, stressing attitudes and work habits as well as specific skills. Employers want people who can take responsibility, who will be interested in improving themselves on the job. Good health and recreational habits and an understanding of working conditions are considered important. The skills demanded are those that belong to families of occupations, such as typewriting, and shorthand skills for a large number of clerical jobs, or knowledge of farming and ability in farm practices for a large number of related jobs in the field of agriculture. Many employers and labor unions prefer to have the training in particular skills given on the job through apprenticeship.

Youth who plan to go directly into community occupations from the secondary school can profit by some opportunity to work in the community as a planned part of their education for vocation. These job experiences can give the training in skills that cannot be provided by the school. The necessary equipment is available in the shop or place of business. Moreover, the real situation is provided. Contacts with people must be made, production schedules must be met, or customers must be satisfied. Proper work habits can be developed through actual performance.

The advance of the beginning employment age is an important social trend. Employers prefer more mature individuals. Trade union restrictions as well as employment practices tend to raise the age of entrance into employment. These are but manifestations of social changes such as a gradual increase in the average age of the population and the mechanization of industry, requiring fewer man-hours to perform a specific job. The restrictions on child labor through social legislation tend to prevent pupils from having these experiences before they are eighteen years of age. For youth, therefore, the learning of vocational skills needs to come near the time of transition from school to work. The young worker should be able to put them to use immediately on the job and receive further upgrading through part-time adult education programs conducted by high schools, junior colleges, or special adult schools.

As youth are placed on the job full time by a secondary school, the school still has a responsibility to assist these young people through evening classes, guidance services, and other means. Part of the experience of youth in education for vocation should be assistance in adjustment to the job and further skills training after full-time work has begun. To carry out such a program, a new concept of the secondary school is called for, one in which transition from school to work may be a gradual process without emphasis on graduation.

Even though most of the vocational courses should be placed in the later years of secondary school or in the junior college, the number of drop-outs before that time is not inconsequential. For them, the training in vocational skills would need to come earlier. It would seem to be sound to plan for this group opportunities to take classes in the evening or part time while they are employed.

In developing the kinds of vocational education to be offered, the school will need to survey the community needs and employment conditions. In some manner, the school should keep in touch with employers and labor unions in the community to secure their advice as to the types of experiences to give youth as job preparation. In an agricultural community, agriculture will find a place. In an industrial community, there will be other types of vocational needs. In other words, the community needs should determine the type of vocational education. The community should be considered as the area served by the high school, regional school, or junior college. To a greater extent than any previous time in history, the school will also need to consider what types of occupations its former students have entered, for migration enters definitely into the picture today.

All pupils—whatever their individual talents, interests, educational and vocational goals, physical and mental handicaps, or learning limitations may be—should be integrated into the total life of the school as much as is reasonably possible.

The total program of the school takes care of individual differences. The specialized learnings, such as vocational skills and advanced scientific studies, are only one means; grouping in or among classes is another. The general education courses, the extra class activities, the guidance service all help to provide for these differences that exist. This book attempts to set forth the various ways by which the school can do so: through varied instructional procedures, through adaptation of the curriculum, through specialized learnings, through administrative devices. These are the ways by which schools can take care of individual interests, needs, and abilities.

When pupils are grouped into special types of classes, such as an honors group or a mentally retarded group, they should be scheduled with as many courses and activities with their age mates as possible or educationally desirable. They should not figuratively or literally be put in a corner of the building and left there.

Even blind children can have many of their daily educational experiences with their normally sighted classmates. They learn to live in a world of "seeing" people. Honors classes, as is the case of any course in the specialized learnings, are scheduled together for only a minor portion of the day. It is not advocated here that pupils who are exceptional in any manner be segregated from their fellow class-mates throughout the day.

SOME COMMON PRACTICES

To what extent are individual differences provided for in second-ary schools? Does the typical high school have opportunities for spe-cialization that consider the pupils' abilities, handicaps, peculiar tal-ents, and future educational and vocational plans? While it is neither possible nor the intent to present a picture of a "typical school," some practices and trends can be pointed out. The next chapter dis-cusses some of the more promising practices.

LIMITED OPPORTUNITY FOR CREATIVE TALENTS. The small high school generally does not provide youth with enough opportunities to explore their talents in art, creative writing, drama, speech, the dance, crafts, and to a lesser degree, music. Music has found its way into most secondary schools, first as an extraclass activity and then as a course with a regular place in the school schedule, offered for credit. Both instrumental and vocal groups have been accorded that privi-lege in many schools. In larger schools pupils in various curricula are usually allowed to participate in music groups.

In small secondary schools there is a dearth of opportunity for special exploration in any of the other creative areas as a class activ-ity, although many are often included in the extraclass activities. Larger high schools offer courses in creative writing and drama where pupils may develop their talents in writing and acting. Cre-ativity through the dance is an infrequent experience in physical education classes. The development of special talents in speaking is left largely to the extraclass category in the smaller schools. Ad-vanced arts and crafts are more expensive offerings that have found room neither in the budget nor in the curriculum of many a small high school.

In large secondary schools, the curriculum may be as barren and void of art experiences for most pupils as in the small school, for their program may be filled with required and recommended courses. We need to look at the course program that pupils follow, not what is offered in the program of studies, in order to get the real picture.

In the academic courses, creativity may be a liability rather than an asset to the student. In a study of two groups, the first rating very high in intelligence but not nearly as high as the other in creativity, and the second rating very high in creativity but not as high in intelligence, it was found that each group exhibited certain characteristics. In contrast to the ability to follow the unusual and to enjoy the risk and uncertainty of the unknown for the creative group, the high I.Q. group tended to work toward the security of the socially rewarded response and the "right" answers. Both groups, despite differences in I.Q., were equal on standardized achievement tests in school subjects. In spite of this fact, the high intelligence student was considered by teachers as more desirable than the average student, but the creative student was not. The researchers concluded that, "Whereas the high I.Q. student wants the qualities he believes make for 'success' and the qualities that are similar to those he believes the teachers like, the high creativity student favors personal qualities having no relationship to those he believes make for 'success,' and in some ways the reverse of those he believes teachers favor. In effect, he does not like the same thing his teachers like; his teachers, as we have seen, do not especially like him either." [1]

INCREASED PROVISIONS FOR ACADEMICALLY TALENTED. The proportion of secondary schools offering special learning experiences for bright youngsters has increased considerably. In recent years, much stress has been placed on provisions in the secondary school curriculum to meet the needs of the "gifted" student. Up to the middle of the twentieth century, except for the usual enrichment for faster learners in classes and the courses for college-bound pupils, little attention was given to the pupil gifted intellectually. A study of special provisions for the exceptionally able child in Ohio in 1950, for example, reported that only 2 per cent of the schools had special classes and 9 per cent had enriched programs for this group. [2] Even less attention was given to those with other outstanding talents. Even early in 1958 at a conference on the academically talented sponsored by the National Education Association, one speaker found it necessary to say that "so far as we have been able to determine, however, not more than 5 per cent of our country's high schools now employ systematic programs to encourage superior students to develop their academic potential." [3]

Although the various studies referred to here were probably not

[1] J. W. Getzels, "The Problem of Values, Value Change, and Personal Identity in Education: Some Recent Studies," in *Frontiers of Secondary Education IV*, Paul M. Halverson, ed., Syracuse: Syracuse University Press, 1960, p. 33.

[2] A. Harry Passow and Others, *Planning for Talented Youth*, New York: Bureau of Publications, Teachers College, Columbia University, 1955, pp. 4-5.

[3] Lyle Spencer, "Implementation—The Effective Use of Identification Techniques," in *The Identification and Education of the Academically Talented Student in the American Secondary School*, Washington, D.C.: National Education Association, 1958, p. 40.

using the same definition of "gifted" or "academically talented," nor interpreting special programs or experiences in the same way, the comparisons with late figures are indicative of the trend. In May, 1960, the National Education Association's research department reported that almost 80 per cent of the urban schools sampled (population 2,500 to 500,000 and over) were providing some specialized learning experiences for talented students. In senior high schools, about 10 per cent of the schools surveyed had special classes only; approximately 25 per cent, enrichment only; 1.3 per cent, acceleration only; about 40 per cent, various combinations of the three; and about 25 per cent, no provisions. These figures did not differ substantially for junior high schools.[4] The larger the school system, the more likely that special provisions of some type are made.

QUANTITY EQUATED WITH QUALITY. There has been some tendency to equate more work and more required academic courses with improved learning experiences for the academically talented. Secondary schools that have been more concerned about the pressures placed upon them to do something to "toughen up" courses for the able pupil have tended to take short cuts by requiring more work rather than to make thorough studies of how experiences for fast-learning pupils could be made more challenging. Some teachers have given a greater number of problems to be solved or pages to be read. Homework of the assigned type has become more popular in the junior high school. The fundamental question of how content and learning experiences should differ for those more fortunately endowed intellectually has not been considered frequently enough.

Some have assumed that the academically superior student will have a program suited to his needs if he is scheduled into five solid subjects instead of four. Undoubtedly, he can successfully complete additional work in his high school years. This has been done by many high school pupils for a number of years. Adding more problems for homework or more courses may improve very little the quality of the program for the able student.

VARIETY OF VOCATIONAL OFFERINGS. The American secondary school offers a variety of opportunities for vocational education. Two patterns of school organization for vocational education offerings have evolved in this country. One is the special vocational high school, found only in larger urban communities or operated in regional areas of the state. In the majority of secondary schools of the country, some type of vocational education is offered. Agriculture courses

[4] "What's New in the Schools?," *NEA Research Bulletin*, 30:47-48, May, 1960.

and farm shopwork are found in many small rural high schools. Business subjects, such as typewriting, are quite common in all but the smallest schools. Home economics courses are frequently offered. Less common are the vocational shop courses, such as printing, automotive mechanics, and the like. Distributive education in the business field is offered mainly in the larger high school, generally restricted to the eleventh and twelfth grades.

One of the main factors that has stimulated development of vocational education has been the underwriting of the program by the federal government brought about by the demands of the people for education suited to the times. Through the Smith-Hughes Act passed by Congress in 1917, the George-Deen Act, and other subsequent acts, grants of money were provided to the states for specific purposes of promoting instruction in agriculture, home economics, distributive education, and trades and industries. Depending upon the particular state plan developed, the local school receives money for a certain portion of the cost of conducting courses in these fields. In turn, the school must meet specified standards for its facilities and instruction.

Generally, specialization in a vocational field is confined to the upper years of secondary school although courses in agriculture, business training, and home economics are frequently offered in the ninth grade. At that level, and in the other junior high school grades, home economics is considered as general education. Beyond the junior high school, it becomes a specialized area open to election mainly by girls.

LIMITED ELECTIVES FOR COLLEGE-PREPARATORY STUDENTS. Courses such as typewriting, industrial arts, home economics, and cooperative work experience have been infrequently elected by college-bound pupils. One reason has been the barriers constructed by the multiple curriculum type of organization of the school program. Pupils have been rather limited in the extent to which they have been allowed to take courses outside of those listed for a particular curriculum.

Some teachers of subjects in these special fields have not seen the possibilities for stimulating intellectual content in fields of business, agriculture, industrial arts, and home economics. The fact that these areas are majors in college should be ample evidence that the content has innumerable possibilities for the study of research methods, performing laboratory experiments, and examining sociological and economic issues involved. An unfortunate attitude has developed that such courses are for pupils who cannot master academic content.

EXPERIENCE-CENTERED APPROACH IN SPECIAL FIELDS. In the vocational areas, the very nature of the course and the fact that a certain amount of actual experience is required by the federal laws setting up the program have been conducive to pupil participation. For many, these courses have been an experience in learning by doing. Projects have been constructed with the hands, skill in the handling of tools has been learned through actual use, working plans have been made and put into action. Part of the vocational work has been experience on the job. The work in the school shop has been organized to resemble the situation in the industrial shop. There is closer touch with the community and a closer relation to real life experiences than is generally true in the academic areas.

Teachers of agriculture use the pupils' home farms as a laboratory for learning good agricultural practices. The teachers under this federally operated program are employed full-time and spend the summer supervising the projects that the boys have selected to carry out on their home farms. The project becomes a year around one, for which planning and gathering information is a part of the organized classroom work. Typically, agriculture classrooms are workrooms, with tables and chairs, an abundance of state and national agricultural bulletins, filing equipment, laboratory equipment such as a milk testing machine and a soil testing kit, and farm shop equipment.

For many students, the areas of industrial arts and home economics fill specialized needs and interests. Opportunities are offered in a number of schools for courses throughout the senior high school years. Often, they may choose areas of greater specialization such as metals, electricity, woodworking, or machine shop. Many shop and laboratories are organized so that various pupils take responsibility for the management duties required. In home economics, teachers have developed a unit plan of organization of experiences. The problems studied, home management and decoration, nutrition, foods, clothing selection and care, and child study, represent phases of life that interest the adolescent girl.

Art and music courses of an advanced nature are characterized by direct participation in different art media or in musical groups of special interest to the pupils. Pupils in art classes can be found working at individual projects of their own choosing. Office practice laboratories give the pupil a chance to practice the skills needed in a modern office. Work experience in the community is becoming more common in business education, giving the pupils supervised experience in the actual job situation.

ISSUES AND PROBLEMS

These issues concern the provision of quality experiences for individual pupils of all abilities and interests and give some special attention to the issues concerning gifted pupils.

1. *Should the secondary school curriculum provide for intellectual interests only or also for vocational, social, civic, aesthetic interests?*

The education that is determined good for American children must be judged in terms of American goals. No educational system can be viewed outside of the culture and the society in which it exists. If some people want to adopt a Western European system of education, a Russian system, or any other system it is only fair to ask if they would also adopt their ideals and principles.

In recent years some have advocated that the school should stress only the intellectual objectives. There is no doubt that the modern technical age, with the rapidly accelerated increase in knowledge, demands an increased need for high-level intellectual achievement. No one has ever questioned whether or not the schools should stress intellectual objectives. The question is, "have we done this task well enough?" More must be known to be an intelligent citizen. There is also a need for more highly trained specialists in different fields, since more well-educated persons will be needed in an age when machines take care of more and more of the labor and routine. There is need for intellectual status in government, in diplomatic service, in medicine, in industry, in education, in the military, in research of all kinds, and in many other phases of life in order to survive.

But the two purposes, intellectual achievement and responsible citizenship, are not necessarily the same. Intellectual training per se does not necessarily improve the individual as a citizen. Depth in specialization is one kind of need; breadth in understanding, commitments to democratic behavior, and some reasonable understanding of oneself and one's fellow man, another.

Restriction of opportunities through a curriculum for the academically talented alone is a negation of a long-believed fundamental principle. Equality of opportunity does not mean that everyone gets an equal dosage. If one believes in equality of opportunity, he must also believe in provision for individual differences, giving each person a chance to develop his own talents and capabilities to the maximum. A large number of pupils need a curriculum in some aspects differentiated from that of those who will specialize further in the study of a profession or in a logically organized discipline. For each, the experience should be fruitful in order to be of the highest quality.

Nor can the community afford to deny young people an equality of opportunity to explore the arts and the humanities, at the expense of specialization. The arts and the humanities contain some of the basic knowledge and interest which make life worth living; the sciences, it is hoped, will help people to enjoy these aspects of living more fully.

The total community sets the limits on its own creativity and the creativity of its schools. Its own intellectual interests are reflected in part by the school curriculum, but even more in the intellectual interests and the attainment of its children. The child who comes from a home where the intellectual interests are not valued is far less likely to go on to college and to enter one of the professions or a field of research.

It is doubtful that the American public would want to drop from its schools the outstanding programs that have been developed in such areas as homemaking, health, agriculture, business, and other vocational skills.

2. Should there be fixed curricular standards or flexible standards according to pupils' abilities?

If the American secondary schools acceded to the demands of those who would have national standards for the curriculum and for school-leaving examinations, education would be moving in the direction of the same expectancies of accomplishment for all. Yet, the ideal of excellence requires that each person perform up to his maximum, not up to the average of what a group can do.

There are advocates of the practice of weeding out along the way of progression in school those who cannot achieve a minimum standard in examinations at various stages in the school program, as in the European concept of education. American public secondary schools have held that they cannot afford to weed out the less academically talented or the so-called "average" student who will eventually become participating citizens determining all of the complex issues involved in local, state, national, and the total international community. It can afford this no more than it can afford to fail to challenge the outstanding student by holding to standards that he as an individual should be able to achieve.

Good teaching increases the differences that exist between students because the good students go much farther beyond the poor students if the instruction is good and challenging. Consequently, a school should strive to spread the achievement among its students rather than attempt to achieve sameness for all through some concept of minimum standards.

Quantity is sometimes equated with quality, for a child may be urged to study harder when he already is doing wrong what he is attempting to do. The same thing may be true in our attempts to make courses tougher to all students. To some teachers this may mean making courses equally tough for all instead of expecting that students work up to their own capacities; yet these same teachers may not be varying at all the kinds of materials that they are giving students to do and the kinds of expectancies they have for them. Spending a greater amount of time on what the student does not understand without further assistance will lead only to undesirable learnings. In a like manner, increasing the number of academic courses required for graduation, as is happening in many secondary schools, will not necessarily increase the quality of work. Merely adding on poorly taught courses in which the quality of experiences is low will not improve standards in the least.

Thus the current emphasis upon improvement of intellectual experiences in school is indeed a promising trend, but this means to stimulate, to challenge the intellect as never before, not to stifle it with dull, repetitive material taught by dull uninspired teachers. The teacher who inspires his students is one who has the love of learning himself, who never ceases to want to learn more about his field and about human behavior.

At times Americans seem to act as though they believe that the democratic principle of equality meant a similar experience and similar expectancies, regardless of variations of abilities and interests. Equality of opportunity demands dissimilar experiences in order for different individuals to succeed. The quality of that experience is the reference point.

3. *Should the secondary school curriculum stress uniformity and conformity or individuality, creativity, and uniqueness of ideas?*

Do the people want a curriculum in their schools that will tend to set conditions which promote uniformity, agreement, and sameness? The determining factor is the kind of experience which is planned for students. In the attempt to achieve homogeneity as a *means* to make teaching the bright youngsters easier, educators should also be fearful lest they achieve homogeneity as a *result* of that instruction. For great scientists, inventors, artists, research workers, and frontier thinkers in any field are basically non-conformists in their outlook and ideas. They have to be in order to break the barriers of knowledge. The stress on learning more subject matter for the purpose of getting into college or obtaining good marks may be the fetter that restrains the young person from being inventive, playing with ideas and experimenting on his own.

Most of all, the talented student needs freedom to be creative, to try things out, to question, to explore. It is not difficult to place a value upon conformity, which all but the intellectual geniuses may learn to accept as the way to get ahead, if students are not allowed to discuss controversial issues nor question traditional practices.

Creativity recognizes no subject barriers. It is not confined to the academically inclined. Creative talents are found in any field of human endeavor: in speech, linguistics, art, music, drama, science, writing, skilled trades and crafts, technical skills, business, politics, as well as in a profession that is a composite of a number of these fields, such as medicine or teaching.

The question of individuality by no means applies only to the gifted. Individual development is needed for any group. Each person can make a contribution in his only way. Uniformity is a far cry from uniqueness of ideas and achievement. It has been shown in a number of studies that girls generally receive higher marks on the average in high school than boys, but girls also generally conform more readily to doing the assigned tasks. In the final analysis, our answer to this question boils down to the value placed on uniqueness and creativity of ideas, ideas that might not even be "in the book." Nonconformity, within limits set by concern for the welfare of others and acceptable behavior, may well have only nuisance value.

A curriculum that stresses the right answer in cases where there may be no answers that are either right or wrong, such as in the social studies, provides little opportunity for creativity and uniqueness of a student's ideas. It is a disturbing fact that students who receive the highest marks tend to be those who conform and that, in a sense, the students who are the most secure tend to be the conforming ones. Does this mean that teachers are tending to mark high those students who agree with them and their points of view and who give the answers that the teacher expects?

4. *Should the academically talented student be accelerated in his school program or should he proceed through the school years at the same pace as other students?*

Educators have generally been opposed to acceleration of bright students by some means through which they would complete college in fewer number of years than their fellow classmates. The social and psychological adjustment of the pupil has been one of the main concerns. In recent years, research results have thrown some doubt on this contention. The following advantages and disadvantages of acceleration, developed by A. Harry Passow of Teachers College, Columbia University, and reported by the National Education Association's Project on the Academically Talented, include the various arguments of both positions:

ADVANTAGES OF ACCELERATION

1. Acceleration provides the gifted with opportunities commensurate with their ability to progress and places them in the grade corresponding to level of maturity rather than to chronological age.
2. Students should be allowed to acquire educational attainments in the shortest time needed. Since research shows little correlation between achievement in a given area and the time devoted to its study, gifted children should be encouraged to proceed at their own rate.
3. Indications are that a person's outstanding creative accomplishments are products of early adult life. This peak of creativity is used to greatest advantage when students are enabled to enter productive careers earlier than would be possible in a rigid system of grade progress.
4. Emotional maladjustments may result from keeping children in classes which do not challenge them. Achieving below potential ability is probably more harmful than the temporary difficulties attendant upon being placed with somewhat older students.
5. Acceleration is a form of enrichment; the time saved in mastering fundamental learnings makes possible more work in the given field, or additional work in other areas of interests.
6. The saving of a year or more enables a student to complete advanced or graduate work without having to delay marriage and independent living.
7. If able students are allowed to save a year or more in their public schooling, the consequent lowering in school years and school costs, and increased man-years of productivity will result in lower costs and significant savings for students, parents, schools, and communities.

DISADVANTAGES OF ACCELERATION

1. Rich learning experiences do not necessarily come from a fixed pattern of subject matter. Although the time spent on particular activities can be decreased, studies in depth and breadth also contribute an essential ingredient to the learning process.
2. There are better ways of eliminating the boredom resulting from lack of challenge than reducing time spent in class.
3. Intellectual maturity may not go hand in hand with social and emotional maturity when younger students are placed with older ones.

This may result in a denial of leadership opportunities to those whose physical or social maturity is less than that of the older students.

4. Acceleration may deny bright students the time and opportunity to think, reflect, explore, and appreciate. The pressures for rapid progress may result in a curtailment of creativity.

5. Students with like mental age but different chronological age may perform qualitatively quite differently; the more difficult work provided for the gifted child through acceleration may not necessarily yield more appropriate experiences.

6. Equal acceleration in all areas does not take into account differences in rates of maturation. A student ready for rapid progress in one area may not be ready for it in another area.

7. Acceleration tends to separate the gifted from his age peers and to emphasize differences in ability. This separation may lead to undesirable social and behavior patterns.

8. Pure skipping may leave serious gaps in the student's learnings, which, in turn, may affect his later educational attainments.[5]

It is doubtful that acceleration, special classes, or enrichment as means for providing for the talented are mutually exclusive. In fact, they are only administrative devices and do not guarantee in themselves the kind of experience that the pupils will have. The accelerated pupil may have a better experience in high school or in college depending upon which institution and faculty make the greatest effort to give him challenging experiences. Certainly, freshmen college courses have no envious record in this respect.

It may well be that greater freedom and independence of pursuit of individual interests may supply the answer. It is very doubtful that segregating bright students entirely from their fellows will be of any advantage to them and will probably have disadvantages.

5. *Should academically talented pupils be segregated for instruction in special classes, or should they be taught in the regular classes with individualized activities?*

The issues involved in this question are well stated by a publication of the Project on the Academically Talented of the National Education Association.

Those who oppose special classes for the academically talented advance the following points:

1. Special classes tend to establish an elite group and to encourage snobbery.

[5] *Administration Procedures and School Practices for the Academically Talented Student.* Washington, D.C.: National Education Association, 1960, pp. 64-68.

2. Students in slow or average classes are likely to feel inferior and antagonistic toward pupils in advanced classes.
3. Many students who would be leaders in average groups are submerged in gifted groups.
4. Students in special classes are subjected to excessive intellectual competition and homework.
5. Homogeneous grouping is impossible; some differences will always exist within a class.

Those in favor of grouping the academically talented advance the following arguments:

1. When the range of differences in a class is narrowed, the teacher can more effectively meet the varied needs of individual students.
2. Superior students can explore advanced concepts and work up to their intellectual capacity without fear of losing status with classmates.
3. When superior students work together, they are able to appraise realistically their own strengths and weaknesses.
4. The bright pupil is more likely to be given leadership opportunities in a special class than in a class with many average and slow students.
5. Teachers of special classes have an opportunity to gain adequate training in the particular skills required for teaching gifted students.[6]

SELECTED REFERENCES

Note: Selected references for this chapter may be found at the end of Chapter 11.

[6] *English for the Academically Talented Student,* Washington, D.C.: National Education Association, 1960, p. 82.

11

QUALITY PROGRAMS FOR THE INDIVIDUAL

A program for the individual within a framework of mass instruction is not only a possibility but a necessity for a democratic society. Specialized types of experiences make possible the fulfillment of each person's special potentialities. The individual learner can be provided for through differentiation within each class, through specialized classes, through grouping for instruction, and through independent kinds of study activities.

The principles discussed in the previous chapter are illustrated here with examples of the more outstanding practices in secondary schools, many of them experimental in nature. Selected references for both chapters are included at the end of this chapter.

IMPLEMENTATION OF THE PRINCIPLES

One of the significant trends in secondary education in the United States is the development of programs and special opportunities for the academically talented and gifted students, beginning in the last half of this century. These developments and the outstanding programs in vocational education, including work experience, and other special learnings are described in this section.

VARIED COURSE OFFERINGS. Of the different ways to provide for individual differences among pupils, the one which has been done best throughout the years by secondary schools is the offering of a variety of courses for pupils of different interests and talents. As noted in Chapter 7, the program of courses in a secondary school of 700 pupils or more generally contains a long list of electives embodying all of the subject fields. The most common are in the foreign languages, the sciences, mathematics, home economics, industrial arts, and business subjects.

Some courses are of recent origin to provide for individual talents and interests. Many of these are rarely offered in small high schools. The following is an illustrative rather than an inclusive list of specialized types of courses. Some indication of the experiences in the course is presented briefly.

1. *Journalism.* In this course, pupils often have the responsibility of producing the school paper or a section of the local paper. In such cases, the course provides firsthand experience in managing, planning, and writing articles.

2. *Drama.* As their work in the course, pupils carry out the production and staging of plays. They have practical experience in selecting the play, applying makeup, designing and constructing scenery, lighting, costuming, directing, and managing the production. Pupils take much of the responsibility for presenting a play. In a few cases, they also write productions.

3. *Creative writing.* In this course, pupils who do superior work in English composition and show imaginative and creative abilities are given further opportunity to explore. The student's own writing, in the different literary forms, provides the basis for discussion and criticism. In a number of cases, students publish their writings in the school paper or magazine.

4. *Speech.* The experiences in speech courses vary with the situation in the school and community. When the school operates a radio station or has access to local stations, speech work may be built around radio programs. Other activities of speech classes include panel discussions before local clubs, discussion groups, assemblies, and practice through various other avenues.

5. *Radio.* Theory is combined with practice as pupils work with radio sets for laboratory experiments and construction. Other similar specialized courses in physical science are aeronautics and electricity.

6. *Latin American history, Far East, international relations, economics, sociology.* These are types of courses in social studies of a more specialized nature that permit students to pursue the study of the field in depth. They utilize a good deal of pamphlet and periodical material and many of the more popular non-fiction books.

7. *Commercial art, industrial design, applied arts, advanced art.* Many different media or activities in arts and crafts classes make it possible for youth to explore their talents: sketching, metal arts, clay, plaster, plastics, graphic arts, lettering, designing, commercial art, puppetry, stage settings, model making, map making, leather work, wood. Comprehensive arts and crafts offerings are being given more frequently and provide for a variety of types of expression.

8. *Harmony, theory, applied music.* Advanced courses in music give

high school youth advantages for intensive study in this special field. Music courses and groups meeting on regular schedule offer innumerable possibilities for pupils to develop proficiency in choral singing, solo singing, performance on various types of instruments, participation in instrumental groups, composing, orchestration, and experience in staging musical productions. Many high schools have highly developed music programs.

Included also are courses of a specialized nature such as the languages of India, China, Russia and Japan. Russian is taught in an increasing number of high schools. The student of education can find others in bulletins on programs of studies published by secondary schools.

DIFFERENTIATION WITHIN COURSES. Adaptation of the curriculum to individual differences in the courses required of all pupils occurs either within each class grouped heterogeneously or among classes grouped according to ability in the subject.

Within a single class that contains pupils of all abilities slower pupils may do more oral work, use textbooks and reference books with a simpler vocabulary, carry out practical projects involving contacts with people or manual skills, or do more specific excrcises or problems of a less difficult nature. The abler pupils may do more research, read widely, lead discussions, work on creative analysis, carry on independent study in the library, put on panels on radio and TV, and serve as resource persons to other students.

In the social studies, enrichment is accomplished by an atmosphere of free inquiry in which critical analysis, creative ideas, and scholarly research is predominant. Combined social studies—English classes may include more independent research in books, current periodicals, and original documents and bibliographical work. Pupils compare and evaluate, summarize, and practice public speaking and discussion procedures.

Grouping within the class to take care of different interests and abilities occurs more often in core, English, and social studies classes. At Germantown Friends School in Philadelphia, a small secondary school with heterogeneous classes, the English classes use a unique form of grouping. They meet four times a week for each section as a whole, with the teacher's fifth day entirely devoted to small reading groups, voluntarily attended and organized around ability and interest. The small groups read and discuss literature as an extension of ideas discussed in the classroom. One of the themes used for reading centered on freedom and responsibility. Books chosen by the abler group included Plato's *Apology,* Shaw's *Saint Joan,* Mill's *On*

Liberty, Anderson's *Barefoot in Athens,* and Forster's *Two Cheers for Democracy.*

Some of the provisions for gifted students within social studies and mathematics class in the Minneapolis public schools point up the fact that the work in these courses is differentiated:

Social Studies
> Providing additional research on topics or problems beyond the usual class work
> Providing leadership opportunities in formulating problems during the pupil-teacher planning period in the development of a unit
> Stressing originality and creativeness in the presentation of material
> Having pupils act as assistants to the teacher
> Helping them to engage in individual or group field trips
> Helping them to arrange interviews
> Encouraging local study of politics
> Engaging in surveys in school and community.
> Arranging for attendance at lectures
> Having students contact and arrange for resource people
> Promoting the development of skills in use of library resources
> Providing opportunities in leadership in service organizations and activities in the classroom, school, and community.

Mathematics
> Doing library research work
> Reading for interest and recreation
> Writing book reports
> Giving oral reports
> Solving additional and more difficult problems
> Investigating topics of special interest
> Making models
> Preparing exhibits for science fairs
> Watching and reporting on mathematics television programs
> Organizing and conducting meetings of a mathematics club
> Preparing lessons to teach to their classes
> Conducting class discussion
> Writing mathematics term papers

RAPID PROGRESS PLANS. The interest in the academically talented youth in secondary school has stimulated experimentation with both administrative and instructional plans that permit more rapid progress in school or in the subject. Some of the administrative adaptations are likely to be a variation of the old idea of skipping a grade. The project for early admission of high school pupils into college at the end of their junior year was supported by the Ford Foundation through a system of scholarships. These students at the end of four years of college did as well or better than those in a control group, in both course grades and various examinations. They also participated extensively in extraclass life.

There is no evidence in research to indicate that taking work earlier in college by skipping a year in high school is superior either to acceleration in college or to acceleration within specific subject areas. The Advanced Placement Plan of the College Entrance Examination Board, which permits high school pupils to earn college credit while still in high school, described in Chapter 18, permits acceleration while allowing the student to stay in high school.

The Baltimore City Schools in three of the city's high schools have an advanced college preparatory course, generally known as the "A course," which has been in effect since 1926. By carrying additional subjects in grades 9 through 11, pupils in the course can devote their senior year (grade 12) to college-level subjects, such as English literature, foreign language, advanced mathematics and science, history, and engineering subjects. Pupils who complete the course and are recommended by the principal are admitted with advanced standing to the University of Maryland and a number of other colleges and universities. This is a sequential and coordinated program extending over a full four-year span from grade 9 through grade 12.

In Torrance, California, selected high school students may enroll in courses in the junior college in the district, and advanced eighth-grade pupils may take one course in high school. In New York City, junior high school students also may take advanced courses in senior high school.

Other types of acceleration include summer session courses, taking two sequential full-year courses in two semesters, or moving at a faster pace within a subject by more fundamental reorganization of the content.

In the field of mathematics, more acceleration within the subject throughout the high school years has been done than in other fields. The Walnut Hills High School in Cincinnati has seventh-grade sections which ordinarily complete the work normally covered in seventh- and eighth-grade mathematics. Algebra is given at the eighth-grade level in a number of junior high schools. In North High School, Denver, seniors can enroll in a course which consists of trigonometry, analytical geometry, and calculus, if they have completed the usual mathematics sequence by the end of the eleventh grade. Sometimes the courses in plane and solid geometry are combined in the tenth grade and advanced algebra and trigonometry in the eleventh grade, as in several of the Minneapolis high schools.

In some cases, a reorganization of the content in mathematics provides for more rapid progress and more content from modern mathematics for the abler students. In the Connersville Senior High School, Connersville, Indiana, a selected group of pupils take plane geometry in the first semester of the sophomore year emphasizing the logic of proofs. During the second semester they study measurement, plane and solid geometry, mensuration, statistics, percentage, functional notation, and literal numbers. In the junior year, the content consists of real-number axis, linear equations, areas, volumes, ratio and proportion, vector analysis, reasoning, exponents and laws, logarithms, slide rule, number systems, circular functions, and historical development of mathematics. The work in the senior year consists of a similar combination of advanced topics in mathematics analysis.

Acceleration of learning is accomplished by a continuous sequence of foreign language courses from the seventh grade, or earlier, through the twelfth grade. The Denver Public Schools begin conversational language in the fifth grade and the more formal sequence in the eighth grade. A ten-year foreign language program of a continuous nature beginning at the third grade was advocated by a conference sponsored by the NEA's Project on the Academically Talented Student.

In other fields, numerous examples can be found. In science, Stratford High School, Stratford, Connecticut, begins biology in the ninth grade for the honors group gifted in science; elementary chemistry and physics are offered in tenth grade; and advanced courses in chemistry and physics in the eleventh and twelfth grades. In the Denver public high schools, in the field of English, the three-year sequence is compressed into two years for a small group of students, permitting more advanced work in the senior year. In social studies, acceleration is accomplished by granting credit to a few students who achieve above the 95th percentile on a standardized American history test given in the ninth grade. Neither the fields of social studies nor English have been modified, however, to the extent the mathematics and science have.

SPECIAL TYPES OF CLASSES FOR THE TALENTED. Administratively, these are ways of grouping, but they are more than that. The programs presented represent enriched experiences for secondary school pupils. These special classes or groups use individual study, laboratory work, research papers, research projects, wide reading, original writing and compositions, discussion of ideas, speakers, community study, and evaluating learning activities to a greater extent than most classes. They are characterized by more freedom for the pupil to schedule his learning activities. The content is at a more advanced level, in many instances, the equivalent of, or even beyond, what freshmen study in some colleges.

Most of the newer types of programs are for the academically talented, although a number of special opportunities have long been provided for pupils with talents in the fine arts. Most of these provisions are found in the large high schools.

Conant has recommended that no high school be smaller than one which can have a graduating class of 100 pupils. He believes that high schools smaller than this cannot without excessive cost provide classes in advanced subjects for the academically talented.[1] A survey in the state of Maryland revealed that there were only 129 academically talented students enrolled in 95 high schools with graduating classes fewer than 100. In this survey only about 10 per cent instead of the top 15 or 20 per cent of the pupils were included. There was considerable variation among high schools. One school had 22 per cent of the total number in the graduating class in the academically talented category, while some had less than 1 per cent. In addition, it was found that academically talented students are concentrated in large suburban and metropolitan high schools.[2] Consequently, many of these special provisions will not apply to the smaller high schools.

Seminars, honors classes, and advanced classes are special types of courses to which academically talented students are admitted on the basis of achievement tests, intelligence tests, previous records, and teacher recommendation. Many schools have a plan for identification and placement of pupils in these courses. They may be a part of the general grouping scheme for a particular grade. However, in most cases they represent a special grouping. Many excellent programs, some of which are described briefly, keep pupils of all abilities together for some of the basic general education courses and offer these special classes for the select group of pupils. The distinction among the uses of the term "seminar," "honors course," and "advanced course," is not clear cut.

1. *Seminars.* Seminars are likely to be small, informal in nature, concerned with ideas, and drawing from the subject matter of one or more fields. They are modelled after the college seminar idea in which experiences are planned by the group and in which student

---

[1] James B. Conant, *The American High School Today,* New York: McGraw-Hill Book Co., Inc., 1959, pp. 37, 76-85, and 119.

[2] Thomas G. Pullen, Jr., "What the Academically Talented Study," *Public Education in Maryland,* Vol. VII, No. 3, February 1959, Baltimore: Maryland State Department of Education, not paged.

participation is at a maximum. Sometimes the seminars go into content not usually studied in high schools, such as, psychology, sociology, and philosophy. Swarthmore, Pennsylvania, High School, has a seminar in contemporary problems which deals with the nature of critical thinking, semantics, logic, the historical approach to problems, research and writing techniques, and problems facing twentieth-century America. Great Neck High School, Great Neck, New York, offers a seminar in social studies organized around great ideas and issues. A senior seminar in Abraham Lincoln High School, San Francisco, uses more than one teacher to direct the study of philosophy, literary backgrounds, and psychology.

Gifted students in Denby High School, Detroit, are given an opportunity to broaden their experience in a seminar for the select top 1 per cent of the pupils in this large high school. The seminar correlates subject matter from different fields and is assigned to teachers from different subjects. Members of the seminar participate in the selection of subject matter, usually developed around readings and individual projects. For example, one year the seminar selected two survey books as "textbooks": *Basic Teachings of the Great Philosophers* and *Basic Teachings of the Great Psychologists*. Each pupil had a research project on which he worked independently.

One of the most comprehensive studies of a program for talented students has been conducted in the Portland, Oregon, public schools since 1952 in cooperation with Reed College. The term "gifted" as defined by this project included approximately the upper 10 per cent of the academically talented and the same proportion in each of seven special aptitudes: art, music, creative writing, creative dance, dramatics, mechanical talent, social leadership. A variety of screening devices are used. The general term "educational enrichment classes" is applied to a number of types of special classes, which may be special sections of regular classes, seminars in academic subjects, comprehensive seminars, and special talent classes.

The seminars in academic subjects for juniors and seniors are small discussion groups of five to eighteen pupils in English, social studies, science, and mathematics, taken as an extra course or in place of the required course. Pupils have an experience in trying to interpret events in the light of the evidence, requiring them "to define their own problems, to draw their own conclusions, and to focus their expectations on themselves rather than on the instructor." [3]

---

[3] *The Gifted Child in Portland,* Portland Oregon: Portland Public Schools, 1959, pp. 63-64. This 192 page report contains descriptions of seminars in the different subjects, as well as the enrichment classes in regular subjects. The program also includes the elementary schools.

Comprehensive seminars were experimented with for two years in two high schools. Pupils were rotated from teacher to teacher at intervals during the first semester in the fields of English, mathematics, social studies, and science. The pupils spent the second semester of the seminar on the subject of major interest to them. Such topics were studied as semantics, literature and life, origins and causes of war, nuclear physics and astrophysics. Authors read included Bacon, Dewey, Whitehead, Newman, Plato, Mill, Carlyle.

2. *Honors courses.* Honors courses are special classes for the academically talented, given in a certain subject area. In many cases, the rest of the program is taken with the regular group, although the high-level classes which are a part of an ability grouping plan are also sometimes called honor classes. Frequently, they are courses for seniors for which talented students are selected. They are also known by other names such as the educational enrichment classes in Portland, classes for very superior pupils, and starred classes.

For example, Mt. Lebanon High School, Mt. Lebanon, Pennsylvania, offers a program for superior students in English in the tenth through twelfth grades. Flexibility, informality, and independence of thought is stressed. Semantics has replaced formal grammar. Extensive outside reading, analysis of philosophical ideas and other literary content, and independent literary analysis characterize the course. Honors English courses are offered in Coral Gables Senior High School, Florida, where theme writing involves critical analysis, and creative writing in the short story, drama, and poetry. In the San Diego, California, honors English class pupils engage in a mature study of English literature and write weekly on the subjects related to their reading; in composition the emphasis is on substance, organization, logic, and style. New York City conducts honors classes in a number of fields in several of its regular high schools. In social studies honors classes, pupils practice techniques of social research and critical analysis of historical materials.

In junior high schools, honors classes are given in English, mathematics, and social studies at the Plant Junior High School, West Hartford, Connecticut. Additional reading, creative writing, outlining, research, and broadened and accelerated content characterize this work. At the John J. Lynch School, Holyoke, Massachusetts, a ninth-grade English-honors-type course includes a unit on argumentation which stresses teaching youth how to think clearly. Fallacies of thinking, deductive reasoning, the syllogism, the scientific method of thinking are a part of the content of the unit. Classes for the academically talented for seventh- and eighth-grade pupils in Glencoe,

Illinois, provide for advanced work in mathematics, reading, social studies, science, foreign language, dramatics, creative writing, drawing, art, and the like. These classes are changed every nine weeks although a pupil may remain in a class for two or three nine-week periods.

3. *Advanced courses.* Advanced courses of different types are, in a sense, much like the honors class and the terms often are used interchangeably. In smaller secondary schools advanced courses may be offered for pupils from two or three grades. These advanced classes in many outstanding secondary schools give work of a more specialized nature in a field or at a more advanced level than formerly was offered at the secondary school level. They include such courses as microbiology, biological research, field biology, genetics, atomic physics, geophysics, electronics, radio, speech, world literature, humanities, the Far East, calculus, analytic geometry, probability and statistical inference, and more commonly advanced chemistry and physics. The Bethesda-Chevy Chase Senior High School, Montgomery County, Maryland, has a rapid learner program which includes advanced sections in English, physical science, physics, algebra, trigonometry and solid geometry, biology, chemistry. Able students may also elect journalism, Pan American history, Far Eastern Affairs, and advanced courses in languages. Such intellectual abilities as ability to see relationships, learning by complex associative methods, abstract aspects of subject matter, ability to work independently and to think critically, assumption of initiative in planning and carrying out work are considered both in selection of pupils and in selecting experiences for the courses. Boulder High School, Colorado, has an advanced double-period block course in American literature and American history. Oakland, California, offers for talented students advanced physics and electronics in a specially equipped laboratory at the school district's Chabot Observatory science center.

INDEPENDENT AND SPECIAL STUDY OPPORTUNITIES. In addition to special classes conducted regularly on the school schedule, there are both credit and noncredit opportunities for talented students to carry on independent study and research, more or less on their own, and to use special facilities and resources. High achievers are able to take responsibility for studies that are challenging to them, with the necessary guidance and encouragement. Until recent years, however, few schools have provided such opportunities. Some studies have shown that a good proportion of gifted students never use the town or community library, indicating the need for more stress on independent activities.[4]

Some of the types of programs listed here are also utilized by smaller high schools that do not have enough talented students to make up special classes.

1. Shops, libraries, and laboratories are open before school, after school, and during the school day during vacant periods for student use. Sometimes teachers are scheduled to be of assistance during these times or outstanding upper-class students serve as assistants.

2. Language laboratories represent a trend toward individual study and laboratory work in foreign language classes, where today the stress is on communicating in the language rather than on translation. These laboratories, aided by the National Defense Education Act, consist of simple recording and listening devices or more elaborate machines, including in addition film strips, recordings, and other instructional materials. Tape recorders, headphones, microphones, and listening stations are considered basic equipment. Pupils may record their voices for improvement of pronunciation and listen independently to lessons recorded.

3. Teaching machines are just beginning to be used in some schools for self-instruction purposes, as indicated in Chapter 8.

4. Summer projects and programs are used for more than make-up or acceleration purposes. Summer camps, common in some states such as Michigan, serve for enrichment in art, music, and outdoor education and science study. Summer school courses for handicapped, gifted, or a cross-section of pupils are found among the summer programs in public schools described in Chapter 15 and are also frequently utilized in connection with workshops for teachers. Universities and colleges run special programs for high school pupils particularly in science and mathematics, some of which are supported by the National Science Foundation. These may allow some acceleration in college or may be for enrichment purposes. One of these is conducted at Indiana University, a high school science institute consisting of two weeks of scheduled group lectures, laboratory work, demonstrations, and field trips, followed by a six weeks independent student laboratory research assistantship program. A number of universities give selected high school pupils opportunity to work with distinguished scientists on research projects during the summer.

5. University television programs in languages, sciences, and other fields are taken by selected high school pupils by special arrangement. The San Francisco public school system has such an arrangement with San Francisco State College for college credit.

[4] Walter Barbe, "A Study of the Reading of Gifted High-School Students," *Educational Administration and Supervision*, 38:148-54, March, 1952.

Early morning programs are sometimes utilized for independent study purposes under the direction of a high school teacher (see Chapter 8 for further descriptions of these programs).

6. Correspondence courses are used in the same way to provide additional opportunities for students in smaller secondary schools to take subjects not offered by the school. Pupils work under the direction of a teacher, largely independently. Limon High School, Colorado, uses correspondence courses secured through various colleges within the area for broadening the curriculum.

7. A voluntary tutorial plan is used less frequently but offers similar opportunities for independent study.

8. Independent research projects permit pupils to carry on research in the school or community during the school day. The project is generally related to the class work. At Darien, Connecticut, able high school students may be excused from school part of the time to participate in community learning experiences, especially in the arts and sciences. Torrance, California, has a system of contracts for independent study and encourages independent projects and research in connection with class work. In Dade County, Florida, certain selected pupils, because of their high ability in science, are assigned during the last two periods of the school day to work in scientific laboratories of cooperating agencies in the community.

9. Independent study programmed in the schedule is illustrated by the experimental science projects class in Abraham Lincoln High School, San Francisco, in which pupils enroll for credit and conduct independent and group experiments of their choice during vacant periods, before school, and after school, working individually with the teacher. At Cannon City, Colorado, pupils in plane geometry may take work in solid geometry on an independent study basis at the same time.

10. Weekly seminars beyond the regular class work are a part of the experiences of talented students in Centennial High School, Pueblo, Colorado and in Sewanhaka High School, Floral Park, New York. These sessions may include speakers, field trips to the community, discussions, and resource persons from the school faculty. The seminars may be in different fields in the different high schools.

11. Saturday and after-school classes are provided for able learners to supplement the regular program in a few schools. It is the large urban high schools rather than small high schools that have generally taken advantage of these times for enrichment of the program. San Francisco Polytechnic High School conducts a two-hour after-school program in its Lux Electronics Laboratory. Able secondary school (as well as elementary school) students may work twice a week on electronics projects of their own. In the Philadelphia public schools, talented art students have an opportunity to take special classes in eleven art centers on Saturday mornings.

12. Lectures are provided in the evenings for talented students. The San Diego City Schools schedule monthly evening lectures in the fields of science and the humanities for the twelfth-grade student in honors classes, drawing speakers from area colleges and universities as well as from professional and community leaders.

13. Leadership opportunities furnish practice in leadership skills for those with superior talents of various kinds. At Denby High School, Detroit, for example, pupils plan assemblies, serve on student government bodies, man the audio-visual services, serve as shop foremen and speech leaders, promote community drives.

PROVISIONS FOR HANDICAPPED PUPILS. Pupils who are handicapped either physically, mentally, or emotionally to the extent of needing special education provisions are estimated as constituting anywhere from 10 to 15 per cent of the public school population. There are no accurate figures available. In fact, many schools do not have adequate staff for diagnosing these handicaps in the school population.

Much of the special provision for individualization of both instruction and facilities for these children has been done at the elementary school level. In the majority of communities, these youngsters have either been placed in special schools, have dropped out of school before reaching the secondary level, or have been taken care of as well as possible by teachers in the regular classrooms. A startling fact is that of the major textbooks in general secondary school curriculum published up to 1960, not one devoted even a section to the education of the exceptional child.

It is in the large urban and suburban school districts where provisions are made for these youth. These provisions include diagnostic services; psychological, psychiatric, and medical services; special facilities and equipment; and a curriculum adjusted to their needs, often including provision for a part of the day spent in a separate classroom. Most large districts have separate classes for the mentally retarded. In the smaller school districts fewer provide such classes, 48.9 per cent of the urban districts of 2,500 to 4,999 population having limited or full provisions. The small village and rural areas have few if any. In some smaller communities, a few school systems provide these classes and services on a cooperative basis. In urban districts, varying in population from 2,500 to over 500,000, 69.4 per cent offer at least some separate classes for mentally retarded children; 58.1 per cent, for slow learners; 38.8 per cent, for the physically handicapped; 19.2 per cent, for the partially seeing; 19 per cent, for the hard of hearing; and 14.7 per cent, for the emotionally disturbed.[5]

[5]"Special Classes for Handicapped Children," *NEA Research Bulletin,* 39:43-46, May, 1961.

Physical handicaps such as deafness and blindness are provided for in special day or residential schools, although the trend seems to be to include the pupils in this category in the regular public schools, if possible. Pupils with hearing and sight losses are placed in special classrooms, spending part of the day in regular classes. Pupils with these disabilities may be attending regular classes, even in college, once they have mastered Braille or lip-reading. The speech handicapped are assisted by speech therapists in the larger school systems, who work with a number of schools. Other kinds of physical disabilities, such as cerebral palsy, orthopedic handicaps, cardiac disorders, epilepsy, tuberculosis, and glandular disorders present problems which most high schools are not equipped to take care of in any special way. Many of these cases may be homebound. The same is true of the emotionally disturbed child who needs psychiatric care or who may be classified as a delinquent.

More has been done for the mentally handicapped. Although there is no general agreement among specialists dealing with exceptional children, the mentally retarded is usually considered as a pupil with an I.Q. below 75 or 80. The severely mentally retarded of below 50 I.Q. cannot profit by formal education beyond elementary levels. In fact, it is doubtful that a number of the 50 to 70 I.Q. group receive with profit education beyond the elementary school level, no matter where they are placed.

It should be remembered that the I.Q. is a rather tenuous kind of designation of mental capacity, especially among those whose lives and mental processes are complicated by multiple kinds of handicaps. Many a physically handicapped or emotionally disturbed child of good intelligence has been considered by teachers to be mentally retarded.

Most of the young people in the above classifications are placed in special classes part of the day, and in regular classrooms if possible the rest of the day, where good programs exist. We are not speaking here of the slow learner, whose individual needs are taken care of in the regular classrooms or in some form of ability grouping. Provision for placement in special classes is a flexible matter, instruction is individualized in small classes of from five to twenty depending upon the disability, and diagnostic services are provided. These pupils are considered basically like other children with special needs to individualize instruction.

Where special classes are provided, it is on the school district basis with system-wide services and with the classes usually concentrated in one or more secondary schools. Usually these provisions are in junior high schools, although in recent years schools are developing programs in senior high schools, especially in the Midwest. Smaller school districts may band together for these types of facilities since the cases are few for various kinds of physical handicaps. Specially prepared teachers are employed to teach the special classes.

Norwich Free Academy, Norwich, Connecticut, which serves as the semipublic secondary school for the area, has a core program of English-social studies and mathematics-science for the mentally retarded. In the Mt. Lebanon, Pennsylvania, public schools, the special education program extends into both junior and senior high school. Pupils enrolled in the special class in the junior high school continue through the senior high school program. The program in the special classes is an integrated one. All academic work is taken in the special class, and non-academic subjects in junior high school and elective subjects in senior high school are taken with regular groups. The program stresses civic and social skills, physical fitness, the ability to live as a contributing member of a family, vocational skills and attitudes, and leisure time activities.

In the Evanston, Illinois, Township High School, the mentally retarded are in special classrooms part of the day where special materials and teaching aids are used. They are in large homerooms with other pupils part of the day. Besides personal guidance in the tool subjects, emphasis is placed on occupational education. In the eleventh and twelfth grades, work experience is an important part of the curriculum. Field trips to factories, business establishments, and employment agencies help the pupils to understand their community and to learn about its job opportunities. Another unique feature of the program is the opportunity for community service. This may be on an individual basis at a hospital or community nursery school. Group community service includes such activities as a puppet show given for crippled children.

The Indianapolis public schools have special sight-saving classes for the visually handicapped in grades 9 through 12 and secondary school classes for crippled children and for the mentally retarded. Pupils in sight-saving classes work in regular classrooms in all oral subjects, but all written work, reading, and lesson preparation is carried on in their own classroom under their special teacher. The program for crippled children (heart cases, orthopedic, tuberculosis, congenital deformities, cerebral palsy, polio, severe cases of epilepsy, or other cases necessitating special class provisions) include physiotherapy and hydrotherapy for children for whom physicians have so recommended, rest periods, and occupational therapy for selected children.

In Montgomery County, Maryland, the public schools have an

extensive program in special education including psychological, psychiatric, medical, and speech therapy services. Special classes are held for the mentally retarded in the age bracket 13 to 18; for the brain injured, emotionally disturbed, and learning disability groups in the age bracket 11 to 13; in addition to classes for younger pupils.

PROVISIONS FOR VOCATIONAL EDUCATION. Youth in secondary schools in this country are likely to find opportunity to develop vocational skills and understandings if they plan to go to work following the completion of their high school education. Most four-year and senior high schools except the smallest include some work in at least one of the areas of business education, agriculture, cooperative programs, or vocational-industrial education. Schools are adjusting their programs of preparation for entrance into occupations to the realities of the modern economic world and its conditions of employment, industrial processes, and labor organization. Some of the characteristics of programs of education for vocation are described here.

1. *Giving basic skills for families of jobs related to general education in the comprehensive high school.* General shop programs are replacing the specialized shop courses in many secondary schools. In these schools, pupils get varied types of experiences in wood, metal, auto mechanics, drafting, and machine tools rather than specializing in one of these phases. While much of this work is considered as general education, it is also prevocational in nature. In shop courses with vocational objectives, pupils make working drawings of their projects, learn to use hand tools and power machine tools in working with wood; make projects with sheet metal; learn how to use machine tools in constructing items of metal, such as hand tools; work with electric wiring, installation, and repairs; repair autos, often bringing their own to the school shop; do carpentry jobs in constructing actual houses. Blueprint reading, forging, and welding are less common types of experiences provided. The shop experiences are intended to give the pupil basic information, skills, and attitudes.

English, mathematics, science, and social studies are important phases of education for vocation. In addition to improving the individual's competency as a citizen, they often contribute directly to the vocational objective. In agriculture and distributive education programs, special efforts are made to relate these courses to that objective; for example, science is related to the need for scientific knowledge in farming, and economics courses include discussion of employment, labor-management relations, and similar problems.

The Sewanhaka Central High School District No. 2, New York

State, offers at Sewanhaka High School vocational and technical courses in the tenth through twelfth grades which combine academic and vocational or technical education. This is a comprehensive high school. Technical education has a vocational aim for pupils who plan to take further work in engineering colleges or technical institutes. Vocational courses are comprised of agriculture, including work experience for employment as florists, in nurseries, in kennels, on poultry farms, and other related fields of agriculture; automobile mechanics to prepare boys for employment in auto industries; beauty culture for girls who wish to become beauticians or beauty shop operators; machine shop practice in preparation for metal working trades; printing, publishing, and photographic processes to prepare youth for employment in fields of printing, advertising, and press work. Technical courses include architectural drafting and building construction, drafting and mechanical design, technical electricity and electronics, and instrumentation and automation for those who excel in mathematics and science.

Lakeview High School, Decatur, Illinois, has added vocational work in art for students who will go into studios, local agencies, printing departments of industries, department stores and the like. Design, color, drawing, art work and layout, operation of cameras and printing and duplicating machines are a part of the content. In the last two years students spend a daily four-hour block in vocational art class.

2. *Providing vocational education in separate secondary schools.* Although the vocational school has the disadvantage of segregating pupils at an early age and to some extent reinforcing class status, it cannot be denied that some of the vocational schools in large cities have provided the finest technical and vocational experiences for their pupils. Recognition is given, too, in some urban areas to the fact that large numbers leave high school at an early age.

Baltimore City provides a general vocational junior high school designed for pupils interested in exploring the whole field of vocational and trade skills and in acquiring definite occupational skills. Persons on the skilled and semiskilled levels as well as the highly skilled craftsmen can find opportunities for employment in Baltimore's diversified industries: thus the General Vocational Junior High School provides job preparation for the pupils of skilled and semiskilled ability and the vocational-technical high schools offer training opportunities for those pupils interested in the highly skilled and technical fields.

Baltimore City has two schools, The Mergenthaler Vocational-Technical High School and the Carver Vocational-Technical High

School, outstanding in their preparation of pupils for the trade and technical areas and in the stress that is placed on general education throughout their curriculum. In the curriculum, which may be terminal for many pupils, emphasis is placed on maximum development of general skills which prepare for entrance into employment. Course offerings include more than thirty-five trade, business, and industrial subjects some of which are: power sewing, distributive education, dressmaking and design, cosmetology, commercial art, and practical nursing for girls; automotive mechanics, airplane mechanics, brick masonry, trowel trades, carpentry, commercial baking, electric arc and gas welding, machine shop, drafting, printing, and industrial electronics for boys; food preparation and service, business education, tailoring, sign painting, and show-card writing for boys and girls. To meet the rapidly changing industrial pattern, a new series of technician programs has recently been added to the curriculum. These new courses are designed to prepare the pupil for the type of position best described as technician, whose duties will lie between the skilled tradesman and the graduate engineer. These courses, which provide an understanding of the growing field of technology as well as a practical knowledge of the basic trade skills are the following: airframe and powerplant technician, electrical maintenance technician, industrial electronics technician, mechanical technician, and tool design technician.

3. *Emphasizing work habits and attitudes.* In vocational programs, experiences are planned for the care of tools, thoroughness, and accuracy in carrying out projects, careful planning of work, promptness, and other habits and attitudes necessary for success in a vocation. For example, secretarial-training programs in high schools and junior colleges differ considerably in this respect from those in commercial business colleges. The latter teach the skills in the shortest period of time, while the former stress ability to take responsibility, attitudes toward employers, proper dress, background information, and skills in English. In related classes in distributive education programs, proper dress for work, relations with employers, and habits that contribute to success on the job are important problems discussed. In some schools the academic courses also deal with these problems.

4. *Placing vocational skills in upper secondary school years.* Much of the vocational work has tended to be placed in the upper years of the secondary school or in junior college, close to entrance to employment for many pupils. In Grades 7 through 10 pupils are given a well-developed curriculum in the various areas of general education considered essential to the life of every individual. Although the

pupil may have had opportunity to explore his abilities and interests in general shop courses in the first years of secondary school he does not begin to specialize until the later years, in some cases not until the thirteenth and fourteenth years. Some larger high schools receiving federal aid under the Smith-Hughes Act offer courses in skilled trades, such as the auto trades and building trades courses in Highland Park High School, Highland Park, Illinois.

USE OF COMMUNITY IN SPECIAL FIELDS. The entire community is the laboratory for some phases of specialized learnings for pupils of all types of abilities. Pupils learn by participation in the process and engage in experiences that have meaning and purpose. The use of the community is, of course, also a part of experiences in general education. Here the discussion is centered on the areas of specialized learnings.

1. *In many specialized fields.* Schools utilize the resources that exist for development of talents: zoos, botanical gardens, museums, libraries, learned societies, colleges, industrial research laboratories, industries, business places, shops, community theatres, television and radio stations, recreation programs, government agencies, young people's orchestra, reforestation projects, farms, travel to other areas, and people with different backgrounds. While those opportunities may be more restricted in the smaller communities, imagination in using a community as a school laboratory is not restricted by school size.

Vocational education programs are more likely to be closely linked with the community than other specialized areas. Surveys are conducted to determine what are the community needs. A larger community with a number of business establishments, for example, finds that there is a need and a demand for trained stenographers. Agriculture courses are established in farming areas where boys have an opportunity and an interest in farming. Distributive education programs are begun in communities that have a number of retailing establishments which are interested in having the schools develop this type of education.

2. *In agriculture.* In the vocational agriculture programs in secondary schools, the pupil's home farm is his laboratory. Much of the investigation and study that he does at school is centered around acquiring information that will be helpful in carrying on his projects on the farm. These are year-round projects that the farm boy carries through to completion under the supervision of the teacher of agriculture who works with him on the farm and at school.

In production projects, the pupil raises the crops, cattle, hogs, or some other kind of farm produce. He often owns his projects himself or in partnership with his father. For example, a boy will buy some calves, make his plans for raising them, plan how to feed them, keep records of costs, and market them at the proper time. The supplementary farm practices that are a part of his experiences consist of learning, through the actual operation, such skills as caponizing chickens, shearing sheep, or operating an incubator. The farm shop in connection with agriculture programs gives the pupil an opportunity to repair farm machinery that he uses and to learn skills useful to a farming career.

Another type of farm project, known as an improvement project, has as its objective improving the land, farm buildings, or stock. In one instance, farm youth might work for dairy herd improvement, keeping actual milk production and feeding records. At Frost Community School, Navarro County, Texas, the agriculture teacher and the high school boys in his classes have cooperated with the boys' fathers to extend such improvement projects to a community-wide basis. They have built terraces for conservation of the soil, sprayed fruit trees, introduced new crops, culled poultry, and helped in other ways to make their agricultural community a better place in which to live.

In response to a need for improvement in the breeding and care of poultry, the eighth grade of Plainview-Rover School, Plainview, Arkansas, constructed a poultry house and raised a flock of purebred chickens. In this community, the project supplied the lunchroom with eggs. It illustrates that in junior high school grades also, outside the federal vocational program, significant experiences in the area of agriculture are provided as an integral part of the life of the school. In some sections of the country where forestry is a source of livelihood, the school may own a forest, or the state may lease land to the school for forestry instruction. Elma High School, Elma, Washington, for example, owns several tracts of forest land where youth acquire firsthand laboratory experience in forestry practices.

3. *In business education.* Business education programs make good use of the school community as a laboratory for preparation in vocational skills and attitudes. Pupils serve as receptionists and typists in the school office, cashiers in the cafeteria, file clerks in the nurse's office, assistants in the guidance office. In the school community, teachers make good use of the lunchroom, the accounting of funds, and the planning and executing of pupil safety programs. They experience learning situations in books that must be checked and distributed, supplies that must be sold, and equipment that must be constructed. Often, these activities are tied in with the classroom work.

An example of training in the handling of money is found in

Weatherwax High School, Aberdeen, Washington, where the book-keeping classes take charge of activity accounts. The classroom here has become an integral part of the ongoing life of the school community.

4. *In service activities.* In some secondary schools, especially in rural areas of the South, activities in specialized areas are an integral part of a worthwhile program of experiences for both vocational and general education purposes. Pupils run the school store, run the feed and grist mills, work in the cannery, work in the slaughterhouse, or maintain the school grounds. Care is taken that pupils are not exploited and that such experiences are not merely drudgery and hard work.

5. *In home economics.* For many high school girls, home economics is a specialized phase of study, which the federally aided programs consider as having the objective of homemaking as a vocation. They may take courses for four years in order to develop their competencies as a homemaker. In the well-developed programs are found a wealth of firsthand experiences that are actually a part of the homemaker's life. Home economics teachers work with their pupils for more than nine months of the year. The best programs have more actual laboratory experiences than just in the areas of foods and clothing. In these schools, the girls take care of children, manage a house, prepare meals for outside groups, and do upholstering, wallpapering, painting, and the like. In South Philadelphia High School, girls have the opportunity to get firsthand information about children through participation in the child-care program in nursery schools.

Home nursing classes, as well as the more common homemaking classes, use the homes of the community for laboratory experiences. The pupils learn skills which they practice in their own and other homes of the community.

PART-TIME COOPERATIVE WORK PROGRAMS. One of the significant developments in American secondary education is the part-time cooperative program in which the school and business or industry cooperate in providing the education for youth. The plan has been given an impetus through federal aid to the school under the George-Deen Act of 1936.

The general plan. Pupils spend part of the time at school and part of the time on the job. In some cases, they alternate a few weeks at school and at work, in others, a half a day is spent at school and half a day on the job. During the time at school, pupils receive training related to the job and take other related courses. In retailing programs, the related work may consist of show-card lettering, salesmanship, and other skills useful to the job. Related study may include employer-employee relationships and conditions that promote successful employment. A coordinator employed by the school supervises the pupils on the job and serves as contact person with the employers. At the school, he gives the related training courses. Pupils and teacher plan their work together to fit the needs of the particular job. Each pupils will have individual goals, for no two jobs will be exactly the same.

In this type of plan, the school gives the general education and the broad, general vocational education, while the community provides the laboratory for actual work experience. It is fundamentally an educational program, for no employer is obligated to hire any of the trainees as his regular employees after they have completed training. It is realistic, for it meets community needs and is set into the community rather than apart from it. It holds promise for the future, since it does not require huge outlays of funds for equipping elaborate school shops designed to give training in specific skills.

Distributive education. One type of federally aided program, known as distributive education, deals with retailing and other distributive occupations. The school and the place of business cooperate in the education program. In Suffolk High School, Suffolk, Virginia, the pupil works at a store, which serves as his laboratory for vocational education, for fifteen to twenty-five hours a week. He learns the different aspects of the work and is supervised by the coordinator from the school. At school, he studies salesmanship, advertising, display, business English, store- and stockkeeping, and related work as a part of a course in retail selling.

The cooperative retail selling program at Springfield High School, Springfield, Vermont, is planned by the coordinator and the merchants of the community. Pupils work afternoons in the stores during their senior year for fifteen to eighteen hours a week. They are at school during the morning for English, social studies, physical education, and the related subjects. Apprenticeship wages, determined cooperatively by the school and a Merchants' Advisory Committee, are paid to pupils for their work. The merchant trains the pupil in various phases of retail selling as a part of his experience on the job. This training includes use of the cash register, the writing of sales slips, wrapping, filling orders, marking merchandise, inventory, store arrangement, window display, sales technique, and the like. The store manager reports to the school coordinator on the student's progress. In addition, the Springfield public schools have planned with industry another type of cooperative education program in the machine shop and technical education area.

Diversified occupations. Another type of common vocational program is cooperative training for specified occupations, in some states called a "diversified occupations" program. This is a form of part-time education adaptable to smaller communities, since no elaborate equipment is needed in the school. It involves a cooperative arrangement between the school and local businesses and industries. In this plan there is a variety of types of jobs in which the pupils may receive their training, such as, foods, printing, electrical repair, shipping clerk, automobile body repair, cleaning and pressing, jewelry repair, and general store work.

At Evanston Township High School, Evanston, Illinois, a cooperative training program is offered for students interested in entering a skilled trade or industrial occupation. This program in diversified occupations offers an opportunity for junior and senior boys and girls to train part time at the career of their choice. The school provides the related instruction and the employer trains the student-learner in the job skills and procedures as he progresses on the job. Some typical occupations in which the student-learner may be trained are: automotive mechanics, commercial art, radio and television repair, electrical appliance repair, machinist, laboratory technician, photography, building trades, and nursery work. The students are employed and placed in a learning situation for a minimum of three hours per day and fifteen hours per week at a salary comparable to that paid other beginning workers in that field.

Montgomery Blair High School, Montgomery County, Maryland, offers three types of work experience programs in which seniors and a limited number of juniors attend classes half of the school day (English, job problems and electives) and work the other half-day for employers selected for adequate training programs. Students earn two and one-half to three and one-half credits for supervised work experience including job problems, and two or three credits for the other two or three general subjects. The program consists of distributive education, commercial work experience, and diversified occupations.

Office practice work. In many instances where secondary schools may not have a part-time cooperative education program under the federal plan, they have established cooperative working relations with the business offices of the community. The office practice course, usually offered in the senior year to pupils preparing for stenographic work, is an example of that type of plan. In connection with this class, pupils may receive work experience on the job, either through part-time work or work in an office over an extended number of days, such as during vacation periods.

SELECTED REFERENCES

Administration of Vocational Education. U.S. Department of Health, Education, and Welfare, Office of Education, Vocational Education Bulletin, 1948, No. 1, General Series No. 1, Washington, D.C.: Government Printing Office, 1949, 112 pp.—Presents a brief, convenient description of the various kinds of federally aided vocational education programs.

AMERICAN ASSOCIATION OF SCHOOL ADMINISTRATORS AND OTHERS. *Labels and Fingerprints.* Washington, D.C.: The Association, 1960, not paged.—A cogent statement on individualizing the school program and the threats to uniqueness and individuality in certain school practices.

ASSOCIATION FOR SUPERVISION AND CURRICULUM DEVELOPMENT. "Creativity." *Educational Leadership,* 18:3-42, October, 1960.—This issue of the journal is devoted to the theme of creativity with articles on creativity in language arts, dramatics, science and mathematics, art.

Catskill Area Project in Small School Design. Oneonta, N.Y.: The Project, 1959, 25 pp. —This report of the project describes some ways by which small secondary schools can provide for special needs of pupils through correspondence courses, equipment, and use of the community's resources.

DOUGLASS, HARL R. (ed.). *The High School Curriculum.* New York: The Ronald Press Co., 2nd ed., 1956, Chaps. 8, 22-30.—Different chapters are written by specialists in science, foreign languages, mathematics, home and family living, business education, music, industrial arts, and art. Includes some discussion of education for vocation.

CHASE, FRANCIS S. and ANDERSON, HAROLD A. (eds.). *The High School in a New Era.* Chicago: University of Chicago Press, 1958, pp. 362-379, 433-446.—Programs for the gifted and for low-ability students and in vocational education are examined in these sections.

EVERETT, SAMUEL (ed.). *Programs for the Gifted: A Case Book in Secondary Education.* (Fifteenth Yearbook of the John Dewey Society). New York: Harper & Brothers, 1961, Chaps. 7-12.—Contains a number of descriptions of programs in secondary schools especially developed for the talented youth.

FORD FOUNDATION, FUND FOR THE ADVANCEMENT OF EDUCATION. *They Went to College Early.* New York: The Fund, 1957, 80 pp.—Evaluation of the early admission program to college.

GARRISON, IVAN K., "The Mentally Retarded in the Secondary School," in *Frontiers of Secondary Education I,* Paul Halverson, ed. Syracuse: Syracuse University Press, 1956, pp. 77-95.—Discusses kind of program developed, some of the psychological facts related to teaching the mentally retarded, and the organization of programs for this group.

GAVIN, RUTH WOOD (ed.). *The Social Education of the Academically Talented.* Curriculum Series, No. 10, Washington, D.C.: National Council for the Social Studies, 1958, 101 pp.—Describes practices in both secondary and elementary schools in the broad area of social education. Valuable for other fields than social studies, especially in its discussion of issues and principles.

HAVIGHURST, ROBERT J. and OTHERS. *A Survey of the Education of Gifted Children.* Supplementary Educational Monographs, No. 83, Chicago: University of Chicago Press, 1955, 114 pp.—Summaries of programs in some forty-five school systems.

278 CURRICULUM AND INSTRUCTION

JOHNSTON, MARJORIE C. and SEERLEY, CATHERINE C. *Foreign Language Laboratories in Schools and Colleges.* U.S. Department of Health, Education, and Welfare, Office of Education, Bulletin 1959, No. 3, Washington, D.C.: Government Printing Office, 1958. 86 pp.—Describes the growth of language laboratories and gives examples of the modern approach in foreign languages.

KELLER, FRANKLIN J. *The Double-Purpose High School.* New York: Harper & Bros., 1953, 207 pp.—Discussion and descriptions of curricula in comprehensive and in vocational high schools. Emphasis on relation of vocational to academic education.

MORSE, ARTHUR D. *Schools of Tomorrow—Today,* Garden City, New York: Doubleday & Co., Inc., 1960, 191 pp.—This paperback volume reports experiments conducted by schools, some of which describe projects in searching for talented students, specialized kinds of activities and facilities for the talented, and summer programs for the abler student.

NATIONAL EDUCATION ASSOCIATION.
Administration Procedures and School Practices for the Academically Talented Student. 1960, 223 pp.
Identification and Education of the Academically Talented Student in the American Secondary School. 1958, 160 pp.
Art for the Academically Talented Student. 1961, 112 pp.
English for the Academically Talented Student. 1960, 128 pp.
Guidance for the Academically Talented Student. 1961, 144 pp.
Mathematics for the Academically Talented Student. 1959, 48 pp.
Modern Foreign Languages for the Academically Talented Student. 1960, 89 pp.
Music for the Academically Talented Student, 1960, 127 pp.
Science for the Academically Talented Student. 1959, 63 pp.
Social Studies for the Academically Talented Student. 1959, 42 pp.
Summary of Research on the Academically Talented Student. 1959, 42 pp.—Washington, D.C.: National Education Association.
These are excellent statements on the different subject fields developed by experts in the field, and on some general issues and administrative problems.

NATIONAL ASSOCIATION OF SECONDARY-SCHOOL PRINCIPALS. *Modern Foreign Languages in the Comprehensive Secondary School.* Washington, D.C.: The Association, 1959, 16 pp.—A position paper on the program of foreign languages developed by the Association's Committee on Curriculum Planning and Development.

NATIONAL ASSOCIATION OF SECONDARY-SCHOOL PRINCIPALS. "Secondary Education for Mentally Retarded Pupils." *Bulletin of the National Association of Secondary-School Principals,* 39:1-162, January, 1955.—A review of the national status of education for mentally retarded at the secondary school level.

NATIONAL ASSOCIATION OF SECONDARY-SCHOOL PRINCIPALS. "Seeking Improved Learning Opportunities." *Bulletin of the National Association of Secondary-School Principals,* 45:1-285, January, 1961.—In this fourth report of the Association's staff utilization studies are some good articles describing independent study plans in secondary schools.

PASSOW, A. HARRY and OTHERS. *Planning for Talented Youth.* New York: Bureau of Publications, Teachers College, Columbia University, 1955, 84 pp.—This pamphlet discusses succinctly information on the issues and practices in providing for abler students. Based on research in the field.

12

EXPERIENCES IN EXTRACLASS ACTIVITIES

In the last fifty years a considerable change has taken place in the point of view concerning "extracurricular" activities. More and more it is realized that these activities can make a significant contribution to the educational growth of the child. For instance, the pupil may make far more growth in oral expression on the debating team than in an English class; his growth in music appreciation as a member of the band or orchestra may be greater than in the more formal music class; he may have more opportunity to develop writing skills as a reporter for the school paper than in the English class; and his growth in certain citizenship qualities from participation in school clubs may be as significant as in the social studies class.

The realization that extraclass activities have significant educational values has encouraged educators to attach increasing importance to them. Educators today believe that these activities should not be considered "extra," but that they should be considered part of the school curriculum, the educational activities provided under the supervision of the school. In harmony with this point of view, activities are called "extraclass" rather than "extracurricular," to distinguish them from those activities which form a part of the usual classroom program.

In many schools it is difficult to distinguish between "class" and "extraclass" activities. For instance, such music organizations as band, orchestra, choir, and glee club are frequently scheduled in the program of the school much like any other subject. Similarly, the student council may be given a place in the regular daily schedule, the staff for the newspaper and yearbook may be given credit toward graduation for this work, and intramural sports may be included as part of the physical education program. It should be recognized therefore, that the designation of activities included in the present chapter as "extraclass" is to some extent an arbitrary one and can be justified only as a basis for discussing these activities.

BASIC PRINCIPLES

Certain principles are basic to a forward-looking and effective program of extraclass activities in the secondary school. These principles are appropriate to all the different types of activities. They apply at both the junior and the senior high school levels.

Extraclass activities should be considered a significant part of the total educational experience of the child in school and should, therefore, be included as an integral part of the total educational program.

The justification of extraclass activities in the program of the school is the same as for any subject in the curriculum; namely, that they contribute to the educational growth and development of children. Only those activities, therefore, should be introduced into the program of the school which clearly can make such a contribution. Furthermore, the emphasis on each of these activities should be governed by their importance to the educational program. In other words, social activities are justified not as entertainment, but because they provide learning experiences for children not offered elsewhere in the school program. Similarly, sports activities, assembly programs, clubs, and student publications—these activities, and others, are justified as part of the program of the secondary school because they help youth develop in health, citizenship skills, character, basic language, and in other important ways.

The more important objectives of the program of extraclass activities are as follows:

1. To help pupils develop qualities of leadership, group cooperation, and other qualities essential to effective democratic living.
2. To help pupils acquire certain personal and character qualities, such as self-confidence, poise, initiative, resourcefulness, courtesy, and self-control.
3. To help pupils explore various interests, talents, and abilities, in a manner which would be difficult in the usual classroom program.
4. To assist pupils to be active and creative, and to gain the satisfaction that comes from accomplishing things that to them are interesting and worth while.
5. To give pupils an opportunity to apply many of the fundamental skills and much of the knowledge which they acquire in other ways in the classroom program.

The extraclass activities should be closely correlated with other aspects of the school's instructional program.

When extraclass activities were first introduced into the secondary school program, they were clearly "extra" in every sense of the word. Participation was often confined to a few pupils, the activities took place after the regular school hours, and in other ways these activities were set apart from the educational program. Educators today believe that the instructional program of the school should be planned as a whole, with every part of that program closely correlated with every other. For instance, the clubs, the classes, and the homerooms should prepare and present assembly programs; the English and social studies classes should prepare pupils for responsibilities as officers of clubs and the student council; the homerooms, homemaking classes, and English classes should give pupils backgrounds in etiquette and social practices for more effective participation in school parties; and in other ways the work in the various classes and in extraclass activities should contribute to each other.

With careful planning, some extraclass activities may provide excellent opportunities to apply the basic skills and knowledge taught in the regular class program. For instance, experience in oral expression may be provided by the student council, clubs, assemblies, debating teams, and dramatic productions; written expression may become more functional through participation on the school newspaper or the yearbook; basic knowledge in science may be extended through photography clubs, science clubs, and science fairs; and music and art skills may be developed through the clubs, organizations, and activities in these subjects. In fact, the motivation provided by extraclass activities can make a tremendous contribution to the growth of pupils in the skills and knowledge taught in the classroom program.

The program of extraclass activities should be sufficiently broad and varied to provide for the needs, abilities, and interests of all the pupils in school.

If the program of extraclass activities is to serve the purposes for which it is intended, it is essential that there be clubs to interest every pupil, sports activities for every boy and girl, music organizations for pupils at different levels of ability, and assembly activities that appeal to every interest. This indeed presents a challenge to every teacher and administrator in the secondary school. That it can be done is evident from the practices found in many junior and senior high schools today, some of which will be presented later in this chapter.

For some pupils, the major motivation in school may well come from their participation in one or more of the extraclass activities. This is particularly true of boys during adolescent years when their interests in academic activities may not as yet have matured. For instance, a boy who plays football may well find all his school work more interesting because of his enthusiasm for this sport. Similarly, participation in music organizations, "pep" squads, student council, dramatics, and numerous other activities provide tremendous interest for some pupils.

The management of extraclass activities should provide for pupil participation and responsibility in their control, administration, and planning.

Pupils should participate in developing the extraclass program as a whole. For instance, they should be consulted when the offering of a new club is being considered; they should help plan the assembly activities for the year; and they should offer suggestions for the year's social functions. What is more, pupils should have a considerable part in planning and carrying on the specific activities, once the program is under way. In the clubs, the members should plan the activities, the projects, and the meetings. Pupils should serve on committees for planning school parties, they should participate in policy decisions in the student council, and they should make decisions concerning school publications and prepare the materials for them. Such pupil participation should always take place under competent faculty supervision.

These activities provide an excellent laboratory for skills in democratic living. As pupils assume responsibility for the various activities, they learn how to make and carry out group decisions, to organize group activities, to work democratically with their fellows, and to evaluate their successes and failures in group activity. Pupil participation in the government of the school should involve some real responsibility, and not be limited to petty tasks the administration may want to have done. Only if they assume important responsibilities will pupils experience the satisfaction of making a significant contribution to the life of the school, and thus have enthusiasm for further participation.

The pupil's school experience outside of class should be planned as carefully by administrators, teachers, and pupils as any other phase of the instructional program.

The idea that these activities were "extra" has had considerable bearing on the attention which has been given to planning and organizing them. Planning for them after the "regular" school work is done too often results in little actual planning by either teachers or pupils. Where this attitude persists, much of the educational value of extraclass activities will not be realized. The principal and faculty should plan the entire program of extraclass activities for the school, having pupils participate as much as their time and ability permit. Faculty sponsors working with pupil officers and committees should carefully prepare the program and organization of each individual activity. The same principles of organization and planning which pertain to English, the social studies, and other subjects, are equally appropriate for assemblies, student publications, clubs, speech activities, and the student council. The thorough planning of extraclass activities in terms of specific educational objectives is essential if these activities are to contribute significantly to the education of youth.

Extraclass activities should be carried on at a time and administered in such a way that all interested pupils may participate.

According to this principle, the educational values of extraclass activities are realized to the fullest extent only if all interested pupils can participate. This does not mean that extraclass activities must necessarily be confined to the regular school day. For some activities, such as intramural and interscholastic sports, it is difficult to provide sufficient time either for practice or for games during regular school hours. This principle does suggest, however, that the arrangements for extraclass activities should not exclude anyone who is interested in participating.

The arrangements that need to be made to implement this principle must vary a great deal from school to school. In rural communities, where all pupils come to school by bus, a longer school day may be necessary, special buses may have to be arranged for pupils who participate, or the activities may be scheduled at other times when pupils can participate. In urban communities, where all pupils live within walking distance of the school, some activities may be carried on after school or on Saturdays. If extraclass activities have significant educational values for youth, these activities need to be arranged in such a way that pupils may take part in them.

The extraclass activities should be evaluated continually in terms of the educational goals they are to achieve.

Continuous evaluation is essential to the success of any part of the educational program. This is true for extraclass activities fully as much as for other parts of the curriculum. Answers are needed for questions such as: What activities particularly contribute to the educational growth of children? What activities apparently make little contribution to such growth? How well are the principles for an effective extraclass program being implemented? How can the effectiveness of the various activities be improved? What new activities should be added to the program? What proportion of the student body takes part in extraclass activities? Everyone who is in any way concerned with the extraclass activities should participate in evaluating them. This includes the principal of the school, the supervisors, teachers, parents, and pupils. Pupils especially should take a significant part in evaluating the effectiveness of the activities in which they participate. It is through continuous evaluation that the extraclass activities may be improved so as to contribute increasingly to the educational growth of children.

The interests and the needs of individual pupils should be the primary prerequisites to participation in extraclass activities.

The pupil with poor speech habits, the one who has little musical talent, or the one with mediocre athletic ability, as well as the talented youth, should have the opportunity to improve himself through participation in extraclass activities. This does not mean that every pupil should play on the first team, represent the school in interscholastic debate, or have the lead in the class play. That would hardly be desirable, if it were possible. This principle does mean, however, that the sports program should have a team for every pupil; that the music organizations should provide a place for pupils of various talents; that there should be numerous activities in speech and dramatics so that every interested pupil may participate; that elective offices are distributed so that many pupils may gain experience in leadership positions; and that clubs, assemblies, and school publications are so planned that all pupils who may profit from them are encouraged to take part.

The principle suggests, furthermore, that it is not desirable to have school clubs or other organizations elect their members, like college fraternities and sororities, or to place other blocks in the way of participation. The pupil's interest in the activity and his ability to participate satisfactorily should be the primary prerequisites for membership. If extraclass activities are truly educational in nature and purpose, then they, like class activities, should be available to all pupils who may profit from them.

SOME COMMON PRACTICES

VARIETY OF ACTIVITIES. The outstanding characteristic of extraclass activities in the secondary schools today is the variety and number of these activities. This is true of activities in all types of secondary schools—junior high schools, senior high schools, and four-year high schools. A typical program of activities in a secondary school includes interscholastic and intramural athletics, clubs, assemblies, dramatics, music organizations, school newspaper and periodical, yearbook, student council, social functions, debating teams, declamation and oratory, cheer leaders, baton twirlers, and a host of others.

The traditions of a secondary school are centered to a large extent in the program of extraclass activities. At least that is true of those which give character to the student life of the school. The extraclass activities of a school, consequently, have a tremendous influence on the morale of the student body, its loyalties and school spirit, and its attitude toward the total educational program. There is little doubt but that the attitude of pupils toward the curriculum program, and their success in it, are influenced by their interest in extraclass activities.

In many secondary schools, the great number and variety of extraclass activities, desirable as they may be, also present some problems. Frequently, the activities have been introduced one after another, but without much thought to their place in the educational program as a whole. Then, too, some pupils engage in too many activities at one time, while the participation of others who need these educational experiences is limited. If these activities are to contribute to worth-while educational goals, definite leadership for the entire program of activities is essential. In many schools, however, there is no such leadership. The principal usually assumes this responsibility with a multitude of other duties. In some schools, a professional staff member who has the experience, the interest, and the time for it is specifically designated as the director of extraclass activities.

EXTENSIVE CLUB ACTIVITIES IN JUNIOR HIGH SCHOOL. In both junior and senior high schools, pupil clubs are a significant part of the program of extraclass activities. Practices governing these activities vary widely from school to school. In junior high schools, it is common to offer a considerable variety of club activities so that every child may find one of interest. In these schools, clubs usually meet during an activities period which is part of the regular school day, every pupil is expected—though not required—to belong, and the dues and other costs are held to a minimum. There are seldom prerequisites for membership, other than the pupil's interest in the club. In the junior high school, election by the present club group as a requirement for membership is seldom permitted.

One characteristic of club activities common to both junior and senior high schools is the attempt to meet the interests of all pupils. Half a century ago, clubs were limited largely to debating and literary societies. Today, many large schools have a club for every conceivable interest of boys and girls. The clubs include school service clubs, such as leadership, safety patrol, and "pep" leaders; hobby and special interest clubs, such as marionette making, wood carving, stamp collecting, bird study, and photography; and subject area clubs, such as French, Spanish, and Latin. Later in this chapter, a comprehensive club program in a specific secondary school will be described.

There is the possibility, however, that club activities may prove to be little more than busy work for the pupils. In fact, this characterizes the club activities in some secondary schools. In other schools, the faculty sponsor of a club has a particular responsibility for avoiding this possibility. He should help pupils plan the activities of the club with definite educational objectives in mind. The faculty sponsor and the pupil members should continually evaluate the effectiveness of the club in terms of the educational purposes it is intended to serve.

DISCOURAGEMENT OF FRATERNITIES. One of the most difficult problems for the faculty and administration in some secondary schools is secret societies such as fraternities and sororities. Often they meet away from the school building with no supervision from teachers or parents. Not only are they undemocratic in their selection of members, but it is doubtful that they serve any worth-while educational purpose. Still, they have existed for years in some schools, and continue to do so despite objections from school administrators, teachers, and parents.

In some states, fraternities and sororities at the secondary-school level have been declared illegal by legislative statute. Courageous school administrators and interested parent groups have attacked the problem with varying degrees of success. One positive approach is to have an excellent program of club activities and social functions which will appeal to every pupil who might have an interest in belonging to a fraternity or sorority. Under intelligent supervision from faculty and parents, clubs and social activities can do much to satisfy those desires and interests of pupils to which fraternities and sororities in the secondary schools have such a strong appeal.

FORMAL SPEECH ACTIVITIES. The speech activities in the secondary school usually include debate, oratory, interpretative reading, and extemporaneous speaking. In the junior high school, these activities tend to be conducted on an informal basis, with much emphasis on wide pupil participation, non-competitive activities, and activities confined largely to the regular school day. Speech activities in the junior high school are carried on in assemblies, clubs, and English and social studies classes. In some communities, there is interschool competition in speech at the junior high school level, although it is usually between schools in the same system. Some junior high schools, however, have interscholastic competition in speech activities, much like the senior high school, a practice not generally encouraged in the junior high school. Such a program with emphasis on winning may interfere with the development of speech activities for all interested pupils.

The activities in the senior high school differ sharply from those in the junior high school. In the senior high school, the speeches are usually quite formal, with participation limited to a few able pupils; there is considerable interschool competition in debate, oratory, and declamation; and much attention is given to the audience situation. Although competitive speech activities are more appropriate in the senior than in the junior high school, even there they may not serve the needs of pupils in a comprehensive secondary school. Competitive speech activities often reach only a limited number of all the pupils in schools. These activities should be a part of a broad speech program in which every interested pupil may participate in some way.

ATHLETICS FOR THE FEW. The program of athletics in the secondary school attracts more interest among the student body and the public than any other pupil activities. At the same time, it is also the most controversial part of the entire educational program of the secondary school. There are reasons for this. In many senior high schools, interscholastic competition is strongly emphasized, with less attention to intramural activities in which every pupil may participate. Teams other than the varsity often exist primarily to provide training for boys who later may make the varsity squad. Limited attention is given to sports for adult life, such as swimming, golf, and tennis. Girls frequently have little, if any, place in the senior high school sports program. Furthermore, the interest of sports fans in the community in building winning teams may overshadow the educational purposes that the program of athletics should serve.

The only justification for any activity in the program of a secondary school is the contribution it makes to the educational growth and development of youth. Measured by this criterion, the athletics program in some senior high schools is indeed found wanting. It is true that more and more schools are developing broad intramural programs. This is good. Too often, however, the demands of the varsity teams on the time of the faculty and on the physical facilities of the school are so great that intramural activities are far too limited. Examples of broad sports programs are given later in this chapter.

In the junior high school, there is often a broad sports program which has a place for every interested boy and girl. Intramural activities tend to predominate in the junior high school, with competition carried on between grades, homerooms, or physical education classes. Usually these activities come in the afternoon rather than the evening; participation by many pupils is emphasized; and there are sports activities for girls as well as boys.

In the past decade, interscholastic athletics have been greatly expanded in the junior high school. A recent study reveals that more than 85 per cent of the junior high schools in the United States have some type of interscholastic athletics. About one-third of the junior high schools with an interscholastic program, however, play only schools within the same system. The sports most popular in the interscholastic program of the junior high schools include, in order of popularity: (1) basketball, (2) track, (3) football, (4) baseball, (5) softball, and (6) swimming.

There are mixed opinions regarding the growth of interscholastic athletics in the junior high school. The majority of the principals of schools that have such programs favor them. There are many educators, however, who strongly oppose interscholastic sports competition for junior high school pupils. This group includes many junior high school principals, specialists in physical education and health, and other leading educators. Conant, after studying the programs of 237 junior high schools in the United States by visiting them and observing their programs, said in his report: "Interscholastic athletics . . . are to be condemned in junior high schools; there is no sound educational reason for them and too often they serve merely as public entertainment."[1] Both the proponents and opponents of interscholastic athletics in the junior high school do agree, however,

[1] James B. Conant, *Education in the Junior High School Years*, Princeton, N.J.: Educational Testing Service, 1960, p. 42.

that there should be a broad intramural sports program in junior high schools, and that these activities should not be overshadowed by interscholastic competition.

In both junior and senior high schools, girls are badly neglected in the sports program. In many schools, there are no activities at all for girls, except in the physical education classes. Frequently, the gymnasium, swimming pool, and playgrounds are just not available for a girls' sports program. Although it need not be as extensive or as strenuous a program as that for boys, the better school situations recognize that there should be some sports activities which meet the needs and interests of secondary school girls.

RESPONSIBILITIES OF STUDENT COUNCILS. The participation of pupils in the administration of the school is most commonly provided through the organization of a student council. The council is usually a representative pupil body elected by grades or homerooms and serves under a constitution which defines its duties and responsibilities. Usually, its authority is limited to such activities as (1) the direction of corridor traffic, (2) cafeteria supervision, (3) supervision of pupil elections, (4) the sponsoring of assemblies, parties, and field days, and (5) service as an advisory body to the principal and faculty.

The student council, more than any other student organization, can contribute to the development of good school morale, loyalties to the school and its traditions, and wholesome school citizenship attitudes among pupils. These factors may in turn be reflected in desirable attitudes toward the total educational program and, ultimately, in better achievement by pupils in their studies. In some schools, the effectiveness of the student council is limited because its meetings are too infrequent. In most schools, the student council meets once a week, but in others only every other week. A few schools schedule student council meetings daily or several times weekly just like any class. Deliberation and study by the student council of important school problems requires more time than an occasional meeting affords.

The student council as an organized activity has developed much farther in senior than in junior high schools. In fact, some junior high school principals and teachers question the maturity of early adolescents to assume responsibility for student council activities, although the success of student councils in some junior high schools refutes this point of view. In the latter schools pupils have the experience of engaging in student council activities at a level that is appropriate for early adolescents.

PUPIL PUBLICATIONS AS AN EXTRACLASS ACTIVITY. The most common pupil publications in the secondary school are the school paper, yearbook, magazine, and pupil handbook. These publications are usually prepared by editorial staffs composed of pupils working under the supervision of a faculty committee or adviser. In large schools, the paper and the magazine are usually issued on a regular schedule, although in small schools this is not always possible. In some schools, these publications are the work of the English classes, while in others they are an extraclass activity with an editorial staff chosen from the student body. Especially in the senior high schools, the latter practice is common.

The pupil handbook is usually prepared to inform pupils about the traditions, administrative practices, and regulations of the school. Usually there is one issue a year. In some schools the same handbook is used for several years. The handbook may be prepared by the faculty or the principal purely as an administrative device to help orient new pupils to the school. Sometimes the student council prepares the handbook, making this one of its major projects for the year. Other pupil groups that prepare the school handbook are a citizenship club or a school service club.

Pupil publications can make a significant contribution to the educational program of the secondary school. In many schools it is considered desirable to have close correlation between these publications and the work in certain subject areas, especially English. Although competent faculty supervision of school publications is considered desirable, such supervision should not discourage freedom of expression by pupils. Pupil publications are a part of the total program of instruction in written expression and should provide opportunities for many pupils to apply writing skills developed elsewhere in the school program.

SOCIAL ACTIVITIES AS ENTERTAINMENT. The social functions in the secondary school frequently provide entertainment activities for pupils, and nothing more. As such it is difficult indeed to justify the time and attention which these activities receive. Social activities should help boys and girls develop desirable personality qualities; acquire skills in music, art, and dramatics; gain confidence, poise, and skill in various social situations; and form wholesome boy-girl relationships.

In many schools, the program of social activities is much too limited to provide the experiences that adolescents need to develop these qualities. These activities may consist of only two or three evening dances during the school year. Sometimes the pupils who attend are those least in need of social development, while pupils from poor backgrounds stay away. Some schools have many informal social activities, such as parties during the club and homeroom periods, informal dancing during the noon hour and after school, and social activities for special groups like the athletic squads, play casts, and the student council. Such informal social activities may reach many pupils who do not have the money, the clothes, and the social poise to attend more formal affairs.

The effectiveness of social activities depends to a large extent on how well they are planned and carried on. Much help should be given pupils to learn how to participate in these activities. Various aspects of the social graces should be studied in homerooms, clubs, and other activities—how to ask a girl for a "date," courtesies toward one's "date," and courtesies toward the chaperones. In the junior high school, attention should be given to table manners, what to wear, and how to conduct oneself at a party. Before dancing parties, there should be instruction in social dancing. In schools where such preparation for social activities is given, these activities contribute more fully to the wholesome growth of boys and girls.

MAJOR PRODUCTIONS IN DRAMATICS. The presentation of a play by the junior class and the senior class has become the accepted practice in most senior high schools. Most senior high schools have a dramatics club, which presents programs for school assemblies, social functions, and parents' groups. In most senior high schools, the opportunity to participate in dramatics productions is limited to a few pupils, with many others who need this experience having no opportunity for it.

In junior high schools, dramatics activities are much more informal than in the senior high school. In few junior high schools, for instance, are there major productions like the junior or senior class play. The dramatics activities emphasize presentations at club meetings, school parties, and school assemblies. These activities may be centered in a dramatics club, though in some schools they are part of the oral expression work in the English classes. The informal dramatics activities of the junior high school have the advantage of distributing participation among more pupils. In both junior and senior high schools, however, dramatics activities could be used more extensively than at present to teach oral expression, to help pupils gain confidence before an audience, and to develop certain personality qualities.

IMPLEMENTATION OF THE PRINCIPLES

Some secondary schools have made definite strides in applying the principles concerning extraclass activities suggested earlier in this chapter. The activities are being correlated more closely with the classroom program; they are being expanded to provide better for the needs and interests of all pupils; and they are being planned increasingly to achieve educational objectives.

INTEGRATION WITH CLASSROOM ACTIVITIES. Some pupil activities in secondary schools are correlated closely with the regular class work in certain subjects. The school publications, such as the paper, the yearbook, and the magazine, are the best examples of such correlation. At Central High School, Aberdeen, South Dakota, classes in journalism edit the paper and the yearbook. Two years of journalism are offered, one year of which may be substituted for the English requirement in the twelfth grade. Every interested pupil with sufficient skill in writing to qualify for the classes in journalism can participate in these activities.

In the Louis Pasteur Junior High School, Los Angeles, California, pupils in eighth-grade arithmetic classes take turns serving as cashier in the school cafeteria and in operating the school store, which sells school supplies at certain hours of the day. The business-education classes at Windham High School, Willimantic, Connecticut, are in charge of the school bank, where pupils purchase tickets for various school activities. Class and club dues, tickets for various events, and supplies and equipment needed for clubs and other activities, are paid for at the school bank. The business-education classes at Windham keep the records for classes, clubs, and other school organizations. These pupils are under the supervision of a teacher of business education, who likewise serves as the central school treasurer.

In the Herman Ridder Junior High School, New York, New York, pupils are placed in English classes according to their interest in journalism, dramatics, or speech activities. They carry on the usual work of the English class, but in addition they emphasize the activity in which they have an interest. At the Sierra Junior High School, Riverside, California, pupils carry on a well-planned election campaign for school officers, which includes campaign speeches that are given before the student body. The teachers of English help pupils prepare these speeches and give them an opportunity to practice in their English classes. In well-planned election campaigns like those at Sierra Junior High School, pupils have an excellent experience in citizenship as well as in oral expression.

School clubs are frequently correlated with the work that pupils do in certain subjects. The Wilson Junior High School, Philadelphia, Pennsylvania, has an extensive offering of school clubs, most of which meet once a week. Although the list of clubs includes many that meet special interests of pupils, there are also clubs in various subject areas that may be closely correlated with the work in those subjects. The subject-area clubs include creative writing, book lovers, dramatics, German, Latin, French, Russian, newspaper, algebra, advanced science, history films, science experiments, instrumental, mathematics puzzle, art, electronics, and woodwork. Clubs such as these may do a great deal to motivate the interest of pupils and to supplement the work of certain subject areas.

CREDIT TOWARD GRADUATION. In some schools, participation in extraclass activities counts toward graduation requirements. At Central High School, Aberdeen, South Dakota, pupils are required to earn 18 extracurricular points in addition to the 16 units in subject areas to meet graduation requirements. The extracurricular points consist of a minimum of 180 clock hours of participation in various types of activities.

At the Oakland High School, Oakland, California, some extraclass activities which are scheduled during the regular school day may count toward the 24 units required for graduation. The student council at Oakland High School meets daily as a regularly scheduled class in leadership, with pupils studying ways of planning and carrying on student council activities. Another student group at Oakland that meets as a regular class is the youth council, which is composed of class and club officers and other pupil leaders. Although activities such as these count toward graduation requirements, they are usually in addition to requirements in the regular school subjects. When credit is given for such activities, it not only gives them more status, but it is possible to demand more thorough preparation and participation on the part of the pupils. Consequently, the activities are more likely to contribute to the educational growth of pupils.

ADEQUATE TIME FOR ACTIVITIES. The most common method of providing time for pupil activities is to have an activities period in the regular daily schedule. At the Franklin Junior High School, Aurora, Illinois, there is a thirty-minute activity period at the end of each day for club meetings, homeroom activities, and assemblies. At the Norwich Free Academy, Norwich, Connecticut, there is a full class period for activities five days a week. The Como Park Junior High

School, St. Paul, Minnesota, has a rotating schedule which provides for two full class periods each week for clubs, assemblies, and other activities.

There are numerous other ways of providing adequate time for pupil activities. Some schools have an extended period which is considered a part of the regular school day, but in which not all pupils participate each day, as, for example, the Edwin O. Smith School, Storrs, Connecticut. Clubs, sports, and other similar activities are scheduled for the extended period. The Manatee High School, Bradenton, Florida, has a study day twice a month, when assemblies are held and most clubs meet. (See Chapter 15 for explanation of the study day.) At Bradenton, therefore, clubs and assemblies do not interfere with the regular classes.

In some communities, where pupils do not come to school on buses, activities are carried on after school hours, usually in the afternoon or on Saturday morning. At the Melbourne High School, Melbourne, Florida, many of the activities are held in the evening. For instance, on a Monday evening the honor society may have its meeting at 6:30, with other clubs meeting at 7:30. Many assembly programs also are held in the evening. Participation in evening activities at Melbourne High School has been exceedingly satisfactory.

DISTRIBUTED PARTICIPATION AMONG PUPILS. Some secondary schools have taken definite steps to distribute participation in activities among as many pupils as possible, as well as to limit the participation of those pupils who may become involved in too many activities. If all pupils are to participate, there must be a wide variety of activities which appeal to every interest. Many schools have a sufficiently broad offering of clubs, interscholastic and intramural sports, and music organizations, to provide a place for every interested pupil. Assemblies, social activities, school service organizations, and publications likewise should satisfy the interests of most pupils in these areas.

Especially in large schools, definite provision needs to be made so that participation is extended to as many pupils as possible. At the New Trier Township High School, Winnetka, Illinois, a large four-year high school, it is the practice to have more than one cast for some of the productions presented by the music department and the drama department. The pattern which is used varies from one activity to another, but the intention is to provide participation for as many pupils as possible. Some secondary schools have a program of interscholastic and intramural sports which provides a place for every pupil. These are described later in this chapter.

In schools organized on the little-school plan, it is easier to distribute activities among interested pupils. For instance, the Stanforth Junior High School, Sewanhaka Central High School District, Floral Park, New York, has a student council, separate assemblies, intramural athletic teams, and similar activities for each of the three little schools. (See Chapter 15 for a description of the little-school plan.) The O'Farrell Junior High School, of San Diego, California, another school organized on the little-school plan, has a student council for each of the three grades. One of the definite advantages frequently cited for the little-school plan of organization is the opportunity it gives in large schools for more pupils to participate in certain school activities.

Some schools have a definite plan to limit the participation of those pupils who may engage in too many activities. The most common plan for this purpose is the point system. The Manatee High School, Bradenton, Florida, has a point system for regulating the number of elective offices a pupil may hold and the number of school organizations to which he may belong. Each pupil office and other activity is assigned a number of points based on the amount of time the activity is likely to require. The total number of points a pupil may carry is based on his previous semester's marks, with an "A" receiving four points, a "B" three points, a "C" two points, a "D" one point, and an "F" a minus one point. A pupil may not exceed 20 points except with special permission, while he is allowed five points regardless of his marks. Furthermore, a pupil may hold only one of certain major offices, such as president of a club, class or other organization, editor of the yearbook, or editor of the school paper. The point system is one way of controlling the extent of participation in activities by individual pupils.

In many schools, participation in activities by individual pupils is considered primarily a counseling rather than an administrative matter. That is, the pupil and his counselor plan his total school program for a given semester, including participation in extraclass activites. Some schools have a rotation plan for certain school offices, with pupils not permitted to succeed themselves. This plan is used especially for club, class, and homeroom offices.

CLASS STATUS FOR MUSIC ACTIVITIES. Such music organizations as band, orchestra, glee clubs, and choir, are frequently placed in the daily schedule and are given the same status as any other subject. In schools with this practice, music organizations are not really considered to be extraclass activities. They meet several times weekly, they may be counted toward graduation requirements, and they often require outside preparation like other subjects.

Many secondary schools also provide a sufficient number of music organizations for every pupil who would like to participate. This means that, for the instrumental groups, several organizations appropriate for various pupil ability levels are needed. The Roosevelt Junior High School, Cleveland Heights, Ohio, has eight organized music groups meeting on a daily basis, with more than 40 per cent of the 900 pupils in school participating. There are beginning, intermediate, and advanced groups for both orchestra and band, an eighth-grade chorus, and a ninth-grade choral group. The beginning orchestra and band are instructional classes in the instruments concerned, but the intermediate and advanced orchestra and band groups present assembly and evening programs throughout the year.

Many junior and senior high schools, especially in the Middle West and the South, have extensive music programs similar to the one at Cleveland Heights. In these school systems, instrumental instruction is given in small groups or to individual pupils as part of the regular school program, beginning in the elementary grades and extending through the senior high school. Vocal and piano instruction are frequently given, as well as instruction on the wind and string instruments. In the Philadelphia public schools during the present year more than 7,000 pupils in the elementary, junior and senior high schools are enrolled in instrumental music classes. Some of these classes meet on Saturday morning, while others are scheduled during the regular school day. In addition, hundreds of pupils participate in the music program of the Philadelphia public schools as members of orchestras, bands, choirs, and other music groups. In school systems with broad music programs, such as those in Philadelphia and Cleveland Heights, all interested pupils can find a music activity in which they can participate.

SPORTS PARTICIPATION FOR ALL PUPILS. A broad program of intramural and interscholastic sports, with a place for all pupils, is offered in many schools. The Aberdeen, South Dakota public schools have such a program. The senior high school at Aberdeen has three football teams, three basketball teams, and two track teams which engage in interscholastic competition. The varsity team for each sport competes with other large high schools in the state which are classified on the basis of enrollment as "A" schools. The second teams, composed largely of juniors, compete with "B" schools, while the third or sophomore teams compete with "C" schools. The senior high school also has intramural teams in touch football, basketball, wrestling, tennis, and golf. The two junior high schools have formed a league with two parochial schools in the city, and have a regular schedule of games in football, basketball, and track. In both the junior and senior high schools of Aberdeen, a sufficient number of teams are provided so that every interested and physically able boy may participate. Approximately 50 per cent of the boys in the junior and senior high schools engage in some sport during the year.

The four junior high schools of Sioux Falls, South Dakota, have both intramural and interschool competition for every interested boy in football, basketball, volleyball, and track. Contact football is limited to eighth- and ninth-grade boys. Boys are assigned to squads on the basis of a classification chart which takes into consideration their age, height, and weight. More than 60 per cent of the boys in the Sioux Falls junior high schools participate in this program.

The Cherry Creek Junior High School, Cherry Creek School District, Arapahoe County, Colorado, has an extensive intramural sports program for both boys and girls. The sports for boys include flag football, tennis, horse shoes, basketball, volleyball, table tennis, wrestling, bowling, track, softball, croquet, golf, and badminton. For girls, the sports are line soccer, field soccer, tennis, table tennis, basketball, volleyball, shuffleboard, newcomb, bowling, track and field, softball, tennis, golf, badminton, and croquet. Some of these activities are corecreational, with boys and girls participating together. The corecreational activities include table tennis, shuffleboard, box hockey, bowling, croquet, tennis, and badminton. The Cherry Creek program is carried on after school hours, with a late bus schedule provided for pupils who participate. More than 75 per cent of the pupils in the Cherry Creek Junior High School engage in one or more sports.

The Windham High School, Willimantic, Connecticut, has an exceptionally good intramural program for girls. The teams usually represent the various classes, although some activities may cut across class lines. The sports for girls at Windham High School include softball, basketball, swimming, field hockey, volleyball, badminton, and others which may be added when enough pupils demonstrate an interest in them. There is a wide participation in the girls' intramural sports program at the Windham High School. The sports program of the secondary school is not adequate unless there is opportunity for participation for girls as well as boys.

PUPIL SELF-GOVERNMENT IN THE SCHOOL. Some secondary schools have pupils participate in developing policies and regulations concerning certain aspects of the administration of the school. These policies and regulations usually are related to pupil activities and other aspects of the school program which may appropriately be controlled and administered by pupils. These activities usually include assemblies, social functions, clubs, and school publications. Control of corridor traffic, cafeteria conduct, and safety patrols also are frequently in charge of pupils. The student council is usually the organization which assumes these responsibilities. The Woodrow Wilson High School, Middletown, Connecticut, has such pupil participation in the administration of certain aspects of the school program. Every pupil at Woodrow Wilson High School is a member of the student association, with the student council serving as its representative group. The student council, which consists of twenty elected members, determines policies for certain pupil activities, supervises school elections, plans and finances assembly programs, and sponsors an annual scholarship for a worthy senior.

In addition to the student council, Woodrow Wilson High School has a student advisory board which supervises pupil conduct in corridors, study halls, and the cafeteria. The advisory board is parallel to the student council in its authority and, like the council, is responsible to the officers and executive committee of the student association. The board formulates policies and makes regulations concerning pupil conduct, and, through the student squads in charge of study halls, the corridors, and the cafeteria, is responsible for enforcing those regulations. Uncooperative pupils are referred to the student advisory board by squad members. The advisory board does not discipline pupil offenders, but uses a counseling approach to help them.

Pupils who persistently violate conduct regulations at Woodrow Wilson High School are referred by the advisory board to a student court, composed of a judge, jury, and prosecutor. The student court, whose sessions are open to the student body, is the only student group that imposes penalties, such as removing the offender from study hall, depriving him of school privileges, or placing him in the custody of a member of the advisory board. The pupil's parents are informed of any penalty imposed by the court and it is placed in the pupil's cumulative record. Only a few cases are referred to the student court each year, most of them being cared for on a counseling basis by the advisory board. The mature behavior of pupils at Woodrow Wilson High School is attributed in large part to the sense of responsibility which they acquire from participation in the student organizations.

CO-OPERATIVE SCHOOL-COMMUNITY DEVELOPMENT OF RULES FOR SOCIAL CONDUCT. The social activities of secondary school youth present serious problems in many communities today. Out-of-school social functions frequently are not properly supervised. Late parties which follow school social functions have become the tradition in many high schools. A big fling for seniors following graduation exercises is a rather common practice and is especially difficult to control because the pupils are no longer subject to school regulations. With most boys driving automobiles, greater freedom for youth, and loose supervision for out-of-school activities, the social life of secondary school youth is of great concern to teachers and parents.

In some communities, suggestions for social functions both in and out of school have been prepared cooperatively by parents, pupils, and teachers. In Mt. Lebanon, Pennsylvania, a statement entitled, "Our Social Code," was developed cooperatively by pupils, parents, and teachers from all of the junior and senior high schools of the city, including both public and parochial schools. The social code, which was printed in attractive booklet form and distributed to parents and pupils, suggests the importance of family cooperation, the kinds of social activities which are appropriate, suitable hours for terminating social functions at different grade levels, and appropriate conduct for youth in such matters as driving, drinking, and smoking. A Parent-Youth Guide, similar to the one in Mt. Lebanon, was prepared by parents, teachers, and pupils in Sioux Falls, South Dakota. This printed booklet, distributed to pupils and parents, has suggestions for conduct at social functions, dating at various age levels, closing hours for parties, appropriate dress and personal grooming, the responsibilities of the home, and personal attitudes and habits related to social life. Statements such as those at Mt. Lebanon and Sioux Falls suggest some agreement among parents and teachers on the types of activities, hours for parties, and the conduct considered appropriate for secondary school youth.

In some communities the Parent-Teachers Association or some civic organization sponsors a party for seniors following graduation exercises to discourage unsupervised parties which may be arranged by the pupils themselves. Many parents have small groups in their homes following school parties, with food, soft drinks, and music enjoyed by secondary school youth. There needs to be much cooperation between parents, teachers, and pupils to provide social activities which appeal to youth, are properly supervised, and may contribute to the enjoyment and wholesome social development of the participants.

PROVISION FOR EVALUATING EXTRACLASS ACTIVITIES. It was suggested earlier in this chapter that there should be continuous evaluation of the effectiveness of extraclass activities. In some schools teachers and pupils are being asked to evaluate the activities program, usually at the end of the year. Sometimes this evaluation covers the entire program, but more often it concerns only those activities for which the teacher is responsible. In the Middlebury High School, Middlebury, Vermont, every teacher evaluates at the end of the year the activities for which he was the sponsor. A two-page questionnaire is used for this purpose, in which questions such as these are asked:

> What were the main objectives of the group?
> What principal projects did the group engage in?
> What major difficulties did the group encounter in meeting its objectives?
> What were the chief accomplishments of the group during the year?
> What suggestions do you have for improving the activities of the group in another year?

Sometimes the evaluation of activities is made by pupils as well as teachers. At Central High School, St. Joseph, Missouri, the student council requests each member to evaluate each activity of the council and indicate which ones should be continued another year. Before the close of school, the outgoing and the incoming officers meet to discuss the results of this survey as a basis for planning council activities for the next year. A similar evaluation of student council activities is made at the Jessup W. Scott High School, Toledo, Ohio, where the members evaluate the work of the council in a questionnaire, including their own contribution as members of the group. They also give suggestions for improving the work of the council. In other secondary schools, similar evaluations are made, usually by questionnaires which apply to certain activities, such as clubs, assemblies, and homerooms.

ISSUES AND PROBLEMS

Some of the issues and problems concerning the extraclass activities of the secondary school today are of recent development, while others are of long standing. The following are some of the more important ones:

1. *Should it be recognized that extraclass activities make a significant contribution to the educational development of youth, or should these activities be considered primarily as recreational activities for youth?*

In the past the position of educators on this issue has been clear. They have held that extraclass activities are a significant part of the pupil's total educational experience in the secondary school. They believed that these activities gave opportunities for developing character, personality, citizenship, and leadership qualities of importance to youth. Furthermore, they believed that some activities were important in developing fundamental learning skills, especially the language skills. Assemblies, dramatics, publications, student council, and speech activities especially contributed to the development of such skills. Most educators still hold the same point of view.

The emphasis in recent years on academic achievement and preparation for college admission has raised serious questions in the minds of some teachers and parents about the place of these activities in the program of the secondary school. There are demands that extraclass activities be curtailed, that they be conducted during out-of-school hours, and that they be clearly subordinated to the classroom program. It is important, therefore, that the entire program of extraclass activities be carefully evaluated to determine its importance as compared with other aspects of the program of secondary education. The kinds of activities, the purposes they serve, the thoroughness with which they are planned, and the contribution of each to the classroom program of the school—these are some things which may have a bearing on this problem.

2. *How should extraclass activities be financed? Should the board of education provide for all or most of the cost; should the pupils who participate support the activities; or should the total program be supported by admission fees to those activities which attract spectators?*

For many years, this has been an important problem in planning for extraclass activities. Some pupils find it difficult to participate in certain sports, for instance, if they must purchase much or all of the equipment. In some schools the cost is borne in part by the board of education, with pupils and spectators providing the remainder. Some schools have activity tickets for pupils which entitle them to attend events as spectators, receive the school paper and yearbook, and participate in social functions. The activity ticket reduces the cost for pupils and still provides a substantial total fund. Even so, the cost to pupils to attend school parties, participate in music organizations, pay class and club dues, and purchase class rings—all these quickly mount up so that some pupils may find it difficult to participate, as data presented in Chapter 4 indicated. The pupils who are excluded may be the very ones who need most the experience of participation in certain activities.

The spectators at school events are an easy way of obtaining financial support for extraclass activities, but this also creates problems. If spectators become unduly important to the activities program, there is the danger that emphasis on good performance may require too much time from the participants and that participation may be limited to a few talented pupils. The financing of a broad and varied program of extraclass activities is a serious problem for parents, pupils, and educators.

3. *Should the time teachers devote to extraclass activities be considered a part of their regular teaching load or should they receive additional compensation for supervising such activities?*

Today this is one of the thorniest problems in the administration of the secondary school. It is quite a common practice, though not a universal one, for coaches of athletic teams to receive additional compensation for this responsibility. For other extraclass activities, this is less common. Some schools reduce the class load of teachers who have major extraclass responsibilities. In a few schools, teachers receive extra compensation for all major extraclass responsibilities in proportion to the time devoted to them. Activities for which additional compensation is paid, other than athletics, usually include dramatics, school publications, and speech activities. However, administrators and teachers in general do not agree on whether there should be extra compensation or released class time for supervising extraclass activities.

4. *How extensive a program of interscholastic athletics is appropriate in the secondary schools?*

This issue presents a number of specific problems: (1) are tournaments and postseason games desirable in the secondary school; (2) should there be interscholastic athletics in junior high school; and (3) is interscholastic competition for secondary school girls desirable? Each of these problems in some communities is the subject for heated and emotional discussion. Many educators and parents agree that too much emphasis is being placed on interscholastic athletics. They do not agree, however, on the extent to which such activities should be limited. Furthermore, there is strong opposition to interscholastic sports activities for junior high school boys and also to such competition for girls at both junior and senior high school levels. These problems need to be studied in terms of their bearing on the health of pupils and on the total educational program for youth.

SELECTED REFERENCES

BERKLEY, DEAN F., and DIEL, W. M. "Junior High School Athletics—A Program for All," *Bulletin of the National Association of Secondary-School Principals*, 42:116-118, May, 1958.—A description of the program of athletics in the junior high schools of Sioux Falls, South Dakota.

BOSSING, NELSON L. *Principles of Secondary Education*. Englewood Cliffs, N.J.: Prentice-Hall, Inc., 1955, Chap. 14.—A brief discussion of the organization of student activities in the secondary school.

FAUNCE, ROLAND C., and CLUTE, MORREL J. *Teaching and Learning in the Junior High School*. San Francisco: Wadsworth Publishing Co., Inc., 1961, Chap. 6.—Discusses the program of student activities in the junior high school.

FORSYTHE, CHARLES E. *Administration of High School Athletics*. Englewood Cliffs, N.J.: Prentice-Hall, Inc., 1954, Chaps. 13-16.—A comprehensive discussion of the program of athletics in high schools.

FREDERICK, ROBERT. *The Third Curriculum*. New York: Appleton-Century-Crofts, Inc., 1959, 454 pp.—A comprehensive discussion of extraclass activities in secondary schools, including all major kinds of activities.

FRENCH, WILL, HULL, J. DAN, and DODDS, B. L. *American High School Administration: Policy and Practice*. New York: Holt, Rinehart & Winston, Inc., 1957, Chap. 11.—A summary statement of administrative practices related to various types of extraclass activities.

GRUBER, FREDERICK C., and BEATTY, THOMAS B. *Secondary School Activities*. New York: McGraw-Hill Book Co., Inc., 1954, Chaps. 6, 9, 11, 12, 14.—A discussion of various aspects of the program of extraclass activities in the secondary school.

GRUHN, WILLIAM T., and DOUGLASS, HARL R. *The Modern Junior High School*. New York: The Ronald Press Co., 1956, Chap. 13.—Presents an overview of extraclass activities in the junior high school.

McKOWN, HARRY C. *Extracurricular Activities* (rev. ed.). New York: The Macmillan Co., 1952, 666 pp.—A comprehensive treatment of extracurricular activities, including the philosophy, organization, and types of activities.

MILLER, FRANKLIN A., MOYER, JAMES H., and PATRICK, ROBERT B. *Planning Student Activities*, Englewood Cliffs, N.J.: Prentice-Hall, Inc., 1956, Chaps. 7-18.—A comprehensive discussion of the major types of extraclass activities, including basic point of view, administration, and finances.

NATIONAL EDUCATION ASSOCIATION, EDUCATIONAL POLICIES COMMISSION. *School Athletics: Problems and Policies*. Washington, D.C.: the Association, 1954, 116 pp.—A statement of policy for athletics in junior and senior high schools, including intramural and interscholastic activities.

SMITH, JOE. *Student Councils for Our Times: Principles and Practices*. New York: Bureau of Publications, Teachers College, Columbia University, 1951, 110 pp.—A comprehensive discussion of student councils in secondary schools, including their purposes, procedures, and organization.

THOMPSON, NELLIE ZETTA. *Your School Clubs: A Complete Guide to 500 Activities for Group Leaders and Members*. New York: E. P. Dutton & Co., Inc., 1953, 317 pp.—A discussion of the school club program, including the administration of the club program and the planning of club activities.

TOMPKINS, ELLSWORTH, and ROE, VIRGINIA. "A Survey of Interscholastic Athletics Programs in Separately Organized Junior High Schools." *Bulletin of the National Association of Secondary-School Principals*, 42:1-47, November, 1958.—Reports the results of a survey of the status of interscholastic athletics in junior high schools of the United States.

13

A COMMUNITY INSTITUTION

The secondary school in the United States has tended to become increasingly a center for the cultural, recreational, and educational life of the total community. It serves these purposes not only for youth in the secondary school years, but it extends its influence to young people and adults of all age levels. It is the purpose of this chapter to examine the ways in which the secondary school may best serve these functions.

BASIC PRINCIPLES

The educational program of the secondary school should be developed with the participation of parents and other citizens.

If the secondary school is to function best in the education of youth, it seems essential that the parents of those youth should have a part in developing the educational program. There should be, therefore, continuous and frequent communication concerning the program of the school between the faculties and the parents. Furthermore, citizens who do not have children in school also have a deep interest in the education of those youth who will be the workers, the labor leaders, the businessmen, the scientists, the physicians, the teachers, and the statesmen of tomorrow. The early leaders in American education recognized the keen interest of the community in the public schools by placing the responsibility for those schools in the hands of elected citizen groups, usually called boards of education. The boards of education have the responsibility for formulating educational goals, developing educational programs, defining school policies, and employing the staff for the schools. In the early years of public education in America, the community was sufficiently small so that parents could keep closely in touch

304

with members of boards of education, with the administrative officials of the schools, and with the teachers of their children. With the growth of urban communities, school officials, teachers, and parents have grown increasingly distant from each other. Both parents and educators believe today that ways must be found for reestablishing and maintaining close working relationships between the school and the home; they believe that parents and citizens should participate in formulating the goals of education and in developing the educational program; and they believe that teachers, parents and other citizens should evaluate the educational program continually and cooperatively as a basis for modifications and improvement.

The educational program of the secondary school should utilize the cultural, civic, economic, and other resources of the community.

The educational program of the secondary school today goes far beyond textbook learning alone. It is a broad program which is concerned with the intellectual growth of youth, with their development as effective citizens, and with their vocational, family and leisure-time activities. Such a broad educational program can be more effective if it brings youth into contact with the cultural, civic, economic, and social life of the community while they are still in school. Furthermore, there are many educational resources in the community which are readily available to the school and which may enrich greatly the learning activities in which pupils participate.

The resources on which the school may draw differ considerably from one community to another. In some cities, such cultural centers as a public library, museums, and art galleries are available. Historical places, government agencies, industrial establishments, and business firms may also contribute to the program of the school. Every community is rich in human resources which may be helpful to the school, such as business leaders, labor leaders, government officials, professional people, people with special hobbies and interests, and teachers in other schools or colleges. The secondary school faculty should identify such community resources and find ways of utilizing them in the instructional program of the school.

The educational program of the secondary school should be extended for those youth who drop out before graduation to help them prepare for a vocation and for more effective citizenship while they are employed.

Recent statistics on retention in school reveal that about one-third of secondary school youth drop out between the eighth grade and the end of the twelfth grade. In other words, according to present-day standards, more than one-third of our youth leave school before they are adequately prepared to earn a living, to establish homes, and to assume the responsibilities for citizenship. The secondary school has a responsibility to these youth for providing further educational opportunities while they are employed.

Although the educational program for out-of-school youth should emphasize vocational preparation, it should not be limited to this. These youth, as much as those who remain in school, need further preparation for citizenship, for home and family living, for participation in church, civic, and social activities, and for leisure-time activities. The secondary school should develop an educational program that will meet the needs of out-of-school youth.

The educational opportunities of the secondary school should be continued beyond graduation for those youth who do not expect to attend a four-year college or university.

There was a time when a secondary-school education was considered adequate for all youth except those who were clearly pointing toward the professions. That is not true any more today. All aspects of the life of citizens are demanding continually more skills and knowledge. Although scientists may develop the theories underlying the developments of the space age, they cannot build the precision machines demanded by that age without the help of skilled and devoted technicians, stenographers, skilled tradesmen, and other workers. Never before in our history has the need been greater for highly skilled workmen.

The secondary school provides the foundations in mathematics, science, the language arts, and the industrial arts that skilled workers need. Furthermore, citizens in all walks of life need today more than ever an understanding of and a commitment to the ideals of democracy which have made America great. They also need to know more about the world in which America must take an increasingly strong position of leadership. These backgrounds, understandings, and skills demand a program of education that extends beyond the traditional secondary school grades into the community college years.

The facilities of the secondary school should provide educational opportunities for adults to prepare for community responsibilities, vocational advancement, and leisure-time activities.

The point of view that education is a life-long process is generally accepted in the United States today. We believe that men and women not only can profit from further education after their period of formal schooling has ended, but that for many adults such further education may actually be a necessity. The type of educational activity appropriate for different adults varies greatly. For many adults, further training in their vocation may be desirable; automation may compel them to prepare for new vocations; they may aspire to positions of leadership in community organizations and in civic affairs; or they may wish to develop interests and skills for wholesome leisure-time activity.

The facilities of the secondary school, which are used by youth during the school day, should be available for adult education programs during late afternoons, evenings, and summer months. Appropriate programs of adult education may enhance greatly the effectiveness of citizens in their activities, in their vocations, and during their leisure hours.

The secondary school should serve as a recreational center for youth and adults during after-school hours, week ends, and vacation periods.

The secondary school has excellent facilities for recreational activities of both youth and adults. These facilities include the gymnasium, the athletic fields, the auditorium, the arts and crafts rooms, the industrial arts shops, and the library. Since these facilities are already available, a broad recreational program during out-of-school hours can be developed at relatively little additional cost to the community.

The need for recreational activities for youth today is particularly urgent because employment opportunities during vacations are limited. Child labor laws, union regulations, the employment policies of large companies, and the attitudes of parents toward employment for their children—these factors limit vacation employment opportunities for youth. Furthermore, the parents of today work much shorter hours than a generation or two ago. Consequently, both children and their parents have much time for recreational activities together.

The secondary school should be a center for the cultural life of youth and adults in the community.

The youth of today develop many cultural interests during their secondary school years in such areas as music, art, dramatics, and the dance. It is unfortunate, indeed, for youth to develop these interests and skills, and then have little opportunity to pursue them after leaving the secondary school. There is every reason why cultural facilities in the secondary school should continue to be available to youth and adults.

The citizens of every community today should have the privilege of contact with such professional and semi-professional groups as symphony orchestras, choirs and choruses, dance groups, and dramatics organizations. What is more, youth and adults who have developed some interest and skill in music, dramatics, or the dance, should have the opportunity to participate in such organized activities. The facilities of the secondary school should be available for performances by both professional and amateur groups.

SOME COMMON PRACTICES

COMMUNITY INTEREST IN INTERSCHOLASTIC ATHLETICS. The interscholastic athletics program of secondary schools frequently is a great source of entertainment and interest for the community as a whole. The community supports the athletic teams of the school and takes great pride in their achievements. This is true not only of parents but also of other citizens. Small and medium-sized communities especially find that school athletic events are a source for community entertainment. In many rural communities the high school basketball games are a chief source of entertainment for both youth and adults during the winter months.

This interest of citizens in the sports events of the secondary school are desirable indeed. It is good for the school at the same time that it provides wholesome recreation for the community. But the interest of the public in interscholastic athletics also creates some problems. The chief justification for interscholastic athletics is their contribution to the educational growth and development of secondary school youth. The community, in its enthusiasm for a winning team, may not recognize the responsibility of the school for the educational welfare of the participants. Secondary school authorities, therefore, have the responsibility for helping parents and other citizens see that interscholastic athletics are primarily an educational activity, and that their entertainment value for the community as a whole is definitely a secondary consideration.

CULTURAL PROGRAMS FOR THE COMMUNITY. In most secondary schools, certain pupil activities have, for many years, made a considerable contribution to the cultural life of the community. The music organizations of the school, such as the band, orchestra, glee clubs, and choir, are a rich source of cultural interest for youth and adults. In many communities, concerts by school groups, music festivals, and other music performances are as well attended as the major interscholastic athletic events. For rural communities, programs by school music groups frequently are the only cultural opportunities of this kind available. The dramatics presentations of the senior class, the dramatics club, and other school groups, much like the music performances, are highlights in the cultural life of the community. Art exhibits, talent nights, puppet shows, dance festivals, variety shows—these and other school activities contribute to community cultural life. These activities are a significant and desirable part of the total recreational and cultural life of any community.

However, these activities are provided in the secondary school primarily because of their importance in the education of youth, a point not always recognized by school authorities. The cultural interests for the community as a whole, important though these may be, are not the major responsibility of the secondary school. The participation of pupils in music, dramatics, and other cultural activities in the better school situations are encouraged for educational purposes rather than for the entertainment of parents and other citizens.

PARENT-TEACHER ASSOCIATIONS. The most active organization in the United States for bringing the home and the school together in a working relationship on problems of education is the Parent-Teacher Association, usually called the P.T.A. At the national level, this organization developed from the National Congress of Mothers, which was founded in 1897 for the purpose of studying the care and training of children. The National Congress of Mothers encouraged the organization of local groups of mothers to study the child. Some of these local groups were associated with the schools and included teachers as well as mothers. Because of this association with local parent-teachers groups, the name of the national organization was changed in 1908 to The National Congress of Mothers and Parent-Teacher Associations, and in 1924 to its present name, The National Congress of Parents and Teachers.

The purposes of the P.T.A. are stated by the National Congress as follows:

> To promote the welfare of children and youth in home, school, church, and community.
> To raise the standards of home life.

To secure adequate laws for the care and protection of children and youth.

To bring into closer relation the home and the school that parents and teachers may cooperate intelligently in the training of the child.

To develop between educators and the general public such united efforts as will secure for every child the highest advantages in physical, mental, social, and spiritual education.[1]

In local communities, the P.T.A. has been most active through its meetings, usually monthly, when programs are presented which help parents and teachers with problems of education. In some communities, however, the programs are presented for entertainment rather than for purposes of promoting school-community understanding. The P.T.A. in many communities sponsors specific projects that are of benefit to children and the school, such as providing playground equipment, sponsoring lunch programs, furnishing libraries, giving scholarships and student loans, and assisting youth-serving agencies in the community. At times these activities are overdone and relieve the school board of its rightful responsibility.

Membership in the P.T.A. is open not only to parents and teachers, but also to others who are interested in problems of children and the schools. Some schools have parent-teacher-student associations, with membership available to interested students as well as adults. There are today more than 42,000 local associations which belong to the National Congress of Parents and Teachers, with more than 11,000,000 members, including several million men and several hundred thousand administrators and teachers. The P.T.A. has been more active in elementary schools than in secondary schools.

IMPLEMENTATION OF THE PRINCIPLES

In recent years, secondary schools have been introducing many new practices to become the educational, cultural, and recreational center of the total community. Practices to implement this role of the secondary school include: (1) cooperation between school and community agencies in developing activities for youth and adults, (2) increased parent participation in the program of the secondary school, (3) recreational and enrichment programs during vacation and out-of-school hours for youth and adults, (4) upward extension of education for all youth beyond the twelfth grade, (5) the de-

---

[1] National Congress of Parents and Teachers, *The Parent-Teacher Organization: Its Origins and Development,* Chicago: National Congress of Parents and Teachers, 1944, p. 1.

velopment of adult education programs, and (6) the development of the school as a cultural center for the community. Some of the practices to achieve these goals are presented in this part of the chapter.

COOPERATION WITH COMMUNITY AGENCIES. If the secondary school is to serve as a center for community life, it is essential that satisfactory rapport be established between the faculty of the school and the professional, business, industrial, civic, and labor leaders of the community, as well as the parents of school children. Without such rapport, the understanding between teachers and citizens so essential for school-community cooperation may be lacking. If the secondary school teachers came largely from the local community, this would not be a difficulty. However, they seldom do. The faculties of most schools are drawn from many communities, sometimes from distant states. When teachers first arrive in a new location, the traditions, backgrounds, and customs of a community, as well as individual citizens, are strange to them. It is important that they become acquainted, feel at home, get to know the community and its people, and participate in the life of the community.

Some communities establish rapport with new teachers through civic organizations sponsoring activities for welcoming them to the community which will be their new home. In Riverside, California, the Chamber of Commerce entertains new teachers the first day of orientation week with a breakfast at a local inn, a tour of interesting places, and a luncheon with leading citizens. Circulars and bulletins with information about Riverside and copies of the local newspaper are given teachers. In Providence, Rhode Island, the Chamber of Commerce sponsors a luncheon for new teachers early in the year, in order to give them an opportunity to meet local citizens. Churches, service clubs, women's organizations, and fraternal groups in many communities are particularly attentive to new teachers. Helping teachers get acquainted and feel at home is the first step toward wholesome school-community relationships.

The Committee on Education of the Chamber of Commerce of the United States has taken an aggressive part in recent years in establishing closer working relationships between the school and the community by encouraging its member organizations in local communities to sponsor a business-education day. Providence, Rhode Island, for example, recently held its Seventh Business-Education Day when forty-five business and industrial firms were hosts to more than 600 school administrators and teachers. Each teacher spent the entire morning on a tour of one of the participating firms to gain an understanding of its place in the economic life of the community. The teachers were guests of the firm at a luncheon followed by a discussion and question-and-answer period at which the work of the firm was explained. Most areas of the business and industrial life of Providence were represented in the program. In some communities which have a business-education day, the teachers are hosts to business and industrial leaders one year, while the next year teachers spend a day visiting business and industrial firms. Activities such as these contribute to closer understanding between the school and the community.

CITIZEN PARTICIPATION IN STUDY OF SCHOOL PROBLEMS. Parents and other citizens frequently participate in planning the curriculum of the secondary school and in making changes in its program. Such participation takes different forms. Some communities have organized groups of citizens who serve over a period of time in an advisory capacity in curriculum development, while in others such groups are formed to assist with specific problems as they arise. The Edwin O. Smith School, a six-year secondary school at Storrs, Connecticut, has a permanent citizens' curriculum committee which meets regularly with the principal and selected faculty members to study curriculum problems. Problems may be suggested to the citizens' committee by the principal or may be raised by the committee itself. The curriculum committee works with the principal and faculty in formulating proposals for curriculum change.

Although some avenues of communication between school and community are constantly kept open in the best situations, citizens participate in developing the program of the school most often when new schools are being built. Sometimes they work with the professional staff in formulating a program as a basis for planning a new building, or they may serve on a curriculum planning committee once the building is underway. In Wethersfield, Connecticut, a group of citizens served with the faculty of a six-year high school for a year and a half in developing the curriculum for separate junior and senior high schools that were to replace the combined school. The citizens contributed their thinking concerning the kind of a junior-senior high school curriculum which they considered desirable for their children.

The practice in some communities is to appoint parents to faculty study groups on specific school problems. The Newton, Massachusetts, public schools have done this for many years. In Newton, parents are invited to participate on study groups concerned with such city-wide school problems as building programs, salary studies, and curriculum development. They also serve on committees concerned with specific problems in a single school. At the Weeks Junior High School in Newton, for instance, eighteen parents representing the six elementary schools in the Weeks district spent two years working with the junior high school faculty in developing a plan for reporting pupil progress to parents. During this period, the parent-faculty study group formulated a statement of philosophy for the school, developed suggestions for implementing that philosophy, and prepared a plan for evaluating and reporting pupil progress which was based on the accepted philosophy.

Parents in many communities are participating in ways such as these in developing the curriculum and in making changes in the program of the secondary school. Such participation by parents and other citizens is by no means a passive one, with parents merely approving the suggestions and recommendations of the professional staff. They participate actively in the work of the study groups, taking a positive part in formulating programs and assuming some responsibility for the decisions that are made. Citizens who participate in curriculum study groups are especially helpful in bringing the citizens' point of view to bear on curriculum development and, later, in supporting the decisions of the study group when they are presented to the community.

INSTRUCTIONAL ASSISTANCE BY BUSINESS AND INDUSTRY. In the past several years, the sharply increased interest in science and mathematics instruction in our schools has encouraged cooperation in these subjects between the schools and industry. This cooperation has expressed itself in a number of ways, such as field trips by pupils to science laboratories in local industries, lectures to school groups by representatives of industry, summer employment for selected pupils in industries related to science, participation by local scientists in secondary school seminars, and summer work experience for science teachers in industrial laboratories. Representatives of industry have participated especially in after-school, Saturday, and summer programs for secondary school youth—particularly for talented youth in science.

A good example of cooperative activities in science and mathematics are those in the Los Angeles city schools. A joint committee of teachers and scientists developed the Los Angeles program, which includes: (1) teams composed of teachers and scientists who prepare demonstration-lectures for high school classes, (2) summer work experience in industry for teachers, and (3) summer employment for pupils in industry where they can be associated with scientists. During the years the Los Angeles program has been in effect, many demonstration-lectures have been presented by the teams of teachers and scientists, and a considerable number of teachers and pupils have participated in the summer employment program where they have had direct contact with science in industry.

The cooperative program in Los Angeles has also led to the development of well-equipped science club centers at a junior high school and one senior high school. Local industrial firms donated the equipment and the supplies to establish the laboratories and other facilities for the center. Several manufacturers have also given equipment and materials, as well as other aid, to science departments in the Los Angeles high schools. For instance, manufacturers of electronics equipment have helped teachers develop units on electronics for physics classes, build teaching aids and other equipment, and in other ways to aid teachers keep their classes up to date.

As in Los Angeles, leaders in business and industry in other cities are assisting secondary school teachers with instructional activities in the field of science. In Baltimore, Maryland, scientists from industry, colleges, and universities participate in the summer science program of the public schools as consultants and instructors. (See Chapter 15 for discussion of summer program in Baltimore.) The flexibility of the summer science program in Baltimore, which is on a non-credit basis, lends itself particularly to co-operation with industry and nearby colleges and universities. The program is limited to pupils with talent in science and is much more informal than the science program during the school year. The program includes seminars with scientists from industry and universities as consultants, field trips to laboratories in industry and universities, and informal contacts by pupils with scientists.

Participation in the secondary school program by resource people in the community is not limited to the field of science. In social studies, leaders in local and state government may participate; in English, journalists may be of help; and in music, art, and drama, talented people may contribute to the program. Resource people can be found for almost every subject in the program of the secondary school.

Participation by professional, industrial, labor, and business leaders has been carried further in the vocational education and work experience activities than in any other part of the secondary school program. In fact, it would be difficult, if not impossible, for the school to offer vocational education and work experience programs without the co-operation and support of leaders in business and industry. Some schools have citizens' advisory committees on vocational education or work experience programs; secondary school youth frequently are placed in business and industrial firms to gain work experience; skilled tradesmen assist secondary school teachers in developing programs in some occupations; and representatives from business and industry help teachers evaluate the effectiveness of these programs. Chapter 12 has descriptions of some outstanding programs in which the school uses the community as its laboratory.

SCHOOL-COMMUNITY RECREATIONAL PROGRAMS. The facilities of secondary schools are available in some communities for recreational activities during out-of-school hours and summer vacations. These activities are primarily for children and youth of school age, but in some communities they include out-of-school youth and adults as well. The summer enrichment programs offered by the public schools in Florida provide splendid recreational activities for children and youth during summer months. In Volusia County, Florida, recreational and enrichment activities offered by the schools during the summer include a variety of sports and games, such as softball, baseball, horseshoe, table tennis, archery, volleyball, shuffleboard, tennis, golf, croquet, relays, kickball, swimming, day camping, water skiing, paddleball, weight lifting, and roller skating. There is instruction in beginning, intermediate, and advanced swimming, as well as diving instruction and a junior lifesaving course. The summer program also includes such activities as woodworking, arts and crafts, and music.

The San Francisco, California, public schools have recreational activities at school playgrounds throughout the city after school hours and all day Saturday during the school year and all day during the summer months. The program includes games, team sports, and arts and crafts for school age children. During the summer vacation the program is supplemented with weekly outings to places of interest, day camps, and special programs. The gymnasiums which are open evenings throughout the year offer a program for both children and adults. In addition to the recreational activities of the public schools, the San Francisco Recreation and Park Department has an extensive recreation program for all ages.

In some communities, the recreation department of the city government and the public schools have a cooperative recreation program. Berkeley, California, has such a program, with the city department of recreation and parks using the school playgrounds. The recreation program in Berkeley comes after school hours and on Saturdays and Sundays during the school year, as well as during vacation periods. Many activities are also offered in parks and playground areas of the city recreation department. These include a wide offering of sports, hiking, camping, arts and crafts, and other special interest activities. In many activities of the Berkeley program children and their parents participate together.

Although it may be easier to develop recreational programs for youth and adults in the far western and southern states, some schools in the less temperate climates also have such programs. The Sewanhaka Central High School District No. 2, Nassau County, New York, has an extensive sports program on Saturdays throughout the school year and daily during the summer, including almost every sport in which youth ordinarily are interested. Some activities are on an informal basis, while there are organized teams in the competitive sports.

After-school and vacation activities for youth offered by the schools in some communities, in addition to sports, include bands, orchestra, choir, dance instruction, dramatics, and arts and crafts. In Berkeley, an annual program is presented by a young peoples' symphony orchestra in the Berkeley High School Community Theater, but under the auspices of the city recreation department. Dramatics presentations in Berkeley may include both youth and adults, and even parents and their children. Such a variety of cultural activities for different age groups is being offered increasingly through the secondary schools and the community recreation agencies.

SECONDARY SCHOOLS AS COMMUNITY CENTERS. Some communities have established the secondary school in a formal way as a community center. This center is primarily for youth of secondary school age, but sometimes its services are extended to adults as well. The Shorewood High School, Shorewood, Wisconsin, a six-year secondary school, has a youth center which is open certain hours after school and on days when school is not in session. The Shorewood youth center is a place where youth come together for various kinds of social and recreational activities under appropriate supervision. A center such as this serves the same purposes for youth as the club or fraternal organization does for adults, providing a gathering place for young people to visit, meet their friends, and participate in both informal and planned activities.

In Atlanta, Georgia, a community center with services and activities for youth and adults has been established at the Bass High School by an organization called the Bass Community Council. The council is composed of representatives from the churches, schools, P.T.A.'s, and civic groups in the Bass High School area. This council is not primarily a school organization, but it is school centered in many of its activities, which include a health clinic, dental clinic, and recreation center. During the summer months, the council offers an extensive program of activities for children and youth, including crafts, sewing, cooking, dancing, music, and sports. Although the Bass Community Council is the sponsor of the community center, the teachers and recreation directors are supplied by the Atlanta public schools and the city recreation department. The activities of the council are not limited to those of interest to youth alone, but are concerned with the total life of the community in the vicinity of Bass High School.

ADULT EDUCATION PROGRAMS IN SECONDARY SCHOOLS. Educational programs for out-of-school youth and adults are frequently offered through the secondary schools in the late afternoons, evenings, and Saturdays. Adult education programs serve a number of purposes, including the opportunity to complete the requirements for a high school diploma, to prepare for a specific vocation, to develop skills and background for vocational advancement, to gain general education for better living, and to acquire cultural improvement. Some communities also have naturalization classes for foreign-born people who want to become citizens. Although adult education programs are most extensive in the cities, they are also offered in many small urban and rural communities, frequently with financial aid from the state.

Dade County, Florida, is a good example of an urban school district which has an extensive adult education program, much of it offered through its secondary schools in the late afternoon and evening. In Miami, which is part of the Dade County school system, there is a wide offering of courses the year around for youth and adults at the Lindsey Hopkins Education Center, which is primarily a center for vocational education. The Dade County public schools also offer courses in law enforcement at the Dade County Police Academy and specialized courses in aviation mechanics at the Aviation School. In recent years, the vocational and adult education program in Dade County has enrolled as many as 50,000 students.

Another extensive program of adult education, much of it offered through the secondary schools, is the one in Rochester, New York, where the Department of Adult Education of the City School District in a recent year offered more than 600 classes, employed over 300 instructors, and enrolled approximately 17,000 students in non-credit courses. The adult education offerings in Rochester are exceedingly broad, including classes in general academic education,

Americanization, arts and crafts, business and distributive education, technical and vocational education, home economics, parent and family life, health and physical education, music and drama, safety and driver education, remedial instruction, education for older citizens, and courses for the handicapped.

In addition to the non-credit program for adults, Rochester has the East Evening Adult High School where a broad program is offered which may lead to a high school diploma, prepare a high school graduate more adequately for college, or give adults an opportunity to improve themselves in cultural and vocational areas. Furthermore, the East Evening Adult High School has an adult guidance and counseling center, where out-of-school youth and adults may have the help of qualified counselors with their educational and vocational problems. The East Evening Adult High School in a recent year had an enrollment of 4,200 students in high school credit courses alone. As in most cities, adult students in Rochester are particularly interested in vocational and technical education, although many of them also enroll for general education courses.

In a suburban area in a smaller community, the Sewanhaka Central High School District No. 2, Nassau County, New York, has an extensive educational program for adults during the evening in five of its high schools, offering courses which lead to a high school diploma, as well as self-improvement courses in foreign languages, current affairs, hobbies, music, art, homemaking, driver education, English and citizenship for new Americans, and a variety of special interest areas. Several community organizations have cooperated with the secondary schools of the Sewanhaka district in developing a program for senior citizens, with offerings in music, contract bridge, dancing, gardening, golf, and hobbies.

Rural communities with excellent adult education programs include Washingtonville, New York, which has a program of vocational, Americanization, and home and family living courses, courses leading to a high school diploma, and many special interest classes. Spencer Central School, Spencer, New York, is another rural school which is open to citizens and community groups most evenings in the week. A teacher devotes half of his time to planning an adult education program. In addition to the classes in the adult education program, community organizations use school facilities for their meetings and activities.

CENTER FOR CULTURAL ACTIVITIES. There are many activities in adult education programs other than formal courses, such as lectures on subjects of current interest, performances by music organizations, and dramatics presentations. Whittier, California, a suburban community in the Los Angeles area, which has an excellent program of adult education, presents each year a series of lectures on problems facing America and the world. This series is part of an extensive program for adults which extends throughout the school day and evening and includes both credit and non-credit offerings. The White Plains public schools, White Plains, New York, sponsored a series of weekly discussion groups on national goals of the United States. The program also has included several series of lecture-discussions on such subjects as the appreciation of modern art, world affairs and anthropology, and a course on group leadership for people interested in learning how to become an effective officer of an organization, a group chairman, or a discussion leader. These adult education classes in White Plains are part of a broad program of vocational and general education and special interest courses.

These are some examples of the variety of cultural activities for adults in the late afternoon and evening which are offered through the secondary schools. In addition, some schools have a dramatics group for adults, such music organizations as a band, orchestra, and choir, and social dancing classes. Activities such as these extend the influence of the secondary school for the cultural development of out-of-school youth and adults.

COMMUNITY COLLEGES AS EXTENDED SECONDARY EDUCATION. The community college, much like the secondary school, is intended to offer programs of education for all youth regardless of their individual abilities or their ultimate educational and vocational goals. The community college offers programs for college-bound youth, for those who want a year or two of general education beyond the twelfth grade, and for those seeking vocational education below the college level. The community college also provides further education for employed youth who did not finish high school, courses for adults leading to a high school diploma, and vocational education for adults. Many community college programs also include courses for personal development, citizenship education, and cultural activities and interests. The community college therefore offers both formal courses and informal educational activities; credit courses leading to certificates, diplomas, and further college work; and a variety of lectures, discussion groups, and activities in almost every area of interest of youth and adults.

The purposes of the Pasadena City College, a two-year public junior college, which is a part of the Pasadena, California, city school system, are an example of the broad functions served by the American community college. They include: (1) general education, (2) occupational education, (3) college education—lower divisions, (4) refresher and remedial education in basic skills, (5) adult education through short-term courses, lecture series, and workshops, (6) counseling and guidance services, and (7) community service through contributions to the cultural, civic, social and economic life of the community.

Not all community and junior colleges in the United States have purposes as broad as those of Pasadena City College, partly because many of these institutions are still too new and their enrollments too limited to justify such a program. Pasadena City College, one of the older and better established community colleges in the United States, in 1959-60 had more than 5,200 full-time students, 4,100 part-time students, and 13,000 in adult education classes. With a total enrollment exceeding 22,000 students, Pasadena City College can offer a broad program of education for both youth and adults. Although many community colleges have more limited programs, their ultimate purposes are similar to those at Pasadena City College.

TRANSFER PROGRAMS IN COMMUNITY COLLEGES. Community colleges usually provide two-year college programs for youth who plan to transfer to a four-year institution. The Joliet Junior College, Joliet, Illinois, the oldest public junior college in the United States, is one of the well-established institutions with many curricula leading to advanced work at a four-year college or university. The college transfer programs offered at Joliet Junior College include the following areas: agriculture, art, business, chemistry, chiropody, conservation, dentistry, engineering, forestry, home economics, journalism, law, liberal arts and sciences, medicine, medical technology, music, nursing, pharmacy, physical therapy, physical education, teacher education and veterinary medicine.

The college transfer programs in the community colleges make it possible for some students who would not otherwise be able to do so to continue their education while living at home. The crowded situation in recent years at the four-year colleges and universities is a further reason for having community colleges. By reducing the freshmen-sophomore enrollments at the four-year colleges and universities, more room should be available for students at the junior, senior, graduate, and professional levels.

TERMINAL PROGRAMS IN COMMUNITY COLLEGES. The terminal programs in the community college are of two kinds: (1) general education programs for students who do not plan to transfer to a four-year college or university; and (2) vocational education programs for students who intend to enter employment directly from the community college. Most of the terminal programs require two years to complete and lead to the Associate in Arts degree. The requirements for this degree ordinarily include courses in such subjects as English, physical education, social studies, psychology, health education, science, mathematics, philosophy and the fine arts. In addition to general education courses, students are expected to meet special requirements of the particular curriculum in which they are enrolled. Community colleges also may have curricula of less than two years, usually in the vocational areas, which lead to a certificate rather than the Associate in Arts degree.

The curricula leading to the Associate in Arts degree at the San Diego City College, San Diego, California, are an example of the broad offerings in some community colleges. Most of the curricula at San Diego qualify students for immediate employment, but some may be used for transfer to four-year institutions by those students with sufficiently high scholarship records. At San Diego City College, the Associate in Arts degree is offered in the following curricula:

Accounting
Aircraft Accounting
Aircraft Manufacturing
Airframe & Aircraft
  Power Plant
  Mechanics
Apprenticeship
Architectural Drafting
Auto Body
Auto Mechanics
Bookkeeping Machine
Business Management
Carpentry
Commercial Art
Cosmetology
Data Processing
Dental Assisting
Diesel
Dressmaking
Electricity
Electronics Technician
Electronics (General)
Electronics (Industrial)
Electronics Communications
Engineering Technician
English
Fine Arts
Fire Science

Foreign Language
General Office
Inspection
Machine Calculation
Machine Shop
Mathematics
Mechanical Drafting
Medical Assisting
Mill Cabinet
Music
Photography
Police Science
Radio Arts
Radio and Television Repair
Recreational Leadership
Refrigeration
Sales Management
Science
Secretarial Training
Social Studies
Speech Arts
Supervision
Technical Illustration
Tool Design
Tool Planning
Transportation Management
Vocational Nursing
Welding

Community colleges with programs of this nature work closely with civic, labor, business, and industrial leaders in developing terminal programs, especially those with vocational objectives. At the

Long Beach City College, Long Beach, California, more than 400 representatives of labor, business, and industry serve on over forty advisory committees representing such widely different occupations as boat building, carpentry, custodial engineering, electronics, garment manufacturing, life insurance, medical office assisting, painting and decorating, public service, publications, retail education, technical writing and illustrating, traffic and transportation, and welding. Similar advisory committees representing business and industry are frequently found at community colleges in other cities.

Guidance and counseling services for students are an important part of the community college program. This service is especially helpful to students because of the wide variety of curricula and courses which are offered. Help to students in locating jobs and follow-up of graduates are usually part of the guidance services. Long Beach City College has an especially effective guidance program, with counselors to assist both day and evening students with planning their junior college programs, to advise them concerning employment opportunities, and to help them obtain employment. The counselors at Long Beach City College also conduct follow-up studies of graduates to find out how well their programs have prepared them for job responsibilities.

ADULT EDUCATION PROGRAMS IN COMMUNITY COLLEGES. From the beginning of the community college movement in the United States, one purpose of these institutions has been to provide opportunities for adults to continue their education. Most community colleges therefore offer extensive programs of adult education. In Long Beach, California, one adult out of every five over eighteen years of age, according to a recent report, was enrolled during the year in some phase of the adult education program at the city college. At Pasadena City College more than half of the student body recently was enrolled in the adult education program. The community college movement in some states is so new that programs for adults have not been as fully developed as those in California. However, community colleges in Maryland, Florida, Texas, Illinois, and in other states are also developing extensive programs of adult education.

The breath of adult education programs in community colleges is revealed by a recent publication of the Long Beach City College, where the offerings of the general adult division include: (1) classes for adults with little schooling, including education beginning with the fourth-grade level; (2) a high school diploma program for adults; (3) programs leading to the Associate in Arts degree; (4) naturalization training classes for the foreign born; (5) programs for those who wish to become better informed about the history and institutions of their own country and other nations; (6) home and family living courses on foods, clothing, family economics, marriage and the family, and child study; (7) preschool parent education classes; (8) cultural and creative expression offerings in arts, crafts, drama, photography, creative writing, music, and foreign languages; and (9) forums and lectures on art, health, investments, world geography and culture, psychology, science, and current events.

There has been a tremendous growth in the enrollments in adult education programs of community colleges throughout the United States in recent years. In some communities the adult education activities of the community college are rapidly replacing those which in the past have been offered in the secondary schools. The community college, therefore, may well achieve the original purpose of its founders who considered a broad educational program for both youth and adults as the major function of this institution.

COMMUNITY COLLEGES AS CULTURAL CENTERS. An interesting development in community colleges has been the offering of cultural opportunities for youth and adults other than through formal courses. These cultural opportunities are available through a variety of activities. At Pasadena City College, a weekly forum offers lectures, panels, and films on developments in science, world relationships, political and social problems, and foreign affairs. The Montgomery Junior College, Takoma Park, Maryland, has a symphony orchestra for youth and adults of the community who are competent musicians. The Montgomery Light Opera Association is likewise sponsored by the junior college, and is open to interested and qualified youth and adults. Students at the college may receive college credit for participating in these organizations. At Long Beach City College, Long Beach, California, in a recent year, more than 14,000 adults participated in discussion groups on national and world affairs and attended lectures on topics of current interest. The community college is therefore becoming a cultural as well as an educational center for youth and adults of all age levels.

ISSUES AND PROBLEMS

A number of issues and problems are of concern to educators as they plan to extend the influence of the school to out-of-school youth and adults. There is a sharp division both in practice and point of view concerning some of these issues, partly because a number of them involve the expenditure of additional public funds. Several of the issues, however, raise questions concerning the relationship between the school and the community in the development of the school program and in the use of school facilities.

1. *How far should the secondary school go in having parents and other citizens participate in the development of the curriculum and in the formulation of school policies?*

Some educators contend that parents and other citizens are no more qualified to participate in developing the school curriculum than they are in helping a physician diagnose and treat their children when they are ill. They contend that the program of the secondary school is so complex that only professional educators are qualified to determine the purposes of secondary education, develop the curriculum, and formulate school policies.

Other educators and citizens contend, however, that the secondary school, in effect, belongs to the community. They point out that although a person may select his own physician and hospital, the school which his children attend and the teachers who teach them are maintained, administered, and employed by a board of education which represents the local community. Furthermore, many educators and citizens believe that laymen can make a definite contribution to the development of the secondary school program, and that the program is likely to be a better one if it is developed cooperatively by teachers, parents, and other citizens.

Although this issue continues to be debated in many communities, there is today a definite trend toward lay participation in developing the program of the secondary school. It seems reasonable that the public should participate in formulating the broad objectives of secondary education and the essential nature of the total programs and that lay groups should work with public schools in an advisory capacity.

2. *Should the facilities of the secondary school be available outside school hours and during vacation periods for civic, social, and cultural purposes and groups in the community or should they be used solely for educational purposes?*

Some educators believe that the schools are established and maintained primarily for educational purposes and that school facilities should be available outside school hours only for activities that are specifically educational. They also believe that the concept of the community-centered school goes far beyond the purposes for which secondary school facilities are maintained. For instance, this group contends that amateur musical and dramatics organizations in the community, unless specifically sponsored by the school, should not use school facilities. Furthermore, these educators hold that various civic organizations, such as fraternal groups, luncheon organizations, and community service groups, ordinarily should not be permitted to use the facilities of the school.

In many communities, however, both educators and citizens hold another point of view. This group contends that the school should be the center of educational, recreational, and cultural activities for the community in every way that is reasonably possible. They would make school facilities available to any civic and community group either free of charge or at a nominal cost. These educators and citizens contend that the facilities of the school should serve as the center of community life during times when they are not needed for school purposes. Although this concept of the community-centered school is not a new one, it is implemented at present in only a few communities.

3. *Should a broad program of education for all youth be provided at public expense beyond the twelfth grade?*

In a few states, such as California, Florida, Maryland, and Texas, this is not today a serious issue. In these states, the public has already taken a definite stand in favor of extending education to all interested youth into the community-college years. In a number of other states, there is definite interest in establishing community colleges. In most of the fifty states, however, the public has at this time reached no decision concerning this issue.

With the increased enrollments at both public and private colleges and universities, all states are facing the problem of providing additional facilities for higher education. This is also an appropriate time to study the need for educational opportunities for youth who do not have the ability nor the interest to attend a four-year college or university. In school systems which do not have a community college, educational opportunities beyond the secondary school for those youths who want further education below the college level are either very limited or totally lacking. Because of the demand for competent people in business and industry, a program of education is needed beyond the secondary school for those youth who will not attend a four-year college or university. In the next decade or two, many states and local school systems must decide whether they are going to provide educational opportunities for all interested youth beyond the twelfth grade.

4. *Should the secondary school provide recreational and cultural opportunities for out-of-school youth and adults of all age*

levels or should it provide these opportunities only for in-school youth?

It is true that at present some communities provide recreational and cultural opportunities for people of all ages, especially those communities which have public community colleges. In some communities, however, it is believed by educators and citizens that the secondary schools have no responsibility for the recreational and cultural activities of out-of-school youth and adults. The concept of the community-centered school holds that the recreational and cultural life of the total community should be centered in the school, and that the facilities of the school should be used for planned activities for people of all ages. The facilities of the school are established and maintained by all the citizens. If the recreational and cultural life of these citizens can be made a richer one by the use of school facilities during out-of-school hours, it would seem that this is a desirable thing to do.

5. *Should the secondary school continue to provide educational opportunities to youth who have already graduated from the secondary school and are currently employed or does it have responsibility only for youth of secondary school age?*

Some secondary schools provide extensive programs of vocational education for employed youth beyond the secondary school age. Educators and citizens generally agree that such educational opportunities should be offered by the secondary school, but they do not agree that these opportunities should be provided entirely free or at a nominal cost. Some educators and citizens contend that once youth are employed they should pay the major cost of those educational programs that are designed to improve their vocational skills and prepare them in other ways for better living. This problem has become particularly urgent in some communities because the popularity of broad programs of adult education has sharply increased the total cost of education.

Although this issue is a debatable one, there are strong arguments for making education at all levels available to citizens in a democracy. If adults improve their skills as citizens and workers, this should be of benefit to the community as a whole. It is important therefore to offer educational opportunities in such a way that all citizens may take full advantage of them. The distinction between in-school youth and out-of-school youth is gradually fading with the increased attendance by employed youth in all kinds of evening programs, both for high school credit toward graduation and for part-time college work.

SELECTED REFERENCES

AMERICAN ASSOCIATION OF SCHOOL ADMINISTRATORS. *The High School in a Changing World.* (Thirty-sixth Yearbook). Washington, D.C.: National Education Association, 1958, Chap. 4.—A discussion of the extension of the program of the high school into the community.

ASSOCIATION FOR SUPERVISION AND CURRICULUM DEVELOPMENT. *Creating a Good Environment for Learning.* Washington, D.C.: National Education Association, 1954, Chap. 16.—Describes projects in the community carried on by a senior-high-school class in Problems of American Democracy.

BOREN, CLAUDE B. "Why a Junior College Movement?" *Junior College Journal,* 24: 345-57, February, 1954.—Considers some of the social factors which have contributed to the development of junior colleges in the United States.

CUONY, EDWARD R. "Helping Parents Understand Adolescence," *Bulletin of the National Association of Secondary-School Principals,* 45:27-30, May, 1961.—Describes an evening course of six meetings on adolescence given for parents at Geneva Junior High School, Geneva, New York.

FAUNCE, ROLAND C., and CLUTE, MORREL J. *Teaching and Learning in the Junior High School.* San Francisco: Wadsworth Publishing Co., Inc., 1961, Chap. 12.—Suggests ways in which junior-high-school pupils may participate in community life.

HILLWAY, TYRUS. *The American Two-Year College.* New York: Harper & Brothers, 1958, Chaps. 1-4.—A comprehensive treatment of the development and program of junior colleges in the United States.

HYMES, JAMES L., JR. *Effective Home-School Relations.* Englewood Cliffs, N.J.: Prentice-Hall, Inc., 1953, Chaps. 1-5.—The relationship of parents and teachers concerning the problems of children in school are discussed.

McCLOSKEY, GORDON. *Education and Public Understanding.* New York: Harper & Brothers, 1959, Chap. 11.—Presents an overview of ways in which citizens may participate in developing the program of the school.

MEDSKER, LELAND L. *The Junior College: Progress and Prospect.* New York: McGraw-Hill Book Co., Inc., 1960, Chaps. 2-4, 8.—A comprehensive discussion of the purposes of the public junior college, its curriculum, and growth in the United States.

NATIONAL CONGRESS OF PARENTS AND TEACHERS. *Working With Youth Through the High School P.T.A.* Chicago: The Congress, 1958, 64 pp.—A pamphlet which gives suggestions for P.T.A.'s in secondary schools.

NATIONAL SOCIETY FOR THE STUDY OF EDUCATION. *The Community School.* (Fifty-second Yearbook, Part II). Chicago: University of Chicago Press, 1953, Chaps. 4, 6, 12.—A discussion of various aspects of community-centered schools presented by leading educators.

NATIONAL SOCIETY FOR THE STUDY OF EDUCATION. *The Public Junior College.* (Fifty-fifth Yearbook, Part I). Chicago: University of Chicago Press, 1956, Chaps. 4-8.—Presents a discussion of junior college education in the United States by leading junior-college educators.

SHEATS, PAUL H., JAYNE, CLARENCE D., and SPENCE, RALPH B. *Adult Education: The Community Approach.* New York: The Dryden Press, 1953, Chap. 7.—A comprehensive treatment of programs of adult education in the public schools.

THORNTON, JAMES W., JR. *The Community Junior College.* New York: John Wiley & Sons, Inc., 1960, 300 pp.—A discussion of the backgrounds, organization, operation, and problems of community junior colleges.

Part III

ORGANIZATION AND LEADERSHIP

14

LEADERSHIP AMONG TEACHERS AND PUPILS

The kind of leadership that a secondary school receives in a large measure determines whether or not it will make progress in achieving changes to keep up with the rapidly accelerating pace of sociological and technical innovations. Leadership may be effective or ineffective, depending upon its purpose. If our secondary schools are to help youth understand, preserve, interpret, and improve the American way of life, then it obviously becomes essential that such schools reflect democracy in every aspect of their organization and program. What kind of leadership can the beginning teacher expect on his first job? Will he find opportunity to exercise responsibility and to try out some of his ideas that he has learned in his teacher education program? Or must he be prepared to find that his principal may talk democracy but practice little of it day by day?

This chapter applies equally to the teacher's leadership, as it does to that of the principal or supervisor. The teacher exercises leadership in numerous ways in the schools with both his fellow-teachers and with his pupils. It is important, too, for the teacher to understand the leadership structure and the problems faced by status leaders in the schools.

BASIC PRINCIPLES

There has been evolving in recent years a considerable body of literature describing the research on leadership in the fields of business administration, psychology, sociology, and education. Industry, too, has paid a great deal of attention to the process of leadership. Basic principles that operate in an effective leadership situation in a school that believes in the concepts of democracy can be identified.

The primary function of educational leadership is the improvement of the learning process.

Any leader, whether he serves in a status leadership role or as a leader of children in the classroom, should keep in mind that the primary purpose of whatever he does is to promote the growth and learning of the pupils in the school. Buildings, schedules, the organization of the curriculum, textbooks, regulations regarding attendance, and all of the routines of the school exist for the purpose of promoting learning. Many of these matters are mechanical and can be routinized.

The modern secondary school principal puts his main effort into giving leadership toward improving the instructional program. As the status leader in the building he plays the major role in the improvement of the learning process. Unless he has a keen interest in what goes on day by day in the classroom, less attention will be paid in the school as a whole to improvement of curriculum and instruction. His attitude needs to be positive toward the improvement of learning, rather than the kind of attitude that focuses on the weaknesses found either among youngsters or teachers.

Leadership should help people determine their goals and move toward those goals.

This principle stands in sharp contrast to the idea that the leader's function is to get things done. The older concept of leadership exhibited particularly in business management, centers around having a strong person who sees that other persons carry out orders. This is also the concept prevalent in a military organization.

The modern theory of leadership is oriented toward the service function. The status leader works with people. He serves as a member of the group to define what the group goals should be. This concept can be applied especially to the field of instruction and curriculum, but it functions as well in the area of administrative policies. Leaders of the old school would take issue with this principle and undoubtedly would be completely unable to implement such a concept.

The principle implies that any leader has faith in people and in the decisions that they make. A leader who behaves in a manner that can be described as democratic will be willing to abide by the decisions that a group has made after it has carefully studied the problems concerned. This theory of leadership has significant implications for the teachers as leaders of pupils in the classroom and in extra-class activities.

*All individuals in the school faculty affected by school poli-
cies should have a part in making them.*

The principal is the administrative leader of his school, delegated
this responsibility by the superintendent of schools. Most principals
clearly understand this role. The superintendent in turn has legal
responsibility directly to the board of education. Therefore, one
might correctly assume that the high school principal has direct
authority over the teachers of the school. Legally this line and staff
organization (borrowing a concept from business) still exists in
American school administration. The important question is how this
authority is used. The more autocratic concepts of leadership are
being challenged by research findings and by practice in many secondary schools. Administration based upon shared leadership is
proving its worth and contributing directly to the basic goals of a
democratic society.

Leadership based upon delegated legal authority is called "status
leadership." The high school principal is a status leader because of
his legal or appointive position within the school system. As a status
leader he can improve human relations among teachers and pupils,
provide certain types of expertness, and promote and coordinate
leadership within the faculty. While he cannot legally delegate his
basic responsibility for administering a school, he may in practice
permit his many leadership functions to be shared.

Implementing this principle means that pupils, teachers, parents,
dietitians, cooks, and custodians all share in some way in making decisions that directly affect them. Curriculum change is carefully
planned by teachers, administrators, and others concerned. Once a
policy has been determined cooperatively, the status leader is the
one to administer the policy to the best of his ability.

Shared leadership also provides for the development of leadership
skills within a group. Teachers who aspire to be leaders will learn
how to function effectively as a status leader if they are given responsibility within a school system or school building. In addition,
teachers who are not at all interested in becoming status leaders have
various kinds of abilities that can contribute to the leadership that
emerges from any decision-making group. Research shows that the
interest members have in an organization depends upon the extent
to which they have a part in making significant decisions for that
organization.

*Leadership should focus on the mutual growth of all con-
cerned.*

This is an extremely difficult principle for some people to understand. They hold to the concept that the status leader works on others to improve them. To these people it is pure nonsense to consider that the leader also will improve himself in the process. Actually, research shows that when the status leader is a part of a study carried on by a group, willing to improve along with others, a great deal more improvement occurs than when he stays apart from the group.

The most effective kind of supervision is that which serves to help the teachers achieve mutual goals that have been arrived at by the supervisor and the teacher. The principle applies to teacher-pupil relationships also. Often supervisors function as though they want to improve someone else but are not willing to improve themselves. Such a position considerably weakens the effectiveness of the supervisor. Some schools have changed the role of the supervisor to that of "consultant.' A consultant is regarded more as a helper, in fact, sometimes being called a "helping teacher."

Leadership that focuses on mutual growth, concerned with human relations and the way people interact with each other, is at the very heart of responsibility in school and classroom. Administrators or teachers who are effective leaders must provide conditions which will release the creative potential of all faculty members or pupils. Freeing people to be creative means to put a minimum of regulations in their way and to encourage them to try out new ideas.

Pupils in the secondary school should be given practice in leadership in which genuine authority resides.

In the secondary school the pupil is an apprentice citizen. It is the schools function to induct him properly into the civic role that he will perform as an adult in his community. The only way by which we can do this effectively is to give him responsibility in his own school society where he achieves practice as a citizen at his age level. Thus, he has a chance to test out his own assumptions as to leadership behavior and to have the assistance of a competent teacher in evaluating that behavior.

Pupil participation in leadership activities in secondary schools should give them genuine authority for managing the affairs or developing the policies that are entrusted to them. Even though they will make mistakes, this is a part of the learning process for pupils who are guided by the teacher in analyzing and correcting those mistakes. This principle is discussed further in Chapter 12.

Leadership is a function of the situation and a product of interaction.

In early studies of leadership, personal qualities or characteristics were stressed. However, research that was conducted did not describe adequately leader behavior. This approach to analysis of what constitutes leadership is static rather than dynamic since it describes an individual at any one time. It does not indicate how he would function under different conditions. Different persons will function effectively in a leadership capacity in different situations. Consequently, the modern theory of leadership is called the situational theory.

Status leaders do not actually lead unless they are recognized as leaders by the group. A particular group of teachers may recognize someone other than a principal as their leader. Leadership is actually derived from the group and depends upon the group's perception of the leader. In other words, leadership is not a product of status but is a matter of how a person behaves when confronted with a particular situation. A leader in one instance will not necessarily be a leader when placed with a different group demanding solutions of different kinds of problems or work toward different kinds of goals. Thus, the supervisor or teacher must be perceived as a leader in order to be most helpful to the group with which he works in promoting improvement of instruction or learning.

Leadership, therefore, is a product of interaction between the person who does the leading and the group. The status leader who denies cooperation in sharing of policy-making is blocking satisfactory interaction. The cooperative kind of working situation in which a leader is recognized as such by the people participating furnishes a high level of interaction.

SOME COMMON PRACTICES

Although many secondary schools are characterized by democratic leadership behavior in administrator-teacher and teacher-pupil relations, the beginning teacher might well find himself in a school where telling is more prevalent than sharing. American secondary education has moved consistently toward providing education for a greater number of young people. It has not moved as rapidly in exemplifying the ideals of democracy in its administrative decision-making as a free people can expect from their schools. There have been serious set-backs caused by forces both in schools and in communities that demand an acceleration of change or a return to a static program that can more easily be administered from the top down.

These demands call for a different kind of leadership from the concept outlined in the foregoing principles. Consequently, both teachers and pupils, under pressure from many sides, may tend to succumb to what seems to be the easier, less time-consuming and troubling way of getting things done.

Principals and other status leaders are not entirely responsible. Public apathy, inadequate financial support, teachers who believe in authoritarian principles may all be contributing factors. Yet the school administrator is responsible for what happens in the school under his jurisdiction. He has both the responsibility and the authority to overcome most of the factors impeding educational improvement. More than anyone else, his concept of leadership and his ability to put that concept into effect will show through the daily events of the school.

LEADERSHIP AS MANAGEMENT. The concept of leadership as managing people has in the past been the prevalent one in school administration as well as in business and industrial management. The head man hires and fires the employees. He or his subordinates exercise the judgment as to important decisions to be made. This concept is typified by the principal who takes pride in running a "smooth" school, wherein he derives the greatest satisfaction when he knows that schedules, programs, and classes are running like clockwork. He does not delegate administrative responsibilities nor permit any sharing of leadership.

Townville Junior-Senior High School has an enrollment of 250 pupils. It is Friday at 9:15 A.M. and the student body marches into the auditorium under the watchful eyes of the faculty. They find seats quietly as the principal comes to the center of the stage—alone. Whispering and giggling cease as he stands waiting attention. He then gives a series of announcements, explains schedule changes, and calls attention to violations of rules. He eventually gives over the platform to the music teacher for group singing. This a regular weekly routine in this school, varied by occasional seasonal pep sessions, band music, athletics awards, and guest speakers. But always the principal presides. He holds teachers' meetings for the purpose of making announcements, calling attention to matters that need to be taken care of, and discussing some forthcoming school event for which details must be arranged. At the beginning of the year, he hands out the textbooks at the opening teachers' meeting the day before school begins in September.

The criterion of good administration is the degree to which the principal secures cooperative efforts in improving learning. In applying this criterion to the sample of administrative practices revealed by this principal, the appraisal seems fairly clear. He operated upon the elite concept of leadership. He seemed to make most of the decisions, and he personally saw that each was executed. Pupils apparently carried out orders. It might be asked what happens in this high school when the principal is absent. This example illustrates, in part, autocratic administration. From the sketchy picture given, there is little direct evidence of the principal's role in curriculum improvement, but there is undoubtedly little sharing in arriving at decisions concerning programs, textbooks, or any other significant matters.

This kind of administration sets the tone for the whole school. The teacher soon perceives the principal as someone who is the doorkeeper of rules and regulations of the school, legislator, and executive wrapped up in one package. He does not see the principal as someone who can be of assistance in planning an individualized reading program or adapting the mathematics curriculum to modern developments in the field. In turn, the teacher is likely to behave in the same manner in working with pupils.

The principal who leaves teachers alone, who believes that the least-interfered-with teacher is the happiest and consequently the most productive one, can also be found in high schools, small or large. There is little coordination of program in his school. Each teacher is more of a law unto himself in curriculum matters. Curiously enough, a principal who exhibits such behavior, often gives another kind of leadership in daily routine affairs. These are his forte and in these matters he may exercise direct control.

PRIORITIES FOR ADMINISTRATIVE FUNCTIONS. Some secondary school principals spend an excessive amount of time in administering various mechanical and routine details. These principals are so busy with absence slips, basketball schedules, assembly programs, honor rolls, discipline violations, attendance records, service club programs, reports, and the like, that they have little time or energy left for working directly with pupils, parents, and teachers to improve the curriculum and instruction. One reason is that the administrative activities are immediate concerns that cannot be safely neglected; the improvement of the curriculum is a long-range activity often with no apparent pressures demanding that it be done.

There are other reasons for this prevailing condition. One must recognize the fact that a large majority of communities fail to provide anything approaching adequate clerical and secretarial assistance for their schools. In small high schools, the superintendent usually functions as the principal. In such schools, the principal is a designated teacher who keeps certain records and may have a few other similar routine administrative duties. Any consistent leadership in curriculum improvement is consequently difficult if not impossible.

These conditions and pressures explain much but not all administrative neglect of curriculum improvement. There are many secondary schools, both large and small, where fairly adequate clerical assistance is available and the principal either does not have a heavy teaching load or does no teaching. Principals may not know how to assist teachers in the important function of teaching. Some are psychologically unwilling or unable to delegate duties to others.

Rural High School, situated seven miles from the county seat, is a four-year secondary school with only 125 pupils. The four full-time teachers and the superintendent teach the classes. The superintendent acts as principal. He must also be responsible for the elementary teachers, and advise the senior class. The many problems of a lunchroom, building repairs, equipment and supplies, operating five school buses, and planning the budget are among his general administrative duties. Miss Jones, the new inexperienced English and social studies teacher, is handed a state required course of study at the first teachers' meeting in September and is told by the principal-superintendent to "follow it in every detail." Subsequent meetings discuss certificates, discipline, textbook accounting, the Christmas program, salaries, county tests, and the proposed new gymnasium. Miss Jones is visited twice for a few minutes during the year by the superintendent, but she is not assisted with her problems, nor does the superintendent actually know what she is doing. He is so busy with the mechanical and routine details of "running a school" that he has practically no time to help teachers improve the educational program of the school. This example typifies one type of secondary school administration: a conflicting welter of opposing ideals resulting from pressure and expediency.

COMPLEXITY OF ADMINISTRATIVE FUNCTIONS. The beginning teacher may find that his principal has many responsibilities in the operation of a modern secondary school. In addition to implementing curriculum policies he must see that policies affecting building and grounds, use of library and other facilities, athletic programs, the distribution of textbooks, faculty committees, publications and dramatics, and the like, are carried out effectively. The principal serves as the direct official representative of the superintendent in all except very small high schools. Although democracy and autonomy should reside in each high school faculty unit, beginning teachers must recognize that in some situations many decisions are made by the superintendent and passed down the line as policy for the principal and faculty. The principal may act as official school and faculty representative to the community in medium-sized and large high schools. He often represents his school officially in P.T.A. activities, service clubs, youth-serving agencies, and system-wide administrative meetings.

The typical secondary school of 100 to 250 enrollment will have a principal who teaches part time. In addition, he has many administrative duties and little assistance, although he may have one teacher who gives limited time to counseling, another to visual education, athletics, clubs, and the like.

In large city secondary schools ranging from 1,500 to 3,000 pupils, the administrative organization will be rather complex. An assistant or vice-principal is the rule; sometimes more than one may be found. The assistant principal usually has responsibility for discipline, attendance, and daily schedules. He may also serve as the guidance coordinator. Some schools call their counselors deans of boys and girls, although these titles are slowly disappearing. Large schools frequently have permanent department heads who may perform some administrative functions. They coordinate instruction, represent their department at meetings, requisition supplies, and possibly supervise instruction. Directors of guidance, audio-visual aids, music, dramatics, athletics, health, and art may also have numerous administrative duties.

Most large secondary schools have a head clerk or secretary who may be given considerable responsibility for supplies, equipment, books, attendance, reports, budget, and other details. School physicians, chief nurses, dietitians, lunchroom managers, librarians, and chief engineers always exercise considerable authority in their fields.

Heavy Administrative Responsibilities of Teachers. One of the justifiable criticisms of the school of today is that the teacher has to perform too many functions that are non-instructional in nature. Some of these result from the schools' taking on added responsibilities that the critics contend do not belong to the schools. These duties tend to place a greater burden on the teacher. Of course, one of the reasons for the burden is the lack of clerical assistance. Some schools are experimenting with the use of teacher's aides to perform non-teaching duties in order to release the time of qualified teachers for teaching and planning, as described in Chapter 7.

There are three broad areas in which the teacher may expect to carry on certain administrative duties. First, within his own homeroom or classroom he is expected to keep attendance records; to record grades, marks, test scores; and to write pupil reports to parents. He must coordinate school drives and campaigns among his pupils. Often he may have to order, account for, and distribute supplies, equipment, and textbooks.

Another responsibility of the classroom teacher is to serve on certain school administrative committees. These committees may be primarily service agencies, but they perform administrative functions as well. Typical committees commonly found in medium-sized and large secondary schools include those which help administer the lunchroom, assemblies, athletics, musical organizations, library, and ticket sales.

A third area of administrative responsibility in which teachers participate is that of representing their department or school at city-wide, regional, or state meetings. Thus a teacher may be selected to explain the purposes of the school honor society to a city service club. He may represent his school at a community meeting to plan drives for the Red Cross or Community Chest. He may also be called upon to do hall duty, lunchroom duty, and perform other functions as needed in the school.

Studies of teacher participation in the determination of administrative policies in some schools reveal a number of interesting conditions. A large proportion of teachers help determine the content of individual courses of study in the curriculum. In only a few functions do a majority of the teachers feel that they participate directly. Few teachers indicate that they cooperate directly with administrators in determining policies in several of the functions studied. Administrative areas in which most cooperative policy formulation exist are in community relations, use of buildings and equipment, school control, reports, and records. Areas in which relatively little cooperative participation is found include faculty administration and school finance.

CONFUSION IN ROLE EXPECTANCIES. Either the teacher's or the administrator's perception of his own role in the school determines how he behaves in that role. Expectations by others of their roles also influence their behavior. The picture of "administrator" for a principal may mean a clarifier of issues, a coordinator of instructional activities, and a leader of group goals. This concept may conflict directly with the way the superintendent, or the community, sees his role. Thus, the principal may be considerably confused by what others expect of him, as opposed to what he expects of himself. Teachers may expect him to be a demorcratic person, the opposite of what the superintendent expects. Research shows that persons who experience role conflicts are less effective than those who do not.[1]

Self-perception influences action; many a principal or supervisor spends time in making textbook inventories instead of in leading a group to develop its own goals because he sees himself in the former role.

There is a close relationship between the teacher's evaluation of leadership of administrators and the teacher's satisfaction with working in the school system. Research shows that a divergence of a teacher's role expectations of an administrator and his perceptions of that administrator's behavior is accompanied by dissatisfaction on the part of the teacher. In other words, in many cases the teacher is unhappy with what he sees in his administrator because he expects something different.

The teacher's own leadership with pupils is subject to the same kinds of conflicts. He may perceive of himself as a guide of the pupils in their search for learning, someone who can work with them rather than on them. The principal may, however, perceive of "teacher" as a lecturer, a drill-master, a disciplinarian, and a dispenser of knowledge. The way in which a teacher's role is viewed affects the kind of leadership given by the principal, as well as the effectiveness of the teacher.

PUPIL LEADERSHIP IN CIRCUMSCRIBED AREAS. The extent and degree of the pupils' activity in various aspects of organization and administration varies markedly from school to school. Frequently, they have no voice in helping to plan the curriculum or in carrying out learning activities. In other cases, they may be full participants in every phase of the learning process. In many schools, pupils have a responsibility in determining school policies and practices through student councils; however, in too few are they delegated real responsibility.

The school is a social institution in which pupils live a considerable portion of their lives. Too seldom have teachers seen the possibilities for use of the ongoing activities in and outside the classroom as a laboratory for learning the important skills of democratic leadership. Often the pupils' leadership may be confined to extraclass activities, or, in some cases, to certain kinds of such activities. The pupils may not exercise leadership skills in the many opportunities that exist in the classroom. Whether they do or not relates to how the teacher views his own role. If he views the teacher as someone

[1] J. W. Getzels and E. G. Guba, "Role, Role Conflicts, and Effectiveness," *American Sociological Review*, 19:164-75, April, 1954.

who maintains the direct control of the learning situation at all times, he will allow little or no practice for pupils in leadership.

It is common practice in many high schools, regardless of size, for pupils to work in offices, libraries, lunchrooms, gymnasiums, and in custodial jobs. Hall traffic, safety, discipline, clubs, and publications are frequently pupil-sponsored and administered. These practices are described in the following section and in Chapter 12.

Frequently, students are perceived of as having the ability to perform only the tasks which may be somewhat custodial or managerial in nature. The policies for clubs, school social affairs, safety, and other functions of the school society are legislated by the faculty and executed by the students. In such a situation leadership cannot be said to focus on the mutual growth of all concerned; the students are the ones who need most the experiences to help them grow to be effective leaders in a democratically oriented culture.

Much greater attention should be paid to the quality of interaction among pupils and among pupils and teachers that is demanded of highly complex cooperative decision-making.

IMPLEMENTATION OF THE PRINCIPLES

The principles outlined at the beginning of this chapter refer to leadership exercised by those in status positions and by teachers. Superintendents, assistant superintendents, curriculum directors, guidance directors, and supervisors, through the kind of leadership they give, help to determine the working climate for teachers and the progress toward instructional improvement. In schools large enough to have a supervising principal, it is his leadership that is of greatest concern to the teacher.

COOPERATIVE DETERMINATION OF SCHOOL SYSTEM POLICIES. In any good school system that has a number of individual school buildings, attempts are made to coordinate the work throughout the system. This is especially true in the area of curriculum and instruction. One way this is achieved is by means of a central coordinating council, which in turn appoints committees of teachers and administrators from the different school units to work on system-wide problems. Often, the council conducts some kind of survey in the school units, in order to determine the problems that need study. Thus, through representatives from the buildings and through discussion of district-wide problems in the building faculty meetings, many people participate in developing policy.

In the Indianapolis public schools, a central coordinating committee sets up continuing study committees, coordinates their activities, and serves as a liaison between study committees and the administration of the school system. Its membership represents the central administration, the supervisors, the consultant staff, special services, and both high school and elementary school teachers and principals.

This committee and seven standing committees on curriculum, pupil personnel, high school load and program, elementary school load and program, in-service, public relations, and staff personnel were recommended through a workshop for teachers held a number of years ago. The procedure of operation is designed to give teachers these opportunities:

1. To share in making decisions and policies that affect their destiny and that of the school children of Indianapolis
2. To accept greater responsibility for building high morale in the teaching staff
3. To devise effective in-service training programs that contribute to improved instruction and learning
4. To recommend curriculum revision based on educational research and the interest and needs of children
5. To develop greater skill in the problem-solving techniques.[2]

The standing of study committees, made up of almost two hundred persons representing every segment of the professional staff, carry on studies throughout the year and recommend solutions to problems.

The following statement from a bulletin of the Minneapolis public schools indicates how another school system involves teachers in planning for instructional improvement:

Curriculum development in the Minneapolis public schools may be initiated in a number of ways: by individual teachers; by school faculties; by department committees, either in schools or system-wide; by principals' groups; by the Elementary School Planning Committee or the Secondary School Planning Committee; by the permanent and special commissions which report to the Curriculum Coordinating Council; and by the Curriculum Coordinating Council itself.

In whatever way a curriculum proposal originates, however, it is channeled through a Planning Committee or the Curriculum Coordinating Council for study and authorization. It is one of these three groups which approves the appointment of production committees and makes recommendations to the administration and the Board of Education for the adoption of completed curricula.

The Elementary School Planning Committee and the Secondary School Planning Committee have the major responsibility for curriculum development at their respective levels; the Curriculum Coordinating Council has as its chief con-

---

[2] "Study Committee Roster," Indianapolis, Indiana: Indianapolis Public Schools, 1956-57, not paged (mimeo.)

cern all system-wide projects and those which extend through all grades. The Council, however, has the duty of coordinating all curriculum development work. It must know about all projects which are under way, suggest ways in which groups can work together, and see to it that school personnel are informed about developments which concern them.

In order that it may carry out its coordinating function adequately the Council has a widely representative membership. Included are six elementary school teachers and six secondary school teachers nominated from the membership of the Planning Committees and elected by a city-wide teacher vote. Representing other groups are two elementary school principals, one junior and one senior high school principal, two members of the consultant staff, and two members of the faculty of the University of Minnesota. Consultants in curriculum, library service, and publications attend meetings as ex-officio members. The administration is represented by the assistant superintendents in charge of elementary and secondary education, and by the superintendent of schools, the chairman of the Council.[3]

Each year the Council publishes its long-range plans for curriculum development.

DEMOCRATIC PARTICIPATION OF THE SECONDARY SCHOOL FACULTY. In forward-looking secondary schools, the beginning teacher can expect to find a principal who is skilled in human relations. The principal in such a school is a person who knows how to administer a secondary school but does not attempt to do it all himself. He knows his faculty members and gives them an opportunity to take responsibility where they are able to do so. He understands that morale will be highest and people will best carry out policies if they have a part in making them.

The vice principal, the guidance director, the athletic director, the student council, and the teachers are all given freedom to make their own decisions within the sphere of activity in which they operate and within the general policies developed by the group as a whole. In such a situation, the principal has a part in selecting his own faculty and, in turn, his teachers assist him in this responsibility. In large secondary schools, administrative councils of teachers are becoming more common.

The principal takes time to work with teachers in improving the instructional program, his most important job. He works with committees, has conferences with his teachers, takes extension courses with them, and serves as consultant to summer workshops participated in by the teachers of his school.

In the Joliet Township High School and Junior College, Illinois, the total professional staff is organized to share in planning, evaluat-

[3] *Progress in Curriculum Development: Annual Report of the Curriculum Coordinating Council, 1957-58*, Minneapolis, Minnesota: Minneapolis Public Schools, Dec. 10, 1958, p. 1.

ing, and policy-making. Such areas as instruction, curriculum development, guidance, student services, extraclass activities, discipline, and staff welfare are dealt with. Face-to-face communication is planned for.

The department organization takes care of quality control of instruction, courses of study, and the development of curriculum. Regular meetings are scheduled each month. Homeroom teachers meet regularly with counselors. Groups of teachers rendering special services are scheduled in such a way that those performing the same or similar tasks work together and meet regularly. Special meetings are arranged when special tasks are to be performed or when extra time is needed beyond the regularly scheduled meetings. In addition, special arrangements are made for each group or its representatives to carry on intensive study and consequent action when opportunities are available to communicate with and receive communications from other interested or similarly involved groups. Extensive communication between working groups and the entire staff is accomplished by general faculty meetings.

The plan results in new advances each year and in high staff morale. It delivers decisions of the policy-making levels and program plans worthy of action. It has caused staff to feel that they are living by decisions they helped to make. Administrative and teacher leadership play a significant part.

Smaller secondary schools, too, have many examples of good leadership. The faculty of the Floodwood Community School in northern Minnesota for many years played a vital part in planning the total activities and program of the school. Staff meetings were held weekly, usually after school, but sometimes partly on school time. The agenda were usually not planned in advance, but teachers and administrators informally presented problems pertaining to the schedule, extraclass activities, discipline, classwork, school-wide projects, and the like. Decisions were reached democratically and the principal, a teacher, or a committee was delegated to carry out the decision for the group.

Three or four monthly staff meetings were usually devoted to curriculum planning under the leadership of an elected curriculum chairman. These meetings were often conducted as workshops in which class units were preplanned, test data analyzed, and parent reports prepared. The expenditure of large budgetary items for textbooks and supplies was usually a joint responsibility of the staff and the administration. Teachers worked directly with the superintendent and the board of education in building a salary schedule. When a new superintendent was to be selected, the teachers were asked by the board to appoint a committee to assist in interviewing candidates and in making final recommendation for the position.

The teacher's planning council of the Sunnyside, Washington, High School is an organization composed of all regular faculty members of the high school. The purpose of this council is the promotion of good student-teacher relationships; democratic teacher-administrator relationships; and a better understanding among pupils, parents, teachers, and administrators.

A chairman and secretary are elected annually by the council; these two officers, two elected board members, and the principal as an ex-officio member compose the executive planning board. The board meets prior to regular council meetings to discuss problems, issues, and suggestions emanating from pupils, parents, or school staff; it prepares the agenda for the planning council which is made available in advance to the faculty.

The planning council meets regularly twice each month and more frequently when necessary. It considers carefully the items on the agenda, and all faculty and administrative personnel are given opportunity to express themselves. Special committees are sometimes appointed to investigate problems and to report to the council. A consistent effort is made to use group process techniques in order that the council may make decisions representing the unanimous approval of all teachers and administrators.

PRE-SCHOOL CONFERENCES TO ASSIST NEW TEACHERS. Fortunate, indeed, is the beginning teacher who has opportunities for orientation, planning, and cooperative study with his colleagues before school opens in the fall. These are usually on a system-wide basis. Only a decade before World War II, the inexperienced teacher typically arrived at his new teaching environment the weekend before classes began, desperately sought a "rooming house," probably attended a short Saturday morning teachers' meeting, and then reported for his first day's work on Monday along with the pupils!

The Portland, Oregon, public schools have a well-organized program for welcoming, assisting, and orienting the new teacher. Special assistance is given in finding a place to live and in getting adjusted to school and community. A teachers' handbook gives pertinent information about the school and community. One person in the central office has been assigned to this duty as one of his main responsibilities.

The School District of Greenville County, Greenville, South Carolina, requires ten days of in-service activities for all professional school personnel. As a general rule, five of these days make up the pre-school conferences, and the other five are interspersed throughout the school year with students not in attendance on those days. Frequently, faculties work within their own buildings; two of the pre-school days invariably follow this pattern. The approach is flexible and usually varies from year to year depending upon the expressed needs of teachers. A district-wide in-service committee consisting of teachers, principals, and staff members develops and coordinates the over-all plan for the year. The plan is democratically developed, and each teacher is given an opportunity to make known his views and feelings before the plan is completed. Consultants are brought in to work with the local staff and teachers' study groups. Included in the plan are both general sessions and small work groups.

The Rochester, Minnesota, public schools, where 65 per cent of the teachers are employed eleven months, hold a two-week orientation and planning period for teachers. One of the functions of these types of conferences is orientation for new teachers.

At Stanford Junior High School, Long Beach, California, various aspects of helping the new teacher are conducted under the direction of the principal, vice-principal, and counselor. For example, the principal on the first two days of the orientation period prior to the opening of school leads discussion on these topics: forms (credentials, oath, health experience, credit union, and the like); data peculiar to the school (history, traditions,); administrative organization and duties of functionaries; school community (type, size, background); basic philosophy of Long Beach schools; purpose of the junior high school and how it seeks to meet the needs of pupils in Long Beach; organization of the school (homerooms, guidance periods); grouping—how and why it works in this school; democratic procedures used; teacher assignments (service load, master program, conference period, length of day, pupil accounting); extra assignments and duties; and professional responsibilities (institutes, P.T.A., local, state, and national organizations).

Handbooks, such as, *Guideposts for New Teachers*, developed by the faculty of the East Hartford, Connecticut, schools are often used for orientation of teachers to the school and the community (see Chapter 13 for ways in which the community helps to orient new teachers).

LEADERSHIP FOR IN-SERVICE GROWTH. While many of the activities discussed above are of benefit for in-service professional growth of the teaching staff, a number of school systems have what they term an "in-service education program." The status leadership of the school does a great amount of planning within its own supervisory staff, with colleges and universities, and with consultants and other resources in order to develop such a program. A number of school systems have in-service education planning committees in which there are teacher members.

Frequently, courses offered by a nearby university are scheduled in the local school district for purposes of in-service growth and obtaining credit toward certification. The courses may be in the nature of cooperative workshops planned and directed jointly by the school and the institution. These may be offered both during the regular year and the summer. The University of Maryland, through its University College, offers to teachers nearly 300 courses each semester in education and the teaching fields in various centers of the state. The College of Education and the University College, through surveys conducted by the counties of the state, plan with the schools the courses desired and needed over a three-year period. Most state institutions of higher learning and a number of private ones now conduct in-service programs in cooperation with the schools.

Summer workshops are often conducted by the school system itself, without college credit, for two to six week's periods, as described in Chapter 15. The Milwaukee, Wisconsin, public schools, is an example of a school system that provides an extensive list of in-service courses, offered for in-service credit through University of Wisconsin, Milwaukee; Marquette University; and Milwaukee-Downer College. While credit is certified through local colleges, it is not college credit but serves as a basis for salary increment in the teachers' salary schedule. One semester's schedule listed the following eight-week classes of one two-hour session each week:

Art for Primary and Intermediate Grades
Aviation in Education
Better Health in the Classroom
Civil Defense Today
Great Orchestral Music
Home Relations Education Workshop
Independent Work Activities in the Primary School
Interpretation of Psychological Tests
Issues in American Foreign Policy (16 sessions)
Mental Health in Education
Methods of Teaching Spelling
Methods of Teaching Tumbling and Self-Testing Activities
Milwaukee's City Government
Music for Primary Grades
Nature Study and Science in the Primary School
Outdoor Education
Photography for Teachers
Science in Grades 4 through 8
Teaching Arithmetic in Intermediate Grades
The Kindergarten Program Today
Today's Isms

In addition, a large variety of courses are offered for college credit on the colleges' campus locations in Milwaukee.

SUPERVISORY LEADERSHIP. In an increasing number of schools the teacher will receive helpful, sympathetic assistance. The fact that in recent years there have been greater numbers of teachers who have lacked the necessary training has caused school systems to develop various kinds of programs of assistance to these teachers. Many school systems have well-planned programs for helping the beginning teacher.

The principal of the school may do the majority of the supervision himself. He must, however, be a person who is trained in supervision and understands teachers' problems, teaching methods, and materials. In cases where he feels that he cannot help the teacher, he calls upon the supervisor from the central school office or the instructional consultant. In some secondary schools, the vice-principal may perform this function or there may be a special curriculum or instructional consultant in the school building.

Available to help the new teacher in some school systems are the helping teachers who are released from their classroom duties for one or more years to spend time in working with other teachers. They do not have any responsibility for evaluating or rating the teachers with whom they work. Such teachers are found, for example, in the schools of Newton, Massachusetts; Portland, Oregon; and Seattle, Washington.

The kinds of supervisory leadership for instructional improvement that outstanding principals give stem largely from their continuous work with teachers in curriculum improvement.

More specifically, some of the types of assistance given by either the principal, the central supervisory staff, or the instructional consultant, are these: helping teachers find materials, helping them to develop new materials, talking over plans with the teachers, conducting teachers' meetings, holding conferences with the teacher to discuss any assistance that the teacher may wish to have, developing plans for the year, interpreting the curriculum guides used by the school, planning the graduate work that the teacher will take, and assisting the teacher with special problem children.

The principal who works closely with the teacher has plenty of opportunity to get into the teacher's classroom and hold conferences with him concerning his ongoing program. He discusses parent conferences with the teacher, assists him with ongoing projects, and even assists him by taking over his classroom or working with him in the classroom at times. Good human relations are the fundamental basis for supervision. The teacher has confidence in the principal whom he respects and who he knows can be helpful. The teacher also knows that he can call upon other specialists in the school system if he wishes, or he can receive help from other teachers who have certain specialties. These are means of sharing leadership roles and responsibilities.

The 1960 Yearbook of the Association for Supervision and Curriculum Development lists a number of ways by which the supervisory staff members are of assistance to teachers.

1. Organizing classrooms, including grouping of children, setting up interests centers, advising on programs, and developing materials
2. Helping teachers develop better teaching techniques
3. Observing teachers and pupils at work and conferring with the teacher following the observation
4. Interpreting curriculum guides and assisting with lesson planning
5. Helping to establish standards of work and behavior
6. Arranging visitations for teachers within or between schools
7. Acquainting teachers with supplementary materials
8. Helping in the development of good human relationships among children, parents, and school personnel
9. Encouraging teachers to share abilities and talents
10. Helping administer tests and interpret scores
11. Helping teachers to solve problems of pupil control and discipline
12. Demonstrating techniques through actual teaching
13. Serving as resource person in before-school and after-school building meetings and areas meetings.[4]

DEFINITION OF ROLES OF SCHOOL PERSONNEL. In a school in which the status leader is working to improve the quality of interaction, he is concerned with the clarification of the roles and the authority of the administrator, the supervisor, and the teacher. In a number of school systems a good deal of thought has been given to the interrelationship of roles within that school. These schools clarify the question as to what relationship the supervisor should have to the principal and to the teacher. In some instances, this question has been solved by giving the supervisor a role as consultant. When an outstanding teacher is brought into the central office for relatively short periods of time, teachers tend to identify this person as one of themselves and feel more comfortable in working with him.

In the Torrance Unified School District in Torrance, California there are no supervisors as such. Consultants with an office in the central administrative building are resource persons available to the principals on call. They work as "staff" members normally and as a preference, but they also work as "line" administrators and exercise

[4] Association for Supervision and Curriculum Development, *Leadership for Instruction,* Washington, D.C.: National Education Association, 1960, p. 114.

administrative authority where the situation calls for it in the execution of district policy or by specific instruction from their assistant superintendent. They are considered as a valuable resource by the principals and the teachers and are used frequently by them. They are sometimes scheduled to specific principals for periods of time as well as being on call.

SHARED LEADERSHIP WITH TEACHERS. The sharing of leadership roles is a factor in the improvement of the climate of the school. Opportunity is presented for leadership to emerge from among the teachers since they serve as chairmen of curriculum committees, committees that develop administrative policy, and committees that deal with relationships with the community. They are given time to carry out these leadership functions and are not merely assigned routine and disagreeable tasks. They may, for example, serve as chairman for a committee that makes recommendations to the faculty concerning what shall be considered as in-service education activities for meeting in-service growth requirements determined by the school faculty.

In the environment in which emerging leadership is encouraged, status leaders and teachers recognize that persons differ in the kinds of contributions they have to make. Those in status leadership positions assist individual teachers in realizing their potential and utilizing their strengths. They organize conditions in the schools so as to make it possible for each teacher to do his best work. In such a school, associations are on a friendly and informal basis, cliques are few, people like to work together, and feel free to disagree without fear of personal offense to others.

SCHOOL AS LEADERSHIP SKILLS LABORATORY. The school offers a wide variety of opportunities for assisting youngsters to learn leadership skills. The pupil may exercise leadership responsibilities in the classroom where he may be in charge of a study committee to investigate some question, of an administrative committee that deals with the planning and care of the bulletin board, or of explaining to visitors what is happening in the class.

The student in the good school also has innumerable opportunities to exercise leadership in extraclass activities where he may serve as president, chairman, committee member, or in some other capacity. In the school that actually searches for these kinds of opportunities, one will find pupils doing many of the kinds of things that in other schools teachers routinely do. Included would be supervision of the library; supervision of the study hall, supervision of halls; in charge of activities in the lunchroom; in charge of the bookstore, the school bank, or other kinds of functions. The student in such a school may also have responsible duties in connection with the school orchestra or band, the school play, parent-teacher association meetings, school assemblies, and other leadership functions of the school society that one would expect a person in his own society to exercise. The most obvious of these is the student government field. This question is discussed further in Chapter 12, where a number of examples of outstanding practices are presented.

ISSUES AND PROBLEMS

Although there tends to be more agreement in recent writings concerning leadership, both in the field of education and in related areas, in practice it is by no means clear cut as to what kinds of leadership should be exercised to improve instruction in the schools. Some of the main issues and problems are pointed up here.

1. *What kind of leadership do the times demand in American secondary education?*

There are those who hold that in order to effect improvement in American education there must be strong leaders who are not afraid to make decisions and who will stay with those decisions. They believe that since changes come about slowly such strong leadership is needed to facilitate those changes.

Those who believe that a democratic type of leadership is best in a critical situation as well as in an easier one, believe first of all that leadership in today's troubled world demands knowledge. Someone who would lead his colleagues needs to be a generally well-informed person. He needs to have the facts about problems, or he needs to be able to secure those facts. They believe that such leadership demands a vision far beyond that required in times past. For the rapid changes of today's world demand insight into possible alternative actions. They believe these changes call for flexibility, for it is difficult to predict what the political and technical changes will mean for tomorrow. They believe such leadership demands standing by one's principles rather than compromising with the pressures that exist to change a program even though one does not agree with that change. In recent years, there have been many examples of pressures exerted on school administrators to abandon their beliefs in individualization of instruction and in understanding the child as a fundamental basis to successful learning.

The times demand complete understanding as never before that leadership cannot reside in only one person in a given situation; that leadership must be shared; that persons with various kinds of abilities exercise leadership in different ways. There is always a temptation toward authoritarianism in order to accomplish something hurriedly. The answer to what kind of leadership to use depends on whether ones goal is to display results to the public or to develop the good in people.

2. Is there a genuine commitment to democratic leadership?

There are numerous pseudodemocratic practices which have a facade of democracy. Some who mouth democratic principles are not really willing to trust people to make decisions. They have no real commitments to group intelligence. Students of human behavior realize that increased skills are needed by those who wish to be the leaders in this day and age and that these are important skills that must be worked at. For example, an important skill is to develop a sensitivity to people's feelings. The one who calls himself a leader cannot hope to run roughshod over the people with whom he works.

One can question whether there is a genuine commitment to democratic leadership, for much that is done in the name of leadership takes a negative approach, rather than a positive approach that develops the potential strength of people. Cited as examples can be merit plans, promotion plans, supervision that aims to improve others only, checking to see if regulations are enforced—all of these concepts are essentially negative in their application, focused on people's weaknesses.

3. Should the leader develop his own ideas or utilize only those developed by the group?

To what extent is the effective leader permissive? There has been a great deal of misconception on this particular point. Some have the concept that a status leader in a democratic form of leadership does not have ideas, that he does not present plans or programs. Others hold that a status leader has a real responsibility for developing proposals that can be freely and frankly discussed by the group. The latter concept of leadership holds that a person abdicates leadership unless he has the vision and perspective to develop proposals for consideration.

Some people conceive of leadership as a way to "get things done." Whose things? Whose goals are to be achieved? Some teachers feel that a person in status leadership is not a leader unless he gets "my" objectives furthered. They approach the matter from a selfish angle and criticize the leader unless he is willing to support their personal goals.

4. *Should the leader follow his own concept of leadership or that of his superiors?*

An important question is whether or not the leader must follow the top status leader's concept of leadership or his own. It is likely to become uncomfortable for the principal or teacher as a leader if he holds conflicting views concerning leadership from those who are part of the central administration. Should the administration of the school take the position that others may have differing concepts of leadership and that each person may be most successful in implementing that concept that he finds most nearly satisfies his own convictions?

A really great leader facilitates freedom for development of ideas among his colleagues who are assigned to work under him. He considers them more in terms of a partnership than in terms of an inferior status position. However, this concept is not widespread in schools, for the theory is still held of a line and staff concept of administration, where certain members follow a line of authority from the top down and others hold so-called staff positions which carry no administrative authority.

5. *Does the situational theory of leadership disregard the individual or emphasize individual strengths?*

This theory, simply stated, is that a person may be a leader in one situation and not in another. It calls for a sharing of leadership among different individuals. Does this mean the principal does not need to have a good background of knowledge about curriculum and instruction? A number of principals in schools cannot give effective leadership to instructional improvement. Usually someone such as curriculum coordinator, supervisor, or perhaps the assistant principal in charge of instruction may be one who has knowledge and skills that will cause him to be regarded as an effective leader in this important function. However, if the principal is not perceived as a leader, he has little chance to assist the faculty in forwarding their own goals since they will tend to resist him rather than to work with him.

The theory recognizes individual differences in that some people can help the group move toward their goals in one kind of problem situation and other persons can help them move ahead in other instances. An example of this would be the kind of person who can effectively take over in case of an extreme emergency to life, in contrast to someone who can effectively help a group in analyzing and defining what it wishes to accomplish. The two kinds of situations are entirely different and require some differences in abilities in leadership. It follows that a status leader should not be asked to fit into a universal mold which disregards his individual personality, background, and makeup.

6. *What problems in leadership do growth in size of an institution create?*

It is often thought that as the school system increases in size many problems are solved. It is true that such a school can offer a richer curriculum than a small school district. However, there are obstacles that arise to effective functioning of the unit. There is a growing realization that the large school system, either a public school or an institution of higher learning, tends to develop an administrative hierarchy. Administrative positions are multiplied so that the teacher in the classroom is subject to a number of administrative personalities, each one who feels that he must justify his position by requiring reports or demanding certain things of the teaching personnel.

One can note a tendency for the top administrators to get further and further removed from the teaching staff in a large institution. Consequently, they are fed information by others, by which they begin to make decisions independent of the people who are most keenly affected by those decisions—the teachers. Basically, the teacher becomes so far away from the decision-making, even though there are central councils, that he does not feel a part of those decisions or know why they are made. Although communication is one of the big problems involved here, it is not the basic one. The problem is one of attaining a close relationship between an administrator and the teaching staff within units in a large administrative situation without a great deal of control from the top.

SELECTED REFERENCES

ANDERSON, VERNON E. *Principles and Procedures of Curriculum Improvement.* New York: The Ronald Press Co., 1956, Chap. 3.—How the teacher can utilize group process skills for leadership in curriculum study.

ANDERSON, VIVIENNE and DAVIES, DANIEL R. *Patterns of Educational Leadership.* Englewood Cliffs, N.J.: Prentice-Hall, Inc., 1956, Chap. 1.—Presents case studies that illustrate human relations problems of teacher and administrator. A unique organization for the study of leadership problems.

ASSOCIATION FOR SUPERVISION AND CURRICULUM IMPROVEMENT. *Leadership for Improving Instruction.* (1960 Yearbook). Washington, D.C.: National Education Association, 1960. 198 p.—A significant statement of the modern concept of leadership, leadership roles, and the development and appraisal of leadership. Shows how teacher leadership is utilized in the school in curriculum study.

DOUGLASS, HARL R., BENT, R. K., and BOARDMAN, C. W. *Democratic Supervision in Secondary Schools.* Boston: Houghton Mifflin Co., 2nd ed., 1953, Chap. 14-15.—Deals with assisting teachers with curriculum problems and materials.

EASTMOND, JEFFERSON N. *The Teacher and School Administration.* Boston: Houghton Mifflin Co., 1959, 522 p.—The whole book gives insight into the various roles for the teacher in his administrative retlationships. Chapter 8 is especially pertinent to the teacher's participation in school administration.

HAMMOCK, ROBERT C. and OWINGS, RALPH S. *Supervising Instruction in Secondary Schools.* New York: McGraw Hill Book Co., Inc., 1955, Chap. 11.—Presents a summary of how modern administration and supervision function cooperatively, with illustrations of promising practices.

MACKENZIE, GORDON N. and COREY, STEPHEN M. *Instructional Leadership.* New York: Bureau of Publications, Teachers College, Columbia University, 1954, 209 pp.—An action research study on how school leaders improved their leadership through evaluating their effectiveness. A good source of information on leadership concepts and practices in schools.

MITCHUM, PAUL M. *The High School Principal and Staff Plan for Improvement.* New York: Bureau of Publications, Teachers College, Columbia University, 1958, 103 pp. —From this booklet the future teacher can gain a picture of how the principal exercises his leadership functions in a secondary school.

NATIONAL SOCIETY FOR THE STUDY OF EDUCATION. *In-Service Education for Teachers, Supervisors, and Administrators.* (Fifty-Sixth Yearbook, Part I). Chicago: University of Chicago Press, 1957, Chaps. 5-6.—These two chapters concern principles of how a faculty works together productively in in-service education and the role of the teacher in these programs.

PRESTWOOD, ELWOOD L. *The High School Principal and Staff Work Together.* New York: Bureau of Publications, Teachers College, Columbia University, 1957, 96 pp.— Presents information on the factors that influence principal-teacher working relationships and the many ways in which they work together.

ROMINE, STEPHEN A. *Building the High School Curriculum.* New York: The Ronald Press Co., 1954, Chap. 16.—Presents a general picture of leadership in the administration of curriculum revision.

SAYLOR, J. GALEN and ALEXANDER, WILLIAM M. *Curriculum Planning for Better Teaching and Learning.* New York: Holt, Rinehart & Winston, Inc., 1954, Chap. 16—Shows the opportunities for teacher participation in curriculum improvement and the possibilities for leadership.

15

ADMINISTRATIVE ORGANIZATION

The administrative organization of a secondary school is an important factor in determining how fully the objectives of the educational program may be achieved. The arrangement of the school year, the nature of the weekly and daily schedule of classes, the size of classes, the provisions for the use of the library, laboratories, and other learning facilities, the opportunity to come into contact with teachers, the schedule for extraclass activities—these are some aspects of the administrative organization of the secondary school which influence the nature of the educational program and the conditions for learning in the school. It is the purpose of this chapter to develop a statement of desirable principles for the administrative organization of various types of secondary schools.

BASIC PRINCIPLES

The administrative organization of a secondary school exists primarily to provide the best possible educational program for the pupils.

This is the predominating principle which should shape the entire administrative organization of a secondary school. All the other principles are secondary to it. The organization of the school has no importance whatsoever except to provide the best possible conditions for learning within the framework of the educational program of the school. In other words, the educational program should not be made to fit into the daily schedule, the building, or any other administrative practices of the school. Rather, the organization of any secondary school should be shaped, insofar as that is possible, by the needs of the instructional program of that school.

The administrative organization of a secondary school should make it possible to offer a broad educational program which meets the needs, interests, and abilities of all pupils in the school.

In the first secondary schools in the United States more than a century ago, the curriculum was a narrow one indeed. The subjects in the early schools were primarily college preparatory, with little attention given to physical education, music, art, industrial arts, and home economics. Extraclass activities were limited or non-existent. The administrative organization for schools with such a limited program could be a simple one.

As children not planning to go to college began to attend the public high school, a broader curriculum became necessary. Besides the college-preparatory subjects, business subjects, industrial arts, homemaking, music, art, and physical education were added. The administrative organization of the early public high school, however, was not appropriate for some of the new subjects. For instance, the length of the class period appropriate for English, Latin, and mathematics was not equally suitable for physical education, home economics, industrial arts and laboratory sciences. Then, too, the growing number of electives and the introduction of a variety of extraclass activities presented problems for the administrative organization.

It has become increasingly important, therefore, to have an organization which is sufficiently flexible to offer a broad program of subjects and activities. The length of the school year, the length of the day, the nature of class periods, the possibility of after-school and evening activities, and other aspects of the administrative organization of the school have a direct bearing on the breadth of the curriculum and the kinds of learning activities that can be offered. The need for flexible organization in secondary schools is essential if they are to provide an adequate educational program for all youth.

The administrative organization of a secondary school should make it possible for the principal, counselors, and teachers to know and to work effectively with individual pupils on their educational and personal problems.

Individual pupils have different backgrounds and problems, and they learn in different ways. The program of the school should recognize these differences. The administrative organization of a secondary school is an important factor in determining how well the instructional program is suited to the differences that are found among pupils. For instance, the size of the school has a direct bearing on meeting individual pupil needs. It is easier in a large school to provide a broad educational program with elective courses and activities for pupils of all interests and abilities. But in a large school the personal interest in individual pupils may not be readily maintained.

In many ways other than the size of the school, the administrative organization has a bearing on the individual problems of youth. The departmental organization of a school, for instance, may give teachers such heavy pupil loads that it is difficult for them to know their pupils well. A rigid daily schedule that permits teachers little time to visit with pupils in informal situations outside the classroom is another limiting factor in teacher-pupil relationships. Every effort should be made to develop an administrative organization in a secondary school which permits the faculty to work effectively with all pupils as individuals.

The administrative organization of a secondary school should encourage correlation between the learning activities and outcomes of different subjects and extraclass activities.

It is important for pupils to see the relationships between the learning activities in the various subjects. The skills in reading, writing, and oral expression which pupils develop in the English class should be applied in history, science, and mathematics. The work in mathematics bears a close relationship to the learning activities in science. Art and music may be important to the study of home and family living. Likewise, the extraclass activities in which pupils participate may contribute to the learning that takes place in the classroom. The departmental organization of a school, however, may discourage the correlation of learning activities and outcomes in the various subjects. Each teacher may be responsible for a small part of the child's educational program, with little opportunity to relate it to other learnings in that program.

There should be ways provided in the administrative organization for teachers of English and social studies to plan together the learning activities for a group of pupils. The school paper, speech activities, assemblies, pupil elections, and other extraclass activities should be closely correlated with the work of the English and social studies classes.

The administrative organization of a secondary school should be sufficiently flexible so that a variety of learning activities may be carried on in classes and elsewhere in the school program.

Educators generally believe that there should be a variety of learning activities in the instructional program—different from subject to subject. Within any subject area, learning activities should be adapted to the particular purpose to be served. For example, there should be such activities as field trips, community surveys, interviews with people in the community, laboratory activities, talks by resource people from outside the school, the use of audio aids and visual materials, and dramatic presentations by the pupils. Some of these, such as field trips, require special arrangements and may take more time than the typical class period allows. For certain activities within the school, such as a speaker, a demonstration, or a dramatic presentation, it may be desirable to have several class groups come together. Likewise, with other types of activities, deviation from the usual pattern of administrative organization for the school may be necessary.

A rigid daily schedule makes it difficult to employ certain types of learning activities. The administrative organization of the school should be sufficiently flexible so that pupils may go on field trips, that some learning activities may extend beyond the usual class period, and that several classes may come together for a large group activity.

The administrative organization of a secondary school should make it possible for all pupils to participate in any part of the educational program in which they may be interested and for which they are qualified.

The administrative organization of the school may limit pupils too much to one aspect of the school's program. Pupils in the college preparatory curriculum, for instance, may find it difficult to take subjects that are not clearly college preparatory. They may wish to take typewriting for personal use, pursue an interest in art or music, or broaden their education through courses in industrial arts or home economics. Likewise, pupils in a vocational curriculum may wish to take a foreign language or some other subject in the college preparatory curriculum. The administrative organization of the school should permit pupils to participate in any part of the total educational program.

Participation in extraclass activities also may be either encouraged or limited by the administrative organization of the school, as discussed in Chapter 12. The administrative organization of the school should place these activities at a time when all interested pupils can take part or make other arrangements so that participation for all pupils is possible.

The administrative organization of a secondary school should provide adequate time for teachers to develop the curriculum, to plan learning activities, and in other ways to prepare for their participation in the instructional program.

The effectiveness of a teacher's contribution to the program of a secondary school depends to a large extent upon the imagination and thoroughness with which he plans his work. This is true for all his responsibilities, including both the class and extraclass program. The planning which teachers need to do involves more than the preparation of lessons day by day. It includes developing the total curriculum of the school, planning extraclass activities, studying individual pupils, preparing units of study, planning for specific learning activities, locating instructional materials, developing evaluation and testing devices, and maintaining records of pupil achievement and progress. This may include planning time before the opening of school, during the school year, and after the close of school in the spring.

As discussed in Chapter 6, teachers in a school need to do much cooperative planning, both in the same subject and for different subjects at a grade level. This must be done in order to develop a well-coordinated program, with all teachers understanding their responsibilities for the program as a whole. Such planning requires time when pupils are not in school, so that teachers may give it their full attention. It also requires time day by day, with teachers of all subjects and grade levels frequently in touch with each other. The effectiveness of the total educational program depends in a large measure upon the provision which is made in the organization of the school for planning and preparation time for teachers.

SOME COMMON PRACTICES

The principles discussed above suggest that the administrative organization of a secondary school should be such that it will assure the most desirable conditions for learning. Some of the more common administrative practices in secondary schools of the United States will be examined and critically evaluated to see how they may influence the effectiveness of the program of secondary education.

INFLUENCE OF ENROLLMENTS ON PROGRAMS. In a comprehensive study James B. Conant (see *The American High School Today*) indicated that a high school, if it is to have a diversified curriculum to meet the needs of all pupils, should have at least 100 pupils in the graduating class. When Conant made the study, however, almost three-fourths of the high schools in the United States were smaller than the size which he recommended. In fact, in several states, such as Iowa, Mississippi, Nebraska, North Dakota, and South Dakota, less than 5 per cent of the high schools had as many as 100 pupils in the twelfth grade. This high percentage of small secondary schools in the United

States persists in spite of the fact that there has been considerable consolidation of secondary schools in recent years.

The small secondary school is handicapped particularly by the fact that only a limited curriculum can be offered. With at least 100 pupils in a grade, as recommended by Conant, it would be possible to have four class groups of twenty-five pupils each. With four classes in a grade, a school could offer courses for pupils who are pointing toward college, general courses for those who do not plan to continue in school after graduation, and a limited offering of vocational courses to prepare pupils for immediate employment. In small secondary schools, the number of elective offerings is usually limited because there are not enough pupils to justify them. Furthermore, in small schools it is expensive to offer subjects for which special facilities are required, such as industrial arts, the laboratory sciences, music, and art. The curriculum in small schools therefore is usually so limited that it fails to meet the needs, interests, and abilities of all the pupils.

Although in large secondary schools it is easier to offer a broad program of curricula and courses, these schools also have certain disadvantages. The chief objection to large schools is that teacher-pupil relationships may become quite impersonal. As a result, pupils in large schools may not receive the individual attention that is needed to help them achieve the most success in school. This is particularly true of schools that exceed 1,200 to 1,500 pupils. These schools are found in large cities in all parts of the United States. In the large cities of the East, there are some secondary schools with enrollments of more than 5,000 pupils. In some large schools, steps are being taken to assure the attention to problems of individual pupils which is desirable for their success in school. These practices will be discussed later in this chapter.

INFLUENCE OF GRADE ORGANIZATION ON PROGRAMS. For many years, the four-year high school, including grades 9 through 12, was the most common type of secondary school in the United States. The four-year high school was preceded by an elementary school, which in the South included seven grades, and in the North and West, eight grades. In the seven-four and the eight-four plans of grade organization, the program in the upper elementary grades was an exceedingly narrow one. Pupils usually had one teacher who taught all subjects in one classroom. Even in schools where a limited amount of departmentalization was introduced in the upper elementary grades, it was difficult to provide the facilities and equipment for such subjects as science, industrial arts, home economics, art, and music. Furthermore, the enrollments in these grades were usually so limited that special opportunities could not be provided except at an unreasonably high cost for such pupils as the gifted, the mentally retarded, and those with particular learning deficiencies.

The junior-senior high school plan of grade organization was introduced primarily to provide a broader program of education in the early adolescent years, as discussed in Chapter 2. In communities with a sufficiently large enrollment, separate junior and senior high schools were established. In the separate junior high school, it is possible to provide a curriculum which is sufficiently broad to meet the needs, interests, and abilities of all pupils. There can be remedial and developmental reading classes, corrective physical education classes, special classes for mentally retarded pupils, programs for gifted pupils, and other opportunities for pupils who need special attention. In the junior high school, it is also easier to justify subjects which require special building facilities and teachers with specialized preparation and skills, such as the foreign languages, science, industrial arts, home economics, music, art, and physical education. In the combined junior-senior high school, which is most appropriate in small communities, it is likewise possible to offer at a reasonable cost those subjects and programs for which specialized staff and facilities are required.

The junior-senior high school plan of grade organization today is the most prevalent one in the United States. In 1959, according to the United States Office of Education, 75 per cent of the secondary schools in the United States were organized on some form of the junior-senior high school plan, and more than 80 per cent of all pupils in grades seven through twelve were enrolled in these schools. Consequently, today more pupils than ever before are attending secondary schools in which broad programs of education are possible from grades 7 through 12.

INFLUENCES OF PUPIL-TEACHER RATIO ON INSTRUCTION. The pupil load which a teacher carries during a school day has a direct bearing on the effectiveness of his instructional activities. If the load is heavy, a teacher may find it difficult to become acquainted with the backgrounds and abilities of individual pupils and to give them the individual help which they may need. Educators usually recommend that, in most subjects, teachers should have an average enrollment in their classes of twenty-five pupils, with thirty as the maximum number. Furthermore, they recommend an average of five classes per day, or twenty-five classes per week, as a reasonable class load for teachers. A teacher with five classes a day may, therefore, be responsible for supervising the work of 125 to 150 different pupils. Some of the more creative concepts of scheduling and varying the numbers of pupils in classes for different purposes are discussed in Chapters 7 and 8 under team teaching.

The number of pupils for which teachers in actual practice are responsible differs greatly from school to school and from subject to subject. In the large cities, it is not at all uncommon for classes in such subjects as English, social studies, science, and mathematics to have an average enrollment of forty or more pupils. In physical education, classes frequently are even larger, with enrollments extending upwards of fifty pupils in a class. In rural and small urban communities, where total enrollments are not so large, teachers may be responsible for a smaller number of different pupils. However, in these communities this advantage may be more than offset by teachers being assigned a larger number of classes and requiring more preparation in different subjects.

There is little doubt that the heavy pupil load which teachers carry in secondary schools limits the effectiveness of their work. In English, for instance, it is impossible for a teacher to require much written work if he has more than 100 different pupils in his classes. The time it takes to read even 100 papers, to correct errors, and to make suggestions for improvement is staggering indeed. The oral and written activities in social studies and the demonstrations, projects, and activities in science likewise place a heavy burden on teachers of these subjects who carry heavy pupil loads.

In certain subjects where pupils need much individual help, the teacher-pupil ratio frequently is smaller than in English, social studies, and science. These subjects are industrial arts, home economics, art, and crafts. Remedial classes in certain subjects and classes for the mentally retarded and other atypical pupils likewise are smaller, with classes of fifteen to twenty pupils not uncommon. In most regular subjects, however, secondary school teachers have a pupil load which is too high for satisfactory attention to the needs of individual pupils.

INFLEXIBILITY OF DAILY SCHEDULES. It is difficult to characterize the daily schedule for secondary schools in the United States because practices differ so widely from school to school. Several examples of typical school schedules may suggest the more common practices. Urban Junior High School, with an enrollment of 1,500 pupils in grades 7, 8, and 9, is located in a city of 75,000. Although the majority of the pupils live in the city, many of them are transported by school bus. School opens at 8:25 A.M. with a five-minute morning devotional period. There are six regular class periods beginning at 8:30, each one fifty-five minutes in length, with five minutes for passing. At 10:30 every day there is a thirty-minute homeroom period for activities and group guidance. Pupils go to lunch in three shifts beginning at 11:00 o'clock, with thirty-five minutes for each lunch period. Some classes are interrupted by the lunch period, with the first half of the class period preceding lunch and the second half following it. There is a five-minute interval at 2:30 for making afternoon announcements. School closes at 3:30 P.M. This school, which is located in the West, has a longer day than many schools elsewhere in the United States.

Suburban Senior High School, a medium-sized school including grades 10, 11, and 12, has an eight-period day beginning at 8:38 A.M. and closing at 3:52 P.M. Each class period is forty-two minutes long, with a three-minute passing interval. Since most of the pupils go home for lunch, the noon hour is seventy minutes long. There is no regularly scheduled time during the school day for such activities as clubs, assemblies, and group guidance. Both in the morning and the afternoon, there is a brief homeroom period which is used primarily to take attendance and make announcements.

Rural High School, a four-year school in a rural area, has an enrollment of sixty-five pupils, all of whom come on school buses. School opens at 9:00 A.M. and closes at 4:00 P.M., with a lunch period that extends from 12:00 noon to 1:00 P.M. There are eight class periods during the day, each forty-five minutes long, with just a minute or two allowed for passing. At 10:30 in the morning there is a ten-minute snack and recess period, the time for which is taken from the second and third class periods. Since there is no cafeteria or lunch room, the pupils bring their lunches and eat them in the regular classrooms. Most of the extraclass activities are carried on during the noon hour, except for a limited program of interscholastic sports which is scheduled at the close of the school day. Pupils who participate in the after-school sports program must provide their own transportation. Because the enrollment in Rural High School is small, such activities as assemblies, clubs, and field trips are arranged on an informal basis as convenient during the school day.

Although these three schedules differ in some details, they are similar in that they permit little adaptation to the needs of different subjects and different types of learning activities. The same time is allowed for physical education, industrial arts, laboratory sciences, mathematics, English and social studies. Yet the nature of these subjects differs so much that the same amount of class time is not equally appropriate. Field trips and other activities that require more than one period are difficult to arrange without interfering with the total schedule.

In some schools which have a seven- or eight-period day, double periods are allowed for certain subjects, such as industrial arts, laboratory science, and physical education. Another common practice is to have a different bell schedule on days when there are assemblies, clubs, or other extraclass activities. In small schools, flexibility in the schedule may be introduced on an informal basis by arrangements with the principal or other teachers. The daily schedule in most secondary schools, however, is too inflexible for the class and extraclass activities of a forward-looking program of secondary education.

VARIED LENGTH OF SCHOOL DAY. The amount of time which pupils spend in school has some bearing on the effectiveness of the educational program. In a long school day, as compared with a short one, pupils can take more subjects, participate in more activities, and receive more help from teachers. In the secondary schools of the United States, there is wide variation of practices. In some schools in New England, where the school day is particularly short, pupils attend school for only five to five-and-a-half hours, not counting lunch time. In schools in the Middle West, the Far West, and the South, the six-hour day is most common. In many schools in the Middle West and the South, moreover, the school day extends to six-and-a-half hours or more, not including the lunch period. Even in the same states, however, the length of the school day varies tremendously from one community to another.

In schools with a short day, as in New England, the offering of subjects and extraclass activities is necessarily limited. In these schools pupils are usually given more homework, less time is devoted to music, industrial arts, home econmics and similar subjects, and most extraclass activities are carried on after the regular school day. Class periods also are shorter, with pupils spending less time under the supervision of each teacher.

In senior high schools of the United States, the school day has been increased slightly during the past twenty years, according to a recent survey made by the Research Division of the National Education Association. During the same period, the average length of the school day in junior high schools has been slightly decreased. In both junior and senior high schools, however, the average length of the school day for teachers has been increased in recent years, with teachers becoming more available for conferences with pupils and parents and for preparation and planning activities. The tendency to increase the length of the school day for both pupils and teachers has been great-

est in those communities where in the past the day has been exceptionally short.

The number of days in the school year also varies. Although in
most states 180 days is recognized as the desirable length for the
school year, in some states certain holidays, teacher institute days,
and other days when pupils are not present may be counted as part
of the 180 school days. In 1957–58, the average length of the school
year for the forty-eight states and the District of Columbia was 176.6
days. In Missouri, with the longest year, schools were in session on
the average 182.1 days, while Arizona and Mississippi had the shortest school term with an average of only 170 days. In recent years
there has been some tendency to increase the number of days in the
school year, although the communities which have lengthened the
year have usually added only a few days.

DEPARTMENTALIZATION IN SECONDARY SCHOOLS. In most secondary
schools in the United States, the program is highly departmentalized,
with teachers who are specialists in the different subjects. In large
secondary schools, pupils usually have a different teacher for every
subject. In the hundreds of small secondary schools, found especially
in the rural communities, a teacher may be responsible for several
different subjects. For instance, in schools with a total enrollment of
less than 200 pupils, one teacher may be responsible for general science, chemistry, physics, and mathematics; another may teach much
of the work in English and social studies; and teachers of foreign
languages, industrial arts, home economics, music, and art may teach
other subjects as well.

The departmentalization of the secondary school has certain advantages. Teachers can be specialists in their subjects, they usually
have fewer preparations, and they need to keep informed in a more
limited subject area. In the departmentalized school, therefore,
teachers should be better qualified in their respective subjects, the
preparation of learning activities should be more carefully done, and
the instruction should be more thorough.

The departmentalized secondary school, however, also has disadvantages. The most serious is the lack of correlation which one
finds among the learning activities in the various subjects. Each
teacher in a departmentalized school tends to plan for his own classes
with little or no reference to the learning that takes place in other
subjects. The lack of correlation between subjects is particularly serious in large schools, where teachers may have little direct contact
with each other.

In many junior high schools today there is some form of block-time scheduling, especially in the seventh and eighth grades, with English, social studies, and the homeroom usually combined and taught by the same teacher. The purpose of this block of time is to make it possible for pupils to have one teacher for a good part of the day who gets to know them well and to whom they can go with their educational and personal problems. The block of time or the core class, discussed in Chapter 7, encourages greater correlation between the language arts, the social studies, and the group guidance activities. Block-time classes are not widely used in the senior high school grades.

IMPLEMENTATION OF THE PRINCIPLES

Many secondary schools today are employing new approaches to administrative organization in an effort to provide a better educational program. These new approaches are not confined to one section of the country nor to one type of school. Furthermore, one finds new administrative practices in all types of secondary schools—senior high schools, junior high schools, six-year high schools, and four-year high schools. Examples of administrative practices that are being introduced to improve the educational program are presented in this part of the chapter.

PERSONALIZATION OF LARGE SCHOOLS. In many large schools, real concern is being shown for the individual student and his place in the program of the school. This is being done by placing students in small administrative units within the framework of the large school. This type of organization is called a "school within the school," the "little-school plan," or the "house plan." Whatever it is called, the purpose of this plan of organization is to give more attention to the guidance of individual pupils and still provide the broad curriculum and program which are possible only in the large secondary school.

In some communities, school buildings are being designed with the little-school plan in mind. The Newton South High School, Newton, Massachusetts, a new three-year senior high school organized on this plan, has three separate houses, each designed to accommodate about 500 pupils. Each house is located in a separate unit of the building, with classrooms for the basic subjects and offices for the house master and counselors. The staff for each house includes a house master, a part-time administrative assistant, counselors, a secretary, and a house aide who assists with office activities. Each house has pupils from all three grades who take their basic subjects with teachers on the faculty of the house in so far as that can be arranged. Exceptions include the sciences, art, physical education, advanced-placement courses, and other subjects which, because of the staff and cost of facilities, cannot be readily placed in each house. Pupils have contact with pupils of other houses through the latter subjects, some all-school activities, and their class organizations. Activities which are separate for the three houses include assemblies, some social activities, teams for intramural sports, and a student council. Although Newton pupils are encouraged to have loyalties to their house, they also develop loyalties to the school as a whole through participation in such all-school activities as interscholastic athletics, social functions, music activities, and school publications.

In the Citrus Union High School District, Azusa, California, two four-year high schools, the Azusa and the Glendora High Schools, are each organized into four little schools on a grade basis. Each little school has its own physical facilities, an administrator, a counselor, and teachers. In the Citrus Union High School District, much emphasis is placed on improving the instructional program through the little schools, with the administrator, the counselor, and the faculty developing a curriculum and planning the instructional program for each little school on a grade basis.

The little-school plan is also being used in some junior high schools. The O'Farrell Junior High School, San Diego, California, a three-year school with an enrollment of 2,200 pupils, is divided into six little schools, two for each grade. In addition to the principal and assistant principals, who are responsible for the total school program, each little school has an instructional coordinator, a counselor, and its own faculty. In the O'Farrell Junior High School, the little-school plan is used particularly for cooperative planning by teachers, getting to know pupils better, and improving contacts with parents. This is accomplished in part by giving most teachers in each little school the same preparation period, so they can meet with the instructional coordinator and counselor, have group meetings with parents, and do much cooperative planning.

The Williamsville Junior High School, Williamsville, New York, like the O'Farrell Junior High School in San Diego, is organized into little schools on a grade basis, with approximately 300 pupils in each little school. In the Williamsville school, as in San Diego, the instructional program is strengthened because teachers of different subjects can plan their work together, thereby correlating learning activities more effectively in the various subject fields. It is also possible for teachers to study pupils with unique problems through group discussions with the counselors, administrators, and parents.

The Stanforth Junior High School, Sewanhaka Central High School District No. 2, Nassau County, New York, is divided into three little schools with pupils from grades 7, 8, and 9 in each. The administration and faculty at the Stanforth Junior High School believe that the younger pupils profit from contact with the older ones. Although the building was not designed for the little-school plan, this type of organization has been introduced effectively in this school. Each little school has its own assemblies, student council, newspaper, clubs, and intramural athletic teams. There is much emphasis at the Stanforth Junior High School on better understanding of pupils as a basis for guidance, on close working relationships between the administrator, the counselor, and the teachers, and on frequent contacts with parents.

The little-school plan has been used sufficiently long in some communities so that educators and parents have had an opportunity to evaluate its effectiveness. They report a number of advantages. In some schools there was a sharp decline in the number of serious discipline problems in the first year or two after the introduction of the little-school plan. Others report that parents come more frequently to school for conferences with counselors and teachers; that more pupils participate in extraclass activities; and that teachers, counselors, and administrators work more closely with each other. With the little-school plan, it is possible to provide the broad educational offerings of the large school, and yet retain the personal interest in individual pupils which is characteristic of the small school.

MULTIPLE CLASSES IN SMALL SCHOOLS. In most states, there has been a decided trend toward the consolidation of small secondary schools into schools sufficiently large to offer a broad educational program. Under consolidation, two or more school districts combine for the purpose of establishing one central school with better facilities, larger enrollments, and a more adequate program. In different states, these schools are called by such names as regional, union, central, or consolidated schools.

Office of Education statistics on school enrollments for the United States reveal that there has been a decided trend toward larger secondary schools for the past twenty years. In 1939, more than two-thirds of the secondary schools in the United States had less than 200 pupils, while in 1959 less than 40 per cent had enrollments under 200. The percentage of schools with enrollments from 200 to 2,500 pupils increased sharply during this period, but the number of very large schools, those with more than 2,500 pupils, actually showed a slight decline. This increased enrollment in secondary schools makes it possible for more schools to offer a richer program for pupils of all interests and abilities.

Although the size of secondary schools has been increasing, the problem of the small school will be with us for many years, especially in rural communities where the population is so sparse that consolidation is difficult. Some attention, therefore, needs to be given to ways of expanding the curriculum in small schools. Progress is being made with this problem in a few communities. In Oswego County, New York, experiments are being made to expand the limited curriculum of small schools by offering courses in multiple classes, with one teacher directing the learning activities of two or more groups of pupils in one room during the same period. Called the Catskill Area Project in Small School Design, the twenty-five schools participating in the project during 1960–61 included kindergarten through grade 12, and all except one were small consolidated schools. The median enrollment of the twenty-five schools for that year was 220, with 496 pupils in the largest school and eighty in the smallest.

The schools participating in the Catskill Area Project have multiple classes in several different subjects. A recent class in mathematics, for instance, had six pupils in one group studying algebra, while ten other pupils were studying arithmetic. In a French class, nine pupils were studying French I, and five were studying French II. A class in business education had a group of six pupils in typewriting, four pupils using dictating machines, and two others studying shorthand. Other subjects in which these schools have had multiple classes include industrial arts, home economics, art, social studies, and several foreign languages. The Catskill Area Project in multiple classes is not intended to serve as an argument against the consolidation of small schools. It does show, however, that small secondary schools can offer a more diversified curriculum in certain subjects with multiple classes.[1]

COOPERATIVE PLANNING PERIODS FOR TEACHERS. Some schools meet the problem of the disadvantages caused by departmentalization by providing time when teachers of the various subjects can get together for cooperative planning of learning activities. At the Weeks Junior High School, Newton, Massachusetts, a period in the morning before pupils arrive at school is set aside for teachers of different subjects to meet for cooperative planning. Teachers do not meet every day, but they are able to do so as often as needed. At the O'Farrell Junior High School, San Diego, California, the teachers in each little school have the same preparation period during the day

[1] The Catskill Area Project in Small School Design, *Multiple Classes: Learning in Small Groups,* Oneonta, New York: The Catskill Area Project in Small School Design, 1961, 33 pp.

to make cooperative planning possible. In some schools, teachers meet for planning purposes during a long noon hour or after school.

In the departmentalized secondary school, many recognize the value of a definite time when teachers can meet for cooperative planning of learning activities. For instance, the teacher of English assists pupils with oral and written activities for their social studies and science classes. The work in art and music is planned so that it will contribute to related learning activities in English and social studies. Teachers of science, home economics, and physical education plan learning activities together in the area of health and hygiene. Through cooperative planning of learning activities there is some assurance of correlation between the various subjects in the departmentalized secondary school.

FLEXIBLE DAILY SCHEDULES. Earlier in this chapter, it was suggested that the daily schedule of classes in most secondary schools is not as flexible as desired for the variety of learning activities that are carried on. A few secondary schools have made the daily schedule sufficiently flexible so that class periods may vary for different subjects, extraclass activities may be offered during the school day, and a large number of subjects may be taken at one time by individual pupils.

A rotating schedule is used in some secondary schools to make the schedule more flexible. At the Norwich Free Academy, Norwich, Connecticut, which has a rotating schedule, a class which meets the first period on Monday, comes the second period on Tuesday, the third period on Wednesday, and so on through the week. The rotating schedule at Norwich makes it easier to have some classes meet once or twice a week, while others may have four or five periods a week. Furthermore, the weekly schedule at Norwich includes several periods for assemblies, homeroom guidance, and other activities. Although the Norwich schedule has only six class periods each day, pupils may carry in addition to assemblies, guidance, and other activities as many as six subjects with the flexibility the rotating schedule provides.

In several junior high schools in St. Paul, Minnesota, a six-period rotating schedule permits pupils to carry seven subjects, each one meeting four times a week. The St. Paul plan also has two periods during the week for extraclass activities and homeroom guidance. Besides the flexibility in arranging classes, another advantage of the rotating schedule is that pupils do not have the same subject every day during the lunch period and late in the day when their interest and attention might be at a low ebb. This is a feature of the rotating schedule which appeals to teachers, as well as pupils.

Another plan for making the daily schedule more flexible is to develop it around a short basic period. At the Joliet Township High School, Joliet, Illinois, which has used such a plan since the early 1920's, the daily schedule has sixteen periods, each twenty-two minutes long, plus a fourteen-minute homeroom period. The time assigned to each subject during the day consists of multiples of the twenty-two-minute periods. For instance, English may have two such periods, chemistry three periods, and certain shop subjects four or more periods.

The Meadowbrook Junior High School, Newton, Massachusetts, has a similar plan with a daily schedule of twelve thirty-minute intervals, as the basic period is called. The class time for the various subjects consists of one or more intervals, depending upon the needs of the subject. Sixteen thirty-minute intervals per week are devoted to English, social studies, and guidance, all taught by the same teacher. Eight intervals are assigned to mathematics and science. In the seventh and eighth grades, four intervals each week are scheduled for conversational French; there are two intervals weekly for typing in the eighth grade; and similar multiples of the thirty-minute interval are assigned to other subjects.

At the Northeast Junior High School, Bethlehem, Pennsylvania, a plan similar to the one at Meadowbrook is used to provide flexibility in the schedule, with twelve thirty-minute "modules," as they are called there. As in Joliet and Newton, the daily schedule in Bethlehem consists of different multiples of the thirty-minute modules for the various subjects. In daily schedules based on multiples of a short period, as in Joliet, Newton, and Bethlehem, the amount of class time can be varied to meet the needs of different subjects.

Flexibility of scheduling makes it possible to have large group and small group classes and independent study, as in the programs of Evanston Township High School, Illinois; Ridgewood High School, Illinois; Jefferson County, Colorado; Newton High School, Massachusetts; and other secondary schools. In the Covina Valley Unified School District, California, a new high school was built around the idea of such flexible scheduling. (See New Approaches to Staff Utilization, Chapter 8, p. 189.)

EXTENSION OF THE SCHOOL DAY FOR FLEXIBILITY. For many years, secondary schools have had a fixed opening and closing time for the school day. Outside these hours, little use has been made of the facilities of the school, except for certain extraclass activities. Some secondary schools are now extending the use of school facilities to pupils beyond the regular school day. The Edwin O. Smith School, Storrs, Connecticut, where the regular day closes at 2:15 P.M., has an extended period of seventy-five minutes after 2:15 P.M. when pupils may take certain elective subjects, participate in extraclass activities, and work with teachers for special help. For instance, pupils who are not able to take some subjects during the regular schedule can do so during the extended period. Pupils who do not have a reason for remaining during the extended period may leave. Since most pupils arrive at school by bus, it is necessary to have two bus trips, one at the close of the required day and the second after the extended period.

Some secondary schools introduce flexibility into the schedule by conducting certain activities after school, in the evening, or on Saturday mornings. At Melbourne High School, Melbourne, Florida, assemblies, the student council, and clubs meet in the evenings, the school library is open several nights a week, and many pupils do individual work in the science laboratories in the afternoon and evening. (See Chapter 12 for discussion of extraclass activities in the evening at Melbourne High School, Melbourne, Florida.) In several senior high schools in Montgomery County, Maryland, the school library is open for pupils in the evening and Saturday mornings. The Ann Arbor High School, Ann Arbor, Michigan, has had a Saturday morning program in science and mathematics for selected pupils interested in independent study. In Baltimore, Maryland, science laboratories in some schools are available after school and Saturday mornings for pupils with high interest in science to work on special projects.

An interesting and well-organized after-school program is the one in science at the Galileo High School, San Francisco, California, offered as "Planned After-School Laboratory Sessions," conveniently abbreviated to the "PALS Program." Pupils participating in this program, which is voluntary and non-credit, come from schools throughout the city for a two-hour session one afternoon a week. They may elect classes in marine biology, chemistry, mathematics skills, geology, astronomy, and other similar subjects. Although the after-school program in San Francisco was initiated by a grant from the Miranda Lux Foundation, its immediate success has led to its continuation with financial support from the local school district. Programs such as these which make the library, science laboratories, and other facilities available to pupils after school, in the evening, and Saturdays introduce flexibility into the organized program of the school so that richer and more varied learning activities can be offered.

PROVISION OF INDIVIDUAL HELP FOR PUPILS. One of the difficult problems in the secondary school is to provide time when pupils may see teachers for individual help. Such help is important for pupils who are having difficulty in a subject and for those who have missed work because of absence. The most common practice is to have an extended period at the end of the day, as at the Edwin O. Smith School, Storrs, Connecticut, when teachers are available to provide special help for pupils. But there are also other practices to provide time for teachers to work with individual pupils.

At the Manatee High School, Bradenton, Florida, certain days in the school year are designated as study days when pupils do not have their classes but may go to teachers for individual help. A day or two preceding study day, pupils plan a schedule for each period of the day. Those pupils who are doing poor work in a subject are required to spend at least one period on study day with the teacher of that subject. If pupils do not need the help of a teacher on study day, they may work in the library or engage in other activities that require more freedom than is possible on a regular school day. Study day is scheduled about once every two weeks throughout the year. The flexibility which the study day introduces into the regular school schedule permits pupils to see teachers for special help, to take field trips, and to have activities that are difficult to arrange on regular school days.

SECONDARY SCHOOL SUMMER PROGRAMS. It is becoming increasingly difficult for secondary school pupils to include in their program of studies all the subects and activities in which they are interested. This is true for the gifted as well as the slow-learning pupils. Many schools throughout the United States therefore are offering summer school programs. According to the National Education Association, more than 40 per cent of the urban school districts over 2,500 in population in 1959 had summer programs at the secondary school level. The purposes given most often for summer school programs are to provide remedial work for pupils with deficiencies in certain subjects, make-up work for pupils who failed subjects, courses that enable pupils to graduate earlier, enrichment of the pupil's program, advanced work for gifted pupils, and such courses as driver education which cannot always be taken during the school year.

Summer sessions differ so much from one community to another that it is difficult to characterize them. In some communities, comprehensive programs are offered for periods extending from six to eight weeks, tuition-free, with full credit given toward graduation requirements. In other communities, summer sessions are primarily for pupils who desire to make up failures or do remedial work. In still other communities, emphasis in the summer session is on enrichment activities which pupils have difficulty including in their regular school programs. The trend is away from make-up work and toward enrichment.

The secondary schools of Oakland, California, have a comprehensive summer program which carries full credit toward graduation. The junior high school session is six weeks long, while that of the senior high school is eight weeks, with a four-and-one-half hour day in both schools. Courses are offered in most of the subjects, with attention to remedial work, make-up work, and enrichment. There is no tuition fee.

Glastonbury, Connecticut, has a four-weeks summer session for junior and senior high school pupils which emphasizes enrichment and remedial work. There is no tuition fee for the summer session and credit is not given. In addition to regular course offerings in English, mathematics, and science, the Glastonbury program provides opportunities in driver education, little theater, music, and woodworking. Many secondary schools in Florida emphasize enrichment during the summer session, with emphasis on sports, music, arts and crafts, industrial arts, and homemaking. The regular school subjects are also offered in many of the Florida summer sessions.

In some communities, advantage is taken of the summer session to provide special opportunities for superior pupils. In Baltimore, Maryland, a program in grades seven through twelve for pupils with talent and interest in science has been offered during a six-weeks summer session, with pupils in attendance only during the morning. Emphasis is on laboratory activities, seminars, and field trips. Leaders from industry and nearby colleges assist in the program. In the Los Angeles, California, secondary schools special summer programs are offered for superior pupils in English, science, mathematics, and social studies. Pupils are admitted to the program on the basis of mental and achievement tests, high motivation, previous achievement, and the recommendations of administrators and teachers. There is also a theater-arts workshop for pupils with special talent in drama, art, dance, and music. As in Baltimore and Los Angeles, many secondary schools in other communities are using summer sessions to offer talented pupils special educational opportunities.

The program of summer offerings in many secondary schools of the United States is so new that it is difficult to predict what they may be like in the years ahead. It is certainly true that enrollments have been expanding rapidly, course offerings have been increasing, more emphasis is being given to enrichment, and many schools are providing special opportunities in the summer for gifted pupils. Besides enrichment opportunities, courses in remedial and developmental reading, typing, and driver education are especially in demand during the summer.

EXTENSION OF THE SCHOOL YEAR FOR TEACHERS. The term for secondary school teachers in most communities has been similar to that for pupils. Many educators believe that this practice is not satisfactory. They feel that teachers should have time to work together in planning the school program when pupils are not present. Many school systems in the United States today have teachers return a week or two before school opens for pre-school planning, and remain after school closes to prepare records and reports and to leave school equipment, books, and other materials well organized. In the state of Florida, it is the practice to have teachers in attendance a minimum of 196 days, while the school year for pupils is only 180 days. Some Florida school districts also have teachers new to the system come several days before the returning teachers. In the Austin, Texas, public schools, the school year for teachers is 190 days, while for pupils it is 180 days. In Cherry Creek School District, Arapahoe County, Colorado, teachers are in attendance 192 days, which is twelve days more than for pupils. Descriptions of pre-school activities designed to help the new teacher are contained in Chapter 14.

The calendar for some school districts gives an indication of how teachers use this extended time. In Brevard County, Florida, teachers have nine days for pre-school planning, nine days for post-school planning, three days for teacher-parent conferences, and one work day between semesters. Teachers new to Brevard County report two days earlier than returning teachers. In Hillsborough County, Florida, teachers have eleven days for pre-school planning, two days for conferences during the year, and four days for post-school planning. Similar uses are made of the extended school year for in-service education of teachers in other school systems.

PROFESSIONAL SUMMER ACTIVITIES. Some school systems have summer courses or workshops for teachers, while others have teachers work on curriculum projects during the summer, receiving extra pay or credit on the salary schedule. In Montgomery County, Maryland, there is a well-planned program of summer activities for teachers, including workshops on special problems, content courses in subjects with new developments, curriculum research and development projects, and administrative and supervisory workshops. Most of the courses and workshops for teachers are four weeks long, but curriculum research and development projects may continue all summer. Teachers who are selected to participate in some of these activities may be employed on an eleven- or twelve-month basis, while for some activities there is extra compensation on a weekly basis. Teachers are selected for summer activities on the basis of special talent and achievement in their profession. Teachers may elect to take certain courses and workshops without compensation, but instead may receive credit toward renewal of certification. (See Chapter 14 for further descriptions of in-service activities.)

In Rochester, Minnesota, teachers who have given evidence of professional maturity and competence may choose an eleven-months contract with additional compensation. Teachers are eligible for the longer contract after two years' experience in Rochester and upon the recommendation of their administrators. Teachers on the eleven-months basis may teach in the elementary or secondary summer school, participate in workshops on professional problems, or prepare curriculum materials. With the approval of the board of education some teachers on the eleven-months basis may attend a university summer session or travel. All Rochester teachers are required to earn four semester credits at a college or university every five years. Many other school systems have teachers work on professional projects during the summer, usually for additional compensation, although only a few systems have professional development programs as extensive as those in Montgomery County and Rochester. The program of secondary education today is so complex that it requires much study and planning by administrators, supervisors and teachers. The extended year for teachers and professional summer activities are ways of providing adequate planning time. Schools with time for teachers to plan instructional activities, prepare curriculum materials, and improve themselves professionally should have more effective programs of secondary education.

PROVISION OF INSTRUCTIONAL MATERIALS CENTERS. Teachers need to have a variety of instructional materials for the kinds of learning activities that are being developed in secondary schools. Some of the instructional materials may be in the school library, but others must be sought elsewhere. Teachers need to have readily available the textbooks and other reference materials in their subjects, the basic textbook materials used at all other grade levels in the school system, courses of study and curriculum guides in the different subjects from other school systems, audio-visual materials of various kinds, bulletins and pamphlets in the various subjects, and professional books and materials for teachers. Every school should also have a center where teachers may, with professional help, prepare instructional materials, such as graphs and charts, mounted materials, transparencies, tapes, slides, films, and filmstrips.

Some school systems are developing instructional materials centers for teachers usually on a system-wide basis. The Portland, Oregon, public schools have a department of instructional materials which includes textbook, library, audio-visual, and radio-television divisions. It furnishes all the materials used in the elementary schools and all materials except textbooks for the secondary schools. There is a professional library for teachers and a curriculum laboratory which has samples of textbooks and many courses of study, curriculum guides, and other curriculum materials from other school systems. The department also prepares instructional materials, such as radio and television programs, a series of booklets on Portland and the Northwest, filmstrips, recordings, and other audio-visual materials. Teachers are encouraged to come to the center to locate and prepare instructional materials and frequent meetings of teacher groups are held there.

The Sewanhaka Central High School District No. 2 in New York has an instructional materials center which has charge of audio-visual equipment and materials, prepares transparencies for use with overhead projectors, has a professional library for teachers, provides samples of many textbooks and reference materials, prepares tape recordings, and orders and distributes on a loan basis such materials as films, filmstrips, recordings, art prints, slides, and many types of display materials.

ISSUES AND PROBLEMS

A number of issues and problems in the administrative organization of the secondary school have a direct bearing on the effectiveness of the instructional program. These problems are of concern to teachers as well as administrators.

1. *How should we modify or expand the administrative organization of the secondary school so that pupils may take a more enriched program?*

At present pupils are under serious pressure to take heavier loads of academic subjects, especially those who are planning to go to college. With increasing competition for college admission, it is desirable for pupils to take more work in the foreign languages, mathematics, and science. At the same time, they should continue to take other subjects of cultural interest and practical value, such as music, art, typing, industrial arts, and homemaking. These subjects help all pupils acquire a broader educational background, both pupils who are going to college and those who plan to take immediate employment upon leaving secondary school.

In many schools pupils take five regular subjects a year, instead of the four that were customary in the past. Even though five subjects may not be required of all pupils, the college-bound pupils may be encouraged to carry such a load. A longer school day, a longer year, and summer schools are other ways to provide more time for the programs for secondary-school youth.

The number of years in the total program of elementary and secondary education can be extended beyond the twelfth grade, as is being done in school systems with a community college. Whatever is done, the amount of work which pupils take in the secondary school cannot be expanded indefinitely without increasing the time which pupils have to devote to that program.

2. *Should the summer session program for secondary school pupils be free, or should parents pay part or all of the cost of summer school instruction?*

Although most educators and parents seem to agree that an optional summer session is desirable for secondary school pupils, there is a lack of agreement concerning the means of paying for it. Summer schools in some communities are tuition free, in others pupils share the cost with the community, and in still others summer schools are supported entirely by tuition fees. If summer sessions are to be a significant part of the program of secondary education, one cannot justify charging pupils for that instruction. In fact, with the school buildings, equipment, facilities, and instructional materials already available, the summer session is the least expensive part of the secondary school program. We need to review the policies with respect to financing summer schools and find ways of supporting them as an integral part of the total program of education.

3. *How much time should teachers, supervisors, and administrators devote to planning the instructional program outside the regular school year?*

A task as complicated as that of teaching in a secondary school demands much careful preparation and planning. Teachers need to have time, therefore, to plan together the total program of the secondary school and to prepare specifically for their individual responsibilities in that program. In several states there is a clear trend toward having planning time for teachers when pupils are not in school. This time may come before school opens in the fall, on certain days during the year, and at the close of school in the spring. It seems essential that such time be available for teachers if there is to be adequate planning in the instructional program.

Planning time for teachers, however, raises some questions. For instance, how much time is it reasonable to expect that teachers will give to planning activities? Should teachers receive extra compensation for such planning activities, or should they be included as a part of their total contract? Most school systems that have a planning period for teachers consider this to be a normal part of a teacher's work, but a few provide additional compensation for it. The most desirable plan would seem to be to have all the professional responsibilities of teachers covered by the salary provisions of the regular teachers' contract.

SELECTED REFERENCES

ASSOCIATION FOR SUPERVISION AND CURRICULUM DEVELOPMENT. *Balance in the Curriculum* (1961 Yearbook). Washington, D.C.: National Education Association, Chap. 7.—Discusses new approaches in organizing the school, such as grouping, the little school plan, block scheduling, etc.

ASSOCIATION FOR SUPERVISION AND CURRICULUM DEVELOPMENT. *Extending the School Year*. Washington, D.C.: National Education Association, 1961, 60 pp.—Presents current developments in summer programs in public school systems for both students and teachers, with numerous examples.

CHASE, FRANCIS S., and ANDERSON, HAROLD A. (eds.). *The High School in a New Era*. Chicago: The University of Chicago Press, 1958, pp. 225-248.—A discussion of ways of organizing large high schools to make them more personal and suggestions for the buildings for such schools.

CONANT, JAMES B. *The American High School Today*. New York: McGraw-Hill Book Co., Inc., 1959, pp. 11-96.—Discusses the comprehensive high school, size of the high school, and makes recommendations for organization.

CONANT, JAMES B. *Education in the Junior High School Years*. Princeton, N.J.: The Educational Testing Service, 1960, 46 pp.—Presents fourteen recommendations for improving the junior high school, including certain administrative practices.

FITTS, DANIEL B. "The House Plan as a New Concept in Secondary School Organization." *Bulletin of the National Association of Secondary-School Principals*, 42:155-63, March, 1958.—Describes the "schools within a school" plan of organization of the Andrew Warde High School, Fairfield, Connecticut, and gives the advantages of this plan.

FORD, EDMUND A. "Organizational Pattern of the Nation's Public Secondary Schools." *School Life*, 42:10-12, May, 1960.—Gives data on percentages of secondary schools organized as four-year high schools, junior high schools, junior-senior high schools, and according to other patterns, and by numbers of pupils enrolled in the different types.

FRENCH, WILL, HULL, J. DAN, and DODDS, B. L. *American High School Administration: Policy and Practice*. New York: Holt, Rinehart & Winston, Inc., 1957, Chaps. 12 and 13.—A discussion of the conventional daily schedule of classes, the modified school day, and the extended year.

GRUHN, WILLIAM T., and DOUGLASS, HARL R. *The Modern Junior High School*. New York: The Ronald Press Co., 1956, pp. 340-52.—A discussion of certain aspects of the administrative organization of junior high schools.

GRUHN, WILLIAM T., TOMPKINS, ELLSWORTH, TRUMP, J. LLOYD, and ROE, VIRGINIA. "The Junior High School Grades in the Six-Year School." *Bulletin of the National Association of Secondary-School Principals*, 44:46-78, November, 1960.—Reports the findings of a survey of the administrative organization of six-year high schools in the United States with particular reference to the junior-high-school grades.

McDOWELL, ARCHIE. "The Santa Cruz Schedule," *Bulletin of the National Association of Secondary-School Principals*, 42:72-76, March, 1958.—Describes the rotating period class schedule used in the Santa Cruz, New Mexico, High School.

NATIONAL EDUCATION ASSOCIATION, AMERICAN ASSOCIATION OF SCHOOL ADMINISTRATORS AND RESEARCH DIVISION. *Length of School Day and Class Periods in Urban School Districts, 1958-59*. Educational Research Service Circular No. 7, Washington, D.C.: the Association, 1960, 62 pp.—Gives data on length of school day and class periods in elementary, junior high, and senior high schools, for 271 cities arranged by population.

NATIONAL EDUCATION ASSOCIATION, AMERICAN ASSOCIATION OF SCHOOL ADMINISTRATORS, AND RESEARCH DIVISION. *Summer School Programs in Urban School Districts*. Educational Research Service Circular No. 7, Washington, D.C.: the Association, 1959, 41 pp.—Gives information about summer school programs for elementary and secondary schools in 302 school systems, including information on length of program, types of courses offered, and practices concerning tuition fees.

NATIONAL EDUCATION ASSOCIATION and NATIONAL ASSOCIATION OF SECONDARY-SCHOOL PRINCIPALS. *Administration: Procedures and School Practices for the Academically Talented Student*. Washington, D.C.: the Association, 1960, 223 pp.—Presents numerous examples of administrative practices for meeting the needs of academically talented pupils.

TRUMP, J. LLOYD, AND BAYNHAM, DORSEY. *Focus on Change: Guide to Better Schools*. Chicago: Rand McNally & Co., 1961, 147 pp.—Presents new ways of organizing the staff for teaching in secondary schools.

16

THE GUIDANCE PROGRAM

The guidance program in the secondary school has never been more important than it is today. There are a number of reasons for this. First, the world in which we live has become increasingly complex, making it more difficult for youth to make intelligent decisions and satisfactory adjustments. Second, the secondary school has been retaining a much larger percentage of youth than was true early in the present century, many of them with little academic ability and interest. Third, the program of the secondary school itself has become increasingly complex. When there was only one curriculum for all pupils in the secondary school, there was no problem of educational guidance in so far as the planning of pupil programs was concerned. In many schools today pupils may choose from a broad offering of curricula and courses, as well as numerous extraclass activities. Fourth, we have learned much in recent years about the psychology of the adolescent, the nature of the learning process, and the mental and emotional development of children. This information has not only emphasized the need for more guidance activities; it has also given us a background for more effective guidance. Fifth, the emphasis in the secondary school in recent years has been on working with children as individuals and helping them select educational goals and plan their programs in terms of their individual interests and abilities.

In the past decade, the pressures for higher academic achievement and for admission to prestige colleges and universities have further intensified the importance of guidance services. The acceptance by individual pupils and their parents of reasonable educational goals, the selection of pupils for honor classes, the choice of colleges appropriate for the ability levels of individual pupils—these are some of the problems that today demand the help of competent and understanding counselors. There are also many problems with which pupils need help that are not necessarily school-centered—problems of boy-girl relationships, emotional problems arising from difficult home situations, and conduct problems of pupils in the community.

Growth in guidance problems such as these has brought an expansion in the guidance services in many schools. The facilities for guidance, the administration of tests, the keeping of more complete school records for individual pupils, the preparation of pupil records for college admission, the placement and follow-up of pupils on jobs, and individual counseling of pupils and parents—all these have been greatly expanded in recent years. It is the provision for activities such as these in the secondary school which is designated as the guidance program.

BASIC PRINCIPLES

The guidance program should be sufficiently broad and comprehensive in the backgrounds, interests, and talents of its staff and in the counseling activities and services which it provides to help all pupils with their many different problems, choices, and decisions.

The need for guidance exists because pupils differ greatly from each other in their backgrounds, their educational goals, their vocational aspirations, and their temperaments. They have problems that differ greatly, both in the nature of the problems and in the solutions that may be most appropriate. As the pupil population in a secondary school becomes more diverse, the problems increase in diversity.

The increasing heterogeneity of the secondary school population and the greater diversity of the problems which the pupils present demand a broad and comprehensive guidance program. There needs to be a guidance staff with many interests and talents. The counselors must comprehend the problems of youth from wealthy homes and those from the "wrong side of the tracks." They must help youth who are pointing toward the prestige colleges, those who are seeking the best college, those of lesser college ability, and those who are looking toward vocational school, apprenticeship, or immediate employment. They must give encouragement to youth of low academic ability, security to youth with emotional problems, and understanding to youth who are socially maladjusted.

The guidance program should be well coordinated and integrated with all other aspects of the educational program of the school.

The guidance department should not be set apart from the rest of the school. Where that situation pertains, guidance activities fail to achieve their maximum effectiveness. Instead, the program should extend into every classroom and every pupil activity.

The guidance staff likewise should be a well-integrated part of the school's professional staff. They should know the problems of teachers as they work with pupils, and they should work closely with teachers in helping individual pupils with their problems. In some schools, counselors are expected to teach part time in order to bring about better coordination between guidance and class activities. Whatever approach may be used, the effectiveness of the guidance program can be measured in large part by its coordination with all other aspects of the school's program. All guidance and pupil service personnel should work as a team in order to achieve a coordinated program of pupil personnel services for a school system, including psychologists, psychiatrists, doctors, nurses, visiting teachers, speech therapists, guidance supervisors and directors, placement officers, pupil attendance officers, and other specialized personnel.

The guidance program should draw on all the resources of the school and of the community which may contribute in some way to the guidance services.

Both in the school and the community there are unlimited resources which may contribute materially to the effectiveness of the guidance program. It is in part through the use of these resources that the guidance program becomes a well-integrated part of the total educational program of the secondary school. In the school, the human resources include the physician, the nurse, the psychologist, the librarian, the principal, the superintendent, the coaches, the secretaries, and all the teachers. The background and interest of each staff member should be examined for the particular contribution that he can make to the guidance services. The contribution of some staff members to guidance may be a formal one, while others may participate only in an informal way. The director of guidance should be sure that the talents of every staff member are identified and that, when it is appropriate, they are used in the guidance program.

In the community, there are also many resources that may contribute to the guidance program. In guidance on vocational problems, persons engaged in almost every profession and occupation may be of service; in guidance concerning post-secondary education, local graduates of various colleges, universities, business colleges, trade schools, and other post-secondary schools are valuable resource people; and in guidance concerning mental and emotional adjustment, many professional people in the community may be helpful.

The material resources in the school which may prove helpful in guidance include books in the school library, films, film strips, and recordings. Such agencies as the public library, Chamber of Commerce, government agencies, business firms, factories, transportation companies, labor unions, and service clubs can provide a wealth of information that may be used in guidance. These resources should be located through a careful community survey, studied for their contribution to the guidance program, classified and catalogued, and utilized whenever they are appropriate.

The guidance program should utilize all avenues and channels for guidance, both in the school and in the community.

Every subject and activity in the program of the school may serve as an avenue for guidance. In the curriculum, such subjects as English, social studies, business, industrial arts, homemaking, and the vocational subjects are particularly appropriate for exploratory activities and for the dissemination of information that is basic to effective guidance on educational, vocational, and personal problems. Among the extraclass activities, clubs, the school newspaper and handbook, and assemblies offer opportunities for giving pupils information that may be important in guidance. The homeroom is another avenue which is appropriate for group and some individual guidance activities.

In the community, the local newspaper may bring pupils information on guidance problems, including information about college admissions problems, employment opportunities, and post-secondary schools below the college level. Local newspapers can be of value especially in presenting guidance information of importance to parents as well as pupils. Various business and industrial firms, as well as certain community agencies enable pupils to gain work experience before making educational and vocational plans and decisions. The effective guidance program utilizes to advantage all these school and community resources and agencies to give pupils the best guidance services.

Adequate and up-to-date information and records for individual pupils are essential for a comprehensive guidance program.

Adequate information about pupils should be conveniently available to anyone who participates in guidance and counseling. This information should include the pupil's home and family background, out-of-school activities and interests, vacation and part-time work experience, intelligence test scores, educational, vocational, and avocational interests, previous achievement in school, participation in school activities, social and emotional development, physical characteristics, health problems, and any unusual problems, successes, and failures of the pupil. A system of records should be established which permits the accumulation in a systematic manner of such information about each child in school.

The backgrounds of individual pupils are changing continually. The pupil's family may be broken through divorce, separation, death or serious illness; his interests in present school activities and in further education may shift greatly from month to month; the vocational areas that are attractive to him one year may be far from his thoughts the next; and the activities in which he takes part in school, the church, and the community may not long remain the same. In short, the information that the school has about individual pupils must be continually modified and expanded lest it become out of date.

Once the school has accumulated adequate information about individual pupils, counselors and teachers need to acquire skill in using it. This skill is not acquired as easily as one might think. Teachers and counselors need to know what intelligence scores mean; how interest inventories may be used in guidance; what bearing certain health information may have on the child's success in school; and what approach concerning education beyond secondary school is appropriate for pupils of various home and out-of-school backgrounds.

Provision for guidance activities should encompass all areas of problems concerning which adolescents need to make decisions and adjustments.

In the discussions on guidance early in the present century, so much emphasis was placed on vocational guidance that, in the thinking of many educators at that time, this was the sole purpose of the guidance program. Today, it is generally recognized that helping pupils with vocational plans and decisions is only one aspect of a comprehensive guidance program. In addition to vocational guidance, there should be guidance concerning the educational plans and decisions of pupils, social, emotional, and personality development, and their growth in health, personality, and character qualities. The guidance program in the secondary school today is concerned with any decision, problem, or adjustment which must be made by secondary school youth.

Adequate information should be available to pupils concerning vocational and educational opportunities beyond the secondary school.

In the counselor's office, the library, or elsewhere in the school, there should be a file of catalogs, bulletins, and other materials from universities, colleges, community and junior colleges, business schools, trade schools, and other post-secondary schools that might be of interest to pupils. The school should also have an occupational file in which pamphlets and bulletins are accumulated for every conceivable occupation which might attract youth upon leaving the secondary school. These files should be easily accessible to pupils and members of the professional staff. The school should also have many fiction and non-fiction books on vocational activities, preferably on an open shelf where they may be readily available to pupils.

It is important that adequate time for group and individual guidance activities be provided in the program of the secondary school.

There should be time for guidance activities in the regular school schedule and at times outside school hours when pupils are available. A period daily or several times weekly may be set aside especially for guidance or time may be designated for that purpose during the year when guidance problems arise. For instance, when pupils are planning their programs for the next semester, teachers may discuss in all classes the relation of their respective subjects to the curricula, courses, and activities which will be available in the coming year. Specific time for helping pupils plan their total programs may be set aside in homerooms, core or block-time classes, or in English and social studies classes. These discussions may serve as a basis for counseling individual students concerning their educational plans and programs. Individual counseling should be carried on during the school day for pupils who leave on buses or have after-school activities or employment, but out-of-school time for counseling is appropriate for pupils who can be available. The important thing is to have adequate time definitely provided for both group and individual guidance activities.

An effective placement and follow-up service for pupils leaving school or graduating should be a part of a comprehensive guidance program in the secondary school.

The responsibility of a secondary school for its pupils does not end when they drop out of school or graduate. For pupils who do not continue their education, there should be assistance in finding employment and succeeding on the job. Furthermore, the school should help its graduates locate better positions as they gain experience and grow in vocational competence. The guidance staff of a secondary school should also follow-up on the success of its graduates at universities, colleges, and other post-secondary schools. The information gained from follow-up studies of pupils should be summarized and studied by counselors to improve the guidance program and by teachers to improve the instructional program. Both pupils who drop out and those who graduate should be included in the placement and follow-up services.

Specialists should be available to assist counselors and teachers with planning and carrying on guidance activities and with guidance problems that require special skills and backgrounds.

Expert advice and assistance are essential to the success of any guidance program. Whether full-time specialists are employed by the school system or are available only on request is not of particular importance. It is essential, however, that the administrators, the counselors, and the faculty of a school should be able to request the services of specialists as they are needed. The specialists most often needed are a physician, nurse, psychologist, psychiatrist, visiting teacher, speech therapist, and a specialist in measurement, evaluation, and statistics.

These specialists should understand the unique problems of secondary school youth, they should appreciate the purpose and nature of a secondary school program, they should know the demands on the physical and emotional health of youth by today's program of secondary education, and they should have a sincere interest in youth and in the guidance program of the secondary school. Certainly, not every physician, nurse, psychologist, psychiatrist, or other guidance specialist has these qualifications. These specialists should therefore have education and experience which qualify them particularly for guidance responsibilities in a secondary school.

There should be competent leadership for the guidance program of a secondary school.

Leadership is needed to develop the guidance program as a whole, to give it perspective, purpose, and direction, to develop and carry on guidance activities, to promote in-service education activities for counselors and teachers, and to evaluate the program continually as a basis for improvement. Since the principal is responsible for the total program of the schools, he must provide much of that leadership. He should be thoroughly sympathetic with the need for guidance in the secondary school and should be informed regarding the purpose and nature of the guidance program.

The principal cannot, however, be sufficiently competent in guidance to provide the specialized leadership which is needed. For that purpose, a secondary school should have a specialist in guidance with experience as a teacher and broad preparation in guidance and counseling. In a large secondary school, a staff member should devote full time to such leadership for the guidance program, while in a small school a part-time guidance director may be satisfactory. The selection of the guidance director should be given careful consideration, since the effectiveness of the guidance program will largely depend upon his leadership.

SOME COMMON PRACTICES

SHORTAGE OF GUIDANCE STAFF. Educators generally agree that a junior or senior high school should have at least one counselor for every 250 pupils, and in addition have other guidance specialists available. In 1959, however, 40 per cent of the secondary schools in the United States had an enrollment of less than 200 pupils. By the recommended standard, therefore, 40 per cent of the secondary schools were too small to justify even one full-time counselor.

In many small schools, either the principal provides the leadership in guidance or a teacher is assigned part time to this responsibility. This person does much of the guidance, including the placement of pupils in colleges, the vocational placement of graduates and pupils who drop out of school, the follow-up of graduates, and the counseling of pupils on a variety of educational, social, emotional, and personal problems. All teachers usually share in the counseling of pupils. In most small schools, the counseling staff is meager indeed for the wide variety of guidance problems that arise.

In many medium-sized and large secondary schools, there is also a shortage of guidance staff. In one junior high school in the East with an enrollment of 600 pupils, there is no person on the staff with specialized preparation for guidance, nor is anyone designated for this responsibility even on a part-time basis. In a junior high school of 1,500 pupils in a city in the Middle West, there is only one counselor for the entire school. Schools such as these are not rare. They can be found in all parts of the United States—in rural areas, suburban communities, and large cities. Although the counseling staff in many schools has been increased in recent years, there are still hundreds of secondary schools in the United States which have only a token guidance staff.

SPECIALIZED GUIDANCE SERVICES. There is no limit to the kinds of specialized help that is needed for the variety of guidance problems that may arise in a junior or senior high school. In addition to a director of guidance, schools most often have a nurse, physician, and dentist available. In many medium-sized and large schools, a nurse is in the school either part or full time, while a physician and a dentist are available for the health examination of pupils and on call. Many large city systems employ physicians and dentists full time, while in medium-sized and small systems they serve on a part-time basis. In small systems and in rural schools, health specialists are usually available only for periodic health examinations and for emergencies. In such schools they are of little help in the guidance program.

Secondary schools often lack the needed specialists in evaluation and measurement to identify gifted pupils, mentally retarded pupils, pupils with emotional and personality problems, and pupils with learning deficiencies in a basic subject. A few pupils also need the help of specialists in speech, hearing, and visual problems; others need guidance because of orthopedic and other physical handicaps; while a few should have the services of psychiatrists and psychologists. In the small schools, these are not likely to be provided. Although only a few pupils need such specialized help, those who need it may indeed need it desperately lest they be handicapped during their entire school careers, and even throughout life.

Some large cities do provide an adequate staff of guidance specialists, but many cities with enough pupils to justify these specialists do not have them. Usually it is lack of funds, not of professional foresight, which deprives children of such guidance help. In rural communities, it is difficult to provide the specialists needed for guidance, though in some areas several school districts cooperate to provide such services.

ORGANIZATION FOR GUIDANCE. Large schools usually have a definite organizational plan for their guidance program, although it varies greatly from school to school. A typical plan of organization in large schools is given in the diagram below.

Medium-sized schools often have some definite organization for the guidance program, with the line of responsibility usually proceeding from the principal to the director of guidance, and then to the homeroom teachers. Some medium-sized schools have a nurse either full time or part time, but other guidance specialists, if available at all, are on call. Small schools usually have an informal staff organization for guidance. For small schools this may be the best practice.

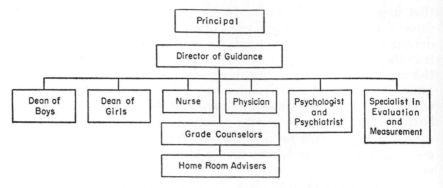

Typical Guidance Organization in Large High Schools

PROVISION FOR CUMULATIVE RECORDS. Most secondary schools have some type of cumulative records in which information for individual pupils is kept in convenient form. The cumulative records usually include information about the pupil's achievement in his classes, test scores, home and out-of-school backgrounds, health record, participation in school activities, and work experience. A few schools include information about the personality and character qualities of pupils, and some have anecdotal information. Most schools have the cumulative records in the principal's office, while others keep them in the guidance office. In some schools the homeroom teacher or other key teacher in the guidance program has a duplicate of the cumulative records for his pupils, while in a few schools all teachers have a summary of information on the cumulative records for their pupils.

Practices concerning cumulative records vary greatly from school to school. It is considered a desirable practice to have all essential information about pupils, elementary as well as secondary, on the cumulative records. Some schools, however, include information about the pupil only for their secondary school years. The nature of the record form is often a large folder 8½ by 11 inches in size. Other types of forms used in some schools are a large envelope with the printed form on the outside, and the inside for anecdotal information; a packet type, with separate cards for achievement marks, test scores, health information, and other kinds of information about pupils; a single card type, with the record forms printed on both sides; and a loose-leaf type which may be kept in loose-leaf record books.

MAINTENANCE OF CUMULATIVE RECORDS. It is exceedingly important that cumulative records be kept up to date if they are to be most useful in guidance. This is a continuous job, since information about individual pupils keeps changing. Information that needs to be recorded periodically includes scores on standardized tests, marks earned in various subjects, information from health examinations, and pupil participation in extraclass activities. There are also many changes which take place in the pupil's personal background that should be recorded, such as changes in his educational and vocational goals, illness, death or separation in the family, illness of the pupil, and work experience. These data may be lacking in some schools for one reason or another. In small schools, the principal, the counselor, and the teachers may be close enough to the pupils to be aware of these personal changes. In a large school they may easily be overlooked unless there is an organized plan to keep in touch with individual pupils and keep their cumulative records up to date.

In many schools the clerical staff for this purpose is inadequate and teachers must assume much of this responsibility. With many different teachers assisting with keeping cumulative records up to date, it is easy for errors to be made in these records. In schools where teachers share this responsibility, they should exercise promptness and accuracy in recording information on cumulative records.

ORIENTATION ACTIVITIES. An important aspect of the guidance program is the orientation which is provided for pupils who are just entering the secondary school. Orientation activities are provided in junior high schools for seventh-grade pupils and in senior high schools for those entering the tenth grade. These activities are usually more extensive in junior than in senior high schools. The purpose of these activities is to help pupils become oriented to the program, activities, and administrative practices of the school.

The more common orientation activities for pupils entering the junior high school include handbooks and mimeographed materials on the program and activities of the school which are given to entering pupils; talks by the principal, director of guidance, and teachers to sixth-grade pupils during their last semester in the elementary school; and visits by sixth-grade pupils to the junior high school. After pupils enter the junior high school, they usually discuss school traditions, the curriculum, extraclass activities, and school rules and regulations in their homerooms or classes. In some schools, eighth- and ninth-grade pupils help seventh-graders get acquainted. Most senior high schools have orientation activities for entering classes similar to those in junior high schools, although they are usually not as extensive.

Although most secondary schools have orientation activities for entering classes, the orientation of new pupils in the upper grades or of pupils who enter during the year may be neglected. These pupils have all the adjustment problems of pupils who come with an entering class, and in addition they may not have any friends in the school. A student handbook containing the traditions and administrative practices of the school usually is given such pupils and the counselor may give them some assistance. The homeroom and classroom teachers need to give such pupils particular attention to be sure that they make friends, become acquainted with the program of the school, and adjust to administrative practices which are new to them.

ASSISTANCE IN PLANNING PUPIL PROGRAMS. In most secondary schools, pupils are given some help in planning their programs of curricula and courses for the secondary school and in making plans for post-secondary education. Both junior and senior high schools have such activities, though in some schools they are quite limited. These activities include discussions of elective curricula and courses in the homerooms; handbooks and other materials explaining the program of the schools; group and individual conferences with parents; and individual counseling of pupils by their counselors and homeroom teachers. In most schools homeroom teachers take considerable responsibility for helping pupils plan their curricula and courses. The leadership for these activities is usually provided by the director of guidance, except in small schools where the principal assumes this responsibility.

One of the serious difficulties in helping pupils plan their educational programs in the secondary school is the lack of time for individual conferences with pupils. Counseling on such matters cannot be hurried. In some schools, time for such counseling is set aside in homerooms or in classes. If the planning of the pupils' elective curricula and courses is begun early enough in the year, there should be sufficient time to give individual pupils the help they need.

LIMITED GUIDANCE ON HEALTH PROBLEMS. Guidance concerning health problems is important for pupils at all grade levels in the secondary school. In most schools there are periodic health examinations by a school physician and nurse. Following these examinations, reports are usually sent to parents, while health records for individual pupils are kept in the nurse's office.

The health guidance of pupils in many schools, however, is not adequate. The shortcomings lie most often in the following: (1) health examinations are too hurried and superficial, (2) there is insufficient follow-up with parents, (3) teachers are not fully informed about the health problems of individual pupils, and (4) there is insufficient counseling of pupils on matters of health. In some schools there is a shortage of staff for adequate health counseling; in others there is not sufficient communication between the school physician and nurse on the one hand and counselors and teachers on the other.

Health counseling in the secondary school is improved by developing a closer working relationship between the nurse, the counselors, and the teachers. Teachers in the better situations have information about the health of pupils which has a bearing on learning problems, and know how to help those pupils. The school nurse recognizes her responsibility for helping teachers understand their pupils and counsels pupils in matters of health.

EMOTIONAL PRESSURES INCREASING. The pressure for academic achievement in secondary schools is greater today than at any previous time in the history of American education. More parents than ever before are financially able to send their children to college, and particularly to the private colleges where enrollments are limited and admissions standards are high. The pressure for achievement in the secondary school is further intensified by the sharp increase in the number of children born during recent years who are now competing for admission to college.

There is also tremendous interest today in the education of the more able pupils in the secondary school. Many schools have honors classes for these pupils in one or more subjects. The ambition of some parents to have their children in the honors classes places further pressure for achievement on secondary school pupils. Then, too, the amount of homework is increasing; the requirements for graduation from the secondary school are being raised in some communities; and more pupils are competing for college scholarships.

The growing pressures on pupils in the secondary school have produced a sharp need for guidance in matters of emotional and mental health. In some schools, counselors keep in close touch with the activities of those pupils who are most likely to be affected by these pressures. In many schools, however, the counseling staff is inadequate for these new problems. In fact, in some secondary schools the principal, the counseling staff, and the faculty are not fully aware of the growing pressures on secondary school youth. Psychologists, psychiatrists, and other specialists in emotional and mental health problems are needed in the secondary schools today more urgently than ever before. Teachers should be aware of these pressures and be alert to pupils who may respond unfavorably to them.

IMPLEMENTATION OF THE PRINCIPLES

COMPREHENSIVE GUIDANCE PROGRAMS. Earlier in this chapter it was suggested that secondary schools should have comprehensive guidance programs closely integrated with all class and extraclass activities to help pupils with all kinds of educational, vocational, and personal programs. Such a comprehensive program of guidance and counseling services has been developed for the Indianapolis public high schools, Indianapolis, Indiana. The guidance and counseling services for the Indianapolis public high schools include: (1) cumulative records for each pupil which provide information about him from the first grade, (2) a comprehensive testing program, (3) group and individual counseling of pupils throughout their school careers, (4) guidance at major transitional periods in the pupil's school experience, such as between elementary and high school, high school and college, and high school and employment, (5) orientation of pupils new to the high school, (6) in-service guidance training for teachers, (7) coordination of school and community guidance agencies, (8) placement of present and former pupils in colleges and universities, in other post-secondary schools, and in gainful employment, and (9) follow-up studies of graduates who enter college, gainful employment, or homemaking A guidance program which provides for such comprehensive services should be effective indeed in helping pupils with their plans, decisions, and problems.

GUIDANCE THROUGH WORK EXPERIENCE PROGRAMS. In recent years, work experience education has been offered in many secondary schools as a part of the school program. Although it is considered a part of the curriculum like other course offerings, it is also closely related to the program of guidance and counseling. Work experience programs were described in Chapter 11. Pupils receive credit for work experience toward graduation like any other course for which they are enrolled.

In Los Angeles city schools there are two kinds of work experience education: (1) general work experience education, which helps pupils acquire desirable work habits, attitudes, and occupational information, and (2) vocational work experience education, which provides supervised employment related to the pupil's curriculum in school and his ultimate vocational goal. Work experience in Los Angeles is ordinarily limited to pupils who have reached the eleventh grade and are at least sixteen years of age.

Work experience programs in Los Angeles, as in other communities, are supervised by staff members of the secondary school. The supervisors and coordinators approve the places of employment, help the pupils adjust to their jobs, and assist employers in planning appropriate work experiences. These experiences are closely coordinated with the total guidance program of the school.

COORDINATED PUPIL PERSONNEL SERVICES. In every secondary school there are typical pupils who present unique instructional and guidance problems. These pupils include those with emotional problems, unusual home backgrounds, physical and mental handicaps, health problems, and hearing, vision, and speech defects. Some of these problems are so serious that the pupils may not be able to continue in the usual school situation. Others merely require specialized services. In many school systems, the services for these pupils are provided by members of the guidance staff.

The San Diego city schools, San Diego, California, have extensive special services for pupils with unusual problems. They have visiting-teacher service for pupils who are not making the best use of their school experience because of social and emotional problems. The visiting teacher works with children and parents on an individual basis. School psychologist services in San Diego provide for testing pupils for special programs for the gifted, mentally retarded, and physically handicapped. The psychologists also serve as consultants to teachers and other members of the guidance staff. The guidance department clinic conducts case studies of pupils with unusual problems who are referred to the clinic by counselors, administrators, or visiting teachers.

The guidance department of the San Diego city schools also provides special services for pupils with unusual instructional problems. It has a pupil study center for gifted pupils in which counseling is provided for those with high ability who have social, emotional, or academic problems. There are programs for handicapped children, including home-teacher service for home-bound or hospitalized children, speech correction programs, instruction in lip reading, and special classes for orthopedically handicapped, mentally retarded, partially sighted, and educable blind children. Guidance programs such as the one in San Diego offer a variety of services which help pupils with unusual problems to continue their education.

Pupil services include those aspects of the instructional program designed to provide ways of studying the needs of pupils and helping them meet those needs. Toward this end all pupil personnel services in some schools are organized into a comprehensive and coordinated program, including guidance services, attendance services, school health services, school psychological services, and school social work services. The Baltimore County Public Schools, Maryland, have such a comprehensive program. The director of pupil services, who is responsible to the assistant superintendent of instruction, has a professional staff which includes supervisors of guidance, school nursing services, clinical services, pupil personnel, visiting teachers, and testing specialists. The county is divided into four regions with visiting teachers and psychologists located in each region.

ADEQUATE GUIDANCE STAFF. The importance of having an adequate staff of counselors, guidance specialists, and teachers qualified for guidance was stressed earlier in the present chapter. In some of the large secondary schools such a staff is being provided. The Pasadena city schools, Pasadena, California, have an especially well-organized staff for guidance and counseling. In the central office of the Department of Guidance and Counseling in Pasadena, there is a coordinator of guidance and counseling who is responsible for the system-wide guidance program. The central office personnel also includes psychologists, who serve the junior and senior high schools, and an occupational information supervisor, who supervises the collection and dissemination of up-to-date occupational information.

In addition to the central office staff in Pasadena, professional staff members in the junior and senior high schools are assigned guidance responsibilities. In the junior high schools, an assistant principal has primary responsibility for the total guidance program, while teacher-counselors who teach part time have supervision of guidance activities at a particular grade level. One period of teacher-counselor time is provided for every hundred pupils. Group guidance in the junior high schools is offered in the two-hour English–social studies period, and is under the direction of the English–social studies teacher. A psychologist from the central guidance office is available to each junior high school one day a week.

In the senior high schools of Pasadena, an assistant principal is in charge of pupil personnel services for the school. A registrar has charge of the registration and attendance records. At each grade level there is at least one full-time counselor, who remains with a group of pupils during their three years in senior high school. Teacher-counselors supplement the work of the grade-level counselor, but they also do part-time teaching. A work-study counselor supervises pupils in the work experience programs. Group guidance is offered in each grade by teachers of English, social studies, or the senior basic course. A psychologist is available from the central guidance office to each senior high school for one-and-one-half days a week.

In Pasadena, the junior college is a part of the regular public school system and provides a broad educational program for students with various educational and vocational goals. The junior college also has a guidance staff, which includes a dean of student personnel, who is in charge of the counseling services, a dean of admissions, a registrar, one full-time counselor for every five hundred students, and a psychologist. Group guidance activities are provided in the basic communications course, which students take in the first junior college year.

A significant feature of the organization of the guidance staff in Pasadena is the fact that teachers have such an important part in the guidance program. Furthermore, in Pasadena the guidance staff is well organized, with definite responsibilities assigned to each.

COOPERATIVE GUIDANCE SERVICES. Schools in small urban and rural communities find it difficult to offer the variety of specialized services that are needed for an effective guidance program. In the state of New York several small school districts can cooperate to provide specialized guidance services through a Board of Cooperative Educational Services, conveniently referred to as BOCES. In northern Westchester County, New York, such a board has been established which has a guidance center for the participating schools. Nine school systems participate in the guidance center project.

The BOCES Guidance Center in northern Westchester County recognizes the school counselor as the key guidance person in the program. The responsibility of the guidance center is to assist and supplement the work of the school counselor. The center provides extensive testing services, trained psychologists, and other specialized counseling services for the participating schools. Pupils from the participating schools are brought to the guidance center on a schedule during the year for testing and counseling services. The BOCES Guidance Center in northern Westchester County is an excellent example of how small communities and rural school districts can provide highly competent guidance services on a cooperative basis at a reasonable cost. BOCES also offers psychiatric consultation services, social worker service, reading service, and other specialized services.

EMPLOYMENT PLACEMENT SERVICES. In a few secondary schools employment placement services are being provided on a well-organized basis. In these schools, a placement counselor is designated to keep in touch with employers, to list part-time jobs for pupils in school, and to assist graduates and pupils who are withdrawing from school to obtain full-time employment.

At the Shorewood High School, Shorewood, Wisconsin, a six-year secondary school, there are such placement services. The placement counselor helps pupils obtain after-school and vacation employment, assists pupils with part-time job experiences as a basis for vocational exploration, locates positions and lists them in the placement office, helps pupils obtain work permits, sets up work experience programs for pupils in local business and industrial establishments, helps pupils obtain interviews with prospective employers, and obtains follow-up information concerning the success of graduates. Other secondary schools, primarily with large enrollments in city systems, have placement services similar to those at the Shorewood High School.

COUNSELING ACTIVITIES FOR COLLEGE ADMISSIONS. American youth today are more interested in college and university education than ever before in our history. The large number of youth applying for admission to college has made it more difficult for them to enter the college which is their first choice. Some secondary schools are planning activities to help youth and their parents make more intelligent plans concerning college. For several years, the Board of Cooperative Educational Services in Westchester County, New York, has had a college conference for pupils in the high schools of the participating school districts. Representatives from colleges in the eastern part of the United States are invited to this conference which meets for an entire day in one of the high schools in the area. High school juniors and seniors attend the conference with their counselors. At the conference they have an opportunity to hear discussions concerning college admissions problems and to meet with several of the college representatives in small discussion groups. Pupils who attend this conference in both their junior and senior years receive considerable help from this contact with the admissions officers of colleges that are represented.

Some secondary schools have prepared handbooks and other printed or mimeographed materials to help pupils and parents make more intelligent choices of colleges and universities. The San Francisco public schools publish a handbook entitled, *Basic Steps for College Preps,* which gives suggestions for planning their high school programs, information about college admissions requirements, estimates of college expenses, and specific information about colleges and universities in the San Francisco area. This booklet is available to pupils in the senior high schools of San Francisco.

In some senior high schools, counselors are being sent to colleges at some distance from the school to locate desirable higher institutions which may have room for entering freshmen. This practice is employed especially by schools in areas where there are few colleges or where the places for freshmen are limited. Conferences to inform parents about college admissions problems, expenses, and programs are being held in many senior high schools. These are a few of the ways in which senior high schools are meeting the urgent need for counseling pupils and parents about college problems.

ISSUES AND PROBLEMS

The secondary school pupil faces many problems which differ in kind and intensity from those of a generation ago. The more complex society in which we live, the diversified program of the secondary school, the pressures attendant to college admission, the decisions related to a vocational career—these are all factors which present certain issues and problems for the guidance program in the secondary school. The following are several of the more urgent ones.

1. *How can comprehensive guidance services be provided in small secondary schools and for schools in rural communities?*

In a large city system it is not difficult to justify the variety of guidance specialists and services that are needed to help secondary school youth with the many problems and decisions they face today. But the majority of the secondary schools in the United States are far too small to justify the psychologists, psychiatrists, specialists in tests and measurements, and other specialists required by a comprehensive guidance program. In fact, many secondary schools in rural areas have enrollments so small that they find it difficult to attract and retain competent counselors. Yet the pupils in these schools, like those in city systems, are confronted with many problems that demand the services of specialists.

Earlier in this chapter, it was suggested that school districts with small enrollments should combine their resources to employ specialists needed in the guidance program, as is being done already in some areas. The approach to this problem must vary with the interests and nature of the communities concerned. Whatever the approach, it is essential that a way be found to provide for every school the specialists that are needed for every type of guidance problem.

2. *How can adequate time be provided in the program of the secondary school for the many group and individual guidance activities that are needed today?*

Providing adequate time for guidance activities has always presented a problem in the secondary school. In recent years the pressures in the secondary school to provide more time for certain academic studies has intensified the problem of finding adequate time for guidance activities. In most junior high schools, pupils carry a full load of studies every day with few, if any, free periods. As more and more senior high schools encourage or require pupils to carry five or more regular subjects, it will become increasingly difficult to find time for guidance and counseling at that level also. Although some guidance activities may come after the regular school day, this is not satisfactory for pupils who work after school, engage in extra-class activities after school, or come on school buses.

Unfortunately, the demands from pupils for guidance services are increasing sharply at the very time that it is more difficult to include them in the school schedule. The difficulty in gaining admission to college alone has forced counselors to spend many more hours with pupils on college selection and admission problems. The time needed for counseling has also increased in recent years because of increased pressures on youth, the demand for broader services as discussed in this chapter, and the many emotional and social problems arising in the home, the school, and the community. The solution to this problem is not a simple one. It demands the attention and cooperation of the administration, teachers, parents, and pupils.

3. *Should secondary schools provide the services of such specialists as psychologists, psychiatrists, and physicians as part of the guidance program or should guidance services be limited to those which are directly related to the learning process and the instructional program of the school?*

Some educators and citizens believe that the secondary school, through its guidance program, is extending services to individual pupils which should rightfully be provided by their parents. For instance, they suggest that if children need the help of a physician, dentist, psychologist, psychiatrist, or other specialist, parents should provide services outside the school. Most citizens agree that the school should help identify those pupils who need such services, but many contend that once the school authorities have notified parents of the child's need for certain services, the school's responsibility has been discharged. For children whose parents cannot afford the services of certain specialists, some educators and citizens suggest that the welfare agencies, not the schools, should assume the responsibility.

There are other educators and citizens who believe, however, that whatever guidance services are needed should be provided by the school for all children. These people believe that the child's total welfare is the concern of the school, including whatever services he may need for his educational, psychological, and physical development. The fact that these services may prove to be too expensive for many parents undoubtedly influences the thinking of some citizens. This issue continues to be debated in many communities, while some pupils fail to receive badly needed guidance services.

> 4. *Should tests and other information that the counselors have accumulated for individual pupils be made available to their parents or kept as strictly confidential information among counselors and teachers?*

Although counselors generally agree that parents should have much information about their children as a basis for helping them make educational and vocational decisions, they do not agree as to how far they should go in this matter. They agree that parents should be fully informed about the health of their children, their achievement in school, their citizenship and conduct qualities, and their social and emotional adjustments. They do not agree, however, concerning the psychological test information that parents should have.

The I.Q. scores have been one specific point of disagreement. Some parents want specific information about the I.Q.'s of their children. In some communities where parents have been given this information, the I.Q.'s of their children have become a competitive matter among neighbors and friends. Some parents have not shown good judgment in the demands they have made on their children for academic achievement, once they were informed about their I.Q. scores.

Some counselors contend that, as a basis for counseling children with respect to achievement in school, choice of college, and other post-secondary school objectives, parents need to know what the intellectual abilities of their children are. These counselors suggest that parents should have all the information about their children in the possession of the school, but that the way in which parents are given this information is important. They believe also that counselors should help parents interpret this information intelligently and suggest to them how to use it in counseling their children. Information about children should, by all means, be properly interpreted in order to be used to the best advantage for counseling purposes.

SELECTED REFERENCES

Association for Supervision and Curriculum Development. *A Look at Continuity in the School Program.* (1958 Yearbook). Washington, D.C.: National Education

Association, Chap. 12.—Discussion of ways of orienting children and youth to new school levels.

BENNETT, MARGARET E. *Guidance in Groups.* New York: McGraw-Hill Book Co., Inc., 1955, Chaps. 4, 5, 7.—A comprehensive discussion of group guidance activities for teachers and counselors in junior and senior high schools.

CROW, LESTER D., AND CROW, ALICE. *An Introduction to Guidance: Basic Principles and Practices.* New York: American Book Co., 1960, Chaps. 7-11.—Discusses major aspects of the guidance program, including organization, guidance and the curriculum, pupil evaluation and recording, and individual counseling.

FOSTER, CHARLES R. *Guidance for Today's Schools.* Boston: Ginn & Co., 1957, Chaps. 4-10.—A discussion of guidance in the schools, including teamwork in counseling, guidance in the classroom, guidance in the community and the home, and testing and evaluation.

HUTSON, PERCIVAL W. *The Guidance Function in Education.* New York: Appleton-Century-Crofts, Inc., 1958, Chaps. 1-5.—Presents an overview of the total program of guidance, including the setting for guidance, components of a guidance program, curricular activities in the guidance program, counseling techniques, and organization of the guidance program.

JOHNSON, MAURITZ, JR., BUSACKER, WILLIAM E., AND BOWMAN, FRED Q., JR. *Junior High Guidance.* New York: Harper & Brothers, 1961, Chaps. 4-6, 8.—A treatment of the guidance program in the junior high school, including orientation, the home room, testing, and individual counseling.

LITTLE, WILSON, AND CHAPMAN, A. L. *Developmental Guidance in Secondary School.* New York: McGraw-Hill Book Co., Inc., 1953, 324 pp.—A discussion of problems of youth which present guidance problems, with suggestions for guidance in secondary schools.

LOUGHARY, JOHN W. *Counseling in Secondary Schools.* New York: Harper & Brothers, 1961, 153 pp.—Presents an overview of the counseling program in secondary schools, with particular attention to counseling techniques.

MCKINNEY, FRED. *Counseling for Personal Adjustment in Schools and Colleges.* Boston: Houghton Mifflin Co., 1958, Chaps. 5-7, 12.—A comprehensive discussion of approaches to counseling, including the counseling relationship, counseling services, and counseling problems of youth.

MILLER, CARROLL H. *Foundations of Guidance.* New York: Harper & Brothers, 1961, Chaps. 1-3, 5.—An overview of the foundations of guidance in our American society of today, including the setting for guidance in the secondary school.

MORTENSEN, DONALD G., and SCHMULLER, ALLEN M. *Guidance in Today's Schools.* New York: John Wiley & Sons, Inc., 1959, Chaps. 8-11.—An overview of the guidance program in the schools, with emphasis on orientation of pupils and counseling individual pupils.

NATIONAL EDUCATION ASSOCIATION AND THE AMERICAN PERSONNEL AND GUIDANCE ASSOCIATION, *Guidance for the Academically Talented Student.* Washington, D.C.: The Association, 1961, 144 pp.—A summary of a conference on the guidance of academically talented students, with many examples of practices in schools.

STOOPS, EMERY, AND WAHLQUIST, GUNNAR L. *Principles and Practices in Guidance.* New York: McGraw-Hill Book Co., Inc., 1958, Chaps. 2, 3, 6-8.—Discussion of the guidance program in the secondary school, including gathering information about pupils, placement service, follow-up, and personnel.

17

THE TEACHER'S ROLE IN GUIDANCE

In the previous chapter, attention was given to the organization of the guidance program as a whole. Little was said about the part that the individual teacher should take in the various guidance activities. It is the teacher, however, who ultimately must bear the brunt of any activities in the secondary school that have a direct relationship to individual pupils. That is true of guidance activities fully as much as any other aspect of the secondary school program. In the present chapter, the place of the teacher in the guidance program will be discussed.

BASIC PRINCIPLES

The teacher is the key person in the guidance program in the secondary school.

The significance of this principle cannot be overstressed. A guidance program can be effective only to the extent that it has the enthusiastic and intelligent support of every teacher in the school. The director of guidance and the other specialists should provide the technical backgrounds and skill needed in planning and conducting the various guidance activities. It is the teacher, however, who has the intimate contact with pupils which is highly essential in guidance. The teacher meets the pupils daily in the homeroom and classes, he has them in clubs and other extraclass activities, and he has opportunities to meet their parents and to become acquainted with their home and out-of-school backgrounds. The teacher, therefore, is in a key position to identify pupils who are in need of guidance services.

It is true, furthermore, that individual pupils may not develop the confidence in guidance specialists to bring to them their most pressing problems. Even in a school that is well-staffed with guidance personnel, the guidance counselor will have at least 250 to 300 pupils for whom he is responsible. During the course of the year he may see each one only a few times, and then sometimes only when a specific problem demands it.

The relationship between counselor and pupil needs to be a very personal one. The personality of one counselor may appeal to some pupils, but not to others. The pupil, therefore, should have some choice among the professional staff to whom he may bring his problems. The teacher-pupil relationship is the one in school which best lends itself to the personal relationship so essential to effective counseling. Consequently, the effectiveness of a guidance program in any secondary school will depend largely upon the interest, the understanding, and the preparation of the individual teacher in guidance activities.

The teacher should have some preparation in the psychology of adolescence, mental hygiene, the gathering and interpretation of information about pupils, and the theory and practice of guidance and counseling.

If the teacher is to participate in guidance activities, he must have some preparation for it. His understanding of adolescents should be broad and thorough, including knowledge about their emotional problems, how they learn, their physiological growth, their social relationships, and their psychological development. He should be able to carry on the study of behavior of pupils in his classroom and to record his observations. The diagnosis of severe maladjustment problems should, of course, be made by a specialist. The teacher must understand adjustment problems sufficiently, however, to identify those pupils who are in need of help and refer them immediately to a guidance specialist. The teacher may need to work cooperatively with guidance specialists in helping pupils make adjustments in school and solve personal and educational problems.

The teacher should also have some understanding of the organization and administration of the guidance program, the types of specialized services that are available, the kinds of problems that demand the services of specialists, and the techniques of counseling. Although the teacher need not have the preparation demanded of specialists in guidance and counseling, he should have sufficient backgrounds in guidance to work effectively with guidance specialists in the counseling program of the school.

The teacher should be assisted in improving his effectiveness for guidance and counseling through a continuous program of in-service education.

The organization of a program of in-service education in guidance for teachers is one of the major responsibilities of the director of guidance and other guidance specialists. Such a program should be carefully planned, continuous, and concerned with all the guidance activities of the teacher. Since the pre-service education of teachers ordinarily provides little experience in guidance, particular attention should be given to the beginning teacher. The in-service education program should be directed particularly toward helping teachers (1) know about the guidance services provided by the school, (2) understand how they may contribute to the guidance program through class and extraclass activities, (3) assume responsibility for group guidance activities in the homeroom, and (4) identify pupils with problems who should be referred to guidance specialists.

A major responsibility of the individual teacher for guidance is the referral of pupils with guidance problems to the appropriate specialists. It is the teacher who has the daily contact with pupils in situations where guidance problems may be first identified. Teachers need to know the symptoms of emotional problems and maladjustments. They also need to know how to establish a rapport with individual pupils in order that they will have the pupil's confidence when guidance problems develop.

The teacher should consider every contact with pupils an opportunity for guidance—in the homeroom, in the classroom, and in extraclass activities.

The teacher's importance to the guidance program lies primarily in the fact that he sees the pupil frequently in various types of learning situations. It is important that the teacher take advantage of the guidance opportunities which these various contacts afford. The homeroom, particularly, is one avenue for guidance where the teacher's contribution can be a significant one. In fact, better guidance is one of the purposes for which the homeroom was originally established. But there are also many situations in the classroom and in extraclass activities where the teacher can be of help to pupils in exploring their potentialities, in making adjustments to new situations, in choosing elective courses and activities, in improving their success in school, and in making plans and decisions concerning further education. Teachers of homerooms, core classes, and block-time classes particularly can be of help to pupils with such problems. Many pupil activities, such as oral reports, panel discussions, committee reports, and written projects, may be used to give information to pupils as a background for guidance and counseling. Helping pupils gain backgrounds of information and explore their interests in various areas through such activities is a significant contribution which can be made by the teacher to the guidance program.

The teacher should have planned conferences with every child under his supervision concerning his educational and personal problems.

Too often, teachers have conferences with pupils only when they are in difficulty. Teachers may be able to help pupils avoid difficulties through conferences that are held periodically even though they may have no specific problem at the time. In fact, the best conference situation between teacher and pupil is likely to pertain when the pupil is apparently getting along well. Furthermore, the teacher may not become aware of maladjustments and problems of pupils until they are revealed through a routine conference. That is especially true in schools where the pupil load for teachers is a heavy one.

The arrangements for teacher-pupil conferences must necessarily vary from school to school. In any situation, however, they should begin early in the year, they should be held preferably during the school day, and they should be held under conditions that assure privacy. In most schools, these conditions may be difficult to achieve. Even so, every effort should be made to provide the most favorable conditions possible for teacher-pupil conferences.

The teacher should establish contacts with the home of every pupil in his homeroom, core class, or block-time class.

Home visitation by teachers is essential as a basis for effective guidance. In a junior or senior high school with a core program or block-time classes where certain teachers have contact with only a limited number of pupils, they should visit the homes of all their pupils. In schools where teachers meet many pupils each day, home visitation may have to be limited to the teachers' homeroom pupils.

Home visitation is not a new practice. In the early schools in America, it was expected that the teacher would become acquainted with the parents of all his pupils and that he would occasionally visit them in their homes. As schools became larger and teaching loads heavier, home visitation became more difficult. Furthermore, the growth of cities created problems for home visitation that did not exist in the early rural communities. Consequently, home visitation by teachers has gradually declined, particularly in the heavily populated centers, until it has practically disappeared.

There are, of course, serious obstacles to home visitation by teachers today. In urban communities, teachers may be reluctant to visit the homes of pupils in certain neighborhoods. In rural communities, the homes may be so widely scattered that the transportation problem may obviate extensive home visitation. In spite of these obstacles, teachers should be urged to visit the homes of pupils in their homerooms or classes insofar as that may be reasonably possible, as a basis for more effective guidance and counseling activities.

The teacher should become well acquainted with the interests, backgrounds, previous achievement, and personal qualities of every pupil in his homeroom and his classes.

Although this may be implied in several of the other principles, it is so important to the teacher's part in the guidance program that it justifies a separate statement. Effective guidance, as well as effective teaching, demands that the teacher know much about each pupil especially in his homeroom, and also in his classes. Much of this information can be obtained from the cumulative pupil records in the principal's or counselor's office. In addition, the teacher should learn much more about his pupils through contacts with them in the homeroom, in classes, and in extraclass activities. The director of guidance and the counselors may also help teachers gain important information about the backgrounds of pupils in their homerooms and classes.

In small schools, teachers see their pupils frequently in various situations, both in school and in the community. In such schools, it is easy for teachers and pupils to become well acquainted. In large schools, it is more difficult for teachers to know their pupils well because the classes are frequently large and teachers may have little contact with pupils, except in homeroom and classes. The departmental schools, where a teacher has 150 or more pupils in five or six different groups throughout the day, has made it especially difficult to implement this principle. In large schools it is therefore important to provide ways for teachers and pupils to meet in situations where they may come to know each other well.

SOME COMMON PRACTICES

EXPLORATORY EXPERIENCES IN JUNIOR HIGH SCHOOL SUBJECTS. All subjects in the secondary school program may be employed as avenues for exploration to give pupils information and backgrounds as a basis for guidance. Exploratory experiences in certain subjects are given especially in the junior high school, and to some extent in the senior high school. Through exploratory activities in certain subjects pupils obtain information concerning educational and vocational opportunities as related to those subjects, an understanding of personal qualities desirable for success in some vocations, information about the educational preparation required for various vocations, and the opportunity to try out individual potentalities and interests. Exploratory experiences in the various subject areas can therefore be exceedingly helpful as a basis for counseling and guidance. In junior high schools, subects which are used for these purposes most often include industrial arts, homemaking, and general science. In the senior high school the subjects where exploration has received the most emphasis are business education, industrial arts, and homemaking.

Many teachers assume that the mere offering of courses in certain subjects will result in exploratory experiences for pupils. Without definite planning, exploration is not likely to occur. Pupil interests and talents are decidedly individual in character. If pupils are to explore those interests and talents, they must have some freedom to decide on the learning activities in which they engage in the various subjects. Such subjects as industrial arts, business, general science, homemaking, English, and mathematics often are too rigidly organized in content and methods to permit pupils the freedom to engage in exploratory activities.

Teachers can develop more opportunities for the exploration of pupil interests and talents in every subject in the curriculum. English and social studies, for instance, offer exploratory opportunities through the reading, the oral work, and the written projects which pupils do. The "outside reading" in English furnishes opportunity to include biographies of leading lawyers, statesmen, doctors, nurses, professional athletes, and labor leaders. For their written and oral work in English, pupils may not use the opportunities to investigate certain vocational fields, the entrance requirements for colleges and professional schools, post-secondary school opportunities of the non-college type, and numerous other matters related to educational and vocational decisions. Too often teachers of mathematics and science neglect to inform pupils about vocational opportunities in these fields and the importance of preparation in these subjects for certain vocations.

OPPORTUNITIES FOR EXPLORATION IN EXTRACLASS ACTIVITIES. The program of extraclass activities is rich in opportunities for the exploration of the interests and talents of pupils. School clubs offer excellent possibilities. Chapter 12 contains descriptions of club activities which may give exploratory opportunities. For example, speech and dramatics clubs permit pupils to try out their talents in these activities, as a basis for vocational decisions related to the law, the ministry, teaching, politics, and the stage; hobby clubs have a bearing on the pupil's exploration of avocational interests; and clubs in art, music, and the dance encourage pupils to explore these interests.

Similar opportunities for exploration as a basis for guidance and counseling may be found in other extraclass activities, such as athletics, student council, music organizations, and school publications. Each of these activities may, under the supervision of an able faculty sponsor, give pupils many experiences in which they can evaluate their interests and abilities as a basis for educational and vocational planning.

At present many secondary school teachers fail to capitalize on the opportunities for exploration and guidance which extraclass activities afford. Frequently the activity becomes an end in itself, serving no long-term purpose in the educational growth of the child. Teachers should examine any activity for which they are responsible to identify the opportunities which those activities afford. They should encourage individual pupils to participate in activities with exploration of their interests and talents in mind.

PERSONALITY DEVELOPMENT IN EXTRACLASS ACTIVITIES. In the secondary school today, extraclass activities provide many opportunities for developing leadership skills, poise, self-confidence, and other character and personality qualities. Activities which contribute especially to character and personality development include social functions, assemblies, speech activities, clubs, and the student council. In the typical secondary school, however, the achievement of such objectives through extraclass activities is incidental rather than the result of careful planning. Although pupils may acquire these qualities and skills incidentally from participation in the activities, by thorough planning there would be more assurance that such objectives would be achieved. The personality and character qualities developed through extraclass activities help greatly in the social adjustments which secondary school pupils need to make. Counseling pupils on problems of social adjustment, therefore, can be helped considerably through pupil participation in extraclass activities.

In most secondary schools, little is done in the classroom program to help pupils with social adjustments. The classwork is centered largely in the development of subject-matter skills and backgrounds. Attention in the classroom program to the development of attitudes and skills related to social adjustments is limited to such classes as home economics, core classes, and homerooms. There are opportunities for personality, character, and leadership development in English, social studies, and some other subjects.

EMOTIONAL ADJUSTMENTS INFLUENCED BY CLASSROOM PRACTICES. Some classroom practices in the secondary school have a bearing on the emotional adjustments of pupils. In this respect classroom teachers have a direct influence on some of the guidance problems which emerge among secondary school youth. For junior high school pupils, the policy concerning discipline with its emphasis on quiet and order, may create unnecessary tensions. A marking system with a uniform standard of achievement for all pupils regardless of ability may stimulate competition among pupils that causes emotional upsets for some of them. The amount and nature of homework may limit unduly the pupil's out-of-school time for relaxation and rest. Overemphasis of final examinations, homogeneous grouping, and scholastic honors likewise are common causes of emotional upsets among pupils.

The possibility of emotional upsets resulting from certain school practices does not mean that these practices should be summarily eliminated from the program of the secondary school. It is important, however, that teachers in junior and senior high schools recognize that the practices frequently do cause emotional upsets. Teachers should employ these practices with complete awareness of the problems they may create; they should modify classroom practices when they appear to cause guidance problems that could be avoided; and they should be alert to pupils who reveal emotional maladjustments and consult the school counselor for advice and help. The classroom teacher must assume most of the responsibility for modifying his procedures which may create unnecessary tensions among pupils.

PROBLEMS CREATED BY PRESSURES ON ABLE PUPILS. The special programs to enrich the school experience of the more able pupils, discussed in Chapter 11, may cause undue pressures on the students by overambitious parents, by teachers, and by the competitive situation with regard to college admission. This in turn may lead to guidance problems as discussed in the previous chapter. Some teachers of the more able pupils merely increase the amount of work pupils are expected to do, rather than to present them with more challenging activities.

Teachers in programs for the more able pupils should recognize the problems which these programs may present. They should select for these programs only pupils with the physical vitality, as well as the intellectual motivation and ability, to carry the work load that will be expected of them. Teachers should examine their approach to teaching these classes to be sure that it is consistent with the health interests of the pupils. Teachers of programs for the more able pupils should keep closely in touch with the counselors concerning the response of pupils to the pressures which the special programs may present.

IMPLEMENTATION OF THE PRINCIPLES

HOMEROOM AS A CENTER FOR GUIDANCE. The homeroom was introduced into the secondary school about fifty years ago primarily to provide a center for guidance activities. In many schools it continues to this day to serve this purpose. The homeroom teacher has daily contact with his pupils, he keeps in touch with their progress in school, and he coordinates many of the guidance activities and services for individual pupils.

The homeroom in effect is the center of the life of the total school community of which pupils and teachers are loyal, active and contributing members. At the Upper Darby High School, Upper Darby, Pennsylvania, this concept of the homeroom is stated as follows: "In a few years each student will become an active participant in community, state, and national affairs. He will also select a vocation or profession through which his special talents, skills, and abilities may find expression. The homeroom is a small social unit in the school community—a practice field for the ideals, principles, and theories acquired in history, civics, English, business, and other school subjects." [1] In keeping with this purpose the homeroom elects officers and has committees to give leadership to its own activities, it sends representatives to the student council, encourages pupil participation in all school activities, and develops support for the total program of the school. With this as its background, the homeroom provides a setting which is conductive to effective guidance and counseling.

If the homeroom is to serve effectively for this purpose, teachers need to have time to spend with their pupils. In some schools adequate time is provided in the homeroom for both individual and group guidance activities. At the Collinwood High School, Cleveland, Ohio, there is a fifteen minute homeroom period daily. At the Joliet Township High School, Joliet, Illinois, pupils have a homeroom period of fourteen minutes every morning. At the David Crockett Junior High School, Amarillo, Texas, there is a thirty-minute homeroom period at 2:00 every afternoon. The Norwich Free Academy, Norwich, Connecticut, has a daily homeroom period of twenty minutes, and one or more full class periods of fifty minutes each week for guidance and counseling activities.

[1] *Handbook of Information*, Upper Darby Senior High School, Upper Darby, Pennsylvania, 1957-1958, p. 31.

HOMEROOM GROUP GUIDANCE ACTIVITIES. The group guidance activities that are carried on in the homeroom are intended to provide pupils with background information in their plans for further education and for vocational decisions. In most secondary schools, the group guidance activities in the homeroom include such topics as orientation to the school, planning pupil programs for junior and senior high school, making a success of one's school work, social manners and skills, how to study, school citizenship, and personality and character development. In some schools a definite outline of topics has been prepared for the guidance of the homeroom teacher, while in other schools these activities are planned from time to time during the year under the direction of a school counselor or by the teacher and his homeroom pupils.

The homeroom guides developed for the junior high schools of Riverside, California, are an excellent example of well-planned group guidance activities. In the junior high schools of Riverside, the guidance and counseling program is centered largely in the homeroom. Four large areas of study serve as a basis for the group guidance activities in the homeroom: (1) orienting the pupils to school, (2) helping pupils with the exploration of interests and talents, (3) helping pupils with self-understanding, and (4) looking ahead to further education in the senior high school.

The topics that are included in the homeroom guide for the seventh grade serve as a specific example of the nature of total group guidance of the Riverside junior high schools. The seventh-grade topics include: getting acquainted, organizing the homeroom, getting started in junior high school, following school rules and regulations, learning to study, taking part in extraclass activities, choosing a hobby, looking over your report card, respecting school property, practicing safety, getting along with others, learning about good manners, managing your money, joining the family team, understanding yourself, planning ahead, looking forward to eighth grade, and planning your vacation. The homeroom guides such as the *Seventh Grade Homeroom Guide*, published by the Riverside City Schools, Riverside, California, suggest books, pamphlets, and other materials that are available to teachers and pupils; specific methods and activities for the homeroom; and ways of adapting the guidance activities to the academically talented, the slow learners, and other groups of pupils.

The guidance program in the junior high schools of Sioux Falls, South Dakota, is another example of a well-organized program that is centered largely in the homeroom. The program in Sioux Falls emphasizes flexibility in the activities, the topics, and the materials that are to be covered. The homeroom guidance program in Sioux Falls includes specific topics and activities that are decided upon in advance, guidance topics that are based on resource materials and booklets that are available to the homerooms, topics which arise from time to time during the school year, and topics and activities that may be initiated by the homeroom teachers and pupils themselves. There are well-developed guidance outlines for all three junior high school grades in Sioux Falls which suggest ways of organizing the homeroom, group guidance topics to be covered, methods for carrying on these activities, resource materials that are to be available to homeroom groups, and such supplementary materials as pamphlets, film strips, movies, and other guidance materials. The program in the junior high schools of Sioux Falls, like that in Riverside, is characterized by thorough planning for all three years, the availability of reference and resource materials, and guidance and direction of the program from the department of guidance services.

GUIDANCE ACTIVITIES IN CORE CLASSES. In many secondary schools the functions of the homeroom have been combined with those of the core or block-time class. In these schools the core class therefore becomes the center of the guidance and counseling program. This practice is more common in junior than in senior high schools, primarily because it is in junior high schools that the core or block-time class has been most widely introduced. For example, in the West Junior High School, Kansas City, Missouri, the core classes in all three grades keep pupils together with the same teacher for English, social studies, and homeroom. The teacher has two such groups, including a total of approximately sixty pupils. The core teacher is largely responsible for the guidance and counseling activities of these pupils. The core teacher has available the services of a school counselor, nurse, and other guidance specialists, much like homeroom and classroom teachers in schools which do not have core or block-time classes.

In the junior and senior high schools of Pasadena, California, the guidance and counseling program in grades 7 through 10 is centered in a two-hour block class which includes English, social studies, and guidance. The teacher has two such classes during the day, thus serving as the homeroom adviser for two groups of pupils. In the eleventh grade in Pasadena the English classes are designated as the place where group guidance activities are centered. In the twelfth grade, the senior basic course gives attention to group guidance activities. At Folwell Junior High School, Minneapolis, the core teacher is provided with an extra period daily for guidance and counseling.

Conferences with parents and with pupils are scheduled during that period.

The group guidance activities in schools with core or block-time classes are similar to those with a homeroom plan of organization. In some of these schools the group guidance activities are well outlined, but in others they are left largely to the judgment of the teacher. In Pasadena, definite group guidance activities are suggested for the block-time classes at each grade level. The emphasis in group guidance at each grade level in Pasadena is as follows: in the seventh grade, orientation to the school, planning for the eighth grade, and evaluation of one's success in school; in the eighth grade, planning a program for high school; in the ninth grade, personal and social adjustments and planning for the senior high school; in the tenth grade, orientation to high school; in the eleventh grade, a unit on occupations in the English classes; and in the twelfth grade, a senior basic course which offers a unit on planning for college, other post-secondary school education, and employment.

Placing the guidance and counseling program largely in the core or block-time class has some distinct advantages. Under this plan guidance activities are usually well integrated with other aspects of the program of the school. The teacher of the core class, for example, may correlate guidance activities with oral and written work, suggest readings on educational and vocational subjects, and introduce other activities that may provide backgrounds for counseling. He can also become well acquainted with his pupils since he has them in class for two or more periods each day. Another advantage of the core class is that more time is available for individual counseling of pupils.

TEACHER GUIDANCE IN LITTLE-SCHOOL PLAN. One of the advantages of the little-school plan of organization (see Chapter 15) is that it makes possible better guidance of individual pupils, usually accomplished by making the classroom teacher the key person in the guidance program. At the O'Farrell Junior High School, San Diego, California, which is organized on the little-school plan, the guidance and counseling program is centered in the block-time classes. The teacher of the block-time class, called the counseling teacher, is responsible for the counseling activities of two groups of pupils. He remains with a group of pupils for two periods a day in English and social studies in grades 7 and 8 and in mathematics and science in grade 9. A major responsibility of the counseling teacher is that of guidance and counseling for pupils in his block-time classes.

In the little-school plan at O'Farrell Junior High School there is, in addition to the counseling teachers, a guidance counselor for each little school. The guidance counselor is free much of the day to work with teachers on counseling problems and to help pupils with problems referred to him by the counseling teachers. The teachers for each little school have a preparation period at the same time so that they can have conferences with the teaching counselors and the guidance counselor to discuss the guidance problems of their pupils. These conferences of all teachers make it possible for the counseling teachers to be well informed concerning the progress of their pupils in school. The responsibility for guidance which is given teachers at the O'Farrell Junior High School is typical of schools that are organized on the little-school plan.

ASSISTANCE TO TEACHERS IN UNDERSTANDING PUPILS. If the core, the homeroom, and the other classroom teachers are to function effectively in the guidance program, they should be well informed about individual pupils for whom they are responsible. In some schools seventh-grade teachers are informed about pupils when they first enter junior high school from the elementary grades. In Williamsville, New York, where the junior high school is organized on the little-school plan, seventh-grade teachers spend part of a school day in the spring with sixth-grade teachers to learn about the new pupils they will have in the fall. In some schools, where teachers have a planning period for several days before school opens in the fall, teachers from various grades meet to help each other get acquainted with new pupils they are to receive. These conferences for teachers are particularly helpful when pupils go from the elementary to the junior high school, or from the junior to the senior high school.

Teachers in these schools receive certain kinds of information about individual pupils before school opens in the fall, such as, the health of pupils, their emotional problems, unusual home and out-of-school backgrounds, psychological test scores, previous achievement, deficiencies in basic skills, in-school and out-of-school interests and activities, and personality and character qualities. In school systems where teachers return in the fall several days before school opens for preparation and planning activities, they use part of this time to study the cumulative records of pupils they expect to have in homeroom and classes. The school counselors sometimes meet with teachers in small groups to discuss with them the pupils they will have during the coming year. In some schools teachers are given essential information about individual pupils in the teacher's handbook or a mimeographed bulletin. This information is usually marked "confidential," and teachers are urged not to leave it where pupils might see it.

Teachers also receive help in administering tests and interpreting test results, especially in schools that have extensive testing programs. The junior high schools of Dade County, Florida, have a counselor in each school who is a specialist in testing and evaluation. He is in charge of the total testing program for a school, which includes the scheduling of tests, helping teachers to administer tests, having tests scored promptly, and assisting teachers in interpreting and using test results as a basis for counseling pupils. Cherry Creek School District, Arapahoe County, Colorado, a small suburban community, has a psychometrist who is in charge of the testing program for the entire school system. Besides his responsibility for the selection and administration of tests at all grade levels, the psychometrist assists counselors and teachers in interpreting and using test results to the best advantage in both teaching and counseling. The director of guidance, the school nurse, the physician, the psychologist and other guidance specialists help teachers understand and interpret information about individual pupils as a basis for guidance and counseling.

PUPIL INFORMATION GATHERED BY TEACHERS. Secondary school teachers do not rely only upon the cumulative records in the office for all information they need about individual pupils as a basis for counseling. Regardless of how up to date the cumulative records may be, the interests, backgrounds, and activities of pupils are always changing. Furthermore, teachers may want information about individual pupils which the cumulative records do not contain. Teachers use a variety of practices to gain information about pupils beyond that on the usual school records. Homeroom teachers and teachers of core classes have conferences with pupils early in the year to get acquainted. They sometimes call on the parents in their homes or invite parents to come to school for conferences.

Teachers also become acquainted with pupils through oral and written activities in their classes. Teachers of English, social studies, and core classes frequently have pupils write autobiographies to gain a better understanding of their interests, backgrounds, and educational and vocational goals. They sometimes have pupils fill in interest and activity questionnaires to reveal changes in their interests. Panel discussions, committee reports, and oral presentations by individual pupils on educational and vocational interests also reveal much valuable information about pupil interests. They participate in child study programs to learn to observe and gather data about children, such as the programs conducted in many school systems of Maryland with the assistance of The Institute for Child Study of the University of Maryland.

PARENT PARTICIPATION IN GUIDANCE. A recent development in the guidance and counseling program of the secondary school is the increasing participation of parents. Parent participation has been especially extensive in the orientation activities when pupils enter junior high school from the elementary grades. In Cherry Creek School District, Arapahoe County, Colorado, junior high school counselors call at the homes of all entering seventh-grade pupils during the weeks before school opens to discuss junior high school problems. At the Colonel Joseph M. Belt Junior High School, Montgomery County, Maryland, parents of entering seventh-graders visit school for an evening in the spring to become acquainted with teachers and the program of the school. The evening visit by parents follows a daytime visit by the sixth-grade pupils. At the Alfred Plant Junior High School, West Hartford, Connecticut, parents of entering seventh-grade pupils visit the school for a morning session soon after school opens in the fall. They meet the principal, teachers, and grade counselor; visit classes; and remain for lunch with the pupils.

In some schools participation by parents in guidance and counseling is encouraged at times other than the orientation period for new pupils. At the Colonel Joseph M. Belt Junior High School parents of eighth-grade pupils come to school for an evening to discuss the progress of their children in school as a basis for planning high school programs. In this conference teachers give parents information about the achievement of their children as measured by standardized tests and in other ways. Parents have the opportunity to compare the achievement records of their children in the eighth grade with their previous records in the sixth grade.

In some school systems parents also are invited to come to school for conferences with teachers and counselors by appointment on designated conference days during the year. In many of the Florida schools several parent conference days are included in the school calendar, with pupils not attending on those days. For instance, in the Brevard County, Florida, public schools three days are designated as parent conference days, when parents come by appointment for conferences with teachers and counselors. At the Shorewood High School, Shorewood, Wisconsin, pupils are included in conferences with parents and counselors on certain days in the afternoon when pupils are dismissed an hour early. Conferences with parents at times when their children do not have any serious problems may do much to prevent problems from arising.

IN-SERVICE EDUCATION IN GUIDANCE. The importance of in-service education in guidance and counseling for homeroom, core, and classroom teachers is being recognized in some secondary schools. The most common practice for helping teachers with guidance is to have publications prepared by the guidance staff which give suggestions on guidance and counseling. In large city systems, such publications are essential to give teachers an understanding of their responsibilities for guidance in the total guidance program. The Los Angeles City School District, for instance, has an excellent bulletin entitled, *Coordination of Guidance in the Junior High School,* which explains the responsibilities for guidance of the guidance specialists, the homeroom teachers, and the classroom teachers. The Pleasantville, New York, Junior High School has a mimeographed publication on homeroom guidance entitled, *Junior High School Guidance Program,* which was prepared by the principal and homeroom teachers during a summer workshop. This publication presents outlines of topics, activities, and materials for group guidance in the homeroom. Such publications can be exceedingly helpful in improving the teachers' contribution to the guidance program especially when they participate in preparing them.

Some schools have child study groups, seminars, and workshops to prepare teachers for guidance and counseling responsibilities, such as those previously mentioned. The study groups and workshops usually are under the direction of the counseling staff of the school system, often with the assistance of universities or colleges. In the Bay County public schools, Panama City, Florida, a two-day guidance workshop was held as part of the pre-school planning session for the professional staff. All guidance workers in the county attended and interested teachers were encouraged to participate. In the Sewanhaka Central High School District No. 2, Floral Park, New York, committees of teachers and counselors work during the summer to prepare guidance activities that are appropriate in the various subject areas. These materials are concerned especially with the relation of the respective subjects to different educational and vocational goals.

Courses on guidance are another approach to the in-service preparation of teachers for guidance. Some school systems have their own in-service programs for teachers in which guidance courses are offered. The Sewanhaka Central High School District has such an in-service program in which courses related to guidance are included. Colleges and universities likewise offer courses in guidance for teachers which may be taken in the evening, on Saturdays, or during summer sessions.

ISSUES AND PROBLEMS

There are certain issues and problems in guidance and counseling which are of particular concern to the professional staff of the secondary school. Some of these problems are rather technical and are of interest primarily to specialists in guidance. Many of them, however, are of direct concern to administrators and teachers as well. The following are some of the more important ones.

1. *Should guidance and counseling be considered a specialized activity in the secondary school which should be assigned primarily to guidance specialists or to homeroom and classroom teachers with the assistance of guidance specialists?*

There is a definite trend in the thinking of many guidance specialists that guidance and counseling is a specialized function which should be assumed only by people with particular preparation, experience, and training for it. The guidance specialists who hold this point of view suggest that homeroom and classroom teachers do not have sufficient background and preparation to assume definite guidance responsibilities.

Some educators, however, feel that this is an unrealistic approach to the whole concept and problem of guidance in the secondary school. This group contends that actually homeroom and classroom teachers, by necessity, must be the key people in the guidance program. They point out that secondary school youth are more likely to turn to teachers with whom they have had close contact, rather than to guidance specialists, when they face a personal problem. These educators contend that much guidance must begin with the homeroom and classroom teacher, but that the teacher should quickly evaluate the seriousness of the problem and refer it, if necessary, to a specialist for further study. Most educators would agree, however, that teachers and guidance specialists should work together in helping pupils with guidance problems.

2. *Should guidance be considered primarily in terms of individual counseling, or should there also be group guidance activities?*

Some specialists in guidance contend that guidance consists primarily of individual counseling, and that there are few, if any, guidance activities that can be carried on in a group guidance situation. Many of the guidance activities carried on by the core, the homeroom, and the classroom teacher are group activities. If guidance is primarily individual counseling, this would eliminate much of the guidance participation of these teachers.

Some educators contend that much of the exploratory work that serves as a basis for guidance and counseling can be carried on appropriately in group situations. Furthermore, these educators hold that group situations are the most efficient approach to certain guidance activities. It is probably true that a middle ground between these points of view is appropriate. That is, there may be some problems that demand individual counseling either by the teacher or a specialist, while for others a group situation would be appropriate. It is the latter type of activity to which we ordinarily refer as group guidance.

3. *How much information concerning pupils should be given the core, the homeroom, and the classroom teacher?*

This subject usually brings sharp division of opinion among teachers. Some teachers prefer to know little about the pupils' backgrounds until they have become acquainted with them. These teachers contend that it is better to obtain information about pupils as one works with them. They suggest that teachers may be prejudiced against a child if they know that his I.Q. is low, that he has been a poor student in previous years, and that he has had emotional, social, and citizenship problems.

Other teachers contend that it is important for them to know much about their pupils before they meet them in class or homeroom. They would examine the cumulative records of pupils, discuss them with previous teachers, and obtain information about them from the counselor, the nurse, and other guidance specialists.

Certainly teachers need some information about the health of the child, his previous achievement records, and his social and emotional adjustment. Information about the conduct and school citizenship problems of individual pupils may be withheld until after teachers know the pupils. If records are objective and factual reporting of behavior rather than teacher opinions, this problem will be largely solved. Counselors and teachers need to resolve this problem so that teachers may be sufficiently well informed about their pupils to work with them effectively from the opening of school.

4. *Should conduct and school citizenship problems be considered as disciplinary problems which are not the concern of the guidance specialist or should they be considered as counseling problems with the counselor assuming some responsibility for these problem cases?*

Some guidance specialists urge that a sharp line be drawn between those problems which are clearly guidance and those which may be designated as disciplinary. This group contends that counselors should be concerned only with guidance problems, and that discipline problems should be referred to the principal, the assistant principal, the dean of boys, the dean of girls, or some other designated person.

Other educators contend that most, if not all, pupil behavior problems in school should be approached as counseling problems. They believe that the approach to any conduct problem should be that of helping pupils study themselves in relation to the social group, rather than from the punitive approach. There is reason to believe, according to these educators, that problems of pupil misconduct could be improved more readily if they were considered counseling rather than discipline problems.

SELECTED REFERENCES

ARBUCKLE, DUGALD S. *Guidance and Counseling in the Classroom.* Boston: Allyn & Bacon, Inc., 1957, 397 pp.—A comprehensive discussion of the teacher's responsibility for guidance and counseling, with suggestions on the teacher's preparation for guidance, teacher counseling, tests and measurements, and working with student groups.

ASSOCIATION FOR SUPERVISION AND CURRICULUM DEVELOPMENT. *Guidance in the Curriculum.* (1955 Yearbook). Washington, D.C.: National Education Association, 228 pp.—Discussion of the relation between guidance and the curriculum, with particular attention to the teacher's part in guidance.

BUCHER, GORDON E. "Home-Room Guidance Reborn," *The Clearing House,* 35:361-65, February, 1961.—A description of the group guidance activities in the home room at Pleasantville Junior High School, Pleasantville, New York.

CUNNINGHAM, RUTH, AND ASSOCIATES. *Understanding Group Behavior of Boys and Girls.* New York: Bureau of Publications, Teachers College, Columbia University, 1951, 446 pp.—A comparison treatment of group behavior of boys and girls of value especially to teachers in studying behavior of individuals within the group and how to work effectively with groups.

GORDON, IRA J. *The Teacher as a Guidance Worker.* New York: Harper & Brothers, 1956, Chaps. 7-9.—A comprehensive discussion of the teacher's responsibilities for guidance, with emphasis on an understanding of human development concepts as related to the classroom.

HYMES, JAMES L., JR. *Effective Home-School Relationships.* Englewood Cliffs, N.J.: Prentice-Hall, Inc., 1953, 264 pp.—A comprehensive discussion of the importance and techniques of home-school relationships, of special value to homeroom and classroom teachers.

LIFTON, WALTER M. *Working With Groups: Group Process and Individual Growth.* New York: John Wiley & Sons, Inc., 1960, 238 pp.—A discussion of theories of the group process, techniques for working with groups, typical problems in the group process, and evaluation of the effectiveness of the group process.

PRESCOTT, DANIEL A. *The Child in the Educative Process.* New York: McGraw-Hill Co., Inc., 1957, Part 2.—This book is helpful to the teacher in understanding his guid-

ance function of gathering and interpreting data about the child. Describes child study programs.

SANDERSON, HERBERT. *Basic Concepts in Vocational Guidance.* New York: McGraw-Hill Book Co., Inc., 1954, Chaps. 1, 2, 11.—A discussion of vocational guidance with particular reference to its place in the secondary school.

WHITE, VERNA. *Studying the Individual Pupil.* New York: Harper & Brothers, 1958, 238 pp.—Written particularly for the teacher, this book suggests how information may be collected about individual pupils, how it should be synthesized and interpreted, and how teachers should use it.

WILLEY, ROY D., and STRONG, W. MELVIN. *Group Procedures in Guidance.* New York: Harper & Brothers, 1957, Chaps. 7-9, 13, 14.—A discussion of guidance in groups including classes, homerooms, and the core class.

18

RELATION TO ELEMENTARY SCHOOL AND COLLEGE

The public secondary school in America from the very beginning has been related in one way or another to other schools in our educational system. The first secondary school—the Latin grammar school —served almost exclusively as a college-preparatory institution. The purposes and program of the Latin grammar school, therefore, were closely related to those of the colleges, although the support and control of these two institutions were completely separate. The next secondary school to develop in America, the academy, as originally established, was separate from both the elementary school and the college of its day. As the Latin grammar school declined, however, the academy rapidly took over its college-preparatory function. Therefore the academy, like the Latin grammar school, quite early in its history established a close relationship with the colleges. Neither the Latin grammar school nor the academy, however, were closely related to the elementary schools of their time, either in purpose, program, support, or control.

The first public high schools in America were considered to be a continuation of the elementary school. The purpose of the early high school, like that of the elementary school, was to provide education in the vernacular, its support and control came from the community, and it was intended to meet the educational needs of those youth who were not going to college. Early in its history, however, the high school took over the college-preparatory function of the academy. Like the academy, the early high school therefore developed a program which was intended primarily to prepare youth for college. At the same time, the early high schools neglected to develop the close ties with the elementary school which one might have expected because of the purpose which these two schools at the beginning had in common.

425

Since about 1900 a change has gradually come about in the relations between the public high school and the elementary school. The early high schools had admissions examinations and took from the elementary schools only those pupils who performed satisfactorily on the examinations. Early in the present century this practice was discontinued and the high schools began to accept all pupils promoted by the elementary school. Since the high schools and elementary schools were governed by the same public authority, the teachers from both levels have come together increasingly to study curriculum problems and develop educational programs that are continuous from the elementary through the secondary school.

In spite of the tendency to bring about closer working relationships between the schools at various grade levels, there continues to persist a lack of articulation in the educational program which is of concern to both educators and parents. The American school system still exists largely as three rather distinct administrative units—elementary, secondary, and higher education—which develop and carry on their educational programs much too independently of each other.

Not only is there no justification for any lack of articulation in our educational system, but it is becoming increasingly urgent that steps be taken to correct it. It is the purpose of this chapter to present principles that are basic to improved articulation between the secondary school on the one hand and the elementary school and the college on the other, and to suggest practices that are or should be employed for the implementation of those principles.

BASIC PRINCIPLES

The educational program from kindergarten through the community college should be developed as one well-articulated and continuous program.

In Chapter 1 it was pointed out that the growth of the individual is gradual and continuous from birth to adulthood; there is no sharp separation in his growth characteristics from early to middle childhood, from middle childhood to adolescence, and from adolescence to adulthood. His development from year to year is a gradual one—physically, physiologically, psychologically, emotionally, and socially. In addition, children do not grow in the same way or at the same pace, and at every age level there are wide variations in the growth characteristics of individuals.

The nature of human growth and development has a direct bearing on the total program of education. The total program of education should likewise be continuous, with no abrupt breaks from grade to grade and school to school. From kindergarten to college, there should be satisfactory articulation in all aspects of the educational program—in the philosophy and purposes of education, the curriculum, the administrative organization and practices, the materials and methods of instruction, and in the special services offered as part of the school program.

Satisfactory articulation in the educational program requires more than agreement on the course content that is taught at the various grade levels. It means that teachers at all grade levels understand the philosophy, the purposes, and the methods of teaching for grades other than their own; that the administrative organization from one school level to another is not too sharply different; that the attitude toward youth in the senior high school is similar to that toward pupils in the upper grades of the junior high school; and that the approach to teaching freshmen college students recognizes the way those students were taught in the last year of the senior high school. In all aspects of the educational program, there should be coordination from grade to grade and school to school if there is to be satisfactory articulation in our school system.

The junior high school, the senior high school, and the community college should accept pupils at the level in the fundamental skills, attitudes, and understandings which they have achieved in the various subjects at the time that they enter each of these schools.

There is a wide range of differences in the achievement level of pupils in every subject and in every grade of the entire school system. When pupils enter the tenth grade of the senior high school, for instance, some of them may be reading at the level of the typical fourth- or fifth-grader, while the reading skills of others may exceed that of the average high school senior or college freshman. The achievement of pupils in other subjects, such as mathematics, history, spelling, and speech, likewise may show a wide range of differences in every grade. These differences in achievement are perfectly normal and, since there are great differences in the native abilities of pupils, in their home backgrounds, and their intellectual interests, wide differences in individual achievement will always exist.

The educational program in every grade of the school system should make provision for these differences in the achievement level of individual pupils. There should be appropriate curricula for pupils of different abilities and interests, special help for pupils who are deficient in certain basic skills, and opportunities for superior pupils to move ahead as rapidly as their abilities and interests may warrant. It is especially important that every teacher be aware of the differences in the previous achievement of his pupils and that he recognize that such differences are perfectly normal for any typical group. As pupils enter the junior high school from the elementary school, or the senior from the junior high school, teachers need to identify the achievement levels of individual pupils and then plan learning activities to help each one make reasonable progress in terms of his previous achievement.

Teachers of all grade levels within a school system should meet together frequently to discuss the philosophy, the content, and the methods of the educational program at the various grade levels.

Teachers in the public schools are frequently critical of the instructional program in the grades below. The teacher of college freshmen is notoriously critical of instruction in the fundamentals in the senior high school; the senior high school teacher feels that the junior high school has not properly prepared pupils in his subject; and the junior high school teacher is often dissatisfied with the start which his pupils have been given in the elementary grades. Yet, it is reasonable to assume that the teacher at any grade level is better qualified than the teachers in the grades above or below to decide what learning activities, subject content, and standards of achievement are appropriate for pupils in his grade or course.

If there is to be satisfactory articulation in the educational program, it is important that teachers have mutual respect for and confidence in each other's professional ability. They should assume that pupils who come to them have gone as far in their achievement in the previous grades as was reasonably possible. Mutual confidence and respect among teachers at the various grade levels can be achieved only if they come together frequently to get acquainted, to discuss common problems, and to plan together the total educational program. These meetings should be held at a time when teachers are free to give the problems under discussion their full attention.

There should be satisfactory articulation between the college-preparatory program of a secondary school and the programs of institutions of higher education which most of its graduates attend.

The articulation of the program of secondary schools with those of colleges and universities is particularly difficult because these institutions are usually under different administrative control. Furthermore, the graduates of a secondary school may attend any one of dozens of colleges and universities throughout the United States and even in other countries. It is this very situation, however, which makes some attempt at articulation between secondary schools and institutions of higher education so important. The fact that students in their first year at college may be away from home for the first time intensifies the need for a close working relationship between secondary schools and colleges.

The responsibility for effecting improved articulation rests with both the secondary schools and the colleges and universities. Leadership in developing a closer relationship between these institutions should be provided by the professional organizations in which the secondary schools, the colleges, and the universities are represented. The secondary school, however, should not wait for the colleges and universities to act in this matter. Administrators, counselors, and teachers in secondary schools should take the initiative in establishing a close relationship between their own school program and those of the higher institutions that most of its graduates attend.

The administrative and counseling staff of the secondary school should establish a sufficiently close relationship with post-secondary schools other than four-year colleges or universities to make the transition of pupils to such schools as satisfactory as possible.

The graduates of a secondary school, as well as many who drop out before graduation, may attend a number of different kinds of post-secondary schools. In school systems with a public community college, articulation between the program of the secondary school and that of the community college should not be difficult. Their administrators, counselors, and faculties should be able to meet together and take appropriate steps to provide continuity in the total educational program. But there are many post-secondary schools other than community colleges which high school graduates attend, most of them under private control with no direct connection with the public secondary schools. Some are established as commercial ventures, others are non-profit private schools, and still others are organized by business or industry to train their own employees. There are trade schools, business schools, barber schools, beauty schools, and a variety of others. They may be day schools, evening schools, short-term schools or correspondence schools.

Administrators and counselors in secondary schools should help their graduates meet the admissions requirements for all kinds of post-secondary schools in their vicinity, assist them in their choice of such schools, guide them with admissions procedures, and help them to become oriented and to adjust to the schools they enter. Secondary school authorities should also provide leadership in promoting articulation in so far as that is possible between the program of the secondary schools and those of the various post-secondary schools in the vicinity.

A sound program of general education in high school constitutes a desirable preparation for college.

At times there has been apparent conflict between the college preparatory and the life preparatory functions of secondary education. Originally the principal aim of the early American secondary school was preparation for college. Slowly, this function was modified to include considerable emphasis upon life functions. Today, the college preparatory function is still dominant and growing in importance.

Research indicates that the nature of the high school pattern of courses is not a significant factor in determining college success. Able students pursuing college-preparatory curricula generally succeed in higher education, but so, too, do superior students who take vocational courses in high school. Research reveals that such factors as high school rank, recommendation of high school principal, general scholastic aptitude, study habits, interests, and such basic skills as reading are related fairly closely to college success. Such competencies as the last three on this list can be developed through a great variety of learning experiences and from different types of curricular practices.

Stress should be placed in the college preparatory programs on attaining a high quality general education, with such outcomes as the ability to write well, to think clearly in both writing and speaking, and to present thoughts effectively in speaking; competence and understanding in using library resources and references; the ability to read and comprehend materials of varied difficulty with the speed of reading adapted to the type of material and the purpose of reading; broad cultural interests; and wide reading and interests in many fields. The understanding of mathematics has become more essential for effective college preparation. Of course, students should be counseled to take subjects that fit in with occupational objectives and future college careers, such as, mathematics, sciences, and foreign languages for specialization in one of the scientific branches.

SOME COMMON PRACTICES

PREVIOUS DIFFERENCES IN PREPARATION OF TEACHERS. There are several reasons why in the past there has been such serious lack of articulation between the elementary and the secondary schools. One reason is the sharp difference that existed for many years in the preparation of elementary and secondary school teachers. Until recent years secondary school teachers came almost entirely from liberal-arts colleges and universities where they completed a four-year program with strong preparation in subject matter, but with a minimum of professional education. Teachers in the early elementary schools were prepared primarily in "normal schools," in a program of one to two years which emphasized a review of elementary school subjects and methods of teaching those subjects. Elementary school teachers, therefore, lacked the broad general education which secondary school teachers received in the liberal-arts colleges. These differences in the character and amount of preparation for elementary and secondary school teachers continued well into the present century.

The cleavage between elementary and secondary school teachers was further accentuated by the fact that in the past the salaries of teachers at the secondary level were usually higher, sometimes considerably so. The differences in salaries were probably justified because of the more extensive education required of secondary school teachers. Even so, the salary policies, like the differences in education, did not contribute to the mutual confidence, understanding, and respect among teachers which are essential to satisfactory articulation between the elementary and the secondary schools.

Since about 1920, the differences in preparation between elementary and secondary school teachers have gradually changed. The early normal schools, with their one- and two-year programs, have become teachers colleges, state colleges, and in some cases universities, with four-year programs of teacher education, a large part of which is devoted to the liberal arts. These institutions today prepare many teachers for the secondary as well as for the elementary schools. The separate institution devoted solely to teacher education has largely disappeared from the educational scene. The liberal-arts colleges and the universities likewise are not only requiring more professional education of secondary school teachers than in the past, but they are also preparing many teachers for the elementary schools.

With the extension of the normal school program to four years, the various states have been increasing certification requirements to teach in elementary schools, with most of them today requiring four years of college work for an elementary teacher's certificate. There are still many teachers in elementary schools with less than four years of preparation, but mainly they entered the profession before the requirements were raised. The growing similarity in the preparation of elementary and secondary school teachers and the equalization of salaries should help to increase the mutual confidence and respect among teachers of all grade levels and should lead to better articulation between the elementary and secondary schools.

ARTICULATION PROMOTED BY JUNIOR HIGH SCHOOLS. In Chapter 2, it was pointed out that in their early history the elementary and secondary schools in the United States developed independently of each other. The seven- and eight-year elementary schools that prevailed until about 1910 were clearly separate and distinct in organization and program from the four-year high schools. There was much difference between the elementary and secondary schools in the subject matter that was taught, in the methods of teaching that were employed, and in the administrative organization and practices of the schools.

The introduction of the junior high school beginning in 1910 was motivated to a large extent by this lack of articulation between the elementary and secondary schools. In fact, better articulation in the educational program was one of the strongest arguments for the reorganization of the 7-4 and 8-4 plans which was presented by early advocates of the junior high school. They pointed out that, under the junior-senior high school plan, pupils can be introduced gradually to departmentalized teaching; that the methods of teaching may gradually be changed from those prevalent in the elementary grades to those of the secondary school; that the amount and nature of independent study required of pupils can be gradually increased; and that such subjects as foreign languages, science, and algebra may be introduced earlier. The administrative and counseling staffs of the junior high school have also considered it to be one of their major responsibilities to promote better articulation between the elementary and the secondary schools. The junior-senior high school plan of grade organization, therefore, has focused attention on the problem of articulation in our schools and has contributed materially toward bringing about a closer relationship between the elementary and secondary schools.

LIMITED ARTICULATION PRACTICES. It would be an exaggeration to suggest that the introduction of the junior high school in the American school system led immediately to satisfactory articulation between the elementary and secondary schools. The junior high school idea has been introduced gradually in the United States, and only in the last few years have a majority of our secondary schools been organized on the junior-senior high school plan. Although, in communities with junior high schools articulation between elementary and secondary education has received increased attention, even in these schools many practices conducive to improved articulation are being introduced less rapidly than is desired. A study of articulation practices in school systems with junior high schools in various parts of the United States revealed that, under the junior-senior high school plan, certain relatively simple articulation practices should be employed more extensively than they are at present.[1] The articulation practices which need increased attention are (1) visitation by junior high school teachers to the elementary and the senior high schools to become acquainted with teaching methods used in these schools, (2) making courses of study for the elementary and senior high schools, as well as the basic textbooks, and other instructional materials, available to teachers in the junior high school for their respective subjects, and (3) having teachers from all grade levels get together in workshops or study groups on common instructional problems.

The Byers study revealed that many school systems have an assistant superintendent or a curriculum director who has some responsibility for supervising the instructional program at all grade levels. Such leadership in curriculum and instruction for the entire school system is desirable. It is equally important, however, to have the teachers at all grade levels get acquainted with each other and be familiar with the philosophy, content, and methods of instruction employed in grades other than their own. Practices which help bring teachers together and help them understand each other should, therefore, be emphasized if articulation between elementary and secondary education is to be satisfactory.

SCHOOL-COLLEGE PARTICIPATION IN PROFESSIONAL ORGANIZATIONS. Early in the history of the National Education Association (first organized as the National Teachers' Association in 1857), college and university professors, as well as elementary and secondary school teachers, were prominent in its activities. Both college and public school educators belonged to the Association, participated in its activities, and served on its committees. An example of this participation is found in the work of the Committee of Ten on Secondary School Studies, appointed by the National Education Association in 1892, with Charles W. Eliot, president of Harvard University, as chairman and composed of both university and secondary school teachers. The purpose of this committee was to bring about more uniformity in high school studies and thereby to improve the preparation of youth for college work. The report of the Committee of Ten,

[1] Richard S. Byers, "Articulation in the Junior High School," Unpublished Doctoral Dissertation, Storrs, Connecticut: University of Connecticut, 1955, 268 pp.

presented to the Association in 1893, in addition to making recommendations concerning the content of each of the major subject areas, urged that there be closer articulation between the programs of the colleges and the secondary schools. The report of the Committee of Ten had tremendous influence in bringing about better understanding between secondary school and college teachers concerning the nature and content of high school studies.

The early participation of college and public school teachers together in some state and national education organizations unfortunately has not continued to the present time. Although both groups of educators continue to be qualified for membership in the National Education Association and in the state education associations, the college and university teachers, except for those at teacher-education institutions, do not participate as extensively as they did half a century ago. Both secondary school and college teachers do participate actively, however, in many national professional organizations in the various subject fields, such as the National Council for the Social Studies, American Historical Association, National Council of Teachers of English, National Council of Teachers of Mathematics, National Science Teachers Association, Modern Language Association, and others. Besides the national associations, many professional organizations in the subject fields are also organized on state and regional levels, with college and public school teachers participating. Some of these organizations have been exceedingly active in conducting research, providing professional leadership, and encouraging interest in the more effective teaching of their subjects in both the colleges and the secondary schools. These organizations have been of benefit in developing better articulation between the colleges and the secondary schools.

SCHOOL-COLLEGE RELATIONSHIPS IN ACCREDITING ASSOCIATIONS. For many years the regional accrediting associations in the United States, whose membership includes both colleges and secondary schools, have had considerable influence on the articulation between the programs of these institutions. The history of the regional accrediting associations dates back to 1895, when two associations were established—the North Central Association of Colleges and Secondary Schools, which includes states from West Virginia to Arizona in the Southwest and Wyoming in the West, and the Southern Association of Colleges and Secondary Schools, including states in the South from Virginia to Texas. In 1918, the Northwest Association of Colleges and Secondary Schools was formed, patterned after the North Central Association. Two other regional associations likewise include in their membership both colleges and secondary schools. The New England Association of Colleges and Secondary Schools was organized in 1885. The Middle States Association, organized in 1892, did not begin accrediting schools until 1928, while the New England Association only recently has taken steps to accredit schools. There is a Western College Association, which includes colleges in California, Hawaii, and Guam, but it does not at present accredit secondary schools, though it is developing plans to do so.

The regional associations have exerted much influence over a period of many years in encouraging a closer working relationship between the colleges and secondary schools in the states where they have jurisdiction. The accrediting process alone does much to develop better articulation between the colleges and secondary schools because the standards for accreditation are developed cooperatively by representatives of the schools and colleges. (See discussion on accreditation by regional associations in Chapter 19.) The regional associations assist further in the articulation of school and college programs because through their annual meetings, their committees, and other activities, they bring together representatives of the colleges and the secondary schools. These representatives usually are the administrative officers of the member institutions, rather than teachers; but even so, the activities of the associations provide a channel of communication between the colleges and secondary schools which is conducive to better articulation in their programs.

SCHOOL-COLLEGE RELATIONSHIPS IN ADMISSIONS EXAMINATIONS. The admissions examinations, which colleges and universities have been giving to secondary school graduates for many years, are helpful in encouraging some coordination between the programs of the colleges and the secondary schools. The most widely-used examinations are those prepared and administered under the direction of the College Entrance Examination Board. The Board, which was founded in 1900, is a non-profit association of public and independent colleges, universities, secondary schools, and educational organizations, whose expressed purpose is to "provide direction, coordination, and research in facilitating the transition from secondary school to institutions of higher learning."

The College Entrance Examination Board has a number of tests which are administered to secondary school students who plan to seek admission to colleges and universities. The admissions examinations include the Scholastic Aptitude Test, which is designed to provide some indication of a student's ability to do college work, and the achievement tests, which at present include examinations in thirteen different subjects. The admissions examinations are given at some 1,400 centers in the United States and in forty foreign countries. Results of the admissions examinations are sent to the colleges requested by the candidates. Each college establishes its own criteria for admission and therefore makes its own interpretation of the test scores for individual applicants.

In addition to the admissions examinations, the Board offers a Preliminary Scholastic Aptitude Test, which may be taken by high school juniors for early guidance regarding college admissions. The Board also has placement tests, which are administered by colleges and universities as an aid to counselors in helping students plan their college programs. Other services of the Board which are helpful in establishing a better transition from secondary school to college are an advanced placement program which permits able students to take college-level work while still in the secondary school; a college scholarship service which enables parents of applicants for financial aid to submit a single confidential statement to be sent to designated colleges; a program of research and special studies of problems concerning the transition from secondary school to college; and conferences and seminars in which college and secondary school representatives discuss problems of college admission, guidance, and testing. Without a doubt, the College Entrance Examination Board has exerted a strong influence over the high school curriculum, sometimes to the disadvantage of experimentation in the secondary school.

INFLUENCE OF COLLEGE ENTRANCE REQUIREMENTS. Perhaps the most direct influence which colleges and universities have had on the programs of secondary schools is through the entrance requirements which they demand of secondary school graduates. These requirements are largely a product of the present century. Before 1900, there was little uniformity in the requirements which various colleges and universities in the United States demanded of entering students. Relatively few colleges and universities had admissions requirements that would be considered at all adequate by present-day standards, and even these colleges frequently waived those requirements if necessary to fill their freshmen classes. Furthermore, many colleges had preparatory departments which were not always distinctly separate from the college program itself.

One of the serious problems in establishing college-entrance requirements was the lack of a standard by which the completion of a secondary school program could be measured. The Carnegie Foundation for the Advancement of Teaching took steps to establish such a standard when, in 1909, it proposed that a "standard unit" of high school work be used as a basis for transferring credits from secondary schools to colleges, and this unit should consist of 120 sixty-minute hours of study, or their equivalent, in any major subject. The Carnegie Foundation based its standard on the program of the four-year high school, which was the prevailing type of secondary school in the United States at that time. As a basis for measuring a unit of high school work, the Carnegie Foundation assumed that the length of the school year was from thirty-six to forty weeks, that a class period was from forty to sixty minutes long, and that a subject was studied from four to five periods a week. The College Entrance Examination Board approved the "Carnegie unit," as it came to be called, in November, 1909. Within the next few years the Carnegie unit was rapidly adopted by both high schools and colleges throughout the United States as the standard unit of measure for high school work. It remains so to this day.

When the Carnegie unit was first recommended by the Carnegie Foundation, it was suggested that in four years of high school a pupil might be expected to complete a minimum of fourteen units of work. This minimum requirement was soon raised by colleges, high schools and state departments of education. By 1928, the requirement for a high school diploma was fifteen units in eleven states, sixteen units in thirty-five states, and seventeen units in one state. By 1961, only one state still required as little as fifteen units for a high school diploma, one state required fifteen-and-one-half units, sixteen units were required in thirty-two states, and seventeen units or more were required in eleven states. In 1961, six states announced a further increase in the units required for graduation from high school. Many high schools have requirements that exceed the minimum imposed by the various states, as noted in Chapter 7. The Carnegie unit which originally was established by college and university people, therefore, has had much influence on the nature and standards of the requirements for a high school diploma.

The Carnegie unit is not the only aspect of college-entrance requirements which has had widespread influence on the educational program of the secondary school. Many colleges and universities require the completion of certain subjects in high school as a basis for admission, usually stating such requirements in terms of the Carnegie unit. The subjects most often required for college entrance are English, history, mathematics, science, and a foreign language. Although these requirements vary greatly among colleges, they have had a marked influence on the subjects which are required for completion of high school programs. State departments of education and legislatures in some states have formulated minimum subject requirements for a high school diploma. These have been influenced by the subjects which colleges demand for admission. Although many secondary schools today have multiple curricula which provide a place for both college- and non-college-bound youth, the influence of the Carnegie unit and the college-entrance requirements continue to influence the content, nature, and organization of the programs of secondary schools in the United States.

THE COLLEGE ADMISSIONS SCRAMBLE. The scramble—or college "squeeze" as principals may prefer to think of it—for high school graduates to get into colleges poses some serious threats to improved secondary school–college relations. At the same time the situation presents challenges to faculties of both types of institutions.

The expanding secondary school enrollment, the increasing proportion of high school graduates who go on to college, the lack of adequate college facilities to take care of the burgeoning population, the shortage of well-prepared college teachers, and the increasing demand for a college education in various occupations, all have combined to influence the problems of college admission. Colleges have raised their entrance requirements and so have become more selective in admission policies. This is true of state universities and colleges as well as private institutions of higher learning. Influenced by their parents who are anxious to get their sons and daughters into the best possible college, many students apply for admission to several colleges before high school graduation, much to the dismay of college admissions officers who no longer can expect that once they admit a student he will show up on the campus the next fall.

The pupil in his last year of high school may live in an atmosphere of tension, strain, and uncertainty because of the fiercely competitive scramble for admission to college and the fear of not getting into the college of his first choice.

Still, many colleges are not yet crowded. The situation places on the high school counselor greater responsibility than in the past for knowing the standards, admission requirements, and programs of the various colleges so that he may counsel both pupils and parents effectively.

IMPLEMENTATION OF THE PRINCIPLES

There has been much attention in recent years to improving the relationships of the secondary schools with the elementary schools from which pupils come and the colleges and universities to which they go. Some of these practices are the result of definite attempts by school authorities to bring about better articulation from school to school, while others have come about through recent developments in secondary and higher education. In this section of the chapter, some of the recent practices to improve articulation from the elementary school to the college and university are discussed.

EARLIER INTRODUCTION OF SECONDARY SCHOOL STUDIES. In recent years there has been a decided trend toward introducing earlier in the school program some studies that in the past were considered to be primarily secondary school subjects. Some school systems today offer a foreign language as early as the lower elementary grades, and in most junior high schools a foreign language is introduced as early as the seventh or the eighth grade.

Science is also being taught increasingly earlier than the senior high school. Many school systems have well-developed science programs which begin in the lower elementary grades and extend through the senior high school. Although science instruction in the elementary grades is exceedingly elementary, it does provide pupils with certain backgrounds of knowledge and understandings in science before they reach the secondary school. Furthermore, the amount of time devoted to science in the seventh and eighth grades of the junior high school has increased greatly. The science facilities, equipment, and instructional materials in the junior high school have also been considerably improved. For the more able students, some junior high schools offer biology or earth science in the ninth grade in place of the usual course in general science.

Changes have also taken place in the teaching of mathematics in the junior and senior high schools. In junior high schools, the more able pupils frequently study elementary algebra in the eighth grade, followed by intermediate algebra or plane geometry in the ninth. Some schools permit pupils who are highly gifted in mathematics to study beyond algebra and geometry on an individual basis before they leave the ninth grade.

Many junior and senior high schools have also introduced new approaches to teaching mathematics which are sharply different from that of the past. The new mathematics programs have been discussed in Chapter 9. The new approaches to teaching mathematics may be used with pupils of various ability levels and are being developed as well-coordinated programs for the junior and senior high school grades.

The earlier introduction of secondary school subjects has intensified the importance of closer articulation from grade to grade and school to school in the total instructional program. If pupils come to the secondary school with several years of background in a foreign language, the language program in the secondary school grades needs to be modified accordingly. Since the conversational approach is used most often in foreign-language instruction in the elementary and junior high school grades, the methods as well as the content in the foreign-language program of the senior high school need to be modified accordingly. Teachers of foreign languages at all grade levels should therefore plan the total language program together and should keep in frequent touch with each other. Changes in the science and mathematics programs likewise demand closer working relationships among teachers in the elementary school, the junior high school, and the senior high school.

EXTENSION INTO HIGH SCHOOL OF ELEMENTARY SCHOOL STUDIES. Just as some secondary school studies are being introduced in the elementary grades, so studies which in the past have been identified with the elementary school are being taught increasingly for some pupils in the secondary school and even the community college. Several decades ago, algebra was a standard requirement in the ninth grade with plane geometry in the tenth. For some years now general mathematics and arithmetic have been offered in the ninth and sometimes in the tenth grade for pupils who are not ready for algebra and geometry. Reading also is being taught increasingly in the secondary school as pointed out in Chapter 9. Most junior high schools offer reading instruction, usually a program in developmental reading for all pupils and special instruction for pupils with reading deficiencies. "Power" reading and "speed" reading are also being offered increasingly in the junior high school for pupils who want to improve their reading skills, even though they are not deficient in reading.

Reading instruction is also being introduced in the senior high school, though not as widely as in the junior high school. At the Ramona High School, Riverside, California, all pupils in the tenth grade take a developmental reading course in which entire English classes are moved into a well-equipped reading laboratory for a six-weeks' period. Furness Junior High School in Philadelphia has special classes in reading for the more able pupils who want to increase their reading skills as a basis for better work in senior high school and college. Many junior and senior high schools are developing such reading programs. A recent nation-wide study of more than 2,100 six-year high schools reveals that, in 26 per cent of the schools, reading instruction is provided for pupils who need special help at all grade levels. However, the principals of 73 per cent of the schools studied believe that some reading instruction should be offered in both the junior and senior high school grades.[2]

The offering of such studies as reading and arithmetic in the secondary school, which have been in the past considered to be elementary, has encouraged teachers of all grade levels to come together more frequently to develop the instructional program in these areas.

ARTICULATION THROUGH TEACHERS MEETING TOGETHER. Earlier in this chapter, it was suggested that frequent meetings among teachers of various grade levels is essential for satisfactory articulation in the total school program. These meetings should come at a time when teachers are not tired from a day's work. Many school systems in the United States today recognize the importance of providing such planning time for teachers as a basis for better articulation. The provision for such meetings varies considerably. Some systems have teachers return in the fall a week or two before school opens, others provide free days during the school year, while still others have workshops for teachers during the summer as described in Chapter 15.

Cherry Creek School District No. 5, Arapahoe County, Colorado, offers an example of a school system which has regularly planned articulation meetings during the year. Several teachers' study days are designated for articulation purposes so that teachers from all grade levels may devote their time to a study of common problems. In Austin, Texas, teachers have workshop sessions in June following the close of school, with elementary, junior, and senior high school teachers coming together in the same study groups.

The problem of articulation is a particularly difficult one in communities which have only elementary schools, and send their children to another school district for their high school education. The regional high schools in Connecticut and Massachusetts, the township high schools in Illinois, and the union high schools in California are examples of school district organization which provides elementary education for children in one district and secondary education in another. In situations like these, articulation is especially difficult because the elementary and secondary schools are under different administrative and supervisory authorities.

Some secondary schools which take children from several elementary school districts are making an attempt to provide for adequate

[2] William T. Gruhn and Others, "The Junior High-School Grades in the Six-Year High School," *Bulletin of the National Association of Secondary-School Principals*, 44: 46-78, November, 1960.

articulation in the total school program. An example is the Amity Regional High School at Woodbridge, Connecticut, a six-year secondary school which has its own regional board of education and receives children from three elementary school districts, each under a different administrative authority. In order to promote satisfactory articulation, monthly meetings are held which are attended by both elementary and high school teachers. Sometimes these meetings are directed toward a specific subject area and are attended only by teachers of that subject, while others deal with broad articulation problems of concern to all teachers. These monthly meetings are planned well in advance so that appropriate attention may be given to problems of articulation between the elementary schools and the regional high school.

ARTICULATION THROUGH ORIENTATION ACTIVITIES. One aspect of articulation is that of making the transition as easy as possible for pupils when they move from one school to another. For this purpose, orientation activities are provided for pupils in most school systems as they leave the elementary school to enter the junior high school. (Orientation activities, frequently considered a part of the guidance program, are discussed in Chapter 16.) Parents, pupils, and teachers are included in these activities. At the Edison Junior High School, Sioux Falls, South Dakota, the student council has charge of orientation activities for the entering seventh grade. In the spring of the year, sixth-grade pupils and their parents visit Edison Junior High School for an evening program, which includes an explanation of the junior high school program, a tour of the building, and an opportunity to get acquainted with the principal, counselors and teachers. The orientation program at Edison is carried on for several evenings, with a small group of parents and pupils each evening so that they may participate more fully in the orientation discussions.

The Los Angeles City School District suggests a program for articulation between the elementary schools and the junior high schools which goes far beyond orientation activities for pupils and parents. The following articulation activities are recommended in Los Angeles to elementary and junior high school faculties: (1) frequent meetings of elementary and junior high school principals in the various administrative districts of the city; (2) invitations to principals and teachers of junior high schools to attend various activities in the elementary schools; (3) visits by sixth-grade teachers to junior high schools; (4) visits by sixth-grade pupils to junior high schools; and (5) meetings for junior high school teachers with parents of entering seventh-grade pupils.

Orientation activities are also provided in some systems for pupils as they go from junior to senior high school and from senior high school to the community college. These activities are similar to those provided for pupils when they enter the junior high school from the elementary school.

IMPROVED SECONDARY SCHOOL–COMMUNITY COLLEGE ARTICULATION. The public community or junior college (see Chapter 13) has done a great deal to bridge the gap which traditionally has existed between secondary schools and colleges and universities.

The community college in some ways is an upward extension of the secondary school. Many community colleges, when they were first established, were carried on in high school buildings during the late afternoon and evening, with high school teachers responsible for some of the community college courses. Furthermore, the public community college in most states is under the same administrative authority as the secondary school. It is, therefore, not difficult to establish and maintain close working relationships between the secondary school and the community college.

The community college has also tended to bridge the gap between the secondary schools and the colleges and universities because it permits youth to remain at home for the first two years of college, thus delaying one of the most difficult adjustments when they attend college away from home. By the end of the community college years, the academic interests are more fully matured and their educational and vocational goals more clearly defined. The public community college, therefore, serves as a transitional school for youth between the secondary school and the four-year college and university.

In some school systems with community colleges, the more able secondary school pupils may do advanced work at the college level before they graduate from secondary school, as described in Chapter 11. Such opportunities for superior secondary school students to take community-college courses encourages closer working relationships between the faculties of the secondary school and the community college, and consequently should lead to better articulation in the total educational program.

ADVANCED PLACEMENT OPPORTUNITIES IN COLLEGES. The opportunity for secondary school students to take advanced placement courses for which they may receive credit at some colleges and universities is one of the most interesting recent developments in school-college relationships. Advanced placement opportunities are provided on a national basis through a program developed by the Advanced Placement Committee of the College Entrance Examination Board. Any secondary school may participate in this program by offering its more able students the opportunity to do college-level work in certain subject areas in their junior or senior year in high school. The Advanced Placement Committee has prepared suggestions for such courses in certain subjects, with descriptions of the advanced placement examinations for those courses. Beginning as an experiment in 1952 with only a small number of students participating, by 1961 13,500 students took the advanced placement examinations administered by the College Entrance Examination Board.

The Advanced Placement Committee of the College Entrance Examination Board submits the results on the examinations to colleges at the student's request. Each college sets its own standards for granting course credit on the basis of the results of these examinations. More than 400 colleges and universities in the United States at present are using the results of the advanced placement examinations of the College Entrance Examination Board for granting college credit to students for work taken in the secondary school. A recent report of this program reveals that a majority of the students whose scores on the advanced placement tests of the College Entrance Examination Board were submitted to colleges have been receiving credit for this work.

Although many colleges and universities are using the Advanced Placement Program of the College Entrance Examination Board, some institutions have developed their own programs cooperatively with nearby secondary schools. For some years the University of Connecticut has had such a cooperative program. This program, like that of the College Entrance Examination Board, is intended for superior students who, while still in the secondary school, are ready to do some college-level work. The Connecticut program in the beginning was developed cooperatively by representatives of the University and the high schools of the State. There are frequent meetings of principals, secondary school teachers, and members of the University faculty concerning the conduct of this program. Students who complete courses in the program with satisfactory marks receive advanced placement credit at the University of Connecticut. Transcripts of this work will be sent to other institutions which the students may decide to attend. The frequent contact between school and college faculties in cooperative advanced placement programs like the one at the University of Connecticut is contributing to closer working relationships and better articulation between colleges and secondary schools.

Some secondary schools have developed extensive advanced

placement offerings as a regular part of their educational program. The Palo Alto, California, senior high schools have such a program with advanced placement courses in English, science, social studies, foreign languages, and mathematics. In Palo Alto pupils may begin to plan their work with the advanced placement program in mind as early as the tenth grade, accelerating the usual senior high school studies so they may enroll for advanced placement courses in the eleventh and twelfth grades. In Palo Alto, as well as in other school systems, the advanced placement offerings are part of the program for intellectually talented pupils.

COLLEGE SUMMER PROGRAMS FOR SUPERIOR HIGH SCHOOL YOUTH. A number of colleges and universities in the United States have recently introduced summer programs for talented secondary school youth, as described in Chapter 11. Although these programs thus far have been largely experimental, some colleges have had considerable success with them. These programs are usually limited to pupils who have completed their junior or senior year in high school. Colleges and universities in Texas have developed such a summer program for talented high school youth.[3] First introduced as an experiment in 1956 at the University of Texas with twenty-eight high school pupils participating, the program was later extended to other leading Texas colleges and universities with several hundred pupils coming from high schools throughout the state. Science and mathematics have been emphasized in the Texas program, with students working in seminars and carrying on individual projects rather than the more formal activities of the typical high school or college class. The program is for enrichment rather than advanced placement credit. A follow-up study of teachers and students who have participated in the Texas summer program reveals outstanding achievement by students in later work in college and considerable value for articulation between high school and college.

THE MICHIGAN SECONDARY SCHOOL COLLEGE AGREEMENT. Although the colleges still influence the secondary school curriculum, there is increasing evidence of understanding between these institutions. The Eight-Year Study, completed in 1941, gave impetus to the movement to free secondary schools from rigid college entrance requirements and toward greater cooperation between colleges and secondary schools.

The Michigan Study of the Secondary School Curriculum, which began in 1937, represents an agreement made between the Michigan

[3] *The Step Ahead: Report on the Summer Programs for Talented High School Students,* Texas Education Agency, Austin, Texas, 1959, 57 pp.

College Association and the cooperating high schools to admit selected graduates from these schools, regardless of their pattern of courses, upon the recommendation of the school faculty. As a result of the successful operation of this agreement, it was revised in 1946 to include any accredited high school in the state. High schools agreed to observe the following four conditions:

1. To gather significant personal data about each student and summarize it for submission to the college
2. To provide a continuous study and evaluation of the curriculum
3. To carry on a continuous follow-up study of former students
4. To provide a program of vocational orientation and information relating to college courses

Eighty-four high schools were admitted to the program in the first two years of its operation; these represented more than 20 per cent of the secondary school pupils in the state of Michigan. In 1961, 272 high schools were participating in the program, slightly more than half of the eligible high schools.

ISSUES AND PROBLEMS

A number of current issues and problems in the relations of the secondary school to the elementary school, on the one hand, and to the college and university on the other are causing educators serious concern today. The following are some of the more important ones.

1. *How can teachers be encouraged not to criticize the instructional program and the achievement of pupils in previous grades?*

Teachers at each grade level tend to be unduly critical of the instructional program and the achievement of pupils in previous grades. This is true of teachers in the university, the secondary school, and the elementary grades. The problem cannot be solved by administrative regulation alone. It is far too deep-seated for that. Teachers need to recognize that the instructional program in all grades is equally important and that there are teachers at all levels who have professional skill and competence. The development of desirable professional attitudes toward their colleagues at other grade levels needs to begin in the teacher-education institutions; administrators, supervisors, and curriculum consultants should emphasize such professional attitudes; and local, state, and national professional organizations should study this problem and contribute to its solution. Until there is mutual confidence, understanding, and respect among teachers of all grade levels, satisfactory articulation in the total educational program will not be achieved.

2. *Can teachers keep informed concerning the content, methods, and materials of instruction for their subjects at other grade levels by reading courses of study and textbooks from other levels only or do they also need to meet with teachers of the other levels?*

This problem is especially serious in large cities where it is difficult for teachers from different grade levels to get together; in school districts with only elementary schools which send pupils to other districts for their high school education; and in sparsely settled rural communities where the distances are great between schools.

Some educators feel that if printed or mimeographed courses of study and curriculum guides are available, they will provide teachers with information about the course content and approaches to teaching at other grade levels and the problems will be solved. They feel teachers can also gain much help from studying the textbooks, reference materials, tests, and other instructional materials used at the various grade levels.

These materials for all subjects should, by all means, be placed in the teacher's professional workroom in every school or be given to every teacher for his subject area. Teachers should have easy and continuous access to all instructional materials used elsewhere in the educational program.

But many educators contend that this is not enough. They believe that the best way for teachers to keep informed about the instructional program at other grade levels is to have frequent contact with the teachers through workshops, study groups, and visitation. Teachers of English, mathematics, and other subjects in the secondary school should engage in a continuous program of class visitation in the elementary grades and the community college, as well as in other grades of the secondary school. There is no adequate substitute for personal contact among teachers as a way to keep informed about the instructional program elsewhere in the school system.

3. *How can better articulation in the administrative policies and practices of the elementary, the junior, and the senior high school be achieved?*

Pupils have difficulty in adjusting to certain administrative policies and practices as they go from school to school, including homework, marking, pupil progress reports, the class schedule, and discipline practices. For instance, conscientious pupils may become seriously upset if the marking system is sufficiently different in the senior from the junior high school so that what was previously considered to be A work, now becomes B or C work. Teachers in the upper grades sometimes justify this difference in practice in terms of a nebulous thing which they call "higher standards." Yet, it is hardly that. Rather, it indicates a difference in marking practices from one school to another. Similar differences are found from school to school in other administrative policies and practices.

The difference in practice from school to school is not in itself a serious matter. But it becomes serious if the transition from one administrative practice to another is too abrupt and if pupils are not adequately prepared to adjust to the change. The leadership in improving articulation in these policies and practices must come from administrators and supervisors. However, teachers have much responsibility for the implementation of certain administrative policies. They too need to participate in any efforts to bring about better articulation from the elementary school through the senior high school.

4. *How can the articulation between secondary schools and colleges and universities be improved?*

This problem is especially difficult because the graduates of a secondary school may matriculate at any one of hundreds of public or private colleges and universities located anywhere in the United States. Increasingly fewer secondary school graduates will attend the college of their first choice. Many of them may matriculate at institutions at a greater distance from their homes than in the past. Furthermore, the higher standard of work which is being required to remain in college may reduce the length of time students will be retained, and consequently give them less time to make an adjustment to the college program. The problem is also intensified by the higher entrance requirements of the colleges.

If the school and college faculties recognize the seriousness of the articulation problem, there are many things they can do to improve the present situation. School and college teachers can participate increasingly in the same professional organizations and, therefore, meet more often to study common problems; representatives of schools and colleges in the same region can meet regularly to discuss problems of articulation; teachers of such basic subjects as English, mathematics, science, and foreign languages in schools and colleges in the same region can develop courses in these subjects that are well coordinated in philosophy, content, methods, and instructional materials; representatives of schools and colleges can come to some agreement on the responsibilities of each for teaching certain fundamental skills and knowledge; and teachers in schools and colleges can establish mutual respect for each other's professional competence and judgment by meeting together more frequently. The lack of articulation between secondary schools and colleges is so serious that action on this matter cannot be delayed. Ways of establishing better coordination between the programs of the secondary schools and the colleges and universities must be found.

SELECTED REFERENCES

ASSOCIATION FOR SUPERVISION AND CURRICULUM DEVELOPMENT. *A Look at Continuity in the School Program.* Washington, D.C.: National Education Association, 1958, 305 pp.—A comprehensive treatment of the subject of continuity in the program of the total school system. These Chapters describe school practices in providing continuity.

COLLEGE ENTRANCE EXAMINATION BOARD. *The College Board Today.* New York: The Board, 1960, 40 pp.—A description of the organization, membership, services, and programs of the College Entrance Examination Board.

COLLEGE ENTRANCE EXAMINATION BOARD, COMMITTEE ON ADVANCED PLACEMENT. *Advanced Placement Program: Course Descriptions.* New York: The Board, 1960, 139 pp.—Describes the Advanced Placement Program and contains suggestions for courses in the program.

FUESS, CLAUDE M. *The College Board.* New York: Columbia University Press, 1950, 222 pp.—Presents a history of the activities of the College Entrance Examination Board during its first fifty years.

GRUHN, WILLIAM T., and DOUGLASS, HARL R. *The Modern Junior High School.* New York: The Ronald Press Co., 1956, pp. 352-57.—Suggests ways of improving articulation in school systems with a junior-high-school plan of grade organization.

Michigan Secondary School—College Agreement: Analysis of 1960 Reports. Bulletin No. 43, Lansing, Michigan: State Department of Public Instruction, 1960, 31 pp.—Report on the progress of this most significant plan of cooperation of secondary schools and colleges with regard to college admissions.

NATIONAL ASSOCIATION OF SECONDARY-SCHOOL PRINCIPALS. "Advanced Placement Programs in Secondary Schools." *Bulletin of the National Association of Secondary-School Principals,* 42:1-171, December, 1958.—Much of this issue is devoted to a discussion of the advanced placement programs in secondary schools, including an explanation of the program developed by the College Entrance Examination Board, descriptions of courses prepared by the Board, and descriptions of advanced placement programs at selected secondary schools.

NEVINS, REV. JOHN F. *A Study of the Organization and Operation of Voluntary Accrediting Agencies.* Washington, D.C.: The Catholic University of America Press, 1959, 401 pp.—A comprehensive research study of the history, purposes, organization, and policies of the regional accrediting associations of colleges and secondary schools in the United States.

TOMPKINS, ELLSWORTH, and GAUMNITZ, WALTER H. *The Carnegie Unit: Its Origin, Status, and Trends.* U.S. Department of Health, Education, and Welfare, Office of Education, Bulletin 1954, No. 7. Washington, D.C.: Government Printing Office, 1954, 58 pp.—Presents the origin and development of the Carnegie unit, its influence on secondary education, and efforts to improve or displace it.

TRAXLER, ARTHUR E., and TOWNSEND, AGATHA. *Improving Transition from School to College.* New York: Harper & Brothers, 1953, 165 pp.—A discussion of current problems with respect to college admissions and the transfer of students from high school to college.

WRIGHT, GRACE S. *Requirements for High School Graduation in States and Large Cities.* U.S. Department of Health, Education, and Welfare, Office of Education, Bulletin 1961, No. 2. Washington, D.C.: Government Printing Office, 1961, 29 pp.—Reviews changes in high-school graduation requirements in 50 states and in 50 representative cities in the United States with a population of 50,000 and over.

Part IV

IMPROVEMENT OF PROGRAMS

19

EVALUATING THE SECONDARY SCHOOL PROGRAM

A public secondary school is always in the limelight. It is good that it is so. The school belongs to the public. The better informed the people are about its program, the more intelligently they can make decisions either over the backyard fence or in the voting booth. In fact, alert secondary school principals are always working at keeping the parents and other citizens informed as to developments in the school. All of this is a form of evaluation, for somehow or other citizens make judgments regarding what they hear about a school, regardless of their sources of information.

The public will make judgments whether or not it is well informed. There always have been and always will be self-appointed judges of the schools, both local people and those who gain a national audience through their own publications and through the press. They set themselves up as judge and jury, and sometimes as prosecuting attorney as well. The school that has allowed its communication channels to deteriorate and never makes any attempt to gather systematic evidence about the success of its program should not be surprised that the public accepts these judges' evaluations. For the school may have no evidence to refute their accusations—at least no collected and analyzed data.

What is required in order to have the facts regarding the success of the school's program, both for the school and for the community to use in making their value judgments, is the theme of this chapter. Some of the deficiencies in this area, kinds of procedures that are being used effectively, the examples from schools that look at themselves critically, and the issues and problems involved are discussed in the following pages.

BASIC PRINCIPLES

The evaluation of a school's program seeks to determine the degree to which the objectives of the school are being attained.

Evaluation of a school has both a purpose and a direction. It tries to discover to what extent a school, a program, or a particular group is moving in the direction intended. How good are our schools, and in what ways? As a good teacher plans experiences for pupils in terms of the desired behavior changes, so should a school clarify first of all what it is trying to do. If it is seeking only to improve the intellectual attainment of its pupils, it will evaluate only those factors that identify such progress. If it seeks also to change pupils' civic behavior, to develop attitudes that deal with human values, and to inculcate a genuine appreciation for the culture of a people, its appraisal will have to be broader in scope.

Sometimes the process of evaluation gets the cart before the horse. Tests are given school-wide, and teachers plan their program and what they will emphasize in terms of preparing pupils to pass the tests. In evaluation, the setting up of objectives is the first step, which should precede, not follow, the gathering of data. The evaluative process is a means of finding out how well goals were achieved.

Evaluation is a continuous, cumulative process with systematic gathering of data for evaluative purposes.

Evaluation is rooted in the philosophy of society, the nature of the individual learner, and the goals of the school. Hence, it is never an isolated process nor an end point, something to be done at the end of a year or when a survey committee comes to the institution. It is not a goal in itself—a mere "test" to be passed. Evaluation is a continuous, cumulative process. Evidence of pupil growth and progress should be gathered daily in reference to goals established by the teacher and the school. Tests are used to determine how much pupils know before beginning the work and to diagnose difficulties.

Since modern secondary schools are attempting to promote many kinds of pupil growth, it is imperative that the school systematically gather evidence regarding a variety of desired behavior changes. Too frequently, schools test only for the retention of information and for the learning of skills, and assume that other goals are likewise being attained. This is a dangerous practice. When teachers try to help pupils develop desirable attitudes, functional skills and information, and vital understandings, a broad program of appraisal is needed to guide learning in all these areas. To secure evidence of growth or of difficulties within these wide areas of significant learnings, a great variety of appraisal instruments need to be used.

A systematic plan for gathering data means looking at the various kinds of objectives and the different facets of the schools' program, facilities, and staff to decide what kinds of information need to be collected about pupils' growth, about teachers, about experiences planned, and about facilities and resources available and how they are used. This kind of a process should go on day by day. The rushing and scurrying to fill in forms when an accreditation evaluation is to be done is not conductive to the improvement that results from constant self-evaluation.

The formulation of criteria as a basis for making judgments concerning the effectiveness of a school's program is an important part of evaluation.

The goals of a school or of a teacher are criteria by which judgments are made. But further standards are needed in order to make the judgment as objectively as possible. What does the objective mean as to the kinds of experiences pupils should have in a classroom? Should bright pupils all be segregated into special schools in order to acquire information more rapidly, or in order to satisfy a segment of the public? What is an adequate library in terms of the kinds and number of books and the way they are organized for use? What are poor, adequate, or excellent facilities for science laboratories? These are the kinds of questions that need to be considered.

The principles in this chapter, and throughout this book, serve as criteria by which practices are evaluated. They represent judgments based upon what is known about the learning process and the process of growth and development, and upon whatever other evidence is available from the behavioral sciences and research in education. They must be based on the kind of society in which the schools exist. Democratic values and purposes, as discussed in Chapters 1 through 3, are bases by which a criterion can be developed and judgments made.

Evaluation of a secondary school, or any segment of it, should have as its goal an objective, rigorous appraisal of practices.

This is the essence of evaluation. The use of reliable and valid instruments, suited to the purpose, is essential. Evaluation is improved when the best instruments available for measurement are used.

This principle presumes that there will be objective evidence on which to base judgments. All available information concerning the pupils that will be useful in the evaluation process should be collected. Individual differences must be discovered and recognized in the appraisal of whatever progress pupils make. There are data to be collected concerning the teachers, the community, the community's understanding of its school system, and the facilities provided. Evidence is also secured from testing out new ideas during ongoing research projects in the school system.

Some types of goals cannot be evaluated as objectively as others. Yet, that is no excuse to neglect finding out to the best of our ability how well they are achieved. Careful observation of behavior in the classroom can be objectified. New evaluating instruments that deal with intergroup relations are being constructed. Some instruments will have to be developed by the school itself. This will mean securing opinions as well as statistical data, for opinions are facts to be dealt with. Pupils' and teachers' perceptions of what a school program or a classroom experience is like are important information to have. So is the information as to how the perceptions of different people, pupils, administrators, teachers, and parents may differ. The aim of evaluation of the school's program should be moving away from the casual type of judgment toward more objective appraisal.

Evaluation should be a planned part of changes in the school's program.

Change is constantly taking place in school systems. In the secondary schools of the United States, the rate of change has been accelerated since the late 1950's. New content, new ways of organizing the curriculum and the school, new instructional procedures with the advent of developments in electronics are all described in this book. Some of these changes are being carefully evaluated, some so-called experiments include a rather shoddy attempt at evaluation, and others are not evaluated at all.

Generally, curriculum changes have been decided upon as a result of committee study, but only infrequently have committees planned ways of testing the innovations. The time to plan the evaluation of changes in the curriculum, or any aspect of the school program, is during the consideration of what the change will be like and how it will be put into effect. Thus, baseline data can be collected from the outset in order to furnish comparisons over a period of time.

The plan for reorganizing a schedule to provide greater flexibility or time for independent study, for introducing new content, for accelerating the bright students' program, or for using new educational media should have written into it the hypothesis as to how the change will affect learning, what data needs to be collected, what instruments are to be used, and how judgments will be arrived at. Otherwise, the school will be operating on the basis of shrewd guesses or someone's subjective judgment.

Usually people who are closely involved in experimentation with new ideas are enthusiastic about them. Unless there is objectivity and a sincere willingness to secure evidence, whether or not it supports the experiment, the school will not actually know whether the procedure is superior to previous practices. Nor will it be likely to know unless evaluation is built into the change.

Evaluation should involve all groups of people who are concerned with the educational program and who may be able to give information or judgments concerning its effectiveness.

Evaluation as an integral part of modern education should be in harmony with democratic principles and procedures. Since many persons jointly share in determining purposes and in planning learning experiences, they should also cooperate in appraising the learning process. This procedure insures efficiency, yet provides both for individual differences and for sharing common social purposes. Teachers who share the planning of a course, and make it a regular practice of meeting together, also evaluate cooperatively the progress made in the course. Evaluation of a school program, on a broader base, is a cooperative job for administrators, supervisors, counselors, teachers, parents, pupils, and citizens.

Each one has something to contribute to the total evaluative process. Parents can provide information with respect to changes in behavior. In the cooperative secondary school evaluation, discussed in this chapter, it has often been found that pupils furnish some perceptive answers and keen insights into the kinds of experiences they have in school. Teachers have various kinds of competencies and information to contribute.

Besides this, the process from the setting up of hypotheses to the judging of results is an educative one. Those who participate in the planning and decisions know and understand the purposes and results of changes. Certainly, this procedure is far superior to having uninformed critics on the outside sniping at any kind of change because of their fear of its costing more money or their fear of its dangerously tampering with the possibilities for their children's receiving a good education.

The various people mentioned can participate in different phases to the extent of their expertness and their sincere willingness to learn and to be objective about results. It is extremely important that school leaders, teachers, and citizens be willing to accept results that may indicate inferiority of a new procedure or program. Otherwise, evaluation becomes mere sham and window dressing.

It is also important that school administrators and supervisors take the lead in rigorous examination of the school program, in cooperation with lay citizens in developing pilot programs that are tested in the school situation.

Evaluation should provide for maintaining effective channels of communication with the community, as a part of the total evaluative process.

Evaluating the school goes on constantly whether or not a school system is in any way involved in studying its practices. The conversations at lunch or at the bridge table may either condemn or praise what the school is doing. Whatever people think about their schools, they have arrived at the opinions by means of hearsay, stories told by their children, newspaper publicity, school reports, demonstrations at the school, discussions in parent study groups, participation in school studies, or in some other way. They are making judgments about the school on the basis of the information they have.

Regular channels of communication need to be established so that the community is well informed about its schools. These are two-way channels, by which schools may also gather information and receive opinions from the community.

There are many ways by which intercommunication can be accomplished. Illustrations of how schools are keeping in close touch with the public are given in this chapter. The strength of the school program, the risk in making changes, and the pride in the schools are closely dependent upon the accuracy and amount of information that people have about their schools. They are also dependent upon the extent to which people's opinions can be made freely and frankly and the extent to which people feel they are a part of the school.

Self-evaluation should be a part of the process of appraisal.

All that has been said about a school system evaluating its practices presumes that principals, supervisors, and teachers will be making judgments about themselves. To be sure, they will often need expert help from research bureaus and consultants. But unless they are closely wrapped up in the process, the probabilities that anything will change as a result of whatever study is made are practically nil. Thick volumes of school evaluations made by some outside firm or expert often have had little influence on the practices of the schools studied. As involvement in studies spreads to the larger "self," the parents and public, the chances are greater that results will be translated into practices.

SOME COMMON PRACTICES

In American secondary education, the appraisal of practices has tended to be done more by outside agencies than by the school itself. The nature of these groups and the kinds of evaluative procedures used by them will be discussed in this section. Also pointed up here are some of the weaknesses in this whole area of determining the effectiveness of a secondary school program. The following list presents some of the difficulties faced in the evaluation of any phase of a school program:

1. Failure to gather data about the present status of the program
2. The lack of evaluative instruments for many types of goals
3. Emphasis placed upon quantitative as contrasted with qualitative factors
4. Reliance upon subjective judgments
5. Resistance to evaluation of many common practices
6. Teachers' unfavorable attitude toward research
7. Lack of time for teachers to do research
8. Lack of skill in research and evaluation
9. Lack of clerical aid
10. Difficulties in communication of findings
11. Difficulties in obtaining assistance in evaluation projects
12. Dearth of funds for evaluation

Some of these problems will be discussed further in this section.

INFREQUENT EVALUATION OF ESTABLISHED PRACTICES. Some practices in the secondary schools tend to resist critical scrutiny. Many practices have never been subjected to testing for experimental evidence. They have been tested in practice only and found to work, but no one knows for sure if they work better or worse than other practices would.

Generally, established practices have not been questioned, a basic step in evaluation. This is particularly true with regard to the methodology and content in subject fields. It took some emergency measures in a world war to convince educators that foreign languages could be taught more effectively a different way. Imagine the opposition encountered in an attempt to teach grammar from a linguistic approach rather than a formal conventional grammar approach (see Chapter 9). A whole host of factors would probably converge in a resistance movement—teachers prepared in the formal approach to grammar, textbook writers and publishers of standard texts, professors in English departments, parents who would fear lack of preparation for college, and many others.

On the other hand, there has been almost a revolutionary change in mathematics content, backed by a national effort on the part of many groups to improve the matematical background of the many people needed in the scientific and engineering professions. These newer program in mathematics are being evaluated in the schools.

It is a fact that newer practices are subject to more rigorous evaluation than are those already embedded in the program. The core curriculum has been evaluated in a number of instances. The use of television is the subject of a number of experimental programs. Team teaching, the use of teaching machines, and different forms of school organizations are being evaluated. Yet, opposition to any one of these practices, even as a danger to the profession, has been heard in professional or lay circles in spite of what the evidence might show. However, it should be pointed out that just as much of a problem is the "holy grail" attitude of some of the proponents of teaching by television, or of other new practices, who have an undeniable enthusiasm for the new approach that in itself limits the possibilities for objective evaluation.

Much of the evaluation of secondary school practices has been characterized by reliance upon subjective judgment. Human judgments enter into any type of appraisal in drawing conclusions from data. The interpretations of results of controlled experiments are subject to human error. However, in the realm of curriculum, instructional practices, and administrative and organizational practices, the evaluation has been mainly subjective because little data for appraisal purposes has been collected. Very often information regarding pupil progress is not systematically gathered or analyzed.

The beginnings of action research studies, which are described in this chapter, are promising. They are still found in only a few schools where there are strong research departments or research-oriented administrators, or where schools and universities are cooperating in studies.

NEGLECT OF EVALUATION OF SOME OBJECTIVES. Numerous kinds of important growth in adolescent behavior are not directly evaluated. While secondary schools may state objectives relating to attitudes, ideals, appreciations, and understandings, and plan pupil experiences relating to them, few teachers attempt to evaluate these behaviors directly. They either take for granted that these objectives are being attained, or else believe that the achievement of skills and facts indicates satisfactory growth in the more intangible goals.

Although this condition is largely due to a failure to see evaluation in terms of appraising growth toward objectives, it must also be attributed to the fact that few written appraisal instruments have been developed for measuring effectively attitudes and appreciations. The improvement of competency in evaluation, through sharpening observation powers and techniques, is just gaining hold in education. Careful observation can yield objective evidence of growth, especially of behavior indicating attitudes and habits.

PERIODICAL SCHOOL SURVEYS BY OUTSIDE AGENCIES. Periodical rather than continuous appraisal has been the rule in American education. Usually, the surveys conducted have been of the school system as a whole. When an accreditation evaluation was imminent, when the citizens of the community were demanding to know the facts, when a state legislature had enacted legislation requiring a study of the state's schools, or when the school wanted to gather data for a specific purpose, surveys have been made, often rather comprehensive in nature. But they have been sporadic, not ongoing as a part of the functioning of a school system.

The school surveys have, in the past, generally been conducted by outside agencies. Most schools were not equipped to conduct surveys of their own. Consequently, they have called in consultants and consulting firms to do the job. The standard procedure for the statewide and school system surveys has been to put the task in the hands of the outside consultants, who proceeded to gather data from the school records, from teachers and principals, from pupils, from the board of education, and from the community. Often pupils were tested with standardized achievement tests. Recent years have seen a change in these procedures in some kinds of surveys.

Large school systems that have research departments have conducted their own surveys. These departments of research or research bureaus have, however, been concerned mainly with surveys such as testing programs. They also collect data of value to the superintendent's office in making decisions. But the continuous research and evaluative studies that appraise practices in school have not, as a rule, been one of their main functions. Bureaus of research and field sservices in universities have also tended to deal more with surveys and testing than with experimental research.

ACCREDITATION AGENCIES AS EVALUATORS. Accreditation of secondary schools requires either visitation by a survey committee or filling out information forms, or both, regarding the extent to which the school meets established standards for organization, administration, personnel, pupils, program of studies, plant, equipment, and other items. This is done by the state agency, the state department of education, or by a regional agency. About 40 per cent of the states require accreditation of secondary schools. In a number of states, the accreditation is voluntary, as a procedure available to schools that wish to have their students accepted for transfer to other schools and colleges. The accreditation of secondary schools is a necessary safeguard for the state.

In recent years, more attention has been given to standards that require qualitative judgments. The primary purpose, according to the various state manuals describing standards for accreditation, is to assist local schools to improve their programs.

The state education agency generally cooperates with one of the regional accreditating agencies for secondary schools and colleges described in the last chapter. Since about 1940, the associations have used the Cooperative Study of Secondary School Standards (now called National Study of Secondary School Evaluation), which embodies a different principle than fixed standards. This procedure is described in the next section of this chapter.

QUANTITATIVE RATHER THAN QUALITATIVE DATA. Yardsticks for the evaluation and accreditation of a school are more quantitative than qualitative. The number of credits required for graduation, the number of academic courses taken, the number of graduates who succeed in college, the degrees attained by teachers, and the number of books in the library illustrate the quantitative measures. They tend to become the symbols for quality. Quantitative differences show only the differences in amount, not in kind or quality. The number of credits taken for graduation may be a significant fact, but it tells nothing about the quality of the program required for graduation. The qualitative differences of whatever is evaluated refer to differences in kind or in quality, such as, the improvements in behavior of pupils that may result from a practice. Pupils may, for example, have a better ability to do research independently if certain practices are instituted in their courses.

The very heart of education is a truly personal matter, the gaining of stature in the art of independent thought and in learning how to discover one's self, develop one's talents, and relate to other people. These ends are not easily subjected to counting procedures. Competence of teachers is more than the number of credits passed successfully or the degrees attained. Many of these aspects are important to be counted, but evaluation needs also to go more deeply into changes that occur.

EVALUATIVE ROLE OF COMMUNITY OPINION-MAKERS. It is a fair question to ask: Who is doing the evaluating of American secondary schools? The state and regional agencies evaluate for accreditation purposes, but they do not evaluate the success of practices within the schools. Only the school itself can and should properly perform that function. But, since few schools do, who is serving this evaluative role in communities where schools have abdicated their responsibility?

It is an interesting question to speculate on, for certainly there is no tangible evidence to furnish the answer. In the first place, every member of the community does his own individual evaluating. Often it may be the small dissatisfied groups, the malcontents, who form "investigating" bodies of their own. They may furnish the community with a type of information based on hearsay or prejudiced toward their own point of view. Such groups may become powerful factors in bond issues. They may be opinion-makers to be reckoned with. State legislative investigating committees may take on the function of evaluating the curriculum and issuing reports of their own, without any professional help.

The self-appointed judges, previously mentioned, gain considerable acceptance for their views through publications that have wide public sale. Frequently, their conclusions are based upon misinformation or lack of information, or are a deliberate attempt to promulgate their point of view. They may discuss even technical subjects such as reading with but little regard for the research in the field.

Learned societies issue statements regarding the weakensses in the secondary school program. Groups of professors of liberal arts, individual scholars, and professors of education pronounce judgments on the strengths and deficiencies of the schools. National agencies carry on scholarship testing programs that select outstanding students, and secondary schools are judged by the number of students who are selected.

These are evaluative judgments of the schools. They may be based on flimsy evidence, bias, misinformation, or on sound evidence. For good or for bad, they represent a form of evaluation of school practices that is likely to fill a vacuum left by the failure of secondary schools to appraise continuously and objectively their own practices.

IMPLEMENTATION OF THE PRINCIPLES

COMPREHENSIVE EVALUATION. An evaluation program in schools that are continuously looking at their program tends to be system-wide in nature. Many of the areas of the life of a school are closely interrelated. Data are usually gathered and studied about the program offered, the learning activities, the pupils, the extraclass activities, the guidance program, equipment and facilities, special services, the community, the graduates, the administration and organization of the school, the supervisory program, public relations, personnel procedures, and other aspects.

Curriculum improvement programs are usually evaluated in terms of the kinds of changes that are sought, such as changes in teachers, in teaching-learning procedures, in behavior of pupils, in community-school relationships, in the organization of the school, in instructional materials used, and in curriculum study procedures.

The National Education Association's pamphlet, *How Good Are Your Schools?* lists for professional and lay groups twelve major aspects of a school's program to be evaluated. It presents criteria for evaluation, with a number of questions under each criterion. Only major questions and the criteria are given here:

1. The School Program as a Whole
   Are the program and the facilities of your school system adequate?
   An effective school program . . .
      Provides an adequate program for all learners
      Recognizes differences in learners
      Provides favorable environment for teaching and learning
      Develops responsible citizens
      Identifies and meets individual needs
      Has home and community support
      Builds high morale
      Is periodically reviewed
2. The Elementary School Program
   Is your program adequately serving the elementary school children of your community?
   An adequate elementary school program . . .
      Is concerned with all aspects of pupil growth
      Develops ability to read, write, spell, speak, and compute
      Teaches children to think critically and imaginatively
      Adjusts the content and methods to the learners
3. The Junior High School

Is your school program adequately providing for the junior high school students of your community?

An adequate program for students of junior-high school age . . .

Strengthens and extends basic skills learned in elementary school

Fosters new interests and extends learnings in areas of special aptitude

Gives special attention to guidance

4. The Senior High School

Does your school program adequately meet the needs of the youth in your community?

An adequate high school program . . .

Offers courses to meet the needs of youth with various ambitions and interest

Adapts courses to the capacities of the learners

Offers guidance services

Provides school-wide activities

5. Education for Older Youth and Adults

Are the educational needs of older youths and adults adequately served by your public schools and/or other community agencies?

An adequate program for older youths and adults . . .

Provides access to opportunity for at least two years of college education

Provides educational opportunities needed by adults of all ages

6. Competent and Qualified Classroom Teachers

Is your school system staffed with a competent and certified staff of teachers?

The staff of a first-rate school system . . .

Is professionally prepared

Is balanced as to experience

Grows in service

Has good working conditions

Is on a professional salary schedule

Has high morale

7. Materials of Instruction

Are the teaching materials and equipment adequate in your school system?

A first-rate school system provides . . .

High quality textbooks and supplementary and reference materials

Other kinds of teaching tools

8. Buildings and Equipment

Do the buildings and equipment in your school system adequately provide an environment for quality education?

The building and equipment of a first-rate school system should . . .

Be up to date, safe, and clean
Provide adequate space for the pupils enrolled
Provide essential special facilities
Have maximum utilization by schools and community

9. A Proficient Administrative and Supervisory Staff
Is the administrative and supervisory staff of your school system adequate to insure a productive educational program?
Administrative leadership . . .
Recognizes the need for qualified staff
Respects and develops the competencies of all staff members

10. Sound and Adequate Finance
Are your schools adequately financed?
A sound school finance program . . .
Utilizes a variety of sources of funds
Provides adequate funds
Receives adequate local financial support
Receives adequate state financial support
Uses available federal funds

11. A Forward-Looking Board of Education
Does your board of education provide the leadership you want for your schools?
The board of education in a community should . . .
Enlist able persons as members
Develop school policies but not administer them
Have community support
Be fiscally independent

12. Citizen Interest
Is citizen interest in your community adequately supporting the schools?
Citizen interest in the schools is . . .
Indicated by parental interest
Shown by active support of community agencies
Aided by information[1]

The National Congress of Parents and Teachers prepared a guide titled *Looking in on Your Schools* for P.T.A. fact-finding groups to use in working with school people. This guide deals with purposes or goals of the school, curriculum, teachers, guidance and counseling services, physical and mental health programs, instructional materials and resources, library services, interpersonal relations, "pursuit of excellence," school plant and facilities, financing, size of the school district, school board, and the parent-teacher association.

One of the significant studies of the American Association of School Administrators in cooperation with the National School

[1] Adapted from *How Good Are Your Schools?* Washington, D.C.: National Education Association, 1958, pp. 6-30.

Boards Association was a special project on evaluating school systems. The study identified a number of school systems that were doing outstanding work in evaluating themselves. An intensive study was made of the procedures used by these schools and published in a series of pamphlets, which present case studies of how twenty-eight different school districts in the United States evalute their schools. These are excellent, comprehensive descriptions to show what practices schools have in self-evaluation.

CHECKLIST OF IMPERATIVE NEEDS. Under the direction of the Committee on Curriculum Planning and Development of the National Association of Secondary-School Principals a statement of ten imperative needs of youth was developed, and a check-list of secondary school curriculum practices organized around these imperative needs. It was an instrument for a principal and faculty to use in looking at its program in terms of analyzing how well it was meeting these needs of youth. The check-list provided for composite judgments on the items, with ratings on a five-point scale from very inferior to very superior. Judgments were the faculty's opinions about characteristics of the school program, but the use of the check-list served to encourage considerable study as a self-evaluative process.

The kinds of practices evaluated can be illustrated by a few examples of statements listed under the imperative needs as items on the checklist:

> The school uses the work experiences of its students to enrich the instructional programs of both employed and unemployed youth in school.
> The school evaluates its health program in terms of better health among its pupils as indicated by means of periodic physical examinations
> The school bases its program of citizenship education on values to which American democracy is committed and on a continuing study of civic, social, and economic problems in our society.
> The school provides situations designed to develop wholesome boy and girl friendships not only in the classroom but also in after-school activities.
> The school uses several areas of the curriculum and a diversity of means to help pupils become alert and responsible consumers.
> The school provides experiences for all students designed to help them develop the habit of searching for reasonable explanations to natural phenomena rather than blindly relying upon superstition and pseudo-science.
> The school provides opportunities for pupils to increase their appreciations through creative work in such areas as landscaping, poetry, the drama, music, etc.

The school maintains developmental reading programs in order that pupils' increased ability to read may also bring satisfaction and enjoyment in this method of using leisure time.

The school provides for the critical examination and evaluation of differing and conflicting value systems.

The school broadens the ordinary work in written expression by providing opportunities for various kinds of writing including creative writing.[2]

PLAN OF SECONDARY SCHOOL EVALUATIONS. The Cooperative Study of Secondary School Standards, mentioned in the previous section of this chapter, represented a considerable step ahead of previous accrediting procedures. The study involved the six regional accrediting associations who entered into a cooperative study of secondary school standards in 1940. In this plan, the single inspector of a school was replaced by a visiting committee composed of faculty members of high schools and colleges, administrative and curriculum specialists, and practitioners. Another significant change is the fact that these committees make their judgments, not on the basis of uniform minimum standards, but upon how well the school is achieving its stated objectives. Stress is placed also on how the secondary school may be helped to improve.

The study, now called the National Study of Secondary School Evaluation, publishes *Evaluative Criteria* for use in the school evaluations. These are used widely by the regional accrediting bodies and by state departments of education for evaluation of secondary schools for accreditation purposes.

The Criteria include forms for entering data and judgments by the school faculty, which are later checked by the evaluating committee. The data forms include philosophy and objectives, school and community, program of studies, student activity programs, instructional materials services—library and audio-visual, health services, school plant, school staff and administration, individual staff members, and statistical and graphical summaries of the evaluation. In addition, there is an evaluation form for each of the subject fields: agriculture, art (including crafts), business education, core program, distributive education, driver education, English, foreign languages, health education, home economics, industrial arts, mathematics, music, physical education for boys, physical education for girls, science, social studies, vocational trade and industrial education.

A third significant development in these procedures is that the

[2] William L. Ranson, "How Well Does Your High School Rate on the Imperative Needs of Youth?" *Bulletin of the National Association of Secondary-School Principals*, 33:13-40, No. 164, October, 1949. (Selected items).

school faculty makes its own self-evaluation first. The faculty forms its own committees and collects data on pupil population, the community, the faculty, the activities, the services, the plant, and the school program. The faculty develops or uses its already developed statement of philosophy and goals of the school against which it evaluates its practices. In the better situation, the school spends at least a year in studying its program before the evaluation committee visits the school. This self-evaluation is perhaps the most valuable phase of the study for purposes of faculty growth.

The evaluating committee spends a number of days in the school interviewing teachers, pupils, principal, and community members. The committee visits classes and activities and meets with groups of faculty members and students. It then gives its judgment as to the various items rated by the faculty, changing the ratings where it feels such change is warranted, and makes its recommendations in the form of both an oral report to the faculty and a written report to the school.

Schools which use these appraisal plans most effectively continuously collect and organize data concerning the various aspects of the pupil growth and the school's program.

EVALUATION PROCEDURES FOR JUNIOR HIGH SCHOOLS. A number of states have developed evaluation plans for junior high schools, for example, California, Utah, Texas, Illinois, Oklahoma, and Connecticut.

The Utah *Junior High-School Evaluative Criteria,* published by the Utah State Department of Public Instruction, developed from a study over a six-year period, is an example of an appraisal instrument planned especially for junior high schools and adapted to their characteristics and purposes. The plan provides for both self-evaluation and evaluation by a visiting committee. It is suggested that faculty, students, and parents participate in the evaluation process. It expresses the point of view that evaluation should be based on the school's objectives. Pupil population and school community data are collected. Included in the evaluation are fourteen subject areas, six service areas, and some general appraisal of the school.

One of its unique features is the basing of evaluation in part on some of the newer concepts and ideas growing out of the studies on staff utilization under the direction of the National Association of Secondary-School Principals, including effective use of teacher competencies, educational materials, and school facilities. The use of flexible class size and grouping, independent study, modern instructional media; stress on individual achievement levels and on maximum development of capabilities are characteristic of these criteria. The publication of the Connecticut State Department of Education, *An Assessment Guide for Use in Junior High Schools,* outlines professional staff evaluation and study of five areas: pupils, philosophy, program, personnel, and plant.

APPRAISAL OF GROWTH IN CITIZENSHIP. Another kind of evaluation study is the one concerned with certain aspects of the secondary school program. An example of such a study that involved the elementary schools as well as the secondary schools is the Detroit Citizenship Education Study, carried on over a period of years. In the study, the schools sought to find out what gains pupils made in the areas of interest and competence in active citizenship and what helped to bring about these results. Data gathered included inventory of values and beliefs concerning democracy and democratic practices.

FOLLOW-UP STUDIES. High schools attempt to appraise their programs by making follow-up studies of former students, both dropouts and graduates. The depression years of the 1930's gave a great impetus to some excellent studies of youth who had dropped out of school. Howard M. Bell's *Youth Tell Their Story* is a classic example. A number of these were done under the auspices of the American Youth Commission, created in 1935 by the American Council on Education to study the problems of youth. These studies generally dealt with civic life, vocation, home and family life, health, education, and recreational and social life. (See Selected References for a list of some of these youth studies.)

Studies of drop-outs more often tend to be concentrated upon why people leave school, while studies of graduates made through contacts with colleges and employers are more likely to include the graduates' evaluation of the school program. Many high schools consistently follow-up their graduates in institutions of higher learning as a part of the evaluation of their programs.

The follow-up studies of the Illinois Secondary School Curriculum Program, under the leadership of the State Department of Public Instruction and the University of Illinois, included sixty-one secondary schools. This program is now known as the Illinois Curriculum Program and located in the State Department of Public Instruction, Springfield, Illinois. Questionnaires to graduates, parents, and teachers dealt with such questions as "What do you think?" "How much real-life help did they get?" "How much were you helped by your high school?" and "How well equipped are you for effective living?"

The areas of their life and activities included earning a living, developing an effective personality, living healthfully and safely, managing personal finances, spending leisure time, taking part in civic affairs, preparing for homemaking, and using educational opportunities.[3]

Follow-up study of evaluation of employers and former students is illustrated by one conducted by the Torrance Unified School District, Torrance, California. Its purpose was to evaluate a new phase of the program, work experience. The distributive and diversified work experience programs had begun as pilot programs. This was a part of the study made to determine whether these experiences should become a total part of the program. Former students of the program were queried as to motives for enrollment in the program, attitudes toward the program, present employment and future plans, what effect the program had on the students' attendance and school citizenship, and a general evaluation of the benefits of the program. The employers answered questions regarding the quality of former students' background in certain skills, their attitudes, their productiveness on the job, the assistance derived by students from the work experience, and the employers' attitudes toward continuing to cooperate in the program.

OPINION SURVEYS. Surveys of opinions used by school systems suffer from some of the same limitations as follow-up studies, since they are made after the events have occurred and are opinions of someone. Yet, the opinions that parents have about their schools are important facts to know since such a survey may uncover a great deal of misinformation that the public has about its schools, or it may lead to more effective communication channels between school and community.

The Illinois Inventory of Parent Opinion, used rather extensively in studies in Illinois as well as elsewhere, inquires about personal facts concerning the responder, his satisfactions or dissatisfactions with the school's program for his child, the teachers' treatment of the child, the amount of time spent in homework, activities and equipment in the school, the parents' visits to the school, information received from the school, and the parents' opinions regarding certain issues in school finance and program. There is a similar Illinois Inventory of Pupil Opinion as well as an Illinois Inventory of Teacher

[3] Kenneth B. Henderson, *Principal Findings of the Follow-Up Study of the Illinois Secondary School Curriculum Program*, Illinois Secondary School Curriculum Program Bulletin No. 17, Circular Series A, No. 51, Springfield, Illinois: Superintendent of Public Instruction, 1951, 88 pp.

Opinion. These inventories are used by school administrators and school boards to gather opinions from the community about its schools, by supervisors to determine teacher opinions and information with regard to their practices, and by teachers to discover more about their pupils' opinions of the school and school practices. These are examples of types of survey forms available for secondary schools to use.

The Denver public schools have conducted opinion surveys of the adult population in the city. Three phases of the 1959 study (*Denver Looks at Its Schools*) dealt with the citizens' opinions about the quality of teaching and learning, their opinions about certain values in education besides subject matter, and their sources of information about the schools.

ACTION RESEARCH AND EXPERIMENTAL PROGRAMS. One of the highest quality forms of evaluation of a school is the process of doing research on practices in the actual school situation. The school builds in the evaluation of a practice when it is established. Some of the research is done on a more formally structured basis, such as an experimental research study in which an experimental group and a control group of pupils are compared, but all of it is an attempt to be more objective and research-minded in finding out the success or failure of an innovation.

A type of research carried on in schools to evaluate practices is called action or operational research. This type of research is carried on by educators in order to study their problems scientifically and, thus, improve their own practices.

Since action research tests out practices in a school situation, it is a way of evaluating the effectiveness of what the school does. For example, on a more simple level, a junior high school teacher may be dissatisfied with the results of the method he uses in the teaching of spelling. Consequently, he studies the various procedures which he might use, discusses them with his principal, and arrives at a method that he decides to use. The next step is to develop an hypothesis which includes both a statement of the goal and the action to be taken to achieve the goal, such as, "If the misspelled words from the writing my pupils do for all their classes are used as a basis for spelling instruction, their spelling will improve." He will then plan what data he needs to collect with regard to spelling before he begins, during the time he is carrying on this study, and at the end of the study. After he has planned how to carry on this action research, what data to gather, and how he is going to use the data to evaluate the results of the action, he begins the actual research in his classroom. He may have decided to have students keep progress charts of their own improvement to involve them in the experiment. At the end of the time set for the study, with the help of his principal, he draws his own conclusions as to whether or not the evidence shows that pupils have made greater progress than over a previous similar period of time using his former procedure.

The process is intentionally simplified in this brief example, in order to give an overview of the steps taken in action research. In many instances, action research studies will involve a number of teachers working together on a study, or an entire department, under the supervision of a principal, department head, or curriculum consultant. In most instances, the teachers or the school will be evaluating a new program or practice that they wish to try out.

In a sense, action research is a rather revolutionary concept applied especially to curriculum and instructional practices. For one thing, those who are to carry out the findings are involved in the doing of the research, including the hypothesizing, the development of the research design, the gathering of data, and drawing conclusions. But even more radical is the notion that those who do the research want to improve their own, not someone else's practices. In this process of more rigorously testing out ideas the researcher (teacher) is personally involved, both an advantage and a disadvantage. The process does not pretend to arrive at final answers, but it does provide for a careful analysis of the results of what one is doing. As in any research, the questioning mind of the teacher involved is a most significant factor. It tests ideas derived from more basic research in the school and classroom situation.

Illustrations of two action research programs in the Indianapolis public schools are presented briefly. The first is an experimental program in remedial reading to meet the needs of underachievers in ninth grade classes. The hypotheses tested was that through a special program of instruction for two periods at the 9B level, most underachievers will attain their levels of expectancy in reading and grammar in one semester and much greater pupil growth in reading and other language skills will be attained than in classes in which one period a day is devoted to reading instruction. The daily double period of instruction was offered with individual and group instruction. Data on the students was collected by diagnostic tests, readiness tests, inventories and questionnaires to identify specific difficulties and interests. Achievement tests were used to measure pupil growth throughout the semester and inventories and questionnaires secured pupil, parent, and teacher evaluations regarding the effectiveness of the plan.

A second research project was a study of the use of calculating machines in teaching general mathematics as compared with the usual method of teaching, testing with eighth grade students the hypothesis that students who use calculating machines in studying portions of a ninth-grade general mathematics course will show significant gains in paper and pencil computation and in arithmetic reasoning over those who do not use the calculating machines. Data were again collected by standardized tests and other means to test the hypothesis.

EVALUATION OF CLASSROOM CLIMATE. Some promising evaluating instruments are being developed to record objectively for evaluative purposes what is happening in the classroom. These generally record teacher and pupil interaction by a competent observer. The goal is to develop a reliable type of observation technique which can accurately describe certain aspects of the human environment within the classroom. For example, the *Classroom Observation Schedule* of the Bureau of Educational Research, University of Illinois, looks at the way the teacher differentiates the work in the classroom, the interactions between teacher-pupil and pupil-pupil, the leadership of teacher and pupils, the use of instructional materials, and the types of activities in which the pupils engage. A number of elements are evaluated as to whether they are negative or positive kinds of actions by pupils and teacher.

ISSUES AND PROBLEMS

There is no doubt that there has been an upsurge of interest of the public in its secondary schools. The greatly increased amount of space devoted to public education in the popular magazines is ample evidence of such interest. Articles deal with "How good are our schools?" "Are the high schools doing the job?" "What are high schools for?" These statements by educators and laymen are evaluative in nature. Many of them are frankly critical. Some compare examination scores of present-day pupils with those of pupils thirty to a hundred years ago. Others compare the success in college of public and private school graduates. Conclusions are drawn to support the particular author's thesis—the great debate goes on.

But is this enough evidence? By what criteria is excellence judged? Do the evaluations in the public media relate to the objectives of the American secondary school for this particular society or to the values inherent in a democratic philosophy of living? These questions relate to some of the major issues in this field.

1. *Should evaluation of a secondary school be done by outside
agencies or by the school and community itself?*

Studies of what happens after a survey by an outside agency has
been completed have thrown considerable doubt on its value for
change in school practices. It seems to take more than facts and com-
parative figures to move a school faculty from its state of equilibrium.
The evidence shows that involvement in an enterprise is directly
related to the factor of willingness to change. The more recent procedures for evaluation of secondary schools have been in the direction of self-evaluation, not as an instrument of inspection, but as an
instrument for improvement. For evaluation without subsequent improvement is a dead end. The facts are nice to know, to take pride
in, or to grumble about but they may not be a means to a better
school system.

To be sure, evaluations conducted by the school itself, with the
assistance of outside consultants and of the community, involve time
and work. Some schools have decided that the effort is worth the
results. Others feel that the evaluation of the school is a job for a
survey done by a state university, a state department of education,
or other outside group. The question that faces any school and its
community is whether the judgments that any formal or informal
outside group makes concerning secondary education shall be accepted verbatim, or used only as ideas for looking at their own
schools.

2. *Who shall determine the criteria for evaluation?*

A closely allied question deals with who sets the standards. Should
these be set by groups that have limited background in and knowledge of the public schools, by the professional staff of the school,
or by the lay public? There have been instances when a group in
the community, such as a group of college professors, have made
recommendations for changes in the school system, such as, the institution of city-wide examinations at the end of certain grades in
order to determine promotions, establishment of separate and fixed
curricula, the elimination of pupils who could not meet certain standards, and the like.

The important questions are: By what criteria did they arrive at
these recommendations? Were they qualified to decide what the
secondary schools should do? One might ask the same questions
concerning any so-called expert, but the point is that reports issued
by any influential community group will have considerable effect on
people's thinking. The public may not stop to question the rationale
upon which these judgments were based.

It is doubtful that any outside group should set up the criteria, for this in effect means that they also set the goals for the schools. Their ideas should be considered in any study, for different people who have some expertness to contribute and community citizens should participate in formulating criteria. Outside consultant help can be secured to assist schools and communities in their study. This does not mean that these consultants set the standards.

3. *Should evaluation of the program of a secondary school be based only upon pupil achievement in subject content or should it also give consideration to various factors that may influence pupil growth and development?*

This is one of the questions that secondary school leaders and faculties will have to decide. Readily quantified types of data have been most popular in evaluative studies. Standardized achievement tests are available and readily administered. When it comes to measuring the quality of a classroom climate, the task is not an easy one. The kinds of instruments that assess growth in areas of human relations, attitudes, and values are still in their infancy. Thus the tendency has been to take the easy way out. The school's goals include international understanding, civic interest, democratic commitments, and scientific inquiry but the behaviors that typify these goals are rarely measured.

One secondary school asked itself the following questions in order to find out if "we cut the mustard?" If this particular school went no further, was it evaluating all of its goals?

1. What is the native ability of the pupils?
2. What was the achievement of the pupils on the survey tests?
3. Are the pupils up to grade level?
4. How well are pupils achieving with respect to their academic ability?
5. Have pupils made a normal growth between test periods?
6. Does the growth vary with the sexes?

The temptation is great to collect only the easily collectible data. The qualitative type of information that gets at feelings, behavior, attitudes, and mental health, may be the most significant both for its own sake and for the effect that such factors have on achievement.

4. *Should evaluation of secondary school practices be based upon opinions and what other schools are doing or upon experimental programs and research?*

It is evident that much of the evaluation of secondary schools rests upon someone's judgment of the situation by the use of certain criteria. The secondary school evaluations have broadened the base of that judgment to include the school faculty itself.

Some of the published reports referred to in this book were based upon visits to schools and discussions with school administrators. They may represent one person's judgment as to what the high school should be like. Others are made by deliberative bodies out of their own experience. These are influential reports but the problem is that they have often been accepted without question as the basis for making appraisals of high school practices. The only evaluation of their program that some high schools have done is to check their practices against these recommendations. If their school compared favorably, then the community was given the impression that the quality of the program was good.

Schools have, in a number of instances, collected a sampling of practices in other secondary schools, and if they found that their practices came up to this level, their judgment was that they had a good school.

Norms were not intended to be absolute standards that fit all cases. This kind of evaluation, while it may be helpful, is far from enough. The issue is whether secondary school evaluations shall be made by such a superficial judgmental means or by the conduct of carefully evaluated experimental programs. Research must become much more prevalent than it has been in the past if the answer is in favor of the latter course. For one-stand surveys characterize secondary school evaluations more accurately than do such comprehensive studies as the Eight-Year Study of the Progressive Education Association, in which a number of secondary schools participated for a period of eight years collecting data on the students in high school and later on in their college careers.[4]

5. *Should the programs of secondary schools be evaluated regularly by state-wide or national testing programs?*

This issue has previously been referred to in this book. It is an extremely significant one which applies both to who determines the curriculum, as discussed in Chapter 6, and to how evaluation of secondary school programs is accomplished.

Some people are urging that state-wide tests be given to pupils every year in order to see how well the pupils in each school do. The community could then judge whether or not it had good schools by comparing these results with those of the neighboring school district and the state as a whole. Both school people and lay citizens

[4] See Wilford M. Aikin, *The Story of the Eight-Year Study*, New York: Harper & Bros., 1942, 157 pp.

are included among the voices raised for state examinations. Some have advocated national testing programs to determine how well pupils and schools meet national standards. In some respects, the standardized college entrance examinations and the merit type scholarship tests are being used for this purpose by schoolmen and by the public.

All of the preceding issues are related to this one. The question of local versus state or national control is involved. So is the question of freedom of schools to be experimental, to do research on new procedures, to change with the times. The answer should lie in what is best for optimum development of the community's children.

2. *Shall the standards by which attainment of an education is judged be (1) credits, degrees, marks, diplomas, and other external evidence or (2) a change of behavior for the pupils?*

The use of credits, marks, degrees, and diplomas pose a dilemma for us in education. They are perfectly good ways which we have invented to provide information as to achievement, but the trouble is some pupils persist in making them the real ends toward which they strive. These pupils have turned the tables on us and have made these external trappings the ends of their education, substituting them for a genuine interest in and a desire to learn. Someone has once said facetiously that perhaps the best thing for colleges to do would be to give each student a degree as soon as he enrolled, and then those would remain who really wanted to attain an education. Undoubtedly there are students in both colleges and secondary schools who are just marking time in their education, getting by with doing the least possible in order to attain the necessary marks or degrees.

The external devises are quantitative aspects of measurement. Looking at a change in behavior involves more of the qualitative aspects of measuring the results of a school curriculum. But quantity and quality should go hand in hand.

In recent years, the school has been moving toward change of behavior as its goal. Questioning minds have rightfully criticized such vague meaningless generalities as "preparation for life" or "life adjustment" as goals which are supposed to furnish direction for the school's general education program. Neither one gives the slightest clue as to the kind of behavior expected of a person who succeeds in life. If we teach for the purpose of changing behavior of pupils, we are inevitably led into consideration of how a person acts, what he says or reads, how he spends his spare time, and how he treats others. Included are questions of behavior that indicates a willingness to act on the bases of carefully weighed evidence, the ability to gather evidence, to reason logically and soundly.

Thus the quality of the experience becomes the standard, and quality is something that cannot be measured numerically. If a student has had a high quality experience he will show it through the way he thinks, acts, and talks about school, his enthusiasm for continued learning, and his very actions in the home and in the school as well as in the community at large.

SELECTED REFERENCES

AMERICAN ASSOCIATION OF SCHOOL ADMINISTRATORS. *American School Curriculum.* (Thirty-first Yearbook). Washington, D.C.: National Education Association, 1953, Chaps. 11 and 12.—These two chapters are on appraising pupil achievement and total effectiveness of the school. Contains a list of opinion survey instruments for judging a school.

AMERICAN ASSOCIATION OF SCHOOL ADMINISTRATORS. *Judging Schools with Wisdom.* Washington, D.C.: National Education Association, 1959, not paged.—A pamphlet developed by this Association and the National School Boards Association that contains twelve criteria for school evaluating programs.

AMERICAN ASSOCIATION OF SCHOOL ADMINISTRATORS. *Quest for Quality.* Washington, D.C.: National School Boards Association and American Association of School Administrators. 1960.—A series of fourteen booklets of about 30 to 40 pages each which describe how a selected group of school districts evaluate their educational programs. The approaches used in evaluation are described by means of case studies of schools in different size and type communities. The last booklet, No. 14 deals with "Keys to Quality," an overall summary of procedures used by these schools.

ANDERSON, VERNON E. *Principles and Procedures of Curriculum Improvement.* New York: The Ronald Press Co., 1956, Chap. 11.—A chapter on evaluating curriculum improvement and conducting action research in the schools.

ASSOCIATION FOR SUPERVISION AND CURRICULUM DEVELOPMENT. *Research for Curriculum Improvement.* (1957 Yearbook). Washington, D.C.: National Education Association, 1957, Chaps. 1-9.—Gives an excellent picture of what research in improvement of curriculum practices is, how it is conducted, how teachers are involved in it as a means of evaluating an important aspect of the school.

COREY, STEPHEN M. *Action Research to Improve School Practices.* New York: Bureau of Publications, Teachers College, Columbia University, 1953, Chaps. 1-3.—A good statement on action research that contains helpful examples of two action research studies.

DIMOND, STANLEY E. *Schools and the Development of Good Citizens: The Final Report of the Citizenship Education Study.* Detroit: Wayne University Press, 1953, 215 pp. —An account of how schools participated in research studies to evaluate the effect on pupils of citizenship education.

HAND, HAROLD D. *What People Think About Their Schools.* New York: Harcourt, Brace & World, Inc., 1948, 219 pp.—A discussion of how schools and teachers can conduct opinion studies. Contains the Illinois inventory of parent and pupil opinions.

NATIONAL ASSOCIATION OF SECONDARY-SCHOOL PRINCIPALS. "Seeking Improved Learning Opportunities." *Bulletin of the National Association of Secondary-School Principals,* 45:1-285, January 1961.—This final report of staff utilization studies conducted in schools contains a number of examples of action research studies which focus on improvement of practices.

NATIONAL SOCIETY FOR THE STUDY OF EDUCATION. *Citizen Cooperation for Better Public Schools.* (Fifty-third Yearbook, Part I). Chicago, Illinois: University of Chicago Press, 1954, Chap. 11.—A chapter on the citizen's participation in evaluating a school program.

NATIONAL STUDY OF SECONDARY SCHOOL EVALUATION. *Evaluative Criteria.* Washington, D.C. American Council on Education, 1960, 376 pp.—A standard set of criteria used in evaluating secondary schools throughout the country.

RICH, WILLIAM B. *Approval and Accreditation of Public Schools: Responsibilities and Services of State Departments of Education.* United States Department of Health, Education, and Welfare, Office of Education, Washington, D.C.: Government Printing Office, 1960, 40 pp.—Gives information on practices of the different state departments of education with respect to accreditation of secondary schools.

SHUMSKY, ABRAHAM. *The Action Research Way of Learning.* New York: Bureau of Publications, Teachers College, Columbia University, 1958, Chaps. 4-10.—Action research for the teacher, including both practical and theoretical analysis of the concept. The author holds that attitudes and personal perceptions of the research do and should enter into the study.

TABA, HILDA and NOEL, ELIZABETH. *Action Research: A Case Study.* Washington, D.C.: Association for Supervision and Curriculum Development, 1957, 58 pp.—Descriptions of action research conducted by teachers.

WILSON, L. CRAIG and OTHERS. *School-Community Improvement.* New York: Harcourt, Brace & World, Inc., 1959, Chaps. 10-16.—A readable account of how a county worked toward improvement of its schools, showing how the school and community work together in a continuous study and collection of information to evaluate what it was doing.

WRIGHTSTONE, J. WAYNE and OTHERS. *Evaluation in Modern Education.* New York: American Book Co., 1956, Chaps. 1-4 and 23.—Part I is helpful for getting an understanding of the nature of evaluation and what it includes. The last chapter concerns the evaluation of school and teaching practices.

YOUTH STUDIES DONE IN THE 1930's

1. AMERICAN YOUTH COMMISSION: *Youth and the Future.* Washington, D.C.: American Council on Education, 1942.
2. BELL, HOWARD M.: *Youth Tell Their Story.* American Youth Commission Study, Washington, D.C.: American Council on Education, 1939.
3. ECKERT, RUTH E. and MARSHALL, THOMAS O.: *When Youth Leave School.* The Regents' Inquiry, New York: McGraw-Hill Book Co., Inc., 1939.
4. FULLER, RAYMOND G.: *A Study of Youth Needs and Services in Muncie, Indiana.* American Youth Commission Study, Washington, D.C.: American Council on Education, 1938.
5. LOVEJOY, GORDON W.: *Paths to Maturity.* Cooperative Personnel Study, Chapel Hill: University of North Carolina, 1940. (North Carolina Youth Study)
6. McGILL, NETTIE P. and MATHEWS, ELLEN M.: *The Youth of New York City.* New York: The Macmillan Co., 1940.
7. PAYNE, STANLEY L.: *Thirty Thousand Urban Workers.* Social Problems Series No. 6, Works Progress Administration, Washington, D.C.: Government Printing Office, 1940. (Interviews with 30,000 youth).
8. RAINEY, HOMER P.: *How Fare American Youth?* New York: Appleton-Century-Crofts, Inc., 1937.

9. SPAULDING, FRANCIS T.: *High School and Life*. The Regents' Inquiry, New York: McGraw-Hill Book Co., Inc., 1939.
10. WILLIAMS, CLAUDIA; BRYANT, DRAYTON S. and JONES, AARON E.: *Youth—California's Future*. Sacramento, California: State Department of Education and State Relief Administration, 1940.

20

A NEW LOOK AT SECONDARY EDUCATION

The secondary school in America is in the process of "becoming." More changes are taking place in secondary schools than in either elementary schools or colleges. It is good that this is so. Free public education through the high school grades has played a major part in making possible the technical and social advances and in developing the greatness of this country, which was molded out of many heterogenous groups with differing backgrounds, purposes, and beliefs. The radical idea that all people need to be educated to a high level and that it is the responsibility of the state to see that they have that opportunity was a center of controversy for many years. Thus, both the idea and the process by which it took form were revolutionary. The high schools set out to do a job that fostered this American dream and that suited the times of a nation growing and expanding in population, wealth, and the provision of a good life for greater numbers of its people.

But we are now living in a revolutionary age in which change not only in science and technology but also in international relations occurs almost overnight and is constantly accelerating. The strides forward in speed of travel are symbolic of what is happening. It is impossible to conceive of where technical and scientific advances will take us in the next ten to twenty years. Changes in political traditions and forms and in social organization will inevitably follow. Ways of dealing with other nations must change in a world where soon even the small nations may have the power of destruction of civilization in their hands. In this most difficult and challenging period, mankind has the power to make the most awesome choice in all history; the choice between total destruction and eliminating war and alleviating the ills of fellow-man. For it is now possible to visualize a comfortable standard of living throughout the world, with a high level of education and eradication of most diseases now prevalent.

It should be obvious that in the face of the revolution in technology and scientific advances, secondary education must change. It must prepare people to assume the responsibilities, the demands, and the self-sacrifices that this country will face if it can hope to exercise leadership for a free world. This means knowledge for the common man far beyond what he now possesses. It means the stretching of our sights to envision opportunities for development of talent wherever it exists, regardless of sex or race. Certainly, these talents will include the scientific and the technical skills but even more the creativity of mind in the humanities, the social sciences, and the behavioral and health sciences.

What will the high school be like in a period of transition and change? What does secondary education need to become to meet the challenges of a new and different world? Since the scientific age precludes soothsaying, necromancy, and astrology, all we can hope for is to find some leads to change and to prepare young people to cope with drastic changes. This country can no longer afford to have secondary education merely reflect the current interests of society, for assuredly if the schools prepare people for a life of more chrome-laden cars, casual suburban living, innocuous slick magazines, more gadgetry to make life easier, gifts for "the man who has everything," and "how to make friends and influence people," our nation will never be great again. Instead, schools need to guide society through reflecting its highest ideals. They need to prepare all young minds for the most searching study of provocative questions of which they are capable, and equip them with the tools and desire for learning throughout a lifetime.

We need to rethink the goals of the secondary school in the last half of the twentieth century. The role of the secondary school is changing. It is becoming to a greater extent, college preparatory, but that fact is no license to return to what was common practice when secondary education had largely a college preparatory function. Instead, we need to think of what can best be accomplished for youth in these six years of a span of education that lasts a lifetime. What is good preparation for future study of any kind in any age which will demand the constant upkeep with changing knowledge and conditions?

Recognition needs to be given to the development of educative communications media, of which only the beginning has been seen. They will in the future serve to a considerably greater extent the purposes of adult education. With the increasing programs of adult education conducted by school systems, other public agencies, and industries and organizations, which are bound to develop further, the secondary school will no longer need to bear all the burdens of education that it previously did. But it will need to bear a tremendously increased responsibility for helping youth to develop independent study skills and the desire to use the new and old media for continued self-education.

It is helpful to look at what secondary education is becoming or shows potential for becoming. Some of the apparent trends as seen throughout this book in the discussion of outstanding practices are bulwarked by developments in the behavioral sciences. They point the way for promising trends that may develop and need to expand in the future. The student of education should be under no illusions that these are characteristic of the majority of secondary schools. But he should also realize that there are secondary school teachers and administrators who have a fundamental understanding of the world in which they live and who are putting their beliefs into practice with intelligent insight into the feelings, realities, and aspirations of human beings.

The discussion of the first two main points in this chapter is based upon the assumption that changes are needed in both the form and the substance of secondary education. If changes are made only in the form, or the organization of the school, the school day, the year, and the curriculum organization—the framework—we may well have only a shallow alteration at best. Modifications of these traditional forms, may, however, facilitate greatly the change in substance, or the quality of experiences, content, and attainment. In addition, certain conditions serve as necessary catalytic agents to change. If these conditions occur, secondary education has a much greater probability of retaining its vitality as a force in American life. This is the third point of the discussion.

THE FORM

There is much concern among leaders in secondary education about the incrusted practices that have resisted innovations. Hopefully, some secondary schools no longer feel that the forty- or sixty-minute daily schedule for classes is sacred. For many years, high school pupils pursued four subjects a year, each year in school. Interestingly enough, only those who had lagged behind were sometimes allowed to take five subjects, and usually did as well as pupils of equivalent ability who were taking four. Pupils now frequently take more academic and other courses for a broader and richer program. Wtih pupils earning twenty to twenty-five units in the four years, more questioning of a practice not substantiated by research has begun. Why should a pupil be in class five times a week instead of one, two, three, or four times? Are there some things that he learns as well, or better, in groups of different size than the traditional twenty-five?

The schedule and the time spent per day in organized class instruction is properly the handmaiden to instructional purposes and procedures. In the promising experimental situations described in this book, a pupil may spend a part of his time in large group situations, another part in small group discussions, and a considerable part doing independent study and research. The vision of some teachers in providing conditions for individual pursuits is helping their pupils to explore in depth subjects of special interest to them. Perhaps *the flexibility of scheduling a particular pupil's time,* depending upon his maturity and progress in independent study skills, will be as characteristic of the future high school as is the familiar pattern of today consisting of four or five periods of classes with one or two periods of study hall. The study room of the future will probably not be a large barren hall but a language laboratory, a science laboratory, a technology center, a human relations center, an industrial arts shop, a foods research center, a music room, or a library, all used before, during, and after the school day.

The studies of the Commission on Experimental Study of the Utilization of the Staff in the Secondary School, described in this book, have shown that flexibility of pupils' schedules and individualization of programs may go hand-in-hand with *more efficient use of the teacher's time and talents.* While little is known from research as to what constitutes competence in teaching, it is a valid assumption that teachers have their own individual strengths. Some can work best in laboratory situations, others in lecture situations, and others in small groups. It is probable that it will be found that some teachers are most effective in conferences with students. We are beginning to act as though we believed that teachers are also different, and that if a teacher is outstanding in some teaching skill, his talents should be utilized to the utmost. These studies, too, are pointing in the direction of using teaching aides, clerks, instructional assistants, and community consultants in order to give the teacher more time for preparation, conferencing, and the significant instructional activities. The hierarchy is one of competence and skill, not of status, and it is high time that we learn to distinguish between the two.

The core curriculum, team teaching, the use of television and other organizational and technical means have helped us to create a situation in which it is possible for teachers to come in more direct personal contacts with students. Savings in time through independent study and large group instruction will give the teacher more time to see individual pupils, when that teacher meets with groups of students fifteen hours a week instead of twenty-five hours or more. Reduction of class size to twenty-five pupils for five periods a day will not solve the problems, because teachers would still work with 125 pupils a day. The more creative means of deploying a teacher's time, discussed in this volume, will make more direct pupil-teacher contact possible. Flexibility and willingness to be experimental in patterns or organization will avoid fastening any of these forms on the secondary school as barnacles difficult to remove.

Broadened responsibilities for guidance, for conferences to plan and evaluate a student's work, more time for study, for community contacts, and for curriculum improvement are in the offing for the teacher, if the non-instructional jobs that the teacher now has to do are reduced.

The use of newer media of instruction, television, teaching machines, and other audio-visual aids constantly being perfected in the electronics laboratory, also fits into this picture. We have nothing to fear from the instruments themselves, only from their unintelligent use without purpose or understanding of when they can best promote learning. We must be on the alert to see that they do not replace valuable experiences of contacts with people. They can in the future supplement the teacher's knowledge and assist him in utilizing both his and his students' time more effectively, but they can also be shunned as once was the violin, in some circles, as "an instrument of the devil" which was used for dances. It all depends on the user.

There is some evidence that education is moving in the direction of *organizational patterns that fit best the concept of understanding, knowing, and respecting the child* and giving him a choice of opportunities to develop his talents. The comprehensive high school with its possibilities for programs to suit many types of abilities is gaining in popularity. The size of the school is being considered in relation to the optimum growth of adolescents. The problem of impersonal relations that plague both suburban living and large high schools is being tackled by the development of organizational patterns within schools, patterns which have many of the advantages without the disadvantages of the small high school. The extension of the school day and of the school year, with some promising different uses of the students' and the teachers' time during the summer seem to be coming.

Programs of courses for pupils are tending toward greater individualization in some quarters, without rigid demarcation lines that cast students of a supposed homogeneous group into the same mold. The programs of study in the future will undoubtedly be planned and programmed on electronic machines on an individual basis, even within multiple curricular patterns, until we see the futility of such meaningless mass grouping. We can perhaps look forward to the day when any elective is available to a student in high school regardless of his grade level. There is not the slightest evidence that some ninth and tenth grade students are not capable of pursuing some twelfth grade elective courses. In fact, what is known about continuity of learning belies such a notion.

There are some promising few beginnings of *breaking down the vertical barriers between school units*. Sixth-grade pupils capable of doing so pursue some of their studies in junior high school; ninth-grade pupils, in senior high school; and twelfth-grade pupils, in junior college, while still remaining as an integral part of the student body in their own school unit. This is the kind of flexibility that a school system creates within its own structure of school organization.

The leveling of artificial fences between school units as barriers to individual progress is consistent with the idea of extending services of the secondary school to out-of-school youth who have not completed high school and youth who have graduated and are working in the community. There is little justification for the secondary school not offering its resources to youth when they drop out of school; guidance services, placement services, shop facilities, recreation facilities, and evening classes are all services that are evident in some communities and in some fields such as agriculture. The all-or-none theory of a student either having to be in school full time or not at all may well be a thing of the past in the future secondary school. There will likely be less emphasis on graduation and leaving school and more on a continuous program of education that may last for an indefinite length of time into adult life.

This trend is apparent already in the extensive programs of adult education and in the excellent programs of terminal education in the thirteenth and fourteenth years in some areas of the country where the community junior college has strongly developed in that direction. Part-time cooperative education and evening classes represent a strong beginning toward that objective. The community college or junior college of the future may well be such an institution that serves all types of community needs. Certainly, this trend is of importance in the area of vocational education with the rising beginning employment age and the trend toward placement of vocational skills courses in the upper years of secondary school. In such a school program, the distinction between in-school and out-of-school youth will be diminished.

THE SUBSTANCE

Should the secondary schools make these organizational changes and then go no further, the prospect for the future would be bleak indeed. There is a considerable danger that this may happen, as has been evident in the discussions in previous chapters. Schools may feel that once setting up opportunities for independent study or programming pupils into more academic courses have been accomplished, they now have a program that will meet the challenges of the times. But they may have merely gone through the motions without fundamentally changing pupils' experiences for the better. The traditional homework of more pages or problems assigned may be disguised as independent study and the increased academic courses required may be poorly taught by teachers who have neither the vision nor the knowledge to teach them.

There are, however, a number of promising trends which seem to portend a real concern for the quality of experiences that pupils have in secondary schools. Once the tendency of equating quantity with quality—adding more courses equated with excellence or making courses "tough," equated with learning—is passed, we will make rapid strides toward improving the intellectual stimulation derived from school. This is happening in a number of schools.

There is a *concern for values in secondary education* in a number of the newer curriculum trends. The teacher-pupil relationship which was characterized by the teacher in the front of the room dispensing factual questions out of a book never came close to the problem of values by which men live or the motives and reasons for their actions. The interest in human relations, intergroup education, citizenship education, economic education have all stressed values in different areas of carrying out social functions. The studies which have indicated that social class relates significantly to marks, school success, participation in extraclass activities, and dropping out of school have made teachers conscious of the attitudes and beliefs that the lower class child brings with him to school from his environment, and the unrealities of some of the demands and expectancies of the school.

School leaders are questioning the practices that strive to enhance these social distinctions. Much effort has gone into the elimination of secret societies, and self-perpetuating clubs of the "elite" type are becoming rare, even though some parents still seem to want to fulfill their needs and cravings for status through supporting these ventures. Multiple curricula are being questioned as instruments of furthering social distinctions that place some people in an inferior class. There is a feeling that they no longer serve any useful purpose in a school that has a good guidance program through which students are counseled each year as to the career best suited to them. Only if we act on the belief that "classifying certain people as 'inferior' but degrades the classifier" will these kinds of practices be questioned.

Complementary to the attention to values by which men's lives are guided is the slowly *increasing tendency to look at goals in terms of behavior changes.* A considerable number of teachers think of social skills, attitudes, and appreciations as behavior patterns that can be evaluated by how a person acts, what he says, does, reads; how he treats his fellow-man; how he can use language effectively; what reading or art forms he likes; to what extent he uses his intellectual capacities in the classroom and laboratory. In the area of citizenship, we have learned to look at what community or political activities the citizen participates in, how he keeps himself informed about issues, what action he takes with regard to community problems. At least some teachers define the behavior components of effective thinking and what it means in terms of behavior to know more about a subject. More and more are conscious of the fact that ability to parrot information in quiz-show fashion is not the understanding that a high order of intellectual experience demands.

There is today less insistence upon a certain number of units in specified high school subjects but greater concern for improved quality of experience of the college-bound student. Many college people are giving careful thought to the question of skills needed for college success, such as skills in writing, expressing oneself clearly, using sources of information, and skills in mathematics. This is another manifestation of interest in change of behavior as the result of secondary schooling.

One of the behaviors considered desirable for pupils is an understanding of what is studied. Everyone has had some experience in formal education where understanding was desired but such curiosity may soon have been deadened by constant demands of memorizing what was said by the author of the book or by the teacher. One of the trends that bodes well for the future is *the increasing emphasis on deriving meanings* from the content studied or the experience undergone.

Meaningless experiences, whether it be theorems memorized, history "recited," statistical data or formulas learned for a test, or literature "learned by heart,'" have no place in education of the future that needs to deal with social, technical, and human problems far more complex than those ever dreamed of twenty years ago. Meaning is related to purpose, to thinking, to maturity, to experience background, to perception, and to utilization. One need only read the "gobble-de-gook" that some children make of the words of the salute to the flag when they are asked to write what they understand them to mean. Word calling, however, is not a phenomenon limited to younger children.

Persons in professional education are guilty of a similar practice when they talk of studying children and *not* subject matter to people for whom these words seem to be utter nonsense. Helping others to derive meanings is to communicate clearly, not just because of what is said and how it is said, but because backgrounds and feelings of the person which whom one communicates are considered.

Today we see, more than ever before in our lifetime, a concentration by learned societies and school people on the revision of content of various subjects in order that it might have more meaning for people and greater relation to the lives they will live in the twentieth century. This is happening especially in the sciences and in mathematics, but also to a lesser extent in the social sciences, in industrial arts, and in English, which undoubtedly will be radically affected by the developments in communication, linguistics, and semantics.

It is indeed heartening to find many teachers expressing *concern for preserving freedom of thought,* in spite of the social pressures for conformity. Librarians have vigorously opposed the bookburnings, both those of an obvious nature and those of a more subtle kind. For the rigidity of conformity is paralyzing to the liberal education that the secondary school seeks to give all youth. In schools of today there is less regurgitation of statements from the book and there are fewer teachers replying to pupils that it is important to study something "because I say so." Both of these practices make for conformity rather than original thinking.

There was a school superintendent who, when high school students questioned what he said in class, shaking his jowls, replied, "I'm a hundred per cent right!" The students appropriately nicknamed him "Whifflesnoozer." So long as students challenge the whifflesnoozers, we need have little fear of placing the cause of freedom in these future citizens' hands, but if they tend to look for someone who can give them the answer, then our charge becomes a greater one.

In an address entitled *"How Fares Freedom in the American High*

School" Paul Halverson, professor of education at Syracuse University, raised some pertinent questions:

> By the very nature of mass education in our country there will be group standards, group restrictions, and group patterns of procedures which limit the freedom of the individual learner and his teacher. Unfortunately, we have gone far beyond these kinds of inevitable limits on complete freedom and individualization of instruction. There has been added a vast network of administrative and supervisory decrees, mandates, and regulations which hedge in the classroom teacher and learners on all sides, preventing autonomous group planning and action for significant learning experiences. Add to that in some states the vast superstructure of state course of study, state examinations systems, and state level inspectional supervision and we end with a minimum of freedom granted to the teacher and learner in the classroom.

✻　✻　✻

> The second principle is one which suggests flexibility in approach to student control. What is the meaning of this for school practice? In the first place, I believe many high schools could provide more freedom in alternatives of behavior consistent with the best interests of all; but in few places is as much of a premium placed on conformity of behavior and on uniformity of disciplinary measures. What would we do without first bells, second bells, tardy bells, passing bells, dismissal bells? Without white slips, red slips, blue slips, and pink slips? Without handbooks? Principals, teachers, pupils, custodians, parents, school boards—all must have them! Without detention halls, first offenses, second offenses, suspensions and expulsions—all administered with deftness as though we are certain of what we are doing? What does it all add up to? [1]

He also speaks of creative, free teachers who are encouraged to experiment; those who are under severe restrictions; and those who "love their chains." It is this third group that should give us concern, for the second seems to find many ways of giving students experiences in creative thought.

Attaining for all secondary school teachers freedom from fear, freedom to discuss all sides of an issue, freedom to give pupils an opportunity to read materials expressing different points of view, freedom to work for the extension of democracy to all people and groups within society is the goal of the secondary schools of the future. Then it will be recognized that it is imperative that controversy and individuality need to be fostered since so much of the pattern of modern society tends to conform.

One of the essential ingredients of a program of education is a *purpose and a sense of direction.* The more true this is for the teacher and for the learner, the more effective will be the learning situation. In a sense, education cannot rightfully be spoken of as having a pur-

[1] Paul M. Halverson, ed., *Frontiers of Secondary Education I,* Syracuse, New York: Syracuse University Press, 1956, pp. 5 and 9.

pose; it is the individual teacher, the administrator or supervisor, who either has a clear-cut sense of direction or follows blindly whatever new movement or device comes along. The "gadgeteers" in education get on a horse and ride off in all directions at the same time. There are many examples, however, of school faculties thinking together about what the school is attempting to do. Through this means, purposes can be clarified and practices evaluated against them.

Questions such as, "Should pupils be grouped in some way for instruction?" cannot be answered by a simple "yes" or "no." Grouping of various kinds can be extremely valuable for instructional purposes, but if we are "groupy," we may tend to herd people into smaller groups on any occasion: buzz, work, or study groups. Each has a definite purpose and is useful for achieving certain objectives. Courses, curricula, groups within classes, classes, grades, and even schools represent a kind of grouping, each for a particular purpose. In a like manner, how can questions concerning the use of lectures as a procedure and the size of the class be answered unless the basic reason for using the lecture or having a certain size class are known?

Some talk as though television were a cure-all for educational ills and others become rather emotional about its possibilities for displacing the teacher. If we examine the purpose that television might serve to facilitate learning, if we examine the reasons why in some situations large classes might be effective and in others, small seminar groups; or if we examine the aims that could be most effectively advanced by aids of some kind to the teacher, human or mechanical, we will be consistent with the experimental attitude so necessary to progress.

Any means for the most effective use of staff and facilities in times of rapidly expanding school population should meet the criterion of purpose. Is it done simply to take care of larger numbers of students or to facilitate the learning process? Truly, as those who guide education clarify their own purposes for what they do, the secondary schools will continue to strengthen their programs.

One promising direction being taken by forward-looking secondary schools is the *focus of attention on the individual,* his uniqueness, his talents whatever they may be, his peculiar contribution, and what makes him capable or incapable of learning. This is one direction in which teachers should not waver in spite of the demands of certain groups for education of an elite at the expense of others. One of the significant contributions of American secondary education is the concept that each child is entitled to a high school education at public expense. As Robert M. Hutchins, former Chancellor of the

University of Chicago, has stated "The conception of a people all devoting the early years of their lives to study with a view to attaining the maximum development of their highest powers is surely one of the grandest that history can show." [2]

Certainly, the increased interest in the study of the pupil and his development is one of the characteristic trends of modern education. But it is not just for the purpose of finding out what he is, but also to discover what he is capable of becoming, and to assist him in making the most of his abilities. The spirit of inquiry that characterizes the best in secondary education is entirely in line with stressing the individual's uniqueness. For conformity tends to lose the individual in the group and is crippling to inventiveness.

The current interest in the student of unusual ability is one expression of concern for the individual and a recognition that programs should be different for people who differ. One of the ways in which secondary schools are experimenting with a great deal of promise is in adapting their programs to students with special talents. In so doing, one of the cautions that needs to be exercised is to avoid lumping pupils under a category such as the "gifted," but instead to consider in what a pupil is gifted and his special degree of ability. The terms "average child" and "the gifted" have no more meaning than "the handicapped" when it comes to considering what kind of special attention a particular pupil needs.

In our anxiety to achieve quality performance, one of the most difficult questions that faces us is who are to be the chosen ones? Ability is only one factor that enters into performance. Motivation, interest, and purpose may be equally important. The fact that some studies show that scientists do not tend to come from those who rank in the highest percentiles in academic ability, should give us food for thought. There are more ingredients than one that contribute to creativity and inventiveness. Even experts are still a far cry from knowing enough to select those who are destined to be outstanding. A genuine respect for individual differences and a regard for personal worth cannot be equated with selection for instructional grouping.

In a number of ways, the American secondary school has chosen to *mitigate class differences* rather than segregate by social class. Segregation by race is painfully, slowly, but surely losing ground. The American people have placed their faith in the comprehensive high school attended by pupils from all social classes. Educators know that social class is closely related to achievement and aspira-

[2] Robert M. Hutchins, *Some Observations on American Education*, Cambridge: Cambridge University Press, 1959, p. 22.

tions in school. Except for a few instances in large cities, most of our high schools are for all of the children living in the community rather than for a selected group who have a certain occupational objective or are within a certain range of ability.

The private secondary school has served as a sort of a safety valve in order to preserve this ideal of a high school for the children of all the people. For parents who preferred to have their children associate only with children of the same religion, race, or social class have always had access to the private school. True, those are rarely the reasons given, but nonetheless they may represent the real motive in some cases. It is well known that private schools may appeal to parents for other reasons as well—such as small classes, experimental nature, religious convictions, and the like.

The secondary school curriculum of the future, it is earnestly hoped, will *place a value upon the means by which it achieves ends, as well as upon the ends toward which it strives.* It is of utmost importance that we as educators are clearly aware of the ends toward which we are working in education. These ends are solidly grounded in the kind of a society wanted and the kinds of skills, values, and understandings which are needed to live in and foster that society, as well as to approach higher levels than mere survival in the world of tomorrow. The ends are interwoven with the means. If we say that we do not care how we achieve our aims, we make the same mistake as the misguided who would use the techniques of communism to fight communism.

A high school student would not be expected to distinguish propaganda from facts and objective information unless he has both kinds of materials placed in his hands and is helped to analyze them. We would not hope to develop in him a love of the beautiful in music, literature, or human relations unless he has some satisfying experiences with the good and the beautiful in each of these fields.

Thus, teachers may also, by the very means that they use, deprive the students of a keen desire and interest for learning. Education needs to work hard at being increasingly effective in influencing the behavior of students in terms of values that are intellectual as well as human, in terms of a desire and a zeal to continue their education. There is little hope of a potential scientist in the young man who said, "I'm glad I got my physics off," no matter what his capabilities.

If we wish to we could settle for less than best in our endeavor to strengthen the secondary school program of the future, or for sameness and conformity, or for judging human worth by differences in intellect alone, or for blind acceptance without questioning. But it is doubtful if the price we would have to pay will be worth it.

THE CONDITIONS

There is no certainty about the direction of change. The trends discussed in the preceding section are possibilities for the future of secondary education. Perhaps further testing of these ideas through methodical evaluation will show that they are not the best means for achieving the results that are wanted. Nor will these changes just happen.

There are hard conditions to meet if secondary education is to make progress. The results, if these conditions are met, may be different from what can now be imagined, but they are also likely to be superior. That is what makes commitment to research and experimentation exciting.

On top of that list of prerequisites to well-ordered change is the type of *leadership that represents some of the best minds in education and that releases the potential for creativity in the faculty of a school.* Such leadership believes in the dignity and the worth of each individual teacher. It does not depend upon artificial status symbols or power for its accomplishments. It harnesses the leadership in the staff. It is founded on the concept that to be a leader a person must have ideas of his own. It conceives of its purposes as assisting others to define their goals and to achieve those goals. This kind of democratically oriented behavior in leadership is evaluated in terms of productivity in achievement of goals, mutuality of goals, and individual creativity of the staff.

The principal of a school who operates in this fashion understands that changes are evoked, not forced. He considers what change means to people. He works with his faculty in studying problems and shows a trust in the decisions of the group. While he may be enthusiastic about teacher involvement in policy-making, he realizes that not all teachers share his beliefs, strange as it may seem, and most of all, he values differences in beliefs among the faculty. All this is to say that the setting which the principal of a secondary school provides is a significant factor in the improvement of the school's program.

A second condition necessary is *enlisting the community in the educational enterprise.* We may know of some secondary school that is considered a "community school." It is close to the people in the community in many ways. In the so-called community schools, the people seem to know a great deal about their schools; they take part in school affairs; they take pride in their schools; they are a part of the school program since both the people and the community agencies are used extensively as resources for education; they contribute ideas and participate in studies; and they support the school for needed bond issues or in times of crisis. Somehow or other they got that way through someone's effective and insightful leadership.

For desirable changes will come about in secondary education as the people who support the school know and understand what it is all about, as an appeal is made to their intelligence, as their intelligence is utilized and they are made to feel that they are partners in this great enterprise. What is meant here is study, hard work at trying to find solutions, not fruitless debate based on either ignorance or prejudices. The two-way lines of communication are essential to get ideas from as well as to the public.

The community includes the scientists, the poets, the leaders in government and in industry, the person who has special knowledge to contribute in any field. It includes the larger community of national organizations representing the academic fields and those in the field of professional education. It includes the professors in academic fields who can contribute much to revising content in their fields. It includes expertness wherever it can be found. The secondary school of the future needs to have better communication with colleges than it ever has had—face-to-face situations, not only transcripts and occasional reports.

A third condition is *keeping the control of the schools close to the public* which they serve. One hazard to these grass-roots contacts is the large suburban school district in which the people may become farther and farther removed as the population grows. Another is the danger of national control of one form or another mentioned in the previous chapters.

There seems to be a considerable movement for national testing programs and the setting of national standards for the curriculum throughout the country. This movement presents one of the greatest hazards to the individuality and versatility of the curriculum developed by local people throughout the country and the control that rests now in the lay boards of education. The curriculum is always influenced by any kind of centralized testing program that compares achievement of school and school or district and district. It is hard to conceive of how national standards could be adaptable to the many kinds of situations that exist in school districts in this country.

One has to but listen to the comments of foreign educators who come to this country to find out that there is a great deal of similarity in the school programs throughout the fifty states. For they are constantly astounded by the fact that they find schools working at the same purposes even though the United States does not have a national department of education that determines the curriculum.

In recent years, too, there has been a development of courses of study by national organizations and learned societies. Such developments should not be feared if these course materials are tested and used intelligently by the schools, modified to fit the particular group of students being taught. Instead, these ideas should be welcome, as well as any other ideas obtained from people who are knowledgeable in any field. National organizations have long made pronouncements about education which have influenced the elementary and secondary school curriculum in this country. Whether the pronouncements come from the National Education Association, or from other professional educational bodies, or from learned societies in the subject fields, they should be studied by local school systems and followed only if the study shows that such action is warranted.

The function of curriculum planning rests largely with the local school staff, working with lay people and using whatever information and talents they can find to aid them in this most important task. There is no more important responsibility in the hands of the school and its professional staff, for this is the heart of the school program. No matter what pronouncements are made by national bodies or what courses are developed, nothing can take the place of qualified teachers, administrators, and supervisors.

This leads us into the fourth condition necessary: *well-prepared teachers*. The amount of preparation required ten or twenty years ago is not an acceptable standard for teaching in the last half of the twentieth century. The futile arguments about how much subject matter knowledge and how much professional knowledge a teacher needs to have cannot be continued. He needs to have as much as he can get of both, and of the right kind. But certainly, if we believe that people differ, some will need far more of some aspects of education for teaching than others. Credits can never satisfactorily measure knowledge and skill which the competent teacher needs.

But there can be no hope of improvement of secondary education of the kind that would excite the imagination unless we set our sights high as to the competence demanded of a teacher. It must be understood, without a shadow of a doubt, that the most important factor in curriculum improvement is the teacher. For petty, critical people, whose horizons are limited, whose vision for the future is dim, whose faith in young people has waned, or who know little about either the subject or the pupils and the learning process are not the hope for the future of the secondary school.

It is time we recognize that teacher preparation is a life-long process, much of it from self-study, and that teachers ought to be drawn from the most capable group of students suited to the task of working with children (or adults) at a certain age level.

The capstone condition essential to improvement of secondary education is *commitment to research and experimentation* in education and in the behavioral sciences. Most practices in secondary schools have been submitted only to the practical test of time. We know they get results but we do not know, in many cases, whether other practices would get better results. Unless we can strengthen the skills in research and the convictions that practices both new and old need to be put to the severe test, we will not be sure that the changes we make are the right ones for the goals we seek. Do they encourage individuality and diversity, or do they compress unique personalities into a common mold? Do they develop the behaviors which characterize a free people? Do they make the most of each individual's potentialities? Upon what well-conceived theory are they based? Are they consistent with what is already known about human development and behavior?

Research depends upon the leadership of ideas. It germinates in a culture of the open and questioning mind. It thrives in an atmosphere free from the emotional and irrational smog of prejudice. At the same time as the secondary school seeks to develop these conditions as means to improve the accomplishments of its goals, it had better be sure to include these behaviors among its goals.

If these provisions can be assured, we can be confident that the secondary schools will continue to adjust intelligently to a rapidly changing civilization, even though the changes may not be either what we might anticipate nor what supports our personal biases. We can also be assured the public will continue to place its confidence in its secondary schools.

SELECTED REFERENCES

ALCORN, MARVIN D. and LINLEY, JAMES M. (eds.). *Issues in Curriculum Development.* New York: Harcourt, Brace & World, Inc., 1959, Chaps. 2, 4, 5, 7, 8, 10.—These chapters are especially pertinent to secondary education. Presents articles by authors taking different sides on a number of issues.

AMERICAN ASSOCIATION OF SCHOOL ADMINISTRATORS. *Labels and Fingerprints.* Washington, D.C.: National Education Association, 1960, not paged.—A challenging, brief statement on the uniqueness of the learner and practices which tend to obscure the individual and promote the group pattern.

ASSOCIATION FOR SUPERVISION AND CURRICULUM DEVELOPMENT. *The High School We Need.* Washington, D.C.: National Education Association, 1959, 28 pp.—A pamphlet prepared by the Association's Commission on the Education of Adolescents which outlines guidelines for the future of secondary education.

ASSOCIATION FOR SUPERVISION AND CURRICULUM DEVELOPMENT. *The Junior High*

School We Need. Washington, D.C.: National Education Association, 1961, 37 pp.—Outlines what the junior high school of the future should be like.

ASSOCIATION FOR SUPERVISION AND CURRICULUM DEVELOPMENT. "The School of the Future—1985." *Educational Leadership,* 17:470-521, May, 1960.—Articles on the education for tomorrow in secondary and elementary schools.

CONANT, JAMES B. *Education in the Junior High School Years.* Princeton, N.J.: Educational Testing Services, 1960, 46 pp.—Makes recommendations, conservative in nature, for junior high school practices in required subjects, skills, departmentalization, extraclass activities, schedules, guidance, etc., growing out of Dr. Conant's study of secondary schools.

CONANT, JAMES B. *The American High School Today.* New York: McGraw-Hill Book Co., Inc., 1959, 140 pp.—An influential report growing out of a Study of the American high school, made by Dr. Conant. Makes recommendations for improving public secondary education and summarizes some of the conditions found in visits to high schools.

EHLERS, HENRY and LEE, GORDON C. (eds.). *Crucial Issues in Education.* New York: Holt, Rinehart & Winston, Inc., rev. ed., 1959, Parts I and III.—These parts are especially pertinent, dealing with freedom and censorship in education, the aims of education, and education for the gifted. Presents differing viewpoints of authors on these issues.

FORD, EDMUND A. *Rural Renaissance: Revitalizing Small High Schools.* U.S. Department of Health, Education, and Welfare, Office of Education, Bulletin 1961, No. 11. Government Printing Office, 1961, 54 pp.—Forward-looking experiments in small secondary schools in order to improve their programs and enrich the offerings.

FEATHERSTONE, WILLIAM. *A Functional Curriculum for Youth.* New York: American Book Co., 1950, Chaps. 5, 7-9.—An older statement that contains some challenging ideas for the secondary school curriculum.

HALVERSON, PAUL M. (ed.). *Frontiers of Secondary Education.* Syracuse: Syracuse University Press.—A series of pamphlets, publishing the lectures given at the annual conference on Secondary Education sponsored by Syracuse University. In 1961, five issues had been published, and presumably others will become available. Stimulating lectures of interest concerning the future of secondary education and trends that can be noted.

MALLERY, DAVID. *New Approaches in Education.* Boston: National Council of Independent Schools, 1961, pp. 3-116.—Describes programs in private schools which have been of an experimental nature.

MORSE, ARTHUR D. *Schools of Tomorrow—Today.* Garden City, N.Y.: Doubleday & Co., Inc., 1960, 191 pp.—Describes a number of experiments conducted in schools in such areas as team teaching, use of teacher aides, use of television, programs for the gifted.

NATIONAL ASSOCIATION OF SECONDARY-SCHOOL PRINCIPALS. "Seeking Improved Learning Opportunities," *Bulletin of the National Association of Secondary-School Principals.* 45:1-285, January, 1961.—These reports of experimental studies in secondary school point to ways in forward-looking trends in scheduling, team teaching, independent study, and other means of organization for instruction.

NATIONAL ASSOCIATION OF SECONDARY-SCHOOL PRINCIPALS. "The Junior High School Today and Tomorrow." *Bulletin of the National Association of Secondary-School Principals.* 44:1-132, November, 1960.—Examines practices and proposals for the junior high schools as developed by The Association's Committee on Junior High-School Education.

NATIONAL COUNCIL FOR THE SOCIAL STUDIES. *Citizenship and a Free Society: Education for the Future.* (Thirtieth Yearbook). Washington, D.C.: National Education

Association, 1960, Chaps. 5, 7, 9, 11, 13.—Looks ahead two decades with optimism and criticizes some of today's practices in citizenship education.

ROCKEFELLER BROTHERS FUND. *The Pursuit of Excellence: Education and the Future of America.* Report V, the Special Studies Project. Garden City, N.Y.: Doubleday & Co., Inc., 1958, 49 pp.—An important statement of the challenge to excellence in the future of American education, of import for secondary schools.

SCOTT, C. WINFIELD and OTHERS (eds.). *The Great Debate: Our Schools in Crisis.* Englewood Cliffs, N.J.: Prentice-Hall, Inc., 1959, 184 pp.—One of the growing numbers of paperbacks on educational topics. Deals with pros and cons on many issues that relate to secondary education. Includes a chapter on proposals for action.

TRUMP, L. LLOYD. *Images of the Future: A New Approach to Secondary Education.* Washington, D.C.: National Association of Secondary-School Principals, 1959, 46 pp. —A challenging statement on the organization for instruction, schedules, use of teacher time, educational facilities, etc. presenting some new concepts and ideas. Written for the Commission for the Experimental Study of the Utilization of the Staff in the Secondary School.

TRUMP, J. LLOYD and BAYNHAM, DORSEY. *Focus on Change: Guide to Better Schools.* Chicago: Rand, McNally & Co., 1961, 147 pp.—Summary statement of the projects of the Commission on the Experimental Study of the Utilization of the Staff in the Secondary School. Portends possible changes for the future.

TRUMP, J. LLOYD. *New Directions to Quality Education: The Secondary School of To-morrow.* Washington, D.C.: National Association of Secondary-School Principals, 1960, 14 pp.—Brief statement of grouping for instruction, team teaching, scheduling, and other aspects of staff utilization as desirable directions in which to move in secondary education, growing out of studies of the Commission on The Experimental Study of the Utilization of the Staff in the Secondary School.

INDEX

Academic achievement, pressures for, 395–96, 412
Academically talented; *see also* Gifted
 curriculum principles for, 236–37, 241
 extent of provisions for, 243–44
 issues pertaining to, 247–48, 250–53
 special classes for, 259–63
 survey of, in Maryland, 260
Academy; *see* Secondary school
Acceleration
 advantages and disadvantages of, 250–52
 rapid progress plans, 257–59
Accrediting agencies
 as evaluators, 461–62
 nature and work of, 122–24, 434–35
 school-college relationships in, 434–35
Action research, 130, 472–74
Activities, extraclass
 administration of, 282, 301–2
 athletics, 287–88, 296–97, 308
 clubs, 285–86, 293
 compensation for sponsoring, 302, 380–81
 cost to pupil, 87
 credit for, 293
 dramatics, 291
 evaluation of, 283–84
 fraternities, 286–87
 guidance, opportunities for, 410–11
 history of, 38–39
 integration with school program, 280–81, 292–93
 issues and problems regarding, 300–302
 in junior high schools, 285–86, 288, 292–97
 music; *see* Music curriculum
 need for variety of, 281–82, 302
 objectives of, 280
 participation in, 89, 283–84, 294–95
 planning for, 282–83
 principles for, 280–84
 publications, 290
 schedule for, 293–94
 social, 290–91, 298–99
 speech, 287
 student participation in control of; *see* Student government
 time for, 283
 variety of, 285–86
Administration of the secondary school; *see also* Leadership
 complexity of, 338–39
 priorities in, 337–38
 pupil participation in, 297–98
 teacher participation in, 333, 339–40
Administrative organization; *see* Organization of secondary school
Adolescents; *see also* Developmental tasks of adolescents, Pupils
 culture conflicts of, 74–75
 needs, 92–100
 normal development of, 15
 principles of growth, 12–17
 problems of, 16, 96–100
 self concept of, 14–15
 unity of growth, 16–17
 variation in rate of growth, 17
Adult education, 306–8, 316–18, 322–23
Advanced placement program, 258, 443–45
Agriculture curriculum, 272–73
Appraisal of school practices; *see* Evaluation of the secondary school program
Appreciation, experiences in, 225–26
Articulation
 through continuous progress, 487–88
 issues and problems of, 446–49
 through junior high school, 432
 limited practices in, 432–33
 through orientation activities, 442–43
 principles of, 146, 426, 430
 of secondary and elementary schools, 426–28, 431–33, 439–43
 of secondary school and college, 428–30, 433–38, 443–46
 through teachers' meetings, 441–42
Arts and crafts curriculum, 225, 255
Athletics, 287–88, 296–97, 308

Beginning teacher, assistance to, 311, 346–47, 377
Behavior changes, teaching for, 5, 112–13, 489
Biological Science Curriculum Study, 215
Block time classes; *see also* Schedule, secondary school
 definition of, 107

501

INDEX OF SCHOOL PRACTICES

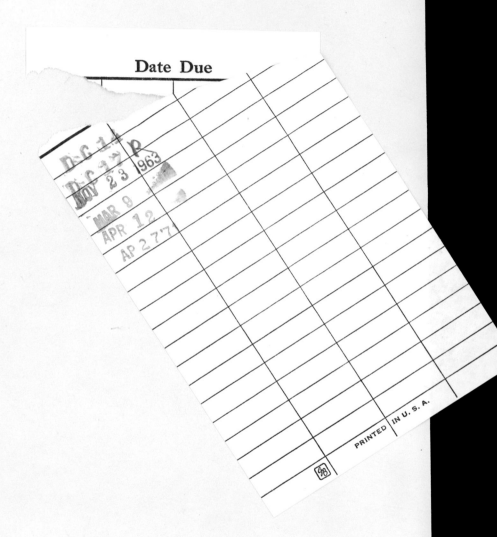

Date Due